THE ILLUSTRATED COLUMBIA ENCYCLOPEDIA

VOLUME

4

Bro-Cha

THE
ILLUSTRATED

COLUMBIA

This edition is published
and distributed by
Rockville House Publishers, Inc.
by arrangement with COLUMBIA
UNIVERSITY PRESS
NEW YORK & LONDON

ENCYCLOPEDIA

EDITED BY
WILLIAM BRIDGWATER
AND
SEYMOUR KURTZ

Picture Editors—Design and Layout   DONALD D. WOLF and MARGOT L. WOLF

Musa metafisica
by Carlo Carrà

Bow River in Banff National
Park, Canada
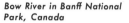

Head of a Centaur

ACKNOWLEDGMENTS

Illustrations courtesy of:

Key to picture position: t-top; c-center; b-bottom; r-right; l-left   Combinations: tr-top right; tl-top left; etc.

American Museum of Natural History - 1002, 1209 r, 1230
American President Line - 1218, 1219 tr
Austrian State Information Office - 942 tr, 1126 t
Belgian Tourist Bureau - 1000
Bemidji Civic and Commerce Assn.
Douglas Scott Bliven - 1176 b
British Information Service - 959, 991 br, 993, 1076 l
B.O.A.C. - 1035 l, 1035 r
Buffalo C. of C. - 969 b
Bulgarian National Committee - 975 l
Raffaelo Busoni - 978, 1130, 1216
California Mission Trails Assn. - 1049 b
Canadian National Film Board - 1085 tl, 1086 tr, 1086 bl
Canadian Pacific Railway - 1085 tr, 1087
Carnegie Institute - 1133 r
Civic-Commerce Assn. - 983
Colorado Dept. of Public Relations - 982 t
Columbia University Press - 962, 963, 964
Cooper Union Museum - 1009 r
Armando Curcio Editore, Rome - All four color illus., plus the following black & white illus. 949, 977 r, 1023 r, 1039, 1041 bl, 1086 tl, 1129 l, 1135, 1146, 1162 t, 1175, 1209 l, 1238, 1110, 1115
Field Museum of Natural History, Chicago - 969 t, 1009 l, 1125 r, 1139 t, 1190, 1231, 1242 t, 1162 bl
French Government Tourist Office - 1038, 1159 l, 1232
Ewing Galloway - 956 l, 1041 r, 1192, 1201 b
German Information Office - 948, 1134, 1137
Glen Orry Cattery - 1176 c
Government of India Tourist Office - 963 tl, 1041 tl
The Granger Collection - 937 b, 937 t, 951, 954 c, 958, 967, 970, 979, 982 b, 995, 996, 997 r, 998, 1012, 1044, 1069 tc, 1070, 1079 l, 1079 r, 1088, 1097 r, 1103, 1120 l, 1136 r, 1140, 1148, 1155 l, 1156, 1160 r, 1164, 1185 b, 1197, 1215, 1226, 1233 r, 1242 b, 1245 t, 1250, 1245 t
Hungarian Committee - 961
Israel Information Service - 953
Library of Congress - 973, 1155 r
Federico Arborio Mella, Milan, Italy - 939 tl, 939 tr, 942 tl, 944, 950 tr, 957 tl, 957 tc, 957 tr, 957 b, 968 b, 974, 975 r, 988, 991 tl, 992, 994, 997 l, 999, 1003, 1005 b, 1010, 1015 l, 1018, 1025, 1031, 1034, 1037, 1052, 1054, 1081, 1091, 1101, 1100 bl, 1100 t, 1107, 1111 l, 1111 r, 1113 t, 1119, 1123 r, 1133 l,
1139 b, 1143, 1144 t, 1144 b, 1154, 1158 l, 1158 r, 1159 bl, 1159 br, 1160 l, 1162 b, 1163, 1165, 1166 t, 1166 b, 1168, 1169, 1171 bl, 1173 b, 1179 l, 1186 r, 1189 r, 1189 l, 1196 l, 1198 l, 1201 t, 1205, 1206, 1207, 1210 t, 1214, 1219 b, 1220 t, 1220 b, 1223, 1224, 1225 b, 1225 t, 1227, 1230 t, 1233 l, 1234 b, 1234 t, 1239, 1243, 1244 l, 1247, 1249, 1224
Metropolitan Museum of Art - 1019 b, 1019 t, 1141 l, 1141 tr, 1244 r
Mother Cabrini High School - 1024 r
National Archives - 1109, 1195
N.A.S.A. - 1105
National Gallery of Art - 955
National Park Service - 952 br, 1048 tl, 1129 r, 1084 l
New York Public Library - 950 l, 1013, 1050, 1057, 1065, 1076 r, 1141 b, 1149, 1172
New York Zoological Society - 1113 l, 1113 br, 1167, 1183, 1196 tr, 1198 l
Nova Scotia Bureau of Information - 1085 b
Ohio State Development Department - 1122
Pan American - Grace Airways - 968 t
Provincial Publicity Bureau, Quebec - 1084 l
Redwood Empire Assn. - 1047 r
Rumanian Legation - 956 l
Sacramento C. of C. - 1046 r
Santa Fe Railway - 1131, 1142
Scandinavian Airlines - 1097 l
So. California Visitors Council - 1046 l
Southern Pacific Company - 1049 c
Spanish Tourist Office - 986, 1028
Standard Oil Co. of N.J. - 977 l, 1090, 1125 l, 1150
Swiss National Travel Office - 1245 b
Tea Council of the U.S.A., Inc. - 1219 tl
T.W.A. - 1049 t
UNATIONS - 981, 992 bl, 992 r
United Artists, Inc. - 1240 r
U.S. Dept. of Agriculture - 1008 bl, 1008 tl, 1008 lc
U.P.I. - 952 l, 954 r, 971, 991 tr, 1001, 1004, 1005 t, 1052 b, 1157, 1096, 1104, 1120 r, 1121, 1123 l, 1136 l, 1145, 1153, 1159 tr, 1196 b, 1210 b, 1222, 1228
Washington Department of Commerce and Development - 1161
Wide World Photos - 1102
Wine Institute - 1048 lc
Margot L. Wolf - 1176 t, 1008 d
Hamilton Wright - 1114

KEY TO PRONUNCIATION

ā fate (fāt), fail (fāl), vacation (vākā'shùn)

â care (kâr), Mary (mâ'rē)

ă bat (băt), add (ăd), marry (mă'rē)

ä father (fä'dhùr), marble (mär'bùl)

ã French tant (tã), Rouen (rōōã'), and similar sounds in some other languages

b back (băk), cab (kăb)

ch chap (chăp)

d dock (dŏk), cod (kŏd)

dh father (fä'dhùr), then (dhĕn). Compare with th.

ē even (ē'vùn), clearing (klēr'ĭng), obvious (ŏb'vēùs)

ĕ end (ĕnd), met (mĕt), merry (mĕ'rē)

ẽ French vin (vẽ), bien (byẽ), and similar sounds in some other languages

f fat (făt), Philip (fĭ'lĭp)

g get (gĕt), tag (tăg)

h hat (hăt). See also ch, dh, kh, sh, th, zh, and hw

hw where (hwâr), what (hwŏt)

ī fine (fīn), buyer (bī'ùr)

ĭ pin (pĭn), pit (pĭt), spirit (spĭ'rĭt), fated (fā'tĭd)

j jam (jăm) edge (ĕj), ginger (jĭn'jùr)

k cook (kŏŏk), tackle (tă'kùl)

kh loch (lŏkh, German Aachen (ä'khùn), Licht (lĭkht), and similar sounds in some other languages

l peal (pēl), pull (pŏŏl)

ḷ crumple (krŭm'pḷ)

m hammer (hă'mùr)

ṃ fanaticism (fùnă'tĭsĭzṃ)

n dinner (dĭ'nùr)

ṇ dampen (dăm'pṇ)

ng singing (sĭng'ĭng), finger (fĭng'gùr), sang (săng), sank (săngk)

ō hope (hōp), potato (pùtā'tō)

ô orbit (ôr'bĭt), fall (fôl)

ŏ hot (hŏt), toddy (tŏ'dē), borrow (bŏ'rō)

õ French dont (dõ), chanson (shãsõ'), and similar sounds in some other languages

oi boil (boil), royal (roi'ùl)

ōō boot (bōōt), lose (lōōz)

ŏŏ foot (fŏŏt), purely (pyŏŏr'lē), manipulate (mùnĭ'pyŏŏlāt)

ou scout (skout), crowd (kroud)

p pipe (pīp), happy (hă'pē)

r road (rōd), appeared (ùpērd'), carpenter (kär'pùntùr)

s saw (sô), case (kās)

sh shall (shăl), nation (nā'shùn)

t tight (tīt), rating (rā'tĭng)

th thin (thĭn), myth (mĭth). Compare with dh.

ū fume (fūm), euphemism (ū'fùmĭzm)

û curl (kûrl), Hamburg (hăm'bûrg), French œuvre (û'vrù), peu (pû), German schön (shûn), Goethe (gû'tù), and similar sounds in some other languages

ŭ butter (bŭ'tùr), suds (sŭdz), hurry (hŭ'rē)

ù affair (ùfâr'), sofa (sō'fù), contravene (kŏntrùvēn'), monopoly (mùnŏ'pùlē), suburban (sùbûr'bùn), callous (kă'lùs), rather (ră'dhùr)

ü French Cluny (klünē'), German Lübeck (lü'bĕk), and similar sounds in some other languages

ũ French Melun (mùlũ'), Chambrun (shãbrũ'), and similar sounds in some other languages

v vest (vĕst), trivial (trĭ'vēùl)

w wax (wăks)

y you (yōō), bunion (bŭ'nyùn)

z zipper (zĭ'pùr), ease (ēz), treads (trĕdz)

zh pleasure (plĕ'zhùr), rouge (rōōzh)

' main accent, written after accented vowel or syllable: Nebraska (nùbră'skù), James Buchanan (jāmz' būkă'nùn)

" secondary accent: Mississippi (mĭ"sùsĭ'pē)

— dash, replacing obvious portion of pronunciation: hegemony (hĭjĕ'mùnē, hē–, hĕ'jùmō"nē, hĕ'gù–)

- hyphen, to prevent ambiguity: Erlanger (ûr'lăng-ùr), dishearten (dĭshär'tùn)

Cross References are indicated by SMALL CAPITALS

Brown, Moses, 1738–1836, American manufacturer and philanthropist, b. Providence, R.I. He was associated with his brothers John, Joseph, and Nicholas Brown in the family's mercantile activities before establishing (1790), with Samuel SLATER, the first water-powered cotton mill in America. The moving of Rhode Island College, later Brown Univ., from Warren to Providence in 1770 was largely due to his influence, and he contributed generously to the college. Moses Brown School in Providence, a leading preparatory institution for boys, was established (1819) by Quakers on land donated by him. See biography by M. E. Thompson (1962).

Brown, Nicholas, 1769–1841, American manufacturer and philanthropist, b. Providence, R.I., grad. Rhode Island College (renamed Brown Univ. in 1804 for him), 1786. He extended the internationally known mercantile business of his father, Nicholas Brown (1729–91). Later his own firm, Brown and Ives, came to control most of the water power on the Blackstone river, where his uncle, Moses Brown, and Samuel Slater had pioneered in the cotton textile industry. He was the treasurer (1796–1825) and long the benefactor of his alma mater. Butler Hospital (1847) was founded by his bequest for the care of the mentally ill.

Brown, Olympia, 1835–1926, American Universalist minister and woman-suffrage leader. b. Prairie Ronde, Mich., grad. Antioch College, 1860, and the theological school of St. Lawrence Univ., 1863. She was one of the first women in America to be ordained (1863) to the ministry. For 30 years she was president of the Wisconsin Woman's Suffrage

Olympia Brown

Association. In 1873 she married Henry Willis, but retained her own name.

Brown, Robert, 1773–1858, Scottish botanist and botanical explorer. In 1801 he went as naturalist on one of Matthew Flinders's expeditions to Australia, returning (1805) to England with valuable collections. In his *Prodromus florae Novae Hollandiae et Insulae Van Diemen* (1810) he described Australian flora. A leading botanist of his day, he served as librarian to the Linnaean Society and to Sir Joseph Banks and later as curator at the British Museum. He observed BROWNIAN MOVEMENT in 1827 and discovered the cell nucleus in 1831. His studies of several plant families and of pollen were also notable.

Robert Brown

Brown, Samuel Robbins, 1810–80, American missionary and educator, b. East Windsor, Conn., grad. Yale, 1832, and studied at Columbia (S.C.) Theological Seminary and at Union Theological Seminary. As missionary (1839–47) to China, he took charge of a school founded by the Morrison Educational Association. When he returned (1847) to the United States, three students accompanied him, the first Chinese to come to America to be educated. Brown had an important part in the founding of Elmira College. From 1859 to 1879 he was a missionary in Japan.

Brown, Thomas Edward, 1830–97, English poet. He wrote, in Manx dialect, a number of narrative and lyric poems, collected in the volumes *Fo'c'sle Yarns* (1881), *The Doctor and Other Poems* (1887), and *The Manx Witch and Other Poems* (1889).

Brown, Walter Folger, 1869–1961, American cabinet officer, b. Massillon, Ohio, grad. Harvard, 1892. A lawyer of Toledo, Ohio, he became prominent in Republican politics and was (1927–29) Assistant Secretary of Commerce. As Postmaster General (1929–33) under President Herbert Hoover, Brown secured a reduction of air-mail rates and a consolidation of air-mail routes—policies which aided the development of commercial aviation.

Brown, William, U.S. banker: see BROWN, family.

Brown, William Hill, 1765–93, American writer; son of a celebrated Boston clockmaker, Gawen Brown. He wrote poems, essays, two plays (one of them a historical tragedy, *West Point Preserved*), and a short novel, *Ira and Isabella*, but he is notable only as the probable author of the first American novel, *The Power of Sympathy* (1789). Because an episode in the book reflected a scandal which involved Perez Morton and his sister-in-law Frances Theodora Apthorp, the novel was long ascribed to Sarah Wentworth Morton, who was a neighbor of Brown. It had little circulation, and a well-authenticated story has it that the Mortons and Apthorps, with the author's consent, bought up the copies and suppressed the book. See Emily Pendleton and Milton Ellis, *Philenia: the Life and Works of Sarah Wentworth Morton* (1931).

brown coal: see LIGNITE.

Brown Deer, village (pop. 11,280), SE Wis., on the Milwaukee river N of Milwaukee; inc. 1955. Meters are manufactured.

Browne, Charles Farrar: see WARD, ARTEMUS.

Browne, Hablot Knight, pseud. **Phiz,** 1815–82, English illustrator. At 21 he was chosen by Charles Dickens to illustrate *Pickwick Papers.* His success was immediate, and in due course he illustrated many of Dickens's novels as well as works of Harrison Ainsworth and Charles Lever. Browne also contributed popular cartoons to *Punch.*

Browne, Robert, c.1550–1633, English clergyman and leader of a group of early separatists popularly known as Brownists. Browne conceived of the Church as a self-governing local body of experiential believers in Christ. Preaching without a license, Browne attacked the forms of government and the discipline of the Established Church; he gathered a congregation at Norwich c.1580. In 1581 he and his followers sought refuge in Holland. There he published (1582) several treatises that are generally regarded as the first expression of the principles of CONGREGATIONALISM. Circulation in England of these tracts was punishable by death. Upon his return to England in 1584, Browne was imprisoned and later was excommunicated. But by 1586 he was sufficiently reconciled with the Church to be made master of the Stamford grammar school, and in 1591 he submitted to episcopal ordination and became rector of Adchurch, Northamptonshire. See biographies by Champlin Burrage (1906) and F. J. Powicke (1910).

Browne, Sir Thomas, 1605–82, English author and physician, b. London, educated at Oxford and abroad, knighted (1671) by Charles II. His *Religio Medici,* in which Browne attempted to reconcile science and religion, was written about 1635. After circulating in manuscript, it was first published in a pirated edition (1642); an authorized edition followed (1643). Inspired by the discovery of funeral urns near Norwich, he wrote *Hydriotaphia: Urn Burial* (1658), a solemn reflection on death and immortality, in which he expressed a belief in the futility of things here on earth. Published with *Urn Burial* was the more optimistic *The Garden of Cyrus,* a work devoted to the mystic symbolism of the number five. Browne's philosophy is now primarily of historical interest. It is the quality of his faith and, particularly, his mode of expression that make him one of the outstanding figures in the history of English literature. His other notable works are *Pseudodoxia Epidemica* (1646), commonly known as *Vulgar Errors,* and *Christian Morals* (1716). See edition of his works (ed. by Geoffrey Keynes, 6 vols., 1928–31); biographies by Edmund Gosse (1905) and J. S. Finch (1950); studies by E. S. Merton (1949), W. P. Dunn (1950), and Joan Bennett (1962).

Browne, Thomas, d. 1825, Loyalist commander in the American Revolution. A resident of Augusta, Ga., he was the victim of patriot violence in 1775, when he was tarred and feathered for ridiculing the Continental Congress. Later he organized (1778) a Loyalist troop in Florida and raided settlements in S Georgia. In 1780 he captured Augusta; in 1781 he was forced to surrender to Andrew Pickens and Henry Lee. After his exchange he was a colonel in the Queen's Rangers in South Carolina and was defeated (May, 1782) by Anthony Wayne. Browne, who was fiercely hated by the patriots, escaped and lived out his life in the British West Indies.

Browne, Thomas Alexander, pseud. **Rolf Boldrewood,** 1826–1915, Australian author. A squatter, a magistrate, and a commissioner in the gold fields, he wrote many books of adventure, such as *Robbery under Arms* (1888).

Browne, William (William Browne of Tavistock) (tăv′ĭstŏk), 1591?–1645?, English poet. An imitator of Spenser, he did his finest work in pastoral poetry, of which *Britannia's Pastorals* (1613, 1616, 1825) and *The Shepherd's Pipe* (with George Wither and others, 1614) are the best examples.

Brownell, Herbert, Jr., 1904–, U.S. Attorney General (1953–57), b. Peru, Nebr., grad. Univ. of Nebraska, 1924, LL.B. Yale, 1927. Admitted to the bar in 1927, he practiced law in New York city and served in the New York state legislature (1933–37). He managed Thomas E. Dewey's campaigns for the governorship of New York in 1942 and for the presidency in 1944 and 1948. From 1944 to 1946 he was chairman of the Republican National Committee. In 1952 Brownell played an important part in securing the nomination and election of Dwight D. Eisenhower as President. Appointed to the cabinet as Attorney General, Brownell figured prominently in the Eisenhower administration's controversial loyalty-security program.

Brownfield, town (pop. 10,286), co. seat of Terry co., NW Texas, in the Llano Estacado SW of Lubbock; inc. 1926. The town's growth has been spurred by the oil industry, cattle raising, and plants processing chemicals and food.

brown hematite: see LIMONITE.

Brownian movement or **motion,** the zigzag, irregular motion exhibited by minute particles of solid matter when suspended in a fluid. It is named after the botanist Robert Brown who observed (1827) the movement of plant spores floating in water. The effect, being independent of all external factors, is ascribed to the thermal motion of the molecules of the fluid. These molecules are in constant irregular motion with a velocity proportional to the temperature. Small particles of matter suspended in the fluid are buffeted about by the molecules of the fluid. Brownian motion occurs for particles which are about 0.001 mm. in diameter; these are small enough to share in the thermal motion, yet large enough to be seen with a microscope. Jean Perrin made a quantitative study of the dependence of Brownian motion on temperature and particle size which is regarded as one of the most direct verifications of the kinetic molecular theory of matter.

brownie, in Celtic folklore, nocturnal creature associated with farmsteads. Although brownies were said to help with churning and other household labors, they were also known to haunt the countryside, particularly old dwellings.

Browning, Elizabeth Barrett, 1806–61, English poet; wife of Robert Browning. A delicate and precocious child, she spent a great part of her early life in a state of semi-invalidism. In 1838 the Barretts moved to 50 Wimpole St., London, where Robert

Browning carried on the ardent courtship with Elizabeth, which resulted in their marriage (1846) in defiance of her tyrannical father. They eloped to Italy, where most of their married life was spent and where their one son was born. Mrs. Browning threw herself into the cause of Italian liberation from Austria. "Casa Guidi," their home in Florence, is preserved as a memorial. Mrs. Browning's health improved in Italy, and her work as a poet gained in strength and significance. Her greatest poetry, *Sonnets from the Portuguese* (1850), was inspired by her own love story. *Casa Guidi Windows* (1851), on Italian liberty, and *Aurora Leigh* (1857), a novel in verse, followed. See *The Letters of Robert Browning and Elizabeth Barrett Browning, 1845–46* (1899); Rudolph Besier, *The Barretts of Wimpole Street* (1930), the most popular dramatization of the Brownings' love story; biographies by Dorothy Hewlett (1952) and G. B. Taplin (1957).

Elizabeth Barrett Browning

Robert Browning

Browning, John Moses, 1855–1926, American inventor, b. Ogden, Utah. His father was a gunsmith, and Browning at 13 invented his first gun in his father's shop. After obtaining a patent on a breech-loading rifle in 1879, he became a small-arms designer for the Winchester arms company. Later he worked for other manufacturers, notably the Colt firm, and still later was in an independent concern. He invented a repeating rifle (1884), a box-magazine rifle (1895), and his patents soon covered a wide field of repeating arms. He also invented the Browning automatic pistol, the Browning machine gun, and the Browning automatic rifle—all standard equipment of the U.S. army in the First World War. The Browning automatic rifle, also called the BAR, is still in use.

Browning, Orville Hickman, 1806–81, U.S. Secretary of the Interior (1866–69), b. Harrison co., Ky. One of the organizers of the Republican party in Illinois, Browning helped secure his friend Lincoln's nomination (1860) for President, but later, as U.S. Senator from Illinois (1861–63), he opposed Lincoln on the emancipation question. After Lincoln's death Browning supported Andrew Johnson's Reconstruction policy in opposition to the radical Republicans. He joined Johnson's cabinet in Sept., 1866, and was one of the President's closest friends and advisers during the impeachment struggle. His diary, edited by T. C. Pease and J. G. Randall (2 vols., 1927–33), is an important and detailed source for the Lincoln and Johnson administrations. See biography by M. G. Baxter (1957).

Browning, Robert, 1812–89, English poet. His remarkably broad and sound education was primarily the work of his artistic and scholarly parents—in particular his father, a London bank clerk of independent means. *Pauline,* his first poem, was published anonymously in 1833. In 1834 he visited Italy, which eventually became his second homeland. He won some recognition with *Paracelsus* (1835) and *Sordello* (1840). In 1837, urged by William Macready, the Shakespearean actor, Browning began writing for the stage. Although not especially successful, he wrote eight verse plays during the next nine years, two of which were produced—*Strafford* in 1837 and *A Blot in the 'Scutcheon* in 1843. The narrative poem *Pippa Passes* appeared in 1841; it and subsequent poems were later published collectively as *Bells and Pomegranates*

(1846). Included were "My Last Duchess" and "Soliloquy of the Spanish Cloister," both dramatic monologues; this form proved to be the ideal medium for Browning's poetic genius. Other notable poems of this kind are "Fra Lippo Lippi," "Andrea del Sarto," and "The Bishop Orders His Tomb." In 1846, after a romantic courtship, Browning secretly married the poet Elizabeth Barrett and took her to Italy, where they lived for 15 happy years. There he wrote *Christmas Eve and Easter Day* (1850) and *Men and Women* (1855). In 1861, after the death of his wife, he returned to England, where he wrote *Dramatis Personae* (1864). This was followed by what is considered his masterpiece, the murder story *The Ring and the Book* (4 vols., 1868–69). Set in 17th-century Italy, the poem reveals, through a series of dramatic dialogues, how a single event is perceived by different people. Browning gained recognition slowly, but after the publication of this work he was acclaimed a great poet. Societies were instituted for the study of his work in England and America. His later works include *Dramatic Idyls* (2 vols., 1879–80) and *Asolando* (1889). Browning's thought is persistently optimistic. His psychological portraits in verse, ironic and indirect in presentation, and his experiments in diction and rhythm have made him an important influence on 20th-century poetry. He was buried in Westminster Abbey. See variously published volumes of his letters; biographies by W. H. Griffin and H. C. Minchin (rev. ed., 1938) and Betty Miller (1952); studies by R. A. King (1957) and Park Honan (1961); bibliography by L. N. Broughton and others (1953).

Browning, town (pop. 2,011), NW Mont., NW of Great Falls, in a ranch and oil-field region; inc. 1919. Near GLACIER NATIONAL PARK, it is the headquarters and trade center for the Blackfeet Indian Reservation.

Brownists: see BROWNE, ROBERT.

Brownlee Park, uninc. town (pop. 3,307), S central Mich., a suburb E of Battle Creek.

Brownlow, William Gannaway (broun'lō), 1805–77, known as the "fighting parson," governor of Tennessee (1865–69), b. Wythe co., Va. He became an itinerant Methodist preacher, noted for his powers of vituperation and won a large following in E

Tennessee by his speeches on public questions. He edited the Jonesboro *Whig* for 10 years and after 1849 made the Knoxville *Whig* one of the most influential papers in the state. Though he did not oppose slavery, Brownlow strongly opposed secession and shared with Andrew Johnson, whom he despised, the Unionist leadership of E Tennessee. His paper continued to express views violently hostile to the Confederacy until Oct. 24, 1861, when it was suppressed. Brownlow fled to the mountains, but was taken, imprisoned for a month, and afterward kept under guard until March 3, 1862, when he was sent within Union lines. He then made an extensive and highly successful speaking tour of the North and also wrote his *Rise, Progress, and Decline of Secession* (1862), which contained a narrative of his experiences. Early in 1865, Tennessee having been completely conquered by Union forces, he was elected governor and instituted his own version of Reconstruction. He disfranchised and persecuted those who had served in the Confederate army, used the state guards against the Ku Klux Klan, and proclaimed martial law in the most turbulent areas. He was elected in 1867, and when his term ended, Tennessee was a broken, impoverished state. Many considered his governorship as destructive as the Civil War itself. He was a U.S. Senator from 1869 to 1875. See biography by E. M. Coulter (1937).

Brownsburg, town (pop. 4,478), central Ind., WNW of Indianapolis. It has a cannery.

Brown-Séquard, Charles Édouard (broun'-sākär', -sākwär'), 1817–94, physiologist, b. Mauritius, of French and American parents. He taught at Harvard (1864–68), practiced medicine in New York city (1873–78), and succeeded (1878) Claude Bernard at the Collège de France. He was known for his research on the functions of the sympathetic nervous system and the spinal cord; he also studied the physiological effects of the injection of genital gland extracts and of the application of heat to the cortex. His most important work was on internal secretions; he is considered a founder of endocrinology, especially organotherapy.

Brownson, Orestes Augustus, 1803–76, American author and clergyman, b. Stockbridge, Vt. Largely self-taught, he became a vigorous and influential writer on social and religious questions. He was a Presbyterian, but left that church to become first a Universalist and then a sort of free-lance minister, working for such socialistic schemes as the short-lived Workingmen's party. Later he was a Unitarian minister until in 1836 he started his own church, the Society for Christian Union and Progress. As founder and editor of the *Boston Quarterly Review* (1838–42) and as editor of the *Democratic Review* (1842–44), he condemned social inequalities. At this time he was one of the transcendentalists and was so interested in Brook Farm as to send his son there. He entered the Roman Catholic Church in 1844, and later, as editor of the new *Brownson's Quarterly Review,* he attacked non-Catholic beliefs. Among his books are *New Views of Christianity, Society, and the Church* (1836); two autobiographical novels, *Charles Elwood; or, The Infidel Converted* (1840) and *The Convert* (1857); *The American Republic* (1865). See biography by his son, Henry F. Brownson (3 vols., 1898–1900), who also edited his works (20 vols., 1882–87), and biographies by Arthur Schlesinger, Jr. (1939) and Theodore Maynard (1943); study by Lawrence Roemer (1953).

brownstone: see SANDSTONE.

Brownstown. 1 Town (pop. 2,158), co. seat of Jackson co., S Ind., SE of Bloomington; laid out 1816. It has canneries. A state forest is nearby. **2** Borough (pop. 1,379), SW Pa., just W of Johnstown.

Browns Valley, village (pop. 1,033), W Minn., on the S.Dak. line and NW of Ortonville; settled 1866. It is a farm trade center. A skeleton known as Browns Valley man was discovered nearby in 1934; its antiquity has been disputed.

Brownsville. 1 City, Fla.: see WEST PENSACOLA. **2** Borough (pop. 6,055), SW Pa., on the Monongahela and SSE of Pittsburgh; laid out 1785, inc. 1815. John A. Brashear and Philander C. Knox were born here. **3** City (pop. 5,424), co. seat of Haywood co., W Tenn., near the Hatchie river and W of Jackson, in a farm and timber area; settled c.1810, inc. 1870. The city has cotton gins and sawmills. **4** City (pop. 48,040), co. seat of Cameron co., extreme S Texas, on the Rio Grande and S of Corpus Christi. Here in 1846 Gen. Zachary Taylor founded Fort Taylor, which was besieged by Mexicans as the Mexican War began. He fought the battles of Palo Alto and Resaca de la Palma in coming to its relief, and he renamed (1846) it for its defender, Major Jacob Brown. Fort Brown was active until 1944, was held briefly by Union forces in the Civil War, and was prominent in the disturbances on the Mexican border. Brownsville, laid out in 1848 and incorporated in 1850, was a cattle-shipping point in the late 19th cent. Today it is one of the chief cities of the rich irrigated section of the lower Rio Grande valley and has many industries, especially those connected with oil and natural gas. The city is a port of entry across the river from Matamoros, Mexico. With the completion (1936) of a deepwater channel it became an important ocean port. A junior college is here. In 1906 a group of Negro soldiers stationed at Fort Brown entered Brownsville to avenge alleged abuses. They fired indiscriminately at townspeople and houses. When investigations failed to reveal the guilty parties involved, President Theodore Roosevelt issued a controversial directive ordering that 167 of the Negro soldiers stationed at the fort be dishonorably discharged.

brown Swiss cattle, one of the oldest breeds of cattle, originated in Switzerland and brought to the United States in 1869. Chiefly a dairy breed, they are large, thick-fleshed cattle and are also used for beef. They are light to dark brown.

brown thrush: see THRASHER.

Brown University, at Providence, R.I.; for men; chartered 1764 as Rhode Island College at Warren, opened 1765. It moved to Providence in 1770 and was renamed for Nicholas BROWN in 1804. Pembroke College, a separate though affiliated college for women, was established in 1891. The John Carter Brown Library (see BROWN, JOHN CARTER) is especially significant for its early Americana.

Brown vs. Board of Education of Topeka, Kansas: see INTEGRATION.

Brownville. 1 Town (pop. 1,641), central Maine, on both sides of Pleasant River and NNW of Bangor, between Sebec and Schoodic lakes; settled 1819, inc. 1824. Wood products are made. **2** Village (pop. 1,082), N central N.Y., on the Black River and WNW of Watertown; inc. 1828.

Brownwood. 1 City (pop. 16,974), co. seat of Brown co., central Texas, SE of Abilene; settled 1856, inc. 1876. A bustling industrial community, Brownwood has small factories, railroad shops, and plants processing pecans, peanuts, cotton, oil, and other products of the region. It has two coeducational colleges, Howard Payne (Baptist; 1889) and Daniel Baker (a branch of Southern Methodist Univ.). Nearby Lake Brownwood is a large reservoir used for irrigation as well as for fishing and boating. **2** Uninc. village (pop. 1,286), SE Texas, Orange co., NNW of Orange.

Bruant, Libéral (lēbāräl′ brüä′), c.1635–1697, best-known member of a French family of architects. He is said to have made the original plans for the Place Vendôme, Paris, which later was designed by J. H. Mansart. Among his works in Paris are the large asylum of La Salpêtrière and the Hôtel des Invalides, Louis XIV's vast project of a hospital for disabled soldiers. He also designed the Church of the Invalides, to which Mansart later added the Dôme des Invalides.

Brubeck, David W., 1920–, American pianist and composer, b. Concord, Calif. He began studying piano at the age of four, and later majored in music at the College of the Pacific. He studied composition with Darius Milhaud and Arnold Schoenberg, and in 1951 organized a modern jazz quartet. His music, influenced by modern classical composers, is distinguished by complex harmony and the use of meters not typical in jazz. He has made numerous foreign tours, and in 1959 his quartet joined the N.Y. Philharmonic-Symphony Orchestra for the premier of *Dialogue for Jazz Combo and Symphony,* composed by his brother, Howard Brubeck.

Bruce, celebrated Scottish family descended from an 11th-century Norman duke, Robert de Brus. He aided William I in his conquest of England and was given lands in England. His son was granted fiefs in Scotland, and accordingly the family rendered homage in both kingdoms. In the Scottish dynastic struggle which followed the death of Margaret Maid of Norway in 1290, the Bruces claimed succession to the throne as a result of the marriage of the 5th Robert the Bruce to Isobel, who was the daughter of David, earl of Huntingdon, brother of William the Lion of Scotland. In 1290 the son of that marriage, Robert the Bruce, was a claimant to the throne, rivaled by John de Baliol, a great-grandson of David of Huntingdon through an older daughter. A grandson of this Robert was the famous Robert Bruce or Robert the Bruce— Robert I of Scotland. The brother of Robert I, Edward Bruce, was crowned king of Ireland in 1316, but was killed in 1318. The young son of Robert I succeeded his father as David II and was in turn succeeded by his nephew, Robert II, son of Robert I's daughter Marjory and the first king of Scotland of the Stuart family.

Bruce, Charles Granville, 1866–1939, British mountaineer, b. Wales. As a British army officer he had a distinguished record in N India and was widely respected by the natives, some of whom he commanded during the First World War. He led the Mt. Everest expeditions of 1922 and 1924.

Bruce, Sir David, 1855–1931, British bacteriologist, b. Melbourne, Australia. He discovered the bacterium of Malta fever (1887) and the cause and mode of transmission of nagana (a disease of horses and cattle) and of African sleeping sickness (with David N. Nabarro and Sir Aldo Castellani). He was head of the Royal Society's commission to study sleeping sickness in Uganda (1903, 1908–10) and Malta fever in Malta (1904–6).

Bruce, Edward, d. 1318, Scottish king of Ireland, brother of Robert I of Scotland. He aided his brother in subduing Scotland and in 1315 was declared heir to Robert's throne. With Robert's approval he then invaded Ulster, to which he had some hereditary claim. He was crowned king of Ireland in 1316 and found many Irish allies against the Anglo-Irish rulers, but he failed to consolidate his gains, even when Robert joined him in 1317. Edward was killed in battle in 1318.

Bruce, James, 1730–94, Scottish explorer in Africa. He examined Roman ruins in North Africa (1755) from Tunis to Tripoli and visited Crete, Rhodes, and Asia Minor. In 1768 he traveled down the Red Sea as far as the straits of Bab el Mandeb. From Massawa he struck inland for Gondar, then the capital of Ethiopia. He rediscovered (1770) the source of the Blue Nile, which he followed (1771) to its confluence with the White Nile. He wrote *Travels to Discover the Source of the Nile, 1768–73* (3d ed., 1813). For his travels in Barbary, see R. L. Playfair, *Travels in the Footsteps of Bruce* (1877).

Bruce, James, 8th **earl of Elgin:** see Elgin, James Bruce, 8th earl of.

Bruce, Stanley Melbourne (měl′bùrn), 1883–, Australian statesman. Educated at Cambridge Univ., he was called to the bar (1906) in England, then returned to Australia to become a Melbourne businessman. After service in the First World War, he entered the commonwealth legislature in 1918, was treasurer (1921–23) in the cabinet of W. M. Hughes, and served (1923–29) as prime minister. He was notable for promoting the closest relations of Australia with the empire compatible with Australian self-government, and he also advocated international cooperation. Bruce was (1921, 1932–38) Australian delegate to the League of Nations and in 1936 president of the council. From 1933 to 1945 he was high commissioner for Australia in London. In 1947 he was made Viscount Bruce of Melbourne.

Bruce, Thomas, 7th **earl of Elgin:** see Elgin, Thomas Bruce, 7th earl of.

Bruce, Victor Alexander, 9th **earl of Elgin:** see Elgin, Victor Alexander Bruce, 9th earl of.

Bruce, William Speirs, 1867–1921, Scottish explorer and authority on the polar regions. He first went to the Antarctic as ship's surgeon in 1892 and later did survey work in Franz Josef Land and oceanographical work in the Arctic Ocean. He led (1902–4) the Scottish National Antarctic Expedition in the *Scotia,* performing much valuable scientific research in the Weddell Sea and discovering Coats

Land. He established a meteorological station on Laurie Island (in the South Orkney group). He edited the reports of the expedition (6 vols.) and wrote *Polar Exploration* (1911). Bruce made a number of voyages to Spitsbergen and became an authority on the islands. See R. N. Rudmose Brown, *A Naturalist at the Poles* (1923).

Bruce, lumber town (pop. 1,698), N central Miss., on the Skuna and SSE of Oxford; inc. 1927.

brucellosis: see CONTAGIOUS ABORTION and UNDULANT FEVER.

Bruce of Melbourne, Stanley Melbourne Bruce, Viscount: see BRUCE, STANLEY MELBOURNE.

Bruceton, town (pop. 1,158), NW Tenn., on the Big Sandy River NE of Jackson; settled 1920, inc. 1925.

Bruch, Max (mäks' brōōkh'), 1838–1920, German composer. He conducted the Liverpool Philharmonic Orchestra (1880–83) and taught at the Berlin Hochschule (1892–1910). His Violin Concerto in G Minor (1868) and his variations on the *Kol Nidre* (1881) for cello and orchestra are his best-known compositions.

brucine: see NUX VOMICA.

Bruck an der Mur (brŏŏk' än dĕr mōōr'), city (estimated pop. 16,101), in Styria, E central Austria, at the confluence of the Mur and Mürz rivers. It has a metallurgical industry and paper mills. There is a 15th-century Gothic church.

Brücke [Ger.,=bridge] German expressionist art movement, lasting from 1905 to 1914. Influenced by the art of *Jugendstil*, Van Gogh, and the primitive sculpture of Africa and the South Seas, the *Brücke* group developed an art of fervent emotionalism. Founded in Dresden by Kirchner, Schmidt-Rottluff, and Heckel, the group invited Nolde and Pechstein to join the following year and Otto Mueller in 1910. They lived and worked communally, periodically issuing portfolios of their graphic art, which at first bore a rather communal style. By 1911 most of them had gone to Berlin. In their exhibitions they displayed brutally deformed, boldly colored portraits, landscapes, and city themes. Like their French fauvist contemporaries, the art of the *Brücke* expressionists was intense and violent but more inclined toward primitivistic and demonic qualities, symbolism, and introspection.

Max Bruch

Anton Bruckner

Bruckner, Anton (än'tŏn brŏŏk'nŭr), 1824–96, Austrian composer. Early orphaned, he taught himself to play the organ so well that in 1856 he was appointed organist at the Linz cathedral. He became court organist in Vienna in 1867, and later he taught at the Vienna Conservatory and at the university there. He established a reputation as a virtuoso organist on trips to France in 1869 and to England in 1871. As a composer he was influenced by the chromatic harmony and orchestral size of Wagner's music, while his contrapuntal complexity and extended melodies are in the formal tradition of Beethoven and Schubert. His outstanding works are the Masses in D Minor (1864), in E Minor (1866), and F Minor (1867–71); a *Te Deum* (1881–84); and nine symphonies, of which the Fourth or Romantic (1874), the Eighth, or Apocalyptic (1884–87), and the Ninth (1895–96) are best known. He also wrote motets, cantatas, chamber music, piano and organ pieces, and pieces for male chorus. See the studies by Dika Newlin (1947), H. F. Redlich (1955), and Erwin Doernberg (1960).

Brudenell, James Thomas: see CARDIGAN, JAMES THOMAS BRUDENELL, 7TH EARL OF.

Bruegel, Brueghel, or **Breughel** (all: brû'gŭl), famous family of Flemish genre and landscape painters. The foremost, **Pieter Bruegel** (pē'tŭr),

Mountain Landscape by Ernst Ludwig Kirchner, one of the members of the Brücke group.

The Shepherd *(detail from a painting by Pieter Bruegel the elder).*

The Holy Family *by Jan Bruegel.*

the elder, c.1525–1569, called Peasant Bruegel, studied in Antwerp with his future father-in-law, Pieter Coeck van Aelst, but was influenced primarily by Bosch. In 1551 he became a member of the Antwerp Guild. Bruegel visited Italy in the early 1550s. However, he did not imitate the greatest Italians. Instead, he remained closer to the Flemish tradition and employed his native powers of minute observation in depicting the whole living world of field and forest and the sturdy race of peasants at work and play therein. Far from being the jolly peasant of popular legend, he was a learned city-dweller and friend of humanists. His pictures of genre subjects may have allegorical or moralizing significance. In his tremendous range of invention, Bruegel approached Bosch in his creation of nightmarish phantasmagorias in such works as *The Fall of the Rebel Angels* (Brussels). He painted the more cheerful, acutely perceived scenes of daily life, e.g., *Peasant Wedding* (Vienna), for which he is best known. The *Fall of Icarus* (versions in Brussels and New York) is his only mythological subject. He painted religious histories— *Numbering at Bethlehem* (Brussels), *Way to Calvary* (Vienna), with figures clothed in contemporary Flemish dress; parables— *The Sower* (Antwerp), *The Blind Leading the Blind* (Naples); genre scenes— *Children's Games, Peasant Dance* (both: Vienna); and landscapes showing the activities of the months—(several in Vienna, *Harvesters* in the Metropolitan Mus.); and other works. A skilled draughtsman and etcher, Bruegel uses a delicate line to define his figures. His people are stubby in proportion, but lively and solid, although he does not emphasize modeling. His color is remarkably sensitive, as is his feeling for landscape. His compositions are often based on diagonal lines, creating gentle rhythms and allowing planes of landscape to unfold into the distance. See studies by F. Grossmann (1957) and Ludwig Münz (Eng. tr., 1961). His son, **Pieter Bruegel** the younger, 1564–1637, often copied his father's works. Two of his paintings are in the Metropolitan Museum. His brother, **Jan Bruegel** (yän), called Velvet Bruegel, 1568–1625, was a better painter who specialized in still life, rendered with extreme smoothness and finesse. He was a friend of Rubens, and occasionally supplied floral ornament for works from Rubens's shop. He was also adept at landscape. Representative works are in Brussels and Berlin.

Bruges (br\=oozh, br\=oo′jĭz, Fr. brÜzh), Flemish *Brugge* (brÜ′gù), city (estimated pop. 52,465), capital of West Flanders prov., NW Belgium. It is connected by canal with ZEEBRUGGE, its outer port. Once the greatest and busiest port of N Europe, it is now a manufacturing center producing lace, railroad cars, textiles, and communications equipment; a tourist center, famed for its medieval architecture; and a market town. It was founded on an inlet of the North Sea in the 9th cent. and became (11th cent.) a center of trade with England. In the 13th cent. it flourished as the major entrepôt port of the HANSEATIC LEAGUE and as one of the chief wool-manufacturing centers of Flanders. New ports were founded to accommodate increasing trade, notably SLUIS. At its zenith (14th cent.), Bruges was one of the great commercial hubs of

The market hall of Bruges, with its famous carillon.

Europe. An early COMMUNE of the Low Countries, the city held extensive political privileges and often played a part in the chronic struggle among England, France, and the counts of Flanders. Its government, first in patrician hands, gradually passed to the trade guilds of the wool industry. When Philip IV of France annexed Flanders in 1301, Bruges led the rebellion against him. The French garrison was massacred (1302), and shortly afterward the citizen-army of Bruges led to victory in the BATTLE OF THE SPURS. Despite frequent political disturbances Bruges continued to prosper until foreign competition caused the decline of the Flemish wool industry in the early 15th cent. When the North Sea inlet silted up, Bruges lost its access to the sea and to its outer ports. By the beginning of the 16th cent. Antwerp had replaced Bruges as the major entrepôt port. Commercial and industrial revival began with extensive harbor repairs (begun 1895) and the opening of the Zeebrugge canal. Bruges became the cradle of FLEMISH ART during the rule (14th–15th cent.) of the Burgundian dukes in Flanders. The Hospital of St. John (12th cent.) contains several masterpieces by Hans Memling. Jan van Eyck, Gerard David, and many other masters are richly represented in the churches, public buildings, and several small museums of the city. Among its noted buildings are the 13th-century market hall or cloth hall, with its famous carillon; the town hall (14th cent.); the Church of Notre Dame (12th–13th cent.), with the tombs of Charles the Bold and Mary of Burgundy and with Michaelangelo's *Virgin;* the Cathedral of Saint-Sauveur (begun 10th cent.); and the Chapel of the

Precious Blood (begun 12th cent.), a major place of pilgrimage.

Brugmann, Karl (kärl′ brŏŏk′män), 1849–1919, German philologist. A professor at Leipzig, he was one of the school holding that scientific rules of linguistics do not admit of exceptions. With the help of others, notably Hermann Osthoff, Wilhelm Scherer, and Berthold Delbrück, he did much work in Indo-European linguistics and issued a large comparative grammar of Indo-European languages, which is still a standard reference.

Brugsch, Heinrich Karl (hĭn′rĭkh kärl brŏŏksh), 1827–94, German philologist. An Egyptologist, he deciphered the demotic and compiled a demotic-hieroglyphic dictionary.

Brühl, Heinrich, Graf von (hĭn′rĭkh gräf′ fŭn brül′), 1700–1763, Saxon statesman. He was adviser to Augustus II, king of Poland and elector of Saxony, and gained control of both governments after the accession (1733) of AUGUSTUS III. Brühl advanced the economic and cultural development of Saxony but did not succeed in making the Polish crown hereditary with the Saxon rulers. An able diplomat, he neglected Saxon military potential and sought powerful allies. When Frederick II of Prussia made (1756) a surprise attack on Saxony, Brühl fled with his king to Poland. There he remained through the Seven Years War, while Frederick exploited Saxony. Charges that Brühl amassed his fortune through fraud have not been proved.

Brulé, Étienne (ātyĕn′ brülā′), c.1592–1632, French explorer in North America. He arrived (1608) in the New World with Samuel de Champlain, who sent him in 1610 into the wilderness to learn about the Indians and the land. He lived with the Huron Indians and c.1612 accompanied a group of them to Georgian Bay of Lake Huron. In 1612 he guided Champlain to that lake, and on the return journey they were (so far as is known) the first white men to see Lake Ontario. Brulé was then sent to the headwaters of the Susquehanna and followed that river to Chesapeake Bay. On his way back he was captured by the Iroquois and tortured, but escaped (1618). He once more lived with the Huron, making many explorations of which no definite record remains. He probably visited Lake Superior and thus saw all the Great Lakes except Lake Michigan—the first white man to do so. In 1629 he piloted the English vessels that captured Quebec and his old commander, Champlain. Then he retired to live an increasingly dissolute life among the Huron. He was killed in an Indian quarrel, and his remains were eaten. See C. W. Butterfield, *History of Brulé's Discoveries and Explorations, 1610–1626* (1898).

Brumaire (brümâr′), second month of the FRENCH REVOLUTIONARY CALENDAR. The coup d'état of 18 (actually 18–19) Brumaire (Nov. 9–10, 1799), engineered chiefly by Sieyès, overthrew the DIRECTORY and established the CONSULATE under Napoleon. It nearly failed because of Napoleon's inept conduct at the Council of Five Hundred, but the situation was saved by his brother Lucien BONAPARTE.

Brummell, George Bryan (brŭ′mŭl), 1778–1840, Englishman of wealth, called Beau Brummell. After a brief career at Oxford and in the army, he became known as a man of fashion especially notable for the exquisite finery of his clothes. He was the intimate of the prince regent (later George IV). Reckless gambling and heavy debt caused his flight to Calais. and there he struggled on for 14 years. He then held (1830–32) a sinécure consulate at Caen. He died in a hospital for the insane. *Male and Female Costume* is a treatise on dress supposedly written by him (ed. by Eleanor Parker, 1932). See biographies by Willard Connely (1940) and C. M. Franzero (1958).

Brunanburh, battle of (brŏŏ′nŭnbûrg), A.D. 937, won by ATHELSTAN, king of the English, over a combination of Irish, Scots, and Strathclyde Britons. The site is on the west coast of England, between Chester and Dumfries. A poem in the *Anglo-Saxon Chronicle* celebrating the battle has been often translated. See edition by Alistair Campbell (1938).

Brundidge (brŭn′dĭj), town (pop. 2,523), SE Ala., SE of Montgomery near Troy; settled c.1810. It is a trade center for a peanut and timber area.

Brundisium: see BRINDISI.

Brunehaut: see BRUNHILDA.

Brunei (brŏŏnī′), sultanate (c.2,225 sq. mi.; pop. 83,869), NW Borneo, under British protection since 1888. Its two parts are both enclosed by SARAWAK. The capital and major port, also called Brunei (pop. c.16,000), lies on the Brunei and

Brunei location map

Bantu rivers. The modern section of the town is dominated by a mosque (1958), while the older part consists almost entirely of houses built on piles. Oil and natural gas are Brunei's major exports. Rubber, coconut, sago, and rice are grown. The Dyaks are the chief native people, Malay the main language, and Islam the dominant religion. After changing hands several times, Brunei by the early 19th cent. was a haven for pirates and a center of the slave trade. In 1888 the British established a protectorate over Brunei. An association of Brunei, North Borneo, and Sarawak, presided over by the British commissioner for Singapore and SE Asia, was set up in 1953. In 1959 Brunei received its first constitution. The sultan, Sir Omar Ali Saifuddin, was given additional powers in local administration, while the British retained control of defense and foreign affairs. In July, 1962, Brunei accepted membership in the proposed Federation of Malaysia. A revolt against the federation was put down by the British late in 1962.

Brunel, Sir Marc Isambard (brŏŏnĕl′), 1769–1849,

BRUNELLESCHI, FILIPPO

Saint Bruno, founder of the Carthusians (painting by Francisco Ribalta).

Filippo Brunellescni's dome on the cathedral of Florence.

English engineer and inventor. Born in France, he was a royalist refugee to America in 1793. He became chief engineer of New York city, built the old Bowery theater (burned in 1821), constructed a canal between Lake Champlain and the Hudson, and carried out other projects. In 1799 he went to England, where he patented machinery for making ships' blocks. He invented many other mechanical labor-saving devices. In 1825 he began the construction of the Thames Tunnel (the first in which a shield was used; see TUNNEL). In 1841 he was knighted. See Richard Beamish, *Memoirs of Sir Marc Isambard Brunel* (1862). In the work on the tunnel Sir Marc was assisted by his son, **Isambard Kingdom Brunel**, 1806–59, English civil engineer and an authority on railway traction and steam navigation. He was engineer of the Great Western Railway, building bridges and docks. Later he constructed railways in Italy and was a consulting engineer in Australia and India. He is best known, however, for his designing and construction of the three ocean steamships, the *Great Western* (1838), which was the first transatlantic steam vessel, the *Great Britain* (1845), the first ocean screw steamship, and the *Great Eastern* (1858), the largest steam vessel of its time. See biography by his son (1870); Celia Brunel Noble, *The Brunels: Father and Son* (1938).

Brunelleschi, Filippo (fēlēp'pō brōōnĕl-lĕs'kē), 1377–1446, the first great architect of the Italian Renaissance, a Florentine by birth. Trained as sculptor and goldsmith, he designed a trial panel, *The Sacrifice of Isaac* (1401; Bargello, Florence) for the bronze doors of the Florence baptistery. The commission, however, was won by Lorenzo GHIBERTI. Thereafter, Brunelleschi became more interested in architectural planning. He made several trips to Rome, where he devoted himself to the study of classical buildings. About 1420 he drew two panels in perspective (now lost) which had important consequences for both architectural and art theory. The Church of San Lorenzo, Florence, reveals his systematic use of perspective in the careful proportioning of the interior structure and in the articulation of spatial volumes. In the Ospedale degli Innocenti (foundling hospital; 1419–45), Brunelleschi introduced a motif that was widely imitated during the Renaissance—a series of arches supported on columns. In 1420 he began to build the dome for the cathedral in Florence. This octagonal ribbed dome is one of the most celebrated and original domical constructions in architectural history. Brunelleschi's other works include the churches of Santa Maria degli Angeli and Santo Spirito and the Pazzi Chapel, all in Florence. His designs exhibit beauty of detail and elegance, as well as mastery of construction.

Brunet, Jacques Charles (zhäk' shärl' brünä'), 1780–1867, French bibliographer. His bibliographical dictionary, *Manuel du libraire et de l'amateur de livres* (1810; 5th ed., 1860–65), is a standard work.

Brunetière, Ferdinand (fĕrdēnă' brünütyĕr'), 1849–1906, French literary critic. An opponent of naturalism, he believed that laws of evolution applied to literary forms as well as to species. His vast learning is evident in the masterly *Manuel de l'histoire de la littérature française* (1897) and in the history of French literature from 1515, most of which was published (1904–17) posthumously from notes. See study by Elton Hocking (1936).

Brunhild (brōōn'hĭld), **Brünnehilde** (brün"ühĭl' dů), or **Brynhild** (brĭn'hĭld), mighty female warrior of Germanic mythology and literature. In the NIBELUNGENLIED she is the warlike queen of Iceland, whom SIEGFRIED defeats in combat and wins for his brother-in-law, Gunther. Hating Siegfried, Brunhild contrives his death at the hands of Hagen. In the Icelandic version of the story, the VOLSUNGASAGA, as Brynhild, she is the chief of the Valkyries. Sigurd (Siegfried) saves her from an enchanted stronghold, and the two fall in love. Gudrun, however, makes him forget Brynhild by means of a magic potion and takes him as her husband; Sigurd then wins Brynhild for Gunnar (Gunther). After bringing about Sigurd's death, Brynhild destroys herself on his funeral pyre. Wagner in his opera cycle *The Ring of the Nibelungs*, in which she is Brünnehilde, makes her a Valkyrie who defies her father, the god Wotan (see WODEN), to help the lovers Siegmund and Sieglinde. Wotan places her sleeping on a fire-surrounded mountain-top, from which she is rescued by Siegfried. He is made by magic to forget her, and for his unfaithfulness she brings about his death, her own death on his pyre, and the burning of Valhalla.

Brunhilda (brŭnhĭl'dů) or **Brunehaut** (brünō'), 534?–613, Frankish queen, wife of SIGEBERT I of Austrasia; daughter of Athanagild, the Visigothic king of Spain. She was a chief participant in the bloody war (561–613) against Neustria that followed the murder of her sister Galswintha—wife of Sigebert's brother Chilperic I of Neustria—and Chilperic's marriage to his mistress FREDEGUNDE. The struggle continued between Brunhilda and Fredegunde after the death of Sigebert and the murder of Chilperic. Throughout the reigns of her son, Childebert II, and of two grandsons, Brunhilda was the actual ruler of Austrasia and, later, of Burgundy, when by her design that country was united with Austrasia after the death (592) of King GUNTRAM. She was endowed with the gifts of a great statesman, but her unscrupulousness in the execution of her plans earned her the fierce hatred of the nobles, whom she nonetheless controlled. She was finally betrayed by them to Fredegunde's son, CLOTAIRE II of Neustria. He put her to a horrible death.

Brünig Pass (brü'nĭkh), 3,396 ft. high, ancient route between the Forest Cantons and the Bernese Alps, central Switzerland. It is crossed by a highway and a railroad.

Brüning, Heinrich (hĭn'rĭkh brü'nĭng), 1885–, German statesman. A leader of the Catholic Center party, he was appointed (1930) chancellor of the Reich to put German finances in order. The Reichstag, which soon failed to support him, was dissolved (1930), and new elections were ordered. The new Reichstag was equally unable to produce a working majority, but Brüning continued to govern by decree. His drastic deflationary measures were very unpopular. In 1932 Brüning dissolved Hitler's militia. Shortly afterward he was abruptly dismissed by President Hindenburg, who appointed Franz von Papen as the new chancellor. Brüning left Germany in 1934 and from 1937 to 1952 was a professor of political science at Harvard. In 1952 he resumed residence in Germany and became a professor at the Univ. of Cologne.

Brünn: see BRNO.

Brünnehilde: see BRUNHILD.

Brunner, Arnold William, 1857–1925, American architect and expert on city planning, grad. Massachusetts Institute of Technology. He practiced in New York. The Pennsylvania capitol building and grounds in Harrisburg, the Cleveland Civic Center, and the Albany water front were his chief achievements in group planning.

Brunner, Emil (ā'mēl brōōn'ůr), 1889–, Swiss Protestant theologian. The clearest and most systematic thinker of the school of dialectical theology, he was a professor of theology at the Univ. of Zurich (1924–53) and Christian Univ., Tokyo, Japan (1953–55). In 1938–39 and again in 1946, 1947, and 1948 he visited and lectured in the United States. Like Karl BARTH he challenged the leaders of modern rational and liberal Christian theology and proclaimed a theology of revelation. The Christian faith, he maintained, arises from the encounter between man and God as He is revealed in the Bible. Brunner, in attempting later to leave a place for natural theology in his system, came into conflict with Barth over the question of natural revelation—Brunner refusing to separate theology completely from the general consciousness of man. His more important works include *Die Mystik und das Wort* (1924), *Der Mittler* (1927; Eng. tr., *The Mediator*, 1934), *Das Gebot und die Ordnungen* (1932; Eng. tr., *The Divine Imperative*, 1937), *Der Mensch in Widerspruch* (1937; Eng. tr., *Man in Revolt*, 1939), and *Wahrheit als Begegnung* (1938; Eng. tr., *The Divine-Human Encounter*, 1943). See Cornelius Van Til, *The New Modernism* (1946); P. K. Jewett, *Emil Brunner's Concept of Revelation* (1954).

Bruno, Saint (Saint Bruno the Great), d. 965, German churchman and statesman; brother of Emperor Otto I. He was made (953) archbishop of Cologne and in the same year became duke of LOTHARINGIA. He held much power both ecclesiastic and secular and, as chancellor (940–53) and as archchancellor (951–65), was his brother's chief adviser. He organized the civil service, led the revival of learning, and reformed the monasteries according to the pattern laid down by the Cluniac reform. Feast: Oct. 11.

Bruno, Saint (d. 1009): see BONIFACE, SAINT.

Bruno, Saint, c.1030–1101, German monk, founder of the CARTHUSIANS, b. Cologne. He studied and taught at Rheims. In 1084 he took six companions and founded a little monastery in the Alps, which became the mother house of the Carthusian order (see CHARTREUSE, GRANDE). In 1090 Urban II, whom Bruno had taught, called him to Rome as a counselor. He died in Italy in retirement at a monastery he had founded. Feast: Oct. 6.

Bruno, Giordano (jŏrdä'nō brōō'nō), 1548–1600,

Italian philosopher, b. Nola. He entered the Dominican order in his early youth but was accused of heresy and fled (c.1576) to take up a career of study and travel. He taught briefly at Toulouse, Paris, Oxford, and Wittenberg, but, personally restless and in constant opposition to the traditional schools, he found no permanent post. His major metaphysical works, *De la causa, principio, et uno* (Eng. tr., *The Infinite in Giordano Bruno*, 1950) and *De l'infinito, universo et mondi* (both 1584), were published in France. Further works appeared in England and Germany. A man of considerable talent, Bruno also wrote satire and poetry. In 1591 he returned to Venice, where he was tried for heresy by the Inquisition. After imprisonment at Rome, he was burned to death. Bruno challenged all dogmatism, including that of the Copernican cosmology whose main tenets, however, he upheld. He believed that our perception of the world is relative to the position in space and time from which we view it and that there are as many possible modes of viewing the world as there are possible positions. Therefore we cannot postulate absolute truth or any limit to the progress of knowledge. He pictured the world as composed of individual elements of being, governed by fixed laws of relationship. These elements, called monads, were ultimate and irreducible and were based on a pantheistic infinite principle, or cause, or Deity, manifest in us and in all the world. He was the first to state what has now become the cosmic theory. Bruno's influence on later philosophy, especially that of Spinoza and Leibniz, was profound. See I. L. Horowitz, *The Renaissance Philosophy of Giordano Bruno* (1952).

Bruno the Great, Saint: see BRUNO, SAINT (d. 965).

Brunschvicg, Léon (lãõ′ brün′shvĕk), 1869–1944, French philosopher, b. Paris. From 1909 until his death he taught at the Sorbonne. Brunschvicg's philosophy, which has had considerable influence on modern European thought, is usually called critical idealism. He extended the teachings of Kant and Hegel and also drew upon Plato, Descartes, Spinoza, and Pascal. He regarded mathematics as the highest level yet reached by human thought, and maintained that judgment preceded all other activities of the mind. For Brunschvicg, God was whatever enables us to live the life of the spirit. His principal works are *La Modalité du jugement* (1897); *Les Étapes de la philosophie mathématique* (1912); *Le Progrès de la conscience dans la philosophie occidentale* (2 vols., 1927); and *La Raison et la religion* (1939).

Brunswick, dukes of: see CHARLES WILLIAM FERDINAND; FERDINAND; FREDERICK WILLIAM.

Brunswick (brŭnz′wĭk), Ger. *Braunschweig* (broun′-shvĭk), former state, N central Germany, surrounded by the former Prussian provinces of Saxony, Hanover, and Westphalia. In 1946 it was included (except for several small territories placed in SAXONY-ANHALT) in the state of LOWER SAXONY. Brunswick (the former capital), Goslar, Helmstedt, and Wolfenbüttel were the chief towns. The region of Brunswick is situated on the North German plain and in the northern foothills of the Harz, where silver, copper, lead, and iron are mined. The land is drained by the Leine and Oker rivers. Grain, sugar beets, and potatoes are the main crops. The duchy of Brunswick emerged from the remnants of the domains of Henry the Lion, to whom Emperor Frederick I left only the territories of Brunswick and Lüneburg (roughly modern Brunswick and Hanover). The Guelphic house repeatedly divided into several branches, the main ones being Brunswick-Wolfenbüttel and Brunswick-Lüneburg. In 1692 the duke of Brunswick-Lüneburg became elector of HANOVER. The Brunswick-Wolfenbüttel line (itself a cadet branch of the Lüneburg line since 1634) ruled over Brunswick and had, among its dukes, the famous generals Charles William Ferdinand and Frederick William. Frederick William recovered (1813) the duchy, which Napoleon I had incorporated (1807) in the kingdom of Westphalia. The line became extinct in 1884, and Brunswick was ruled by regents until 1913, when Ernest Augustus, grandson of King George V of Hanover, was made duke. A member of the North German Confederation after 1866 and of the German Empire after 1871, Brunswick became a republic in 1918 and then joined the Weimar Republic.

Brunswick, Ger. *Braunschweig*, city (pop. 240,431), Federal Republic of Germany, in Lower Saxony, N central Germany, on the Oker. Formerly the capital of the state of Brunswick, it is now an active trade and industrial center with iron, steel, food, and brewery plants. It manufactures pianos. Chartered (12th cent.) by Henry the Lion, it became (14th cent.) an important member of the

Brunswick's famous Till Eulenspiegel fountain.

Hanseatic League. In 1753 the residence of the dukes of Brunswick was shifted here from Wolfenbüttel. The moated old city, with its historic buildings, suffered heavy damage in the Second World War. A 12th-century cathedral (containing the tomb of Henry the Lion), several Romanesque-Gothic churches, and the famous fountain (built

1408) representing Till Eulenspiegel are found
here. The art museum has a fine collection of
paintings. Lessing is buried in Brunswick.

Brunswick. 1 City (pop. 21,703), co. seat of Glynn
co., SE Ga., on the Atlantic coast SSW of Savannah; inc. 1856. Founded in 1771–72, it was named
for George III of the house of Brunswick. The city
is a port of entry, and its sheltered harbor is used by
coastal freighters and a shrimping fleet; naval
stores, lumber and lumber products, canned
shrimp, fertilizer, chemicals, and cotton are exported. Brunswick and the coastal islands offshore (see SEA ISLANDS) are popular resorts. A
large U.S. naval training station for radar operators
is nearby. **2** Town (pop. 15,797), S Maine, on the
Androscoggin and W of Bath, in a resort area.
Settled as a trading post in 1628, it was attacked by
the Indians several times, and Fort Andros (1688;
destroyed by Indians a few years later) and Fort
George (1715; dismantled in 1737) were built for
protection. The town was incorporated in 1738.
Brunswick is the seat of BOWDOIN COLLEGE and a
U.S. naval air station. Shoes, clothing, and
brushes are made. It was here that Harriet Beecher
Stowe wrote *Uncle Tom's Cabin* and that Haw-
thorne's first novel, *Fanshawe* (1828), was printed.
A house that dates from 1808 was once the home of
Longfellow. **3** Town (pop. 3,555), NW Md., on the
Potomac and SW of Frederick; laid out 1780, inc.
1890. It is a railroad center in a farm region. **4** City
(pop. 1,493), N central Mo., on the Grand River
near the Missouri and W of Moberly, in a livestock
and grain area. It was laid out c.1837 on the
Missouri river, which later changed its course.
Pecans are grown here. Nearby is the site of Fort
Orleans, established by the French in 1723. **5** Vil-
lage (pop. 11,725), N Ohio, a suburb SSW of
Cleveland; inc. 1960.

Brusa: see BURSA.

Brush, George de Forest, 1855–1941, American
painter, b. Shelbyville, Tenn., studied at the National Academy of Design and with Gérôme in
Paris. His early, scrupulously realistic paintings of
Indians gave way, in later work, to Italianate figure
compositions. Examples of his work are *Mother
and Child* (Mus. of Fine Arts, Boston), and *Mother
and Child* (Corcoran Gall.)

Brush, shipping town (pop. 3,621), NE Colo., on
Beaver Creek near the South Platte and NE of
Denver, in a farm area; inc. 1884. Milk and sugar
beets are processed.

Brusilov, Aleksey Alekseyevich (ŭlyĭksyā′ ŭlyĭksyā′-
ĭvĭch brōōsē′lŭf), 1853–1926, Russian general. As a
commander in the First World War, he won victories in Galicia. In 1916 the "Brusilov offensive,"
successful at first, cost Russia at least a million
lives. Brusilov was briefly commander in chief
under the Kerensky regime (1917), and in 1920 he
joined the Red Army's staff in directing the war
against Poland.

Brussa: see BURSA.

Brussels (brŭ′sŭlz), Fr. *Bruxelles* (brüsĕl′), Flemish
Brussel (brü′sŭl), city (with suburbs, estimated
pop. 1,407,660), capital of Belgium and of Brabant
prov. It is officially bilingual (French and Flemish). Situated on the Senne, a tributary of the
Dyle, at the junction of the Charleroi-Brussels and
Willebroek canals, Brussels is an important com-

Maison du roi on the Grand' Place in Brussels.

mercial, industrial, and cultural center. Among its
varied manufactures, including pharmaceuticals,
electronic equipment, and machine tools, that of
lace is the oldest and best known. It is the administrative seat of the European Economic Community. It has a university (founded 1834), academies
of arts, sciences, and medicine, a noted conservatory, splendid art collections, and a botanical
garden. Fortified in the 11th cent., Brussels was a
commercial center on the trade route from Bruges
and Ghent to the Rhineland, and in the 13th cent.
it became a center of the wool industry. In the
15th cent., when it was made capital of Brabant,
its arts flourished and many stately mansions (some
still standing) were built. Brussels became the seat
of the dukes of Burgundy and later of the governors
of the Spanish (after 1714 Austrian) Netherlands.
In 1561 the Willebroek Canal, connecting Brussels
with the sea, was completed. Renowned for the
luxury and gaiety of its life, Brussels became in the
late 16th cent. the grim center of the duque de
Alba's reign of terror. The city suffered heavily in
the wars of the 16th, 17th, and 18th cent. that were
fought mostly in the Low Countries. Brussels
changed hands repeatedly in the French Revolutionary Wars; during the Waterloo campaign
(1815) it was Wellington's headquarters. Between
1815 and 1830 it was, with the Hague, the alternate
meeting place of the Netherlands parliament; in
1830 it became the capital of independent Belgium.
Brussels was occupied by the Germans from 1914
until the armistice in 1918, and during the Second
World War from 1940 until its liberation by British
troops in Sept., 1944. The historical nucleus of the
city, the Grand' Place, is the site of the 15th-
century Gothic city hall, the 13th-century Renaissance *Maison du roi* or *Broodhuis*, meeting place of
the old States-General, and of a number of rebuilt
Gothic guildhalls. The Grand' Place is one of the

finest monuments of medieval and Renaissance architecture. The main landmark of Brussels is the Collegiate Church of St. Michael and St. Gudule, founded in the 11th cent. and later rebuilt, which contains many noted Flemish paintings. Other famous buildings are the palace of justice and the royal palace. Most of Brussels, however, is modern, with broad boulevards circling the city along the former ramparts.

Brussels carpet: see CARPET AND RUGS.

Brussels sprouts, variety (*gemmifera*) of CABBAGE producing small edible heads (sprouts) along the

Brussels sprouts

stem. It is cultivated like cabbage and was first developed in Belgium and France in the 18th cent.

Brut, Brute (both: brōōt), or **Brutus** (brōō′tŭs), a Trojan, legendary first king of Britain, descendant of Aeneas. His story appears in Nennius and in Geoffrey of Monmouth, and his name gives the titles to long poems by Wace and Layamon.

Bruttium (brŭ′tēŭm), ancient region, S Italy, roughly occupying the present CALABRIA, the "toe" of the Italian peninsula. It faces Sicily across the Strait of Messina. Inhabited in the interior by the Brutii (whose chief town was Cosenza) and by the Lucani, it was settled (8th cent. B.C.) along the coast by Greek colonists. SYBARIS and CROTONA were among the most prosperous towns of MAGNA GRAECIA. The Romans conquered Bruttium in the 3d cent. B.C. RHEGIUM and VIBO VALENTIA were important Roman cities of Bruttium. The region passed to Byzantium after the fall of Rome and came to be known as Calabria.

Brutus (brōō′tŭs), in ancient Rome, a surname of the Junian gens. **Lucius Junius Brutus,** fl. 510 B.C., was the founder of the Roman republic. He feigned idiocy to escape death at the hands of Lucius Tarquinius Superbus (see TARQUIN). Roman historians tell how he led the Romans in expelling the Tarquins after the rape of Lucrece, how he became one of the first praetors (there were no consuls), and how he executed his sons for plotting a Tarquinian restoration. **Decimus Junius**

Marcus Junius Brutus, one of the assassins of Julius Caesar.

Brutus Gallaecus (dĕ′sĭmŭs, gălē′kŭs), fl. 138 B.C., consul, consolidated the province of Farther Spain and stopped the encroaching Lusitanian tribesmen. **Marcus Junius Brutus,** d. c.77 B.C., was a partisan of LEPIDUS (d. 77 B.C.) in the struggle with CATULUS (d. 60 B.C.); POMPEY had him murdered. His wife Servilia was the half sister of Cato the Younger. Their son was **Marcus Junius Brutus,** 85? B.C.–42 B.C. He and C. CASSIUS LONGINUS were the principal assassins of Julius CAESAR. He had sided with Pompey, but after the battle of PHARSALA, Caesar pardoned him, made him governor of Cisalpine Gaul (46 B.C.), and, in 44 B.C., urban praetor. Nevertheless, he joined Cassius in the plot against Caesar. After the murder of Caesar, Brutus went east and, in the republican cause, joined Cassius and held Macedonia with him. Late in 42 B.C., Octavian (later AUGUSTUS) and Antony arrived, and a battle was fought at Philippi. When it went against the republicans, Brutus committed suicide. Brutus' wife Portia was the daughter of Cato the Younger. Brutus had a contemporary reputation as a Stoic philosopher, and his admirers have regarded him as a second Cato, driven reluctantly to commit murder in order to save the republic. His detractors, on the other hand, have considered his friendship with the self-seeking Cassius as indicative of his true character. A lesser member of the conspiracy was **Decimus Junius Brutus,** d. 43 B.C., a partisan of Caesar against Pompey and a favorite of the dictator. Caesar gave him command in Gaul and appointed him to be his heir in case of Octavian's death. After Caesar's death, Brutus refused to surrender Cisalpine Gaul. In 43 B.C., Antony, to whom the senate had assigned the province, besieged Brutus at Mutina (modern Modena). He tried to escape and was killed.

Brüx: see MOST, Czechoslovakia.

Bruyn, Barthel Bartholomaeus (bär′tŭl bärtōlōmā′ōōs broin), 1493–1555, German Renaissance painter, active in Cologne from 1515. Known especially for his portraits, which combine Northern realism with Italian-inspired monumentality and breadth, Bruyn also painted religious works such as the high altar at Essen Cathedral (1522). A portrait of a man and three religious works are in the Philadelphia Museum; many of his works are in Germany.

Bruyn, Cornelis de (kōr'nā″lĭs dù), 1652–c.1726, Dutch portrait painter and traveler. He painted for some years in Italy, where he was known, in Rome, as Adonis. He is remembered chiefly for the records of his extensive travels in Egypt, Persia, India, and other lands, illustrated with his own designs.

Bry, Théodore de (tēōdôr' dù brē', brī'), 1528–98, Flemish engraver and publisher, b. Liège. He spent most of his life in Frankfurt-am-Main. He visited London, where he executed a series of 12 plates, *The Procession of the Knights of the Garter*, and another of 34 plates, *The Funeral of Sir Philip Sidney*. The British geographer Hakluyt assisted him in obtaining materials for an illustrated collection of voyages and travels, *Collectiones peregrinationum* (1590–1634). Bry also published a series of portraits of famous men and illustrated the works of Thomas Hariot and J. J. Boissard. His son **John Théodore de Bry**, 1561–1623, assisted him and continued or completed several of his works.

Bryan, William Jennings, 1860–1925, American political leader, b. Salem, Ill., grad. Illinois College, 1881, and Union College of Law, Chicago, 1883. He practiced at Jacksonville, Ill., until removing, in 1887, to Lincoln, Nebr. Bryan was a U.S. Representative from 1891 to 1895 but was defeated for the U.S. Senate in 1894. The next two years he spent as editor in chief of the Omaha *World-Herald*. Having ardently identified himself with the silver forces in Congress, he became their most popular speaker in a preconvention drive to control the Democratic national convention at Chicago in 1896. At the convention his famous "Cross of Gold" speech so swayed the delegates that his nomination was assured, even though he was only 36 years old. The POPULIST PARTY also nominated him, but the conservative, gold Demo-

William Jennings Bryan

crats ran John M. Palmer. The chief issue of the campaign was Bryan's proposal for free and unlimited coinage of silver, which he thought would remedy the economic ills then plaguing farmers and industrial workers. In strenuous tours extending over 18,000 mi., he made some 600 speeches for

the silver cause, but lost the bitterly fought contest to Republican William McKinley, whose campaign was skillfully managed by Marcus A. HANNA. He controlled the Democratic convention in 1900 and saved the silver plank from removal by the East, though agreeing to put the campaign emphasis on anti-imperialism. Defeated again by McKinley, Bryan in 1901 started the *Commoner*, a widely read weekly which kept him before the people. His reduced party power in 1904 resulted in the compromise nomination of Alton B. PARKER, a conservative New Yorker, upon a platform dictated by Bryan. Parker, however, disavowed the silver plank, and Bryan unwillingly acquiesced. Parker's overwhelming defeat by Theodore Roosevelt turned the Democrats again to Bryan, who in 1908 was nominated a third time. Roosevelt's candidate, William H. TAFT, defeated him. The last Democratic convention in which Bryan played an important role was that of 1912, where his switch to Woodrow WILSON helped gain Wilson the nomination. Upon his election Wilson named Bryan Secretary of State. Bryan was influential in holding the Democrats together during the first 18 months of Wilson's administration, when unity was essential to enact the President's reform program of legislation. He had little previous experience in foreign affairs but studied international questions conscientiously. With some 30 nations he negotiated treaties providing for investigation of all disputes. Anti-war leanings made Bryan more conciliatory than Wilson toward Germany. His Latin American policies, particularly those involving Nicaragua, caused a good deal of friction. Disliking the strong language of the second *Lusitania* note, drafted by Wilson, he resigned on June 9, 1915, rather than sign it. However, he supported Wilson in the 1916 election and after war was declared. In the 1920 Democratic convention at San Francisco he fought in vain for a prohibition plank, and in 1924 at New York city he supported William G. McAdoo against Alfred E. Smith, but he was no longer the party's leader. In his later years Bryan, a Presbyterian, devoted himself to the defense of fundamentalism. His militancy was one reason for the increased popular attention given to the modernist-fundamentalist controversy, which subsided soon after his death. He addressed legislatures urging measures against teaching evolution and appeared for the prosecution in the famous SCOPES TRIAL in Tennessee. Although he won the case in the trial court, Bryan's beliefs were subjected to severe ridicule in a searching examination by opposing counsel, Clarence DARROW. Five days after the trial, Bryan died in his sleep. Although the nation consistently rejected him for the presidency, it eventually adopted many of the reforms he urged—the income tax, popular election of Senators, woman suffrage, public knowledge of newspaper ownership, and prohibition. In his prime a handsome man, personally charming, and with a voice that made him the greatest orator of his day, he was idolized by the masses (especially in the West), for whom he truly spoke. See the memoirs (1925), begun by Bryan and finished by his widow; biographies by W. C. Williams (1936) and P. W. Glad (1960). His brother, **Charles Wayland Bryan**, 1867–1945, b. Salem, Ill., educated at the

Univ. of Chicago and Illinois College, was for many years W. J. Bryan's political secretary and business agent. He was publisher and associate editor of the *Commoner*, mayor of Lincoln, Nebr., and governor of Nebraska.

Bryan. **1** City (pop. 7,361), co. seat of Williams co., NW Ohio, NNW of Defiance, in a trade and industrial area; laid out 1840, inc. as a village 1849, as a city 1941. Furnaces, automobile and truck parts, and electrical appliances are among its manufactures. **2** City (pop. 27,542), co. seat of Brazos co., E central Texas, NW of Houston. Founded in 1865 in a region of big plantations, it was long a cotton center. Farms producing alfalfa, truck crops, dairy goods, and poultry now occupy much of the land. The city has a variety of light industries, including the production of cottonseed oil, agricultural chemicals, furniture, and aluminum windows. A military school for boys is here.

Bryansk (brēänsk'), city (pop. c.206,000), capital of Bryansk oblast, W central European RSFSR, on the Desna river. A transportation hub, it forms an important industrial district with nearby Bezhitsa, with which it was incorporated in 1956. There are ironworks and locomotive, machine, and cement plants. Originally called Brinyu and later Debryansk, the city was first known in 1146. For a time the capital of a principality, it later passed to Lithuania, and in the 16th cent. was annexed by Muscovy. Bryansk was a fortress until the 19th cent.

Bryant, William Cullen, 1794–1878, American poet and newspaper editor, b. Cummington, Mass.

William Cullen Bryant

Admitted to the bar in 1815 after a year at Williams College and private study, he practiced law in Great Barrington, Mass., until in 1825 he went to New York. By this time he was already known as a poet and critic. Influenced by the English romantic poets, he celebrated the majesty of nature in such poems as "Thanatopsis," "To a Waterfowl," "Inscription for the Entrance to a Wood," and "The Yellow Violet," all written before he was 21. He became associate editor of the New York *Evening Post* in 1826, and from 1829 to his death he was part owner and editor in chief. An industrious and forthright editor of a highly literate paper, he was a defender of human rights and an advocate of free trade, abolition of slavery, and other reforms. He traveled widely, made many public speeches, and continued to write poems (e.g., "The Death of the Flowers," "To the Fringed Gentian," and "The Battle-Field"). His blank-verse translation of the *Iliad* came out in 1870, that of the *Odyssey* in 1872. See biographies by Parke Godwin (1883), John Bigelow (1890), and H. H. Peckham (1950); Allan Nevins, *The Evening Post* (1922).

Bryaxis (brĭăk'sĭs), 4th cent. B.C., Greek sculptor. With Scopas, Leochares, and Timotheus, he was employed, c.350 B.C., upon the sculptures of the Mausoleum at Halicarnassus. Among other works attributed to him were several statues, including one of Apollo in the grove of Daphne, near Antioch. In 1891 at Athens his signature was discovered on a base for a tripod. The base is sculptured in relief with figures of horsemen.

Bryce, James Bryce, Viscount, 1838–1922, British historian, statesman, and diplomat, b. Belfast. After his education at the Univ. of Glasgow and at Oxford, he practiced law in London for a short time before becoming professor of civil law at Oxford. He wrote monumental works in several fields; the first of these was his *History of the Holy Roman Empire* (1864), a book still widely used. He entered politics and became a leader of the Liberal party, occupying a variety of posts, including the presidency of the Board of Trade and the chief secretaryship of Ireland. His interest in sociology and philosophy is evident in the second of his great treatises, *The American Commonwealth* (1888), a classic that is still read and used. As ambassador to the United States (1907–13) he was one of the most popular ever to be in Washington, since his knowledge of Americans, as revealed in his writings, was profound. Other major works were *Studies in History and Jurisprudence* (1901) and *Modern Democracies* (1921). See biography by H. A. L. Fisher (1927); *Bryce's American Commonwealth: Fiftieth Anniversary* (commemorative essays, 1939).

Bryce Canyon National Park, 36,010.38 acres, SW

"Thor's Hammer" in Bryce Canyon National Park.

Utah; est. as a national monument 1923, as a national park 1928. Formation of the Pink Cliffs (c.2,000 ft. high) began almost 60 million years ago, when inland lakes and seas started to lay down deposits of silt, sand, and lime. Rain, frost, and running water, working through alternate strata of softer and harder limestone, have created some of the most colorful and unique erosional forms in the world—miniature cities, cathedrals, spires, chessmen, and other formations. Probably the first Indians to inhabit this area were the Basket Makers, and many of their artifacts may be found.

Bryhtnoth: see BYRHTNOTH.

Bryn Athyn (brĭn" ă'thĭn), residential borough (pop. 1,057), SE Pa., N of Philadelphia; inc. 1910. The Bryn Athyn Cathedral, a center of American Swedenborgianism, is noted for its design.

Brynhild: see BRUNHILD.

Bryn Mawr (brĭnmär', brĭn" mär'), uninc. village, SE Pa., a suburb W of Philadelphia. A junior college is here. Also here is **Bryn Mawr College** (for women), opened in 1885 by the Society of Friends, with a bequest from Joseph W. Taylor of Burlington, N.J. Modeled on a group curriculum plan at Johns Hopkins Univ., Bryn Mawr was one of the first women's colleges in the United States to offer graduate degrees. The library is especially noted for its collection of rare books and medieval incunabula.

bryony: see GOURD.

Bryson, Lyman, 1888–1959, American educator, b. Valentine, Nebr., grad. Univ. of Michigan (B.A., 1910; M.A., 1915). He taught there from 1913 to 1917. From 1918 to 1924 he was active in Red Cross work. He was appointed professor at Teachers College, Columbia Univ., in 1935, and during the Second World War he worked in the Office of War Information. Consultant on public affairs for the Columbia Broadcasting System, he was instrumental in popularizing such forms of adult education as the public forum. Among his books are *Adult Education* (1936), *Which Way America?* (1939), *The New Prometheus* (1941), *Science and Freedom* (1946), and *The Next America* (1952).

Bryson City, town (pop. 1,084), co. seat of Swain co., SW N.C., in the Great Smoky Mts. region, WSW of Asheville. It is a tourist center in a timber, mining, and farming area.

Brythonic (brĭthŏn'ĭk), group of Celtic languages of the Indo-European family. It includes Welsh, Breton, and the extinct Cornish. See LANGUAGE (table).

Bryusov, Valery Yakovlevich (vŭlyĕ'rē yä'kŭvlyĭvĭch brēōō'sŭf), 1873–1924, Russian poet, novelist, and critic. He was the spearhead of the symbolist movement and wrote highly polished and esoteric verse celebrating sensual pleasures. Of his poetry, *Stephanos* (1906) is perhaps best known. *The Fiery Angel* (1903) and *Altar of Victory* (1913) are novels. He became a Communist party member after the Revolution of 1917.

Brzeg: see BRIEG.

Brzesc nad Bugiem: see BREST, Byelorussian SSR.

Bubastis (būbăs'tĭs), ancient city, NE Egypt, in the Nile delta, near the modern Zagazig. Capital of Egypt in the XXII and XXIII dynasties, it began to decline after the second Persian conquest (343 B.C.). Bubastis was the center of the worship of the lion-headed (or cat-headed) goddess Bast. In the time of Herodotus it had an annual Saturnalia. As Pi-beseth, Bubastis is mentioned in Ezek. 30.17. Excavations were made in 1886, 1887, and 1906. Among the finds were a chapel of the VI dynasty (proving that the site dates back to the Old Kingdom) and a great temple built in the 8th cent. B.C.

bubble chamber: see WILSON CLOUD CHAMBER.

Buber, Martin (bōō'bĕr), 1878–, Jewish philosopher, b. Vienna. Educated at German universities, he

Martin Buber

taught philosophy and religion at the University of Frankfurt-am-Main (1924–33). From 1938 to 1951 he taught social philosophy at the University of Jerusalem. Greatly influenced by the mysticism of the HASIDIM which he interpreted in many works and by the Christian existentialism of Kierkegaard, Buber evolved his own philosophy of religion, especially in his book *I and Thou* (2d ed., 1958). Conceiving the relations between God and man not as abstract and impersonal, but as an inspired and direct dialogue, Buber has also had a great impact on contemporary Christian thinkers. An early Zionist, he worked to permeate political Zionism with ethical and spiritual values. In Israel, his home since 1938, he strongly advocated Arab-Israeli understanding. Among his writings are *Jewish Mysticism and the Legends of Baalshem* (1931); *Mamre* (1946); *Moses* (1958); *The Origin and Meaning of Hasidism* (1960). See biography by A. A. Cohen (1957); M. S. Friedman, *Martin Buber; the Life of Dialogue* (1957); M. L. Diamond, *Martin Buber, Jewish Existentialist* (1960).

bubonic plague: see PLAGUE.

Buçaco: see BUSSACO.

Bucaramanga (bōō"kärämäng'gä), city (pop. c.190,-000), N central Colombia. Founded in 1622 in the eastern highlands of the Andes, Bucaramanga developed after 1880 as a coffee and tobacco center. Improved communications have made it a leading commercial center.

Bucareli y Ursúa, Antonio María (äntō'nyō märē'ä bōōkärä'lē ē ōōrsōō'ä), 1717–79, Spanish colonial administrator. He served in the army and as governor of Cuba before succeeding the marqués de Croix as viceroy of New Spain (1771–79). His

Martin Bucer

John Buchan

Franklin Buchanan

administration, one of the most popular in Mexico, brought peace and prosperity. See B. E. Bobb, *The Viceregency of Antonio María Bucareli* (1962).

buccaneer: see PIRACY.

Bucephalus (būsĕ'fŭlŭs), favorite horse of Alexander the Great. There are legends of his speed and the wondrous deeds that Alexander performed while riding him. He died in 326 B.C. after the battle on the Hydaspes River. The city Bucephala was founded there by Alexander in his honor.

Bucer or **Butzer, Martin** (bū'sŭr, boōt'sŭr), 1491–1551, German Protestant reformer. His original name was Kuhhorn [cow's horn], of which Bucer is a Greek translation. At 14 years of age he joined the Dominican order, and he studied at Heidelberg, where he heard (1518) Luther in his public disputation on the doctrine of free will. Influenced by the reformist thought, Bucer left the order and accepted a pastorate at Landstuhl. In 1523 he entered upon the work of the Reformation in Strasbourg—preaching, writing, and helping to lay the foundations of the Protestant educational system. Many of his activities were devoted to attempts to reconcile the differences in regard to the Eucharist (see LORD'S SUPPER) which divided the Lutherans from the Swiss and South German reformers. Bucer's position was closer to that of the Swiss leader, Zwingli, and in this as in other doctrinal matters he is credited with a spiritual kinship to Calvin. In spite of his desire for unity, Bucer rejected the Augsburg Confession (see CREED), drawn up in 1530 in the hope of achieving religious peace. It was not until a personal meeting with Luther in 1536 that, in the Wittenberg Concord, Bucer was successful in securing agreement on the Eucharist among himself, Luther, and the reformers of S Germany. When Bucer failed to subscribe to the Augsburg Interim (1548)—a compromise between Catholics and Protestants proposed by Charles V—he found it expedient to accept the invitation of Cranmer and moved to England. There, highly honored, he taught at Cambridge and tutored Edward VI, at whose request he wrote *De regno Christi*. See Hastings Eells, *Martin Bucer* (1931); Constantin Hopf, *Martin Bucer and the English Reformation* (1946).

Buch, Christian Leopold, Freiherr von (krĭs'tyän lā'ōpôlt frī'hĕr fŭn boōkh), 1774–1853, German geologist and paleontologist, graduate of the mining academy, Freiberg, Germany. One of the most influential geologists of his age, he is noted especially for his study of volcanism. In addition to a valuable geological map of Germany, his works include geological and paleontological studies of several areas in Europe.

Buchan, Alexander (bŭ'kŭn, –khŭn), 1829–1907, Scottish meteorologist. Educated at Edinburgh, he taught from 1848 to 1860; his works include *The Handy Book of Meteorology* (1867). In 1878 Buchan became curator of the library and museum of the Royal Society of Edinburgh. He was responsible for founding the observatory on Ben Nevis (1883).

Buchan, John, 1st Baron Tweedsmuir (bŭk'ŭn, twēdz'mŭr), 1875–1940, British author and statesman, b. Scotland. Included among his works are a four-volume history (1921–22) of the First World War; biographies of Montrose (1913), Scott (1932), and Cromwell (1934); and adventure novels, including *The Thirty-nine Steps* (1915), *The Path of the King* (1921), and *Mountain Meadow* (1941). A member of Parliament from 1927, he was appointed governor general of Canada in 1935 and was raised to the peerage. His administration was popular, and he promoted good relations with the United States. See his autobiography, *Pilgrim's Way* (1940).

Buchan (bŭ'khŭn, –kŭn), district along the rocky coast of Aberdeenshire, NE Scotland, between the Ythan and the Deveron. Called "the cold shoulder of Scotland," it is treeless, windswept, and bleak. The soil is sparse but well cultivated. The ports of Peterhead and Fraserburgh are here. Buchan Ness is Scotland's easternmost promontory.

Buchanan, Franklin (bŭkă'nŭn), 1800–1874, American naval officer, b. Baltimore. Appointed a midshipman in 1815, Buchanan rose to be a commander in 1841. He was chief adviser to Secretary of the Navy George BANCROFT in planning the U.S. Naval Academy at Annapolis and was its first superintendent (1845–47), resigning to fight in the Mexican War. He commanded the *Susquehanna*, flagship of Matthew C. Perry, in the expedition to Japan (1852–54). Buchanan was a captain in the U.S. navy when he resigned in April, 1861. In September he took the same rank in the Confederate navy. With his flagship the ironclad *Virginia* (formerly the *Merrimack*) he attacked and destroyed two of the wooden vessels of the Union blockading squadron in Hampton Roads (March 8, 1863). He was wounded in that engagement and had no part in the epochal battle of the MONITOR AND MERRIMACK the next day. Promoted admiral, Buchanan was ranking officer in the Confederate navy. With the ironclad ram *Tennessee* as his flagship he fought heroically against David G. FARRAGUT in the battle of Mobile Bay (Aug. 5, 1864), but was finally forced to surrender. After the war he was for a time president of Maryland Agricultural College. See biography by C. L. Lewis (1929).

Buchanan, George, 1506–1582, Scottish humanist. After being driven into exile for his Protestant views, he held academic posts on the Continent where he was highly regarded as a Latin poet. In 1560 he returned to Scotland to tutor Queen Mary and later James VI. His *Rerum Scoticarum historia* (1582) is still a useful source of his time, but his most influential work was the *De Jure regni apud Scotos* (1579), which argued that the king rules by popular will and for the general good. See biography by Donald Macmillan (1906).

Buchanan, James, 1791–1868, 15th President of the United States (1857–61), b. near Mercersburg, Pa., grad. Dickinson College, 1809. He read law at Lancaster, Pa., and in practice there gained considerable notice for his wide learning and brilliant oratory. Thus prepared, he went into state politics, then entered the national scene as Congressman (1821–31), and was later minister to Russia (1832–33) and Senator (1834–45). Early a Federalist, he was later a conservative mainstay of the Democratic party. He served (1845–49) as Secretary of State under J. K. Polk, and though Polk exercised a strong personal hand in foreign affairs, Buchanan ably seconded his efforts. The quarrel with Great Britain over Oregon was settled peacefully. That with Mexico after the annexation of Texas led, after the failure of the mission of John SLIDELL, to the Mexican War and the Treaty of Guadalupe Hidalgo (1848). Under President Franklin Pierce, Buchanan was (1853–56) minister to Great Britain. He collaborated with Pierre SOULÉ, minister to Spain, and John Y. MASON, minister to France, in drawing up the OSTEND MANIFESTO (1854), which was promptly repudiated by the U.S. Dept. of State. His open advocacy of acquiring Cuba (which would presumably have come into the Union as a slave state) won him the hatred of the abolitionists, whom he in turn despised as impractical troublemakers. He was nominated as a Democratic candidate for the presidency in 1856, with John C. BRECKINRIDGE as his running mate, and he won the election over John C. Frémont, the candidate of the young Republican party, and Millard Fillmore, candidate of the Whig and Know-Nothing parties. Buchanan did not have the majority of the popular vote, and his moderate views were disliked and mistrusted by extremists both in the North and in the South. Though he attempted to keep the "sacred balance"

between proslavery and antislavery factions, in his administration the United States plunged down through conflict toward the armed strife of the Civil War. Buchanan, who disapproved of slavery as morally wrong, felt that under the Constitution slavery had to be protected where it was established and that the inhabitants of a new territory should decide whether that territory should be free or slave. He angered many in the North by renewed efforts to purchase Cuba and by favoring the proslavery Lecompton Constitution in KANSAS. As his administration drew to a close, after the election (1860) of Abraham Lincoln to succeed him as President, Buchanan was faced with the secession of the Southern states. Very learned in constitutional law, he maintained that no state had the right to secede but he held, on the other hand, that he had no power to coerce the erring states. He believed that the Federal government was authorized to use force only in protecting Federal property and in collecting customs. Therefore the question of the Federal forts in Southern states became of great importance. Buchanan tried desperately to keep peace and promised South Carolina Congressmen that no hostile moves would be made as long as negotiations were in progress. When Major Robert Anderson moved U.S. troops from Fort Moultrie to FORT SUMTER, there was an outcry from South Carolina that the President's promise had been broken. Buchanan defended Anderson but, reluctant to act, sent supplies to Fort Sumter only belatedly. He was battered with criticism from North and South, and shortly after his administration ended, gunfire at Fort Sumter commenced the war. All Buchanan's efforts were lost. The home outside Lancaster, "Wheatland," occupied by Buchanan and by his niece, Harriet Lane, who was

*President
James Buchanan*

BUCHANAN

The Athenaeum in Bucharest.

Buildings of the university of Bucharest.

also his White House hostess, was made a public shrine in 1937. John Bassett Moore edited his works (12 vols., 1909–11). See biographies by G. T. Curtis (1883) and P. S. Klein (1962).

Buchanan. 1 City (pop. 5,341), SW Mich., near the Ind. line SW of Battle Creek; platted 1837, inc. as a village 1863, as a city 1929. Automobile parts and construction and communication equipment are manufactured. Nearby are numerous Indian village sites and mounds. **2** Village (pop. 2,019), SE N.Y., on the east bank of the Hudson and SW of Peekskill; inc. 1928. An atomic power plant here supplies electricity for a wide area. **3** Town (pop. 1,349), western Va., NE of Roanoke and on the James river; inc. 1811. It has limestone quarries.

Buchans, town (pop. 2,493), N.F., Canada, in the interior, W of Grand Falls. It has a large mine yielding lead, silver, zinc, and copper.

Bucharest (bōō′kûrĕst, bū′-), Rum. *Bucureşti* (bōōkōōrĕsht′), city (estimated pop. 1,291,351), capital and largest city of Rumania, in Walachia, SE Rumania, on the Dambovita, a tributary of the Danube. It is the chief industrial and communications center of Rumania, with manufactures of machinery, textiles, metals, and chemicals. It is the seat of the patriarch of the Rumanian Orthodox Church and has a university (founded 1864) and several academies and scientific institutes. The city was first mentioned as *Cetatea Dambovitei* [Dambovita Citadel] in 1368, when it was a military fortress and a trade center. It became in 1459 a residence of the Walachian princes and changed (15th cent.) its name to Bucharest. The city became (1698) the capital of Walachia under Constantine BRANCOVAN, and after the union (1859) of Walachia and Moldavia it was made (1861) the capital of Rumania. The Treaty of Bucharest (1812) ended the Russo-Turkish War of

1806–12. An accord between Bulgaria and Serbia was also signed (1886) here. The Treaty of Bucharest (1913) stripped Bulgaria of her conquests in the Second Balkan War. Bucharest was occupied (1916–18) by the Central Powers in the First World War. After the Rumanian surrender to the Allies (Aug., 1944) in the Second World War, Bucharest was severely bombed by German planes; Soviet troops entered on Aug. 31. It was the headquarters of the COMINFORM from 1948 to 1956. A city of contrasts in the late 19th and early 20th cent., its palatial public buildings standing side by side with destitute hovels, Bucharest today is a modern city with fine parks, libraries, museums, and theaters. Among its most notable buildings are the Metropolitan church (1649), the 17th-century St. George church, the Radu Voda (1649) and the Stavropoleos (1724–30) churches, and the Athenaeum, devoted to art and music.

Buchenwald (bōō′khŭnvält″), village, German Democratic Republic, in the former state of Thuringia, central Germany, in the Buchenwald forest. It was the site of a CONCENTRATION CAMP set up by the Hitler regime.

Buchman, Frank Nathan Daniel (bŏŏk′mŭn), 1878–1961, American evangelist, b. Pennsburg, Pa., grad. Muhlenberg College, 1899. The international movement he founded is variously called First Century Christian Fellowship, Oxford Group, Moral Re-Armament (often known as MRA), and Buchmanism. Buchman was ordained in the Lutheran ministry in 1902. He was in charge (1905–15) of religious work at Pennsylvania State College. In 1921 Buchman, after five years of extension lecturing for the Hartford Theological Foundation, visited England. There he preached "world-changing through life-changing" among the students at Oxford Univ., hence the name Oxford Group. In 1938 he instituted a campaign known as Moral Re-Armament. The work of evangelism for personal and national spiritual reconstruction is conducted informally and intimately in groups gathered in educational institutions, in church congregations, or in homes. "House parties" take the place of conferences, and religious experiences are shared in personal confessions. The evangelists stress absolute honesty, purity, love, and unselfishness. The work has spread to more than 50 countries, and the first world assembly for Moral

Re-Armament was held in 1958. See Buchman's *Remaking the World* (new ed., 1949) and *The World Rebuilt* (1951); A. W. Eister, *Drawing-Room Conversion* (1950).

Buchner, Eduard (ā'dōōärt bōōkh'nùr), 1860–1917, German chemist. He taught at Berlin,

Eduard Buchner

Ludwig Büchner

Breslau, and, from 1911, at Würzburg. He discovered (1896) that alcoholic fermentation of sugars is caused by yeast enzymes and not by the yeast cells themselves. Zymase, part of the enzyme system causing fermentation, was discovered by him in 1903. For this work he received the 1907 Nobel Prize in Chemistry.

Büchner, Georg (gā'ôrk bükh'nùr), 1813–37, German dramatist. He was a student of medicine and a political agitator. Dying at 24, he left a powerful drama, *Danton's Death* (1835; Eng. tr., 1928); a fragmentary tragedy, *Wozzeck* (1850; Eng. tr., 1928), which Alban Berg adapted for his opera; and a comedy, *Leonce and Lena* (1850; Eng. tr., 1928). Büchner greatly admired J. M. R. Lenz, whom he made the hero of a *Novelle* by that name. See study by A. H. J. Knight (1951).

Büchner, Ludwig (lōōt'vĭkh), 1824–99, German philosopher and physician. After being forced to leave his position as instructor at Tübingen because of his philosophical views, he devoted himself to medicine and writing. His doctrine was an extreme materialism developed in protest to idealistic metaphysics. Among his works were *Kraft und Stoff* (1855; Eng. tr., *Force and Matter*, 1864), *Natur und Geist* (1857), and *Darwinismus und Socialismus* (1894).

Buck, Carl Darling, 1866–1955, American philologist, b. Orlando, Maine, grad. Yale (B.A., 1886; Ph.D., 1889). He taught at the Univ. of Chicago from 1892 to 1933. His *Grammar of Oscan and Umbrian* (1904) is still authoritative.

Buck, Leffert Lefferts, 1837–1909, American civil engineer, b. Canton, N.Y., grad. St. Lawrence

Univ., 1863. He designed many notable bridges, including the Verrugas viaduct near Lima, Peru; two bridges at Niagara Falls; the Columbia river railroad bridge at Pasco, Wash.; and the Williamsburg Bridge in New York city.

Buck, Pearl (Sydenstricker), 1892–, American nov-

Pearl S. Buck

elist, b. Hillsboro, W. Va., grad. Randolph-Macon Woman's College, 1914. Until 1934 she lived principally in China, where she, her parents, and her first husband, John Lossing Buck (from whom she was later divorced), were missionaries. Her first novel, *East Wind: West Wind* (1930), was followed by *The Good Earth* (1931), which won the Pulitzer Prize. *The Exile* (1936) and *Fighting Angel* (1936) are biographies of her mother and her father. In 1935 she married Richard J. Walsh. Miss Buck received the Nobel Prize in Literature

Stage design for Georg Büchner's Wozzeck.

in 1938. She has written children's books and plays in addition to such novels as *The Patriot* (1939), *Dragon Seed* (1942), *Peony* (1948), and *Letter from Peking* (1957). Her poignant writings, which accurately describe foreign customs and problems, have helped contribute to racial understanding and to the discussion of those issues which affect all humanity. See her autobiography, *My Several Worlds* (1954) and biography by Cornelia Spencer (1944).

Buckeye, town (pop. 2,286), S central Ariz., W of Phoenix, in an irrigated farming and cattle-raising area; inc. 1929.

buckeye: see HORSE CHESTNUT.

Buckeye Lake, uninc. town (pop. 2,129), central Ohio, SSW of Newark. It is a resort town on Buckeye Lake. Much of the surrounding area comprises a state park.

Buckhannon (bŭk″hăn′ŭn), city (pop. 6,386), co. seat of Upshur co., N W.Va., on the Buckhannon river and S of Clarksburg; settled 1770, inc. 1852. Its principal industries are coal mining and lumbering. West Virginia Wesleyan College (Methodist; coeducational; 1890) is here.

Buckhaven and Methil (mĕth′ĭl), burgh (pop. 21,104), Fife, E Scotland, on the Firth of Forth. Methil is Fife's leading port for the export of coal. Mary Queen of Scots met Lord Darnley at Wemyss Castle, built in the 13th cent.; a more recent castle is nearby.

Buckholdt, Johann: see JOHN OF LEIDEN.

Buckhurst, Lord: see SACKVILLE, CHARLES, and SACKVILLE, THOMAS.

Buckie, burgh (pop. 7,666), Banffshire, NE Scotland, on the Moray Firth. A leading herring port, it has an engineering plant and manufactures whisky and barrels.

Buckingham, dukes of (Stafford line): see STAFFORD, EDWARD; STAFFORD, HENRY; STAFFORD, HUMPHREY.

Buckingham, George Nugent Temple Grenville, 1st marquess of: see GRENVILLE, GEORGE NUGENT TEMPLE, 1ST MARQUESS OF BUCKINGHAM.

Buckingham, George Villiers, 1st duke of (vĭl′yŭrz, bŭk′ĭng-ŭm), 1592–1628, English nobleman. He arrived at the English court (1614) as James I was tiring of his favorite, Robert Carr, earl of Somerset. Villiers was made a gentleman of the bedchamber (1615) and after Somerset's disgrace rose rapidly,

George Villiers, 1st duke of Buckingham

becoming earl of Buckingham (1617), marquess (1618), and lord high admiral (1619). In 1620 he married Lady Katherine Manners, who was daughter of the earl of Rutland and was inclined to Roman Catholicism. By this time Buckingham dispensed the king's patronage; when Parliament in 1621 protested the abuses of monopolies by his brothers and dependents, Buckingham agreed in the censure but prevented possible punishment— a service he was unable to perform for his friend Francis BACON. When negotiations dragged for the proposed marriage of Charles, prince of Wales, and the Infanta Maria of Spain, Buckingham, who favored the match, went (1623) to Spain with the prince incognito. There they found Spanish demands impossible to meet, and on their return Buckingham, now a duke, was a hero in England for having prevented the unpopular marriage. He promoted war with Spain and persuaded James to disregard his promise to Parliament concerning religious restrictions on the proposed match of Charles with Henrietta Maria, sister of Louis XIII of France. In support of FREDERICK THE WINTER KING, he hired Graf von Mansfeld to head troops against the emperor in the Palatinate in the Thirty Years War, but then did not supply him adequately and was held responsible for the expedition's utter failure. After the accession of CHARLES I, Buckingham was still the favorite, and the virtual dictator of English affairs. Parliament resented his power, and suspected him of sacrificing the nation's welfare for his own personal gain. After the complete failure (1625) of an expedition against Cádiz, Buckingham was impeached (1626), and Charles dissolved Parliament to prevent his trial. After the disastrous failure (1629) of Buckingham's attempted relief of the HUGUENOTS on the Isle of Ré off La Rochelle, Parliament delivered another remonstrance against the duke. Buckingham was at Portsmouth preparing another expedition for La Rochelle when he was killed by John Felton, a discontented naval officer. The romantic aspects of the duke's career figure largely in Alexander Dumas's historical novel, *The Three Musketeers.* See biographies by C. R. Cammell (1939) and Hugh Ross Williamson (1940).

Buckingham, George Villiers, 2d duke of, 1628–87, English courtier; son of the 1st duke. Brought up with the royal family and educated at Cambridge, he was a strong royalist in the civil war. He took part in both civil wars. In 1648 he escaped to the Continent, where he was a privy councilor of the exiled Charles II. He fought for the king in the defeat at Worcester (1651), but later intrigues with Cromwell's government estranged him from Charles. Buckingham's estates were confiscated in 1651. In 1657 he returned to England and married Mary, the daughter of the Puritan lord and general, Thomas FAIRFAX OF CAMERON, and was consequently imprisoned until 1659. He served with Fairfax against John Lambert in 1660, but after the Restoration he regained the favor of Charles II and was one of the most powerful courtiers of the reign. Vain and ambitious, his career was marked by his recklessness, quarrelsome temper, and lack of principle. He was a member of the CABAL (1667–73), a bitter rival of his fellow minister, the 1st earl of Arlington. He was furious when he was

Buckingham Palace with the Victoria Memorial in the foreground.

kept in ignorance of the secret provisions of the Treaty of Dover (1670) with Louis XIV, and was even more offended by the loss of his military command in 1673. Also, the House of Commons attacked him for misusing public funds and conducting secret negotiations with France, and the House of Lords reprimanded him for his open liaison with the countess of Shrewsbury, whose husband he had killed in a duel in 1668. In 1674 Charles dismissed him. He joined the enemies of the duke of York (later James II) and participated vigorously in the cry against the Roman Catholic victims of Titus Oates's Popish Plot (though he had earlier been much in favor of religious tolerance). He managed not to vote for exclusion of the duke of York from succession to the throne and in 1684 was restored to favor and retired from politics. He showed the good as well as the bad aspects of the Restoration courtier: he patronized science and literature, had exquisitely refined tastes, wrote poetry, religious tracts, and plays, and dabbled in chemistry. He was producer and partial author of a celebrated satire on heroic drama, *The Rehearsal* (1671; ed. by Montague Summers, 1914), directed in its later version against John Dryden. See biographies by R. P. T. Coffin (1931), H. W. Chapman (1949), and J. H. Wilson (1954).

Buckingham (bŭ′kĭnghăm, bŭ′kĭng-ŭm), town (pop. 7,421), SW Que., Canada, on the Lièvre river and E of Ottawa. The town is in a lumbering and farming region and has a large chemical industry.

Buckingham (bŭ′kĭng-ŭm), municipal borough (pop. 4,377), Buckinghamshire, central England. Stowe School (1923), a public school for boys, occupies the seat of the former dukes of Buckingham.

Buckingham Palace (bŭ′kĭng-ŭm), residence of British sovereigns from 1837, Westminster metropolitan borough, London, England, adjacent to St. James's Park. Built (1703) by the duke of Buckingham on the site of a mulberry grove, it was purchased (1761) by George III and was remodeled (1825) by John Nash; the eastern facade was added in 1847. The great ballroom was added in 1856,

and in 1913 Sir Aston Webb designed a new front. The palace has nearly 600 rooms and contains a collection of paintings, including many royal portraits, by noted artists.

Buckinghamshire (bŭ′kĭng-ŭmshĭr), **Buckingham,** or **Bucks,** county (pop. 486,183), 749 sq. mi., central England. The county town is AYLESBURY. The chief rivers are the Thames, which forms the southern boundary, the Ouse, and the Thame. In the southern part of the county are the chalky Chiltern Hills with their beech forests, and to the north lies the fertile Vale of Aylesbury. The region is chiefly agricultural. Cattle and sheep are raised. There are miscellaneous small manufactures. Roman and pre-Roman remains are extensive; the ancient ICKNIELD STREET and WATLING STREET crossed the county. There are numerous literary associations: at Stoke Poges, Thomas Gray is buried in the country churchyard that inspired his "Elegy," John Milton had a cottage for a time at Chalfont St. Giles, and the poet William Cowper lived for many years at Olney.

Buckland, William, 1784–1856, English geologist. He was dean of Westminster from 1845. First to note in England the action on rocks of glacial ice, he did much to bring physical and natural science into high repute. He wrote *Reliquiae Diluvianae* (1823) and *Geology and Mineralogy Considered with References to Natural Theology* (1836). Francis T. Buckland, English surgeon and naturalist, was his son.

Buckland, town (pop. 1,664), NW Mass., in hills W of Greenfield; inc. 1779. Mary Lyon was born in Buckland and taught school here.

Buckle, Henry Thomas, 1821–62, English historian. Contemptuous of the historical writing of his day with its intense concern with politics, wars, and heroes, he undertook the ambitious plan of writing a history of civilization, treating all men in their relation with each other and with the natural world about them. At the time of his early death he had completed only two volumes of his panoramic *History of Civilization in England* (1857–61; new ed. in one volume, 1904). Attempting to make history a genuine science, Buckle arrived at various "laws" of history by an inductive process. It is easy to point out that these "laws"—e.g., the law of climate, by which he demonstrated that only in Europe could men reach high levels of civilization —were to a large extent only rationalizations of his own progressive and liberal views. Yet the effect that the book had in shaping English liberal thought was immediate and huge. It profoundly influenced later scientific historians, and it helped to fasten attention on masses rather than individuals, on the wide levels of all life rather than on politics, and on the interrelations of man and nature rather than man and morals.

Buckley, town (pop. 3,538), W Wash., near the White River and E of Tacoma; settled 1853, platted 1888, inc. 1890. It is the trading center of a rich farm, timber, and mining region.

Bucknell University: see LEWISBURG, Pa.

Buckner, Simon Bolivar, 1823–1914, Confederate general, b. Hart co., Ky., grad. West Point, 1844. After serving in the Mexican War, he resigned from the army (1855) and entered business, ultimately settling in Louisville. In 1860 Buckner, fearing war, prepared and secured the passage of a bill creating a large Kentucky militia and, as inspector general, trained it. When Kentucky announced its neutrality in May, 1861, Buckner stationed the troops to prevent invasion and unsuccessfully tried to get Lincoln to recognize the neutrality declaration. The legislature became strongly Unionist and assumed control of the state's military affairs, so Buckner resigned and in Sept., 1861, was commissioned a Confederate brigadier general. At FORT DONELSON (Feb., 1862), he surrendered to Grant and was taken prisoner. Soon exchanged and promoted major general, he commanded a division in Bragg's invasion of Kentucky and fought at Perryville (Oct., 1862). He fortified Mobile (Dec., 1862–April, 1863), commanded the Dept. of East Tennessee (May–Aug., 1863), fought around Chattanooga (Sept., 1863), and from 1864 until the end of the war commanded in Louisiana. Returning to Kentucky in 1868, he was editor of the Louisville *Courier* and was later governor of the state (1887–91). See biography by A. M. Stickles (1940).

Buckner, city (pop. 1,198), W Mo., E of Kansas City; founded 1875, inc. 1932. It ships wheat and livestock.

Bucks: see BUCKINGHAMSHIRE.

Bucksport, town (pop. 3,466), S Maine, on the east bank of the Penobscot river and S of Bangor; settled 1762, inc. 1792. The British burned part of Bucksport in 1779 and again in the War of 1812. The town grew as a port in the 19th cent. and now has a large paper mill. The Old Jed Prouty Tavern dates from 1804. Across the river is a state park which includes Fort Knox (1856).

buckthorn, common name for the Rhamnaceae, a family of woody shrubs, small trees, and climbing vines widely distributed throughout the world. The buckthorns (several species of the genus *Rhamnus*) and the jujube (*Zizyphus jujuba*) are cultivated for their ornamental foliage. The jujube was also used locally and exported for use in confectionery and as a flavoring, now largely replaced by artificial flavorings. (The lotus of Tennyson's lotus-eaters is

thought to have been the jujube.) Other members of the family yield dyes and a limited amount of lumber, e.g., cogwood, a hardwood. Other American species of *Rhamnus* are the redberry, the Indian cherry, and, in California, *Rhamnus purshiana*, which yields the purgative CASCARA SAGRADA.

buckwheat, common name for the Polygonaceae, a family of herbs and shrubs found chiefly in north temperate areas and having a characteristic pungent juice containing oxalic acid. Species native to the United States are most common in the West. The largest genus of the family, *Polygonum* (or *Persicaria*), contains the knotweeds and the smartweeds, found in many parts of the world. The common smartweed (*P. hydropiper*) is an annual sometimes called water pepper for its acrid quality. Several species of the dock genus (*Rumex*) are sorrels (the common name used also for the similarly acrid but unrelated OXALIS). The garden or green sorrel (*R. acetosa*) and the sheep, red, or field sorrel (*R. acetosella*) have long been used in Europe for salads and greens. Among the plants used as potherbs are the patience or spinach dock (*R. patientia*) and the tanner's dock (*R. hymenosepalus*); the latter is the source of canaigre (kǔnā′gǔr), used for tanning. Economically the important members of the family are of the rhubarb genus (*Rheum*) and the buckwheat genus (*Fagopyrum*), both native to Asia. Most of the rhubarb cultivated for its edible thick, fleshy leafstalks is *R. rhaponticum*, called also pieplant and wine plant. Medicinal rhubarb is obtained from this and other species of the genus. The cultivated buckwheat (*F. esculentum*) has been grown in the Old World since the Middle Ages as a honey plant and for its characteristic three-cornered grain, utilized for poultry and stock feed. Buckwheat flour is used in the United States; the plant is sown as a cover crop. The *Eriogonum* genus includes the wild or yellow buckwheat (*E. alleni*), restricted to the Appalachian shale barrens, and many Western species, e.g., the desert trumpet (*E. inflatum*), a desert flower of arid plains and plateaus. The interesting *Koenigia* genus has only one species, but it is found in arctic regions, in the Himalayas, and in Tierra del Fuego.

bucolics: see PASTORAL.

Bucuresti: see BUCHAREST.

Bucyrus (būsī′rŭs), city (pop. 12,276), co. seat of Crawford co., N central Ohio, on the Sandusky river and NE of Marion, in a farm area; settled 1819, laid out 1822. It is a trade and industrial center and has varied manufactures, including farm and highway-construction machinery, fluorescent lamps, and roller bearings.

bud, in lower plants and animals, a protuberance from which a new organism or limb develops; in seed plants, a miniature twig bearing compressed rudimentary lateral stems (branches), leaves, or flowers, or all three, and protected in cold climates by overlapping bud scales. In warm climates buds grow all year; in temperate climates they grow in summer and remain dormant in the winter. The winter buds (particularly the larger terminal buds on twigs) of trees and shrubs are almost always so characteristic that they serve to identify the species. The "eyes" of a potato are undeveloped buds. See also BUDDING and STEM.

Budaeus: see BUDÉ, GUILLAUME.

Budapest, the Danube dividing Buda and Pest.

Budapest (bŏŏ′dŭpĕst″), city (estimated pop. 1,807,-300), capital of Hungary, N central Hungary, on both banks of the Danube. The largest city of Hungary and its industrial, cultural, and transportation center, Budapest has varied manufactures, notably machinery, iron and steel, chemicals, and textiles. Together with its industrial suburbs (particularly Csepel, Kispest, Pestszenterzsebet, Pestszentlorinc, and Ujpest, all joined to Budapest in 1949), Budapest accounts for about half of Hungary's total industrial production. It is the seat of the Hungarian Academy of Sciences, of a university, and of many other scientific and educational institutions. Budapest was formed in 1873 by the union of Buda (Ger. *Ofen*) and Obuda (Hung. *Óbuda,* Ger. *Alt-Ofen*) on the right bank of the Danube with Pest on the left bank. The Roman capital of Lower Pannonia, Aquincum, was near the modern Obuda, and Pest developed about another Roman town. Both cities were destroyed by Mongols in 1241, but in the 13th cent. King Bela IV built a fortress (Buda) on a hill here, and in the 14th cent. Emperor Sigismund built a palace for the Hungarian rulers. Buda became the capital of Hungary in 1361, reaching its height as a cultural center under MATTHIAS CORVINUS. Pest fell to the Turks in 1526, Buda in 1541. When Charles V of Lorraine conquered them for the Hapsburgs in 1686, both Buda and Pest were in ruins. They were resettled, Buda with Germans, Pest with Serbs. Buda, a free royal town after 1703, had a renaissance under Maria Theresa, who built a royal palace and in 1777 transferred to Buda the uni-

versity founded in 1635 by Peter Pazmany at Nagyzombat. The university was moved in 1784 to Pest, which in the 19th cent. throve with commerce and was, after the flood of 1838, rebuilt on modern lines. Buda became largely the residential sector. The united city was by 1917 Hungary's leading commercial center and was already ringed by industrial suburbs. Budapest was not only a bustling metropolis but a beautiful city famed for its literary, theatrical, and musical life; it attracted tourists by its mineral springs, its historic buildings, and its parks, notably the large municipal park and the show place of Margaret Island (Hung. *Margit Sziget*), in the Danube, where St. Margaret, daughter of Bela IV, had lived in a convent. With the collapse of the Austro-Hungarian monarchy (Oct., 1918), Hungary, under Count Michael KAROLYI, was proclaimed an independent republic. Budapest became its capital. After the resignation of Karolyi (March, 1919) the Communists led by Bela KUN gained control of the city and established a Soviet republic in Hungary. Following the defeat (July, 1919) of Kun's forces, Budapest was occupied and looted by Rumanian forces. In Nov., 1919, Budapest was seized by forces of Admiral HORTHY, who in March, 1920, was proclaimed a regent of Hungary. In Oct., 1944, Horthy proclaimed Hungary's withdrawal, as Germany's ally, from the Second World War and that same month German troops occupied Budapest. After a 14-week siege, the city fell (Feb., 1945) to Soviet troops. Almost 70 percent of Buda was destroyed or heavily damaged, including the royal palace and the Romanesque Coronation Church. In Jan., 1946, Hungary was proclaimed a republic with Budapest its capital. In 1948 the Hungarian Communists, backed by Soviet troops, seized control of Hungary and proclaimed it (Aug., 1949) a people's republic. Budapest was the center of a popular uprising against the Hungarian Communist regime in Oct.-Nov., 1956 (see HUNGARY).
Budaun (bŭdoun′), town (pop. c.6,000), Uttar Pradesh state, N India. It trades in grain. An important northern military outpost under the Mogul empire, it has the Great Mosque (the Jama Masjid) which dates from 1223.
Buddha (bŏŏ′dŭ) [Sanskrit,=the enlightened one], usual title given to the religious leader who founded BUDDHISM. It is generally believed that he lived from c.563 B.C. to 483 B.C. The story of his life is incrusted with legend, and even the Pali canon, which purportedly conveys the events of his life, was written at least 200 years after his death. He was of noble family of the Kshatryia (or warrior) caste, son of a wealthy ruler of the Sakya clan, whose territory lay along the southern edge of Nepal; the Buddha, it is said, was born in the Terai of Nepal. His given name was Siddhartha, his family name Gautama (or Gotama); later he was called Sakyamuni (sage of the Sakya clan). According to tradition, at Siddhartha's birth it was predicted that he would become either a universal ruler or a universal teacher. His father, wishing Siddhartha to succeed him as ruler, took great pains to shelter the boy from all misery and any omens that would persuade him to become a teacher. Siddhartha spent his youth in great luxury, married and fathered a son. When he was

29, however, he went for a ride in the royal park and saw four signs that were to decide his career—an aged man, a sick man, a corpse, and a wandering religious mendicant. He recognized in the first three signs the presence of suffering in the world, and, in the serenity of the mendicant, he saw his destiny. Renouncing his life of luxury, he left the royal palace, forsaking his wife, Yashodhara, and his infant son, Rahula. For six years, a hermit and a wanderer, he suffered extreme self-mortification. One day he sat down under a bo tree (i.e., pipal tree) at Buddh Gaya determined not to leave his seat until the riddle of human misery was solved. The Bodhisattva (or future Buddha) withstood the temptations and torments cast by Mara, the Evil One, and, on the 49th day, he was rewarded for his holy asceticism by "the great enlightenment," or NIRVANA. He became a teacher, gathered disciples, who were the first Buddhist monks, and spread the results of his vision abroad. The Buddha preached his first sermon in the Deer Park at Sarnath, near Benares. He returned home briefly where he converted his father, wife, and son. His cousin Devadatta, jealous of the Buddha, tried to kill him by loosing a wild elephant in his path, but the Buddha calmed the beast with his gentleness. For 45 years Siddhartha traveled and preached his ministry, and in time he came to be called Bhagava [Sanskrit,=lord], Tathagatha [Sanskrit,=he who

has come], and the Buddha. Early representations of the Buddha often took the form of an empty throne, a pair of footprints, a wheel, or a pipal tree, symbols of his having attained nirvana and having left the world. The Gandhara and Mathura schools of art, which flourished from the 1st and 2nd cent. A.D. and which were much influenced by Western ideas, produced the first images of the Buddha. See E. H. Brewster, *Life of Gotama the Buddha* (1926); E. J. Thomas, *The Life of Buddha as Legend and History* (1931); Maurice Percheron, *The Marvelous Life of the Buddha* (1960).

Buddh Gaya or **Bodh Gaya** (both: bōōd′ gä′yä), village, W central Bihar state, India. BUDDHA according to tradition received enlightenment under a pipal tree (bo tree) here. There are extensive relics of Buddhist sculpture, dating from the 8th to the 12th cent. A.D.

Buddhism (bōō′dĭzŭm, bŭ′–), philosophy and system of ethics, one of the great Oriental religions. Today it numbers many millions of adherents in Ceylon, Nepal, China, Japan, Tibet, Thailand, Burma, Cambodia, Korea, Laos, and Viet Nam. Buddhism arose from the teachings of the Buddha in India during the 6th and 5th cent. B.C. The caste system at that time was still in the making, and, when the priestly Brahmans put forward their claims to spiritual and social supremacy, many individuals in the nobility, such as the Buddha and

THAILAND: Penitent Buddha; medieval period, bronze

JAPAN (left): Daibutsu of Kamakura; 13th cent., bronze, 42 ft. high

GANDHARA, PAKISTAN:
Head of Buddha;
5th cent., limestone

CAMBODIA: Head
of Buddha;
12th cent., stone

THAILAND: Head of
Buddha; 12-14th cent.,
sandstone

CHINA: Meditating Buddha;
11th cent., wood

CEYLON (below): Sleeping
Buddha; 12th cent., rock-
hewn, 43 ft. long

KOREA (right): Standing
Buddha; c. 9th cent., bronze

*Standing bronze Buddha
(India, 5th century).*

Mahavira, founder of JAINISM, disputed these claims and asserted their independent points of view. They resisted the complex ritual of Brahmanism and its emphasis upon sacrifice as a means to salvation; they rejected the sanctity of the Vedas and the importance of caste. Primitive Buddhism was, nevertheless, close to early HINDUISM. It accepted belief in rebirth and the TRANSMIGRATION OF SOULS, as well as the idea that behavior in one life bears some relation to one's condition in future lives (see KARMA), and it defined the goal of religious endeavor as escape from the continuous round of rebirth. The Buddha's interest, however, was largely ethical, not metaphysical. His concern was with human sorrow, suffering and dissatisfaction, which he saw as inherent in life as it is ordinarily lived. These things could be dispelled, he taught, only by abandoning desire, which includes personal ambition, craving, longing, and selfishness of all kinds. The means to this abandonment was neither self-indulgence nor self-mortification, but a middle path of moderate detachment. The *Sermon of the Turning of the Wheel of the Law*, delivered by the Buddha at the deer park at Sarnath, elucidates these points by means of the "four noble truths" which state that existence is sorrow, that the origin of sorrow is desire, that sorrow ceases when desire

ceases, and that the way to achieve cessation of desire is the "noble eightfold path." This eightfold path comprises right belief, right resolve (to renounce sensual pleasure, to harm no living creature and ultimately to attain salvation), right speech, right conduct, right occupation, right effort (to keep the mind free from evil and devoted to good), right contemplation, and right meditation (to achieve a state of selfless contemplation). Disciples of the Buddha took vows against killing, stealing, falsehood, unchastity and strong drink; they practiced confession and lived an austere, world-denying life. The objective of this effort was NIRVANA, a state of complete blissful detachment, which, when attained permanently (parinirvana), brought cessation of rebirth. The spiritual adept who could achieve this goal was known as an *arahat* or *arahant* [worthy]. Buddhism early developed into a monastic church. The Buddha's disciples were ascetic mendicants who settled during the rainy season in fixed sites. In time these monastic communities (*sangha*) became permanent and were regarded as one of the "three jewels" of Buddhism, the others being the Buddha and the Law (*dhamma*). After a long oral tradition, Buddhism also began to develop (c.1st cent. B.C.) a written sacred canon. The Pali scriptures (see PALI LITERATURE) are retained in Ceylon and Sanskrit scriptures have been preserved, largely through translations into Chinese and Tibetan. A portion of the Buddhist canon consists of the Jataka, a collection of over 500 lively folk tales and other stories. Most of the Jataka tales, which have been drawn from many sources, are secular, but they have been given an aura of sanctity by being ascribed to the Buddha, who is said to have told them as recollections of his previous births.

Growth of Buddhism. Buddhism spread rapidly from the place of its origin. Under the emperor ASOKA (d. 232 B.C.), who conceived of it as a world religion, it spread throughout India and was introduced into Ceylon by Asoka's son, Mahinda, according to some legends. Most of the stupas, or Buddhist reliquary shrines, which are found throughout India, were erected in this period. Subsequently, Indian traders and travelers carried Buddhism throughout SE Asia and to S China. It also spread to the northwest among the Greek kingdoms left by Alexander the Great's conquests in present-day Pakistan and Afghanistan. One highly readable piece of early Buddhist literature, *The Questions of Milinda*, relates the conversion of the Greco-Bactrian king, Menander (Milinda), by the Buddhist sage, Nagasena. Kanishka, monarch of the Kushan Empire which dominated (A.D. c.100) N India, was an ardent patron of Buddhism. He championed a new Greco-Buddhist style of sculpture and architecture. The art forms of the Gandhara school, especially the curly-haired, seated Buddhas, became dominant as far away as Japan. Kanishka also led the introduction of the faith into Central Asia, and from there it spread into North China, soon reaching Korea and, by the 6th cent., Japan. The variety of Buddhism which diffused from NW India into this region and, eventually, to such peripheral areas as Viet Nam, differed from the early sects of Buddha's time. It came to be known as Mahayana [greater vehicle], distinguishing itself from the older Hinayana [lesser vehicle], which remained closer to original Buddhism. The latter is still the religion of Ceylon, Burma, Thailand, Laos, and Cambodia, where the less invidious term, Theravada [doctrine of the elders], is used.

Branches of Buddhism. Mahayana Buddhism developed a large body of metaphysical speculation and an extensive pantheon. The meaning of nirvana changed radically in popular Mahayana. Increasingly, it came to denote salvation in a definite afterlife in paradise; paradise and hell also are described vividly in Mahayana writings. In place of the essentially atheistic religion of the historical Buddha, the Mahayanists have a myriad of godlike Buddhas who have appeared on earth, attained enlightenment, taught the faith, and attained nirvana, where prayers cannot reach them. Mahayana also developed a newer type of deity, the bodhisattva [potential Buddha] who, despite enlightenment, remain in this world to help others to salvation. The most famous Bodhisattvas are Avalokiteshvara, the main figure in the Ajanta cave paintings, whose symbol is a blue lotus, and Maitreya, the future Buddha, known in China as Mi-lo-fu. The bodhisattva ideal of aid to others has led to a strong emphasis in Mahayana on charity—good works to help others and to contribute to one's own salvation. In many Mahayana sects it is believed that any individual may become a Bodhisattva if he devotes his life to doing good. A third class of Mahayana deities are the Dhyani or contemplative Buddhas, the most important of whom is Amitabha (in Japan, Amida). He presides over paradise, properly known as the "Pure Land," and his popularity in China and Japan surpasses that of the Buddha Gautama. Mahayana, as it developed and spread, generated dozens of sects which base their differences on divergences in interpretation of ritual, theology, or metaphysics. The Pure Land sects (in China, Ching-t'u; in Japan, Jodo and Shin) promise a heavenly salvation in the Western Paradise of Amitabha for those who give the Buddha complete devotion; faith replaces a strenuous life of good works, and, in the large Japanese Shin sect, priests are allowed to marry, eat meat, and live like the laity. The contemplative sects stress meditative insight as a means to salvation. Derived from the Indian *dhyana* [contemplation] sects, they include Ch'an, introduced to China in the 6th cent. A.D., and its derivative, ZEN BUDDHISM, in Japan. The rationalist sects reject intuition as a means to salvation, advocating rational study and meditation; they include Japanese Tendai and Chinese T'ien-T'ai, the scriptures of which are known as the *Lotus of the True Law*. The mystery of true word sects developed in China in the 8th cent. as Chen Yen and were established in Japan in the 9th cent. as Shingon by Master Kobo Daishi (744–835), reputedly the inventor of Japanese writing. They have elaborate pantheons, extensive temple worship, and a heavy stress on magic. In Japanese Shingon, which has been closely tied to Shinto, the highest deity is the Buddha Dainichi or Vairocana [Great Sun]. The Nichiren [Sun-Lotus] sect, founded by the monk Nichiren (1222–1282), is a solely Japanese development. It espouses active nationalism and

has had, at times, as many as 8,000,000 adherents. A late and degenerate form of Mahayana Buddhism reached Tibet about A.D. 630 and was merged with native demonolatry; this religion is sometimes regarded as a separate "vehicle," Vajrayana [vehicle of the thunderbolt], and is widely known as LAMAISM or tantric Buddhism. Hinayana or Theravada Buddhism of Ceylon and SE Asia still observes the monastic disciplines of early Buddhism. The monk practices solitary meditation and goes out from the monastery every morning, dressed in yellow robes, to beg his food. The Theravada monk is known as Bikkhu and members of the female order are called Bikkhunis. Philosophical Theravada holds that the Buddha no longer exists, as he lost all being or becoming when he entered nirvana. Nevertheless, worship is not absent among Theravadins. Monks and laymen alike revere relics of the Buddha, which are housed in stupas and pagodas, and the layman regularly worships a variety of Buddha images, the hand positions of which indicate the mood of the Buddha. Popular deities, some surviving from pre-Buddhist times, are also worshiped, often being regarded as famous disciples of the Buddha. The future Buddha, Maitreya, who resides in Tushita [heaven], and Buddha Avalokiteshvara are worshiped, as in Mahayana. The best known of the Theravada reliquary shrines is the Temple of the Tooth in Kandy, Ceylon, where, it is said, a tooth of the Buddha is kept in a crystal urn. In many temples in Theravada countries facsimiles of the Buddha's footprints are venerated. Unlike Mahayana, Theravada has few sectarian differences; the Pali canon is accepted by all Theravadins, and variations are primarily in details of ritual. Despite its success elsewhere, Buddhism declined and almost disappeared in India after the 7th cent. A.D. The invasions of the ferocious White Huns in the 6th cent. A.D., which resulted in the destruction of Buddhist monasteries and the disorganization of Buddhist leadership, were partly responsible. Also important was the incorporation by Hinduism of the Buddha as the ninth incarnation or AVATARA of their own god, VISHNU, which seriously vitiated the uniqueness of Buddhism. The Moslem invasions of India from the 11th cent. gradually destroyed the remaining Buddhist centers, and today only a few thousand believers in the foothills of the Himalayas maintain the old Buddhist tradition in India. See T. W. Rhys Davids, trans., *The Questions of King Milinda* (1890–94) and *Buddhism, Its History and Literature* (1926); Caroline Rhys Davids, *Buddhism, a Study of the Buddhist Norm* (1912); H. C. Warren, *Buddhism in Translations* (1922); Charles Eliot, *Japanese Buddhism* (1935); K. P. Landon, *Southeast Asia, Crossroads of Religion* (1949); Edward Conze, *Buddhism: Its Essence and Development* (1953); E. A. Burtt, ed., *The Teachings of the Compassionate Buddha* (1955); K. W. Morgan, ed., *The Path of the Buddha* (1956); A. F. Wright, *Buddhism in Chinese History* (1959); Christmas Humphreys, *A Popular Dictionary of Buddhism* (1962); Erik Zürcher, *Buddhism* (1962).

budding, type of GRAFTING in which a plant bud is inserted under the bark of the stock (usually not more than a year old). It is best done when the bark will peel easily and the buds are mature, as in spring, late summer, or early autumn. Budding is a common means of propagating roses and most fruit trees in nurseries.

Budd Lake, uninc. village (pop. 1,520), N N.J., NE of Hackettstown. It is a lake resort.

buddleja or **buddleia:** see LOGANIA.

Budé, Guillaume (gēyōm′ büdä′), 1467–1540, French scholar, known also by the Latinized form of his name, Budaeus (būdē′ŭs). One of the greatest of humanists and one of the greatest French scholars of all time, he was a towering figure of the Renaissance. He was secretary to Francis I, was busy about royal affairs, and persuaded the king to found the COLLÈGE DE FRANCE. His commentaries on the Pandects virtually introduced textual criticism in the study of Roman law. His treatises on language helped to establish the discipline of philology. He translated and commented on Greek literature and fostered the revival of Greek learning in France. Budé's voluminous writings also dealt with Greek and Roman numismatics, with political and economic theories, and with various other subjects.

Bude (būd), town (pop. 1,185), SW Miss., ESE of Natchez and on the Homochitto, in a timber area; inc. 1912.

Budenny, Semyon Mikhailovich (boōdĕn′ē, Rus. sĭmyôn mēkhī′lŭvĭch boōdyô′nē), 1883–, Russian general. A Don Cossack and a sergeant in the tsarist army, he joined the Communist party in 1919, organized the Red Cavalry, and won dashing victories in the civil war. Made (1935) a marshal, he held a command (1940) in the war against Finland. In the Second World War he was severely defeated (1941) by the Germans at Kiev and was shifted to the rear.

Bude-Stratton (būd′–), urban district (pop. 5,095), Cornwall, SW England. Wheat is the chief product. Bude has a picturesque canal. Stratton village was the scene of a parliamentarian defeat in the Puritan Revolution.

Budge, John Donald (Don Budge), 1915–, American tennis player, b. Oakland, Calif. He won the U.S. and British (Wimbledon) singles titles in 1937 and 1938. Budge also was a member of the 1937 U.S. team that won the Davis Cup from Great Britain. In 1938 he scored the "grand slam" of tennis by winning the U.S., Australian, French, and British singles championships; in the same year he and Gene Mako won the U.S. doubles crown. He turned professional in 1939. He wrote *How Lawn Tennis is Played* (1937) and *On Tennis* (1939).

Budgell, Eustace (bŭj′ŭl), 1686–1737, English essayist. He was a cousin of Addison, through whose aid he obtained several public offices. Budgell contributed to the *Tatler*, the *Spectator*, and the *Guardian*, and wrote pamphlets against the ministry in the *Craftsman*. He lost a fortune in the collapse of the South Sea Bubble and later became involved in the losing end of a controversy over a sum of money left him by Matthew Tindal. He ended his life by suicide.

budgerigar: see PARAKEET.

budget, inclusive list of proposed expenditures and expected receipts of any person, enterprise, or government, for a definite period, usually one year. Budget estimates are based on the expenditures and receipts of a similar previous period, modified by any expected changes. The governmental bud-

get originated in England. In the United States, the President annually submits to Congress a budget which shows the condition of the Treasury at the end of the last completed fiscal year, its estimated condition at the end of the current fiscal year, and its estimated condition at the end of the ensuing year if the budget proposals are carried out; the revenues and expenditures during the last completed year and the estimates thereof for the current year; recommendations of provisions for meeting the revenue and expenditure for the ensuing year; and any other data considered helpful to Congress in its determination of the government's financial policy. No other administrative officer is allowed to make revenue recommendations unless asked to do so by Congress or one of its houses. To help the President, the Bureau of the Budget was created (1921), under the Treasury Dept., to receive, compile, and criticize estimates of expenditure needs submitted by the various governmental services and to study in detail all government services and recommend to the President any changes therein that will increase their economy and efficiency. The bureau was transferred in 1939 to the executive office of the President. The national budget is often regarded as the immediate policy statement of the presidential administration. Since the beginning of the Second World War and through most recent times the national budget has grown immensely because of increased defense requirements. It was estimated that by 1964 the national budget would be ten times as large as the pre-Second World War budget of $9.1 billion in 1940. All the states have some form of budget system. See A. E. Buck, *Public Budgeting* (1929); F. A. Bland, *Budget Control* (4th ed., 1946); A. W. Willsmore, *Business Budgets and Budgetary Control* (4th ed., 1960).

Budweis (bŭd′wīs, Ger. boōt′vīs), Czech Česke Budějovice (chĕs′kĕ boō′dyĕyôvītsĕ), city (estimated pop. 66,323), S Bohemia, Czechoslovakia, on the Moldau. A commercial center, it produces pencils, enamelware, machinery, and beer. It is also an important railway junction and a river port. Founded in the 13th cent., Budweis is noted for its old inner town, with an arcaded square, and for an old castle.

Buel, Jesse (bū′ŭl), 1778–1839, American agriculturist and journalist, b. Coventry, Conn. He published the Kingston *Plebeian* (1803–13) and the Albany *Argus* (1813–20). He wrote tirelessly on agriculture—in his newspapers, in his reports as secretary of the state board of agriculture, and, after 1834, as editor of the *Cultivator*, one of the earliest farm journals to become widely popular. In the sandy land near Albany after 1821 he developed by scientific practices a model farm which yielded him large financial returns. The program he adopted—crop rotation, deep plowing, drainage, and heavy manuring—was widely followed later. He served several terms in the legislature, where he worked for a state agricultural school. He was defeated for the governorship of New York by William L. Marcy in 1836. He wrote *The Farmer's Companion* (1839), which passed through many editions. See *Jesse Buel, Agricultural Reformer: Selections from His Writings* (ed. by H. J. Carman, 1947).

Buell, Abel (bū′ŭl), 1742–1822, American silversmith, engraver, and type founder, b. Killingworth, Conn. He engraved a number of maps, including maps of the Florida coast and a large wall map of the United States, the first produced in America after the Treaty of Paris in 1783. He experimented in type founding, cast the first font of native-made American type (1769), and later supplied type to Connecticut printers. He invented machinery for cutting and polishing precious stones; invented a machine for coining money and for a period produced copper coins for the state; established in 1795, at New Haven, one of the first cotton mills in the country, which, however, soon failed; and was interested in many other projects. All this time he was producing silver and jewelry. See biography by L. C. Wroth (rev. ed., 1958).

Buell, Don Carlos, 1818-98, Union general in the Civil War, b. near Marietta, Ohio, grad. West Point, 1841. Before the outbreak of the Civil War, he had served with distinction in the Seminole and Mexican wars. Buell was appointed brigadier general of volunteers (May, 1861), helped to organize the Army of the Potomac, and was placed in command of the Dept. of the Ohio (Nov., 1861). When Grant moved up the Tennessee and Cumberland rivers, Buell supported him by marching on Bowling Green, and after the fall of Fort Donelson he pursued the retreating Confederates to Nashville. In March, 1862, he was placed under Gen. H. W. Halleck and made major general, commanding the Army of the Ohio. Halleck ordered him to advance on Savannah, Tenn., and Buell came up just in time to save the day at Shiloh (see SHILOH, BATTLE OF). After accompanying Halleck to Corinth, he was ordered to proceed with four divisions to Chattanooga, but Braxton BRAGG reached there before him. When Buell concentrated his forces at Murfreesboro, Bragg marched around his left and headed for Louisville. Buell's rapid marching and Bragg's delay enabled the Union general to reach Louisville first. He fought Bragg at PERRYVILLE on Oct. 8, 1862, and on the next day the Confederates retreated from Kentucky. Buell was dilatory in his pursuit and advanced to Nashville. Dissatisfied with his campaign, the administration removed him in favor of Gen. W. S. ROSECRANS. A military investigation was held (Nov., 1862–May, 1863), and, after a year, Buell was discharged as major general of volunteers. He thereupon resigned his regular commission and took no further part in the war. See J. B. Fry, *The Army under Buell* (1886).

Buena (bū′nù), borough (pop. 3,243), S central N.J., ENE of Vineland; inc. 1848.

Buena Park (bwā′nù), city (pop. 46,401), S Calif., SE of Los Angeles; inc. 1953. Citrus fruit is processed, and electronic equipment and aircraft parts are made. Knott's Berry Farm is here.

Buenaventura (bwā″nävāntōō′rä), city (pop. c. 90,000), W Colombia, a port on the Pacific. Founded c.1540, it was burned by the Indians at the end of the 16th cent. The present port on Cascajal Island in Buenaventura Bay was more recently settled. It is the port of the Cauca valley, and since the completion of the railroad to Cali and the opening of the Panama Canal, it has become increasingly important, exporting coffee, platinum, gold, and hides.

Buena Vista (bwā′nä vē′stä), locality just S of Saltillo, Coahuila, where a battle of the Mexican War was fought, Feb. 22-23, 1847. Gen. Zachary TAYLOR, disobeying orders from the U.S. government, had advanced here. Santa Anna, having gathered a Mexican army, came north by heroic marches and, attacking Taylor's forces furiously, outflanked them. The fighting was hard and at the end of the second day seemed a drawn battle, but on the night of Feb. 23 the Mexican army withdrew, leaving Taylor in control of the north of

Battle of Buena Vista, with General Zachary Taylor on white horse at right (steel engraving 1866).

Mexico. Among the U.S. officers Gen. John E. Wool distinguished himself by his command at Buena Vista.

Buena Vista. 1 Resort town (pop. 1,806; alt. 7,800 ft.), central Colo., on the Arkansas and W of Colorado Springs; founded and inc. 1879. It was once the center of a rich silver-mining region. The gamblers, adventurers, and desperados who had come into the town during the mining boom were driven out by the townspeople in 1880. Today the town raises livestock and grain. **2** City (pop. 1,574), co. seat of Marion co., W Ga., SE of Columbus, in a farm and timber area; settled 1830.

Avenida 9 de Julio and Plaza Republica, Buenos Aires.

Argentina's Parliament in Buenos Aires.

Cotton cloth is made. **3** City (pop. 6,300), western Va., in the Blue Ridge ESE of Lexington; founded 1889, inc. 1891. It manufactures paper, bricks, and plastic and rubber products. A girls' junior college is here. The city is at the edge of George Washington National Forest.

Buenos Aires (bwā′nus ī′rēz, â′rēz, Span. bwā′nōs ī′räs), city (pop. c.3,875,000), capital of Argentina, in the federal district, NE Argentina, on the right bank of the Río de la Plata. The largest city of Latin America, Buenos Aires is the chief port and the financial, industrial, and social center of Argentina. On the eastern edge of the Pampa (see PAMPAS) and connected with Uruguay, Paraguay, and Brazil by a great inland river system, the city is the distribution hub and a trade outlet for those vast regions. Its modern port—one of the busiest in the world—exports chiefly meat, meat products, and grain. The most heavily industrialized city of the nation, Buenos Aires has food-processing plants, large metalworks, automobile factories, oil refineries, textile mills, and printing plants. A city of great wealth, it is modern and well built, with spacious parks, excellent buildings, and some fine streets, such as the Avenida de Mayo. It also has a modern subway system. Among the numerous educational, scientific, and cultural institutions are the Univ. of Buenos Aires (founded 1821) and the National Library. The cathedral, completed in 1804, has the tomb of José de San Martín and is a well-known landmark. Buenos Aires was first founded in 1536 by Pedro de MENDOZA, but because of Indian attacks Domingo Martínez de IRALA ordered (1539) the colonists to move to Asunción; the move was completed by 1541. A second and permanent settlement was planted in 1580 by Juan de GARAY, but it did not become of paramount importance until the latter part of the colonial period. The growth of Buenos Aires, however, was greatly enhanced by the development of trade, much of it contraband. In 1617, at the instance of Hernando Arias de Saavedra, the province of Buenos Aires or Río de la Plata was separated from the administration of Asunción, with Buenos Aires as the seat of the new provincial government. During the 17th cent. the city ceased to be endangered by Indians, but it was frequently raided by the French, Portuguese, and Danes. It became the capital of the viceroyalty of the Río de la Plata in 1776 and shortly afterward was made an open port by Charles III. From that time on it had the hegemony of S South America. In 1806 the city was captured by British troops under Gen. William BERESFORD but was quickly recaptured by Jacques de Liniers; in 1807 a second British attack was repulsed. The defeat of the British attack was significant in its effect on the people of Buenos Aires; it helped to prepare the way for the revolt against Spain, in which Buenos Aires played an important part. In May, 1810, the cabildo deposed the viceroy and established a junta. The winning of independence was followed by a period of confusion and strife in Argentina. A long conflict ensued between the unitarians, strongest in Buenos Aires prov., who advocated a centralized government dominated by the city of Buenos Aires, and the federalists, who supported provincial autonomy and equality. The dictator Juan Manuel de ROSAS ostensibly rejected the unitarian system, but he maintained the dominance of Buenos Aires. Although an attempt was made by Justo José de URQUIZA to establish a federal government, it was under Bartolomé MITRE, the champion of the city, that national political unity was finally achieved. The bitterness between Buenos Aires and the province continued, however, until 1880, when the city was detached from the province and federalized. The spectacular economic rise of Argentina in the second half of the 19th cent. attracted to Buenos Aires capital and immigration from all over the world. The province of Buenos Aires (118,752 sq. mi.; pop. c.5,450,000) is the richest and most populous of Argentina. LA PLATA (since 1882) is the capital. Situated in E Argentina, on the Atlantic, the province forms part of the Pampa and is the major livestock-raising and agricultural region of the country. Beef, mutton, pork, wheat, corn, flax, oats, and barley are the principal products. It has a dense rail network, and industry is mainly concentrated in Zárate, La Plata, Mar del Plata, and Bahía Blanca.

Buer: see GELSENKIRCHEN.

Buffalo. 1 Town (pop. 1,140), E central Iowa, on the Mississippi and WSW of Davenport. **2** Village (pop. 2,322), co. seat of Wright co., E Minn., NW of Minneapolis, in a lake region; settled c.1855, inc. 1887. Clothing and wood products are made. **3** City (pop. 1,477), co. seat of Dallas co., SW Mo., NE of Springfield, in a farm region; inc. 1845. **4** City (pop. 532,759), co. seat of Erie co., W N.Y., on Lake Erie and the Niagara river. In 1803 Joseph Ellicott laid out a village here for the Holland Land Company. Almost destroyed by fire (1813) in the War of 1812, Buffalo was slow in rebuilding until the opening of the Erie Canal in **1825, when it began growing rapidly. By 1832 it**

Buffalo

was incorporated as a city. Transportation was the primary factor in the city's early growth, and it became a major Great Lakes port, one of the largest grain-distributing ports in the United States, and an important railroad focus. Among its industries are flour milling, iron and steel manufacturing, the production of industrial chemicals, and the operation of automobile, aircraft and missile plants. Its educational institutions include the Univ. of Buffalo (see BUFFALO, UNIVERSITY OF), a state teachers college, Canisius College (Jesuit; for men; 1870), and D'Youville College (Roman Catholic; for women; 1908). In Delaware Park are the Albright Art Gallery and a zoo, and in Humboldt Park is the Buffalo Museum of Science. Notable buildings include the city hall (1932); the Prudential Building (1895–96), designed by Louis Sullivan; and the Larkin office building, designed by Frank Lloyd Wright. A state mental hospital and a state institute for the study of malignant diseases are here. Grover Cleveland became mayor of Buffalo in 1882. Here in 1901 President McKinley was assassinated at the time of the Pan-American Exposition, and Theodore Roosevelt took the presidential oath. Millard Fillmore's home was in Buffalo. **5** Town (pop. 1,618), co. seat of Harper co., NW Okla., NNW of Woodward, in a farm and livestock area; founded 1907, inc. 1908. **6** Uninc. village (pop. 1,209), NW S.C., SE of Spartanburg. Textiles are made. **7** City (pop. 1,108), E central Texas, E of Waco, in a farm area; est. 1872. **8** City (pop. 2,907), co. seat of Johnson co., N Wyo., SSE of Sheridan and on Clear Creek; founded c.1880, inc. 1884. Eastern gateway to the Bighorn National Forest, it is the trade center for a ranch, farm, and resort area. To the north lies Lake De Smet.

buffalo, name commonly applied to the American BISON, but correctly restricted to certain related oxlike mammals of Asia and Africa. The Asiatic water buffalo or Indian buffalo stands 5 ft. or more at the shoulder. Its widely spread horns project from the sides of the head and curve backward. For many centuries it has been domesticated as a draft animal and as a source of milk, but wild forms still

Aerial view of Buffalo, N.Y.

exist. The anoa or pygmy buffalo is the wild ox of the Celebes. The fierce Cape buffalo is found in South Africa.

Buffalo, University of, at Buffalo, N.Y.; coeducational; chartered and opened 1846 as a medical school. Its college of arts and sciences was first opened in 1913. Buffalo's modified tutorial system is one of the few systems in the nation to offer individual instruction during junior and senior years.

buffalo berry: see OLEASTER.

Buffalo Bill, 1846–1917, American plainsman, scout, and showman, b. near Davenport, Iowa. His real name was William Frederick Cody. His family moved (1854) to Kansas, and on the death of his father (1857) he set out to earn the family living,

Buffalo Bill

working for supply trains and a freighting company. In 1859 he went to the Colorado gold fields, and in 1860 he rode briefly for the Pony Express. His adventures on the Western frontier as an army scout and later as a buffalo hunter for railroad construction camps on the Great Plains were the basis for the stories later told of him. Ned BUNTLINE in 1872 persuaded him to appear on the stage, and except for a brief period of scouting against the Sioux in 1876, he was thereafter connected with show business. In 1883 he organized Buffalo Bill's Wild West Show, and he toured with it throughout America and Europe for many years. It was imitated by many other wild West shows. Wyoming granted him a stock ranch, on which the town of Cody was laid out. He died in Denver and was buried on Lookout Mt. near Golden, Colo. The exploits attributed to him in the dime novels of Buntline and Prentice Ingraham are only slightly more imaginative than his own autobiography (1920). See R. J. Walsh and M. S. Salsbury, *The Making of Buffalo Bill* (1928); biographies by H. B. Sell and Victor Weybright (1955) and D. B. Russell (1960).

buffalo bur: see NIGHTSHADE.

Buffalo Center, town (pop. 1,088), N central Iowa, NW of Mason City, in a farm area.

buffalo clover: see LUPINE.

buffalo fish: see SUCKER.

buffalo grass, low perennial grass (*Buchloe dactyloides*) of the plains regions, one of the most important range grasses. Its dense matted growth is valuable also in erosion control. Buffalo grass usually grows together with the gramas or mesquite grasses (genus *Bouteloua*), especially blue grama and side-oats grama, taller grasses with the same distribution as buffalo grass.

Buffalo Grove, village (pop. 1,492), NE Ill., NW of Chicago; inc. 1958.

Buffington, Pa.: see NEW SALEM, Fayette co.

Buffon, Georges Louis Leclerc, comte de (zhôrzh′ lwĕ′ lŭklĕrk′ kŏt′ dù büfô′), 1707–88, French naturalist and author. From 1739 he was keeper of the Jardin du Roi (later the Jardin des Plantes) in Paris and made it a center of research during the ENLIGHTENMENT. He devoted his life to his monumental *Histoire naturelle* (44 vols., 1749–1804), a popular and brilliantly written compendium of data on natural history interspersed with Buffon's own speculations and theories. Of this work, the volumes *Histoire naturelle des animaux* and *Époques de la nature* are of especial interest. His famous *Discours sur le style* was delivered (1753) on his reception into the French Academy.

Buford, John (bū′fùrd), 1826–63, Union general in the Civil War, b. Woodford co., Ky., grad. West Point, 1848. His cavalry operations in the GETTYSBURG CAMPAIGN were particularly notable.

Buford, city (pop. 4,168), N Ga., NE of Atlanta, in a farm area; inc. 1872. It has a tannery, established in 1873.

Bug (bōōg, bŭg, Rus. bōōk), Ukr. *Buh*, river, rising E of Lvov in the Volhynian-Podolian hills, NW Ukrainian SSR. It is c.480 mi. long and flows N along the Polish-Ukrainian and Polish-Byelorussian borders past Brest and then NW through Poland to join the Vistula near Warsaw. It is connected with the Dnieper by the Dnieper-Bug Canal via the Pina river and with the Niemen by the Augustov Canal via the Narva. The Bug is also known as the Western Bug.

Bug or Southern Bug, Rus. *Yuzhny Bug* (yōō′zhnē bōōk′), Ukr. *Pivdynnyy Buh*, river, Ukrainian SSR, known to the ancients as Hypanis. It is c.530 mi. long, rises NW of Khmelnitsky, which it passes, and flows SE past Vinnitsa, Pervomaisk, Voznesensk, and Nikolayev into the Black Sea. It is navigable c.97 mi., from Voznesensk to its mouth.

bug, name applied correctly only to the suborder Heteroptera (order Hemiptera), insects characterized by a jointed beak adapted for piercing and sucking and by gradual metamorphosis. The true bugs differ greatly in appearance, but most have long slim legs, smooth bodies, and two pairs of wings. Most bugs feed on plant juices, some eat insects and spiders, and others, e.g., the bedbug, feed on man. Included in the group are the squash bug, the stinkbug, the chinch bugs, and various water bugs.

Buganda (bōōgän′dù), kingdom and federated state (17,311 sq. mi.; pop. c.1,900,000), S Uganda. The capital is Kampala. The kingdom dates from the mid-17th cent., and it had already attained a high level of development when first visited (1862) by Europeans. A protectorate was established (1894) over the region by Great Britain, and in 1900 the kingdom was granted limited internal self-government. Within the protectorate the desire for independence was always strong, and British plans for a unified, independent Uganda were opposed by the

Buganda parliament, which declared (1960) the kingdom's secession from the protectorate. Buganda became a federated state within Uganda, with a large measure of self-government, when the protectorate received its independence in 1962. See D. A. Low and R. C. Pratt, *Buganda and British Overrule* (1960).

Bugayev, Boris Nikolayevich: see BELY, ANDREI.

bugbane, any plant of the genus *Cimicifuga,* tall north temperate perennials of the BUTTERCUP family. The white spirelike bloom has a rank odor that attracts flies, which pollinate the plant. Common in woodlands of E North America is *C. racemosa,* black snakeroot or black cohosh, sometimes gathered for its medicinal root. Other plants are also called bugbane and snakeroot; most plants called cohosh belong to the related BANEBERRY genus.

Bugeaud de la Piconnerie, Thomas Robert (tōmä' rōběr' büzhō' dù lä pēkōnürē'), 1784–1849, marshal of France, duke of Isly, general and administrator in Algeria. He served in Napoleon's Imperial Guard until forced into retirement in 1815. Returning to public life after the July Revolution of 1830, he became a deputy. Sent twice (1836, 1837) to Algeria on special missions, he returned again in 1841 to undertake the pacification of Algeria as governor general. His celebrated victory at Isly (1844) finally broke the power of ABDU-L-KADIR. Bugeaud attempted to cooperate with the Arabs, to promote military colonization, and to encourage French settlers, but the unpopularity of his policies forced his resignation in 1847. He was named commander of the troops in Paris by Louis Philippe during the February Revolution of 1848. A strong general, he was feared in France as a potential Napoleon. He wrote on colonial, military, and economic subjects.

Bugenhagen, Johann (yō'hän boo'gùnhä"gùn), 1485–1558, German Protestant reformer. Born in Pomerania, he is sometimes called Dr. Pomeranus. An ordained priest, he was attracted to the reform movement by Martin Luther's writings. In 1521 he went to Wittenberg and entered upon a lasting friendship with Luther and Melanchthon. He was a lecturer in the university and pastor of the principal church in Wittenberg. Much of Bugenhagen's attention was devoted to ecclesiastical and educational organization in Brunswick, Hamburg, Lübeck, Pomerania, and Denmark. Bugenhagen helped Luther in his translation of the Bible. Of his own literary works the most important is *Interpretatio in librum Psalmorum* (1523). See biography by W. M. Ruccius (1924).

Bugge, Sophus (sō'foos boo'gù), 1833–1907, Norwegian philologist. He made a notable edition of the Old Norse runes, and his was the first critical edition (1881–89; 2d series, 1896) of the poems of the *Eddas.*

bugle, brass wind musical instrument consisting of a conical tube coiled once upon itself, capable of producing five or six harmonics. It is usually in G or B flat. Its principal use is for military and naval bugle calls, such as taps, reveille, and mess, and, in earlier times, for hunting calls. In the early 19th cent., keyed bugles were made in order to obtain a complete scale.

Buhl, André Charles: see BOULLE, ANDRÉ CHARLES.

Buhl (būl). **1** City (pop. 3,059), S Idaho, near the Snake WNW of Twin Falls; founded 1906, inc. 1909. In a reclaimed farm and dairy area served by the Minidoka project, Buhl is an important shipping point for potatoes and has many food-processing plants. **2** Village (pop. 1,526), NE Minn., between Virginia and Hibbing in the Mesabi iron range.

buhrstone (bûr'–), any hard, rough-surfaced, porous, siliceous rock which can be shaped and used as a millstone for grinding cereals, paint pigments, or other materials. The finest variety is a cellular quartz from the Tertiary strata near Paris; coarser buhrstones are quarried in the E United States.

Buisson, Ferdinand Édouard (fěrdēnä' ädwär' büēsō'), 1841–1932, French educator. He studied

Ferdinand É. Buisson

at the Sorbonne and later taught (1866–70) in Switzerland. After 1870 he served in the department of education, first as an inspector of schools and later as a director of primary education, resigning in 1886 to become professor of pedagogy at the Sorbonne. He produced the *Dictionnaire de pédagogie* (1882–93). From 1902 to 1914 and again from 1919 to 1924, he was a member of the chamber of deputies and was also active in working for civil rights. An ardent pacifist, he attended (1867) the first congress of the International Peace League; with Ludwig Quidde of Germany he received the 1927 Nobel Peace Prize.

Buitenzorg (boi'tùnzôrkh) [Dutch, =free from care], Malay *Bogor,* city (pop. 154,092), W Java, Indonesia. At the foot of two volcanoes, it is a summer resort, known chiefly for its magnificent botanical gardens (laid out 1817). Tea is grown on the surrounding highlands; coffee, rice, and spices are also important crops. Automobile tires, machinery, and textiles are manufactured. It has a palace of the former Dutch governor of Java.

Bukavu (bookä'voo), city (pop. c.60,500), capital of Kivu prov., E Republic of the Congo, a port on Lake Kivu. It is an administrative, commercial, and communications center. Agricultural products are processed, notably coffee and hides. Founded in 1901, it was formerly known as Costermansville.

Bukhara (bùkä'rù), city (pop. c.69,000), capital of Bukhara oblast, SE Uzbek SSR, in the Zeravshan river valley. The name is also spelled Bokhara. On the Shkhrud irrigation-canal system, it is the center of a large cotton district and has textile mills. First mentioned in Chinese chronicles in the 5th cent. A.D., Bukhara is one of the oldest trade and cultural centers in central Asia. It came under the Arab caliphate in the 8th cent. and became a major center of Islamic learning. During the 9th and 10th cent. it was the capital of the Samanid state. From the 16th cent. to 1920 it was the capital of the khanate or emirate of Bukhara, which was ceded to Russia in 1868. Until 1924 it was the capital of the Bukhara People's Republic. There are many monuments, including the mausoleum of Ismail Samanid (892–907), the minaret of Kalyan (1127), the mosque of Magoki-Attari (12th cent.), the Ulugbek (1417–18) and Mir-Arab (1535–36) medressehs (schools), and the medresseh of Abdylazizkhana (1651–52). When in the 19th cent. a spur of the Trans-Caspian RR reached Bukhara, the station, by request of the emir, was built at a distance (8 mi. to the southeast) from the city. Around the station grew New Bukhara, renamed (1935) Kagan. Kagan (pop. c.22,500) produces cotton, textiles, and cottonseed oil.

Bukhara, emirate of, former state, central Asia, in TURKISTAN, in the Amu-Darya river basin. Part of ancient Sogdiana, it was ruled (A.D. 709–874) by the Ummayid Arabs and played an important role under the Samanid dynasties (875–1000). It was a trade, transport, and cultural center of the Islamic world. The Seljuks ruled from 1004–1133; later, the realm was conquered by Jenghiz Khan (1220) and in the 14th cent. by Tamerlane. The Timurid dynasties ruled until the invasion of Uzbek tribes early in the 16th cent. The Bukhara emirate was founded by the Uzbek Khan Sheybani, who in 1500–1507 conquered the Timurid domains in Transoxania. In 1555 Abdullah Khan transferred the capital from Samarkand to Bukhara, from which the state then took its name. Internal feuds weakened Bukhara, it split into a number of principalities, and in 1740 it was conquered by Nadir Shah of Persia. In 1753 Bukhara again became an independent emirate but did not recover its supremacy over Khorezm, Merv, Badakhshan, Tashkent, and the Fergana Valley. Bukhara's population consisted principally of Uzbeks (who remained politically dominant), Sarts, and Tadzhiks. Defeated by Russia in 1866, the emirate became a Russian protectorate in 1868. In 1920, after a prolonged battle with Bolshevik forces, the last emir was driven into Afghanistan. The Bukhara People's Soviet Republic was established (1920) and lasted until 1924. In the same year it was proclaimed a socialist republic and was included in the USSR; a few months later, however, it was dismembered and divided between Uzbekistan, Tadzhikistan, and Turkmenistan.

Bukhari (Mohammed ibn Ismail al-Bukhari) (bōōk-härē′), d. 870, Arabic scholar and Moslem saint, b. Bukhara. He traveled widely over Moslem lands and made a tremendous collection of the traditional sayings of the Prophet. It is regarded in ISLAM as the commentary par excellence and the law book second only to the Koran. The tomb of Bukhari, near Samarkand, is a noted place of pilgrimage.

Bukharin, Nikolai Ivanovich (nyĭkŭlī′ ēvä′nŭvĭch bōōkhä′rēn), 1888–1938, Russian Communist leader and theoretician. A member of the Bolshevik wing of the Social Democratic party, he spent the years 1911–17 abroad and edited (1916) the revolutionary paper *Novy Mir* [new world] in New York. He took part in the October Revolution (1917) in Russia and became a leader in the Comintern and editor of *Pravda* [truth]. In 1924 he was made a full member of the Politburo. As STALIN rose to power in the 1920s, Bukharin at first allied with him against KAMENEV and Zinoviev. An advocate of slow agricultural collectivization and industrialization (the position of the "right opposition"), Bukharin lost (1929) his major posts after his view was defeated by the Stalinist majority in the party. He edited *Izvestia* [news] briefly in 1934 but was dismissed. In 1938 he was tried publicly for treason and was executed. He wrote and translated many works on economics and political science.

Bukki (bŭk′ī) [Heb.,=wasting from God]. **1** Descendant of Aaron. 1 Chron. 6.5,51; Ezra 7.4. **2** Danite. Num. 34.22.

Bukkiah (bŭkī′ŭ) [Heb.,=wasting from God], Levite 1 Chron. 25.4,13.

Bukovina (bōōkŭvē′nŭ), Rum. *Bucovina*, Ukr. *Bukovyna*, historic region, E Europe, in W Ukraine and NE Rumania. Traversed by the Carpathians and by the upper Pruth and Sereth rivers, it is heavily forested and produces timber, textiles, grain, and livestock. There are mineral resources, notably manganese, iron and copper, and oil. Chernovtsy, in the Ukraine, is the chief city. The population is largely Rumanian in S Bukovina and Ukrainian in N Bukovina. Before the Second World War, there were a number of Germans and, in the towns, many Jews; most of the Jews were exterminated during the war. A part of the Roman province of Dacia, Bukovina was overrun after the 3rd cent. A.D. by the Huns and other nomads. It later (10th–13th cent.) belonged to the Kievan state (see KIEV) and the Galich and Volhyna principalities. After the Mongols withdrew from Moldavia, Bukovina became (14th cent.) the nucleus of the Moldavian principality. The term Bukovina was first mentioned in the agreement concluded in 1412 between King Ladislaus II of Poland and Sigismund of Hungary. In 1514 Bukovina, then a part of Moldavia, became tributary to the Turkish sultans. Ceded (1775) by the Ottoman Empire to Austria, it was at first a district of GALICIA, but in 1848 it was made, as a titular duchy, a separate Austrian crownland. Under Austria Bukovina won limited autonomy and in 1861 Chernovtsy was made seat of a provincial diet. With the dissolution of the Austrian Monarchy in 1918, the Ukrainian national council at Chernovtsy voted the incorporation of N Bukovina into the West Ukrainian Democratic Republic. The Treaty of Saint Germain (1919) gave only the southern part of Bukovina to Rumania, but the subsequent Treaty of Sèvres (1920) transferred the whole of Bukovina to Rumania. The Rumanian regime suppressed self-government in N Bukovina and pursued a policy of Rumanization. By a treaty of June, 1940, Rumania ceded the northern part of Bukovina (2,140 sq. mi.; pop. c.774,000) to the USSR and it was incorporated into the Ukrainian SSR. From 1941 to 1944 Rumanian troops again occupied N Bukovina, but the Rumanian peace treaty of 1947 confirmed N Bukovina in possession of the USSR. It now forms part of the Chernovtsy oblast in the Ukraine. The remainder (c.1,890 sq. mi.; pop. c.500,000) forms one of the historical provinces of Rumania and is now part of the administrative region of Suceava.

Bulawayo (boōlùwä′yō), city (pop. c.190,000), SW Southern Rhodesia. The most important railroad center in the Federation of Rhodesia and Nyasaland, it also has much industry. Founded by the British in 1893, it was the scene (1896) of a MATABELE revolt.

bulb [Gr.], thickened, fleshy plant bud, usually formed under the surface of the soil, which carries the plant over from one blooming season to another. It may have layers (as in the onion and hyacinth) or scales (as in some lilies)—both of which are highly modified leaves. Many popular outdoor and house plants, such as the tulip and the narcissus, are grown from bulbs, some of them out of their usual season by forcing. Not true bulbs, but often so called, are the CORM of the crocus and the gladiolus, the TUBER of the dahlia and the potato, and the RHIZOME of certain irises and other plants. All such organs are specialized subterranean stems serving for food storage and asexual reproduction. See F. F. Rockwell and E. C. Grayson, *The Complete Book of Bulbs* (1953); P. M. Synge, *The Complete Guide to Bulbs* (1962).

bulbul (boōl′boōl), name for a family of 119 species of medium-sized, dull-colored passerine birds with short necks and wings, native to Africa and S Asia. Bulbuls are famed as songsters and are popular as cage birds in the Orient. Frequently mentioned in Persian poetry, the word bulbul is often mistranslated "nightingale."

Bulfinch, Charles, 1763–1844, American architect, b. Boston. A member of the Boston board of selectmen in 1791, he was chosen chairman in 1799—an office equivalent to mayor and held by Bulfinch for 19 years. Of the numerous structures which he

designed in Boston, the greater number have long been demolished, including the Federal Street Theater (1794), the first theater in New England. His chief monumental works remain—the statehouse in Boston (1799), University Hall at Harvard Univ. (1815), and the Massachusetts General Hospital (1820). From 1818 to 1830 Bulfinch carried to completion the CAPITOL at Washington; of his own contributions there remains the west portico, with the terraces and steps forming the approach to it. In this work and in the Massachusetts statehouse he evolved an architectural composition which has been used for state capitols throughout the country. He designed a memorial column on Beacon Hill (1789), Massachusetts State Prison (1803), a number of Massachusetts courthouses, and Franklin Crescent in Boston (1793). The last was a long curved row of 16 residences, inspired by the continuous block of houses which had been erected by Robert Adam and others in England. The First Church of Christ in Lancaster, Mass. (1816–17), one of the few remaining churches of the many which he designed, is one of his finest productions. While Bulfinch's works fall into the general category of "early American" architecture, they yet bear a distinctive stamp of his own. Their elegance, repose, and refinement of detail rank them among the best products of the nation's early years. See C. A. Place, *Charles Bulfinch* (1925).

Bulfinch, Thomas, 1796–1867, American author, b. Newton, Mass., grad. Harvard, 1814. He wrote a series of works popularizing fable and legend—*The Age of Fable* (1855), *The Age of Chivalry* (1858), *Legends of Charlemagne* (1863), and *Oregon and Eldorado* (1866).

Bulgakov, Mikhail Afanasyevich (mēkhŭyĕl′ ŭfŭnä′-syùvĭch boōlgä′kŭf), 1891–1940, Russian novelist and playwright. He wrote satirical stories (*The Deviliad*, 1925) and comedies (*Zoe's Apartment*, 1926) and the long novel *The White Guard* (1925), in which a Kievan family hostile to the Revolution

Boston's Old State House by Charles Bulfinch (steel engraving from about 1800).

is sympathetically and realistically portrayed. This was dramatized as *The Days of the Turbins* (1926; Eng. tr., 1934). Bulgakov was criticized for this play and for other works in the 1930s.

Bulganin, Nikolai Aleksandrovich (nyĭkŭlī' ŭlyĭksän'drŭvĭch boŏlgä'nyĭn), 1895–, Russian Communist leader. He held posts in industrial management, was mayor of Moscow (1931–37) and chairman of the state bank (1937–41), and became a political army officer in the Second World War. Made a marshal and a deputy premier in 1947 and a full member of the Politburo in 1948, he was also defense minister under Stalin and later under Malenkov. With the support of Nikita KHRUSHCHEV, Bulganin succeeded Malenkov as premier (Feb., 1955–March, 1958). After his retirement he was accused of having sided with the "anti-party faction" opposing Khrushchev in 1957. Bulganin was expelled from the central committee of the Communist party in Sept., 1958.

Bulgari: see BULGARS, EASTERN.

Bulgaria (bŭlgâ'rēù), republic (42,818 sq. mi.; estimated pop. 7,906,000), SE Europe, on the E Balkan Peninsula. It is bounded by the Black Sea on

Bulgaria location map

the east, by Rumania on the north, by Yugoslavia on the west, by Greece on the south, and by European Turkey on the southeast. SOFIA is the capital. Other important cities are Plovdiv, Varna and Burgas (the main Black Sea ports of Bulgaria), and Ruse. Bulgaria is traversed from east to west by ranges of the BALKANS. In the southwest is the even higher RHODOPE range. The Danube, the Maritsa, and the Struma are the principal rivers. Bulgaria has valuable mineral resources, notably brown coal, iron ore, manganese, lead, zinc, copper, and uranium. There are many mineral springs. Traditionally an agricultural country, Bulgaria has been considerably industrialized since the Second World War. The Communist regime has intensified development of mining and of manufacturing, notably of iron and steel, machinery, and chemicals. Major exports are tobacco, clothing, fresh and tinned fruit, metal ores and concentrates, and attar of roses. Agriculture, however, remains the chief occupation; the principal crops are wheat, corn, barley, tobacco, and roses. Grapes and other fruit are grown, and much stock is raised. The population consists chiefly of Bulgars (85.5 percent) and Turks (8.6 percent), with small minorities of Macedonians and Gypsies. About 85 percent belong to the Eastern Orthodox Church, and 13 percent are Moslems. In 1953 the Bulgarian patriarchate was reestablished with its seat in Sofia. Institutions of higher education include the universities of Sofia, Plovdiv, and Varna. Ancient Thrace and Moesia, which modern Bulgaria occupies, were settled (6th cent. A.D.) by Slavic tribes. In 679–80 Bulgar tribes from the banks of the Volga (see BULGARS, EASTERN) crossed the Danube, subjugated the Slavs, and settled permanently in the territory of Bulgaria. The language and culture remained Slavic, and by the 9th cent. the Bulgars had fully merged with the Slavs. The first Bulgarian empire (681–1018), established by Khan Asparuhk or Isperikh (ruled 680–701) and his suc-

Bulgaria's parliament building in Sofia (right), with the Alexander Nevsky Church in the background.

cessor, Terrel (ruled 701–718), soon emerged as a significant Balkan power and a threat to Byzantium. In 809 the khan Krum (ruled 803–814) captured Sofia from the Byzantines, defeated (811) Emperor Nicephorus I, besieged Constantinople, and withdrew only after obtaining yearly tribute. In the 9th cent. Bulgaria became the arena of political and cultural rivalry between Constantinople and Rome, a rivalry resolved in 865 when BORIS I introduced Christianity from Constantinople. Bulgaria received Byzantine culture through the Slavic literary language developed by SS. Cyril and Methodius in Moravia and brought to the Balkans by their disciples. The first Bulgarian empire reached its height under SIMEON I, who took the title tsar. At the same time the heresy of the BOGOMILS began to spread from Bulgaria. In the 10th cent. Bulgaria crumbled under the attacks of a reinvigorated Byzantium, and in 1018 it was annexed by Emperor BASIL II. Byzantine domination was weakened by the invasions of the PETCHENEGS and CUMANS and by internal disorders at Constantinople. In 1186 the second Bulgarian empire (1186–1396) rose when Ivan Asen (Ivan I) was crowned tsar at TRNOVO. His son, Kaloyan, crowned in 1204 with the approval of the pope, defeated (1205) Emperor Baldwin I of Constantinople. The height of Bulgar power was reached under Ivan II (Ivan Asen), whose rule extended over nearly the whole Balkan Peninsula except Greece, but it soon collapsed. In 1330 Bulgaria became tributary to Serbia, and STEPHEN DUSHAN reduced Bulgaria to a Serbian dependency. After the battles of KOSSOVO (1389) and NIKOPOL (1396) Bulgaria was absorbed into the Ottoman Empire. Turkish rule was particularly oppressive, and rebellions were frequent. After many centuries the administration (1864–69) of MIDHAT PASHA made Bulgaria briefly a model province, but by then Bulgarian nationalism was strong; it was increased by the unpopular hold of the PHANARIOTS

over the Bulgarian church. In 1876 a rebellion, led by Stefan STAMBULOV, broke out. The subsequent Turkish reprisals (famous as the "Bulgarian atrocities") served as occasion for the Russians to liberate (1877–78) their Slavic brothers (see RUSSO-TURKISH WARS). The Treaty of SAN STEFANO created a large Bulgaria—a Bulgaria that Russia expected to dominate. In order to avert the expansion of Russian influence in the Balkans, a European congress was called to revise the treaty (see BERLIN, CONGRESS OF). By the new terms N Bulgaria became a tributary principality under Turkish suzerainty, while S Bulgaria—then called Eastern RUMELIA—and Macedonia remained under direct Turkish rule. ALEXANDER (Alexander of Battenberg), first prince of Bulgaria, annexed (1885) E Rumelia and repulsed a consequent Serbian attack. His successor, Prince FERDINAND of Saxe-Coburg-Gotha, profiting from the revolution of the Young Turks in 1908, proclaimed Bulgaria independent with himself as tsar. Bulgaria was victorious in the first of the BALKAN WARS, but claims to MACEDONIA involved it in the Second Balkan War, and it was soon defeated. In the Treaty of Bucharest (1913) Bulgaria lost S DOBRUJA and a large part of Macedonia. The tension over Macedonia was long to continue. In 1915 Bulgaria entered the First World War on the side of Germany and Austria-Hungary, and with the war's end the government collapsed, Ferdinand fled, and BORIS III succeeded (1918). In the peace (see NEUILLY, TREATY OF) Bulgaria lost its outlet to the Aegean Sea to Greece and some territory to Yugoslavia; S Dobruja was confirmed in Rumanian possession. The Agrarian party

Bulgarian peasants harvesting crop of sugar beets.

Trnovo was the capital of Bulgaria during the 12th and 14th centuries.

BULGARIAN

cabinet established (1919) by STAMBULISKI held
power until overthrown (1923) by a military coup
d'état. An era of political confusion ensued,
dominated by the violent activities of the Macedonian terrorist group. In 1934 Kimon Georgiev
became premier with the help of the army, and in
1935 Boris III established his personal dictatorship. Bulgaria saw in the Second World War an
opportunity to satisfy its territorial claims. In
1940 Rumania was forced to restore S Dobruja.
In 1941 Bulgaria joined the AXIS, occupied parts
of Yugoslavia and Greece (including Macedonia),
and declared war on England and the United
States—but not on the Soviet Union. On the
mysterious death (1943) of Boris III, the infant
SIMEON II succeeded. In 1944 the Soviet Union
declared war on Bulgaria, and Soviet troops entered the country. The opposition forces (Communists, Agrarians, and the pro-Soviet army officers), headed by Georgiev, seized power immediately. An armistice followed, after Bulgaria had
declared war on Germany. Pre-war boundaries
were restored. After a short coalition rule the
Communists succeeded in taking over the government. The monarchy was abolished, and in 1946
Bulgaria was proclaimed a people's republic with
Georgi DIMITROV as premier. Industry was nationalized, resistance to collectivization of farms was
broken by the execution (1947) of the Agrarian
leader, Nikola Petkov, and one-party government
was imposed in 1948. The peace treaty with Bulgaria, ratified in 1947, allowed Bulgaria to keep
S Dobruja. Bulgaria closely followed the Soviet
Union in its domestic and foreign policies, and
after the expulsion of Yugoslavia from the COMIN-
FORM in 1948 Bulgaria sided with the USSR. Relations with Yugoslavia improved after Stalin's
death in 1953. In 1950 Bulgaria requested some
250,000 citizens of Turkish origin to emigrate to
Turkey. Relations with Greece and Turkey also
improved somewhat after 1954. Bulgaria joined
(1949) the Council for Economic Mutual Assist-
ance and in 1955 became a member of the Warsaw
Treaty Organization and was admitted into the
United Nations. See W. S. Monroe, *Bulgaria and
Her People* (1914); Ferdinand Schevill, *History of
the Balkan Peninsula* (1922); Steven Runciman,
A History of the First Bulgarian Empire (1930);
L. A. D. Dellin, ed., *Bulgaria* (1957).

Bulgarian, Slavic language (Indo-European). See
LANGUAGE, table.

Bulgarian literature. For early ecclesiastical writings, see OLD CHURCH SLAVONIC. Modern Bulgarian literature stems from the work of Father
Paisi, who in 1762 began his history of the Slav
Bulgarians, in an effort to inspire national feeling
and to stimulate the use of the Bulgarian language.
There was not at that time even a printing press
in Bulgaria. His imitators continued the effort to
make Bulgarian a literary language, but the period
of struggle (1840–75) for political and ecclesiastical
independence saw the real beginnings of a national
literature in the work of the poets Sava Rakovski
(1821–67) and Petko Rachev Slaveykov (1827–95),
the story writer Lyuben Karavelov (1837–79), the
dramatist Vasil Drumev (1841–1901), and the
great national poet Khristo Botev, who died fighting the Turks. Ivan Vazov was the first profes-

sional man of letters. After Bulgaria's liberation
(1876) from Turkish rule, the literature of the
country became less revolutionary. A group of
regional writers of the late 19th cent. included
Todor Genchov Vlaykov (1865–1943), Georgi P.
Stamatov (1869–1942), Anton Strashimirov (1872–
1937), the satirist Stoyan Mikhaylovski (1856–
1927), and Aleko Konstantinov (1863–97), whose
humorous *Bay-Ganyu* is one of the most popular of
Bulgarian novels. The poet Pencho Slaveykov
(1866–1912), a son of P. R. Slaveykov, led in introducing other European literatures and literary
trends into Bulgaria; his *Song of Blood* (1911–13)
is an epic of the struggle against the Turks. Others
of his period were the symbolist poet Peyo K.
Yavorov (1878–1914), the poet and dramatist
Petko Y. Todorov (1879–1916), and the story
writer Elin Pelin (1878–1949). Bulgaria's losses in
the Balkan Wars and the First World War gave
rise to a poetry whose chief quality was mysticism.
Among the poets of this period are the symbolist
Nikolay Liliyev (1886–); Dora Gabe (1886–) and
Elisaveta Bagryans, the first important women
poets; and Dimcho Debelyanov (1887–1916), who
was killed in the First World War. The prose
writers of the early 20th cent. include the novelists
of peasant life Iordan Iovkov (1884–1938) and
Dobri Nemirov (1882–1945), and the psychological
novelist Georgi Raichev (1882–). After 1945, the
writers most admired include the poet Khristo
Smyrnenski (1898–1923), Khristo Radevski
(1903–), and Nikola Vaptsarov (1909–42), and the
prose writers Lyudmil Stoyanov (1880–), Georgi
Karaslavov (1904–), and Dimiter Dimov, author
of the popular novel *Tobacco*. Recent Bulgarian
literature has undergone Soviet influence. Although there was a relaxation of the pressure to
conform to socialist realism after Stalin's death
(1953), controls were reintroduced in 1957. See
Dimitri Shishmanov, *A Survey of Bulgarian Literature* (Eng. tr., 1932); Vivian Pinto, *Bulgarian
Prose and Poetry* (1957); Clarence Manning and
Roman Smal-Stocki, *History of Modern Bulgarian
Literature* (1960).

Bulgarin, Faddey Venediktovich (fŭdyä′ vĭnyŭd-
yĕk′tŭvĭch bōōlgä′rĕn), 1789–1859, Russian journalist and novelist. He was born Tadeusz Bul-
haryn, a Pole. In 1825 he and Nicholas Grech
founded the influential conservative daily *Northern
Bee,* in which he inveighed against liberal writers,
notably Pushkin. He wrote several historical
novels, including *Ivan Vyzhigin* (1830; Eng. tr.,
1831).

Bulgars, Eastern, a Turkic-speaking people, who
possessed a powerful state (10th–14th cent.) at the
confluence of the Volga and the Kama, E European
Russia. The Bulgars appeared on the Middle
Volga by the 8th cent. and became known as the
Eastern, Volga, or Kama Bulgars. Another branch
of the same people moved west into present Bulgaria and merged with the Slavs. The Eastern
Bulgars accepted Islam in the 10th cent. From the
10th to the 12th cent. the Bulgar state was at the
height of its power. Its chief city, the Great
Bulgar, was a prosperous trade center. Destroyed
by the Mongols in 1237, the state flourished again
till it was conquered by Tamerlane in 1361. It
finally disappeared after its capture by the grand

A banderillero plants his banderillas in the bull.

"The moment of truth" in reverse. A matador has missed, dropped the muleta, and the bull attacks.

duke of Moscow in 1431. The modern Tatars and Chuvash may be descended from the Eastern Bulgars. The Great Bulgar and the Bulgars themselves are sometimes called Bulgari or Bolgari.

Bulge, Battle of the: see BATTLE OF THE BULGE.

Bull, Ephraim Wales, 1806–95, American horticulturist. At his vineyard in Concord, Mass., he originated several grape varieties including the Concord (1849), which became the dominant grape in the E United States.

Bull, Ole Bornemann (ō'lù bōr'nûmän), 1810–80, Norwegian violinist. After his debut in Paris (1832) he toured in Europe and in America, playing mostly his own compositions and Norwegian folk music. Very nationalistic, he founded a theater for national drama at Bergen (1849), and he attempted in 1852 to found a Norwegian settlement in Pennsylvania. See biography by Mortimer Smith (1943).

Bull, the: see TAURUS.

bull [Latin, *bulla*=leaden seal], apostolic letter containing some weighty pronouncement of the pope. The papal bull is more solemn than the papal brief or ENCYCLICAL. The letter, traditionally sealed with lead, begins with the name of the pope and his title as *servus servorum Dei* [servant of the servants of God]. Today only the consistorial bull, the weightiest of all papal pronouncements, is signed by the pope and carries the leaden seal. Famous bulls include *Clericis laicos*, 1296, and *Unam sanctam*, 1302, issued by Boniface VIII in his struggle with Philip IV of France; the Bull of Demarcation, 1493, by Alexander VI; *Exsurge Domine*, 1520, by Leo X against Martin Luther; *Unigenitus*, 1713, by Clement XI, against Jansenism; *Dominus ac Redemptor*, 1773, by Clement XIV, suppressing the Jesuits; *Quanta cura*, 1864, by Pius IX, introducing the *Syllabus errorum*; *Pastor aeternus*, 1871, by Pius IX, on papal infallibility; and *Munificentissimus Deus*, 1950, by Pius XII, defining the dogma of the Assumption of the Virgin Mary. Pope John issued a consistorial bull, *Humanae Salutis*, 1961, to convoke the 21st ecumenical council. The papal bull is used to proclaim the canonization of a saint. A bullarium is a collection of papal bulls. The most famous bullaria are the Roman Bullarium (1733–62) and the Turin Bullarium (1857–85).

bullbaiting, 17th-century amusement, particularly popular in England, in which trained dogs (bulldogs) attacked a tethered bull. Bullbaiting, along with bullrunning (in which the bull was run down and killed by humans), bearbaiting, cockfighting, and dogfighting, was prohibited in England by an act of Parliament in 1835.

bull bat: see GOATSUCKER.

bulldog: see NONSPORTING DOG.

Buller, Sir Redvers Henry, 1839–1908, British general. His military career began in China, and he later took part in campaigns against the Kafirs (1878), the Zulus (1879), the Boers (1881), and the Mahdists (1884–85). He served in Ireland and was quartermaster general (1890–97) and commander at Aldershot (1898–99), before he took command of troops in the South African War in 1899. Although he successfully expelled the Boers from Natal, his failure to relieve Ladysmith brought about his supersession by Lord Roberts of Kandahar. See memoir by Lewis Butler (1907); biography by C. H. Melville (1923).

Bullet, Pierre (pyěr' bülä'), 1639–1716, French architect, assistant to François Blondel in the construction of the Porte Saint-Denis, Paris (1672). Among his other works in Paris are the Porte Saint-Martin (1674) and the Church of St. Thomas d'Aquin (1680). Of the private buildings that he designed, the Hôtel d'Evreux (1707) is notable for his ingenious adaptation of the structure to an irregular site.

bullfighting, national sport and spectacle of Spain. The bullfight (in Spanish *corrida de toros*) has been aptly compared to a drama—the death of a fighting bull—in three acts. The drama is preceded by the color and pageantry of a grand ceremonial parade (*paseíllo*) in which the matadors, whose part is to kill the bulls, and the *toreros* take part. In the usual bullfight there are six bulls and three matadors. Each matador contests two bulls, chosen by lot on the morning of the fight. A matador's team consists of five assistants: two picadors, mounted on armored horses, and three *peones* or capemen on foot, also called *banderilleros* because they plant in the bull the short barbed sticks known as *banderillas.* The charging bull has to be "fixed," that is, slowed down and dominated, and its head made to hang low before a clean kill can be made. The president, the official who supervises the proceedings, signals for the first bull to come out, and the capemen wave *capas* at him, getting the bull to charge the capes; this is known as "running" the bull. Then, in Act 1, come the picadors. The bull is kept charging at the horses (before 1928, when they were armored, most of the horses in bullfights were killed by the bulls) until the picadors administer four *pic* (lance) thrusts; there may be more or fewer *pic* thrusts depending on the condition of the bull. In Act 2, which is brief, the *banderilleros* come out and, while on the run, plant the barbed sticks (*banderillas*) on the withers of the bull behind the neck muscle; these sting the bull and often spur him into giving a better charge for the third act. Now comes the matador. He holds a red cloth, the muleta, smaller than a cape, as well as his sword. The matador not only kills the bull but, using the muleta, makes daring passes at the bull which are often of great grace and beauty. He thus works at dominating the bull until the bull stands with his four feet square and his head hung low; then the matador, thrusting at the bull's aorta, administers the kill. If the matador has performed well he may be awarded an ear or the tail of the bull as a token of his craftsmanship. A matador's performance requires great skill and courage, and popular and successful matadors such as Pedro Romero, Juan Belmonte, Joselito, Manolete, and Carlos Arruza reaped immense awards of praise and money. The bulls are bred and selected for strength and spirit. A type of bullfighting was practiced by the Minoans, Greeks, and Romans. The Moors probably introduced the sport into Spain, whence it spread to southern France and Morocco. It is also popular in the Latin American countries of Mexico, Peru, Colombia, Venezuela, and Ecuador. In Portugal there developed a style of bullfighting from horseback (*rejoneo*) in which the bull is not killed. See Ernest Hemingway, *Death in the Afternoon* (1932); Tom Lea, *The Brave Bulls* (1949); Homer Casteel, *The Running of the Bulls* (1953); Barnaby Conrad, *La Fiesta Brava* (1953), *Gates of Fear* (1957), and *Barnaby Conrad's Encyclopedia of Bullfighting* (1961); John Marks, *To the Bullfight* (1953); Kenneth Tynan, *Bull Fever* (1955); Rex Smith, ed., *Biography of the Bulls* (1957); Angus MacNab, *Fighting Bulls* (1959).

bullfinch: see FINCH.

bullfrog, largest North American frog, an aquatic form with fully webbed toes. The common bullfrog is native to the United States E of the Rocky Mts. It utters deep bass croaks and sometimes a piercing cry. It can close its nostrils and lie at the bottom of a pond for some time. Bullfrog tadpoles require two or three years to become adults. Of the edible frogs, the legs of the bullfrog are the only ones marketed in quantity in the United States.

bullhead, name for several species of fish of the CATFISH and SCULPIN families.

Bullinger, Heinrich (hĭn'rĭkh bŏŏ'lĭngùr). 1504–75, Swiss Protestant reformer. After the death of Zwingli in 1531, Bullinger became pastor of the principal church in Zurich and a leader of the reformed party in Switzerland. He played an important part in compiling the first Helvetic Confession (1536), a creed based largely on Zwingli's theological views as distinct from Lutheran doctrine. In 1549 the Consensus Tigurinus, drawn up by Bullinger and Calvin, marked the departure of Swiss theology from Zwinglian to Calvinist theory. His later views were embodied in the second Helvetic Confession (1566), which was accepted in Switzerland, France, Scotland, and Hungary and became one of the most generally accepted creeds of the reformed churches. He wrote a life of Zwingli and edited the great reformer's complete works.

Bullitt, William Christian (bŏŏl'ĭt), 1891–, American diplomat, b. Philadelphia, grad. Yale, 1912. A member of the peace delegation at the end of the First World War, he resigned from service when his report favoring recognition of Russia was disregarded. After 12 years of private life, he was made special assistant to Cordell Hull and served (1933–36) as first U.S. ambassador to the USSR. Later he was ambassador to France (1936–41,) ambassador at large in the Middle East (1941–42), and special assistant to the Secretary of the Navy (1942–43). He enlisted in the French army and served (1944–45) as a major. He is author of a novel, *It's Not Done* (1926).

bullmastiff: see WORKING DOG.

Bull Moose party: see PROGRESSIVE PARTY.

bull nettle: see NIGHTSHADE.

Bullock, William A. (bŏŏ'lŭk), 1813–67, American inventor, b. Greenville, N. Y. He became an expert mechanic and patented various implements before 1850, when he began working on the printing press that bore his name. It was the first to feed automatically from a continuous roll of paper, to print both sides of the sheet in the same operation, and to cut the paper at proper intervals. It revolutionized the printing industry.

Bull Run, small stream, NE Va., c.30 mi. SW of Washington, D.C. Here were fought two important battles of the Civil War, July 21, 1861, and Aug. 29–30, 1862. The **first battle of Bull Run** (or first battle of Manassas) was the first major engagement of the war. On July 16, 1861, the Union army under Gen. Irvin McDOWELL began to move on the Confederate force under Gen. P. G. T. Beauregard at Manassas Junction. Gen. Robert Patterson's force at Martinsburg, which was to

Bullfrog

prevent the Confederate army under Gen. J. E. JOHNSTON at Winchester from uniting with Beauregard, failed, and by July 20 part of Johnston's army had reached Manassas. On July 21 McDowell, turning Beauregard's left, attacked the Confederates near the stone bridge over Bull Run and drove them back to the Henry House Hill There Confederate resistance, with Gen. T. J. JACKSON standing "like a stone wall," checked the Union advance, and the arrival of Gen. E. Kirby Smith's brigade turned the tide against the Federal forces. The unseasoned Union volunteers retreated, fleeing along roads jammed by panicked civilians who had turned out in their Sunday finery to watch the battle. The retreat became a rout as the soldiers made for the defenses of Washington, but the equally inexperienced Confederates were in no condition to make an effective pursuit. The South rejoiced at the result, while the North was spurred to greater efforts to win the war. The **second battle of Bull Run** (or second battle of Manassas) was also a victory for the Confederates. In July, 1862, the Union Army of Virginia under Gen. John POPE threatened Gordonsville, a railroad junction between Richmond and the Shenandoah Valley. Gen. R. E. LEE sent Stonewall Jackson to protect the town, and on Aug. 9, 1862, Jackson defeated N. P. Banks's corps, the vanguard of Pope's army, in the battle of Cedar Mt. (or Cedar Run). When McClellan's army was gradually withdrawn from Harrison's Landing on the James river (where it had remained after the SEVEN DAYS BATTLES) to reinforce Pope, Lee concentrated his whole army at Gordonsville. He planned to strike before Pope could be reinforced. Pope withdrew to the north side of the Rappahannock river. Lee followed to the south side and on Aug. 25 boldly divided his army. By Aug. 28 Jackson had marched to the Union right and rear, destroyed Union communications and supplies, and stationed his troops just west of the first Bull Run battlefield, where he awaited the arrival of James Longstreet with the rest of Lee's army. Pope was attacking Jackson when Longstreet came up on Aug. 29. The attack was repulsed, but Pope, mistaking a re-formation of Jackson's lines for a retreat, renewed it the next day. After the Federals were again driven back, Lee ordered Longstreet to counterattack. That general, supported by Jackson, swept Pope from the field. The Union forces retreated across Bull Run, badly defeated. Lee's pursuit ended at Chantilly, where the Federals stopped Jackson on Sept. 1, 1862. Pope then withdrew to Washington. Both battlefields are included in Manassas National Battlefield Park (1,970.13 acres; est. 1940). See Allan Nevins, *The War for the Union* (Vol. II, 1960).

bull terrier: see TERRIER.

Bulnes, Manuel (mänwĕl′ bōōl′nās), 1799–1866, president of Chile (1841–51). He served in the revolt against Spain and commanded the victorious Chilean forces at the battle of Yungay (1839), where the Peru-Bolivia confederation of Andrés SANTA CRUZ was destroyed. Bulnes, a conservative, was elected president and, through stern and repressive measures, fostered economic and educational progress.

Bülow, Bernhard Heinrich Martin, Fürst von

A contemporary lithograph of the second battle of Bull Run, August 29–30, 1862, by Currier & Ives.

(bĕrn′härt hĭn′rĭkh mär′tĭn fürst′ fŭn bü′lō), 1849–1929, German statesman. He held many diplomatic posts before he became, through the influence of Friedrich von HOLSTEIN, foreign secretary in 1897 and succeeded Hohenlohe-Schillingsfürst as chancellor in 1900. By his failure to gain the friendship of England and by his aggressive foreign policy, especially toward France in the Moroccan crisis of 1905 and toward Russia in the Bosnian crisis of 1908, he increased German isolation and strengthened the Triple Entente (see TRIPLE ALLIANCE AND TRIPLE ENTENTE). Having lost the confidence of Emperor William II and the support of the Reichstag, he resigned in 1909. He later (1914–15) was ambassador to Italy. See his memoirs (Eng. tr., 4 vols., 1931–32).

Bülow, Friedrich Wilhelm, Freiherr von (frē′drĭkh vĭl′hĕlm frī′hĕr), 1755–1816, Prussian general in the Napoleonic Wars. After his victories (1813) over the French at Gross Beeren and at Dennewitz he was created count of Dennewitz. In 1815 he played a conspicuous part in the Waterloo campaign.

Bülow, Hans Guido, Freiherr von (häns′ gē′dō), 1830–94, German pianist and conductor. After hearing *Lohengrin* in 1850 at Weimar under Liszt's direction, he studied piano with Liszt, and later conducted the premières of several of Wagner's operas. In 1857 he married Liszt's daughter Cosima, who left him in 1869 and later became the wife of Wagner (see WAGNER, RICHARD). While retaining his admiration for Wagner's music, Bülow became Brahms's most ardent champion. He framed the aphorism that Bach, Beethoven, and Brahms are the three B's of music. One of the first pianists to be concerned with stylistically proper performances, Bülow made critical editions of the works of many composers. The first of the modern virtuoso conductors, he achieved his greatest distinction as conductor (1880–85) of the ducal orchestra at Meiningen.

bulrush: see SEDGE.

Bultmann, Rudolf Karl, 1884–. German existentialist theologian, b. Oldenburg, educated at the universities of Tübingen, Berlin, and Marburg. He taught at the universities of Breslau and Giessen and from 1921 to 1950 was professor at the Univ. of Marburg. Strongly influenced by the existentialist philosophy of Martin Heidegger, Bultmann is best known for his work on the New Testament, which he reduced—with the exception of the Passion—to basic elements of myth which then have application to contemporary concerns. His approach is termed "demythologization." His classic work is *Theology of the New Testament* (Eng. tr., 1951). Other writings include *Glauben und Verstehen* (1933), *Das Urchristentum in Rahmen der antiken Religionen* (1949), *Jesus* (1951), *Das Evangelium des Johannes* (1953), *Die Geschichte der synoptischen Tradition* (1957), *Jesus and the Word* (1958), and *Existence and Faith* (1960).

Bulwer, Sir Henry (William Henry Lytton Earle Bulwer) (bool'wŭr; lĭ'tŭn), 1801–72, English author and diplomat; brother of the novelist Edward Bulwer-Lytton. Though he sat in Parliament for some years (1830–37, 1868–71), most of his long life was spent in diplomatic work, interspersed with writing. As secretary of the embassy in Constantinople (1837–38) he secured a commercial treaty with Turkey. When he was ambassador to Spain (1843–48), he negotiated peace between Spain and Morocco, but offended the dictator, Ramón Narváez, and was ordered to leave; his conduct was endorsed in England. As minister to Washington (1849–52) he concluded the important CLAYTON-BULWER TREATY of 1850. Among his later diplomatic posts were Florence, Bucharest, and, again, Constantinople (1858–65). In 1871 he was created baron. His writings include *An Autumn in Greece* (1826), *France: Social, Literary, and Political* (1834–36), *Historical Characters* (1867), and biographies of Lord Byron (1835) and Viscount Palmerston (1870–74, unfinished).

Bulwer-Lytton, Edward George Earle Lytton, 1st Baron Lytton, 1803–73, English novelist, grad. Cambridge, 1826. The son of Gen. William Bulwer and Elizabeth Lytton, he assumed the name Bulwer-Lytton in 1843 when he inherited the Lytton estate "Knebworth." He was created Baron Lytton of Knebworth in 1866. His varied and highly derivative novels won wide popularity. Many of his early books—*Falkland* (1827), *Paul Clifford* (1830), and *Eugene Aram* (1832)—reflect the influence of his friend William Godwin. Bulwer, however, is best remembered for his historical novels, particularly *The Last Days of Pompeii* (1834) and *Rienzi* (1835). In 1849, with *The Caxtons,* he began a series of domestic novels, which had recently become the vogue. A member of Parliament from 1831 to 1841, Bulwer was a reformer, but in 1852 he returned to Parliament as a Conservative. In 1858 he was appointed colonial secretary. He was also a successful dramatist. His plays include *The Lady of Lyons* (produced 1838), *Richelieu* (produced 1839) and *Money* (produced 1840). See studies by Michael Sadleir (1933) and S. B. Liljegren (1957).

Bulwer-Lytton, Edward Robert, 1st earl of Lytton, pseud. **Owen Meredith,** 1831–91, English diplomat and poet; son of the novelist. Bulwer-Lytton. He

was in the diplomatic service from 1850 to 1875, when Disraeli appointed him viceroy of India; for his services in the Afghan wars he was created (1880) an earl. He was ambassador to France from 1887. His poems, written at first under his pseudonym, include *The Wanderer* (1858), a collection of lyrics; *Lucile* (1860) and *Glenaveril* (1885), long narrative poems; and *King Poppy* (1892), an epic fantasy. His verse has been criticized for its affectation and prolixity. He also wrote a biography of his father, which appeared in 1883. See studies by Lady Betty Balfour (1899) and A. B. Harlan (1946).

bumblebee: see BEE.

Buna (boo'nů), town, SE New Guinea, in the Territory of Papua, NE of Port Moresby. It is situated near the Yodda gold fields. In the Second World War it was the scene of heavy fighting.

Bunah (bū'nů) [Heb.,=discretion], Judahite. 1 Chron. 2.25.

Buna rubber: see RUBBER, SYNTHETIC.

Bunau-Varilla, Philippe Jean (fēlēp' zhā' bünō'-vărēyä'),1859–1940, French engineer, prominent in the PANAMA CANAL controversy. An engineer after 1884 in the original French company for building the canal, he was chief engineer before the company went bankrupt in 1889 and was the organizer and promoter of the new company that took over the rights of the old in 1894. Unable to develop his plans in France, he undertook to sell the company to the United States. The attention of the U.S. government had been riveted on the alternative canal route through Nicaragua, but Bunau-Varilla, arriving in 1901, soon converted Mark Hanna and President McKinley to the Panama project. After new opposition developed, he persuaded the French directors to reduce the price of the company, and President Theodore Roosevelt was won over to the Panama plan. When difficulties arose with the Colombian government, the resourceful Bunau-Varilla conspired with insurrectionists in Panama and touched off (1903) a successful revolution. As minister from the new Panamanian republic to the United States, he negotiated the Hay-Bunau-Varilla Treaty, which gave the United States control of the Panama Canal. In the First World War he developed a water chlorination process which was used at the battle of Verdun. See his *Panama* (1913) and *From Panama to Verdun* (1940).

bunchberry: see DOGWOOD.

Bunche, Ralph Johnson, 1904–, American government official and United Nations mediator, b. Detroit, grad. Univ. of California, 1927, and Harvard (M.A., 1928; Ph.D., 1934). After study at Northwestern Univ. and the London School of Economics, he did world-wide research in colonial administration and race relations and taught at Howard Univ. after 1928. In government service after 1941, he worked under the joint chiefs of staff and was chief research analyst in the OSS (1942–44). The first Negro to be a division head in the Dept. of State (July–Oct., 1945), he entered the United Nations in 1946 as director of the Trusteeship Division. He became (Dec., 1947) principal secretary of the UN Palestine Commission and helped to bring peace to the Holy Land. For his work there he was awarded the 1950 Nobel Peace

Ralph Johnson Bunche

Prize. In 1958 he became undersecretary for special political affairs.

Buncrana (bŭnkră'nŭ), urban district (pop. 2,960), Co. Donegal, NW Republic of Ireland, on the eastern shore of Lough Swilly. It is a popular seaside resort.

Bundestag (boon'dĕs-täkh') [Ger.,=federal parliament], lower house of the parliament of the Federal Republic of Germany (West Germany). It succeeded the REICHSTAG. It is a popularly elected body which elects the chancellor, passes all legislation, and ratifies the most important treaties. It can remove the chancellor by a vote of no confidence, but only if it simultaneously elects a new chancellor. In the German Democratic Republic (East Germany), the Volkskammer [people's chamber] according to the constitution exercises similar powers. The upper house of the West German parliament, the Bundesrat [federal council], represents the states. It must approve certain laws.

bungalow [from Indian *bangla*,=house], dwelling built in a style developed from that of a form of rural house in India. The original bungalow typically has one story, few rooms, and a maximum of cross drafts, with high ceilings, unusually large window and door openings, and verandas on all sides to shade the rooms from the intense light and tropical heat. Dwellings of this general type became popular in S California, with numerous differences in plan and materials, and were termed bungalows. The word thus came to be used for a cottage or for any small house with verandas covered by low, wide eaves.

Bunin, Ivan Alekseyevich (boo'nĭn, Rus. ēvän' ŭlyĭksyä'yĭvĭch boo'nyĭn), 1870–1953, Russian writer. He was awarded the 1933 Nobel Prize in Literature. In his youth he belonged to Gorki's group of young realists but avoided political activities. His early works include translations, among them one of *Hiawatha*, and poems. *The Village* (1910; Eng. tr., 1923) is a novel in the Turgenyev tradition depicting the ugliness of peasant life before the Revolution of 1905. Many other works, prose and verse, followed in the same vein, of which the story "Dry Valley" (written 1911–12) is available in English in *The Elaghin Affair* (1935). Although Bunin was a poet of distinction he is per-

haps best known for his short stories, especially "The Man from San Francisco" (1916; Eng. tr. in *The Man from San Francisco and Other Stories*, 1923), and for his great autobiographical novel *The Well of Days* (1930; Eng. tr., 1933). *Memories and Portraits* (1950; Eng. tr., 1951) contains reminiscences of Chekhov, Gorki, and A. N. Tolstoy. Bunin opposed the Revolution of 1917 and lived in France from 1919 until his death.

Bunker Hill. 1 City (pop. 1,524), SW Ill., NE of Alton; inc. 1857. **2** Town (pop. 1,049), N central Ind., N of Kokomo, in a livestock and grain area. **3** Uninc. village (pop. 1,655), SW Oregon, on Coos Bay S of Coos Bay city. In a dairy region, it also has lumbering and fishing industries. **4** City (pop. 2,216), S Texas, WNW of Houston; inc. 1954.

Bunker Hill, battle of, in the American Revolution, June 17, 1775. Detachments of colonial militia under Artemas WARD, Nathanael Greene, John STARK, and Israel PUTNAM laid siege to Boston shortly after the battles of Lexington and Concord, but Thomas Gage, British commander in the city, made no attempt to break it until he was reinforced (in May) by troops led by William HOWE, Sir Henry Clinton, and John Burgoyne. The Continental forces learned of the British plan to take the heights of Dorchester and Charlestown, and William PRESCOTT was sent to occupy Bunker Hill outside Charlestown. Prescott instead chose the neighboring Breed's Hill to the southeast. The fight which ensued is often called the battle of Bunker Hill. Howe was ordered to take the position, and after two slaughterous failures a third charge dislodged the Americans, who had run out of powder. The British victory failed to break the siege, and gallant American defense heightened the colonial morale and resistance. See T. J. Fleming, *Now We Are Enemies: the Story of Bunker Hill* (1960); R. M. Ketchum, *The Battle for Bunker Hill* (1962).

Bunkie, town (pop. 5,188), central La., SE of Alexandria, in a cotton, sugar-cane, and oil region; founded 1882.

Bunnell, town (pop. 1,860), co. seat of Flagler co., NE Fla., S of St. Augustine, in a timber and potato area.

Bunner, Henry Cuyler, 1855–96, American journalist, poet, and story writer, b. Oswego, N.Y. He became famous as the editor of *Puck*, 1877–96, and as a writer of *vers de société* in *Puck*. *Airs from Arcady and Elsewhere* (1884) contained a selection of his lyric and graceful verse; his popular short stories were collected in *Zadok Pine* (1891), *Short Sixes* (1891), and other volumes. See biography by G. E. Jensen (1940).

Bunni (bŭn'ī), Levitical name mentioned in confusing passages. Neh. 10.15; 11.15. Once the name seems to be an alternative of BINNUI **1**.

Bunny Run, uninc. village (pop. 1,058), SE Mich., NNE of Pontiac. A ski area is nearby.

Bunsen, Christian Karl Josias, Freiherr von (krĭs'tyän kärl' yōzē'äs frī'hĕr fŭn boon'zŭn), 1791–1860, Prussian diplomat and scholar. He studied theology at the Univ. of Göttingen. He was a friend of King Frederick William IV and urged him to accept liberal ideas. Bunsen was minister at Rome (1827–38) and ambassador to Berne (1839–

41) and to London (1841–54), but was recalled from London because he supported alliance with the western powers in the Crimean War. A most learned man, Bunsen wrote on religion, language, literature, history, and law.

Bunsen, Robert Wilhelm (bŭn′sŭn, Ger. rō′bĕrt vĭl′hĕlm bŏn′zŭn), 1811–99, German scientist, educated at the Univ. of Göttingen, where he received his doctorate in 1830. He served on the faculties of several universities and was at Heidelberg from 1852 to 1889. His first important contribution to chemistry came with his investigation of certain organic compounds of arsenic. From his studies of the gaseous products of blast furnaces he evolved a method of gas analysis. With Kirchhoff at Heidelberg he discovered by spectroscopy the elements cesium and rubidium. Besides many articles he wrote *Gasometrische Methoden* (1857) and, with Kirchhoff, *Chemische Analyse durch Spektralbeobachtungen* (1861). His important contributions to petrology and chemicogeology include the explanation of geyser action (see GEYSER). As an inventor he is best known for the Bunsen cell (see CELL, in electricity), the Bunsen photometer (see PHOTOMETRY), and the **Bunsen burner**. This gas burner, commonly used in scientific laboratories, consists essentially of a hollow tube which is fitted vertically around the flame and which has an

Robert Wilhelm Bunsen

opening at the base to admit air. A smokeless, nonluminous flame of high temperature is produced. The underlying principle of the Bunsen burner is basic to common gas stoves and lamps.

Bunshaft, Gordon, 1909–, American architect, b. Buffalo, N.Y., grad. Massachusetts Institute of Technology, 1933. As chief designer for the architectural firm of Skidmore Owings & Merrill, Bunshaft was responsible for Lever House, Manhattan's first glass-curtain-wall skyscraper (1952). Among his other works are the Manufacturers Trust Company building on Fifth Avenue at 43d Street, New York city, and a complex of buildings including office space and recreational facilities (near Hartford) for the Connecticut General Life Insurance Company.

bunt: see SMUT.

bunting, small, plump bird of the FINCH family.

Bunting

Among the American buntings are the indigo bunting, in which the summer plumage of the male reflects light as a rich, metallic blue; the painted bunting or nonpareil, with showy red, blue, and green plumage; the hardy snow bunting, whose winter plumage is white marked with light brown on the head and sides; and the lazuli bunting of the West, turquoise above with a chestnut breast and white wing bars. European buntings include the corn, snow, and cirl buntings, the yellowhammer, and the ortolan, which is caught and fattened as a table delicacy.

Buntline, Ned, pseud. of Edward Zane Carroll Judson, 1822?–1886, American adventurer and writer. In 1845 he founded in Nashville *Ned Buntline's Own,* a sensational magazine. After being lynched (1846) for a murder, but secretly cut down alive and released, he went to New York, where he resumed the magazine. He led a mob in the Astor Place riot of 1849 against the English actor Macready. He turned up in St. Louis in the '50s as an organizer of the Know-Nothing movement. After 1846 Buntline wrote trashy novels, forerunners of the dime novels. Typical are *The Mysteries and Miseries of New York* (1848) and *Stella Delorme; or, The Comanche's Dream* (1860). In 1872 he persuaded W. F. Cody (Buffalo Bill) to act in his play, *The Scouts of the Plains,* which started Cody on his stage career. See biography by James Monaghan (1952).

Buñuel, Luis (lwēs′ bŏō′n'ūĕl), 1900–, Spanish film director. He collaborated with Salvador Dali on early surrealistic films, notably *Un Chien andalou* (1928). With *Las hurdes* (1932), a documentary of Spanish agrarian poverty, Buñuel turned to more realistic presentation. *Los olvidados* (1949), produced in Mexico, is a powerful and even brutal portrayal of the irrational responses of society to juvenile delinquency. Later films include *Viridiana* (1961), an allegorical reflection of modern Spanish society, charged with symbolism of universal moral connotation.

bunya-bunya: see MONKEY-PUZZLE TREE.

Bunyan, John, 1628–88, English author, b. Elstow, Bedfordshire; son of a tinsmith. After a brief period at the village free school, Bunyan was set to learn the tinker's trade, which he followed intermittently throughout his life. Joining the parliamentary army in 1644, he served until 1647. The reading of several pious books owned by his first wife and a constant study of the Bible intensified his religious beliefs, and in 1653 he began acting as lay preacher for a congregation of Baptists in Bedford. In this capacity he came into conflict with the Quakers led by George Fox and turned to writing in defense of his beliefs. In 1660 agents of the restored monarchy arrested him for unlicensed preaching, and he remained in prison for the next 12 years. During this period he wrote nine books, the most famous of which is *Grace Abounding to the Chief of Sinners* (1666), a fervent spiritual autobiography. Soon after his release in 1672 he was reimprisoned briefly and wrote the first part of *The Pilgrim's Progress from This World to That Which Is to Come*, published in 1678. This allegory recounts Christian's journey from the City of Destruction to the Celestial City. A second part—describing the manner in which Christian's wife, Christiana, makes the same pilgrimage—appeared in 1684. *Pilgrim's Progress* is remarkable for its simple, biblical style and for its vivid presentation of character and incident. It is often considered one of the world's great books and has been translated into many languages. By the time Bunyan was released from his second imprisonment, he had become a hero to the members of his sect, and he continued preaching and writing until his death. The principal works of these latter years are *The Life and Death of Mr. Badman* (1680) and *The Holy War* (1682). Bunyan's continued popularity rests on the spiritual fervor which permeates his works and on the compelling style in which they are written. His prose unites the eloquence of the Bible with the vigorous realism of common speech. See biography by O. E. Winslow (1961); studies by W. Y. Tindall (1934), H. A. Talon (1951), and Roger Sharrock (1954).

Bunyan, Paul, American legendary lumberjack. He was the hero of a series of "tall tales" current through the timber country from Michigan westward. Known for his fantastic strength and gigantic size, he is said to have ruled his Gargantu-

Statue of Paul Bunyan and his ox at Bemidji, Minn.

an lumber camp between the winter of the blue snow and the spring that came up from China. His prized possession was Babe the Blue Ox, which measured 42 ax handles and a plug of tobacco between the horns. In Southern lumber camps a similar legendary figure is known as Tony Beaver. See study of the legend by D. G. Hoffman (1952).

Bunzlau (boonts'lou) or **Boleslawiec,** Pol. *Boleslawiec* (bôlĕswä'vyĕts), town (estimated pop. 20,300), SW Poland (since 1945), in the former Prussian province of Lower Silesia, on the Bober. Chiefly noted for its pottery, it is also a trade center in a copper-mining and marble-quarrying region. Here, in 1813, a Prussian army defeated the French. The poet Martin Opitz was born here.

Buonaparte: see BONAPARTE and NAPOLEON I.

Buonarroti, Michelangelo: see MICHELANGELO BUONARROTI.

Buoninsegna, Duccio di: see DUCCIO DI BUONINSEGNA.

Buononcini, Italian musicians: see BONONCINI.

buoy (boi, boo'e), float anchored in navigable waters to mark channels and indicate dangers to navigation (isolated rocks, mine fields, cables, and the like). The shape, the color, the number, and the marking of the buoy are significant, but unfortunately the significance varies in different countries, and the system devised by the International Maritime Conference at Washington in 1889 and based on color was not adopted. Though the spar buoys (upright posts) used in northern latitudes are of wood, large buoys generally are of steel or iron. Nun buoys have conical tops; can buoys, flat tops. Buoys may be fitted with bells or whistles (usually operated by motion of the waves), and battery-powered light buoys are much used; radio buoys came into use in 1939. There are also mooring buoys, used for the anchoring of ships.

bur, or **burr,** popular name for fruits that have barbed, pointed, or rough outgrowths; by clinging to the fur or hair of animals and the clothing of man they are transported from the parent plant. Some common burs include those of the chestnut, burdock, bur marigold, and cocklebur. Burs are particularly obnoxious to sheep growers because of the difficulty of removing them from wool.

Buraimi (boori'mi), collective name of several oases lying between Oman and Saudi Arabia, SE Arabia. The region is potentially rich in oil, and the oases are disputed by Oman and Saudi Arabia.

Burano (boorä'no), town (estimated pop. 7,422), in Venetia, NE Italy, built on four islets in the lagoon of Venice. It has been famous for its lace since the 15th cent.

Buras (byoo'rus), uninc. town (pop. 4,908 including Triumph), SE La., SE of New Orleans.

Burbage, Richard, 1567?-1619, first great English actor. He was the leading tragedian of the CHAMBERLAIN'S MEN and was the original player of Shakespeare's *Hamlet, Lear, Othello* and *Richard III*. He also appeared in many of the first productions of Thomas Kyd, Beaumont and Fletcher, Ben Jonson, and John Webster. His father, James Burbage, had built the first permanent theater in London in 1576 called the Theatre. In 1598 the building was removed to Bankside and set up as the GLOBE THEATRE by his brother, Cuthbert, on the death of their father. The brothers also inherited shares in the Blackfriar's Theatre, built by their father in 1596, which became the winter home of the company.

Burbank, Luther, 1849–1926, American plant breeder, b. Lancaster, Mass. He experimented with thousands of varieties of plants and developed many new ones, including new varieties of prunes, plums, raspberries, blackberries, apples, peaches, and nectarines. Besides the Burbank potato, he produced new tomato, corn, squash, pea, and asparagus forms; a spineless cactus useful in cattle feeding; and many new flowers, especially lilies and the famous Shasta daisy. His methods and results are described in his books—*How Plants Are Trained to Work for Man* (8 vols., 1921) and, with Wilbur Hall, *Harvest of the Years* (1927) and *Partner of Nature* (1939)—and in his descriptive catalogues, *New Creations*. After 1875 his work was done at Santa Rosa, Calif. See D. S. Jordan and Vernon Kellogg, *The Scientific Aspects of Luther Burbank's Work* (1909); E. B. Beeson, *The Early Life and Letters of Luther Burbank* (1927); W. L. Howard, *Luther Burbank* (1945).

Burbank, city (pop. 90,155), S Calif., N of Los Angeles; laid out 1887, inc. 1911. Its manufactures include aircraft, electronic equipment, and metal products. There are motion picture and television studios here.

burbot: see COD.

Burchell, William John (bûr′chŭl), 1782?–1863, English explorer and scientist. He was schoolmaster (under the East India Company) at St. Helena (1805–10), whence he sailed for South Africa. His journey (1811–15) across the Karroo desert to Griqualand and Bechuanaland is described in his *Travels in the Interior of Southern Africa* (1822–24). His African collections comprised 63,000 natural objects and much astronomical and meteorological material. He traveled in Brazil (1825–29), gathering over 15,000 natural species. Many plant and animal species discovered by him bear his name.

Burchfield, Charles, 1893–, American painter, b. Ashtabula, Ohio, studied at the Cleveland School of Art. From 1921 to 1929 he worked as a wallpaper designer. His paintings, predominantly in water color, fall into three periods: from 1916 to the early 1920s, poetic evocations of nature; from the early 1920s to the early 1940s, bold, somber landscapes and urban scenes; and after 1943, a return to lyrical expressions of nature. Burchfield is widely known for his depiction of crumbling Victorian mansions, false-front stores, and other relics of the late 19th cent. Weather and sunlight effects are important in all his work. Among his many works in museums are *Setting Sun through the Catalpas* (Cleveland Mus. of Art), *Freight Cars Under a Bridge* (Detroit Inst. of Arts), and *An April Mood* (Whitney Mus. of American Art, New York). See study by John Baur (1956).

Burckhardt, Jacob Christoph (yä′kôp krĭs′tôf bŏork′härt), 1818–97, Swiss historian, one of the founders of cultural history. Of patrician background, he studied under Ranke at the Univ. of Berlin and taught (1844–53, 1858–93) art history and history at the Univ. of Basel. His best-known work is *Die Kultur der Renaissance in Italien* (1860; *The Civilization of the Renaissance in Italy*, available in many English editions). It remains the great classic on the subject, though its primarily political and cultural interpretation of the Renaissance period is a controversial issue among historians. Believing in a pattern of culture peculiar to each age, Burckhardt found the shift from corporate medieval society to the modern spirit in the history of Italy in the 14th and 15th cent. The strife between empire and papacy had created a political and moral vacuum, which resulted in the birth of the modern self-conscious state and in the liberation of the creative individual. Burckhardt saw Renaissance humanism as the revival of classical antiquity, and he conceived the era as one of man's joyous new discovery of himself and the world about him. He profoundly influenced his friend Nietzsche, and the work of J. A. Symonds is based largely on Burckhardt's synthesis. In *The Age of Constantine the Great* (1852; Eng. tr., 1949), Burckhardt analyzed the transition from classical times to the Middle Ages. He also wrote *Cicerone* (1855), a guide to Italian art, and other works on history and on art. Burckhardt feared that the spiritual and esthetic human values were doomed to submersion by the rise of industrial democracy.

Burckhardt, John Lewis (bûrk′härt), 1784–1817, explorer, b. Switzerland, educated in Germany. Supported by an English association for promoting African discovery, he visited Egypt and Syria (1809–13), rediscovered PETRA (1812), then, posing as a learned Moslem, he became the first Christian to reach Medina. He died while preparing to set out from Upper Egypt for his original goal, the Niger river. Included in his *Travels in Arabia* (1829) is a notable account of Mecca. His journals, published by the African Association, include *Travels in Nubia* (1819), *Travels in Syria and the Holy Land* (1822), *Notes on the Bedouin and Wahábys* (1830), and *Arabic Proverbs* (1830).

Burckmair, Hans: see BURGKMAIR, HANS.

burdock, any plant of the genus *Arctium* of the COMPOSITE family, coarse biennials indigenous to temperate Eurasia and mostly weedy in North America. The flowers, usually purple, are followed by roundish many-seeded burs. The great burdock (*A. lappa*) has been used medicinally and (in Japan) cultivated as a vegetable called gobo. The common burdock is *A. minus*. The cocklebur is sometimes confused with burdock.

Burdwan (bûrdwän′), town (pop. 75,376), West Bengal state, NE India, near the Damodar river. It has cutlery and tool manufactures, but is chiefly known for its 108 linga temples dedicated to Siva. It is also spelled Bardwan.

bureaucracy, widely speaking, the body of officeholders of the executive arm of government. The term is often applied to the administrative structure of any large organization, whether public or private. It usually carries a suggestion of reprobation and implies incompetency and parasitism among the functionaries. Bureaucracy existed in imperial Rome and China and in the national monarchies of Europe. The revolutions of the 17th and 18th cent. emphasized the rule of the national legislatures, but in modern states complex industrial and social legislation has called for a vast growth of administrative functions of government. The power of permanent and nonelective officials to apply and even initiate measures of control over the national administration and economy has raised the bureaucracy to critical importance in the life of the state. Critics still object that bureaucracy is powerful and largely unresponsive to control by the people or their elected representatives. Administrative bureaucracies in private organizations have also grown rapidly, especially since the development of the corporation. See CIVIL SERVICE. See J. D. Kingsley, *Representative Bureaucracy: an Interpretation of the British Civil Service* (1944).

Bureya (bōōrā′ä), mountain range, SW Khabarovsk Territory, RSFSR, extending into N China as the Lesser Khingan range. The site of the Bureya coal basin, it rises to c.7,150 ft. and yields iron and coal. The Bureya river, c.445 mi. long, rises in the N Bureya range and flows southwest to join the Amur.

Burgas (bōōrgäs′), city (pop. 72,526), SE Bulgaria, on the Black Sea. It is a seaport and a commercial center, the chief export port of Bulgaria. It was founded (18th cent.) on the site of a 14th-century fortified town.

Burgaw (bûr′gô), town (pop. 1,750), co. seat of Pender co., SE N.C., N of Wilmington, in a farm area. It has sawmills.

Burgdorf (bōōrk′dôrf), Fr. *Berthoud* (bĕrtōō′), town (estimated pop. 13,900), Bern canton, NW Switzerland, on the Emme river. It is a textile center. It has an old castle in which Pestalozzi held (1799–1804) his first school.

Burgenland (bûr′gŭnländ, Ger. bōōr′gŭnlänt), province (1,530 sq. mi.; estimated pop. 270,875), E Austria. Its capital is Eisenstadt. It is a long, narrow, hilly region bordering on Hungary in the east and indented by the NEUSIEDLER LAKE. Primarily an agricultural area, it produces fruit, vegetables, and wine. There is also some mining. A battleground for nearly 1,000 years, Burgenland has many castles, fortified churches, and walled villages. The newest of the Austrian provinces, the territory was transferred from Hungary by the treaties of Saint-Germain (1919) and Trianon (1920). SOPRON, its leading town, was returned (1921) to Hungary after a plebiscite.

Bürger, Gottfried August (gôt′frĕt ou′gōōst bür′gùr), 1747–94, German poet. He is best known for his ballads in folk-song style; the famous *Lenore* (1773) was widely translated and had far-reaching influence. Bürger edited and wrote for the Göttingen *Musenalmanach* and taught aesthetics at the Univ. of Göttingen. He translated many works of Homer, Shakespeare, and others, as well as the famous stories of Baron MUNCHAUSEN. His unconventional approach to poetry was severely criticized by Schiller.

Burges, William (bûr′jĭz), 1827–81, English architect. An ardent proponent of medievalism, he was prominent in the GOTHIC REVIVAL. He is known for his designs for Cork Cathedral (1862) and Trinity College, Hartford, Conn., and for the rebuilding of Cardiff Castle (1865).

Burgess, Gelett (Frank Gelett Burgess) (bûr′jĭs), 1866–1951, American humorist, b. Boston, grad. Massachusetts Institute of Technology, 1887. His ability as an illustrator led him into magazine work, and he was soon writing humorous articles and stories to accompany his illustrations. His best-known poem, "The Purple Cow," first appeared in the San Francisco periodical the *Lark* (1895–97), of which he was an editor and steady contributor. Among his books are *Goops and How to Be Them* (1900) and *Are You a Bromide?* (1907).

Burgess, John William, 1844–1931, American educator and political scientist, b. middle Tennessee. He served in the Union army in the Civil War and after the war graduated from Amherst (1867). He was admitted to the Massachusetts bar in 1869, but did not practice. That same year he joined the faculty of Knox College. In 1871 he went to Germany, where he studied at the universities of Göttingen, Leipzig, and Berlin. He returned in 1873 to teach history and political science at Amherst. In 1876 began his long connection with Columbia Univ. (then Columbia College); he was professor of political science and constitutional law until 1912. Burgess, with Nicholas Murray BUTLER, was a major influence in the creation (1880) of a faculty and school of political science, the first such faculty organized for graduate work in the country and the chief step in changing Columbia College into a university. He was dean of the Faculty of Political Science from 1890 until his retirement. In 1906–7 he served as first Roosevelt professor at the Univ. of Berlin. Burgess's fundamental political philosophy was expressed in *Political Science and Comparative Constitutional Law* (1890–91), the more permanently valuable portions of which were republished as *The Foundations of Political Science* (1933). He interpreted American history in *The Middle Period, 1817–1858*, *The Civil War and the Constitution, 1859–1865*, and *Reconstruction and the Constitution, 1866–1876*, a trilogy published between 1897 and 1902, to which was added *The Administration of Rutherford B. Hayes* (1915). In *Recent Changes in American Constitutional Theory* (1923) he protested against the encroachment of the Federal government upon state and individual rights and immunities. He founded the *Political Science Quarterly*. See his autobiography, *The Reminiscences of an American Scholar* (1934); R. G. Hoxie, *A History of the Faculty of Political Science, Columbia University* (1955).

Burgettstown (bûr′jĭts-), borough (pop. 2,383), SW Pa., near the W.Va. line, W of Pittsburgh; laid out 1795, inc. 1881.

Burgh, Hubert de: see HUBERT DE BURGH.

Burgh, Ulick de, earl of Clanricarde: see CLANRICARDE, ULICK DE BURGH, 5TH EARL OF.

Burghers (bûr′gùrz), a party of the Secession Church of Scotland, or Associate Synod, resulting from one of the "breaches" in the history of Presbyterianism. To qualify as a burgess in certain burghs one was required to take an oath accepting the "true religion presently professed within this realm." Opinion differed as to whether this referred to Protestant religion in general or to the Established Church. Those in the Secession Church who understood the oath in the former sense were the "Burghers," of the Associate Synod. Opposed to them were the Anti-Burghers, of the General Associate Synod, who refused to take the oath. The two bodies mutually excluded each other in 1747. By the end of the century both divisions were further split apart into "Old Light Anti-

Burghers" and "Old Light Burghers" and "New Lights" in each division, over questions of civil magistracy. In 1820 Old Lights and New Lights were brought together again in the United Secession Church.

Burghley or **Burleigh, William Cecil, 1st Baron** (both: bûr′lē), 1520–98, English statesman. He first rose to power in 1548 when Edward Seymour, duke of Somerset, was protector, and he served as secretary of state (1550–53) during the duke of Northumberland's ascendancy. He was not in the favor of Mary I, but was reappointed to office by Elizabeth I, whom he served faithfully for 40 years. He became her principal adviser and in 1572 was made lord high treasurer. His clever, often bold, diplomatic policies contributed greatly to the rise of England as a leading European power. Cautious, as was Elizabeth, he could, nevertheless, act with decision. He took the responsibility for the execution of Mary Queen of Scots and worked tirelessly for the peaceful solidification of Protestantism in England. Burghley's advice was not always followed, but his hand can be seen in most of the important policies of Elizabeth's reign. See Conyers Read, *Mr. Secretary Cecil and Queen Elizabeth* (1955) and *Lord Burghley and Queen Elizabeth* (1960).

Burgis, William (bûr′jĭs), fl. 1717–31, American engraver and publisher of maps and views, b. London. His name appears as publisher on the views *South Prospect of ye Flourishing City of New York* (1717; copy, N.Y. Historical Society); *The New Dutch Church in New York City; A Prospect of the Colledges in Cambridge in New England* (only known copy, Massachusetts Historical Society, Boston); *A South East View of the Great Town of Boston;* and *Plan of Boston in New England* (copy, Library of Congress, Washington, D.C.). The mezzotint *The Boston Light House* is the only plate which contains Burgis's name as engraver (copy, U. S. Lighthouse Board, Washington, D.C.).

Burgkmair or **Burckmair, Hans** (both: häns′ bŏŏrk′mĭŭr), 1473–1531, German engraver and painter of Augsburg. His work shows the influence of his friend Dürer, whose enthusiasm for the Italian Renaissance he shared. Among his well-known paintings are the *Rosary Altar* (Augsburg) and *Holy Family* (1511; Berlin). After c.1508 he executed designs for woodcuts for Emperor Maximilian I; among these prints a series of episodes in the emperor's life is well known. Other famous works of graphic art are *Death as Destroyer* (1520) and *Virtues and Vices.*

burglary, according to common-law definition, the breaking and entering of a dwelling house of another at night with the intent to commit a FELONY, whether the intent is carried out or not. This definition has been generally adopted with some modifications in the criminal law of the various states of the United States. At common law burglary is an offense primarily against the security of habitation, not against the property as such, but today by statute burglary usually includes breaking into places other than dwellings. Breaking as well as entering is essential to commission of the crime; to constitute a breaking, the use of physical force is necessary and sufficient, even though the amount of force may be slight, e.g., turning a key, opening a partly closed window, pushing out a windowpane. Entry through FRAUD (as by posing as a guest), through THREAT, or through CONSPIRACY with servants is deemed by the law equivalent to breaking and is called "constructive breaking." By statute most states do not restrict burglary to action at night, as the common law does. Burglary under common law requires that the intent be to commit a felony, but some statutes declare that the intent need only be "to commit some crime."

Bürglen (bürk′lŭn), town (estimated pop. 3,200), Uri canton, central Switzerland. It is the legendary birthplace of William TELL and has a 16th-century chapel built on the supposed site of Tell's house.

Burgos (bōōr′gōs), city (pop. 66,477), capital of Burgos prov., N Spain, in Old Castile, on a mountainous plateau. It is an important trade center. It was one of the ancient capitals of Castile but is chiefly known for its outstanding architecture and great historic tradition. Founded c.855, it was the seat of the county of Castile under the kings of Leon and became the capital of the kingdom of Castile under Ferdinand I (1035). The royal residence was moved (1087) to Toledo, and Burgos lost some of its cultural importance. The Cid lived and is buried here. In the civil war of 1936–39 Burgos was the capital of Franco's regime. Its most notable building is the cathedral of white limestone, begun in 1221, one of the finest examples of Gothic architecture in Europe; its lofty, filigree spires dominate the city. Among the many other landmarks are the castle, atop a hill overlooking

The cathedral at Burgos.

the city; the Gothic Church of San Estebán; and the Arco de Santa María, a 16th-century gateway.

Burgoyne, John (bùrgoin'), 1722–92, British general and statesman. In the Seven Years War, his victory over the Spanish in storming (1762) Valencia de Alcántara in Portugal made him the toast of London. Elected to Parliament (1768) he helped to reform the East India Company's rule of India. As the American Revolution was beginning, he arrived (1775) with the reinforcement sent to General Gage at Boston. Burgoyne witnessed the battle of Bunker Hill and returned home in disgust (Nov., 1775). He joined (1776) Sir Guy Carleton in Canada and served at Crown Point, but, critical of Sir Guy's inaction, Burgoyne returned to England to join Lord George Germain in laying the plans that resulted in the SARATOGA CAMPAIGN. Burgoyne began (June, 1777) the ill-fated expedition with an army poorly equipped, untrained for frontier fighting, and numbering far less than he had requested. After minor initial success, stiffened American resistance coupled with the failure of Barry ST. LEGER and Sir William HOWE to reach Albany led to his surrender at Saratoga (Oct. 17, 1777). He returned to England, was given (1782) a command in Ireland, and managed the impeachment of Warren HASTINGS. Burgoyne wrote several plays of which *The Heiress* (1786) is best known. See biography by F. J. Hudleston (1927).

bur grass: see SANDBUR.

Burgundians, in French medieval history: see AR-MAGNACS AND BURGUNDIANS.

Burgundii: see BURGUNDY.

Burgundy (bûr'gùndē), Fr. *Bourgogne* (boŏrgô'nyù), region, E France. The name also applied to several kingdoms, to a free county (see FRANCHE-COMTÉ), and to a duchy, all of which embraced large territories outside the present region, which is identical with the province of Burgundy of the 17th and 18th cent. Burgundy is now administratively divided into four departments—Yonne, Côte-d'Or, Saône-et-Loire, and Ain. Burgundy W of the Saône river is generally hilly; in the southeast it includes the southern spurs of the Jura mts.; the center is a lowland, extending south almost to the junction of the Saône and Rhone rivers (see BRESSE). A rich agricultural country, Burgundy is especially famous for the WINE produced in the CHABLIS region, the mountains of the CÔTE D'OR, and the SAÔNE and RHONE valleys. DIJON is the historical capital; other cities are Autun, Auxerre, Beaune, Bourg-en-Bresse, Chalon-sur-Saône, and Mâcon. The territory, conquered by Julius Caesar in the GALLIC WARS, was divided first between the Roman provinces of Lugdunensis and Belgic Gaul, then between Lugdunensis and Upper Germany (see GAUL). It prospered, and Autun became one of the Roman Empire's chief intellectual centers. In the 4th cent. Roman power dissolved, Christianity became widespread, and the country was invaded by Germanic tribes. It was finally conquered (c.480) by the Burgundii, a tribe from Savoy. The Burgundii accepted Christianity, established their *Lex Burgundionum* and formed the **First Kingdom of Burgundy**, which at its height comprised SE France and reached as far south as Arles and W Switzerland. Conquered (534) by the FRANKS, it was throughout the Merovingian period

subjected to numerous partitions. Burgundy nevertheless survived as a political concept, and after the partitions of the Carolingian empire, two new Burgundian kingdoms were founded, Cisjurane Burgundy, or PROVENCE, in the south (879) and Transjurane Burgundy in the north (888). These two were united (933) in the **Second Kingdom of Burgundy** (see ARLES, KINGDOM OF). A smaller area, corresponding roughly to present Burgundy, was created as the **duchy of Burgundy** by Emperor Charles II in 877. In 1002, King Robert II of France made good his claim to the duchy, but his son, Henry I, gave it in 1031 as a fief to his brother Robert, whose line died out in 1361. The golden age of Burgundy began when (1364) JOHN II of France bestowed the fief on his son, PHILIP THE BOLD, thus founding the line of Valois-Bourgogne. Philip and his successors, JOHN THE FEARLESS, PHILIP THE GOOD, and CHARLES THE BOLD, acquired—by conquest, treaty, and marriage—vast territories, including most of the present Netherlands and Belgium, the then extensive duchy of Luxembourg, Picardy, Artois, Lorraine, S Baden and Alsace, the Franche-Comté, Nivernais, and Charolais. In the early 15th cent. the dukes of Burgundy, through their partisans in France, dominated French politics (see ARMAGNACS AND BURGUNDIANS). England, at first supported by Burgundy in the HUNDRED YEARS WAR, suffered a crucial setback when Philip the Good withdrew that support in the Treaty of Arras (1435). A great power, Burgundy at that time had the most important trade, industries, and agriculture of Western Europe. Its court, a center of the arts, was second to none. Yet the ambitions of Charles the Bold, opposed by the determination and resourcefulness of Louis XI of France, came crashing down with his defeats by the Swiss at Grandson, Morat (1476) and Nancy (1477), where he lost his his life. His daughter, MARY OF BURGUNDY, by marrying Emperor Maximilian I, brought most of the Burgundian possessions (but not the original French duchy) to the house of Hapsburg. The duchy itself was seized by Louis XI, who incorporated it into the French crownlands as a province, to which Gex, Bresse, and Charolais were added later by Henry IV and Louis XIV. See Arthur Klenclausz, *Histoire de Bourgogne* (1909); Otto Cartellieri, *The Court of Burgundy* (1929).

Burgundy, Free County of: see FRANCHE-COMTÉ.

Burgundy Gate: see BELFORT.

Burgundy mixture: see BORDEAUX MIXTURE.

Burgundy pitch: see RESIN.

Burhanpur (bûr'hänpoŏr"), town (pop. 70,066), Madhya Pradesh state, W central India. It trades in cotton. Founded c.1400, it has a partly ruined palace (c.1610) of Akbar.

burial, the disposal of a corpse in a GRAVE or TOMB. The first evidence of deliberate burial was found in European caves of the late Paleolithic period. In earlier times, however, man may have buried his dead in sites less favorable to preservation, for respect and care for the dead seem to be specifically human traits. Prehistoric finds include both individual and communal burials, the latter indicating that pits or ossuaries were unsealed for later accommodation or that servants or members of the family were slain to accompany the deceased. Both practices have been followed by various peoples into modern times. The word *burial* has been applied to funerary practices other than interment, such as sea burial, or tree burial (which usually precedes later interment). Secondary burial frequently occurs to terminate a period of mourning (see FUNERAL CUSTOMS). Since graves are less often disturbed than former habitations, and since they often contain artifacts, they provide invaluable material for the archaeologist. See also CEMETERY.

Buriat-Mongolia: see BURYAT AUTONOMOUS SOVIET SOCIALIST REPUBLIC.

Buridan, Jean (byŏŏ'rĭdùn, Fr. zhā' büredā'), d. c.1358, French scholastic philosopher. Rector of the Univ. of Paris, he was a follower of William of Occam and a nominalist. His theory of the will was that choice is determined by the greater good and that the freedom man possesses is the power to suspend choice and reconsider motives for action. Traditionally but almost certainly erroneously he is supposed to have used the simile of "Buridan's ass"—an unfortunate animal midway between two identical bundles of hay and starving to death for want of power to choose between them.

Burin (bū'rĭn), town, S N.F., Canada, on the southwest coast of Placentia Bay. Burin Peninsula lies between Fortune Bay and Placentia Bay. The town has a large fish-processing plant.

Burkburnett (bûrkbûrnĕt'), city (pop. 7,621), N Texas, N of Wichita Falls and near the Red River; settled 1907, inc. 1913. An oil strike in 1918 brought a boom which transformed the quiet little town of Burkburnett into an oil-mad community—one of the wildest and roughest of them all. Speculators, drillers, saloon keepers, gamblers, and adventurers all flocked in, raising the town's population to almost 30,000. Today the city also handles farm produce and cattle.

Burke, Edmund, 1729–97, English political writer and statesman, b. Dublin, grad. Trinity College at Dublin, 1748. The son of a Protestant father and a Roman Catholic mother and himself a Protestant, he never ceased to criticize the stupidity of the English administration in Ireland and the galling discriminations against Catholics. He began the study of law in London but abandoned it to devote himself to writing. His satirical *Vindication of Natural Society* (1756) attacked the political rationalism and religious skepticism of Henry St. John, Viscount Bolingbroke, and his *Philosophical Enquiry into the Origin of Our Ideas of the Sublime and Beautiful* (1756) was a study in the aesthetics of romanticism. In 1759 he started the *Annual Register*, to which he contributed until 1788. Burke was a member of Samuel Johnson's intimate circle. His political career began in 1765 when he became secretary to the 2d marquess of Rockingham, then prime minister, and formed a lifelong friendship with that WHIG leader. He also entered Parliament in 1765 and there defended Rockingham's repeal of the Stamp Act (1766) and strove for a wiser treatment of the American colonies. In 1770 his pamphlet *Thoughts on the Cause of the Present Discontents*, a justification of the value of parties, helped mold the Rockingham Whigs into a cohesive parliamentary opposition. His famous speeches on American taxation (1774) and on conciliation with the colonies (1775) were only the best

Edmund Burke

known of his efforts to oppose the king's course in America. Burke aimed at limiting the patronage of the crown by his economic-reform bill, which was passed in the short Whig ministry of Rockingham in 1782, and by the India bill, drafted by Burke and presented by Charles James Fox, which was not passed. Under the Tory ascendancy of William Pitt the younger, Burke instigated the impeachment and long trial of Warren HASTINGS, and though Hastings was not convicted, Burke's speeches created an awareness of the responsibilities of empire and of the injustices perpetrated in India previously unpublicized in England. Though he championed many liberal and reform causes, Burke believed that political, social, and religious institutions represented the wisdom of the ages; he feared political reform beyond limitations on the power of the crown. Consequently, his *Reflections on the Revolution in France* (1790) made him the spokesman of European conservatives. His stand on the French Revolution—and, by implication, against parliamentary reform—caused him to break with Fox and his Whigs in 1791. Burke's *Appeal from the New to the Old Whigs* (1791) shows how closely he approached William Pitt's Tory position. Burke left, in his many and diverse writings, a monumental construction of British political thought which had far-reaching influence among conservatives in England, America, and France for many years. He held unrestricted rationalism in human affairs to be destructive and affirmed the utility of habit and prejudice and the importance of experiment in political experience. He withdrew from political life in 1795. Work on a complete collection of Burke's correspondence has been started; the first three volumes appeared 1958–61. See selections edited by W. J. Bate (1960); studies by T. W. Copeland (1949), Charles Parkin (1956), C. B. Cone (1957), and P. J. Stanlis (1958).

Burke, John, 1787–1848, Irish genealogist. He issued (1826) *A Genealogical and Heraldic Dictionary of the Peerage and Baronetage of the United Kingdom.* He published this guide irregularly until 1847; since then it has been an annual, commonly called *Burke's Peerage.* This was edited from 1847 to 1892 by his son, **Sir John Bernard Burke,** 1814–92, who was knighted (1854) and appointed (1855) keeper of the state papers in Ireland. As a companion to Burke's peerage, he established the regular issuance of another work begun by his father, commonly called *Burke's Landed Gentry*. His other works include *The Romance of the Aristocracy* (1855) and *Vicissitudes of Families* (1883).

Burke, Robert O'Hara, 1820–61, Irish explorer of Australia. After service in the Belgian and Austrian armies he went (1853) as inspector of police to Melbourne. In 1860, with W. J. Wills and eight other whites, he left Menindee, on the Darling river, to cross the continent. Dissensions broke up the party, but the leaders reached the estuary of the Flinders river, in the Gulf of Carpentaria. On the return journey both Burke and Wills died from famine and exposure. Though the geographical achievements of the expedition were few, rescue parties seeking it added much to the knowledge of central Australia. See C. G. D. Roberts, *Discoveries and Explorations in the Century* (1906).

Burkesville, city (pop. 1,688), co. seat of Cumberland co., S central Ky., on the Cumberland river near the Tenn. line, SE of Bowling Green; inc. as a town 1810, as a city 1926. It is a resort in the Cumberland foothills.

Burlamaqui, Jean Jacques (zhä′ zhäk′ bùrlämäkē′), 1694–1748, Swiss jurist. His chief works are *Principes du droit naturel* [principles of natural law] (1747) and *Principes du droit politique* [principles of political law] (1751). He attempted to demonstrate the reality of natural law by tracing its origin in God's rule and in human reason and moral instinct. He believed that both international and domestic law were based on natural law.

Burleigh, Henry Thacker (bûr′lē), 1866–1949, American Negro baritone and composer, b. Erie, Pa.; pupil of Dvorak at the National Conservatory, New York, where he later taught. He was soloist at St. George's Church, New York, from 1892 to 1946 and also at Temple Emanu-El for 25 years. His concert arrangements of Negro spirituals such as *Deep River*, employing chromatic harmonies in the style of art songs, are widely used.

Burleigh, William Cecil, 1st Baron: see BURGHLEY.

Burleson, Albert Sidney (bûr′lùsùn), 1863–1937, U.S. Postmaster General (1913–21), b. San Marcos, Texas, grad. Baylor Univ., 1881, and Univ. of Texas law school, 1884. A grandson of Edward Burleson, he was a lawyer of Austin, Texas, and a member of the House of Representatives (1899–1913) before resigning to take a cabinet post under President Wilson. His methods of administering communications in the First World War angered businessmen, who charged him with inefficiency and interference with private business; of labor unions, because he forbade strikes of postal employees; and of liberals, whose anti-war periodicals he banned from the mails. Burleson continued to exercise strict control and to advocate government ownership of communications. In 1918 he established air-mail service.

Burleson, Edward, 1798–1851, pioneer of Texas, b. Buncombe co., N.C. After living in Tennessee and serving under Andrew Jackson in the war against the Creek Indians (1813–14), he moved to Texas. He distinguished himself in the Texas Revolution and was later (1840) successful commander in the warfare against the Cherokee in East Texas. He was a senator, then vice president of the Texas republic, but was defeated for the presidency in 1844. He also served in the Mexican War.

Burleson, city (pop. 2,345), N central Texas, S of Fort Worth; est. 1881.

burlesque (bûrlĕsk′) [Ital.,=mockery], form of entertainment differing from comedy or farce in that it achieves its effects through caricature, ridicule, and distortion. It differs from satire in that it is devoid of any ethical element. The word first came into use in the 16th cent. in an opera of the Italian Francesco Berni, who called his work *burleschi*. Beaumont and Fletcher's *Knight of the Burning Pestle*, Gay's *Beggar's Opera*, Sheridan's *Critic*, and Fielding's *Tom Thumb* may be classed as dramatic burlesque. American stage burlesque (from 1865), often referred to as "burleycue" or "leg show," began as a variety show, characterized by vulgar dialogue and broad comedy, and uninhibited audiences. Such stars as Al Jolson, W. C. Fields, Mae West, Fannie Brice, Sophie Tucker, Bert Lahr, and Joe Weber and Lew Fields began their careers in burlesque. In c.1920 burlesque began to refer to the "strip-tease" show, which created its own stars, such as Gypsy Rose Lee; in c.1937 burlesque theaters in New York city were banned. See historical studies of the literary burlesque by R. P. Bond (1932) and C. V. Clinton-Baddeley (1952); Bernard Sobel, *Pictorial History of Burlesque* (1956).

Burley, city (pop. 7,508), co. seat of Cassia co., S Idaho, on the Snake and ESE of Twin Falls; founded 1905, inc. 1906. In a farm area irrigated by the Minidoka project, it has mills processing sugar beets, alfalfa, and potatoes. The city is the headquarters of the Minidoka National Forest.

Burlin, Natalie Curtis, 1875–1921, American writer and musician, b. New York city, studied music in France and Germany. She was one of the leading transcribers of the primitive music of America and Africa, and it was through her efforts that Indian music was encouraged, rather than forbidden by law, in government schools. She visited the Navaho, Zuñi, Hopi, and other Indian tribes, recording words and music with fidelity. Songs of African tribes and American Negroes are also included in her works—*Songs of Ancient America* (1905), *The Indians' Book* (1907), *Hampton Series Negro Folk-Songs* (4 vols., 1918–19), and *Songs and Tales from the Dark Continent* (1920).

Burlingame, Anson (bûr′lĭng-gām), 1820–70, American diplomat, b. New Berlin, N.Y., grad. Univ. of Michigan. After studying law at Harvard, he became a lawyer in Boston and later (1855–61) a Congressman. Defeated for reelection, he was made (1861) minister to China. By his tact and understanding of Chinese opposition to the autocratic methods of foreigners in the treaty ports, he won a place as adviser to the Chinese government. China sent (1867) him as head of a mission to visit foreign lands in order to secure information and sign treaties of amity. He visited Washington, London, and capitals on the Continent. One result was a treaty between China and the United States, supplementary to the 1858 treaty. This, usually called the **Burlingame Treaty**, was signed in 1868. It was a treaty of friendship based on Western principles of international law. One clause encouraged Chinese immigration—laborers were then much in demand in the West; later the heavy influx of Chinese under its provisions caused friction on the West Coast and led to the exclusion of Chinese immigrants (see CHINESE EXCLUSION). See biography by F. W. Williams (1912).

Burlingame. 1 Residential city (pop. 24,036), W Calif., on San Francisco Bay and SSE of San Francisco; founded 1868, inc. 1908. **2** City (pop. 1,151), NE Kansas, SSW of Topeka, in a farm area; founded 1855 as Council City, inc. 1861.

Burlingame Treaty: see BURLINGAME, ANSON.

Burlington, Richard Boyle, 3d earl of, 1694–1753, English patron and architect of the Neo-Palladian movement. Even before age 21, when he became a member of the Privy Council and Lord High Treasurer of Ireland, he showed an interest in architecture. In 1714 Burlington made a tour of Italy and also subscribed to the *Vitruvius Britannicus* of Colin CAMPBELL. He employed (c.1717) Campbell to remodel the Burlington House in London. In 1719 Burlington was again in Italy, specifically to study the architecture of Palladio. Through his patronage of other artists, notably William Kent, and in his own buildings, he furthered the revival of an architecture based on the styles of Palladio and Inigo Jones. The most important of Burlington's own works are the villa for his estate at Chiswick (begun 1725) and the Assembly Room, York (1730).

Burlington, town (pop. 47,008), S Ont., Canada, on Lake Ontario NE of Hamilton, in a fruitgrowing area. This residential town attracts many tourists.

Burlington. 1 Town (pop. 2,090), co. seat of Kit Carson co., E Colo., near the Kansas line, ESE of Denver, in a grain and livestock area; inc. 1888. **2** Town (pop. 2,790), central Conn., W of Hartford; settled 1740, inc. 1806. It has a state trout hatchery. **3** City (pop. 32,430), co. seat of Des Moines co., SE Iowa, on four hills overlooking the Mississippi (spanned here by a toll bridge), SSW of Davenport. Platted in 1833 on the sites of an Indian village (Sho-quo-quon; 1820) and a trading post (1829), it was named Burlington in 1834, incorporated as a town in 1836, and chartered as a city in 1838. It is a shipping and manufacturing center with railroad shops and docks. Tractors, steam turbines, explosives, furniture, and electrical and electronic equipment are manufactured. Burlington was the temporary capital of Wisconsin Territory (1837) and of Iowa Territory (1838–40). One of the oldest newspapers in the state, the Burlington *Hawk-Eye*, is still published. The city has a junior college and is the site of the Tri-State Fair (held in August). Nearby is Geode State Park. **4** City (pop. 2,113), co. seat of Coffey co., E Kansas, S of Topeka; inc. 1870. It is the trade center of a farm and dairy region. **5** Town (pop. 12,852), E Mass., NW of Boston; settled 1641, inc. 1799. Wood and gypsum products and machinery are made. Its pre-Revolutionary meetinghouse, remodeled, still stands. **6** City (pop. 12,687), W N.J., on the Delaware (bridged here to Bristol, Pa.) between Trenton and Camden; settled 1677 by Friends, inc. 1733. It grew mainly as a port; it was capital of West Jersey from 1681 until the union of East and West Jersey (1702), and thereafter until 1790 alternate capital with Perth Amboy. It was on a Philadelphia-New York coach line, and

railroad tracks were laid down Broad St. in 1834. G. W. Doane, long rector of old St. Mary's (built 1703), founded St. Mary's Hall for girls here (1837). The newer St. Mary's church was designed by Richard Upjohn. Burlington is the birthplace of James Fenimore Cooper and of James Lawrence. The first colonial money was printed here by Benjamin Franklin in 1726, and the first newspaper in New Jersey appeared in 1777. The Friends' school (1792; now the Y.W.C.A.) and meetinghouse (1784) still exist. Typewriters and iron products are made here. **7** Industrial city (pop. 33,199), N N.C., E of Greensboro and on the Haw river; chartered 1858, inc. 1893. It manufactures hosiery, textiles, electrical equipment, and wood products. **8** City (pop. 35,531), co. seat of Chittenden co., NW Vt., on Lake Champlain, S of St. Albans; chartered 1763, settled 1773, inc. 1865. The largest city in the state, it is a port of entry and an industrial center. Missile and ordnance parts, data-processing machinery, textiles, canned goods, and wood and steel products are among its manufactures. The city is the seat of the Univ. of Vermont (see VERMONT, UNIVERSITY OF) and Trinity College (Roman Catholic; for women; 1925). Ethan Allen spent his last years near Burlington village (part of his farm is included in Ethan Allen Park), and he is said to be buried nearby. The Burlington *Free Press* (founded 1827) became Vermont's first daily newspaper in 1848. John Dewey was born in Burlington. **9** City (pop. 2,968), NW Wash., SE of Bellingham; settled 1882, inc. 1902. It is the trading center of the fertile Skagit valley. **10** City (pop. 5,856), SE Wis., on the Fox and WSW of Racine; settled 1835, inc. as a village 1896, as a city 1900. Floor covering is made. A Mormon colony was (1844–49) near here.

Burma, Union of, republic (262,000 sq. mi.; pop. c.20,000,000), SE Asia. The capital is RANGOON. Burma is bounded on the west by the Bay of Bengal, East Pakistan, and Assam (India), on the north by Tibet, and on the east by Yünnan prov. (China), Laos, and Thailand. The most densely populated part of the country—Burma proper—is the valley of the Irrawaddy river with its vast delta, one of the main rice-growing areas of the world. The valley is surrounded by a chain of mountains stemming from the Eastern Himalayas and spreading roughly in the shape of a giant horseshoe; the ranges and the river valleys of the

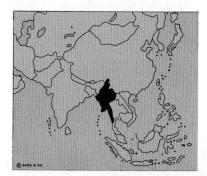

Burma location map

Burmese Buddhist monks.

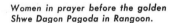

Women in prayer before the golden
Shwe Dagon Pagoda in Rangoon.

Chindwin, the Sittang, and the Salween trend from north to south. In the high mountains N of Myitkyina (rising more than 19,000 ft.) and along the Assam-Burma frontier (from 8,000 to 10,000 ft.) live various Mongoloid tribes, of which the most important are the Nagas, who still practice head-hunting; the Kachins, who came down from Tibet in the 8th cent. A.D.; and the Chins (in the Chin Hills). These tribes raise rice and millet and cut teak in the forests. Gems (notably rubies and sapphires) are found near MOGOK, and since the 13th cent., Burma has exported to China the jade that is mined in the Hukawng valley and in the Jade Mines Tract (a central mountain range). ARAKAN, a narrow coastal plain between the Bay of Bengal and the hills of the Arakan Yoma, produces rice and rubber; it centers around the port and capital, Akyab. To the east on the Shan Plateau is the SHAN STATE, the home of the Shans (a Tai race closely linked to the Siamese). The Bawdwin mines near Lashio, worked by the Chinese since the 15th cent., produce much iron, as well as lead, silver, and zinc. South of the Shan States is the mountainous Kayah State; the KARENS, who inhabit this region, are of Tai-Chinese origin, and many are converts to Christianity. The Mawchi mines there provide a large portion of the world's tungsten. South of Kayah and cut off by the Salween river is Tenasserim, a narrow strip of coast that extends south. It has heavy rainfall (about 200 in. a year) and produces rice, rubber, and fruit. Tin is mined at Tavoy, and there is fishing in the Mergui archipelago. The Dry Zone (annual rainfall 20–40 in.) lies north of the hills of PEGU and is centered around MANDA-LAY and the Irrawaddy river. It is the home of the Burmese proper, a Mongoloid race who came down from Tibet before the 9th cent. and settled in the fertile plains which today produce rice (one third of the area is under paddy), groundnuts, cotton, tobacco, and sesamum. More than 50 percent of

Bazaar in Rangoon.

the Burmese are found here. Most of them are farmers. Their early history was mainly the story of their struggle with the Mons or Talaings (of Mon-Khmer origin, now assimilated). In 1044 Anawratha established Burmese supremacy over the Irrawaddy delta and Thaton (capital of the Talaing kingdom). He introduced Hinayana Buddhism, which is today the prevalent religion. Pagodas, monasteries, and temples are to be found in most communities, and Buddhism has made the rate of literacy high. Anawratha's capital PAGAN, "the city of a thousand temples," was the seat of his dynasty until conquered by Kublai Khan in 1287. Then the Shans, who obtained the rule as tributaries of Peking, maintained it until 1546, when new Burmese dynasties arose, with seats at Ava, Pegu, and Toungoo. The Burmese ruler Tabinshweti once more unified the country (16th cent.), but in the 18th cent. the Talaings of the Irrawaddy delta overran the Dry Zone. Alaungpaya in 1758 rallied the Burmese, crushed the

Burmese dancers perform a classical dance.

Dyed silk is dried outdoors in a Burmese village.

Glazing of pottery in a street of Twante, Burma.

Talaings, and established his capital at Rangoon. Burma was still ruled by his successors when it was annexed piecemeal (1824, 1852, and 1885) by the British, who made it a dependency of India. Under the British, the natural resources of the country were developed. The rice crop in the delta was increased to a point where 7 million tons were grown yearly and over 3 million tons were exported, mainly through Rangoon. Rubber, sugar cane, and cotton were introduced. Over 2,600 mi. of railroads were built. Exploitation of the rich oil deposits of Yenangyaung in central Burma began in 1871. Generally under British rule the distinction was made between the coastal areas, Lower Burma, and the hill country, Upper Burma. In 1937 Burma seceded from India and obtained, as far as internal affairs were concerned, the equivalent of dominion status. In the Second World War, the country was invaded and occupied early in 1942 by the Japanese who set up an "independent" Burmese regime. In the north British and U.S. troops raided enemy lines (see STILWELL, JOSEPH WARREN), and in Dec., 1944, four allied armies, including Chinese forces, started a drive down the central plains, and in May, 1945, they captured Rangoon. After the war, Burma obtained complete independence from Britain. On Jan. 4, 1948, the Union of Burma was set up as a republic with a president and a bicameral legislature; less-developed areas outside Burma proper were made autonomous states (with representatives in parliament) and national territories. The strongly socialistic Anti-Fascist People's Freedom League, which maintained a precarious hold on the government in a confused political situation, was soon faced with armed risings of the Communists and of the Karen tribesmen. In 1949 the Karen rebels forced the government to offer a larger degree of autonomy. Troubles with Communist rebels and Karen nationalists continued to plague Burma after 1950. International tension grew over the presence in Burma of Chinese Nationalist troops who had been forced across the Yünnan border by the Communists in 1950. They made forays into China, and Burma took the matter up with the United Nations, which in 1953 told the Nationalists to leave Burma or be interned. The United States undertook to transport them to

Aerial view of Burma Road between Muse and Kutkai.

Taiwan (Formosa), and the Chinese Nationalist government disavowed those who would not leave Burma. Nevertheless several thousand refused and continued depredations until they were forced to disperse to Laos and Thailand. The elections of 1951–52 ended the transition period for the 1947 constitution. The Anti-Fascist People's Freedom League triumphed, and in 1952 Ba U was chosen first president of Burma. U Nu, of the same party, was premier. The government followed a socialistic plan, and Burma became the first Asian country to curb child labor, set salary minimums, and put the 40-hour week into general effect. Japanese reparations were used to build hydroelectric plants. U Nu, a devout Buddhist, sought to harmonize relations between the various hill peoples and political groups. Internal dissensions, however, forced him to make an alliance in 1958 with the partly Communist National Unity Front party. In 1959 he stepped down in favor of a military government led by Gen. Ne Win. The army restored a measure of stability and efficiency to the country. In April, 1960, Ne Win resigned and U Nu, victorious in a general election, returned to office. Reforms promised in the election campaign were not pressed dynamically, and U Nu's establishment of Buddhism as the official religion met resistance. In March, 1962, a coup d'état again established Gen. Ne Win in power. U Nu and other leaders were arrested. Ne Win suspended the constitution, dissolved the national assembly, and imposed stringent military rule. Official observance of the Buddhist sabbath was canceled. Students were put under curfew and repressive measures against minority agitators were begun. Cultural activities by foreign philanthropic agencies in Burma were prohibited. Foreign aid, however, was accepted from Communist China and the United States. In Jan., 1961, China and Burma reached agreement on an old border dispute. Ne Win's military regime has met much resistance among students and the hill tribes of Upper Burma. See D. G. E. Hall, *Europe and Burma* (1945); F. T. Jesse, *The Story of Burma* (1946); Maung Maung, *Burma in the Family of Nations* (1957); J. F. Cady, *A History of Modern Burma* (1958); F. N. Trager, *Building a Welfare State in Burma* (1958); Hugh Tinker, *The Union of Burma* (3d ed., 1961).

Burman: see BURMESE.

bur marigold or **sticktight,** any species of *Bidens,* a genus of chiefly weedy North American composite plants with pronged burlike fruits (achenes) that have gained various species such additional names as beggar-ticks, Spanish needles, tickseed, and bootjacks. A few showy yellow species are occasionally cultivated. Many of the common names are also used for other weeds with burs.

Burma Road, in China and Burma, extending from the Burmese railhead of Lashio to Kunming, Yünnan prov., China. About 700 mi. long and constructed through extremely rough mountain country, it was a remarkable engineering achievement. Undertaken by the Chinese after the outbreak of the Sino-Japanese war in 1937 and completed in 1938, it carried war supplies landed at Rangoon and shipped by railroad to Lashio. This traffic increased in importance to China after the Japanese took effective control of the Chinese coast and of Indo-China. The Ledo Road (later called the Stilwell Road) from Ledo, India, into Burma was begun in Dec., 1942. In 1944 the Ledo Road reached Myitkyina and was joined to the Burma Road. Both roads have lost their former importance and are in a state of disrepair.

Burmese or **Burman,** Sino-Tibetan language. See LANGUAGE (table).

Burne-Jones, Sir Edward, 1833–98, English painter and decorator, b. Birmingham. Intended for the church, he went to Exeter College, Oxford, where he met his lifelong friend, William Morris. He left Oxford to study painting with Rossetti in London and joined the Pre-Raphaelites. His early work shows Rossetti's strong influence, which is replaced by his emulation of Botticelli and Mantegna. Burne-Jones rose to success in 1877 with the opening of the Grosvenor Gallery. Well-known paintings are *King Cophetua and the Beggar Maid* (Tate Gall., London); *Depths of the Sea*; and *Star of Bethlehem* (Birmingham Gall.). His designs for stained glass, executed by Morris and Company, may be seen in churches throughout England. In his day he enjoyed the highest honors, and many still admire his delicate, though mannered work. See Lady Burne-Jones, *Memorial of Edward Burne-Jones* (1904).

Burnes, Sir Alexander, 1805–41, British traveler in India. As an army officer in India, he studied Oriental languages. In 1832 he left Lahore in Afghan dress and traveled via Peshawar and Kabul across the Hindu Kush to Balkh and thence by Bukhara, Asterabad, and Teheran to Bushire. On his return to England (1833) he was honored. In 1839 he was appointed political resident at Kabul, where he was assassinated two years later. See his *Narrative of a Visit to the Court of Scinde* (1830), *Travels into Bokhara* (1834), and *Cabool* (1842).

Burnet, David Gouverneur, 1788–1870, provisional president of Texas (1836), b. Newark, N.J.; son of William Burnet (1730–91). He went (c.1817) to Texas; and his legal training enabled him to become a spokesman of the American settlers there as trouble with the Mexican government grew. Though appointed (1834) a district judge, he opposed the measures of the Mexican government and was gradually led to favor the independence of Texas from Mexico. In 1836 he drew up the declaration of independence at the convention at Washington-on-the-Brazos, where he was made president ad interim of Texas. His eight-month administration in the chaotic times during and after the revolution (see TEXAS) was not effective. He quarreled bitterly with Sam Houston and thereafter opposed him in politics. Burnet was vice president under Mirabeau B. Lamar, was defeated by Houston for the presidency in 1841, and was chosen in 1866 (because he had opposed secession) U.S. Senator from Texas in the Reconstruction era but was denied his seat.

Burnet, Gilbert (bûr′nĭt), 1643–1715, British bishop and writer. He studied abroad, held (1665–69) the living of Saltoun in Scotland, and was appointed (1669) professor of divinity at Glasgow Univ. In London in 1673 he was well received by Charles II and was lecturer at St. Clements until his defense of his friend Lord William Russell made it unsafe for him in England after the Rye House Plot executions. During James II's reign Burnet's anti-Catholic writing and preaching barred him from court, and he found favor and friendship with William of Orange at The Hague. Accompanying William to England, he was a trusted adviser to William III and Mary (and later to Queen Anne) and was made bishop of Salisbury. His celebrated *History of My Own Times* (published only in 1723–24; ed. by M. J. Routh, 6 vols., 1833) is fiercely biased against James II, but it is also the most informative contemporary source for the period. Burnet made a translation of Sir Thomas More's *Utopia.* He also wrote a *History of the Reformation in England* (3 vols., 1679–1714; abridged ed., 1719), notable for its cognizance of the economic, social, and cultural causes and effects of the Reformation, and many lesser works on history and theology.

See biograpy by T. E. S. Clarke and H. C. Foxcroft (1907).

Burnet, John, 1863–1928, English classical scholar, b. Edinburgh. He was the editor of the Oxford edition of Plato's works (6 vols., 1902–10). His works on Greek philosophy include *Early Greek Philosophy* (1892) and *Greek Philosophy: Thales to Plato* (1914).

Burnet, Sir Macfarlane, 1899–, Australian virologist and physician, grad. Geelong College, M.D. Univ. of Melbourne, 1923. He was resident pathologist (1923–24) at the Royal Melbourne Hospital

Sir Macfarlane Burnet

and a Beit fellow (1926–27) at the Lister Institute, London. He became assistant director (1928) and director (1944) of the Walter and Eliza Hall Institute at the Royal Melbourne Hospital. From 1944 he was professor of experimental medicine at the Univ. of Melbourne. He lectured at several universities in the United States, including Harvard (1944), Johns Hopkins (1950), and Vanderbilt (1958). An expert on viruses and virus diseases, Burnet made important contributions to the understanding of influenza and the development of immunity against it. He shared the 1960 Nobel Prize in Medicine and Physiology with P. B. MEDAWAR for their work in immunological tolerances, or the reactions of the body to the transplantation of foreign living tissues. His writings include *Natural History of Infectious Disease* (rev. ed., 1953) and *Viruses and Man* (1953).

Burnet, William, 1688–1729, English colonial governor in America; son of Gilbert Burnet. As governor of New York and New Jersey (1720–28), he advocated extending the trade with the Indians, seeking to bind the Iroquois to the British and keep them from French influence—a move which was to be of great significance in the French and Indian Wars. He had the first English fort on the Great Lakes built at Oswego. His efforts to regulate trade were opposed by Albany merchants who made great profit in selling English goods to French traders. Burnet was embroiled with the assembly in arguments over policies and finance. After he dissolved the assembly in 1727, he was transferred to govern Massachusetts and New Hampshire.

Burnet, William, 1730–91, American Revolutionary

patriot, b. near the present Elizabeth, N.J., grad. College of New Jersey (now Princeton), 1749; father of David G. Burnet. A doctor of Newark, Burnet was chairman of the Revolutionary committee of safety there. He set up (1775) a military hospital and helped to furnish troops and supplies for the patriot forces. He became surgeon general of the army for the eastern district and was also a member of the Continental Congress in 1776 and in 1780.

Burnet (bûr'nĭt), town (pop. 2,214), co. seat of Burnet co., central Texas, NW of Austin; inc. 1885. It grew about Fort Croghan, a frontier military post established in 1849. The courthouse and other buildings are made of the granite for which the county is famous (see MARBLE FALLS). Limestone is also quarried, and wool and mohair as well as cattle are shipped. Burnet's tourist trade is enhanced by nearby reservoirs, impounded by Buchanan Dam (150 ft. high; 11,200 ft. long; completed 1936) and Roy Inks Dam (98 ft. high; 1,550 ft. long; completed 1936) on the Colorado river. Longhorn Cavern also attracts many visitors.

burnet (bûr'nĭt), hardy perennial herb of the ROSE family found in temperate regions, usually with white or greenish flowers. The European species are sometimes cultivated for the leaves, used in salads, for flavoring, and formerly as a poultice to stop bleeding—hence the botanical name *Sanguisorba* [from Latin, =sucking in blood].

Burnett, Frances Eliza Hodgson (–nĕt'), 1849–1924, American author, b. Manchester, England. She came to Knoxville, Tenn., in 1865 with her family. She is famous for her children's books, particularly *Little Lord Fauntleroy* (1886), *Sara Crewe* (1888), and *The Secret Garden* (1911).

Burnett, James: see MONBODDO, JAMES BURNETT, LORD.

Burney, Charles, 1726–1814, English musician and music historian, Though a composer and organist by profession, his *General History of Music* (1776–89; 2d ed., 1935) and Sir John Hawkins's *General History of the Science and Practice of Music* (1776) were the first important music histories in English. He wrote *The Present State of Music in France and Italy* (1771) and *The Present State of Music in Germany* (1773). They were published together as *Dr. Burney's Musical Tours in Europe* (1959). It

Charles Burney

describes European society, life, and customs as well as music and important musicians. His daughter Frances compiled his memoirs (1832). See P. A. Scholes, *The Great Dr. Burney* (1948).

Burney, Frances (Fanny Burney), later **Madame D'Arblay** (därblä'), 1752–1840, English novelist; daughter of Charles Burney. Although her first novel, *Evelina* (1778), was published anonymously, Miss Burney soon acknowledged its authorship and achieved literary prominence. She became an intimate friend of Johnson and his circle. Her second novel, *Cecilia*, appeared in 1782, *Camilla* in 1796, and *The Wanderer* in 1814. The theme of her books is the entry into society of a virtuous, but inexperienced young girl, her mistakes and her gradual coming of age. Miss Burney spent five unhappy years (1786–91) as a member of Queen Charlotte's household. In 1793 she married General D'Arblay, a French émigré. Her diary and her letters give an excellent account of English culture and society from 1768 to 1840. See biography by Emily Hahn (1950); study by Joyce Hemlow (1958).

Burney, uninc. village (pop. 1,294), N Calif., ENE of Redding, in the Cascade Range. It is a resort and trade center in a timber and farm region. A state park is nearby.

Burnham, Daniel Hudson, 1846–1912, American architect and city-planner, b. Henderson, N.Y., d. Heidelberg, Germany. He was trained in architects' offices in Chicago. With John W. Root he established in Chicago a partnership (1873) which gained many of the most important architectural commissions of the day. The Chicago works included the Monadnock Building; the 20-story Masonic Temple Building (1892), the first important skeleton skyscraper; the Reliance Building, and the "Rookery" offices, the first suitably planned modern office building. Other works were the Flatiron Building and the Wanamaker store in New York, the Union Passenger Station in Washington, and buildings in Cleveland, Buffalo, and San Francisco. Burnham and Root designed the general plan for the Columbian Exposition at Chicago (1893), exerting through it an enormous influence upon contemporaneous civic design. In 1901 Burnham served with C. F. McKim, F. L. Olmsted, Jr., and Augustus Saint-Gaudens on the Senate Park Commission in planning for the future beautification of Washington, D.C. With E. H. Bennett he created a civic improvement plan of great importance for Chicago (1907), much of which has since been put into execution. He also prepared plans for Baltimore, Duluth, and San Francisco and was commissioned by the U.S. government to design plans for Manila and for other cities in the Philippines, including Baguio, the summer capital.

Burnham, Sherburne Wesley, 1838–1921, American astronomer, b. Thetford, Vt. After serving as observer at Dearborn Observatory, Chicago (1877–81, 1882–84), and as astronomer at Lick Observatory (1888–92), he was from 1893 astronomer at Yerkes Observatory and professor of astronomy at the Univ. of Chicago. Although his interest in astronomy had begun with amateur observations, he became outstanding in the field, especially through his discoveries of double stars. He wrote *General Catalogue of Double Stars* (1906) and *Measures of Proper Motion Stars* (1913).

Burnham. 1 Village (pop. 2,478), NE Ill., a suburb S of Chicago and near the Ind. line; inc. 1907. **2** Borough (pop. 2,755), S central Pa., a suburb NNE of Lewistown; founded 1795, inc. 1911. Metal products are made.

burning bush, name for a North American plant of the STAFF TREE family. The scriptural burning bush not consumed by fire (Ex.3.2) is sometimes associated with a bramble or thorn and was adopted by the Presbyterian Church as an emblem of its early persecution.

Burnley, county borough (pop. 80,588), Lancashire, N England, near the junction of the Brun or Burn with the Calder. It is one of the largest centers for cotton cloth production in the world and has such associated industries as calico printing and the manufacture of textile machinery. There is coal in the vicinity. The 14th-century Townley House is of interest.

Burns, John, 1858–1943, British socialist and member of Parliament. A factory worker as a child, he was largely self-educated and was led by his reading to radical socialism. Burns became an outstanding orator, and in 1889 he was leader, with Tom Mann and Ben Tillett, of the London dock strike, an attempt to organize the ill-paid unskilled laborers. Burns was elected (1892) to Parliament among the first labor representatives, but he quarreled with James Kier Hardie and soon abandoned both socialism and the trade union movement. Henceforth associated with the Liberals, he was president of the local government board (1905–14), but resigned from the cabinet in protest against Britain's entering the First World War. He retired from Parliament in 1918. See biographies by G. D. H. Cole (1943) and William Kent (1950).

Burns, Otway, c.1775–1850, American privateer, b. Onslow co., N.C. At the outbreak of the War of 1812, he outfitted the Baltimore clipper *Snap-Dragon* as a privateer and began one of the most spectacular privateering careers in American history. He destroyed and captured millions of dollars worth of British shipping and had a $50,000 price set on his head by the crown. After the war, Burns turned to shipbuilding and later served (1821–35) in the North Carolina legislature. See biography by W. F. Burns (1905).

Burns, Robert, 1759–96, Scottish poet. The son of a hard-working and intelligent farmer, Burns was the oldest of seven children, all of whom had to help in the work on the farm. Although always hard pressed financially, the elder Burns, until his death in 1784, encouraged his sons with their education. As a result, Burns as a boy not only read the Scottish poetry of Ramsay and the collections compiled by Hailes and Herd, but also the works of Pope, Locke, and Shakespeare. By 1781 Burns had tried his hand at several agricultural jobs without success. Although he had begun writing, and his poems were circulated widely in manuscript, none were published until 1786. At this time he had already begun a life of dissipation, and he was not only discouraged but poor and was involved simultaneously with several women. He decided to marry Mary Campbell and migrate to Jamaica. To help finance the journey, he published at Kilmarnock *Poems, Chiefly in the Scottish Dialect*

Robert Burns

(1786), which was an immediate success. Mary Campbell died, and Burns changed his mind about migration. He toured the Highlands, brought out a second edition of his poems at Edinburgh in 1787, and for two winters was a figure of social prominence in the Scottish city. In 1788 he married Jean Armour, who had borne him four children, and retired to a farm at Ellisland. By 1791 Burns had failed as a farmer, and he moved to nearby Dumfries, where he held a position as an exciseman. He died at 37 after a severe attack of rheumatic fever. Burns is supreme in songs such as "Flow Gently, Sweet Afton," "My Heart's in the Highlands," and "John Anderson My Jo." Two collections contain 268 of his songs—George Thomson's *Select Collection of Original Scottish Airs for the Voice* (6 vols., 1793–1811) and James Johnson's *Scots Musical Museum* (5 vols., 1787–1803). Some of these, such as "Auld Lang Syne" and "Comin' thro' the Rye," are among the most familiar and best-loved poems in the English language. But his talent was not confined to song, and two descriptive pieces, "Tam o' Shanter" and "The Jolly Beggars," are among his masterpieces. Burns had a fine sense of humor which he used with equal skill for satire, description, and plain wild fun. His great popularity with the Scots lies in his ability to depict with loving accuracy the life of his fellow rural Scots, as he did in "The Cotter's Saturday Night." His use of dialect brought a stimulating, much needed freshness and raciness into English poetry, but Burns's greatness extends beyond the limits of .dialect. His poems are written about Scots, but, in tune with the rising humanitarianism of his day, they apply to man's universal problems. See his poems (ed. by J. L. Robertson, 1953); his letters (ed. by J. De Lancey Ferguson, 1931); biographies by F. B. Snyder (1936) and J. M. Lindsay (1954); studies by David Daiches (1950) and Thomas Crawford (1960).

Burns, city (pop. 3,523), co. seat of Harney co., E central Oregon, on the Silvies river and N of Malheur; inc. 1899. The livestock center of Oregon, it also has lumber mills.

Burns Flat, town (pop. 2,280), SW Okla., SW of Clinton, in a cotton, cattle, and oil area.

Burnside, Ambrose Everett, 1824–81, Union general in the Civil War, b. Liberty, Ind., grad. West

Ambrose Burnside

Aaron Burr

Point, 1847. He saw brief service in the Mexican War and remained in the army until 1853, when he entered business in Rhode Island. In the Civil War, Burnside commanded a brigade at the first battle of Bull Run and was made (Aug., 1861) a brigadier general of volunteers. His expedition to the North Carolina coast (1862), resulting in the capture of Roanoke Island, New Bern, Beaufort, and Fort Macon, won him a major generalcy and much prestige. He commanded under G. B. McClellan in the ANTIETAM CAMPAIGN and shortly afterward succeeded that general in command of the Army of the Potomac. After a costly defeat at the battle of Fredericksburg (see FREDERICKSBURG, BATTLE OF) in Dec., 1862, Burnside asked the President either to sustain him in dismissing Joseph HOOKER and several other generals who opposed his plans, or to remove Burnside himself. Lincoln relieved him in favor of Joseph Hooker. As commander of the Dept. of the Ohio (March–Dec., 1863), he occupied E Tennessee, took Knoxville, and repulsed Longstreet's attempt to recapture the town. In 1864 he commanded under Meade and Grant in Virginia. Held partially responsible for the mine fiasco at PETERSBURG, he was relieved. Burnside was elected governor of Rhode Island in 1866 and was reelected in 1867 and 1868. From 1875 to his death he was a U.S. Senator. He originated the fashion of wearing long side whiskers, thus the term *burnsides* or *sideburns*. See biography by B. P. Poore (1882); K. P. Williams, *Lincoln Finds a General* (Vol. II, 1950).

Burnsville, resort town (pop. 1,388), co. seat of Yancey co., W central N.C., NE of Asheville, in the Blue Ridge.

Burntisland (bûrntĭ′lŭnd, brŭntĭ–), burgh (pop. 6,036), Fife, E Scotland, on the Firth of Forth opposite Edinburgh. A seaport and resort, it has large shipyards and aluminum works. Here is Rossend Castle, scene of the famous incident (1563) involving Pierre de CHASTELARD.

Burr, Aaron, 1756–1836, American political leader, b. Newark, N.J., grad. College of New Jersey (now Princeton Univ.), 1772. A brilliant law student, he interrupted his study to serve in the American Revolution and proved himself a valiant soldier in the early campaigns of the war for independence. In 1779 ill-health forced him to leave the army. Upon admission (1782) to the bar, he plunged with characteristic energy into practice of the law and politics. He served as member (1784–85; 1797–99) of the New York assembly, as state attorney general (1789–91), and as U.S. Senator (1791–97). Defeated for reelection to the assembly in 1799, he set about organizing the Republican (see DEMOCRATIC PARTY) element in New York city for the election of 1800, for the first time making use of the Tammany Society for political purposes. The result was an unexpected victory for the Republicans, who gained control of the state legislature. Since the legislature named the presidential electors and New York was the pivotal state, Burr's victory insured the election of a Republican President. The intention of the party was to make Thomas JEFFERSON President and Burr Vice President, but confusion in the ELECTORAL COLLEGE resulted in a tie vote. This threw the election into the House of Representatives, dominated by the Federalist Alexander HAMILTON. Hamilton, who regarded Jefferson as the lesser evil of the two Republicans, helped to secure Jefferson the presidency, and on the 36th ballot Burr became Vice President. Burr presided over the Senate with a dignity and impartiality that commanded respect from both sides, and in 1804 his friends nominated him for the governorship of New York. Hamilton again contributed to his defeat, in part by statements reflecting on Burr's character. Burr challenged Hamilton to a duel and mortally wounded him. The circumstances of Hamilton's death brought Burr's political career to an end. Soon after, he left Washington on a journey to New Orleans, at that time a center of Spanish conspirings for possession of the lower Mississippi valley. Burr, unaware that Gen. James Wilkinson was in the pay of the Spanish, laid plans with him that recognized the possibility of war with Spain. What exactly Burr's plans were has never been made clear. Speculation ranges from the establishment of an independent republic in the American Southwest to seizure of territory in Spanish America. With money secured from Harman BLENNERHASSETT, Burr acquired the Bastrop grant on Washita river to serve as a base of operations. In the autumn of 1806, he and his party of 60-odd colonists, well-armed and supplied, began the journey downstream from Blennerhassett Island. The motives behind Burr's earlier trip to New Orleans had come under suspicion; now distrust became widespread. Wilkinson, in an effort to save himself, turned against Burr, fanned the distrust, and in dispatches to Washington accused Burr of treason. Burr was arrested. He was tried in the U.S. Circuit Court at Richmond, Va., Chief Justice John MARSHALL presiding, and found not guilty of an "overt act" of treason. Popular opinion nonetheless condemned him, and his remaining years were spent out of public life. He was married in 1833 to the famous Madame Jumel; they were divorced in 1834. See his correspondence with his daughter, Theodosia (ed. by Mark Van Doren,

1929); biographies by S. H. Wandell and Meade Minnigerode (1925), Holmes Alexander (1937), and Nathan Schachner (1937); T. P. Abernethy, *The Burr Conspiracy* (1959); H. C. Syrett and J. G. Cooke, eds., *Interview in Weehawken* (1960).

Burr, Theodosia, 1783–1813, beautiful and accomplished daughter of Aaron Burr, b. Albany, N.Y. She was educated under her father's strict and competent tutelage and after her mother's death became the admired social mistress of the Burr home at Richmond Hill on Manhattan island. In 1801 she married Joseph Alston, later governor of South Carolina. She made frequent visits to her father's home in the North and, when his name was under a cloud, stood loyally by him. She smoothed the way for his return from exile in Europe but did not live to welcome him home. The ship on which she took passage from Charleston to meet him was lost at sea. See Gamaliel Bradford, *Wives* (1925).

Burr, William Hubert, 1851–1934, American civil engineer, b. Watertown, Conn., grad. Rensselaer Polytechnic Institute, 1872. Professor of civil engineering at Columbia Univ. (1893–1916), he served on many important engineering commissions, including those for the Isthmian Canal (see PANAMA CANAL) and for the Port of New York Authority. His works include *Ancient and Modern Engineering and the Isthmian Canal* (1902) and *Suspension Bridges, Arch Ribs, and Cantilevers* (1913).

burr, in botany: see BUR.

Burra (bŭr'ù), town (pop. 1,599), South Australia, Commonwealth of Australia, in a pastoral and agricultural area. Marble and mineral pigments are obtained in the area. It was (1844–78) the mining center of the Burra Burra copper field.

Burrell, George Arthur (bŭ'rŭl), 1882–1957, American chemical engineer, b. Cleveland, Ohio, grad. Ohio State Univ. (Chem.E., 1918). A specialist in petroleum engineering and the discoverer of helium in Texas, he invented the Burrell gas detector and the Burrell pipette and wrote *Handbook of Gasoline* (1917) and *Extraction of Gasoline from Natural Gas* (1925).

Burrill, Thomas Jonathan (bûr'ĭl), 1839–1916, American botanist, horticulturist, and one of the first of the modern microscopists. He was a pioneer in the study of bacterial diseases of crop plants. For an appraisal of his work, see E. F. Smith, *Bacterial Diseases of Plants* (1920).

Burrillville, town (pop. 9,119), extreme NW R.I., on the Mass. and Conn. lines, NW of Providence; set off from Glocester and inc. 1806. A textile town since the early 19th cent., it includes the villages of Pascoag (păs'kōg") (pop. 2,983), a resort area, and Harrisville (pop. 1,024). A state tuberculosis sanatorium is in Wallum Lake village.

Burritt, Elihu, 1810–79, American worker for world peace, "the learned blacksmith," b. New Britain, Conn. While an apprentice and workman at the forge, he studied mathematics, languages, and geography and amassed a great store of knowledge. Profoundly idealistic, he supported many reform causes—antislavery, temperance, and self-education—and he pleaded for them when he edited (1844–51) the weekly *Christian Citizen* at Worcester, Mass. Most of all, however, he worked for the promotion of peace and the abolition of war. He aided Anglo-American friendship in the days of the Oregon crisis, and he tried to avert the Civil War by a scheme of compensated emancipation. Burritt argued for cheaper international postal rates and greater intellectual exchange among nations. Among his much-read books were *Sparks from the Anvil* (1846) and *Ten Minute Talks* (1873). See Merle Curti, *The Learned Blacksmith* (1937).

burro: see ASS.

Burroughs, Edgar Rice, 1875–1950, American novelist, creator of the character Tarzan. He is the author of *Tarzan of the Apes* (1914) and numerous other jungle and outer-planetary thrillers.

Burroughs, John (bûr'ōz), 1837–1921, American naturalist and author, b. Roxbury, N.Y.; son of a farmer. He became in turn a journalist, a treasury clerk in Washington, and a bank examiner and in 1874 settled on a farm near Esopus, N.Y., where he devoted his time to fruit culture and literature. In his first book, *Walt Whitman, Poet and Person* (1867), he was the first to give adequate recognition to the genius of his poet friend. In the bulk of his prose he made widely popular the type of nature essay which Thoreau had written. His best-known books are *Wake Robin* (1871); *Locusts and Wild Honey* (1879); *Fresh Fields*, a travel book (1884); *Signs and Seasons* (1886); and his one volume of poems, *Bird and Bough* (1906). A growing interest in philosophy and in science is evident in *Time and Change* (1912), *The Summit of the Years* (1913), *The Breath of Life* (1915), and *Accepting the Universe* (1922). "The Sage of Slabsides" became the friend of John Muir, Theodore Roosevelt, Edison, Ford, and other important men of his day. Though attached to his farm home, he traveled to the Pacific coast, the South, the West Indies, Europe, and (with the Harriman expedition) Alaska, observing natural phenomena

John Burroughs

everywhere and recording them in simple, expressive prose. See his autobiography, *My Boyhood* (1922); biographies by Clara Barrus (1925) and Elizabeth Burroughs Kelley (1959).

burrstone: see BUHRSTONE.

Bursa (bōōrsä'), city (pop. 153,574), capital of Bursa prov., NW Turkey. The market center of a rich agricultural region, Bursa is a commercial and in-

Bursa, the capital of Bursa Province.

dustrial center, noted for its textiles. Founded at the end of the 3d cent. B.C. by the king of Bithynia, Prusias I, it was called Prusia ad Olympium. It was captured by the Seljuk Turks in 1075, taken by the Crusaders in 1096, and in 1204 passed to the Byzantines. Captured in 1326 by the Ottomans under Sultan Orkhan, it became the Ottoman capital and was embellished with mosques, baths, a caravanserai, and many other public buildings. It was sacked by Tamerlane in 1402, and Adrianople became the new capital of the Ottomans. There are many fine old mosques, notably the Green Mosque (1421) and the mosque of Bejazit I (1399). The town is sometimes called Brusa or Brussa.

Burschenschaft (boor'shünshäft), student organization in the German universities. The first was founded at Jena in 1815 to foster patriotism and to improve student morals, and the idea spread rapidly to other universities. Soon the nationalist ideals of Friedrich JAHN became the creed of the Burschenschaften. At the Wartburg festival (Oct. 18, 1817), the first general assembly of Burschenschaften met, and the next year a united national organization, the Allgemeine Deutsche Burschenschaft, was formed. It adopted as colors black, red, and gold. After the murder (1819) of August von KOTZEBUE by a student, the Burschenschaften were dissolved by the CARLSBAD DECREES. Although they were reorganized as secret nationalistic societies, their influence on the Revolution of 1848 was minor. By 1849 all government restrictions had been lifted. The Burschenschaften continued as purely social organizations, devoted for the most part to dueling, drinking, and other "manly" pursuits. Burschenschaften also existed in Austria. They were dissolved in Germany in 1935 but reappeared after the Second World War.

bursitis, acute or chronic inflammation of a bursa, or fluid sac. Bursae are present in joint cavities and help prevent friction in the movement of the joints. Sacs of fluid may also develop about a joint in response to irritation or injury, as in a bunion, and may become inflamed causing pain, restricting motion, and producing more fluid than can be absorbed readily. Bursitis is treated with rest, antibiotics, X-ray therapy, diathermy, or cortisone, depending upon the cause and the degree of involvement. Superficial bursae, not necessary to the function of a joint, may be excised.

Burslem: see STOKE-ON-TRENT.

Burt, John, 1814–86, American surveyor; son of William A. Burt. Trained by his father, he surveyed the northern peninsula of Michigan and was influential in developing the iron mines, ironworking, lumbering, and other industries of N Michigan.

Burt, William Austin, 1792–1858, American surveyor and inventor, b. Petersham, Mass. He settled in Michigan Territory in 1824. From 1833 to 1855 he was U.S. deputy surveyor, spending much of his time on the frontiers, surveying in Iowa, Wisconsin, and the Upper Peninsula of Michigan. He completed the geological survey of the Upper Peninsula started by Douglass Houghton and was the discoverer of iron ore in the region. He was the inventor (1836) of the solar compass. His typographer, patented in 1829, was America's first writing machine, ancestor of the American typewriter. Later he invented the equatorial sextant. He wrote *Key to the Solar Compass* (8th ed., 1909). Of five sons whom he trained as surveyors, John Burt became the most famous.

Burton, Ernest DeWitt, 1856–1925, American biblical scholar, b. Granville, Ohio, grad. Denison Univ., 1876, and Rochester Theological Seminary, 1882. From 1882 to 1923 he served as professor of New Testament literature and interpretation at the Univ. of Chicago, of which he became president in 1923. He wrote *A Short Introduction to the Gospels* (revised by H. R. Willoughby, 1926); with E. J. Goodspeed, *Harmony of the Synoptic Gospels* (1917) and *Harmony of the Synoptic Gospels in Greek* (1920); and, with Shailer Mathews, *The Life of Christ* (rev. ed., 1927). See biography by T. W. Goodspeed (1926).

Burton, Harold Hitz, 1888–, Associate Justice of U.S. Supreme Court (1945–58), b. Jamaica Plain (now part of Boston), grad. Bowdoin College, 1909, and Harvard Law School, 1912. A prosperous Cleveland lawyer and a law instructor (1923–25) at Western Reserve Univ., he served as a representative (1929–31) in Ohio and as a reform mayor (1935–40) of Cleveland. He was (1941–45) U.S. Senator before he was appointed to the Supreme Court bench.

Burton, Sir Richard Francis, 1821–90, English explorer, writer, and linguist. He joined (1842) the service of the East India Company and, while stationed in India, acquired a thorough knowledge of the Persian, Afghan, Hindustani, and Arabic languages. In 1853, in various Moslem disguises, he made a famous journey to Mecca and Medina, about which he wrote the vivid *Personal Narrative of a Pilgrimage to El-Medinah and Meccah* (3 vols., 1855–56). With John Speke he took a party to Somaliland; he alone, disguised as an Arab merchant, made the journey to Harar, Ethiopia, where he talked with the local ruler. He went with Speke to uncharted E central Africa to discover the source of the Nile; he found Lake Tanganyika (1858) but abandoned the attempt to reach Lake Nyasa. After a visit to America, Burton published an account of the Mormon settlement at Utah in his *City of the Saints* (1861). While consul (1861–65) at Fernando Po, off W Africa, he explored the Bight of Biafra and conducted a mission to Dahomey, Benin, and the Gold Coast. He explored Santos, in Brazil, while consul (1865) there, and after crossing

Location map of Burundi

Tribal festivities near
Ursumbura, Burundi.

the continent wrote *Explorations of the Highlands of the Brazil* (1869). After a short period (1869–71) as consul at Damascus he was consul (1872–90) at Trieste, where he died. His last years were devoted chiefly to literature. He published remarkable literal translations of Camões and of the *Arabian Nights* (16 vols., 1885–88). See biographies by Lady Burton (1893), G. M. Stisted (1896), Seton Dearden (1937), and Alfred Bercovici (1962).

Burton, Robert, 1577–1640, English clergyman and scholar, b. Leicestershire, educated at Oxford. His famous work, *The Anatomy of Melancholy,* appeared in 1621 under the pen name Democritus Junior. Enlarged and revised several times before his death, this treatise originally set out to explore the causes and effects of melancholy, but it eventually covered a wide range of topics, including science, history, and political and social reform. See studies by W. R. Mueller (1952) and Lawrence Babb (1959).

Burton. 1 Uninc. town (pop. 4,635), central Calif., SE of Tulare. **2** Village (pop. 1,085), NE Ohio, E of Cleveland, in a farm area; inc. 1908.

Burton-on-Trent, county borough (pop. 50,766), Staffordshire, W central England. It is known for its breweries. There are remains of a Benedictine abbey founded in 1002.

Buru or **Boeroe** (both: boō′roō), island (c.3,668 sq. mi.; pop. c.21,000), E Indonesia, in the Moluccas, W of Ceram. Namlea is the chief town and port. The terrain is wooded and mountainous, rising to c.7,874 ft. in the northwest. Cajuput oil, resin, copra, and sago are exported. The Cutch occupied Buru in 1658; it became part of East Indonesia in 1946 and of the republic of Indonesia in 1949.

Burujird or **Burujerd** (both: boōroōjĕrd′), city (pop. c.47,000), W Iran, in Luristan. It is a textile and commercial center in a fertile plain at the edge of the Zagros mts. The Trans-Iranian RR passes through nearby Dorood.

Burundi (bŭrŭn′dē), kingdom (10,747 sq. mi.; pop. c.2,213,000), E central Africa. The capital is Usumbura. Formerly part of the Belgian colony of RUANDA-URUNDI, Burundi (the native name for Urundi) is bordered by Rwanda on the north, by Tanganyika on the east and south, and by the Republic of the Congo on the west. The country is a high plateau region, dissected by deep valleys. Coffee, the principal crop, and cotton are grown, and some minerals are mined. Burundi achieved independence in July, 1962, after a UN–supervised election. Although the country is mainly inhabited by Bahutu people, the Watutsi king, Mwami Mwambutsa IV, was chosen as monarch of Burundi. His son, Louis Rwangasore, became premier but was assassinated soon after he took office; the assassination caused much friction with Belgium. Burundi became a member of the UN in Sept., 1962.

Burwell, city (pop. 1,425), co. seat of Garfield co., central Nebr., NNW of Grand Island, in grazing country; platted 1883.

Bury, John Bagnell (băg′nŭl byōo′rē), 1861–1927, Irish historian, an authority on the East Roman Empire. He was professor at the Univ. of Dublin from 1893 to 1902 and at Cambridge from 1902. Bury considered history a science—"not less, and not more." He stressed historical continuity, and he thought that accident was a frequent determinant in the history of premodern societies. His breadth of viewpoint is reflected in his attention to administration, institutions, topography, and the arts, which contributed to his unrivaled knowledge of late Roman and Byzantine times. *History of the Eastern Empire from the Fall of Irene to the Accession of Basil I, A.D. 802–867* (1912) is but one of his many outstanding studies. Bury also wrote authoritatively on ancient Greece, and his works include as well *History of Freedom of Thought* (1913), *The Idea of Progress* (1920), and a scholarly *Life of St. Patrick* (1905). His edition (7 vols., 1896–1900) of Gibbon's *Decline and Fall* was masterful. Bury edited Pindar's Nemean and Isthmian odes and was an editor of and contributor to *The Cambridge Ancient History.*

Bury, Richard de: see RICHARD DE BURY.

Bury (bĕ′rē), county borough (pop. 59,984), Lancashire, N England, on the Irwell and connected by canal with Bolton and Manchester. A textile city since the time of Edward III, when wool weaving was introduced by the Flemings, it now has factories for the spinning, weaving, and bleaching of cotton. Hats, paper, machines, and boilers are among its other manufactures. Sir Robert Peel and the inventor John Kay were born here.

Buryat Autonomous Soviet Socialist Republic (booryät'), autonomous republic (c.135,560 sq. mi.; pop. c.671,000), SE Asiatic RSFSR. It is a mountainous and heavily forested area, N of Mongolia, extending between Lake Baikal and the Yablonovy range. Ulan-Ude, the capital, and Kyakhta are the major cities. The Trans-Siberian RR crosses the republic, and there is a branch from Ulan-Ude to Mongolia. The mountains have rich deposits of coal, iron ore, tungsten, molybdenum, and gold. Towns, industries, and cultivated farms are largely concentrated in the valley of the Selenga river. The large nomadic population raises cattle and sheep. The republic's industries produce locomotives, lumber, and textiles, and there are fisheries and canning plants at Lake Baikal. Over half the population are Buryats; the rest are Russians, Evenki, and Tuvinians. Known since 1207, the Buryats are descended from Huns, Mongols, Evenki, and Turks. After the treaties of 1689 and 1727, Russia annexed the area and began intensive colonization. The Buryat-Mongol ASSR was formed in 1923, and was so named until 1958. In 1937 two small districts, now constituted as the Aga Buryat National Okrug (in Chita oblast) and the Ust-Orda Buryat National Okrug (in Irkutsk oblast), were detached from the republic. The Buryats speak a Mongolian language. Most of them are today Russian Orthodox, though there are some shamanists. Their folk culture features the recitation of tales and epic poems. Buryat craft excels in carving, engraving, and embroidery. The name is sometimes spelled Buriat.

Bury Saint Edmunds, municipal borough (pop. 21,144), administrative center of Suffolk West, E England. It is the market and processing center for the surrounding rich farm region. There is also some light industry. In 903 the remains of King Edmund were interred here in a monastery, founded c.630, which later became a famous shrine and Benedictine abbey. Among the buildings of historical interest are a Norman gate, ruins of St. James Cathedral, and a 15th-century church. Moyses Hall, a Norman construction, is now a museum.

bus [from *omnibus*, Latin,=for all), public conveyance. A horse-drawn urban omnibus was introduced in Paris in 1662 by Blaise Pascal and his associates, but it was operated for only a few years. The omnibus reappeared c.1812 in Bordeaux, France, and in Paris c.1827, London in 1829, and New York in 1830. It often carried passengers both inside and on the roof. Buses were motorized early in the 20th cent.; motorbus transportation increased rapidly and is now used in most countries. A number of railroad companies operate subsidiary lines. A network of bus lines links all parts of the United States. Buses with sleeping berths for intercity runs in the United States were used in the 1930s, then abandoned. Bus lines have grown at the expense of railroads in intercity travel and of street railways in local travel. Power plants are gasoline or diesel engines, or electric motors fed from overhead wires. Maximum capacity is about 55 passengers.

Busaco: see BUSSACO.

Busch, Adolf (ä'dôlf boosh'), 1891-1952, German-Swiss violinist, studied at the Cologne Conservatory. From 1919 to 1935 he headed outstanding chamber music groups, and, with his brother Hermann Busch (hĕr'män), cellist, and his son-in-law Rudolf Serkin, pianist, he played many trio recitals. In his early compositions he was influenced by his friend Max Reger. Another brother, **Fritz Busch,** 1890-1951, was musical director of the opera in Stuttgart (1919–22) and in Dresden (1922–33), afterward conducting in Europe and particularly at the Glyndebourne Festivals in England and later at the Metropolitan in New York (1945–50).

Busch, Wilhelm (vĭl'hĕlm boosh'), 1832–1908, German cartoonist, painter, and poet. After studying at the academies of Antwerp, Düsseldorf, and Munich, he joined the staff of the *Fliegende Blätter*, to which he contributed highly popular humorous drawings from 1859 to 1871. His humorous, illustrated poems for children, such as *Max and Moritz* (1865; Eng. tr. by Christopher Morley, 1932), are simply drawn, yet highly spirited. Busch's delightful series of wordless pictures were highly influential in the development of the comic strip.

Büsching, Anton Friedrich (än'tōn frē'drĭkh büsh'-ĭng), 1724–93, German geographer and educator. He was professor of philosophy in Göttingen, was a Protestant minister, and was director of a Gymnasium in Berlin. The most important of his many works is *Neue Erdbeschreibung* (10 vols., 1754–92; Vol. XI was written after his death), six volumes of which, describing the geography of Europe, were translated into English as *A New System of Geography* (1762).

Bush, Vannevar, 1890–, American electrical engineer and physicist, b. Everett, Mass., grad. Tufts College (B.S., 1913). He went to Massachusetts Institute of Technology in 1919; there he was professor (1923–32) and vice president and dean of engineering (1932–38). From 1939 until 1955 he was

Vannevar Bush

president of the Carnegie Institution. He also became director of the Office of Scientific Research and Development and was consequently a leading figure in the development of the atomic bomb. He designed calculating devices, including a differential analyzer, and conducted work in power transmission.

bushido (bōō'shĕdō, booshĕdō') [way of the warrior], the code of honor and conduct of the Japanese nobility. Of ancient origin, it grew out of the old feudal bond, which required unwavering loyalty on the part of the vassal. It borrowed heavily from Zen Buddhism and Confucianism, and in its fullest expression the code emphasized, besides loyalty to one's superior and personal honor, the virtues of austerity, self-sacrifice, and indifference to pain; for the warrior, commerce and the profit motive were to be scorned. The code was first formulated in the Kamakura period (1185–1333), put into writing in the 16th cent., and termed *bushido* in the 17th cent. It became the standard of conduct for the DAIMYO and SAMURAI under the Tokugawa shoguns and was taught in state schools as a prerequisite for government service. After the Meiji restoration (1868), it was the basis for emperor worship.

Bushire (booshēr'), city (pop. c.30,000), SW Iran. The chief port of Iran, it lies on an island in the Persian Gulf and is the terminus of a trade route from Shiraz, Isfahan, and Teheran. Opium, carpets, agricultural products, raw cotton, and wool are exported. Founded in 1736 by Nadir Shah, it became a major port in the 19th cent., replacing Rishire and Bander Abbas. The name formerly appeared as Abushehr.

bushmaster, largest venomous snake of the New World, member of the pit VIPER family, found in the tropics of Central and South America. Unlike the related rattlesnake, it lays eggs. It reaches a length of from 8 to 12 ft.

Bushmaster

Bushmen, a people of the southern part of Africa related to the Pygmies and speaking a tongue related to that of the Hottentots. Bushmen of pure blood are seldom over 5 ft. in height, are yellowish brown in color, and have broad noses, flat ears, bulging foreheads, prominent cheekbones, and small cranial capacity. They are nomadic hunters, their favorite weapon being the poisoned arrow. The social unit is the small hunting band; larger organizations are loose and temporary. Caves and rock shelters are used as dwellings. Though the Bushmen are in some ways among the most primitive of men, they have a rich folklore, are skilled in drawing, and have a remarkably complex language. See Isaac Schapera, *The Khoisan Peoples of South Africa* (1951); E. M. Thomas, *The Harmless People* (1959).

Bushnell, Horace (boosh'nul), 1802–76, American Congregational minister, b. Bantam, Conn., grad. Yale, 1827. He became (1833) pastor of the North Church, Hartford, Conn. He wrote *Christian Nurture* (1847) and *God in Christ* (1849). Because of certain views of the Trinity allegedly expressed in the latter, unsuccessful attempts were made to bring him to trial for heresy. Bushnell's dignified reply was made in *Christ in Theology* (1851). His repudiation of the austerity of Calvinism and his stress on the presence of the divine in humanity and nature had profound influence in shaping liberal Protestant thought. Ill health obliged him to retire from the active ministry in 1859, but he continued to write. His works include *The Vicarious Sacrifice* (1866), in which he developed the well-known "moral influence theory" of the atonement; *Sermons on Living Subjects* (1872); and *Forgiveness and Law* (1874). See the *Life and Letters* (ed. by his daughter, Mrs. M. B. Cheney, 1880, 1903); biography by T. T. Munger (1899); studies by A. J. W. Myers (1937) and B. M. Cross (1958).

Bushnell, city (pop. 3,710), W Ill., WSW of Peoria; inc. 1865. It is a rail center in a farm and livestock region.

bushrangers, men following lawful or unlawful pursuits in the wild lands of Australia, but more particularly bandits who terrorized rural areas in the 19th cent. The first bushrangers (c.1806–44) were mainly escaped convicts who fled to the bush and soon organized gangs. Their crimes were checked effectively by various Bushranging Acts passed after 1830. With the discovery of gold, however, bushrangers of a new type appeared and flourished from 1850 to 1870, largely brigand-adventurers who attacked gold convoys. The last of the bushrangers were the men of the Kelly gang. This band of desperados was exterminated in 1880 when three members were trapped and killed at a hotel in Glenrowan, Victoria, and Edward (Ned) Kelly was hanged at Melbourne.

business cycle: see DEPRESSION.

Buskerud (boos'kurood), province (5,728 sq. mi.; pop. 167,796), SE Norway. Drammen is its capital. Extending from the Oslo Fjord in the southeast to the Hardanger plateau in the northwest, it includes the Hallingdal and Numedal valleys.

Busoni, Ferruccio Benvenuto (fär-root'chō bänvä-noo'tō boozō'nē), 1866–1924, Italian pianist and composer. At the age of eight he gave a concert in Trieste, which was followed by many appearances as a child prodigy. His style of piano playing was similar to that of Liszt, whom he greatly admired. He taught at the conservatories in Helsinki and Moscow and from 1891 to 1894 at the New England Conservatory of Music. He transcribed for piano many of the organ works of J. S. Bach and edited his *Well-tempered Clavier*. His own compositions include piano pieces, a piano concerto, a violin concerto, and operas. A writer on musical and aesthetic subjects, his *Sketch of a New Esthetic* (Eng. tr., 1911) contains many provocative ideas. See his letters to his wife (Eng. tr., 1938); biography by E. J. Dent (1933).

Busra: see BASRA.

Bussaco or **Busaco,** Port. *Buçaco* (all: bōōsä′kō), locality, W central Portugal, near Coimbra and around Mt. Bussaco. Now a summer resort, it was formerly a place of seclusion and penitence for monks. Here, in 1810, British and Portuguese troops under Wellington decisively defeated the French in the Peninsular War.

Bussora: see BASRA.

Bustamante, Anastasio (änästä′syō bōōstämän′tä), 1780–1853, Mexican general and president (1830–32, 1837–41). He served in the royalist army against Hidalgo y Costilla and Morelos y Pavón, but his adherence to the Plan of Iguala in support of Agustín de Iturbide was a decisive factor in the latter's success. Vice president under Guerrero, he engineered a successful revolution (1829–30) with the aid of SANTA ANNA. At Bustamante's injunction Guerrero was captured and shot, but he fell from power when Santa Anna seized the government (1832). When Santa Anna's failure to crush the Texas Revolution temporarily weakened his political hold, Bustamante returned from exile in France and was again president. His regime was reactionary, plagued by revolution, by trouble with the French, by the blockade of Veracruz (1838) and especially by Santa Anna, who had recovered popularity. Seizing control, he forced Bustamante again into exile. He returned to serve in the Mexican War.

Bustamante, Antonio Sánchez de (äntō′nyō sän′-chäs dä bōōstämän′tä), 1865–1951, Cuban authority on international law, author of the Bustamante Code. A delegate to the Paris Peace Conference (1919), he was later justice of the Hague Tribunal (Permanent Court of Arbitration). He was also president of the .Pan American Congress (1928) which ratified his monumental code of private international law, coordinating legislation applying to the international security of person and property.

Bustanai ben Chaninai: see BOSTANAI BEN CHANINAI.

Busto Arsizio (bōō′stō ärsĕ′tsyō), city (estimated pop. 57,962), in Lombardy, N Italy. It is an important center of the Italian cotton industry. The church of Santa Maria di Piazza was designed by Bramante.

Busuanga (bōōswäng′ä), island (344 sq. mi.; pop. 14,269), largest of the Calamian Islands, the Philippines, between Mindoro and Palawan islands. Coron is its chief town. A fertile island, Busuanga produces coconuts and rice. Manganese is mined, and fishing is important.

Butades of Sicyon (bū′tŭdēz, sĭ′shĕŏn),c. 600 B.C., semi-legendary Greek sculptor, supposed to have been the first to model in clay.

butane, gaseous chemical compound, a hydrocarbon obtained by "cracking" petroleum. It is used mainly as a heating fuel. Its molecule, which has four carbon and ten hydrogen atoms, exists in two structural forms or isomers. In normal or n-butane, the carbon atoms are arranged in a continuous chain. In isobutane, three carbons are attached to a single carbon atom.

Butaritari: see MAKIN.

Butcher, Samuel Henry, 1850–1910, English classical scholar, b. Dublin, grad. Cambridge, 1873. He taught at Oxford and for 21 years at the Univ. of Edinburgh. Among his standard works on Greek civilization are *Some Aspects of Greek Genius* (1891) and translations of the *Odyssey* (with Andrew Lang, 1879) and *Aristotle's Theory of Poetry and Fine Art* (with a critical analysis, 1895).

butcher bird: see SHRIKE.

Bute, John Stuart, 3d earl of (būt), 1713–92, English statesman. He was prominent at court as early as 1747 and became the tutor and close friend of the impressionable prince of Wales. On the accession of the prince in 1760 as George III, Bute was appointed a privy councilor and first gentleman of the bedchamber. George III's policies of destroying the Whig monopoly of political power, of making the monarch supreme over Parliament, and of ending the war with France were pursued largely under Bute's influence. Bute obtained control of an electoral bloc in Parliament which helped to force William Pitt, 1st earl of Chatham, from office, and Bute was made principal minister. Though he achieved a good settlement for England in the Treaty of Paris (1763), parliamentary opposition to his other policies mounted. After Bute resigned in the face of attack, George III rapidly outgrew his youthful dependence on his friend. See biography by J. A. Lovat Fraser (1912); Romney Sedgewick, ed., *Letters from George III to Lord Bute, 1756–1766* (1936).

Bute, island and county: see BUTESHIRE.

Adolf Butenandt

Butenandt, Adolf (ä′dôlf bōō′tŭnänt), 1903-, German biochemist. He determined the chemical structure of the female sex hormone progestin and later, in 1931, isolated and named the male sex hormone androsterone. Because of a Nazi decree he declined the 1939 Nobel Prize in Chemistry awarded to him jointly with Leopold Ruzicka.

Buteshire (būt′shĭr) or **Bute** (būt), county (pop. 15,129), 218 sq. mi., W Scotland, in the Firth of Clyde. The county consists primarily of the islands of ARRAN, Bute, and the CUMBRAES. Bute, though smaller than Arran, is the most important island and has the county town, ROTHESAY. Agriculture (potatoes, oats, and barley), the main occupation of the county, is chiefly concentrated in the less hilly southern and central portions of Bute. Cattle and sheep are raised, and fishing (herring and whitefish) is of some importance. The islands are popular with tourists for their scenery and for the bracing climate.

Butler, Alban, 1710–73, English Roman Catholic priest, educated at Douai. He was president of the English seminary at Saint-Omer. His monumental work, *The Lives of the Fathers, Martyrs, and Principal Saints* (4 vols. in 7, 1756–59), was the basis for the enlarged edition, *The Lives of the Saints* (12 vols., 1926–38), and for the completely revised work, *Butler's Lives of the Saints* (ed. by Herbert Thurston, S.J., and Donald Attwater, 4 vols., 1956), which is a good, popular reference book.

Butler, Benjamin Franklin, 1795–1858, American political leader and cabinet officer, b. Columbia co., N.Y. Butler like his former law partner, Martin Van Buren, was a member of the ALBANY REGENCY, and he devoted himself and his considerable power to reform politics. He was Attorney General (1833–37) and also Secretary of War (1836–37) under Andrew Jackson and Attorney General (1837–38) under Van Buren but refused later cabinet appointments. He helped to revise (1825) the New York state statutes and organized what is to-day the law school of New York Univ.

Butler, Benjamin Franklin, 1818–93, American politician and Union general in the Civil War, b. Deerfield, N.H., grad. Waterville (now Colby) College, 1838. He moved to Lowell, Mass., when a youth and later practiced law there and in Boston. He was elected to the state legislature in 1852 and 1858 and ran unsuccessfully for governor in 1859 and 1860. Butler was a Democrat but a strong Unionist. At the beginning of the Civil War his contingent of Massachusetts militia was one of the first to reach Washington. He restored order (May,

Benjamin Franklin Butler

1861) in secessionist Baltimore and was given command at Fort Monroe. He commanded the troops that accompanied Admiral Farragut in taking New Orleans and was made military governor of the city. There his highhanded rule (May–Dec., 1862) infuriated the people of New Orleans and the South and earned him the name "Beast." The government, severely criticized both at home and abroad for his actions, finally removed him. In May, 1864, as commander of the Army of the James, Butler was defeated by Beauregard at DREWRYS BLUFF,

and was bottled up at Bermuda Hundred until Grant crossed the James in June. After he failed to take FORT FISHER in Dec., 1864, he was relieved of further active command. From 1867 to 1875 Butler, now a rabid radical Republican, was in Congress. He was one of the House managers who conducted the impeachment proceedings against President Johnson, and he ardently advocated the party's Reconstruction policy. He was said to have great influence with Grant. Butler was (1877–79) an independent Greenbacker in Congress. After several unsuccessful attempts to secure the governorship of Massachusetts, he was elected by the Greenbackers and Democrats in 1882. In 1884 he received the nominations of the Antimonopoly and Greenback parties for President. Regarded by many as an unprincipled demagogue of great ability, Butler aroused intense antagonisms and was nearly always in controversy. See his autobiography (1892); biographies by R. S. Holzman (1954) and H. L. Trefousse (1957).

Butler, James: see ORMONDE, JAMES BUTLER, 12TH EARL AND 1ST DUKE OF.

Butler, John, 1728–96, Loyalist commander in the American Revolution, b. New London, Conn. He served in the French and Indian War and distinguished himself especially by leading the Indians in the successful British attack (1759) under Sir William Johnson against Niagara. Electing the British side after the Revolution broke out, he became a deputy to Guy Johnson at Niagara and worked to keep the Indians friendly to the British. In the Saratoga campaign (1777) he and Indian troops accompanied Gen. Barry St. Leger in the unsuccessful expedition down the Mohawk valley. Later he organized a Loyalist troop called Butler's Rangers, and with them he and his son, Walter BUTLER, attacked the frontier settlements. John Butler in 1778 raided the Wyoming Valley, defeated Zebulon BUTLER, took Forty Fort, and then was unable to keep his Indian allies from perpetrating the Wyoming Valley massacre. Later that year Walter Butler and Joseph Brant led a similar raid on Cherry Valley, and this also ended in a massacre. The name of Butler was thereafter anathema to the patriots. John Butler was defeated (1779) by the expedition of Gen. John SULLIVAN at Newtown near the present Elmira, N.Y.; later in the war Butler joined with Sir John JOHNSON in frontier raids. See Howard Swiggett, *War Out of Niagara* (1933).

Butler, Joseph, 1692–1752, English bishop, theologian, and moralist. He was preacher (1718–26) at the Rolls Chapel, London; his tenure there produced the noted *Fifteen Sermons* (1726). While rector of Stanhope (1725–40), he was also prebendary of Salisbury and, later, of Rochester. In 1738 he was made bishop of Bristol and in 1740 became dean of St. Paul's. In 1750 he was translated to the see of Durham, one of the richest in England. He also served as clerk of the closet to Queen Caroline and later to King George II. It is as a writer that he is chiefly remembered. His great book, *The Analogy of Religion, Natural and Revealed, to the Constitution and Course of Nature* (1736) was aimed at combating the influence of deism in England by demonstrating the reasonableness of Christianity. *The Dissertation of the Nature of Virtue,* published as an appendix to the *Analogy*, is a major document in the development of English ethical theory. See biographies by E. C. Mossner (1936) and W. J. Norton (1940).

Butler, Nicholas Murray, 1862–1947, American educator, president of COLUMBIA UNIVERSITY. (1902–45), b. Elizabeth, N. J., grad. Columbia (B.A.,

Nicholas M. Butler

1882; Ph.D., 1884). Holding a Columbia fellowship, he studied at Paris and Berlin, specializing in philosophy. Beginning in 1885 he was made successively assistant, tutor, and adjunct professor of philosophy at Columbia. He became (1886) president of the Industrial Education Association, reshaped it into what is today Teachers College of Columbia Univ., and was (1889–91) the institution's first president. He was intimately associated with John W. BURGESS in the struggle to integrate a university organization and was largely responsible for the expansion of Columbia College into Columbia Univ. In 1890 he became professor of philosophy and education and dean of the Faculty of Philosophy and in 1901 acting president of Columbia. The next year he formally succeeded Seth Low as president. He instituted the Summer Session, University Extension (now the School of General Studies), the School of Journalism, the Medical Center, and other units which have contributed to the magnitude of present-day Columbia. An advocate of peace through education, he helped to establish the Carnegie Endowment for International Peace, of which he was a trustee and later president (1925–45). His efforts in behalf of disarmament and international peace won him international prestige, and he shared with Jane Addams the 1931 Nobel Peace Prize. Prominent in national, state, and New York city politics, he remained a regular Republican party member despite differences with its platforms. Though a close friend of Theodore Roosevelt, he refused to join the Progressive movement of 1912 and that year received the Republican electoral votes for Vice President after the death of Vice President James S. Sherman, the regularly nominated candidate. He later was the leading Republican advocate of the repeal of the Eighteenth Amendment, urged economy in government, and supported local reform movements. He was (1928–41) president of the American Academy of Arts and Letters. His books include *Education in the United States* (1910), *The International Mind* (1913), *The Meaning of Education* (rev. ed., 1915), *Scholarship and Service* (1921), *The Faith of a Liberal* (1924), *The Path to Peace* (1930), *Looking Forward* (1932), *Between Two Worlds* (1934), and *The World Today* (1946). See his autobiography, *Across the Busy Years* (2 vols., 1939–40); see also *Bibliography of Nicholas Murray Butler, 1872–1932* (1934).

Butler, Pierce, 1866–1939, Associate Justice of the U.S. Supreme Court (1923–39), b. Dakota co., Minn., grad. Carleton College, 1887. Admitted (1888) to the bar, he practiced in St. Paul, specialized in railroad law, and became an expert in railroad-valuation cases, serving (1913–22) both the U.S. and Canadian governments. In the Supreme Court he generally opposed the New Deal.

Butler, Richard Austen, b. 1902–, British statesman, b. India; educated at Cambridge. He entered Parliament in 1929 as a Conservative. In 1944, as minister of education, he piloted through Parliament the Education Act, which provided free primary and secondary education for all. Thus he established his reputation as a leading Tory advocate of social reform. From 1945 to 1951, with his party in opposition, he devoted himself to revising its policies. As chancellor of the exchequer from 1951 to 1955, he led the country out of wartime austerity but opposed major reduction in social services. In 1955 he became leader of the House of Commons and lord privy seal. In 1959 he was made chairman of the Conservative party.

Butler, Samuel, 1612–80, English poet and satirist. During the Puritan Revolution he served Sir Samuel Luke, a noted Puritan and officer of Cromwell. After the restoration of Charles II, he wrote his famous mock-heroic poem *Hudibras* (pub. in 3 parts, 1663, 1664, 1678), an envenomed satire against the Puritans in which Luke was the model for the butt Sir Hudibras. He was also the author of several other verse satires, some of them not published until the 20th cent. See editions of his works by A. R. Waller (1905, 1908) and René Lamar (1928).

Butler, Samuel, 1835–1902, English author, grad. Cambridge, 1858. He was the son and grandson of

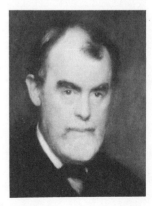

Samuel Butler

eminent clergymen. In 1859, refusing to be ordained, he went to New Zealand, where he established a sheep farm and in a few years made a modest fortune. He returned to England in 1864 and devoted himself to a variety of interests, including art, music, biology, and literature. Besides exhibiting (1868–76) at the Royal Academy, he composed several works in collaboration with Henry Festings Jones, among them the Handelian *Narcissus: a Dramatic Cantata* (1888). His version of Utopia, *Erewhon*, a satire on social and economic injustices, appeared in 1872. *Erewhon Revisited* was published in 1901. He opposed Darwin's explanation of evolution finding it too mechanistic, and he expounded his own theories in *Evolution Old and New* (1879), *Unconscious Memory* (1880), and *Luck or Cunning as the Main Means of Organic Modification?* (1887). In his single novel, the autobiographical *The Way of All Flesh* (1903), he attacked the Victorian pattern of life, in particular the ecclesiastical environment in which he was reared. His notebooks were published in 1912. See biography by J. F. Harris (1916); studies by C. E. M. Joad (1924), Philip Henderson (1953) and Basil Willey (1960); bibliography by S. B. Harkness (1956); Arnold Silver, ed., *The Family Letters of Samuel Butler, 1841–1886* (1962).

Butler, Smedley Darlington, 1881–1940, U.S. Marine Corps general, b. West Chester, Pa. He entered the Marine Corps in 1899 and served in the U.S. occupation of Veracruz, Mexico, in 1914 and with the marines in Haiti and in most other marine campaigns. He was a commander in France in the First World War and retired in 1931 as a major general. He was out of the service nearly a year to direct the cleanup of vice in Philadelphia (1924). General Butler was notable for his violent opinions and flamboyant quarrels and, after his retirement, for his campaign against war and for isolationism. His autobiography, *Old Gimlet Eye*, as told to Lowell Thomas, appeared in 1933.

Butler, Thomas: see OSSORY, THOMAS BUTLER, EARL OF.

Butler, Walter, 1752?–1781, Loyalist officer in the American Revolution, b. New York state; son of John BUTLER. He was an officer in his father's Loyalist troops, Butler's Rangers. He was captured (1777) by the patriots and sentenced to death, but the sentence was commuted. He escaped and in 1778 led the Rangers in a raid. This ended with the CHERRY VALLEY massacre, for which his Indian commander, Joseph BRANT, blamed Butler. Walter Butler was killed in a skirmish with patriot troops under Marinus WILLETT in the Mohawk valley. See Howard Swiggett, *War out of Niagara* (1933).

Butler, William Orlando, 1791–1880, American general and political leader, b. Carrollton, Ky., grad. Transylvania Univ., 1812. He served in the War of 1812 and distinguished himself in the battle of New Orleans. He was a Congressman from 1839 to 1843. In the Mexican War he was a major general of volunteers and was second in command to Zachary Taylor at Monterrey, where he was wounded. After the fighting was over he succeeded Winfield Scott as commander in chief and superintended the evacuation of the U.S. soldiers from Mexico. In 1848 he was vice presidential candidate on the unsuccessful Democratic ticket. Though a slaveholder, he opposed secession and supported the Union cause in the Civil War.

Butler, Zebulon, 1731–95, American colonial leader, b. Ipswich, Mass. After serving in the French and Indian Wars, Butler led a group of Connecticut settlers to the WYOMING VALLEY in N Pennsylvania. He was military leader of the Connecticut settlers in the Pennamite Wars and served as director of the SUSQUEHANNA COMPANY. Butler represented (1774–76) the Wyoming Valley in the Connecticut assembly. A colonel in the Revolution, he was defeated (1778) by Loyalists under John BUTLER and fled to Forty Fort; the Wyoming Valley massacre followed. Butler escaped and later was military commandant of the region.

Butler. 1 Town (pop. 1,765), co. seat of Choctaw co., W Ala., WSW of Selma and near the Miss. line; formed 1819, inc. 1848. Lumber, peanut, and textile products are made here; oil and minerals are in the vicinity. **2** Town (pop. 1,346), co. seat of Taylor co., W central Ga., SW of Macon, in a farm area; inc. 1854. **3** City (pop. 2,176), NE Ind., NE of Fort Wayne, in an agricultural area; settled 1841, inc. 1866. Automotive equipment is manufactured. **4** City (pop. 3,791), co. seat of Bates co., W Mo., NE of Fort Scott, Kansas; laid out 1854. It is known for its livestock auctions and annual horse show. Optical lenses are made. **5** Borough (pop. 5,414), N N.J., NW of Paterson; settled 1695, inc. 1901. Rubber goods are produced. St. Anthony's Monastery (Franciscan) is here. **6** City (pop. 20,975), co. seat of Butler co., W Pa., N of Pittsburgh; settled c.1800, inc. as a borough 1803, as a city 1917. Rich in coal, natural gas, oil, and limestone, it has manufactures of steel, glass, machinery, and railroad cars. **7** Village (pop. 2,274), SE Wis., W of Milwaukee; inc. 1913. Metal products are made.

Butler University: see INDIANAPOLIS.

Buto (bū′tō), ancient city, N Egypt, in the Nile delta. The precise location is uncertain. Capital of Lower Egypt in prehistoric times (before 3100 B.C.), it had a temple dedicated to the serpent-goddess Buto. During the Saïte period (663–525 B.C.) it was revived as an important religious center.

Bütschli, Otto (ô′tō büch′lē), 1848–1920, German zoologist. He was professor of zoology at the Univ. of Heidelberg. His researches on invertebrate animals advanced knowledge of the development of gastropods, insects, and other forms; the structure of nematode worms; and processes of division of the nucleus and cell. A significant contribution was his theory (1878) of the structure of protoplasm, which suggested that it is alveolar or foamlike; he helped to establish that it is fluid in nature.

Butt, Dame Clara, 1873–1936, English contralto, of rich and powerful voice. She made her debut in 1892 and was Orpheus in the opera by Gluck, but was principally heard in concerts and oratorios. She was made Dame of the Empire in 1920. See biography by Winifred Ponder (1928).

Butte (būt), city (pop. 27,877; alt. 5,775 ft.), co. seat of Silver Bow co., SW Mont., SSW of Helena; founded 1862 as a mining camp, inc. 1879. First a gold-mining town, then a silver-boom center, Butte gained its real importance when copper was discovered (c.1880) and Marcus Daly with his Ana-conda Copper Mining Company began to exploit what was boastfully called the "richest hill on earth." Butte, which acquired a reputation as a wide-open town, has ever since been dominated by the mining industry (zinc, silver, manganese, gold, lead, and arsenic, as well as copper) with consequent periods of prosperity and depression and labor troubles. It is also the commercial center for a farm and livestock area. Columbia Gardens recreational area was given to the city by William A. Clark. The Montana School of Mines is here. Butte is headquarters for Deerlodge National Forest.

butte, an isolated hill with steep sides and a flat top, left by the more rapid erosion of the surrounding areas. Buttes are characteristic of the plains of the W United States. See also MESA.

butter, dairy product obtained by agitating cream or milk to unite the fat globules. In America and England the milk of cows is generally the basis, but elsewhere that of goats, sheep, and mares has been used. Butter was known by 2000 B.C., though it was anciently used less as a food than as an ointment for the bath, a medicine, or an illuminating oil. At first it was rudely churned from milk in skin pouches thrown back and forth or swung over the backs of trotting horses. Later, as butter became a staple food, various sorts of hand churns were devised, including rotating, swinging, and rocking barrels or boxes and cylindrical vessels operated by dashers or plungers. Buttermaking requires immaculate cleanliness of all utensils and a cool temperature, often provided on the farm by a milk house with a spring or running water. Formerly the daily milk was set to cool in pans, and the cream, rising to the top because of the low specific gravity of the fat globules, was skimmed off, left to ripen by natural fermentation, and churned until small granules of butter appeared. The buttermilk was drained off and the butter washed, usually salted, and worked into a smooth mass with wooden paddles. Exclusively farm made until c.1850, butter has become increasingly a factory product. The centrifugal cream SEPARATOR, introduced into the United States c.1880, and a method, devised in 1890 by S. M. BABCOCK, to determine the butterfat content of milk and cream gave impetus to large-scale production. The application of principles of chemistry and bacteriology facilitates the making of butter of uniform quality. Most cream is inoculated with a starter culture of bacteria which convert lactose to lactic acid and of other organisms which attack citric acid to produce volatile oils and diacetyl for imparting desirable butter flavors. The percentage of fat extraction and the time required for churning depend on the composition of the butterfat (see FATS AND OILS); the temperature, acidity, richness, and viscosity of the cream; the speed and motion of the churn; and the size of the fat globules. Butter should contain at least 80 percent of fat and not more than 15 percent of water; the body should be close, firm, and waxy; the color uniform. Sweet-cream butter is made from cream to which no starter was added. Sweet, or unsalted, butter is favored in Europe, but other markets prefer at least 2 percent salt. Renovated or process butter is made

from rancid or inferior butter, melted and refined, then rechurned. Whey butter, made from cream separated from whey, is usually oily and of inferior quality. The natural color of butter, derived from the carotene of green plant fodder, ranges from pale yellow to deep gold. Artificial coloring, commonly the oil of the annatto seed, carotene extract, or harmless coal-tar derivatives, is used to keep the tint uniform throughout the year. Butter made from pasteurized cream may be stored for several months with little deterioration, thus augmenting the winter supply with butter made around the peak season (June in the Northern Hemisphere). The United States, Russia, Denmark, Australia, Canada, New Zealand, and Belgium are the leading producers; Denmark, New Zealand, and Australia, the chief exporters; and the United Kingdom, a heavy importer. Although butter is made in every state of the United States, production centers in the northern Middle West, especially Minnesota, Iowa, and Wisconsin. Clarified butter, butterfat separated by heat, is useful in cooking and has good keeping qualities. It is made in quantity in Egypt and in India, where it is known as GHEE. The high dietary value of butter is due to its large proportion of easily digested fat and to its vitamin A content.

butter-and-eggs, common name for a plant of the FIGWORT family and sometimes also for other yellow flowers.

buttercup or **crowfoot,** common name for the Ranunculaceae, a family of chiefly annual or perennial herbs of cool regions of the Northern Hemisphere. Thought to be one of the most primitive families of dicotyledenous plants (see PLANT), the Ranunculaceae typically have a simple flower structure in which each flower part is separate rather than fused into a single organ (see FLOWER). Some botanists believe that the preference of this family for swamps and wet places also indicates its evolutionary position. The family includes numerous familiar wild flowers and many cultivated ornamentals. Well-known representatives are the ACONITE, ANEMONE, BANEBERRY, BUGBANE, CLEMATIS (one of the few vine species), COLUMBINE, GLOBEFLOWER, HELLEBORE, HEPATICA, LARKSPUR, LOVE-IN-A-MIST, MARSH MARIGOLD (the American cowslip), MEADOW RUE, and PEONY. The largest genus, *Ranunculus*, is comprised of the buttercups and crowfoots, names often used interchangeably. Found throughout arctic, north temperate, and alpine regions, with species in the Andes and in subantarctic areas, this genus is characterized by glossy yellow flowers (hence the name buttercup) and deeply cut leaves (supposedly resembling crows' feet). Like some other members of the family, species of this genus contain an acrid juice that makes them unpalatable for livestock and in some cases poisonous. A dozen or more species are common in every part of the United States. Among those cultivated for garden and cut flowers are some double-blossomed Old World species, e.g., the turban or Persian buttercup (*R. asiaticus*), valued for the variety of its colors (all but blue), and the creeping buttercup (*R. repens*), native to both North America and Europe. *R. ficaria*, of Eurasia, is the lesser celandine—a name more commonly applied to some plants of the poppy family, which it

Pearly-eye
butterfly

White peacock
butterfly

Tortricid caterpillar

Thistle butterfly feeding

resembles. Many buttercups are aquatic plants, hence the Latin name for the genus Ranunculus [little frog].

Butterfield, Herbert, 1900–, English historian. He became professor at Cambridge in 1944. His works cover a variety of topics in modern European history; outstanding are his volumes on 18th-century English history and historiography and his *Origins of Modern Science* (1949). *The Whig Interpretation of History* (1931) showed that many accepted views of English history had grown from the bias of such Whig historians as T. B. Macaulay. In *George III, Lord North, and the People* (1948), Butterfield traced political reform ideas in England in the era of the American Revolution. A critic of the historical method of L. B. Namier, Butterfield emphasizes great ideas as being central to man's development.

Butterfield, John, 1801–69, American stagecoach proprietor and expressman, b. near Albany, N.Y. Beginning as a stage driver out of Albany, he rose to ownership of a large network of stage lines. He helped to merge his express company with others to form (1850) the American Express Company. In 1857, when Congress established the overland mail route to Los Angeles, Butterfield was given the mail contract. He organized the service on the 2,800-mile southern route efficiently and continued it until 1861, when the stages were moved to the central route. He also promoted the development of telegraph lines and railroads, and in 1865 he was elected mayor of Utica, N.Y.

Butterfield, William, 1814–1900, English Gothic-revival architect. Favored by the Ecclesiological Society for his Pugin-like correctness in recalling Gothic forms, Butterfield rose to prominence in the middle of the 19th cent. The brilliant polychromy which he created through his combinations of brick, stone, and tile (e.g., All Saints' Church, London; 1849–59) introduced the High Victorian Gothic manner. The softer hues of the interior and the variously textured stone of the church at Baldersby St. James near Beverley in Yorkshire (1856) mark what is perhaps Butterfield's finest church. General interest in polychromy soon waned, but Butterfield continued in this mode with Keble College, Oxford (1868–70), and several buildings at Rugby School (1868–72).

butterfish: see HARVEST FISH.

butterfly, any of a large group of insects found in all parts of the world which, with the MOTH group, comprises the order Lepidoptera. Members of this order have coiled, sucking mouth parts and broad, membranous wings covered with scales which come off as dust if the insect is handled. Red, yellow, black, and white pigments are found in the scales. Blues, greens, and the metallic, iridescent hues, found especially in the tropical species, are caused chiefly by refraction. Butterflies can be distinguished from moths in several ways: the antennae of the butterfly are enlarged at the tip, while those of the moth almost never have terminal knobs but are often threadlike or feathery; the butterfly is chiefly diurnal, the moth largely nocturnal; when at rest most butterflies hold the wings vertically, most moths hold them horizontally; the body of a butterfly is more slender and usually smoother than that of the moth. The life history is divided into four stages: egg, larva, pupa, and adult. The eggs, which hatch in from 2 to 30 days, are usually laid on a plant that the larva (caterpillar) uses for food. After the last of several molts the butterfly larva forms the pupa case, or chrysalis, inside which its body changes to the adult form. Except in those species which winter in the pupa stage, the adult usually emerges from the chrysalis in two or three weeks. Some winter in the egg stage, others as larvae or as adults. Those which migrate usually travel toward the equator in the fall and away from it in the spring. Examples of MIMICRY and of protective coloration are found among butterflies. Among the most beautiful are the swallowtails, which are found all over the world, the North American monarch, and the peacock and the tortoise-shell butterflies. See A. B. Klotts, *A Field Guide to the Butterflies* (1951).

butterfly fish, member of a family of reef-dwelling tropical fishes which also includes the angelfishes and is closely allied to the spadefishes and the tangs. All have compressed bodies and small mouths and teeth and are carnivorous, feeding on crabs, barnacles, and other invertebrates. The fast and aggressive common butterfly fish, 5 to 8 in. long, is marked by dark lines through the eyes and near the tail. The angelfishes have spines on the gill covers and long filaments on the dorsal fins. The queen angelfish, a good food fish that reaches 2 ft. in length, is colored in blues and yellows; the more numerous but smaller common angelfish is similar. The French angelfish is black with yellow

scale edgings; the black angelfish is solid black; and the bizarre rock beauty has a black body with yellow head, fins, and tail. The spadefishes are larger (up to 3 ft.) and faster than the angelfishes and are valued both as food and game fishes. They are barred in black and white. The tangs have variable coloration. They include the violet-brown doctorfish or surgeonfish, the 8-inch blue tang, and the larger and more abundant ocean tang of deep waters.

butterfly flower, fringeflower, or **poor-man's-orchid,** any of the showy plants of the genus *Schizanthus* of the NIGHTSHADE family, native to Chile but grown elsewhere as garden or greenhouse annuals. The flowers resemble butterflies and come in a variety of colors, usually mottled.

butterfly weed: see MILKWEED.

Butterick, Ebenezer, 1826–1903, American inventor of standardized paper patterns for dressmaking, b. Sterling, Mass. He was a tailor and shirtmaker, and c.1859 he or his wife conceived the idea of graded shirt patterns to simplify their work, making it possible to cut the garments on a large scale. In 1863 the first pattern, cut from stiff paper, was placed on the market. Patterns for children's clothes and later for women's followed. Beginning in 1864 these were made of tissue paper. In 1869 a factory was established in Brooklyn and a fashion magazine, later the *Delineator*, was started. Branches were established in London, Paris, Berlin, and Vienna.

butternut: see WALNUT.

buttons, knoblike appendages used on wearing apparel either for ornament or for fastening. Although buttons were sometimes used as fasteners

French decorative silk button, 18th century.

by Greeks and Romans, they were more often merely ornamental disks. They first became important when fitted garments came into use in the 13th cent., and their use has varied with the changes in fashion. In the 16th cent. they became magnificent and were classed among the vanities; of silver or gold and jeweled, they were often set in a long row touching one another. In the 17th cent. cloth covered buttons with embroidered decoration were popular; buttons appeared on everything, even handkerchiefs. The Puritans, considering buttons a vanity, used hooks and eyes. Early American settlers often used buttons in trading with the Indians. In c.1826 the manufacture of buttons began in the United States. Buttons, originally made of bronze or bone, have also been made of materials such as metal, porcelain, paste, wood, ivory, horn,

Butterfly fish

pearl, glass, and plastic. There are two main types, those made with holes and those with shanks. The latter have a loop of metal let in through a hole or soldered into place.

buttonwood: see PLANE TREE.

buttress, mass of masonry built against a wall to strengthen it. It is especially necessary when a vault or an arch places a heavy load or thrust on one part of a wall. In the case of a wall carrying the uniform load of a floor or roof, it is more economical to buttress it at certain intervals than to make the entire wall thicker. Even when a wall carries no load, it is usually buttressed rather than uniformly thickened. In the case of a load-bearing brick wall more than 8 ft. high a buttress is used every 20 ft. The decorative possibilities of the buttress were early discovered in the ancient temples at Abu Shahrein in Mesopotamia (3500–3000 B.C.), where they were used both as utilitarian and decorative forms. The Romans employed buttresses, which sometimes projected from the exteriors of the walls and were then left as mere piles of masonry, without architectural treatment. But in the large structures, such as basilicas and baths, the buttresses which received the thrusts from the main vaulting were confined to the interior of the building, where they served also as partition walls. The basilica of Constantine in Rome (A.D. 312) exemplifies this arrangement. In the medieval church, the groined vaults, concentrating their great lateral thrusts at points along the exterior walls, required

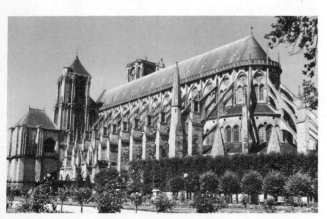

Flying buttresses on the cathedral at Bourges.

buttresses as an essential element to achieve stability. Beginning with Romanesque architecture about A.D. 1000, a steady evolution of buttresses can be traced, from the simple, slightly projecting piers of the 11th cent. to the bold and complex Gothic examples of the 13th, 14th, and 15th cent. Builders in England, Germany, and N France achieved striking architectural effects. They devised the flying buttress, an arch of masonry abutting against the wall of the nave; the thrust of the nave vault could thus be received and transferred to the vertical buttress built against the outside walls of the side aisles. These flying arches, at first

concealed beneath the roofs, began to be exposed outside the roofs in the mid-12th cent. Later they were enriched with gables, stone tracery, and sculpture and were topped with pinnacles to give them extra weight. They constitute, especially in such French cathedrals as Amiens, Beauvais, and Notre Dame de Paris, the true expression of the elasticity and equilibrium which were the basic principles of the Gothic structural system.

butyl rubber: see RUBBER, SYNTHETIC.

Butzer, Martin: see BUCER, MARTIN.

Buxar or **Baxar** (both: bŭksär′), village, West Bengal state, NE India. Here, in 1764, a British victory over the Nawab of Oudh assured British control of the Bengal area.

Buxtehude, Dietrich (dē′trĭkh bŏŏks″tŭhōō′dŭ), 1637–1707, Swedish composer and organist. From 1668 until his death he was organist at Lübeck, where he established a famous series of evening concerts which attracted musicians from all over northern Germany. J. S. Bach walked 50 miles to hear these concerts, and his own style was much influenced by Buxtehude's choral, orchestral, and organ music. His best-known works are freely developed organ fugues and concerted choral music.

Buxton, Sir Thomas Fowell, 1786–1845, English social reformer. As a member of Parliament (1818–37) he began his reform activities immediately with the publication of *An Inquiry Whether Crime and Misery Are Produced or Prevented by Our Present System of Prison Discipline;* this led to the establishing of the Society for the Reformation of Prison Discipline. An abolitionist, Buxton succeeded William Wilberforce as leader of the antislavery group. His efforts resulted in the passage of an act (1833) abolishing slavery in the British colonies. He wrote *The African Slave Trade* (1839) and *The Remedy* (1840). See his memoirs (ed. by his son Charles Buxton, 1872).

Buxton, municipal borough (pop. 19,236), Derbyshire, central England, on the Wye and in the Peak district. It is c.1,000 ft. high; the "old town" is on a hill above it. The center of a great lime industry, Buxton is primarily a year-round resort, with mineral springs and baths. It is the site of a hospital for rheumatic patients.

Buxton, town (pop. 2,339), SW Maine, near the Saco river and W of Portland; settled c.1748, inc. 1772. Shoeboard is made here.

Buxtorf, Johann (yō′hän bŏŏks′tôrf), the elder, 1564–1629, German Hebraist. He was first of a celebrated family of scholars who through four generations occupied the chair of Hebrew at the Univ. of Basel. He entered his professorship there in 1591 and was recognized as the foremost student of rabbinical literature among Protestants. He defended the original text of the Old Testament as the most reliable authority. Among his works was a great rabbinical Bible. Two others, left unfinished, were a concordance to the Hebrew Bible and a Chaldaic, Talmudic, and Rabbinic lexicon, both afterward completed and edited by his son, **Johann Buxtorf,** the younger, 1599–1664, Orientalist. He succeeded his father at Basel in 1630 and from 1654 held in addition the chair of Old Testament exegesis. Besides editing and publishing some of his father's writings, he produced several controversial treatises and other learned works.

The market of Bydgoszcz.

Buys Ballot, Christoph Heinrich Diedrich (krĭs'tôf hĭn'rĭkh dĕd'rĭkh bois'-bälō'), 1817–90, Dutch meteorologist. He was after 1854 director of the Dutch Royal Meteorological Institute. He strove to organize and standardize a system for representing meteorological findings and formulated Buys-Ballot's law: if one stands with his back to the wind, the area of low pressure is to his left. This is true in the Northern Hemisphere; the reverse is true in the Southern Hemisphere. The explanation lies in the deflection, caused by the earth's rotation, in the movement of air from areas of high to areas of lower pressure. Ferrel's law (see FERREL, WILLIAM) is related.

Buz (bŭz) [Heb.,=contempt]. **1** Son of Nahor and Milcah. Gen. 22.21. He was apparently eponym of an Arabian tribe. Jer. 25.23. The term Buzite is probably derived from his name. Job 32.2. **2** Gadite. 1 Chron. 5.14.

Buzau (boōzû'oō), city (estimated pop. 51,075), SE Rumania, in Walachia, on the Buzau river, a tributary of the Sereth. It is an industrial center with oil refineries, foundries, and manufactures of knitwear. It was first mentioned in 1431 and has long been the residence of an Orthodox bishop. The city has an episcopal palace and a 16th-century cathedral, restored in 1740.

Buzi (bū'zĭ), father of Ezekiel. Ezek. 1.3.

buzzard, name commonly applied to various hawks and New World vultures. Old World buzzards include hawks of the genus *Buteo* and the genus *Pernis*, or honey buzzard, which feeds on insects, wasp and bumblebee larvae, and small reptiles.

Buzzards Bay, inlet of the Atlantic Ocean, 30 mi. long and 5 to 10 mi. wide, SE Mass., connected with Cape Cod Bay by the Cape Cod Canal and bounded on the southeast by the Elizabeth Islands. Its shores are very irregular. New Bedford is near the head of one of the larger inlets. The village of **Buzzards Bay** (pop. 2,170), seat of Cape Cod Canal administration, is in the town of Bourne. The Massachusetts Maritime Academy is here.

Byblos (bĭb'lŭs), ancient city, Phoenicia, a port near modern Beirut, Lebanon. The principal city of Phoenicia during the 2d millennium B.C., it long retained importance as an active port under the Persians. Byblos was the chief center of the worship of Adonis. It also, because of its papyri, was the source of the Greek word for book and, hence, of the name of the Bible. Excavations of Byblos, especially since 1922, have shown that trade existed between Byblos and Egypt as early as c.2800 B.C. A syllabic script found recently at Byblos dates from the 18th to the 15th cent. B.C. The name of the modern town Jebail preserves the form Gebal, the name given the city in the Old Testament. Ezek. 27.9. The inhabitants are called Giblites. Joshua 13.5. The Gebal of Ps. 83.7 is almost certainly not the same city; it is otherwise unknown.

Bydgoszcz (bĭd'gôshch), Ger. *Bromberg* (brôm'bĕrk), city (pop. c.229,000), N central Poland, on the Brda river, a tributary of the Vistula. A river port and railway center, it has manufactures of electrical equipment, precision instruments, machine tools, and chemicals. The Bydgoszcz Canal (built 1773–74) links the Brda and the Notec rivers and is part of the Vistula-Oder waterway. Chartered in 1346, it suffered much damage in the Northern War. It passed to Prussia in 1772, but was restored to Poland in 1919. Its most notable building is a 15th-century Gothic church. The city is the capital of Bydgoszcz prov. (8,031 sq. mi., pop. c.1,704,000), formerly called Pomorze (until 1950), a low-lying region drained by the Vistula, Brda, and Notec rivers. Rye, potatoes, and oats are the principal crops. Chief industrial products include paper, rubber, chemicals, and machinery. Its main cities are Bydgoszcz, Torun, Inowroclaw, Grudziadz, Wloclawek, and Chelmno.

Byelo-. For some names beginning thus, see BELO-; e.g., for Byelorussia, see BELORUSSIA.

Byesville (bĭz'vĭl), village (pop. 2,447), E Ohio, S of Cambridge; inc. 1889. Agriculture and coal mining predominate in the area.

Byles, Mather, 1707–88, American clergyman and poet, b. Boston, grad. Harvard (B.A., 1725; M.A., 1728). Famous minister of the Hollis St. Congregational Church, Boston, from 1732, he was dismissed for his Tory sympathies after the British evacuation of Boston. From his uncle, Cotton Mather, he inherited a valuable library, to which he added his own unique collection. His poetry, imitative but witty, appeared in *Poems on Several Occasions* (1744) and other volumes; his prose includes sermons and *The Flourish of Annual Spring* (1741). See A. W. H. Eaton, *The Famous Mather Byles* (1914).

bylini (bĭlē′nē) [Rus.,=what has happened], Russian scholarly term first applied in the 1840s to the great body of narrative and heroic poems which are called by the folk *stariny* (stärē′nē) [Rus.,=what is old]. Most *bylini* are loosely connected with historical events dating from the 11th to the 16th cent. and have been handed down by word of mouth. The poems were first collected and studied in the 18th cent. The largest of the *bylini* cycles is that originating around Kiev and having for its hero Prince Vladimir, the Little Sun. Here the favorite character is the Old Cossack warrior Ilya of Murom. Of importance also is the Novgorod cycle, concerning the adventures of the merchant prince Sadko and Vasily Buslayevich. To a third cycle of Older Heroes belongs the strong plowman Mikula. The characters of the *bylini* all possess supernatural powers. Though modified by foreign borrowings—Scandinavian, Byzantine, Oriental—*bylini* are typically and strikingly Russian and have had an enriching influence on Russian literature, music, and art. See N. K. Chadwick, *Russian Heroic Poetry* (1932); Nikolai Gudzy, *History of Early Russian Literature* (1949).

Byng, George: see TORRINGTON, GEORGE BYNG, VISCOUNT.

Byng, John, 1704–57, British admiral; son of George Byng, Viscount Torrington. Ordered to relieve the French siege of Minorca (1756), his inaction and retreat resulted in a court-martial. His conviction and execution for neglect of duty brought charges that Byng's death was a cloak for ministerial failure and neglect. See study by D. B. E. Pope (1962).

Byng, Julian Hedworth George, 1st **Viscount Byng of Vimy,** 1862–1935, British general. He served in India and South Africa and had several commands in the First World War. The Canadians in April, 1917, took Vimy Ridge under his orders. For his distinguished services he was made a baron and, in 1926, a viscount. He was governor general of Canada from 1921 to 1926.

Bynkershoek, Cornelius van (kôrnā′lĭŭs vän bĭng′-kûrshōōk), 1673–1743, Dutch writer on international law. His *De dominio maris* (1702; Eng. tr., 1923) is a classic on maritime law, and he also wrote on diplomatic rights and, in *Quaestiones juris publici* (1737), on public law. It was Bynkershoek who first proposed the "three-mile limit" rule, which states that a nation may claim sovereignty over territorial waters to a distance of three miles from shore.

Bynner, Witter (bĭ′nùr), 1881–, American poet, b. Brooklyn, N.Y., grad. Harvard, 1902. His first significant book of verse was *Grenstone Poems* (1917), followed by the equally lyric *Canticle of Pan* (1920). Bynner had a remarkable facility in catching the cadences of other writers and cultures. Under the pseudonym Emanuel Morgan he collaborated with Arthur Davison Ficke in writing *Spectra* (1916), a satiric literary hoax (see SPECTRA HOAX). *The Jade Mountain* (1929) is a translation with Kiang Kang-hu of 300 Chinese poems. He produced the quality of Southwestern primitive life in *Indian Earth* (1929). Other works include several plays, essays, *Selected Poems* (ed. by Robert Hunt, 1943), later poems in *Take Away the Darkness* (1947), and *Journey with Genius* (1951), which recalled his association with D. H. Lawrence.

Byrd, Harry Flood (bûrd), 1887–, U.S. Senator from Virginia (1933–), b. Martinsburg, W.Va.; brother of Richard E. Byrd. Educated at Shenandoah Academy in Winchester, Va., he became publisher of the Winchester *Star* and was a figure in state politics. His administration as governor (1926–30) was marked by development of the state highway system. Appointed Senator in 1933, he has been continually reelected. Byrd has taken the lead among conservative Democrats, opposed the New Deal and the New Frontier, and has advocated government economy. For many years he was chairman of the Senate Finance Committee.

Byrd, Richard Evelyn, 1888–1957, American aviator and polar explorer, b. Winchester, Va., grad. Annapolis, 1912. He took up aviation in 1917, and after the First World War he gained great fame in the air: he commanded the naval air unit with the arctic expedition of D. B. MacMillan in 1925; he and Floyd Bennett flew from Spitsbergen to the North Pole and back in 1926 (the first men to fly over the pole); and in 1927 he and three companions made one of the spectacular flights across the Atlantic. His record of flight was presented in *Skyward* (1928). Two years later he led a well-equipped and efficiently organized expedition to Antarctica. Establishing a base at LITTLE AMERICA, he discovered the Rockefeller Range and Marie Byrd Land, and late in 1929 he and Bernt BALCHEN flew to the South Pole and back. The large party gathered much scientific information. In 1930 Byrd was promoted rear admiral, and his *Little America* was published. His second large expedition was organized in 1933, and headquarters were

Admiral Byrd

established once again at Little America. As winter approached, he set up an advance base 123 mi. closer to the South Pole and stayed there alone for several months making observations. *Discovery* (1935) and *Alone* (1938) were records of this fruitful expediton. In 1939–40 he was again in the antarctic commanding a government expedition, and in 1946–47 he headed the U.S. navy expedition, the largest yet sent to the region (see ANTARCTICA). In 1955 Byrd was placed in command of all U.S. antarctic activities, and in 1955–56 he led his fifth expedition to the region. Due mainly to his efforts, the U.S. navy organized (1955–59) Operation Deep Freeze. Byrd's explorations form much of the basis for U.S. claims in Antarctica. See Martin Gladych, *Admiral Byrd of Antarctica* (1960).

Byrd, Byrde, or **Bird, William** (all: bûrd'), 1543–1623, English composer, organist at Lincoln Cathedral and, jointly with Tallis, at the Chapel Royal. Although Roman Catholic, he composed English anthems and services in addition to his great Roman Masses and Latin motets. He was highly esteemed by his contemporaries and was favored by Queen Elizabeth I, who, in 1575, granted to Byrd and Tallis a patent for the exclusive printing and selling of music. Byrd also composed music for the virginal and other instruments. See E. H. Fellowes, *William Byrd* (2d ed., 1948).

Byrd, William, 1652–1704, English planter in early Virginia. He came to America as a youth and took up lands he had inherited on both sides of the James, including the site of later Richmond. In 1691 he moved to "Westover," long famous as the Byrd family home. His landed fortune was increased by his interest in trade, and he served (1703) as president of the Virginia council. Byrd's wealth, culture, and character made him the ideal tidewater aristocrat. He was the father of William Byrd (1674–1744).

Byrd, William, 1674–1744, American colonial writer, planter, and government official; son of William Byrd (1652–1704). After being educated in England, he became active in the politics of colonial America. He served as member of the house of burgesses, as receiver-general of Virginia, as Virginia council member, and as colonial agent in England. Byrd inherited a great estate from his father and ultimately owned over 179,000 acres. In 1737 he had the city which was to be Richmond laid out on one of his estates. His service in 1728 as one of the commissioners to survey the North Carolina-Virginia boundary and his many trips into the backwoods provided the material for much of his writings; *A History of the Dividing Line, A Journey to the Land of Eden,* and *A Progress to the Mines,* were all based on his diaries. Byrd's polished style and crisp wit, in addition to his valuable record of Southern life, have won him a reputation as one of the foremost colonial authors. At his death he left a library of some 4,000 volumes at his Westover estate. See his diaries and other writings (1941, 1942, 1958).

Byrde, William: see BYRD, WILLIAM (1543–1623).

Byrhtnoth (bĭrkht'nŏth) or **Bryhtnoth** (brĭkht'nŏth), d. 991, alderman of the East Saxons. Leader of the English forces in the battle of MALDON, he was killed in the battle and was buried at Ely.

Byrnes, James Francis, 1879–, U.S. Secretary of State (1945–47); governor of South Carolina (1951–55), b. Charleston, S.C. He studied law while working (1900–1908) as a court reporter, owned and edited a newspaper in Aiken, S.C., and represented (1911–25) South Carolina in the House. As Senator (1931–41), Byrnes, a Southern Democrat, became budgetary expert for the New Deal. He served as an Associate Justice of the Supreme Court (1941–42) but resigned and became director of economic stabilization (1942) and later (1943) director of war mobilization. As Secretary of State he tried to mend post-war differences with the USSR. Elected governor of South Carolina, he opposed further Federal centralization and what he called "statism." See his *Speaking Frankly* (1947) and *All in One Lifetime* (1958).

Byrom, John, 1692–1763, English shorthand expert and poet, educated at Trinity College, Cambridge. He devised an early shorthand system and taught it in Manchester. *The Universal English Shorthand* was posthumously published. He was a great admirer of William Law, and much information about Law is found in Byrom's *Private Journal and Literary Remains* (1854–57). He wrote *Seasonably Alarming and Humiliating Truths in a Metrical Version of Certain Select Passages Taken from the Works of William Law* (1774) and other facilely rhyming, rather eccentric religious verse.

Byron, George Gordon Noel Byron, 6th Baron (bī'rŭn), 1788–1824, English poet; son of "Mad Jack"

George Gordon,
Lord Byron

Byron and Catherine Gordon of Gight. His father died in 1791 and Byron, lame from birth, was alternately subjected to the excessive tenderness and to the violent temper of his mother. In 1798, after years of poverty, Byron succeeded to the title and took up residence at the family seat, "Newstead Abbey." He subsequently attended Dulwich school and Harrow (1801–5) and then matriculated at Trinity College, Cambridge. His first volume, *Fugitive Pieces* (1806), was suppressed; revised and expanded, it appeared in 1807 as *Poems on Various Occasions.* This was followed by *Hours of Idleness* (1807), which provoked such severe criticism from the *Edinburgh Review* that Byron replied with *English Bards and Scotch Reviewers* (1809), a satire

The "Cave of Byron" at Portovenere, La Specia, Italy, named in Byron's honor.

in heroic couplets which immediately shot him to fame. He left England this same year for a grand tour through Spain, Portugal, Italy, and the Balkans. He returned in 1811 with Cantos I and II of *Childe Harold* (1812), which made him the social lion of London. It was followed by the verse tales *The Giaour* (1813), *The Bride of Abydos* (1813), *The Corsair* (1814), *Lara* (1814), *The Siege of Corinth* (1816), and *Parisina* (1816). Byron's name at this time was linked with those of several women, notably, Lady Caroline Lamb. In 1815 he married Anne Isabella Milbanke. In 1816, however, she secured a separation for obscure reasons. A theory advanced by Harriet Beecher Stowe was that Lady Byron discovered the existence of improper relations between Byron and his half sister, Mrs. Augusta Leigh. At any rate, Byron, a social outcast, left England and passed some time with Shelley in Switzerland, writing Canto III of *Childe Harold* and *The Prisoner of Chillon*. Settling in Venice (1817), he led, for a time, a life of dissipation, but produced Canto IV of *Childe Harold* (1818), *Beppo* (1818), and *Mazeppa* (1819) and began *Don Juan*. In 1819 he formed a liaison with the Countess Teresa Guiccioli, who remained his acknowledged mistress for the rest of his life. In 1823 Byron was induced to interest himself in the cause of the Greeks. He accordingly sailed for Missolonghi, where he arrived in 1824. He worked unsparingly with Mavrocordatos to unify the divergent Greek forces, but died as a result of exposure. Byron's poetry covers a wide range. In *English Bards and Scotch Reviewers* and in *The Vision of Judgement* (1822; his counterblast to Southey's adulatory poem on George III), he wrote 18th-century satire. He created the "Byronic hero" who

appears consummately in the Faustian tragedy *Manfred* (1817)—a mysterious, lonely, defiant figure whose past hides some great crime. *Cain* (1821) raised a storm of abuse for its skeptical attitude toward religion. The verse tale *Beppo* is in the *ottava rima* which Byron later used for his acknowledged masterpiece *Don Juan* (1819–24), an epic-satire combining Byron's art as a storyteller, his lyricism, his cynicism, and his detestation of convention. See his selected letters (ed. by Jacques Barzun, 1953); biographies by André Maurois (1930), Peter Quennell (1935, 1941), L. A. Marchand (3 vols., 1957), and Doris Langley Moore (1961); study by G. W. Knight (1953).

Byron, John, 1723–86, British vice admiral and explorer. Sailing in 1740 with Admiral George Anson on a voyage around the world, he was shipwrecked off Chile. His *Narrative of Great Distresses on the Shores of Patagonia* (1768) is said to have been used by his grandson, the poet George Gordon, Lord Byron, in writing *Don Juan*.

Byron. 1 Town (pop. 1,138), central Ga., SSW of Macon. **2** City (pop. 1,578), N Ill., SW of Rockford, in a farm area; founded 1835, inc. as a village 1878, as a city 1904.

Bystrom, John Niklas (bü'strûm), 1783–1848, Swedish sculptor. He spent part of his life in Rome. He made colossal statues of kings of Sweden for Stockholm, but he was most successful in portraying women and children.

Bytom: see BEUTHEN.

Bytown, Ont.: see OTTAWA.

Byzantine art and architecture. Included are not only works produced in Byzantium after Constantine had made that city the capital of the Roman Empire (A.D. 330) but also the work done under Byzantine influence, as in Venice and Ravenna and in Syria, Greece, Russia, and other Eastern countries. For over a thousand years, until the conquest of Constantinople by the Turks in 1453, Byzantine art retained a remarkably conservative orientation; the major phases of its development emerge from a background marked by adherence to classical principles. Artistic activity was temporarily disrupted by the Iconoclastic controversy (726–843), which resulted in the wholesale destruction of figurative works of art and the restriction of permissible content to ornamental forms or to symbols like the cross. The pillaging of Constantinople by the Frankish Crusaders in 1204 was perhaps a more serious blow; but it was followed by an impressive late flowering of Byzantine art under the Paleologus dynasty. Byzantine achievements in mosaic decoration brought this art to an unprecedented level of monumentality and expressive power. Mosaics were applied to the domes, half-domes, and other available surfaces of Byzantine churches in an established hierarchical order. The center of the dome was reserved for the representation of the Pantocrator, or Christ as the ruler of the universe, whereas other sacred personages occupied lower spaces in descending order of importance. The entire church thus served as a tangible evocation of the celestial order; this conception was further enhanced by the stylized poses and gestures of the figures, their hieratic gaze, and the luminous shimmer of the gold backgrounds. Because of the destruction of many major monuments in Constantinople proper, large ensembles of mosaic decoration have survived chiefly outside the capital, in such places as Salonica, Nicaea, and Daphni in Greece and Ravenna in Italy. An important aspect of Byzantine artistic activity was the painting of devotional panels, since the cult of icons played a leading part in both religious and secular life (see ICON). Icon painting usually employed the encaustic technique. Little scope was afforded individuality; the effectiveness of the religious image as a vehicle of divine presence was held to depend on its fidelity to an established prototype. A large group of devotional images has been preserved in the monastery of Saint Catherine on Mount Sinai. The development of Byzantine painting may be seen also in manuscript illumination. Among notable examples of Byzantine illumination are a lavishly illustrated 9th-century copy of the Homilies of Gregory Nazianzus and two works believed to date from a 10th-century revival of classicism, the Joshua Rotulus and the

Paris Psalter. Enamel, ivory, and metalwork objects of Byzantine workmanship were highly prized throughout the Middle Ages; many such works are found in the treasuries of Western churches. Most of these objects were reliquaries or devotional panels, although an important series of ivory caskets with pagan subjects has also been preserved. Byzantine silks, whose manufacture was a state monopoly, were also eagerly sought and treasured as goods of utmost luxury. The architecture of the Byzantine empire was based on the great legacy of Roman formal and technical achievements. Constantinople had been purposely founded as the Christian counterpart and successor to the leadership of the old pagan city of Rome. The new capital was in close contact with the Hellenized East, and the contribution of Eastern culture, though sometimes overstressed, was an important element in the development of its architectural style. The 5th-century basilica of Saint John of the Studion, the oldest surviving church in Constantinople, is an early example of Byzantine reliance upon traditional Roman models. The most imposing achievement of Byzantine architecture is the Church of Holy Wisdom (see HAGIA SOPHIA). It was constructed in a short span of five years (532–

Belltower of Caorle, near Venice (11th-century Byzantine architecture).

Church of St. Theodoros at Mistra, Greece (13th-century Byzantine architecture).

537) during the reign of Justinian. Hagia Sophia is without a clear antecedent in the architecture of late antiquity, yet it must be accounted as culminating several centuries of experimentation toward the realization of a unified space of monumental dimensions. Throughout the history of Byzantine religious architecture, the centrally planned structure continued in favor. Such structures, which may show considerable variation in plan, have in common the predominance of a central domed space, flanked and partly sustained by smaller domes and half-domes spanning peripheral spaces. Although many of the important buildings of Constantinople have been destroyed, impressive examples are still extant throughout the provinces and on the outer fringes of the empire, notably in Bulgaria, Russia, Armenia, and Sicily. A great Byzantine architectural achievement is the octagonal church of San Vitale (consecrated 547) in Ravenna. The church of Saint Mark's in Venice was based on a Byzantine prototype, and Byzantine workmen were employed by Arab rulers in the Holy Land and in Ottonian Germany during the 11th cent. Secular architecture in the Byzantine Empire has left fewer traces. Foremost among these are the ruins of the 5th-century walls of the city of Constantinople, consisting of an outer and an inner wall, each originally studded with 96 towers. Some of these can still be seen. See Alexander van Millingen, *Byzantine Churches in Constantinople* (1912); André Grabar, *Byzantine*

Painting (Eng. tr., 1953); D. T. Rice, *Art of Byzantium* (1959); William MacDonald, *Early Christian and Byzantine Architecture* (1962).

Byzantine Empire, successor state to the Roman Empire (see under ROME), also called Eastern Empire and East Roman Empire. It was named after Byzantium, which Emperor CONSTANTINE I rebuilt (A.D. 330) as CONSTANTINOPLE and made the capital of the entire Roman Empire. A division into Eastern and Western empires became permanent after the accession (395) of HONORIUS in the West and ARCADIUS in the East, but the permanent split was not foreseen at the time. Throughout its existence the Byzantine Empire was subject to important changes of its ill-defined boundaries. The core of the empire consisted of the Balkan Peninsula (i.e., Thrace, Macedonia, Epirus, Greece proper, the Greek isles, and Illyria) and of Asia Minor. The empire combined Roman political tradition, Hellenic culture, and Christian beliefs. Greek was the prevalent language, but Latin long continued in official use. The characteristic Oriental influence began with Constantine I, who also introduced Christianity. Orthodoxy triumphed over ARIANISM under Arcadius' predecessor, THEODOSIUS I, but violent religious controversy was chronic. The reigns (395–527) of Arcadius, THEODOSIUS II, MARCIAN, LEO I, LEO II, ZENO, ANASTASIUS I, and JUSTIN I were marked by the invasions of the Visigoths under ALARIC I, of the Huns of ATTILA, and of the AVARS, the SLAVS, the Bulgars (see BULGARIA), and the Persians. Italy, Gaul, and Spain were, after the Western Empire fell (476) to ODOACER, theoretically united under Zeno but actually dominated by, respectively, the Ostrogoths, the Franks, and the Visigoths, while Africa was under the Vandals. In this period arose the heresies of NESTORIANISM and MONOPHYSITISM and the political parties of BLUES AND GREENS to divide the Byzantines.

An Age of Revival. Under the rule (527–65) of JUSTINIAN I and THEODORA, Byzantine power grew. Their great generals, BELISARIUS and NARSES, checked the Persians, repressed political factions, and recovered Italy and Africa, while TRIBONIAN helped the emperor to codify ROMAN LAW. During

Christ Descending into Limbo
(12th-century Byzantine mosaic in St. Mark's Basilica, Venice).

Christ the Good Shepherd
(5th-century Byzantine mosaic in the mausoleum of Galla Placidia, Ravenna).

Empress Theodora and her ladies-in-waiting (6th-century mosaic in San Vitale, Ravenna).

Justinian's reign a great revival of Hellenism took place in literature; Byzantine art and Byzantine architecture entered their most glorious period. Much was lost again under his successors. The LOMBARDS conquered most of Italy. However, Ravenna and the PENTAPOLIS, Rome, Sardinia, Corsica, Liguria, and the coasts of S Italy and Sicily long remained under Byzantine rule, and the exarchs governed until 751 at RAVENNA. The Persians, under KHOSRU I, made great gains, though Emperor MAURICE temporarily checked them in 591. HERACLIUS I (610–41) defeated the Persians but was barely able to save Constantinople from the Avars. Moslem conquests soon afterward wrested Syria, Palestine, Egypt, Africa, and Sicily from the empire. Heraclius' attempt to reconcile Monophysitism and orthodoxy merely led to the new heresy of MONOTHELETISM. His military reorganization of the provinces into *themes* proved effective and was continued by Constans II (641–

48). CONSTANTINE IV (668–85) saved Constantinople from Arab attack. The 7th cent. was marked by increasing Hellenization of the empire, outwardly symbolized by the adoption of the Greek title Basileus by the emperors. The church, under the PATRIARCH of Constantinople, assumed increasing importance in public affairs. Theology, cultivated by emperors and monks alike, was pushed to extremes of subtlety. Literature and art became chiefly religious. Under JUSTINIAN II and his self-made successors the empire was again menaced by Arabs and Bulgars, but the Isaurian emperors LEO III (717–41) and CONSTANTINE V stopped the Arab advance and recovered Asia Minor. The grave issue of ICONOCLASM, which they precipitated, led to the loss of Rome. In 800, during the reign of IRENE, the Frank CHARLEMAGNE was crowned emperor of the West at Rome. Thus ended even the theoretical primacy of Byzantium over Europe. *The Oriental State.* The political division of East

Byzantine art and architecture
inside San Appollinare Nuovo
(5th century) in Ravenna.

and West was paralleled by the religious schism, intensified by the patriarch PHOTIUS, between the Roman and the ORTHODOX EASTERN CHURCH, later culminating in a complete break (1054). In all aspects the Byzantine Empire, having lost its claim to universality, became a Greek monarchy, though Constantinople was the repository of Greek and Roman civilization. Compared with its savants, artists, writers, and artisans, those of Western Europe were crude and barbarous, though sometimes more vigorous and original. In the empire, the administrative machinery was huge, the competition among courtiers intense. Complex diplomatic maneuver, intrigue, and gross violence marked the course of events. Yet moral decay did not prevent such emperors as BASIL I, founder of the Macedonian dynasty, and his successors (notably LEO VI, ROMANUS I, CONSTANTINE VII, NICEPHORUS II, JOHN I, and BASIL II) from giving the empire a period of splendor and power (867–1025). The eastern frontier was pushed to the Euphrates, the Bulgars subjugated, and the Balkan Peninsula recovered. Russia, converted to Christianity, became an outpost of Byzantine culture. In the unceasing struggle between the great landowners and the small peasantry, most of the emperors favored the peasants. Economic prosperity was paralleled by a new golden age in science, philosophy, and architecture.

The Ebb of Power. With the rule of ZOË (1028–50) anarchy and decline set in. The Seljuk TURKS increased their attacks, and with the defeat (1071) of ROMANUS IV at Manzikert most of Asia Minor was permanently lost. The Normans under ROBERT GUISCARD and BOHEMOND I seized S Italy and attacked the Balkans, Venice ruled the Adriatic and challenged Byzantine commercial dominance in the east, and the Bulgars and Serbs reasserted their independence. ALEXIUS I (1081–1118) took advantage of the First Crusade (see CRUSADES) to recover some territory in Asia Minor and to restore Byzantine prestige, but his successors of the COM-

NENUS dynasty were able at best to postpone the disintegration of the empire. After the death (1180) of MANUEL I the Angelus dynasty unwittingly precipitated the cataclysm of the Fourth Crusade. In 1204 the Crusaders and the Venetians sacked Constantinople and set up a new empire (see CONSTANTINOPLE, LATIN EMPIRE OF) in Thrace, Macedonia, and Greece. The remainder of the empire broke into independent states, notably the empires of NICAEA and of TREBIZOND and the despotat of EPIRUS. The Nicaean emperor MICHAEL VIII in 1261 conquered most of the tottering Latin empire and reestablished the Byzantine Empire under the PALAEOLOGUS family (1261–1453). The reconstructed empire was soon attacked from all sides, notably by CHARLES I of Naples, by Venice, by the Ottoman Turks, by the new kingdoms of Serbia and Bulgaria, and by Catalonian adventurers under Roger de FLOR. Within the empire twilight settled. The capital was at odds with the provinces; ambitious magnates were greedy for land and privileges; religious orders fought each other vigorously; church and state were rivals for power. Eventually the Turks encircled the empire and reduced it to Constantinople and its environs. MANUEL II and JOHN VIII vainly asked the West for aid, and in 1453 Constantinople fell to Sultan Mohammed II after a last desperate defense under CONSTANTINE XI. This is one of the dates conventionally accepted as the beginning of the modern age. The collapse of the empire opened the way for the vast expansion of the Ottoman Empire to Vienna itself and also enabled IVAN III of Russia, son-in-law of Constantine XI, to claim a theoretical succession to the imperial title. Among the many excellent Byzantine historians were PROCOPIUS, Emperor CONSTANTINE VII, Princess ANNA COMNENA, Nicetas ACOMINATUS, John CINNAMUS, George ACROPOLITA, and Emperor JOHN VI. The classic, though biased, work on Byzantine history is Gibbon's *Decline and Fall of the Roman Empire.* More recent standard

works are those of J. B. Bury, Charles Diehl, A. A. Vasiliev, and George Ostrogorsky. See also *Cambridge Mediaeval History*, Vols. II and IV; Steven Runciman, *Byzantine Civilization* (1933).

Byzantine music, the music of the Byzantine Empire composed to Greek texts as ceremonial festival or church music. Long thought to be only a further development of ancient Greek musical practice, it is now regarded as an independent musical culture, with elements derived from Syrian and Hebrew as well as Greek sources. Its beginnings are dated by some scholars as in the 4th cent., after the founding of the Eastern Empire by Constantine I. The Greek kithara and aulos were used, but the principal instrument of Byzantium was the organ. No purely instrumental music is extant, however, and the exact nature of the instrumental accompaniment of vocal music is not certain. The eight *echoi* correspond roughly to the eight modes (see MODE) of plain song, but were groups of melodies made of certain definite formulas characteristic of an *echos*. The Byzantine music which survives is all sacred, with the exception of some acclamations for the emperor. Byzantine chant was monodic, in free rhythm, and often attempted to depict melodically the meaning of the words. The language was Greek. The Byzantine hymn, of which there were three types, was the greatest contribution of this culture. The *troparion*, a hymn, was inserted between the verses of the Psalms, and eventually the *troparia* overshadowed the Psalms. The *kontakion*, a hymn important in the 6th and 9th cent., whose origin is ascribed to Romanus, active during the reign of Anastasius I, consists of 18 or 24 strophes all in similar meter, with a contrasting introductory strophe. The subject matter is usually biblical. Often an acrostic is formed by the first letter of each stanza. The time of Romanus and of Sergius (fl. early 7th cent.) is called the golden age of Byzantine music. In the 8th cent. the outstanding hymn writers were St. John of Damascus and Cosmas of Jerusalem. The chief type of hymn was the *kanon*, a series of odes, theoretically nine but often only eight in number, referring to the nine canticles of the Old and New Testaments. Until the 9th cent., poet and composer were always one; later, hymns were set to already existing melodies. With the codification of the Greek liturgy in the 11th cent. there was a general decline in hymnody. Musical activity ceased with the fall of Constantinople (1453). Russian chant, the chant of the modern Greek Orthodox Church, and to a small extent Gregorian chant all owe something to Byzantine chant. Byzantine notation was originally only a system of *ekphonetic* symbols serving to remind a singer of a melody he already knew. Neumes derived from the ekphonetic notation were in use from c.950 until 1200. From 1110 to 1450 a staffless notation indicating the *echos*, starting note, and subsequent intervals of a melody was in use. It is largely decipherable today. Signs were added to it in the centuries which followed, but the modern notation used in the Greek church today was devised in the 19th cent. by Chrysanthus, a Greek archimandrite, because of the confusion in deciphering the manuscripts of early Byzantine music. See Gustave Reese, *Music in the Middle Ages* (1940) and studies of Byzantine music and hymnography

by H. J. W. Tillyard (1923) and Egon Wellesz (1949).

Byzantine rite: see ORTHODOX EASTERN CHURCH.

Byzantium (bǐzăn′shēŭm, –shŭm, –tēŭm), ancient city of Thrace, on the site of the present Istanbul, Turkey. Founded by Greeks from Megara in 667 B.C., it early rose to importance because of its position on the Bosporus. In the Peloponnesian War it was captured and recaptured by the contending forces. It was taken (A.D. 196) by Roman Emperor Septimius Severus. Constantine I ordered (A.D. 330) a new city built here; this was CONSTANTINOPLE, later the capital of the Byzantine Empire. See Charles Diehl, *Byzantium: Greatness and Decline* (Eng. tr., 1957).

Ivory casket cover (Byzantine, 10th century).

Christ in Majesty (ivory, Byzantine, 10th century).

C, third letter of the ALPHABET. In position and form, but not in meaning, it corresponds to Greek gamma (see G). In English it is used variously, e.g., in *can, cent, church,* and *loch.* In MUSICAL NOTATION it symbolizes a note in the scale. In chemistry it is the chemical symbol of the element CARBON. It is the Roman numeral for 100.

Ca, chemical symbol of the element CALCIUM.

Caaba: see KAABA.

Cabal (kŭbăl′), inner group of advisers to Charles II of England. Their initials form the word (which is, however, of older origin)—Clifford of Chudleigh, Ashley (Lord Shaftesbury), Buckingham (George Villiers), Arlington (Henry Bennet), and Lauderdale (John Maitland). Although they were never a working ministry, one or more of this group dominated court policy from 1667 through 1673.

cabala or **cabbala** (both: kă′bŭlù) [Heb.,=tradition], esoteric system of interpretation of the Scriptures based upon a tradition claimed to have been handed down orally from Abraham. Despite this claimed antiquity, the system was really the product of the Middle Ages, arising in the 7th cent. and lasting into the 18th. It arose as a reaction to the formalism of rabbinical Judaism and reached its greatest popularity in the 12th cent. It reflected strong Neoplatonic influence, especially in its doctrines of emanation and the transmigration of souls. Cabalistic interpretation of Scripture was based on the belief that every word, letter, number, and even accent contained mysteries interpretable by those who knew the secret. The names for God were believed to contain miraculous power and each letter of the divine name was considered potent; cabalistic signs and writings were used as amulets. The cabala was thought to contain Christian doctrines such as that of the Trinity and the atonement and was widely studied in the 15th cent. The system degenerated into juggling with letters and formulas and became the basis of much medieval magic. The Cabala still has adherents among the Hassidic Jews. The two principal sources of the cabalists are the *Sefer Yezirah* (Eng. tr., *Book of Creation,* 1877) and the *Zohar.* The first develops, in a series of monologues supposedly delivered by Abraham, a system of numerical interpretation and the doctrine of emanation. It was probably written in the 6th cent. The *Zohar* (called the "Cabalistic Bible") is a mystical commentary on the Pentateuch. It was written by Moses de Leon (13th cent.) but attributed by him to Simon ben Yohai, the great scholar of the 2d cent. See J. F. C. Fuller, *The Secret Wisdom of the Qabalah* (1937); J. L. Blau, *The Christian Interpretation of the Cabala in the Renaissance* (1944); A. E. Waite, *The Holy Kabbalah* (1960).

Caballero, Fernán (fĕrnän′ käbälyä′rō), pseud. of **Cecilia Böhl de Faber,** 1796–1877, Spanish novelist and folklorist. Born in Switzerland, she spent most of her adult life in Andalusia, which is the setting for her stories. Her sentimental novels are interesting only for their regional quality. The first, *La Gaviota* [the sea gull], was written in French and translated (1849) into Spanish. Others are *La familia de Alvareda* (1856), *Lágrimas* [tears] (1858), and *Clemencia* (1862). Some of her Andalusian folk tales were translated as *Spanish Fairy Tales* (1920).

Cabanel, Alexandre (älĕksä′drù käbänĕl′), 1823–89, French academic painter and teacher, popular in his day. His *Birth of Venus* is in the Louvre, with a replica in the Metropolitan Museum.

Cabanis, Pierre Jean Georges (pyĕr′ zhä′ zhôrzh′ käbänĕs′), 1757–1808, French physician and philosopher. He was professor of hygiene, legal medicine, and medical history in Paris. Active in politics as a revolutionist, he was a member of the Council of Five Hundred. He wrote *Rapports du physique et du moral de l'homme* (1802). See study by François Labrousse (1903, in French).

cabbage, leafy garden vegetable of many widely dissimilar varieties, all probably descended from the wild, or sea, cabbage (*Brassica oleracea*) of the mustard family, found on the coasts of Europe. It is used for food for man and stock, mostly in

Right, cauliflower; far right, Savoy cabbage.

Europe and North America. Well-known varieties of the species include the cabbages, BROCCOLI, BRUSSELS SPROUTS, CAULIFLOWER, collards, KALE, and KOHLRABI. All grow best in cool, moist climates. They are attacked mostly by insect pests. The true cabbages (var. *capitata*) include the white and red types and the Savoy type (grown mostly in Europe), with curly, loose leaves. Inexpensive and easily stored, cabbage is important in the diet of many poorer peoples. Popular cabbage dishes include sauerkraut and slaw (raw cabbage). Chinese cabbage or petsai, chiefly a salad plant, is a separate species (*B. pekinensis*) grown in many varieties, especially in the Far East.

cabbala: see CABALA.

Cabbon (kăb′ŏn), town, SW Palestine. Joshua 15.40.

Cabell, Branch (James Branch Cabell) (kă′bŭl), 1879–1958, American novelist, b. Richmond, Va. A graduate of William and Mary College, in 1896–97 he was an instructor there in French and Greek. After various experiences in journalism and in the coal mines of West Virginia, he began writing fiction of a highly individual kind. Early novels in which he derided conventional history were *Gallantry* (1907), *Chivalry* (1909), and *The Rivet in Grandfather's Neck* (1915). He invented a country of medieval fantasy called Poictesme and there set many of his novels, the best known of which is *Jurgen* (1919); others are *The Cream of the Jest* (1917) and *The Silver Stallion* (1926). After 1930 he wrote as Branch Cabell and continued his ironic novels as late as 1940 with *Hamlet Had an Uncle*. His nonfictional writing includes *Beyond Life* (1919), *Straws and Prayer-Books* (1924), *The St. Johns* (with A. J. Hanna, "River of America" series, 1943), and *Here Let Me Lie* (1947). See biographical studies by Carl Van Doren (rev. ed., 1932), L. D. Rubin (1959), and J. L. Davis (1962).

Cabet, Étienne (ätyĕn′ käbā′), 1788–1856, French utopian socialist and reformer. He was elected deputy in 1831, but his bitter attacks on the government resulted in exile (1834–39). In England he was influenced by Robert Owen, and there he developed his communism as expressed in the famous *Voyage en Icarie* (1840); this described an ideal society in which an elected government controlled all economic activity and supervised social affairs, the family remaining the only other independent unit. The book was extremely popular, and Cabet gathered many disciples. A group of them attempted unsuccessfully (1848) to found an Icarian community on the Red River in Texas. The next year Cabet established a temporary colony at the old Mormon town of Nauvoo, Ill., but serious dissension arose in 1856, and he was not reelected president. He died soon after in St. Louis. Most of the Icarians moved to lands they had bought near Corning, Iowa, where branch communities survived until 1898. Works by Cabet include *Histoire populaire de la Révolution française* (4 vols., 1839–40), *Colonie icarienne aux États-Unis d'Amerique* (1856), and *Le vrai Christianisme suivant Jésus Christ* (1846). See Albert Shaw, *Icaria: a Chapter in the History of Communism* (1884).

Cabeza de Vaca, Álvar Núñez (äl′vär nōō′nyäth käbā′thä dä vä′kä), c.1490–c.1557. Spanish explorer in the American Southwest. Cabeza de Vaca [cow's head] was not truly a surname but a title hereditary in his mother's family; he is frequently called simply Álvar Núñez. He came to the New World as treasurer in the expedition of Pánfilo de NARVÁEZ that left Spain in 1527 and reached Florida (probably Tampa Bay) in 1528. When that expedition was dissolved by hardship and Indian hostility, Cabeza de Vaca was one of the survivors whose barges were shipwrecked on an island on the Texas coast. Later scholars have argued much over the identification of that island, but Galveston Island and Mustang Island are popular candidates. The story is one of the most remarkable in the annals of exploration. After much suffering as slaves of the Indians, Cabeza de Vaca and three other survivors escaped and started a long journey overland. His companions were Alonso del Castillo Maldonado, Andrés Dorantes, and Estevanico (an Arab or possibly a Negro). They gained great repute among the Indians as healers since remarkable cures were attributed to their Christian prayers. The route that they followed westward is disputed as much as the island of the shipwreck, but after much wandering they did get to W Texas, probably into New Mexico and Arizona, and possibly (some argue) even to California before, turning south in 1536, they emerged into the full glare of history again as they told their story to Spaniards in Culiacán in Mexico. They were almost certainly the first white men to see the buffalo, and their stories about the Pueblo Indians gave rise to the legend of the Seven Cities of Cibola, later magnified by Fray MARCOS DE NIZA, and brought explorers in search of El Dorado. Cabeza de Vaca's own account, *Los naufragios* [the shipwrecked men] (1542) is the chief document of the startling adventures of his party. An English translation (1851) by Thomas Buckingham Smith was reprinted in F. W. Hodges, *Spanish Explorers in the Southwestern United States* (1907) and in I. R. Blacker and H. M. Rosen, *The Golden Conquistadores* (1960). After returning to Spain, Cabeza de Vaca was appointed governor of the Río de la Plata region and reached Asunción after an overland journey from the Brazilian coast in 1542. His South American career was sadly different from that in North America. He got into much trouble with the popular Domingo Martínez de IRALA. After he returned from a journey up the Paraná river to Bolivia, he was arrested, accused of high-handed practices, imprisoned for two years, and sent back to Spain. There he was found guilty but was pardoned by the king. Cabeza de Vaca wrote his own account of South American events in his *Comentarios* (1555). See Morris Bishop, *The Odyssey of Cabeza de Vaca* (1933); Haniel Long, *Interlinear to Cabeza de Vaca* (1936); Cleve Hallenbeck, *Álvar Núñez Cabeza de Vaca: the Journal and Route of the First European to Cross the Continent of North America, 1534–1536* (1940); J. U. Terrell, *Journey into Darkness* (1962).

cabildo (käbēl′dō), municipal corporation, lowest administrative unit in Spanish government. In the American colonies it was the only institution in which creoles could participate. Composed usually of councilors and magistrates, the *cabildo* distributed lands, imposed taxes, provided police service, and the like. In discussions of major importance the *cabildo abierto* [open cabildo] was formed by including prominent citizens. In theory, membership in the *cabildo* was elective; in practice, it became appointive, proprietary, and hereditary. Corruption and inefficiency were common. The degree of local autonomy at first granted by the crown was soon hedged in by increasing centralization of power in higher authorities. Nevertheless, when the movement toward independence took root, the *cabildo* was the only self-perpetuating institution around which new forces could rally. The *cabildo* could in case of emergency choose a governor, lieutenant governor, or captain general (e.g., Hernán Cortés). The first *cabildo* in the Americas was that of Asunción founded by Domingo Martínez de IRALA.

Cabinda (kŭbĭn'dŭ), Portuguese enclave (2,794 sq. mi.; pop. c.50,000), W Africa; administered from Angola. Cabinda town is the chief population center. It is bounded on the north by the Congo Republic, on the east and south by the Republic of the Congo, and on the west by the Atlantic Ocean. Cabinda was once geographically part of Angola but was separated from it in 1885 when the Belgian Congo acquired a corridor to the sea along the lower Congo river. Largely tropical forest, the region produces hardwoods, coffee, cacao, crude rubber, and palm-oil products. See F. S. van Dongen, *Cabinda Enclave* (1961).

cabinet, group of advisers to the head of the state who themselves are usually the heads of the administrative government departments. Its nature differs widely in various countries. In Great Britain, where the cabinet system originated, it was at first a committee of the privy council and rose to its present status only after parliamentary sovereignty had been clearly established by the Revolution of 1688 and the emergence of party governments in the 18th cent. Since the time of Robert Walpole the British cabinet has usually been a body of ministers drawn from the party possessing a majority in the House of Commons, responsible to the House for the conduct of the administration. The cabinet is chosen by the prime minister, who is guided by the necessity of choosing a group that will represent the disparate elements in his party and who must fill certain posts with commoners rather than peers. Overthrow of the cabinet follows a division of the House of Commons or a general election adverse to the administration. In continental European countries, where the two-party system is not the rule, the coalition cabinet is more common. Cabinet members need not be selected from the majority party nor necessarily from the legislature, and they may speak in either legislative house. In the United States the members of the cabinet are not members of either house of Congress and are responsible, individually and not as a body, solely to the President, who appoints them with the approval of the Senate and may remove them at will. The United States cabinet member may not speak in Congress, though he is often called before congressional committees. The order of seniority in the U.S. cabinet is according to the creation of the respective government departments, beginning with the Dept. of State and followed by the Secretaries of the Treasury and War, the

Attorney General, the Postmaster General, and the Secretaries of the Navy, the Interior, Agriculture, Commerce, and Labor. The cabinet was reduced to nine members in 1947, when the Dept. of War was abolished and the Secretary of Defense became a member, while the Secretaries of the Army, Navy, and Air Force were not given cabinet rank. In 1953 the Secretary of the newly created Dept. of Health, Education and Welfare became a cabinet member. In case of the death or disability of both the President and the Vice President, the succession to the presidency falls to the speaker of the House of Representatives rather than, as before 1947, to the Secretary of State. See W. I. Jennings, *Cabinet Government* (rev. ed., 1959); Stephen Horn, *The Cabinet and Congress* (1960).

Cabira: see SIVAS.

Cabiri (kŭbī'rī), in ancient religion, nature deities of obscure origin. They were connected with several fertility cults, particularly at Lemnos and at Samothrace, where important mysteries were celebrated. According to one legend they were also patrons of navigation. In Greek religion they were associated with Demeter and were similar to the Corybantes and Dactyls.

Cable, George Washington, 1844–1925, American author, b. New Orleans. He served as a Confederate soldier in the Civil War and afterwards was a writer and reporter for the New Orleans *Picayune*. His short stories of New Orleans culture began to appear in *Scribner's Monthly* in 1873; collected and published as *Old Creole Days* (1879), this work established him as a leader of the local-color movement of the South. The historical romance, *The Grandissimes*, considered to be his best novel, appeared in 1880. It was followed by *Madame Delphine* (1881), a short novel concerning a quadroon. After 1884 he lived in Northampton, Mass. His later work, including *Dr. Sevier* (1884) and the essay *The Silent South* (1885), reveals his concern with social evils, particularly with the racial problem in the South. Cable is remembered primarily for his early sketches and novels of Creole life. See editions of his letters by G. A. Cardwell (1953) and Arlin Turner (1960); also biography by Arlin Turner (1956) and study by P. C. Butcher (1959).

cable, usually wire cordage of great strength or a heavy metal chain used for hauling, for towing, for supporting the roadway of a suspension bridge, or to secure a large ship to its anchor or mooring. A cable may also be a line used for the transmission of messages by telephone or telegraph. Such a cable consists of a core protected by twisted wire strands and suitably insulated, especially when it is used to cross oceans under-sea; a message transmitted thus by cable is a cablegram or cable. The insulated wire that conducts electricity from generator to consumer is also called a cable. France and England were first successfully connected by submarine telegraphic cable in 1845. The first permanent transatlantic cable was laid in 1866 by Cyrus West Field, although demonstrations of its possibility had been made in 1858. A coaxial cable was first installed between New York city and Philadelphia in 1935, and in 1936 the first telephone message was transmitted over it. The coaxial cable consists of a tube made of copper or

Coaxial cable

The cable designed to brake landing planes on an aircraft carrier deck must be especially strong.

other conducting material through the center of which extends a wire conductor held in place by insulating disks. A number of such conducting units are held together by a covering of insulating material. By means of the coaxial cable a large number of telegraph and telephone messages and also television images can be transmitted simultaneously.

Cabochiens (käbōshyĕ′), popular faction in Paris in the early 15th cent. Composed largely of small tradespeople and members of the butchers' and skinners' guilds, it was named after one of the leaders, Simon Lecoustellier, called Caboche, a skinner. Chafing at the ruinous and corrupt fiscal practices of the government and the extravagance of the court, they espoused the cause of JOHN THE FEARLESS of Burgundy in the civil war (1411–13) between ARMAGNACS AND BURGUNDIANS. In 1413 they rebelled, violently seized the government of Paris, and promulgated the so-called *ordonnance cabochienne*, containing radical reforms. They were soon suppressed by the victorious Armagnacs.

Cabool (kŭbōōl′), city (pop. 1,284), S Mo., ESE of Springfield, in a farm and timber area; inc. 1884. A state poultry experiment station is near.

Cabot, George (kă′bŭt), 1752–1823, American merchant and politician, b. Salem, Mass., educated at Harvard. He went to sea and became captain of one of the ships owned by his brothers John and Andrew Cabot of Beverly, who in 1777 took him into their firm. Cabot also helped develop the family's cotton mills in Beverly. A Federalist, he was (1791–96) one of Alexander Hamilton's most trusted followers in the U.S. Senate. Made a director of the Bank of the United States in 1793, he became president of its Boston branch in 1803. In the Federalist discontent at the beginning of the

19th cent., Cabot was a leader of the ESSEX JUNTO and presided over the HARTFORD CONVENTION. See biography by his grandson, Henry Cabot Lodge (1877).

Cabot, John (kă′bŭt), fl. 1461–98, English explorer, probably b. Genoa, Italy. He became a citizen of Venice in 1476 and engaged in the Eastern trade of that city. This experience, it is assumed, was the stimulus of his later explorations. Like Columbus (though there is no evidence either influenced the other), he apparently believed the riches of the Far East might be more easily reached by sailing west. He went to England, probably in the 1480s, and resided chiefly at Bristol, a port then promising as a base for discovery. Under a patent granted by Henry VII (March 5, 1496), Cabot sailed from Bristol in 1497 and discovered the North American coast touching at Cape Breton Island or Newfoundland. In 1498 he again sailed for America to explore the coast. The fate of the expedition is unknown, though there is presumptive evidence it reached America and some of its members returned. The English claims in North America were based on his discovery. His son was Sebastian Cabot. See H. P. Biggar, *The Precursors of Jacques Cartier* (1911); J. A. Williamson, *Voyages of the Cabots* (1929).

Cabot, Richard Clarke, 1868–1939, American physician and educator, b. Brookline, Mass., M.D. Harvard, 1892. He was associated with the Massachusetts General Hospital (1898–1921) and with Harvard, where he taught in the medical school (1899–1933) and was professor of social ethics (1920–34). His works include *Physical Diagnosis* (with F. D. Adams, 1901; 13th ed., 1942), *Social Service and the Art of Healing* (1909; rev. ed., 1928), *Differential Diagnosis* (2 vols., 1911–15; 4th ed.,

1920), *Social Work* (1919), and *Adventures on the Borderlands of Ethics* (1926).

Cabot, Sebastian, b. 1483–86?, d. 1557, explorer in English and Spanish service; son of John Cabot. He may well have accompanied his father on the 1497 and 1498 voyages, and he was long given the credit for his father's achievements. In the 19th cent., scholars, finding discrepancies in the Sebastian stories, branded him an imposter and applied his accounts to the 1498 voyage of John Cabot. However, recent research indicates that the Sebastian narratives relate to a later voyage (1509) made in search of the Northwest Passage. He may have reached Hudson Bay. In 1512 he entered Spanish service and in 1518 became chief pilot. After the return of Magellan's ship *Victoria*, he sailed (1526) from Sanlúcar de Barrameda with the ostensible purpose of loading spices in the Moluccas. Instead he explored the Río de la Plata country, spending several years along the Paraguay, Plata, and Paraná rivers, but the hostility of the Indians and the scarcity of food forced him to leave the country. He returned to Spain in 1530, a distrusted and discredited man. In 1548 he reentered English service, and in 1553 he became governor of a joint-stock company (later the MUSCOVY COMPANY) organized to seek a Northeast Passage and open

Sebastian Cabot

trade with China. Under his instructions an expedition sailed the same year under Sir Hugh Willoughby, who was lost in midvoyage and was replaced by Richard CHANCELLOR. The expedition reached the White Sea, and a commercial treaty was negotiated with Russia, breaking the monopoly of the Hanseatic League. See J. T. Medina, *El veneciano Sebastián Caboto* (1908); J. A. Williamson, *The Voyages of the Cabots* (1929).

Cabot, city (pop. 1,321), central Ark., NE of Little Rock, in a dairy, cotton, poultry, and strawberry area. The streams in the region are noted for their quantity of fish.

Cabral, Pedro Alvares (pä'drō äl'vŭrĭsh käbräl'), c.1467–c.1520, Portuguese navigator. A friend of Vasco da Gama, in 1500 he was sent out by Manuel I as head of a fleet destined for India. Bartolomeu Dias was one of his officers. Cabral went far west of his course and reached the coast of Brazil, which

he claimed for Portugal. Proceeding onward, he reached Madagascar and Mozambique. At Calicut, trouble arose over establishing a post for trade and for converting the Mohammedans. He bombarded the city but had to retreat in order to save his East Indian cargo. The ships returned to Portugal with rich cargoes, but his methods of diplomacy were severely criticized. The old story was that Cabral discovered Brazil because he had been driven off his course by storms. This has been questioned, and it has been urged that even before the Spaniard Vicente Yáñez Pinzón saw the Brazilian coast (Jan., 1500), Portuguese navigators had been there and that Portugal, wishing to obtain the land, had managed to secure a revision of the pope's original demarcation of the world into Spanish and Portuguese zones of exploration. Certainly the Treaty of Tordesillas (1494) adjusted the former line and put Brazil in the Portuguese zone, but the truth is still being debated.

Cabrera, Manuel Estrada: see ESTRADA CABRERA.

Cabrera, Ramón, conde de Morella (rämōn' käbrä'rä kōn'dā dā mō"rĕ'lyä), 1806–77, Spanish Carlist general. A royalist, he was noted for valor and for his cruelty during the civil war. Refusing to accept the Carlist defeat in 1839, he continued the war in Valencia and Catalonia until driven into France in 1840. After a brief reappearance as Carlist leader in Catalonia in 1847, he returned to France and then went to England. In 1875 he recognized Alfonso XII as king.

Cabrillo, Juan Rodríguez (hwän rōdhrē'gäth käbrē'-lyō), Port. *João Rodrigues Cabrillo*, d. 1543, Spanish conquistador and discoverer of California, b. Portugal. In 1520 he landed in Mexico with Pánfilo de Narváez and joined in the conquests of Mexico and Guatemala. Accompanying Pedro de ALVARADO up the west coast of Mexico, he assumed command of the expedition and continued the voyage after Alvarado's death. He discovered San Diego Bay Sept. 28, 1542, landing at Point Lòma Head, now in Cabrillo National Monument. He then sailed on to Northwest Cape beyond San Francisco Bay, which he did not find. Returning to winter on San Miguel Island off the Santa Barbara coast, he died Jan. 3, 1543.

Cabrillo National Monument: see NATIONAL PARKS AND MONUMENTS (table).

Cabrini, Saint Frances Xavier (zā'vyŭr kŭbrē'nē), 1850–1917, American nun, founder of the Missionary Sisters of the Sacred Heart of Jesus, b. near

Saint Frances Xavier Cabrini

Lodi, Italy. Founded in Italy in 1880, her order was expressly for charitable and religious work among the very poor. Advised by Pope Leo XIII, she came to America (1889) to aid Italian immigrants arriving here. She lived mainly in New York and Chicago, directing the establishment of hospitals, orphanages, nurseries, and schools in the United States and in Latin America. Her sanctity, highly regarded in her lifetime, became famous after her death. She was beatified by Pope Pius XI in 1938 and canonized in 1946 by Pius XII. Mother Cabrini was the first U.S. citizen to be canonized. Her principal shrine is the Mother Cabrini High School in New York city, where she is buried. Feast: Dec. 22. See Pietro Di Donato, *Immigrant Saint: The Life of Mother Cabrini* (1960).

Cabul (kā′bŭl), town, NW Palestine, the modern Kabul (Israel). Joshua 19.27; 1 Kings 9.13.

ca' canny: see SABOTAGE.

cacao (kȯ̇kä′ō, -kā′-), tropical tree (*Theobroma cacao*) of the STERCULIA family, native to South America, where it was first domesticated and was highly prized by the Aztec Indians. It has been extensively cultivated in the Old World since the Spanish Conquest. The fruit is a pod containing a sweetish pulp in which are embedded rows of seeds, the cocoa "beans" of commerce. To obtain cocoa, the harvested pods are fermented by naturally occurring bacteria and yeasts to eliminate their bitter, astringent quality. The seeds are

Cocoa fruit
on tree

then cured and roasted. The clean kernels, called cocoa nibs, are manufactured into various products. Their large percentage of fat, removed by pressure, is the so-called cocoa butter used in fine soaps and cosmetics and in medicine for emollients and suppositories; the residue is ground to a powder (cocoa) and used for beverages and flavoring. CHOCOLATE is a product in which the cocoa butter has been retained. Cacao products have a high

food value because of the large proportion of fat, carbohydrates, and protein.

Caccini, Giulio (jōō′lyō kät-chē′nē), c.1546–1618, Italian composer and singer. Some of his songs were included in Peri's *Dafne* (c.1597), the first actual opera on record. Both he and Peri composed settings of Ottavio Rinuccini's *Euridice* (1600), the earliest operas of which the music is extant. *Nuove musiche* (1601), a collection of his madrigals and arias, is the most important collection among the early examples of monodic style.

Cáceres, Andrés Avelino (ändräs′ ävälē′nō kä′sārās), 1836?–1923, president of Peru (1886–90, 1894). He was a commander in the war with Chile (see PACIFIC, WAR OF THE) and continued to wage guerrilla warfare long after Peru had been conquered. Bitterly opposed to the peace made by the government of Miguel IGLESIAS, Cáceres attempted to seize control in 1884, but failed. Gathering more troops, he entered Lima in 1885 and forced Iglesias to hold an election. Cáceres was chosen president. His administration was a time of ruin and reconstruction. In 1894 his party forced congress to elect him president, but Nicolás de PIÉROLA soon overthrew the new government. Cáceres later held important diplomatic posts.

Cáceres (kä′thärās), city (pop. 48,210), capital of Cáceres prov., W Spain, in Estremadura. It is a manufacturing center, with phosphate mines and limestone quarries nearby. Cáceres was an important Roman colony, fell to the Moors in the 8th cent., but was recaptured (1229) by Alfonso IX. The old town, atop a hill and encircled by turreted walls, has some Roman and Moorish remains, two Gothic churches, and many 16th-century houses; the new town lies below.

Cache (kăsh), town (pop. 1,003), SW Okla., WNW of Lawton, in a cotton and cattle area. A nearby Federal wildlife refuge has one of the largest herds of buffalo and longhorn cattle in the country.

Cache (kăsh), river, c.213 mi. long, rising in the hills of SE Missouri and flowing SE into E central Arkansas, where it joins the White River.

Cachin, Marcel (märsĕl′ käshĕ′), 1869–1958, French Communist leader. An early leader of the Socialist party, he was instrumental in bringing many Socialists into the first French Communist party in 1920. Long the leader of the Communists in the chamber of deputies and editor of the Communist daily *Humanité*, he was elected senator in 1935. He was expelled (1940) from his seat after the German-Russian nonaggression pact. In 1945 he was elected to the national assembly, where he sat till his death.

cactus, any plant of the family Cactaceae, a large group of succulents found almost entirely in the New World. A cactus plant is conspicuous for its fleshy green stem, which performs the functions of leaves (commonly insignificant or absent), and for the spines (not always present) of various colors, shapes, and arrangements. Cactus flowers are notably delicate in appearance though usually large and showy; they are commonly yellow, white, or shades of red. Cactus fruits are berries and are sometimes edible. Cacti are sometimes used as a substitute for wood, as stock feed, and for hedges. The plants vary from small round globes to epiphytes, vines, and large treelike forms. The re-

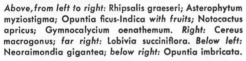

Above, from left to right: Rhipsalis graeseri; Asterophytum myziostigma; Opuntia ficus-Indica with fruits; Notocactus apricus; Gymnocalycium oenathemum. Right: Cereus macrogonus; far right: Lobivia succiniflora. Below left: Neoraimondia gigantea; below right: Opuntia imbricata.

duced leaf surface, the enlarged fleshy stem, which is well fitted to store water and to retain it, and the ramified and extensive root system (much reduced in cultivated cacti) make the plant peculiarly adapted to regions of high temperature and long dry periods. Cacti are not restricted to desert regions, however, for in America they range from the tropics into Canada. A cactus plant appears on the coat of arms of Mexico, and the blossom of the giant cactus or saguaro (*Cereus giganteus*) is the state flower of Arizona. Most cacti bloom in the spring for a very short period, sometimes for only a few hours. The blossoms are noticeably sensitive to light, and often different species blossom only at specific times of the day. One of the most famous of the cacti is the night-blooming cereus (sēr'ēŭs), usually classified as *Selenicereus* or *Cereus grandiflora* (several other night-blooming cactus species bear the same common name). Its fragrant blossoms unfold at a visible rate after sunset and last only a single night. In many of its native habitats the flowering of this cactus is celebrated with festivals. The largest cactus genus is *Opuntia*, jointed-stemmed species recognizable by the fleshy stems made up of either cylindrical (in the cane cacti and the chollas) or flattened (in the prickly pears) joints called pads. The large pear-shaped berries of several of these species are edible, e.g., the cultivated varieties of the Indian fig and the tuna. This fruit is common in Mexican markets; the plants have been widely naturalized in the Mediterranean countries, Australia, and elsewhere as a source of food. Most opuntias grow so rapidly to a large and ungainly size that they are unsuitable for cultivation as ornamentals, and in the wild often become weeds. However, the major economic importance of the cactus family is in the florists' trade. Among those cultivated for their showy blossoms are the Christmas cactus (*Zygocactus*) and species of *Echinocereus* and of *Epiphyllum*, the orchid cactus. The pincushion cacti (*Mammillaria*), the golden ball cactus (*Echinocactus*), and the hedgehog cactus (*Echinopsis*) are among the many grown as oddities for their curious appearance. The nopal (*Nopalea coccinellifera*) is the cactus usually cultivated as a host for the COCHINEAL insect. The hallucinatory drug PEYOTE comes from a cactus of the same name.

Cadalso Vázquez, José de (hōsā' dā kädhäl'sō väth'käth), 1741–82, Spanish poet, critic, and satirist. Distraught over the death of his beloved, the actress Maria Ignacia Ibáñez, he tried to disinter her body. His book of poems, *Noches lúgubres* (1798), adapted from Edward Young's *Night Thoughts*, heralded the Spanish romantic movement. However, he is best known for his prose works, *Los eruditos a la violeta* (1772), a satire on pedantry, and *Cartas marruecas* [Moroccan letters] (1793), an analysis of Spanish society.

Cadamosto or **Cada Mosto, Luigi da** (lwē'jē dä kädämō'stō), 1432?–1488, Venetian navigator in the service of Prince Henry the Navigator of Portugal. He seems to have entered Portuguese service in 1454, and he left a record of a voyage in 1455 which is valuable for the information it gives concerning Portuguese activity in the Canary Islands. He and a Genoese, Antonio de Nola, also in Prince Henry's service, went down the African coast to the Gambia river. In 1456 or 1457 Cadamosto reached the Cape Verde Islands, but the question of discovery of the islands is not settled. They may have been sighted by the Portuguese years before; they may have been discovered just a year before; they may have been first visited by Cadamosto. His name also appears as Alvise da Cadamosto.

Cadbury, Dame Elizabeth Mary (Taylor), 1858–1935, English social worker and philanthropist, studied in France and Germany; wife of George Cadbury. She became interested in social service and was active in many organizations working for improvement in education, housing, and peace. She was a member of the Birmingham Education Committee after 1911 and of the International Council of Women and was city councilor of Birmingham (1919–25), president (1925) of the National Council of Evangelical Free Churches, and a justice of the peace (1926). In 1934 she was made Dame Commander of the British Empire in recognition of her services as a social worker.

Cadbury, George, 1839–1922, English manufacturer and social reformer. In 1861 Cadbury and his brother Richard (d. 1899) assumed control of their father's Birmingham cocoa and chocolate factory. Interested in housing problems, the brothers moved (1880) the plant to Bournville and laid out a garden village. The successful venture influenced European model housing and GARDEN CITY projects. Agitation for national old-age pensions and insurance was financed by Cadbury, who also worked to eliminate harsh labor conditions. See biography by A. G. Gardiner (1923).

caddis fly, any of various insects of the order Trichoptera, with four wings, long antennae, and a short proboscis. The aquatic larvae, food for many fresh-water fishes, are called creepers when used as bait. Many species spin a silken protective case within which the cocoon is spun for pupation.

Caddo (kă'dō), North American Indian tribe, one of a number speaking Caddoan languages. The tribe gave its name not only to the linguistic stock but also to the Caddo confederacy, a loose federation of tribes which in prehistoric times occupied lands from the Red River valley in Louisiana to the Brazos valley in Texas and N into Arkansas and Kansas. The Wichita, the Caddo tribe, and the Waco were the best-known members. Some of the others were the Anadarko, the Nacogdoches, and the Nachitoches. The culture of these loosely knit tribes was similar. Generally they were sedentary, living in villages of conical huts, though they did raise horses. Tattooing and nose piercing were practiced, and distinctive feather mantles were used for ritual. The tribes were bound together by religious rather than political ties.

Caddoan (kă'dōŭn), a group of related North American Indian languages believed by some to form a subfamily of the Hokan-Siouan language family. It includes the Arikara and Pawnee in the north, and the Wichita, Caddo, and other languages in the south. It has been suggested that Caddoan is closely related to the Iroquoian language group.

Cade, Jack, d. 1450, English rebel. Of his life very little is known. He may have been of Irish birth; he himself claimed the name of John Mortimer and cousinship to Richard, duke of York. In 1450 he appeared as the leader of a well-organized uprising in the south of England, principally in Kent, known usually as Jack Cade's Rebellion. The protests were mainly political, not social, although the Statute of Laborers was among the grievances. Others were the loss of royal lands in France, the extravagance of the court, the corruption of favorites, and the breakdown of the administration of justice. The rebels defeated the royal army at Sevenoaks, entered London, executed the ex-minister accused of responsibility for the losses in France, and sacked several houses. The government then offered pardon to Cade's men and so dispersed them. Cade himself was captured and executed. See George Kriehn, *The English Uprising in 1450* (1892).

cadence, in music, the ending of a phrase or composition. In singing the voice may be raised or may be lowered, or the singer may execute elaborate variations within the key. In instrumental music, with development of the theory of harmony, the cadence was made completely dependent on the change of chord. If the dominant chord comes before the tonic, the cadence is authentic; if the subdominant chord comes before the tonic, the cadence is plagal. If the dominant chord leads into another harmony, the cadence is called deceptive. The reverse order of tonic to dominant is a half-cadence. See Walter Piston, *Harmony* (1948).

Cader Idris (kǎ′dùr ĭ′drĭs [chair of Idris], mountain ridge, 2,927 ft. high and c.7 mi. long, Merionethshire, W Wales, near Dolgelley.

cadi: see KADI.

Cadillac, Antoine de la Mothe (kǎ′dĭlǎk, Fr. ätwän′ dù lä môt kädēyäk′), c.1658–1730, French colonial governor in North America, founder of DETROIT. Of the minor Gascon nobility, he came to America in 1683 to seek his fortune and lived for a time at Port Royal (now Annapolis Royal, N.S.) and then on a grant of land in present Maine. He became a favorite of the governor of New France, Frontenac, and in 1694 he was placed in charge of the frontier post at MACKINAC. In 1699 Cadillac went to France to push plans for a post on the Detroit river, which he felt would offer a better strategic position against the English than Mackinac. Receiving a grant of land, trade privileges, and command of the new post, he set out with a band of colonists. Detroit was founded in 1701. Cadillac persuaded many of the Indian tribes to settle near the new colony. In 1711 he was appointed to the governorship of the vast territory of Louisiana. He reached his new post in 1713 to begin an administration that was remarkable only for the frequency and fierceness of internal quarrels. He was recalled in 1716 and spent his last years in Gascony. See biography by A. C. Laut (1931).

Cadillac (kǎ′dĭlǎk), city (pop. 10,112), co. seat of Wexford co., N Mich., on Lake Cadillac and SSE of Traverse City, in a farm area; settled c.1871, inc. as a village 1875, as a city 1877. Heating equipment, boats, and clothing are made. Cadillac is headquarters of the Manistee and Huron national forests. To the west is a winter sports area. Indian mounds are nearby.

Cádiz (kǎ′dĭz, kùdĭz′, Span. kä′dēth), city (pop. 98,754), capital of Cádiz prov., SW Spain, in Andalusia, on the Bay of Cádiz. Picturesquely situated

Old quarters of Cadiz.

on a promontory (joined to the Isla de León, just off the mainland), it is today chiefly an export center and port of call for transoceanic vessels. There is a Spanish naval base here and a U.S. naval base at nearby Rota. The Phoenicians founded (c.1100 B.C.) here the port of Gadir, which became a market for the tin of the Cassiterides and the silver of Tarshish. It was taken (c.500 B.C.) by the Carthaginians and passed late in the 3d cent. B.C. to the Romans, who called it Gades. It flourished until the fall of Rome, but suffered from the barbarian invasions and declined further under the Moors. After its reconquest (1262) by Alfonso X of Castile, its fortifications were rebuilt. The discovery of America revived its prosperity. Columbus sailed from here on his second voyage. In 1587, Sir Francis Drake burnt a Spanish fleet in its harbor, and in 1596 Essex attacked and partly destroyed the city. Cádiz prospered again after 1718 when its port was opened to traffic with the New World, but the loss of the American colonies ruined it once more, and it never recovered its former importance. During the siege by the French—which Cádiz resisted for two years (1810–12) until relieved by Wellington—the Cortes assembled here and issued the famous liberal constitution for Spain (March, 1812). The clean, white city has palm-lined promenades and parks. Its 13th-century cathedral, originally Gothic, was rebuilt in Renaissance style; the new cathedral was begun in 1722. Cádiz has several museums and an art gallery with works by Murillo, Alonso Cano, and Zurbarán. In the church of the former Capuchin convent hangs the *Marriage of St. Catherine* by Murillo, who was at work on this painting when he fell from a scaffold to his death.

Cadiz. 1 (kā′dĭz) City (pop. 1,980), co. seat of Trigg co., SW Ky., W of Hopkinsville near the Cumberland river. It is a trade and shipping center for a tobacco, grain, livestock, and timber area. The Brelsford Caves and a U.S. wildlife refuge are near. **2** (kǎd′ĭz, kā′dĭz) Village (pop. 3,259), co. seat of Harrison co., E Ohio, SW of

Steubenville; laid out 1803–4, inc. 1818. It is the trading and marketing center of a farm area. Coal mining is done.

Cadman, Charles Wakefield, 1881–1946, American composer, b. Johnstown, Pa. Although he is known to the public principally for two songs—*From the Land of the Sky-blue Water*, based on an Indian theme, and *At Dawning*—he composed operas, among them *Shanewis* (1918), *The Sunset Trail* (1925), and his most successful opera, *A Witch of Salem* (1926). He also wrote orchestral music, including *Hollywood Suite* (1932) and *Dark Dancers of the Mardi Gras* (1933), and piano music.

cadmium (kăd′mēum) [from *cadmia*, a Latin name for *calamine*, with which cadmium is found associated], metallic element (symbol=Cd; for physical constants, see ELEMENT, table). It is white, lustrous, very malleable, and ductile. When ignited in air it forms a brown oxide. Cadmium belongs to group II B of the PERIODIC TABLE, and it resembles zinc in chemical properties. It forms complex ions as well as a hydroxide, a carbonate, a chloride, and a sulphide; the last is used as a pigment (cadmium yellow). The element itself is employed in making certain alloys of low melting point, such as Wood's metal, and as a protective plating on other metals, such as steel. Cadmium does not occur free in nature, but in compounds, such as greenockite (a rare sulphide of cadmium), and in zinc ores in the form of a carbonate or a sulphide. It is obtained as a by-product in the extraction of zinc from its ores; the cadmium is distilled off first, since it is more volatile. The element was discovered in 1817 by Friedrich Stromeyer.

Cadmus, in Greek legend, son of Agenor and founder of Thebes. Misfortune followed his family because he killed the sacred dragon that guarded the spring of Ares. Athena told him to sow the dragon's teeth, and from these sprang the Sparti [sown men], ancestors of the noble families of Thebes. Cadmus married Harmonia. At the wedding she was presented with a sacred robe and necklace which later brought misfortune to their possessors. They had four daughters—Ino, Semele, Autonoë, and Agave. Turned into serpents by Zeus, Cadmus and his wife were sent to live in the Elysian fields. Cadmus is said to have introduced the Phoenician alphabet into Greece.

Cadogan, William Cadogan, 1st Earl (kŭdŭ′gŭn), 1675–1726, British general and diplomat, remembered chiefly as the faithful friend and brilliant subordinate of the 1st duke of MARLBOROUGH. The able commander of the dragoons called Cadogan's Horse, he took a distinguished part in the many victories of Marlborough in the War of the Spanish Succession. His early political career was also allied to that of Marlborough, and he fell when the duke fell in 1711. In exile in the Netherlands he conducted dealings with Hanover for the English Whigs, and after George I ascended (1714) the British throne, he won new commands and honors. He helped to suppress the Jacobites in 1715, was created earl in 1718, and was made commander in chief of the army after Marlborough's death in 1722. He also had high diplomatic duties in the resettlements among Great Britain, France, the Netherlands, the Holy Roman Empire, and Spain in the years 1714–20.

Cadorna, Luigi (lwē′jē kädōr′nä), 1850–1928, Italian field marshal. His father, Raffaele Cadorna, was a general in the wars of the Risorgimento and took Rome in 1870. Luigi Cadorna, a count, became the head of the army general staff and reorganized the Italian army before the First World War. During the war he was in fact commander of military operations, King Victor Emmanuel III being nominally commander in chief. Cadorna wrote two military works on the First World War and a biography of his father.

Cadoudal, Georges (zhôrzh′ kädōōdäl′), 1771–1804, French royalist conspirator. A commander of the CHOUANS, he was perhaps the most capable leader of the counterrevolutionists in the VENDÉE. He fled to England in 1801 but returned in 1803 in a plot, financed by England, to drive Napoleon from power and restore the French monarchy. General PICHEGRU participated in the plot, and Gen. Jean Victor MOREAU at least knew of it. Insurrections were planned in Paris and in the provinces, but the conspiracy was uncovered in time by FOUCHÉ. Cadoudal was executed, and the duc d'ENGHIEN, unjustifiably linked with the plot, was kidnaped and summarily shot. The conspiracy, exaggerated in report, was used as a pretext to transform the Consulate into Napoleon's empire.

caduceus (kŭdū′sēŭs), wing-topped staff, with two snakes winding about it, carried by HERMES, given to him (according to one legend) by Apollo. The symbol of two intertwined snakes appeared early in Babylonia and is related to other serpent symbols of fertility, of sun-gods, of wisdom, and of healing. This staff of Hermes was carried by Greek heralds and ambassadors and became a Roman symbol for truce, neutrality, and noncombatant status. By regulation, it has since 1902 been the insignia of the medical branch of the U.S. army. The caduceus is much used as a symbol of commerce, postal service, and ambassadorial positions and since the 16th cent. has largely replaced the one-snake symbol of Asclepius as a symbol of medicine.

Cadwaladr or **Cadwallader** (both: kădwä′lŭdŭr), d. 664?, semilegendary British king, leader against the Anglo-Saxons. Later bards made him a national hero, and Welsh tradition deems him the last king of the Cymry to wear the crown of Britain.

Cædmon (kăd′mŭn), fl. 670, English poet. He was reputed by Bede to be the author of early English versions of the stories of the Old Testament. Cædmon was a herdsman and in his later years became a lay brother in the abbey of Whitby. In 1655 Franciscus Junius, a Dutch scholar, published the text of Old English poems which agreed with Bede's description and which Junius ascribed to Cædmon. See E. V. K. Dobbie, *Cædmon's Hymn and Bede's Death Song* (1937).

Caelian Hill: see *Rome before Augustus* under ROME.

Caelius (Marcus Caelius Rufus) (sē′lēŭs), 82 B.C.–48 B.C., Roman politician. He was an intimate friend of CICERO, in whose collected correspondence many of Caelius' letters are preserved. In 56 B.C. Caelius' mistress, Clodia, sister of CLODIUS, accused him of attempting to murder her. He was acquitted by Cicero's defense in one of the better-known orations, *Pro Caelio*. In the civil war Caelius sided with Julius CAESAR, who made him peregrine praetor in 48 B.C. Later that year, dissatisfied with Caesar's moderate measures to clear debts, Caelius and the tribune MILO made a suicidal attempt at revolt in S Italy. Caelius was apparently acquainted with CATULLUS, who was probably an earlier lover of Clodia.

Caen (kä), city (estimated pop. 67,851), capital of Calvados dept., N France, in Normandy, on the Orne. It is the commercial center of the rich CALVADOS region and has a large textile industry (especially lacemaking). Iron ore is mined and processed nearby. Its importance dates from the time when William I of England (William the Conqueror) made it a favorite residence. The town, an architectural gem, was largely destroyed in the fighting which raged around it during the NORMANDY CAMPAIGN of the Second World War. The Abbaye aux Hommes [men's abbey], burial place of William the Conqueror, who founded it, was preserved; so were the Abbaye aux Dames [women's abbey], founded by Queen Matilda, and the Church of St. Nicholas. All three are outstanding examples of 11th-century NORMAN ARCHITECTURE. The 14th-century Church of St. Peter's lost its famous spire (255 ft. high). The castle of William the Conqueror, the university (founded 1432), and the town hall (17th cent.) were destroyed beyond repair.

Caere (sē'rē), ancient city of Etruria, c.30 mi. N of Rome, Italy. Although a few miles from the sea, it had ports at Alsium (near modern Palo) and Pyrgi (modern Santa Severa). The period of its greatest prosperity was during the 7th and 6th cent. B.C. The cemeteries have been excavated, and the monumental tumuli have yielded vases, pottery, and other art objects, revealing much about ETRUSCAN CIVILIZATION. The modern town here is called Cervetri.

Caerleon (kärlē'ùn), urban district (pop. 4,184), Monmouthshire, W England, on the Usk river. At Caerleon are extensive remains of the Roman fortress Isca, including an amphitheater, soldiers' quarters, walls, and baths. Numerous articles have been collected in a museum. The village is also famed for its connection with the Arthurian legend; it is often identified with CAMELOT.

Caermarthen or **Carmarthen** (both: kùrmär'dhùn), municipal borough (pop. 13,249), county town of Caermarthenshire, S Wales, on the Towy river near its mouth on Caermarthen Bay. It is a port for small vessels, a cattle market, and a dairy center. It stands on the site of the Roman town of Maridunum. The old castle was the headquarters of Welsh chieftains. Caermarthen's parish church of St. Peter is noteworthy, and its museum is second only to the National Museum of Wales. The first art school in Wales was founded here in 1854.

Caermarthenshire or **Carmarthenshire**, county (pop. 167,736), 920 sq. mi., S Wales. The county town is Caermarthen. Largest of the Welsh counties, it is hilly, with lower land along the coast (Caermarthen Bay, off the Bristol Channel) and in the fertile valley of the Towy. The county is generally devoted to agriculture and grazing, but part of the great S Wales coal field extends into the southeast corner of the county around Llanelly. Metals and textiles are manufactured. Caermarthenshire is traditionally the birthplace of Merlin, the wizard of the Arthurian legends.

Caernarvon or **Carnarvon** (both: kùrnär'vùn, kär-), municipal borough (pop. 8,998), county town of Caernarvonshire, NW Wales. It is a seaport on Menai Strait, with slate exports. The castle, begun by Edward I. c.1284, is a fine example of a medieval fortress. The prince of Wales is invested here. The site of the Roman Segontium is nearby.

Caernarvonshire or **Carnarvonshire**, county (pop. 121,194), 569 sq. mi., NW Wales. The county town is Caernarvon. The region is largely mountainous except for the Lleyn peninsula which forms the northern boundary of Cardigan Bay. SNOWDON is the highest mountain in England and Wales. The Conway, chief river of the county, flows along Caernarvonshire's eastern boundary, separating it from Denbighshire. Sheep farming and quarrying (in the largest slate quarries in the world) are the chief industries. Historical remains include evidences of considerable Roman occupation. The county has been important from medieval times as a route to Ireland.

Caerphilly (kärfi'lē), urban district (pop. 36,008), Glamorganshire, S Wales. In a coal area, it is also a market center and is noted for its cheese. Its 13th-century castle is the largest in Wales.

Caer Went: see WINCHESTER, Hampshire, England.

Caerwent (kärwĕnt'), village, Monmouthshire, W England. It is the site of the Roman city Venta Silurum, of which there remain walls, gates, hypocausts, and parts of an amphitheater and temple.

Caesalpinus, Andreas (ăn'drēùs sĕsălpĭ'nùs), Latinized from **Andrea Cesalpino** (ändrā'ä chäzälpē'nō), 1519–1603, Italian botanist and physiologist. He was physician to Pope Clement VIII. He described, in part and as a theory only, the circulation of the blood. His chief work, *De plantis* (1583), contains the first classification of plants according to their fruits, based on a comparative study of his large collection. Linnaeus considered him the first true systematist.

Caesar (sē'zùr), ancient Roman patrician family of the Julian gens. There are separate articles on its two most distinguished members, Julius Caesar and Augustus. Another distinguished member of the family was **Lucius Julius Caesar** (lōō'shùs), d. 87 B.C., consul (90 B.C.). He proposed a law extending Roman citizenship to Roman allies which had not joined in the Social War against Rome (90 B.C.). He was killed in the beginning of the civil war by partisans of MARIUS. His brother **Caius Julius Caesar Strabo Vopiscus** (strā'bō vŏpĭ'skùs), d. 87 B.C., is mentioned as an orator in Cicero's *De oratore*. He was killed with his brother. His name also appears as Vopisius. The son of L. Julius Caesar was **Lucius Julius Caesar**, d. after 43 B.C., one of Julius Caesar's legates in Gaul (52 B.C.). He accompanied the dictator into Italy in the civil war. After the assassination of Julius Caesar he was allied with Marc ANTONY, whose mother, Julia, was his sister. In 43 B.C. he and Antony fell out, and only the pleas of Julia to her son saved her brother in the proscription. When Octavius (later AUGUSTUS) was adopted (44 B.C.) into the Julian gens, he took the name Caesar. His successors as emperors took the name Caesar until HADRIAN, who kept the title Augustus for the emperor and allowed the heir apparent to be called Caesar. This became the custom afterward. The imperial use of the name Caesar was perpetuated in the German *kaiser* and the Russian *tsar*.

Caesar, Julius (Caius Julius Caesar), 102? B.C.–44 B.C., Roman statesman and general. Although he was born of the Julian gens, one of the oldest patrician families in Rome, Caesar was always a member of the democratic or popular party, probably as a result of the example and patronage of his uncle by marriage, Caius MARIUS. In 87 B.C.

Julius Caesar

Marius appointed him *flamen Dialis* [priest of Jove]. Caesar made the most of their relationship, strengthening its political implications when he married (83 B.C.) the wealthy Cornelia, daughter of Lucius Cornelius CINNA, colleague of Marius and enemy of SULLA. In 82 B.C. Sulla ordered Caesar to divorce Cornelia. When he refused, he was proscribed, his property was confiscated, Cornelia's dowry was taken, and he was shorn of his priesthood. He fled Rome (81 B.C.) and went to Asia to serve in the army. On Sulla's death, Caesar returned (78 B.C.) to Rome and began his political career as a member of the popular party. One of his first acts was to prosecute Cn. Cornelius Dolabella, a senatorial governor, for extortion in Macedonia. The case was unsuccessful, but it gained Caesar popularity with his party and repute for oratory. In 74 B.C. he went into Asia to repulse a Cappadocian army. After his return his role was that of the rising young statesman, agitating for the reform of the government on popular lines and helping to advance the position of POMPEY, who had become virtual head of the popular party. Caesar was made military tribune before 70 B.C. As quaestor in Farther Spain in 69 B.C. he helped Pompey to obtain the supreme command for the war in the East. He returned to Rome in 68 B.C. and continued to support the enactment of popular measures and to prosecute senatorial extortionists. In Pompey's absence he was becoming the recognized head of the popular party. At the funerals of his wife and his aunt (68 B.C.), he extolled Marius, the Julian gens, and Cinna. In 65 B.C. or 64 B.C., when he was curule aedile, Caesar had the trophies and statue of Marius set up secretly one night in the Capitol. These two incidents made him popular with the people but earned him the hatred of the senate. In 63 B.C. he was elected pontifex maxi-

mus, allegedly by heavy bribes. He then undertook the reform of the CALENDAR with the help of Sosigenes. The result was one of his greatest contributions to history, the Julian calendar. In Dec., 63 B.C., Caesar advocated mercy for CATILINE and the conspirators and thus increased the enmity of the senatorial party and its leaders, CATO THE YOUNGER and Q. Lutatius Catulus (see CATULUS, family). In 62 B.C. CLODIUS and Caesar's second wife, Pompeia, were involved in a scandal concerning the violation of the secret rites of Bona Dea, and Caesar obtained a divorce, saying, "Caesar's wife must be above suspicion." Having served in Farther Spain as proconsul in 61 B.C., he returned to Rome in 60 B.C., ambitious for the consulate. Against senatorial opposition he achieved a brilliant stroke—he organized the First Triumvirate, made up of Pompey, commander in chief of the army; M. Licinius Crassus, richest man in Rome (see CRASSUS, family); and Caesar himself. Pompey and Crassus were jealous of each other, but Caesar by force of personality kept the arrangement going. In 59 B.C. he married the admirable CALPURNIA. In the same year, as consul, he secured the passage of an agrarian law providing Campanian lands for 20,000 poor citizens and veterans, in spite of the opposition of his senatorial colleague, M. Calpurnius BIBULUS. Caesar also won the support of the wealthy equites by getting a reduction for them in their tax contracts in Asia. This made him the guiding power in a coalition between people and plutocrats. He was assigned the rule of Cisalpine and Transalpine Gaul and Illyricum with four legions for five years (58 B.C.–54 B.C.). The differences between Pompey and Crassus grew, and Caesar again moved (56 B.C.) to patch up matters, arriving at an agreement that both Pompey and Crassus should be consuls in 55 B.C. and that their proconsular provinces should be Spain and Syria respectively. From this arrangement he drew an extension of his command in Gaul to 49 B.C. In the years 58 B.C.–49 B.C. he firmly established his reputation in the GALLIC WARS, in which he reduced all Gaul to Roman control. These campaigns proved him one of the greatest commanders of all time. In them he revealed his consummate military genius, characterized by quick, sure judgment and indomitable energy. The campaigns also developed the personal devotion of the legions to Ceasar. His personal interest in the men (he knew them all by name) and his willingness to undergo every hardship made him the idol of the army—a significant element in his later career. In 54 B.C. occurred the death of Caesar's daughter Julia, Pompey's wife since 59 B.C. She had been the principal personal tie between the two men. During the years that Caesar was in Gaul, Pompey had been gradually leaning more and more toward the senatorial party. The tribunate of CLODIUS (58 B.C.) had aggravated conditions in Rome, and Caesar's military successes could hardly have failed to arouse Pompey's jealousy. Crassus' death (53 B.C.) in Parthia ended the First Triumvirate, and set Pompey and Caesar face to face. The senate began to support Pompey, and in 52 B.C. he was made sole consul. Meanwhile, Caesar had become a military hero as well as a champion of the people. The senate feared him and wanted him to give up his army, knowing that he hoped to be consul when his term in Gaul expired. In Dec., 50 B.C. Caesar, who was in quarters in Ravenna, wrote the senate that he would give up his army if Pompey would give up his. The senate heard the letter with fury, and at the instance of Q. Caecilius Metellus Pius Scipio (see SCIPIO, family) demanded that Caesar disband his army at once or be declared an enemy of the people—an illegal bill, for Caesar was entitled to keep his army until his term was up. Two tribunes faithful to Caesar, Marc ANTONY and CASSIUS (Q. Cassius Longinus), vetoed the bill and were quickly expelled from the senate. They fled to Caesar, who assembled his army and asked for the support of the soldiers against the senate. The army called for action, and on Jan. 19, 49 B.C. Caesar crossed the Rubicon, the stream bounding his province, to enter Italy. Civil war had begun. His march to Rome was a triumphal progress. The senate fled to Capua. Caesar proceeded to Brundisium, where he besieged Pompey until Pompey fled (March, 49 B.C.) with his fleet to Greece. Caesar set out at once for Spain, which Pompey's legates were holding, and pacified that province. Returning to Rome, Caesar held the dictatorship for 11 days in early December, long enough to get himself elected consul, and then set out for Greece in pursuit of Pompey. Having collected at Brundisium a small army and fleet—so small, in fact, that Bibulus, waiting with a much larger fleet to prevent his crossing to Epirus, did not yet bother to watch him—Caesar slipped across the strait. He met Pompey at Dyrrhachium, but was forced to fall back and begin a long retreat southward, with Pompey in pursuit. Near PHARSALA Caesar camped in a very strategic location. Pompey, who had a far larger army, attacked Caesar but was routed (48 B.C.). He fled to Egypt, where he was killed. Caesar, having pursued Pompey to Egypt, remained there for some time, living with CLEOPATRA, taking her part against her brother and husband Ptolemy XII, and establishing her firmly on the throne. From Egypt he went to Syria and Pontus, where he defeated (47 B.C.) Pharnaces II with such ease that he reported his victory in the words "Veni, vidi, vici" [I came, I saw, I conquered]. In the same year he put down, single-handed, a mutiny of his army and then set out for Africa, where the followers of Pompey had fled, to end their opposition led by Cato. On his return to Rome, where he was now tribune of the people and dictator, he had four great triumphs and pardoned all his enemies. He set about reforming the living conditions of the people by passing agrarian laws and by improving housing accommodations. He also drew up the elaborate plans (which Augustus later used) for consolidating the empire and establishing it securely. In the winter of 46 B.C.–45 B.C. he was in Spain putting down the last of the senatorial party under Gaius Pompeius, the son of Pompey. He returned to Rome in Sept., 45 B.C. and was elected to his fifth consulship in 44 B.C. In the same year he became dictator for life and set about planning a campaign against Parthia, the only real menace to Rome's borders. His dictatorial powers had, however, aroused great resentment, and he was bitterly criticized by his enemies, who accused him of all manner of vices. When a conspiracy was formed against him, however, it was made up of his friends and protégés, among them Cimber, Casca, CASSIUS (C. Cassius Longinus), and M. Junius BRUTUS. On March 15 (the Ides of March), 44 B.C. he was stabbed to death in the senate house. His will left everything to his 18-year-old grandnephew Octavian (later Augustus). It is a curious fact that Caesar probably knew of the conspiracy but made no attempt to defend himself. Caesar made the Roman Empire possible by uniting the state after a century of disorder, by establishing an autocracy in place of the oligarchy, and by pacifying Italy and the provinces. It should be noted that he had destroyed an oligarchy, not a democracy, to establish his dictatorship. His success in his dealings with other persons is a testimony to his social grace, and even Cicero (who hated Caesar) said that he would rather spend an evening in conversation with Caesar than in any other way. Caesar has always been one of the most controversial characters of history. His admirers have seen in him the defender of the rights of the people against an oligarchy. His detractors have seen him as an ambitious demagogue, who forced his way to dictatorial power and destroyed the republic. That he was gifted and versatile there can be little doubt. He excelled in war, in statesmanship, and in oratory. His literary works are highly esteemed. Of them his commentaries on the Gallic Wars (seven books) and on the civil war (three books) survive. They are masterpieces of clear, beautiful, concise Latin, and they are among the most reliable histories of antiquity as well as being classic military documents. Caesar wrote poetry, but the only surviving piece is a poem on Terence. A literary classic on Caesar is Shakespeare's tragedy, *Julius Caesar*. Plutarch is the most famous ancient source. See T. R. Holmes, *The Roman Republic* (3 vols., 1923); L. R. Taylor, *Party Politics in the Age of Caesar* (1949); biographies by John Buchan (1936), Guglielmo Ferrero (Eng. tr., 1933), and A. L. Duggan (1955).

Caesar, Lucius Julius: see CAESAR, family.

Caesarea (sĕsûrē´ŭ, sĕzŭ-, sēzŭ-), ancient city and seaport of Mauretania. Juba II changed the name from Iol to Caesarea and made it his capital; it became a large and handsome city, with flourishing trade and arts. It declined after being sacked by the Vandals in the 5th cent. It is the modern Cherchel, Algeria.

Caesarea Libani, ancient city of Lebanon: see ARKITE.

Caesarea Mazaca (mă´zŭkŭ), ancient city of Asia Minor, also called Caesarea of Cappadocia. As Mazaca it was the residence of the Cappadocian kings. The city was renamed (c.10 B.C.) Caesarea by Archelaus, king of Cappadocia. It continued down the ages as a trade center and is today KAYSERI, Turkey.

Caesarean section or **Cesarean section** (both: sēzâ´rēŭn), surgical removal of the child from the uterus through an abdominal incision. The operation is of ancient origin; a Roman law permitted the fetus to be delivered in this manner if the mother died in the last four weeks of pregnancy. The story that Julius Caesar was born thus is probably legendary. The possibility of saving the mother by such an operation was slight until an improved technique was evolved in the late 19th cent. The procedure was also aided by antisepsis and other developments that made surgery as a whole more successful. Caesarean section is performed nowadays when factors that make natural childbirth too hazardous are present, such as an abnormally narrow pelvis, pelvic tumors, and hemorrhage due to accident. The operation can be performed more than once on the same patient.

Caesarea Palestinae (sĕsū̇rē'ū̇ pălĭstĭ'nē, sĕzū̇-, sēzū̇-), old city, NW Palestine, c.20 mi. S of Mt. Carmel. It was taken (104 B.C.) by Alexander Jannaeus, leader of the Maccabees, and was made (30 B.C.) the capital of Herod the Great. The Jewish citizens were massacred by the Romans in A.D. 66. In recent years it has been made into a Jewish colony of Israel, used especially for fishing. Excavations in parts of the city were begun in 1960.

Caesarea Philippi (fĭlĭ'pī), ancient city, N Palestine, at the foot of Mt. Hermon. It was built by Philip the Tetrarch in the 1st cent. A.D. Its site (Paneas) had long been a center for the worship of Pan. Jesus was in the vicinity (Mat. 16.13), but there is no proof that he entered the city. The modern name is Baniyas.

Caesarion: see PTOLEMY XIV.

Caesarius of Arles, Saint (sēzā'rē̇ū̇s, ärl), 470?–543, archbishop of Arles (after 503). He has been called "the veritable teacher of Frankish Gaul." A strict Augustinian, he promoted orthodoxy at six synods, among them the synod of Orange (529) where semi-Pelagianism was condemned. He preached simple, appealing sermons to his diocese of recent converts instructing them in the rudiments of Christianity. These sermons still survive. He founded a monastery for women and wrote rules for the monastic life which had wide influence. Feast: Aug. 27.

cafeteria: see RESTAURANT.

Caffa: see FEODOSIYA.

caffeine, odorless, slightly bitter, crystalline substance composed of carbon, hydrogen, oxygen, and nitrogen. It is an alkaloid found in coffee, in tea (when it is known as theine), in the kola nut and, in small amounts, in cocoa. It can be prepared synthetically from uric acid. When used in moderation, caffeine is a mild stimulant to the nervous system and is generally harmless to most persons. Taken in excess, it can have a deleterious effect on the heart and nervous system.

Caffieri (Fr. käfyārē', Ital. käf-fyā'rē), French family of artists. Philippe Caffieri (1634–1716) left Italy to enter the service of Louis XIV at the Gobelin factory. He and a son, Jacques Caffieri (1678–1755), were employed by the architect Le Brun to make metal adornments for the palace and gardens at Versailles. Jacques's superb creations were chiefly in the rococo style. His son, Philippe Caffieri II (1714–74) worked with him and together they produced an immense volume of metalwork, including sumptuous ormolu mountings for furniture, adornments for several of the royal palaces, e.g., Fontainebleau and Choisy, and casings for clocks—notably a celebrated astronomical clock presented to Louis XV. Another son of Jacques, Jean Jacques Caffieri (1725–92), was a sculptor especially noted for statues and portrait busts.

Caffin, Charles Henry, 1854–1918, Anglo-American writer on art, b. England. He came to the United States in 1892 and was engaged by the decoration department at the Chicago exposition. In 1897 he settled in New York, becoming art critic successively on *Harper's Weekly,* the *Evening Post,* the *Sun,* the *American,* and the *International Studio.* He also wrote many perceptive books on art.

Cagayan (kägī'ū̇n, kägäyän') or **Rio Grande de Cagayan,** river rising in central Luzon, Philippines. It flows c.220 mi. N to the Pacific at Aparri. It is navigable to small sea-going vessels for c.13 mi.

Cagliari (kä'lyärē), city (estimated pop. 160,358), capital of Sardinia and of Cagliari prov., Italy, on the south coast of the island. The chief exports of this modern port are minerals, salt, and cork. A Carthaginian and later a Roman town, it was a Pisan stronghold during the wars with Genoa (11th–14th cent.); its history is that of SARDINIA. A submarine base, it was heavily bombed during the Second World War. There are Roman remains, a medieval castle, Spanish-Gothic monasteries (14th cent.), and a university (founded 18th cent.).

Cagliostro, Alessandro, Conte (äläs-sän'drō kōn'tä kälyō'strō), 1743–95, famous Italian adventurer, magician, and alchemist, whose real name was Giuseppe Balsamo. After early misadventures in Italy he traveled in Greece, Arabia, Persia, and Egypt. While in Italy, he married Lorenza Feliciani, who became his assistant on his trips to the cities of Europe, where he posed as a physician, alchemist, mesmerist, necromancer, and Freemason. He claimed the secret of the philosopher's stone and of miraculous philters and potions. As the Grand Copt of the order of Egyptian Masonry he organized many lodges. His reputation was amazing, particularly at the court of Louis XVI. Implicated in the Affair of the DIAMOND NECKLACE, he was acquitted but banished. Cagliostro returned to Rome in 1789, where the Inquisition charged him with heresy and sorcery and condemned him to die. The sentence was commuted to life imprisonment, and he died in a dungeon. Cagliostro has fascinated later generations as well as his contemporaries, and he appears often in literary works. See biographies by Frank King (1929) and W. R. H. Trowbridge (new ed., 1961).

Caguas (kä'gwäs, kä'wäs), city (pop. 32,015), E Puerto Rico. Founded in 1775, it is the largest of the inland cities and is an industrial and agricultural center. It leads the country in dairy products.

Cahaba (kū̇hō'bū̇), deserted village, S central Ala., near the Cahaba river and SW of Selma. It was the state capital from 1819 to 1826.

Cahaba, river rising in the mountains NE of Birmingham, Ala., and flowing c.200 mi. SW and S to the Alabama river near Selma.

Cahan, Abraham (kän), 1860–1951, American journalist, Socialist leader, and author, b. Vilna. He came to New York city in 1882, entered journalism, and helped found (1897) the *Jewish Daily Forward,* of which he was editor in chief after 1902, making it the most influential Jewish daily in America. He was a founder of the Social Democratic party in 1897 and after 1902 had been a supporter of the Socialist party. Active in spreading socialist teachings among Jewish workers, he encouraged the unionization of East Side garment workers and supported them in their strikes. His writings in English, particularly *Yekl: a Tale of* the New York Ghetto (1896), *The Imported Bride-groom and Other Stories* (1898), and *The Rise of David Levinsky* (1917), have a high place in immigrant literature. He also wrote, in Yiddish, *Blätter von mein Leben* (5 vols., 1926–31), an autobiography.

Cahokia (kủhō'kểủ), village (pop. 15,829), SW Ill., a suburb SSW of East St. Louis; inc. 1927. The first permanent settlement in the state, it was named for a tribe of the Illinois Indians. The French established a mission here in 1699, and later a fur-trading post. The village, with KAS-KASKIA, became one of the chief centers of French influence in the upper Mississippi valley. Cahokia was occupied by the British in 1765 and was later captured by the Americans under George Rogers Clark in 1778. The town has several buildings dating from the 18th cent. Nearby is a state park. See C. W. Alvord, ed., *Cahokia Records, 1778–1790* (1907) and *The Illinois Country, 1673–1818* (1920).

Cahokia Mounds, Indian earthworks near East St. Louis, Ill. There are more than 85 mounds, of which the largest is Monks' Mound (so called from Trappist monks who were settled here early in the 19th cent.), which is 100 ft. high and has a base covering some 17 acres. Considerable excavation has still not settled all questions about the mound builders who constructed these. They were village dwellers and belonged to a culture which flourished c.1300–c.1700. They probably made the mounds as bases for temples and the houses of the chiefs, and it is likely that the largest mounds were erected after Columbus had reached America.

Cahors (kȧȯr'), town (estimated pop. 15,834), capital of Lot dept., S central France, in Quercy on the Lot river. A commercial center, it has canneries and distilleries. It was an important town under the Romans and early became an episcopal see.

Medieval fortified bridge in Cahors

Ruled by its bishops until the 14th cent., Cahors was the capital of QUERCY. Ecclesiastic rule did not prevent medieval Cahors from being one of the major banking centers of Europe, and the Cahors in money lenders were among the most famous. The university of Cahors, founded in 1322 by Pope John XXII (who was born here), was united in 1751 with that of Toulouse. The old part of Cahors is of great architectural interest. Part of the medieval fortifications, including a fortified bridge, still stand. The Cathedral of St. Étienne (12th–13th cent.), with Byzantine cupolas, and the palace of John XXII are among its numerous historic buildings. Clément Marot and Gambetta were born here.

Caiaphas (Joseph Caiaphas) (kā'yủfủs), high priest of the Jews from before A.D. 26 until A.D. 36 or 37, a Sadducee, son-in-law of Annas. He presided at the council which condemned Jesus to death. Later he joined in the examination of Peter and John. Mat. 26.57–68; John 11.47–54; 18.24; Acts 4.6. See also Mark 14.53–65 and Luke 22.66–71.

Caicos Islands: see TURKS AND CAICOS ISLANDS.

Caillaux, Joseph (zhȯzěf' kāyō'), 1863–1944, French statesman. He became finance minister in the Waldeck-Rousseau cabinet (1899) and in the Clemenceau cabinet (1906), winning considerable unpopularity by introducing the income tax. As premier in 1911, he reached a peaceful settlement of the crisis over MOROCCO with Germany. However, he was severely attacked by the nationalists, and his cabinet fell in 1912. In 1913 he again became minister of finance. He resigned in 1914 to defend his wife, who had shot and killed Gaston Calmette, editor of the *Figaro*, for attacking Caillaux's private life. Mme Caillaux was acquitted. Caillaux expressed pacifist sentiments during the First World War and allegedly made contact with the enemy to discuss a negotiated peace. He was arrested (1917) and sentenced (1920) to three years imprisonment for involvement with the enemy. Restored to citizenship in 1925 under the general amnesty, he served as finance minister under Painlevé (1925) and Briand (1926), but each time a hostile chamber of deputies forced his resignation. He was subsequently elected to the senate. See Rudolph Binion, *Defeated Leaders* (1960).

Caillié, René (rȧnā' kāyā'), 1799–1838, French explorer in Africa. He was the first European to visit Timbuktu and return. The son of poor French peasants, he was obsessed with the idea of seeing Timbuktu. After 11 years of preparation, he reached the desert city, disguised as a Moslem trader, and remained there two weeks. See Galbraith Welch, *The Unveiling of Timbuctoo: the Astounding Adventures of Caillié* (1938).

Cain. 1 Eldest son of Adam and Eve, a tiller of the soil. In jealousy he killed his brother Abel and became a fugitive. Gen. 4. **2** City, W Palestine. Joshua 15.57.

Cainan (kā'năn), in the Gospel genealogy. **1** The same as KENAN. **2** Son of Arphaxad. Luke 3.36.

Caine, Hall (Sir Thomas Henry Hall Caine), 1853–1931, English novelist. He lived with Dante Gabriel Rossetti from 1881 until the poet's death and wrote *Recollections of Rossetti* (1882). His novels, some of Manx life, others on biblical themes, include *The Shadow of a Crime* (1885), *The Deem-*

Aerial view of Cairo.

Tinsmith in Cairo's bazaar section.

ster (1887), *The Manxman* (1894), *The Christian* (1897), *The Prodigal Son* (1904), and *The Master of Man* (1921). See his autobiography, *My Story* (1908).

cairn, a pile of stones, usually conical in shape, raised as a landmark or a memorial. In prehistoric times it was often erected over a burial. A BARROW is sometimes called a cairn.

Cairnbrook, uninc. village (pop. 1,100), SW Pa., SE of Johnstown.

Cairnes, John Elliot (kârnz), 1823–75, Irish economist, a follower of John Stuart Mill. His *Slave Power* (1862), a defense of the North in the American Civil War, made a great impression in England. Among his works are *The Character and Logical Method of Political Economy* (1857) and *Some Leading Principles of Political Economy Newly Expounded* (1874).

Cairngorm, group of mountains forming part of the Grampians, central Scotland, on the southwestern border of Aberdeenshire and of Banffshire and the eastern border of Invernessshire and between the Dee and the upper Spey. The name cairngorm is given to an ornamental yellow or brown quartz found in the mountains. The group includes the peaks Ben Macdhui (4,296 ft.), Braeriach (4,248 ft.), and Cairngorm (4,084 ft.).

Cairns, city (pop. 23,800), Queensland, Commonwealth of Australia, on Trinity Bay. It is the principal sugar port of Australia.

Cairn terrier: see TERRIER.

Cairo (kī′rō), Arabic *El Kahirah* [the victorious], city (pop. c.3,100,000), N Egypt, capital of the United Arab Republic. It is on the Nile at the head of the delta. Near this site was the Roman fortress city of Babylon, and almost directly across the river was Memphis, an ancient Egyptian

capital. Cairo, now the largest city of Africa, was founded in 969 by the Fatimite general Jauhar to become the capital of Egypt in place of nearby Fostat (old Cairo). In the 12th cent. it was unsuccessfully attacked by Crusaders, and to defend the city, Saladin erected (c.1179) the citadel, which still stands. Cairo throve under the Mamelukes (13th–early 16th cent.), who added many buildings, but the period of Ottoman rule (1517–1798) saw a decline. Napoleon occupied the city from 1798 to 1801. At this time the city population numbered a quarter of a million. In the 19th cent. it grew in size and commercial importance. The British occupation began in 1882 and did not end until 1936, when Egypt was restored to full independence. In the Second World War it was the Allied headquarters for the Middle East, and in 1943 the Cairo Conference was held here. From 1958 to 1961 it was the capital of the United Arab Republic; Egypt retained the name after Syria withdrew from the alliance. Much of the city is modern with wide streets, but it is in the older sections—Arab and Coptic—that the famed mosques, palaces, and city gates are found. The mosques of Amur (7th cent.), Ibn Tulun (9th cent.), Hasan (1356), and Kait Bey (15th cent.) are especially noted for bold design. The Mosque of El Azhar and adjoining buildings house what is deemed the most important center of Koranic studies in the world. The city is also the seat of Cairo Univ. Khedive Ismail's palace on Gezira Island is a noted 19th-century structure. Cairo has museums of antiquities and an Arab museum. The Nilometer, a graduated column used for over a century to measure the Nile water level, is on Roda Island, where the infant Moses is believed to have been found in the bulrushes. Cairo is the business center of Egypt, and most of its wealth is derived from the transit trade along the Nile and along the railroad, which parallels the river to Aswan. There are extensive railroad facilities and two large airports. The city's industries include steel mills, iron foundries, and cement works; it is also the center of the Arabic motion picture industry.

Cairo (kā′rō, kā′rō). **1** City (pop. 7,427), co. seat of Grady co., SW Ga., near the Fla. line WNW of Thomasville, in a fertile farm area; settled 1866, inc. 1870. It ships quantities of cane sugar and syrup and also processes or ships the area's yield of tung nuts, tobacco, pecans, peanuts, and cucumbers. **2** Residential and industrial city (pop. 9,348), co. seat of Alexander co., extreme S Ill., WSW of Paducah, Ky., on a levee-protected tongue of land between the Mississippi and the Ohio rivers; inc. 1818. A center for shipping by rail, highway, and river, it is the distributing point for a large farm area, popularly called Egypt because of the fertility of the soil and the delta-like geographical similarity. Among Cairo's manufactures are flooring, floor finishes, pipe fittings, automobile parts, and clothing. It was a strategic point in the Civil War and was used as a depot by the Federal government. The Ohio River Highway Bridge connects Cairo with Kentucky, and the Mississippi Highway Bridge extends to Missouri. The city has often been endangered by floods, but a recent Federal flood-control project has decreased the danger.

Cairo Conference, Nov. 22–26, 1943, meeting of U.S. President F. D. Roosevelt, British Prime Minister Winston Churchill, and Generalissimo Chiang Kai-shek of China at Cairo, Egypt, in the Second World War. A joint declaration pledged continuation of the war against Japan until unconditional Japanese surrender, forswore territorial ambitions, and promised to strip Japan of all territory acquired since 1895. Korea was to receive independence "in due course." The TEHERAN CONFERENCE was held immediately.

Cairoli, Benedetto (bānädět′tō kīrō′lē), 1825–89, Italian patriot and statesman, one of five brothers all noted as heroes of the Risorgimento. The only brother to survive the wars, Benedetto took part in the expedition of GARIBALDI to Sicily in 1860 and later became a leftist member of parliament, advocating, with Mazzini, the occupation of Rome. Premier in 1878 and 1879–81, he resigned his office after failing to prevent the establishment of a French protectorate over TUNISIA and after allowing open expression of IRREDENTISM.

caisson (kā′sŭn, –sŏn) [Fr.,=big box], in engineering, a chamber, usually of steel but sometimes of wood or reinforced concrete, used in the construction of foundations or piers in or near a body of water. There are several types. The open caisson is a cylinder or box of size and shape to suit the projected foundation, with a cutting edge around the bottom. This is sunk by its own weight and by excavation and then filled with concrete. Pneumatic caissons are usually used in river-bed work or where quicksand is present. In this type the cylinder or box has an airtight deck high enough above the cutting edge to permit men to work underneath. The air in this chamber beneath the deck is kept under pressure great enough to prevent the entrance of water. Shafts through the deck permit the passage of men, equipment, and excavated material between the bottom and the surface. At the top of each shaft is an air lock to permit communication with the outside without altering the air pressure in the working chamber. As the working chamber moves down, the caisson above the deck and about the shafts is filled with concrete, and when a sufficient depth or bed rock is reached, the working chamber itself is filled, so that there is a solid block of concrete from base to top. A type of caisson often called a camel, used to raise sunken vessels, consists of a cylinder filled with water. This is sunk, attached to the vessel, and emptied by pump or compressed air, so that its buoyancy assists in raising the vessel. Caissons are also sometimes used for closing the entrance to dry docks or instead of gates in canal locks. Workers leaving a caisson after hours of labor under high pressure are given special decompression treatment to accustom them to the lower atmospheric pressure and thus to prevent caisson disease. The addition of nitrogen to the compressed air supplied to the caisson has been found to prevent the disease. See AEROEMBOLISM.

Caithness (kāth′nĕs, kāthnĕs′), county (pop. 27,345), 686 sq. mi., N Scotland, northernmost county of the Scottish mainland. WICK is the county town. The northeastern section of Caithness, flat and treeless, contains most of the county's small percentage of arable land. The southwest is barren with peat moors and sheep runs. Agriculture and fishing are the main occupations, and there is a growing dairy industry. Britain's first large nuclear breeder reactor was opened at DOUNREAY in 1959. Originally part of the Pictish nation, Caithness was absorbed into the viking earldom in the 9th cent. and reverted to Scottish rule only in 1202. It was the scene of constant clan warfare until the end of the 17th cent.

Caius, John (kēz), 1510–73, English physician, studied at Gonville Hall, Cambridge, and at Padua. He practiced in London, where he was court physician. After returning to Cambridge he enlarged and endowed Gonville, renaming it Gonville and Caius College. He promoted the study of anatomy. See his works (with memoir by John Venn, 1912) and *A Boke or Counseill against the Disease Called the Sweate* (1552; facsimile ed., 1937).

Cajal, Santiago Ramón y: see RAMÓN Y CAJAL.

Cajamarca (kähämär′kä), city (pop. c.37,000), N Peru. At an altitude of c.9,000 ft., Cajamarca has a cool, dry climate. Grains and alfalfa are raised in the region, and from nearby mines come gold, silver, and copper. The town was important in Inca times, and it was here Francisco Pizarro captured ATAHUALPA and broke the power of the Incas.

Cajetan, Saint (kä′jŭtăn, kä″yätän′), 1480–1547, Italian churchman and reformer. Son of the count of Thiene, he studied civil and canon law, but abandoned work as a jurist at the papal court to become a priest. He advocated communities of priests who lived in poverty and worked among the people. He was the leader in founding the congregation of the Theatines, formally begun in 1524 and called after a co-founder and first superior, the bishop of Chieti [Latin=*Theate*], who was later PAUL IV.

Calabrian women, on their way to the weekly market, balance baskets of handmade pottery on their heads.

Cajetan's vigor in reform made him a notable figure, and the Theatines were very active in the Catholic Reformation. Cajetan was canonized in 1671. Feast: Aug. 7.

Cajetan (kă'jŭtăn, kä"yātän') [Latin,=from Gaeta], 1469?–1534, Italian prelate, cardinal of the Roman Church, b. Gaeta. His original name was Giacomo de Vio. He joined the Dominicans (c.1484), became general of his order (1508), and was made a cardinal (1517). He played a leading role at the Fifth Lateran Council as an advocate of reform. As papal legate in Germany in 1518 and 1519 he attempted to compose the differences of Martin Luther with the Church. He strongly opposed the divorce of Henry VIII of England from Katharine of Aragon. Cajetan's political skills helped secure the elections of Charles V and Pope Adrian VI. Always a student, he translated parts of the Bible, and his commentaries are published with the *Summa* of St. Thomas Aquinas in the pontifical edition of that work.

Cajuns: see ACADIA.

Cakchiquel: see QUICHÉ.

cake, originally a small mass of dough baked by turning, in present usage a dessert or sweet made of flour, sugar, shortening (preferably butter), eggs, seasonings, and usually some leavening and liquid besides the eggs. The early method of making sweet cake or "fancy bread" was by adding other ingredients to a portion of bread dough. Some cakes, such as fruitcake or poundcake, called for many eggs and for wine, brandy, or sack, these ingredients supplying the leavening agent. Modern cakes are generally raised with baking powder or with baking soda or beaten eggs. Cakes are classed as butter cakes or as cakes made without shortening and depending mainly on beaten eggs for leavening (e.g., spongecake and angel cake).

Calabar (kălŭbär', kă'lŭbär), city (pop c.47,000), a port on an estuary of the Gulf of Guinea, SE Nigeria. Palm products and some rubber and cocoa are exported.

calabash: see GOURD.

Calabrese, Il: see PRETI, MATTIA.

Calabria (kŭlä'brēŭ, Ital. kälä'brēä), region (5,828 sq. mi.; estimated pop. 2,156,821), S Italy. A mountainous peninsula projecting between the Tyrrhenian Sea and the Ionian Sea, it forms the toe of the Italian boot. The southern tip of Calabria is separated from Sicily by the narrow Strait of Messina. Calabria is divided into the provinces of Catanzaro, Cosenza, and Reggio di Calabria, named after their chief cities. Reggio di Calabria is the regional capital. Agriculture, fruit-growing, and sheep and goat raising are the chief occupations. There are several large hydroelectric plants. The ancient BRUTTIUM, the region came to be named Calabria in the early Middle Ages (under the Romans, Calabria designated the present S APULIA). Conquered (11th cent.) by ROBERT GUISCARD, Calabria became part of the Norman kingdom of Sicily and (after 1282) of the kingdom of Naples (see NAPLES, KINGDOM OF). It was conquered by Garibaldi in 1860. Feudal landholding conditions prevailed until modern times. These, added to malaria, frequent earthquakes, droughts, and poor communications, have encouraged large-scale emigration and have held up the social and economic development of the region. Reforms and public works have been in progress since the beginning of the 20th cent.

caladium: see ARUM.

Calah (kā'lŭ) or **Kalakh** (kä'läkh), ancient city of Assyria, S of Nineveh and therefore S of present Mosul, Iraq. Known as Calah in the Bible, it is the same as the ancient Nimrud, named after a legendary Assyrian hunting hero. Calah emerged as a famous city when Ashurnasirpal II chose (c.880 B.C.) the site for his capital. Excavations carried on since the mid-19th cent. have revealed remarkable bas-reliefs, ivories, and sculptures. Also discovered were the palaces of Ashurnasirpal II, Shalmaneser III, and Tiglath-pileser III. Calah continued to be a royal residence even after Nineveh became the political capital. The famous black obelisk of Shalmaneser III was discovered in Calah by A. H. Layard in 1846. Calah is mentioned in Gen. 10.11,12.

Calahorra (käläô'rä), town (pop. 13,183), Logroño prov., NE Spain, in Old Castile, near the Ebro river. It is an agricultural and manufacturing center. Here, in ancient Calagurris, Pompey unsuccessfully besieged the rebel Sertorius in 76 B.C. There are a few Roman ruins and an 11th-century cathedral. Quintilian was born here.

Calais (kă'lā, kălā', Fr. kälä'), city (estimated pop. 60,340), Pas-de-Calais dept., N France, in Picardy, on the Strait of DOVER. Located opposite Dover, Calais has been a major commercial seaport and communications center with England since the Middle Ages. It was fortified (13th cent.) by the counts of Boulogne. In 1347, after a siege of 11 months, Calais fell to Edward III of England. A bronze monument by RODIN commemorates the famous sacrifice of the six burghers of Calais, as related in Froissart's chronicle. Edward III had promised to spare the town if six prominent citizens offered their lives; but Edward spared them and the city when his queen, Philippa, interceded. Calais remained in English hands until it was recovered by the French under François de Guise in 1558. It was the scene of much fighting (1940, 1944) in the

The harbor of Calais.

Second World War and was partly destroyed. Calais preserves a Gothic church.

Calais (kăl′ĭs), city (pop. 4,223), SE Maine, on the St. Croix river opposite St. Stephen, N.B., with which it forms practically a single community; inc. as a town 1809, as a city 1850. On St. Croix, or Dochet, Island in the St. Croix below Calais, Champlain and the sieur de Monts planted a settlement in 1604. Calais was permanently settled in 1779. A port of entry, the city makes wood products and cotton goods and processes food.

calamander wood: see EBONY.

Calamis (kă′lùmĭs), 5th cent. B.C., Greek sculptor at Athens in the period of transition from archaic sculpture to that of Phidias.

Calamity Jane, c.1852–1903, American frontier character, b. Princeton, Mo. Her maiden name was Martha Jane Canary, and the origin of her nickname is obscure. Little is known of her early life beyond the fact that she moved with her parents to Virginia City, Mont., in 1865 and that she grew up in mining camps and rough frontier communities. In 1876 she appeared in Deadwood, S.Dak., dressed in men's clothes and boasting of her marksmanship and her exploits as a pony-express rider and as a scout with Custer's forces. In her later years she toured the West in a burlesque show and appeared at the Pan-American Exposition in Buffalo, N.Y. She died in poverty and obscurity in Deadwood, where she is buried beside Wild Bill Hickock. See biographies by Duncan Aikman (1927) and Mrs. Glenn Clairmonte (1959); R. J. Casey, *The Black Hills and Their Incredible Characters* (1949).

calamus: see ARUM.

Calamy, Edmund (kă′lùmē), 1600–1666, English Presbyterian preacher. For 10 years he was lec-

turer at Bury St. Edmunds until in 1636 his opposition to the observance of certain church ceremonies forced him to withdraw and so identify himself with the Puritan party. He was pastor (1639–62) of the Church of St. Mary Aldermanbury, London. A leader among the Presbyterians, Calamy was a member of the Westminster Assembly (1643). He was one of the five authors of the composite work *Smectymnuus*, directed against Bishop Joseph Hall's apology for a moderate episcopacy. Opposed to the execution of Charles I, Calamy was among those sent to meet Charles II in Holland. At the Restoration, he was made a chaplain to the king, but declined a bishopric. Ejected under the Act of Uniformity (1662), he was imprisoned for a short time for having preached after ejection. A number of his sermons were published. His grandson, **Edmund Calamy,** 1671–1732, nonconformist minister in London, also published many sermons, but he is particularly remembered for his *Account of the Ministers . . . Ejected by the Act for Uniformity* (1702), edited by A. G. Matthews as *Calamy Revised* (1934). His autobiography appeared in 1829.

Calan, Abraham: see CALOVIUS, ABRAHAM.

Calatayud (kä′lätäyōōdh′), town (pop. 18,318), Saragossa prov., NE Spain, in Aragon. It is in a fertile agricultural area and has sugar refineries. Founded (8th cent.) by the Moors and conquered (1120) by Alfonso I of Aragon, it retains a Moorish castle and the collegiate Church of Santo Sepulcro, once the main church of the Knights Templars in Spain. Near Calatayud stood ancient Bilbilis, birthplace of Martial.

Calatrava, Campo de (käläträ′vä, käm′pô dhä), region in Ciudad Real prov., central Spain, in New Castile. It gave its name to the **Knights of Calatrava,** Spain's oldest military order, whose original seat was the fortress of Calatrava la Vieja, now in ruins. Founded in 1158 by the Cistercians as a defense against the Moors, the order was very powerful, holding large possessions until the 13th cent.; later it declined. In 1499, the title of grand master passed to the Castilian and thence to the Spanish crown.

calcareous rock: see LIMESTONE and MARBLE.

calcareous soils, formed largely by the weathering of calcareous rocks and fossil shell beds. They usually contain chalk, marl, and limestone and frequently a large amount of phosphates. They are often very fertile, as in the case of the buckshot soils of the South. Sometimes they are flinty, thin, and dry. They often form a large part of the soil of deserts, which may prove very fertile when sufficient moisture for crops is applied.

Calcasieu (kăl′kùsōō″), river rising in W central Louisiana and flowing S through Lake Charles (see CHARLES, LAKE) and Calcasieu Lake (20 mi. long) to the Gulf of Mexico. It is partly navigable and connects the port of LAKE CHARLES with the Intracoastal Waterway and the Gulf of Mexico.

calceolaria: see FIGWORT.

Calchas (kăl′kăs), in Greek legend, priest whose prophecies aided the Greeks in the TROJAN WAR. In medieval romances, he is the father of Cressida.

calcination, in metallurgy, process of heating solid material to drive off volatile chemically combined components such as carbon dioxide and water. It is sometimes a step in the extraction of metal from ores. Calcination is distinguished from drying, in which mechanically held water is driven off by heating, and roasting, in which the material is heated in the presence of air. Originally calcination meant the method of obtaining lime from limestone by heating it and driving off carbon dioxide.

calcite (kăl′sīt), very widely distributed mineral, commonly white or colorless, but appearing in a great variety of colors owing to impurities. Chemically it is calcium carbonate, but it frequently contains manganese, iron, or magnesium in place of the calcium. It crystallizes in the hexagonal system, its crystals being characterized by highly perfect cleavage. Calcite also occurs in a number of massive forms, in which it may be coarsely to finely granular (as in marble), compact (as in limestone), powdery (as in chalk), or fibrous. One crystalline form, called dogtooth spar because of its dogtooth appearance, exhibits faces of perfect scalene triangles. Another form, satin spar, is finely fibrous and has a satin luster. ICELAND SPAR is nearly pure calcite. Other important forms of the mineral are LIMESTONE, MARBLE, CHALK, MARL, STALACTITE AND STALAGMITE formations, TRAVERTINE, and Oriental ALABASTER. Among the places where calcite is mined are New York and Missouri in the United States; Gunajuato, Mexico; Iceland; Andreasburg, Germany; and the counties of Cumberland, Derbyshire, Devonshire, Durham, and Lancashire in England.

calcium (kăl′sē·ŭm) [from Latin, =lime], silvery-white, relatively soft metallic element (symbol= Ca; for physical constants, see ELEMENT, table). In chemical activity it resembles strontium and barium and is classed with these two as a metal of the ALKALINE EARTHS. Calcium is an active element. It tarnishes rapidly when exposed to air and burns with a bright flame when heated. It reacts directly with water, forming the hydroxide. It combines with several elements, e.g., with oxygen, carbon, hydrogen, chlorine, fluorine, arsenic, phosphorus, and sulphur, forming numerous compounds. Although calcium metal is of little commercial importance, calcium compounds are widely and diversely used. The element is a constituent in LIME, bleaching powder or CHLORIDE OF LIME, MORTAR, plaster, CEMENT, CONCRETE, WHITING, putty, precipitated CHALK, GYPSUM, and plaster of Paris. Calcium carbide, a compound of the element and carbon, is used to prepare ACETYLENE and also calcium cyanamide, which is employed as a fertilizer. The phosphate (composed of calcium, phosphorus, and oxygen) is a major constituent of bone ash. The arsenate (composed of calcium, arsenic, and oxygen) and the cyanide (composed of calcium, carbon, and nitrogen) are used as insecticides. Calcium does not occur by itself in nature, but is found in its widely distributed compounds, e.g., ICELAND SPAR, MARBLE, LIMESTONE, FELDSPAR, APATITE, CALCITE, DOLOMITE, FLUORITE, GARNET, and LABRADORITE. It is a constituent of most plant and animal matter. Calcium is essential to the formation and maintenance of strong bones and teeth. In the human adult the bone calcium is chiefly in the form of the carbonate and phosphate salts. A sufficient store of vitamin D in the body is necessary to the proper utilization of the calcium. Calcium also functions in the regulation of the

heart beat and in the conversion of prothrombin to thrombin, a necessary step in the clotting of blood. As the bicarbonate it is a cause of temporary hardness in water; and as the sulphate, of permanent hardness. Calcium metal is usually prepared by the electrolysis of the fused chloride. Sir Humphry Davy is credited with its discovery in 1808. Calcium compounds, in general, when held in the Bunsen burner flame, show an orange or yellow-red color. Calcium is in group II A of the PERIODIC TABLE.

Calcol (kăl′kŏl), Judahite. 1 Chron. 2.6. Chalcol: 1 Kings 4.31.

calculating machine, mechanical device for performing computation. Calculating machines today include the adding machine, the calculator (used mostly for multiplication and division), and the electronic COMPUTER (applied in complex mathematical problems). Early devices used by man to aid in calculation include the ABACUS (still common in the Orient), and the counting rods, or "bones," of John NAPIER. Much used for occasional approximate calculations is the SLIDE RULE. Blaise PASCAL in 1642 devised what was probably the first simple adding machine using geared wheels. An improved mechanism for performing multiplication by the process of repeated addition was invented (c.1672) by G. W. von LEIBNIZ. The principle of this mechanism, sometimes known as the stepped drum or stepped wheel, is still used in some machines, although it has been modified to reduce its bulk. The stepped drum is a cylinder with nine teeth parallel to the long axis; the length of the teeth is graduated in proportion to the numbers 1 through 9. By means of a cogwheel arrangement the required number of teeth on the drum are engaged, and when the adding wheel is transferred and rotated appropriately each number is added to the one before it. A machine using the Leibniz mechanism was the first to be produced successfully on a commercial scale. Devised (1820) by Charles Xavier Thomas of France, it could be used for adding, subtracting, multiplying, and

Burroughs' adding machine (1888).

dividing. A mechanism permitting construction of a more compact machine than the stepped drum was incorporated in a machine invented (late 19th cent.) by F. S. Baldwin in the United States. Later the machine was redesigned by Baldwin and W. J. R. Monroe. W. T. Odhner of Russia constructed a machine using the same device as Baldwin's at about the same time. Commonly used in modern machines of the barrel, or cylinder, type, Baldwin's device consists of a wheel with nine retractable pins or teeth. In the cover plate of the barrel are nine curved slots, each numbered 1 to 9. The end of a setting lever projects from the wheel through each curved slot. The lever, set at the desired number, causes a corresponding number of teeth to project from the wheel within the machine, and a series of gear actions results in the turning of a number wheel through the required rotations. Some adding machines have, instead of the setting levers, a keyboard with nine rows of keys in each column numbered 1 to 9. In the simplified forms there are 10 keys numbered 0 to 9. There are adding machines that also perform multiplication, division, and subtraction. Some machines are operated by hand levers and others by electric motors. Machines that perform the calculation and record the items and the result on paper are constructed around a so-called key-set mechanism; after the keys are pressed, a second motion—operating a handle or setting the motor in operation—causes the numbers to be printed. Those that perform the calculation without recording it on paper have a key-driven mechanism that requires only the one motion of pressing the keys. Apertures are provided for reading the results. The first key-driven machine was patented in the United States in 1850, and in 1887 D. E. Felt patented a key-driven calculator. In 1888 W. S. Burroughs was granted a patent on a key-set adding machine with a crank. In recent years great advances have been made in the development of machines for performing long and highly complex calculations. Forerunner of these was one designed by Charles BABBAGE in the 1830s. Although he worked on it for years he was unable to complete it because materials and skills essential for its construction were not developed until the 20th cent. A mechanically operated differential analyzer was designed by Vannevar BUSH, who completed it in 1930; an improved design, produced in 1942, could be operated either mechanically or electrically. A machine known as the Complex Computer and based on the principle of the telephone switchboard was perfected in 1940, laying the groundwork for the development of electronic computers. Also among the early complex machines were the Automatic Sequence-Controlled Calculator (1944); the Electronic Numerical Integrator and Calculator (1946), the first to use electronic tubes for calculating; and the Selective Sequence Electronic Calculator (1947). See J. P. Meehan and Gilbert Kahn, *How to Use Adding Machines* (1962); G. R. Brookspear, *The Fundamental Operations of Calculating and Adding Machines* (1962).

calculus: see MATHEMATICS.

calculus or **stone,** in medicine, accumulation of mineral salts deposited in various parts of the body in the form of hard concretions. Common sites for such stony deposits are the gall bladder, kidney, urinary bladder, joints, and salivary ducts. Gallstones are composed of varying amounts of calcium salts, bile pigments, and cholesterin; they vary in size and number. Stones forming in the GALL BLADDER may cause inflammation of the bladder wall, infection, increased secretion of bile, and obstruction of the duct. Blockage of the bile duct may result in acute attacks of COLIC and JAUNDICE, in addition to indigestion. Small stones may pass through the bile ducts into the digestive tract; surgery is indicated, however, in the case of larger concretions. Accumulations of small stones (gravel) in the kidney may cause extreme pain when passing through the ureter. Vesical (urinary bladder) calculi may form as a result of urinary retention and infection. Dental calculus (tartar) is usually deposited around the necks of the teeth; pulp stones are often found in the pulp chambers of the teeth.

Calcutta (kălkŭ′tǔ), city (pop. 2,926,498), capital of West Bengal state, E India, on the Hooghly river 86 mi. from the Bay of Bengal. It is the chief port of E India and its major industrial center; jute is milled, and textiles, chemicals, paper, and metal products are manufactured. Calcutta was founded (1690) by the British East India Company, and from 1833 to 1912 it was the capital of India. In 1756 the nawab of Bengal, Siraj-ud-daula, captured Calcutta and killed most of the garrison by imprisoning it overnight in a small, stifling room, the notorious "black hole." Robert Clive retook the city in 1757. It has the Univ. of Calcutta (founded 1857), several unaffiliated colleges, and the Indian Museum, which has one of the world's outstanding natural history collections. The Maidan, a large river-front park surrounded by government buildings, is the most attractive section. A gigantic 170-year-old banyan tree with foliage extending some 300 ft. in diameter is in the botanical gardens.

Calcutta, uninc. town (pop. 2,221), E Ohio, S of Youngstown.

Caldecott, Randolph (kôl′dŭkǔt), 1846–86, English artist and illustrator. He is famous for his drawings of contemporary English country life and for his charming and humorous illustrations, including those for Washington Irving's *Old Christmas* and *Bracebridge Hall* and Blackburn's *Breton Folk.* Perhaps his best are the colored illustrations for a series of 16 children's picture books, including *The House that Jack Built* and *The Grand Panjandrum Himself.*

Calder, Alexander (kôl′dŭr), 1898–, American sculptor, b. Philadelphia; son of a prominent sculptor, Alexander Stirling Calder. Trained as a mechanical engineer, Calder turned to painting and studied (1923–26) at the Art Students League. In 1930 he went to Paris and was influenced by the art of Mondrian and Miró. In 1932 he exhibited his first brightly colored constellations, "mobiles," painted cut-out shapes connected by wires and set in motion by wind currents. His buoyant inventions, "mobiles" and "stabiles," have become world famous. Calder is also noted for his book illustrations and stage sets. He has studios in Roxbury, Conn., and in Paris. See study by J. J. Sweeney (1951).

Calderón Bridge (kälđärōn′), site of a decisive battle

Jain temple in Calcutta.

The 170-year-old banyan tree in Calcutta's botanical garden.

in the Mexican revolution against Spain, fought on the Lerma river E of Guadalajara, Jalisco, Mexico. On Jan. 17, 1811, insurgents commanded by HIDALGO Y COSTILLA met the royalists under CALLEJA DEL REY. On the point of victory, Hildalgo's men were panicked by the explosion of an ammunition wagon. Their flight led to the collapse of the independence movement under Hidalgo.

Calderón de la Barca, Pedro (pā'dhrō käldärōn' dä lä bär'kä), 1600–1681, Spanish dramatist, last important figure of the Golden Age, b. Madrid. Educated at a Jesuit school and the Univ. of Salamanca, he turned from theology to poetry and was a court poet from 1622. His plays were carefully contrived, subtle, and rhetorical. The earlier plays, of the cloak-and-sword school, include *La dama duende* [the lady fairy] and *Casa con dos puertas mala es de guardar* [the house with two doors is hard to guard]. His finest work is in the *autos sacramentales* (one-act religious plays), among them *El divino Orfeo* and *A Dios por razón de estado* [to God for reasons of state]. Of his philosophical dramas the best known are *El mágico prodigioso* [the wonderful magician]; *El alcalde de Zalamea; La vida es sueño* [life is a dream], one of the masterpieces of the Spanish theater; and *El gran teatro del mundo*. Calderón took holy orders in 1651 and thereafter wrote few plays except the *autos*, of which he supplied two a year for the Corpus Christi festival. See studies by E. J. Hasell (1912) and A. E. Sloman (1958); Salvador Madariaga, *Shelley and Calderón* (1935).

Caldwell, Erskine (kôld'wŭl), 1903–, American author, b. White Oak, Ga. His realistic novels of the rural South include *Tobacco Road* (1932; a dramatized version ran for over seven years on Broadway), *God's Little Acre* (1933), *Tragic Ground* (1944), and *This Very Earth* (1948). His short stories, collected in such volumes as *Jackpot* (1940), are flavored with the same earthy situations and pungent characterizations as his novels.

Caldwell. 1 City (pop. 12,230), co. seat of Canyon co., SW Idaho, on the Boise river and W of Boise; founded 1883, inc. 1890. On the site of an Oregon Trail camping ground, the city is now a processing and shipping point for a farm, dairy, and livestock area in the Boise project. It has an agricultural experiment station. The College of Idaho (Presbyterian; coeducational; 1891) is here. **2** City (pop. 1,788), S central Kansas, SSW of Wichita near the Okla. line, in a farm and grazing area and near oil fields; laid out 1871, inc. 1879. An important point on the old Chisholm Trail, it boomed in the 1880s. **3** Borough (pop. 6,942), NE N.J., NW of Montclair; settled before 1785, inc. 1892. Aviation equipment is made. The Presbyterian parsonage in which Grover Cleveland was born is now a museum. **4** Village (pop. 1,999), co. seat of Noble co., SE Ohio, on Duck Creek and S of Cambridge; inc. 1870. It is in a coal-mining and farming area. **5**

Pedro Calderón de la Barca

City (pop. 2,204), co. seat of Burleson co., E central Texas, ENE of Austin, in a farm area.

Caleb (kā′lĕb) [Heb.,=dog], principal spy sent into Canaan, noted for his faithfulness to God. Num. 13.6; 14; 32.12; Joshua 14.6–14. The name is mentioned elsewhere, apparently in connection with a clan inhabiting S Palestine. 1 Sam. 30.14; 1 Chron. 2.18,19,42,46,48,49. Chelubai: 1 Chron. 2.9. The name **Caleb-ephratah** (–ĕf′rŭtŭ) at 1 Chron. 2.24 is a textual error.

Caledonia (kă″lĭdō′nĕu), Roman name for that part of the island of Great Britain which lies N of the Firths of Clyde and Forth. The name occurs in the works of Lucan (1st cent. A.D.) and is still used rhetorically, usually to mean all of Scotland.

Caledonia. 1 Village (pop. 2,563), co. seat of Houston co., extreme SE Minn., near the Iowa-Wis. line, SW of La Crosse; settled c.1855. It is a trade and manufacturing center in a farm area. A state park is nearby. **2** Village (pop. 1,917), W central N.Y., SW of Rochester, in a farm and dairy region; inc. 1891. Boilers and heating equipment are made.

Caledonian Canal, Scottish waterway 60 mi. long, cutting through Inverness-shire from Moray Firth to Loch Linnhe and following the Great Glen. Built 1803–47 to save ships the circuitous route around the Pentland Firth, it is little used today. Of the waterway, 38 mi. consist of the natural waters of Lochs Ness, Oich and Lochy. The canal has 29 locks.

Calef, Robert (kā′lŭf), 1648–1719, author of *More Wonders of the Invisible World* (1700). A Boston cloth merchant, probably born in England, he bitterly attacked Cotton MATHER for his part in the witchcraft delusion. The book, published in London because no Boston printer would accept it, generally condemned the view of witchcraft then prevailing and had a salutary effect throughout New England. It is reprinted in G. L. Burr, ed., *Narratives of the Witchcraft Cases, 1648–1706* (1914).

calendar [Latin, from Kalends], system of reckoning time for the practical purpose of designating days in order to record past events and to calculate dates for future plans. The calendar is based on noting ordinary and easily observable natural events, the cycle of the sun through the seasons with equinox and solstice, and the recurrent phases of the moon. The earth completes its orbit about the sun in 365 days 5 hr. 48 min. 46 sec.—the length of the solar year. The moon passes through its phases in about 29½ days; therefore, 12 lunar months (called a lunar year) amount to more than 354 days 8 hr. 48 min. The discrepancy between the years is inescapable, and one of the major problems for man since his early days has been to reconcile and harmonize solar and lunar reckonings. Some peoples have simply recorded time by the lunar cycle, but, as skill in calculation developed, the prevailing calculations generally came to depend upon a combination. The fact that months and years cannot be divided exactly by days and that the years cannot be easily divided into months has led to the device of intercalation. The simplest form of this is shown in ancient calendars which have series of months alternating between 30 and 29 days, thus arriving at two mean months of 29½ days each. Similarly four years of about 365¼

days each can be approximated by taking three years of 365 days and a fourth year of 366. This fourth year with its intercalary day is the leap year. If calculations are by the lunar cycle, the surplus of the solar over the lunar year (365 over 354) can be somewhat rectified in three years by adding an extra (intercalary) month of 33 days. Reckoning of day and year is considered necessary by practical peoples to determine sacred days, to arrange plans for the future, and to keep some intelligible record of the past. There were, therefore, various efforts to reconcile the count in solar, lunar, and semilunar calendars, from the Egyptians and the Greeks to the Chinese and the MAYA. The problem was fundamental. So for chroniclers was the establishment of a fixed point in time for calculating years in an ERA.

The Roman Calendar. The prevailing modern method of constructing a calendar in the Christian West came originally from the Egyptians, who worked out a formula for the solar year (12 months of 30 days each, five extra days a year, and an extra day every four years). This was to be later adopted by the Romans. In its most primitive form the Roman calendar had no such refinement. It apparently had 10 months, which were (to use corresponding English terms whenever possible): March (31 days), April (29 days), May (31 days), June (29 days), Quintilis (31 days), Sextilis (29 days), September (29 days), October (31 days), November (29 days), and December (29 days). To fill out the 365 days a number of blank days or occasional intercalary months were used. Later, January (29 days) and February (28 days) were added at the end of the year. In the time of the early republic the so-called year of Numa was added. The Romans thus arrived at a cycle of four years: the first year had four months of 31 days, seven of 29, and one, February, of 28; the second year had a February of 23 days and an intercalary month of 27 days; the third year was like the first; the fourth year had a February of 24 days and an intercalary month. The chief trouble with this system was that in a four-year cycle there were four days too many. What was worse, the pontifex maximus was given the power soon after 200 B.C. to regulate the calendar (which for ordinary civil purposes was expressed in terms of the consulates of whatever men held it). The practice grew up of using the intercalations for the promotion of political ends to lengthen or to shorten an official's term. When Julius Caesar was pontifex maximus, the calendar had been so much abused that January was falling in autumn.

The Julian Calendar. At this point the methods of the Egyptian calendar were borrowed for the Roman. Julius Caesar by the advice of the astronomer Sosigenes added 90 days to year 46 B.C. (67 between November and December, 23 at the end of February). This caused the spring of 45 B.C. to begin in March. To retain this position of the seasons, he changed the length of most of the months: March, May, Quintilis (subsequently named August to honor Augustus), and October he left as they were; he added 2 days each to January and Sextilis (subsequently named July after Julius Caesar himself); February was 28 days long except that in every fourth year a day was inserted between the 23d and the 24th of the month. In Roman computation three days in the month were used for counting the date. These three were the Kalends (first day of the month), the Nones (the seventh day in March, May, July, and October, the fifth in the other months), and the Ides (the fifteenth day in March, May, July, and October, the thirteenth in the other months). The days were counted before, not after, the Kalends, Nones, and Ides. Thus, Jan. 10 was the fourth day before the Ides of January or the fourth day of the Ides of January, because the Romans counted inclusively. Jan. 25 was the eighth of the Kalends of February, Feb. 3 was the third of the Nones of February. Feb. 23 was the seventh of the Kalends of March and remained so when an intercalary day was inserted every fourth year between it and Feb. 24; hence in leap year there were two days counted as the sixth of the Kalends of March. The leap year was therefore called bissextile [Latin,=sixth twice]. There is a legend that alterations in the length of the months were made later by Augustus to flatter his own vanity, but there seems to be no foundation for this story.

The Gregorian Calendar. The Julian year is 365 days 6 hr., hence a little too long. Therefore, by the 16th cent. the accumulation of surplus time had displaced the vernal equinox to March 11 from March 21, the date set in the 4th cent. In 1582 Pope Gregory XIII rectified this error. He suppressed 10 days in the year 1582 and ordained that thereafter the years ending in hundreds should not be leap years unless they are divisible by 400. The year 1600 was a leap year under both systems, but 1700, 1800, and 1900 were leap years only in the unreformed calendar. The reform was accepted, immediately in most Roman Catholic countries, more gradually in Protestant countries, and in the Eastern Church the Julian calendar was retained until the 20th cent. The present generally accepted calendar is therefore called Gregorian, though it is only a slight modification of the Julian.

Old Style and New Style. The reform was not accepted in England and the British colonies in America until 1752. By that date the English calendar was 11 days different from that of the Continent. For the period before the reform was introduced, the Gregorian style is called the New Style (N.S.), and the Julian the Old Style (O.S.). New Style years begin Jan. 1, but Old Style years began usually March 25. Thus Washington's birthday, which is Feb. 22, 1732 (N.S.) was Feb. 11, 1731 (O.S.). Frequently to avoid confusion both styles are given; thus 1731/32 or 1731/2 or 11 Feb. 1731/22 Feb. 1732.

The Christian Ecclesiastical Calendar. The Church calendar with its movable feasts shows an interesting example of a harmony of several different systems. The key to it is the reconciliation of the seven-day week with the Roman calendar (see WEEK). The resurrection of Jesus has always been traditionally reckoned as having taken place on a Sunday (first day of the week); hence the annual feast celebrating the event, EASTER, should fall on a Sunday. The Bible places the Passion with relation to the Passover. Since the Jewish Passover is on the evening of the 14th (eve of the 15th) Nisan

(see below), it may fall on any day of the week, hence Easter must fall on a Sunday near the 14th Nisan. Anciently some Eastern Christians celebrated Easter on the 14th Nisan itself; these were called *Quartodecimans* [Latin,=fourteenth]. In 325 the First Council of Nicaea determined that Easter should fall on the Sunday following the full moon next after the vernal equinox, the full moon being theoretically the 14th day, and Nisan beginning with a new moon in March. The vernal equinox was considered by the Church to fall on March 21. The paschal, or Easter, moon is the moon the 14th day of which falls next after (not on) March 21. Today Easter is calculated mathematically according to a system not taking all factors of the lunar period into consideration, hence it nearly always varies somewhat from what it should be according to true astronomical calculation. Several different systems have been used for determining Easter; today some Eastern Churches use a different one from that of the West. In the 6th and 7th cent. in England, there was a great dispute between Christians who derived their rite from the Celts and Christians who had been converted as a result of the mission of St. Augustine. The dispute over Easter arose because the Celts retained a computation for Easter based on a lunar cycle of 84 years, while the Romans had, in the 5th cent., given up the 84-year cycle for a 532-year cycle. The dispute was settled at the Synod of Whitby in favor of the Roman system, which prevailed from that time over the entire West. For a conventional means of computing Easter, see the Book of Common Prayer.

The Jewish Calendar. The Jewish calendar is today a lunisolar or semilunar calendar, i.e., an adjustment of a lunar calendar to the solar year. The months are Tishri (30), Marheshvan (29 or 30), Kislev (29 or 30), Tebet (29), Sebat or Shebat (30), Adar (29), Nisan (30), Iyar (29), Sivan (30), Tammuz (29), Ab (30), and Elul (29). The intercalary month of 30 days is added after Adar, Nisan being anciently the first month, and the intercalation is arranged to take place seven times in 19 years. The common year is referred to as a defective, regular, or perfect year, depending upon whether its length is 353, 354, or 355 days; the leap year may have 383 (defective), 384 (regular), or 385 (perfect) days. The Jewish civil year begins about the autumnal equinox, with the festival of Rosh ha-Shanah (the first of Tishri), which in 1962 fell on Sept. 29–30, marking the start of the Jewish year 5723.

The Moslem Calendar. The Moslem calendar is the only widely used purely lunar calendar, its year varying from 354 to 355 days. Hence the seasons and months have no connection, and there are about 33 Moslem years to every 32 Gregorian years. The months are Muharram (30), Safar (29), 1st Rabia (30), 2d Rabia (29), 1st Jumada (30), 2d Jumada (29), Rajab (30), Shaban (29), Ramadan (the fast, 30), Shawwal (29), Dhu-l-Kada (30), and Dhu-l-Hijja (month of the pilgrimage, 29 or 30).

Other Calendars. The old Chinese Calendar was devised to have six 60-day cycles, each cycle having 10-day periods and three such periods going to make up a month. By the 5th cent. B.C. the solar year was calculated at 365.2444 solar days and the solar month at 29.53059 days. The difference between solar time and the cycles was adjusted by intercalary months and shorter intercalary periods. The years were arranged in major cycles of 60 years with minor cycles of 5 years each. An interesting calendar is that of the MAYA, who used a year of 365 days divided into 18 20-day periods, with a 5-day period at the end. A recurrent series of 20 days was used also, like our week. A remarkable feature was that the year was never readjusted to the error in its length; instead, the feasts and dates were adjusted to the calendar. The Aztec calendar was very similar. Many attempts have been made to devise new calendars, adjusting the months more regularly to the solar year, discarding the week, making the months equal in length, and the like, but they have never been widely adopted. The most celebrated is the FRENCH REVOLUTIONARY CALENDAR. In the 20th cent. the movement toward calendar reform has been strong, the aim being not to abandon but to refine the intercalary system of the Julian-Gregorian calendar. For the method of computing years from a fixed point (e.g., the birth of Christ and the hegira), see ERA. The adoption of such era systems has made computation of time much easier. The Athenian system of identifying years by archons, the Roman system of identifying them by consuls, and the system used both earlier and later of reckoning by the year of the reign of certain kings offers enormous difficulties, and the establishment of chronology is one of the major problems in ancient and medieval history. The classic work on chronology is that of the Benedictines, first published in 1750, *L'Art de vérifier les dates des faits historiques.* See M. P. Nilsson, *Primitive Time Reckoning* (Eng. tr., 1920); R. L. Poole, *Studies in Chronology and History* (1934); P. W. Wilson, *The Romance of the Calendar* (1937).

calendering, a finishing process by which paper, rubber, or textiles are smoothed, glazed, polished, or given a *moiré* or embossed surface. The material is passed through a series of cylinders, usually of metal or of compressed paper or cotton. The resulting surface depends on the pressure exerted by the cylinders, their temperature, composition, and surface designs and the type of coating or glaze previously applied to the material to be calendered.

calendula (kŭlĕn'dūlů), any species of the genus *Calendula,* Old World plants of the COMPOSITE family. The common calendula (*C. officinalis*), an annual with yellow to deep orange flower heads produced through a long blooming season, was a popular garden flower in Shakespeare's time—his "marigold." Its dried florets have been used as a food coloring and for flavoring stews and soups (whence the name pot marigold) and have also long been used medicinally.

Calera (kůlĕr'ů), town (pop. 1,928), central Ala., S of Birmingham; settled in the mid-19th cent. There are lime kilns here which were worked by the early Spaniards.

Calexico (kůlĕk'sĭkō), city (pop. 7,992), S Calif., at the Mexican border, SSE of El Centro; founded 1900, inc. 1908. It is a port of entry and a trade center in the southern part of the fertile IMPERIAL VALLEY.

calf, golden, idol erected by the Israelites on several occasions. Aaron made one while Moses was on Mt. Sinai. Ex. 32. Jeroboam placed one at Bethel and another at Dan. 1 Kings 12.26–32. Hosea denounced one in Samaria. Hosea 8.5,6. A bull cult was widespread in Canaan at the time of the invasion of the Israelites. The use of such a cult recalls Apis in Egypt and the Minotaur in Crete.

Calgary (kăl'gŭrē), city (pop. 249,641), S Alta., Canada, on the Bow river and near the foothills of the Rocky Mts. A wholesale and processing center for a wide agricultural and stock-raising area, Calgary is also the headquarters of many oil firms. The city began (1875) as a fort of the Northwest Mounted Police.

Calhoun, John Caldwell (kăl″hōōn′), 1782–1850, American statesman and political philosopher, b. near Abbeville, S.C., grad. Yale, 1804. He studied

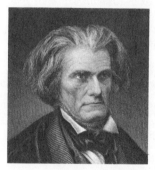

John Caldwell Calhoun

law under Tapping Reeve at Litchfield, Conn., and began (1808) his public career in the South Carolina legislature. Frontier born, he acquired a large plantation by marrying (1811) his cousin, Floride Calhoun. Later he came to represent the interests of the Southern planter aristocracy. A Congressman (1811–17) and acting chairman of the House Committee on Foreign Affairs, Calhoun was one of the leading "war hawks," who whipped up enthusiasm for the War of 1812. He remained a nationalist for some time after the war, speaking for a strong army and navy, for encouragement of manufacturing, for internal improvements, and for a national bank; many of these causes he later opposed. Calhoun was an efficient Secretary of War (1817–25) under President James Monroe and was Vice President (1825–29) under John Quincy Adams. Throughout Adams's administration he opposed the President and aligned himself with the supporters of Andrew JACKSON. An able constitutional lawyer, he made an imposing figure skillfully presiding over the Senate. When the Jacksonians finally triumphed in 1828, Calhoun was again elected Vice President, and it was widely assumed that he would succeed Jackson in office. But relations between the two men soon cooled. Calhoun, largely prodded by his wife, and his supporters offended the President in the Eaton affair (see O'NEILL, MARGARET). Jackson finally became furious when he discovered that years before Calhoun had privately denounced Jackson's conduct in Florida while publicly giving the impression that he had supported the general. Primarily, however, Jackson and Calhoun had come to disagree on the nature of the Union. As the preeminent spokesman for the South, Calhoun tried to reconcile the preservation of the Union with the fact that under the Union the South's dominant agricultural economy was being neglected and even injured at the expense of the ever-increasing commercial and industrial power of the North. When a still higher tariff replaced (1832) the Tariff of Abominations of 1828, Calhoun maintained that the Constitution, rightly interpreted, gave a state the power to nullify Federal legislation inimical to its interests. He returned to South Carolina, had a state convention called, and directed the passage of the famous ordinance of NULLIFICATION. In Dec., 1832, he quit the vice presidency after being elected to the Senate and there eloquently defended his STATES' RIGHTS principles in dramatic debates with Daniel Webster. The firmness of Andrew Jackson and the compromise tariff proposed by Henry CLAY resolved the nullification crisis in 1833, but the larger issue of states' rights persisted, leading ultimately to SECESSION and the Civil War. Meanwhile, Martin VAN BUREN, Calhoun's bitter political enemy, held the vice presidency in Jackson's second term and went on to succeed Jackson in the office Calhoun had long coveted. As the abolitionists grew stronger in the North, Calhoun became an outspoken apologist for slavery and bent every effort to maintain the delicate balance between North and South in the Senate by opposing the prohibition of slavery in newly admitted states. Thus serving briefly (1844–45) as Secretary of State under John Tyler, he completed negotiations for the admission of Texas as a slave state, but later tried to avert war with Mexico. Again (1845–50) in the Senate, he advocated compromise in the Oregon boundary dispute but opposed the admission of California as a free state in the debates over the COMPROMISE OF 1850. In rejecting the Wilmot Proviso, Calhoun set forth the theory that all territories were held in common by the states and that the Federal government merely served as a trustee of the lands. His *Disquisition on Government* and *Discourse on the Constitution and Government of the United States*, both published posthumously, crystallized his political philosophy. The Constitution, he stated, established a government of concurrent majorities composed of two elements—the state governments and the Federal government. Hence the states enjoy the power of veto, or nullification, and the right of secession results necessarily from the origin of the Union as a compact among the sovereign parties. His theories attempted to formulate democracy in terms of protection for a minority, specifically, the South, and they were later embodied in the Confederate constitution. Because they are associated with an institution—slavery—offensive to the idealism of most Americans, Calhoun has never been a popular figure in U.S. history. He was, however, the intellectual giant of political life in his day, and although many of his contemporaries found him arrogant and overbearing, he was not lacking in warm, human qualities. Calhoun's plantation, with his house, Fort Hill, is now the campus of Clemson (S.C.) College. See his works (ed. by R. K.

Crallé, 6 vols., 1851–55); his papers (ed. by R. L. Meriwether, Vol. I, 1959); Biographies by C. M. Wiltse (3 vols., 1944–51), M. L. Coit (1950), and G. M. Capers (1960).

Calhoun, city (pop. 3,587), co. seat of Gordon co., NW Ga., NNW of Atlanta, on the Oostanaula river; inc. 1852. It was destroyed by General Sherman in the Civil War. Nearby is a bronze statue of Sequoyah, near the site of New Echota, once the capital of the Cherokee.

Calhoun City, rail and lumber town (pop. 1,714), N central Miss., NW of Columbus; inc. 1905.

Calhoun Falls, textile-mill town (pop. 2,525), W S.C. near the Savannah river and S of Anderson, in a cotton, peach, and grain area; inc. 1908.

Cali (kä'lē), city (pop. c.591,000), W Colombia. Founded by Benalcázar in 1536 in the upper Cauca valley, Cali (alt. 3,291 ft.) has become the commercial center of the entire region. A railroad connects it with Buenaventura; rail lines and highways tie it with the cities of the cordilleras to the northeast and with Quito (Ecuador) to the south. It ships out livestock, minerals, lumber, and farm products. In the revolution against Spain, Cali remained patriotic in sympathy and was of some prominence.

Caliari, Paolo: see VERONESE, PAOLO.

calico. The cotton cloth of India was mentioned by historians before the Christian era and praised by early travelers for its fine texture and beautiful colors. Block-printed cottons from Calicut imported into England c.1630 were called calicuts. The name calico was soon applied to all Oriental cottons having an equal number of warp and weft threads, then to all plain-weave cottons. In the United States the term is now applied specifically to narrow-width, inferior cottons mainly used for house dresses and aprons.

Calicut (kă'lĭkŭt″, –kŭt), city (pop. c.192,485), Kerala state, S India, on the Malabar coast of the Arabian Sea. Once the leading port of S India, it declined in the 19th cent. and now mainly exports pepper, timber, and rubber. Calicut was (1498) Vasco da Gama's first Indian port of call, and soon the city became a center for European traders. The term *calico* was first applied to Calicut cotton cloth, which was then an important manufacture. Calicut passed to British rule in 1792.

California (kălĭfôr'nyủ), state (156,803 sq. mi.; 1960 pop. 15,717,204), W United States, admitted 1850 as the 31st state (a free state). The capital is SACRAMENTO. The largest cities and major seaports are LOS ANGELES, SAN FRANCISCO, OAKLAND, and SAN DIEGO. California is bounded on the north

California
location map

CALIFORNIA

State Seal of California

State Capitol
in Sacramento

State Capitol
in Sacramento

View of Los Angeles with Wilshire
Boulevard; MacArthur Park at right.

properly the area drained by the Sacramento and the San Joaquin rivers, is sometimes used to mean all the intermontane region. In the southeast lie vast wastes, notably the MOJAVE DESERT. Rising as an almost impenetrable granite barrier E of the Central Valley is the SIERRA NEVADA range, within which are Mt. Whitney, SEQUOIA NATIONAL PARK, and YOSEMITE NATIONAL PARK. The CASCADE RANGE, northern continuation of the Sierra Nevada, includes LASSEN VOLCANIC NATIONAL PARK. East of the S Sierra Nevada is DEATH VALLEY NATIONAL MONUMENT. The coastal region, with a dense but relatively backward native population and no immediate lure of gold, did not attract the conquistadors. The first voyage (1542) to Alta California [Upper California], as the region N of Baja California [Lower California] came to be known, was commanded by Juan Rodríguez CABRILLO, who took possession of the territory for Spain; his report of the venture, however, stirred little interest In 1579 an English expedition, headed by Sir Francis DRAKE, claimed the region for Queen Elizabeth I, exposing Spanish vulnerability in the area and inspiring other raiders, both Dutch and English, to follow. The next display of Spanish interest came in 1602, with the voyage of Sebastián VIZCAÍNO. Colonization was slow to materialize, but finally in 1769 Gaspar de PORTOLÁ established a colony on San Diego Bay. In 1776 Juan Bautista de ANZA founded San Francisco. Already Father Junípero SERRA and other Franciscans had established a string of missions; some of these are today historic shrines. The early colonists, called the Californios, lived a fairly easy, pastoral life. They were not much molested by the central government of New Spain or later of Mexico, but they did indulge in strenuous local politics and in quarrels with their governors, such as Juan Bautista ALVARADO. Many of the Indians were

by Oregon, on the east by Nevada and Arizona, from which it is separated by the COLORADO river, on the south by Mexico, and on the west by the Pacific Ocean. Third largest of the states in area, it has diversified topography and climate. Along the 1,200-mile coast extends a series of low mountains known loosely as the Coast Range, a region which from San Francisco south is subject to tremors and sometimes to severe earthquakes caused by the San Andreas fault. Receiving heavy rainfall in the north, where the giant cathedral-like redwood forests prevail, the Coast Range is considerably drier in S California, and S of the Golden Gate no major rivers reach the ocean. Behind the coastal ranges lie the long alluvial valleys of central California; the Central Valley, meaning

Aerial view of San Francisco, with approach and a part of the San Francisco Bay Bridge. The Golden Gate Bridge is in the background, left.

Annual parade of the Buddha Lion in San Francisco's Chinatown (below).

gathered about the missions, but when these were secularized under the Mexican republic (1833–34) the Indians were dispersed and victimized. Their degradation, which culminated after the Americans came, is pictured by Helen Hunt Jackson in her novel *Ramona*. The Californios offered little opposition to the Russians, who penetrated as far south as Fort Ross (1812), or to the first American settlers, who landed on the California coast in 1816. Jedediah S. Smith and other trappers made the first overland trip in 1826, but colonization of California remained largely Mexican until the 1840s. In 1839 the Swiss John Augustus SUTTER arrived and established his "kingdom" of New Helvetia on a vast tract in the Sacramento valley. He did much for the overland American immigrants, who began to arrive in large numbers in 1841. Some of them, like the DONNER PARTY, met with tragedy. Events moved swiftly in the next few years. After having briefly asserted the independence of California in 1836, the Californios drove out (1845) the last Mexican governor. Under the influence of John C. FRÉMONT the Americans set up (1846) a republic at Sonoma under the Bear Flag. The news of war between the United States and Mexico reached California soon afterward. On July 7, 1846, Commodore John D. Sloat captured Monterey, the capital, and claimed California for the United States; in 1847 Stephen W. KEARNY defeated the Californios in the south. By the treaty of Guadalupe Hidalgo (1848) Mexico formally ceded the territory to the United States. In the same year occurred the most significant event in California history—while establishing a sawmill for Sutter near Coloma, James W. MARSHALL discovered gold and touched off the California gold rush. The forty-niners came in droves, spurred by the promise of fabulous riches from the Mother Lode. Soldiers deserted the ranks, crews

abandoned their ships, farmers left their crops unharvested, merchants closed their stores, and city officials vanished. Waves of overland wagons streamed westward. Writers such as Bret Harte and Mark Twain stayed to write of the color, violence, and human tragedies of the roaring mining camps. San Francisco was quickly catapulted into a boom city, and its bawdy, lawless BARBARY COAST caused the rise of the VIGILANTES. The battle for statehood began in 1849, and after heated

Giant redwood tree in Sequoia National Park.

debate California came into the Union by the COMPROMISE OF 1850. In 1853 Congress authorized the survey of a railroad route to link California with the eastern seaboard, but the transcontinental railroad was not completed until 1869. In the meantime communication and transportation depended upon ships, the stage coach, the PONY EXPRESS, and the telegraph. When railroad construction began, Chinese laborers were imported in great numbers. The Burlingame Treaty (1868) provided, among other things, for unrestricted Chinese immigration. This was at first enthusiastically endorsed by Californians, but a slump in the state's shaky economy transformed the influx of large numbers of Chinese laborers into a threat against white settlers. Ensuing bitterness and friction led to the Chinese Exclusion Act of 1882. A railroad-rate war (1884) and a boom in real estate (1885) fostered a new wave of overland immigration. Vineyards had been planted by 1861, and the first trainload of oranges left Los Angeles in 1886. By the turn of the century the development of petroleum, industrialization resulting from the increase of hydroelectric power, and expanding agricultural development attracted more settlers. Health seekers migrated in large numbers to S California. As industrious Japanese farmers acquired valuable land and a virtual monopoly of California's truck-farming operations, the issue of Oriental immigration again arose. The bitter struggle for their exclusion plagued international relations, and in 1913 the California Alien Land Act was passed despite the efforts of President Wilson's administration to stop it. Successive waves of immigration followed. Settlers were attracted by a new real-estate boom in the 1920s and by promise of work in the 1930s, when the aimless wanderings of migratory workers, depicted by John Steinbeck in *The Grapes of Wrath*, caused profound dislocation in the economy. During the Second World War California was host to well over one million warworkers and service personnel, many of whom later settled in the state. The agricultural and industrial economy, the resources, the water supply, and transportation, public utilities, and educational facilities could not be developed at a pace to keep up with the staggering increase of inhabitants. Although today agriculture is second to industry as the basis of the state's

The finest wines in America are produced and aged in California wineries.

Cabrillo National Monument at right, an old Spanish lighthouse in San Diego. Out of use since 1891, it commemorates the discovery of California in 1542 by Juan Rodrígues Cabrillo.

economy, California produces more fruits and vegetables than any other state. It is a leading producer of barley, sugar beets, lemons, walnuts, almonds, apricots, peaches, figs, olives, and grapes; in 1962 the state contributed more than 50 percent of the nation's wine. Most of the produce comes from small farms, but marketing is generally through cooperative associations. The labor of gathering and packing the produce is done to a large extent by the seasonal migrant farm worker (including thousands of Mexicans), and one of California's major social problems is the improvement of his condition. Much of the state's manufacturing depends upon the processing of the farm produce (milling, canning, and packing) and upon such natural resources as mineral deposits, quarries, and forests. In 1960 California's production of mineral fuel rated third in the nation. Since the Second World War heavy industry has increased enormously—notably in the manufacture of metal products, electronic equipment, machinery, aircraft, and missiles. Defense-contract industries, particularly in S California, represent a major bulk of the region's economy. California is the major center for producing motion-picture and television films in the United States. Most acute of the state's problems is the need for, and control of, water supply. The once fertile Owens valley is now arid, its waters tapped by Los Angeles 175 mi. away, and water is piped to the coast across the Mojave Desert from the Colorado river 200 mi. away. In the lush, fruitgrowing IMPERIAL VALLEY irrigation is controlled by the All-American Canal, which also draws from the Colorado. Far to the north in the Central Valley the problem is not one of too little water but of bad distribution—an imbalance being lessened by the vast CENTRAL VALLEY PROJECT. With more than a thousand new settlers pouring in daily, California claimed in 1963 to have the highest population in the nation. Its pleasant climate and natural beauty have attracted great numbers of retired persons, and "senior-citizen" communities, a recent American innovation, have sprung up in the state. Tourism constitutes an important source of income. Disneyland, the magnificent GOLDEN GATE BRIDGE, the towering bristle-cone pine (called the oldest living thing on earth), the giant SEQUOIA, several national parks and forests, and many beautiful beaches are included in California's numerous attractions. Among the more prominent of the institutions of higher learning are the Univ. of California, with seven campuses (see CALIFORNIA, UNIVERSITY OF); Occidental College and the Univ. of Southern California, at Los Angeles (see SOUTHERN CALIFORNIA, UNIVERSITY OF); STANFORD UNIVERSITY, at Stanford; the CALIFORNIA INSTITUTE OF TECHNOLOGY, at Pasadena; MILLS COLLEGE, at Oakland; and the CLAREMONT COLLEGES, at Claremont. See C. E. Chapman, *History of California: the Spanish Period* (1921); R. G. Cleland, *History of California: the American Period* (1922); Federal Writers' Project,

Death Valley from Dante's View, with Telescope Mountain in background, left.

The torrent of water of Yosemite Falls becomes the placidly flowing Merced River.

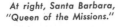

At right, Santa Barbara, "Queen of the Missions."

California: a Guide to the Golden State (1939); J. W. Caughey, *California* (2d ed., 1953); P. F. Griffin and R. N. Young, *California, the New Empire State* (1957); R. G. Cleland, *From Wilderness to Empire* (rev. ed. by G. S. Dumke, 1959); S. T. Harding, *Water in California* (1960).

California. 1 City (pop. 2,788), co. seat of Moniteau co., central Mo., WNW of Jefferson City, in a livestock, dairy, and grain area; founded 1845, inc. 1857. Harnesses, saddles, and pork products are made. **2** Borough (pop. 5,978), SW Pa., S of Pittsburgh; laid out c.1850, inc. 1853. A state teachers college is here.

California, Gulf of, arm of the Pacific, c.700 mi. long and 50 to 100 mi. wide, NW Mexico. It separates the peninsula of Lower California on the west from Sonora and Sinaloa on the east. The Colorado river flows into it at the head of the gulf, and several large rivers empty into it from W Mexico. Because the gulf has the strongest tidal current in the Pacific and unpredictable winds, navigation is risky. Among early adventurers in these waters were Francisco de ULLOA and Hernando de Alarcón. Pearl fishing is important along the shores, and the gulf has some of the finest deep-sea fishing in NE Pacific coastal waters.

California, Lower: see BAJA CALIFORNIA.

California, University of, at seven campuses; land-grant and state supported; coeducational; chartered 1868, opened 1869 when it took over the College of California (est. 1853 at Oakland as Contra Costa Academy). In 1873 it moved to the present Berkeley campus. At Berkeley are the Lawrence Radiation Laboratory, the main library, which houses over 4,000,000 manuscripts and a large number of collections relating to many fields, and an extensive museum system including museums of paleontology, zoology, and anthropology. The Los Angeles campus (est. 1881 as Los Angeles State Normal School, transferred to the university 1919) is known for its theater department. The cancer and brain research institutes are here. At La Jolla is the Scripps Institution of Oceanography (est. 1901, transferred to the university 1912) whose research facilities include eight ships and several laboratories. The San Francisco campus (est. 1864 as Toland Medical College, transferred to the university 1934) is employed exclusively by the medical sciences. Other campuses are at Riverside (est. 1907 as the Citrus Experiment Station), Santa Barbara (est. 1891 as a private school transferred to the university 1944), and Davis (opened 1909). Two additional campuses are being planned in Orange and San Diego counties. The university operates agricultural experiment stations at Berkeley, Davis, and Riverside, and a state-wide extension service.

California Institute of Technology, at Pasadena, Calif.; for men; founded 1891 as Throop Polytechnic Institute; called Throop College of Technology 1913–20. The institute's research facilities include the jet propulsion laboratory (operated in conjuction with the National Aeronautics and Space Administration), the Guggenheim Aeronautical Laboratory, and a cosmic ray laboratory.

California Joe, 1829–76, American frontiersman and scout, whose real name was Moses Embree Milner, b. Stanford, Ky. He went to California in the gold rush, later moving into the Oregon country. He was a sharpshooter during the Civil War, after which he became a scout in the Indian campaigns, serving under George A. Custer and Philip H. Sheridan; both commended him in reports. Custer once appointed him chief of scouts, but California Joe got so drunk within a few hours that he had to be demoted. In 1875 he guided the government expedition led by W. P. Jenny to investigate the mineral resources of the Black Hills. He was shot in a private quarrel. See biography by J. E. Milner and E. R. Forrest (1935).

californium, radioactive metallic element of the ACTINIDE SERIES (symbol=Cf; in group III B of the PERIODIC TABLE; for physical constants see ELEMENT, table). It was first produced (1950) by G. T. SEABORG and co-workers at the Univ. of California by bombarding an isotope of curium with alpha particles. A number of isotopes have been prepared with half lives of 45 min. to 660 years. Although only minute quantities of the element have been obtained, its trichloride, oxychloride, and oxide have been produced.

Caligula (kŭlĭg′yō͞olŭ), A.D. 12–A.D. 41, Roman emperor (A.D. 37–A.D. 41). His real name was Caius Caesar Germanicus, and he was the son of GERMANICUS CAESAR and AGRIPPINA I. When he was a small child with his parents on the Rhine he wore military boots, whence his nickname [*caligula*=little boots]. After the death (A.D. 33) of his brother, Drusus, he and Tiberius' grandson, Tiberius Gemellus, were the heirs apparent. On the death of TIBERIUS the army helped make Caligula emperor. Shortly afterward he became severely ill, and there is a widely accepted belief that he was thereafter insane. He earned a name for ruthless and cruel autocracy, and torture and execution became the order of the day. He was responsible for

Caligula

serious disturbances among the Jews, and he nearly caused a rebellion in Palestine by attempting to erect a statue of himself in their temple. He is reported to have made his horse a consul and a member of a priestly college. His reign ended when a tribune of the Praetorian Guard, Chaerea, assassinated him. CLAUDIUS I succeeded. See J. P. V. D. Balsdon, *The Emperor Gaius* (1934).

Calipatria (kăl'ĭpăt'rêù), city (pop. 2,548), SE Calif., SE of the Salton Sea, in a farm region of the IMPERIAL VALLEY; founded 1914, inc. 1919.

caliphate (kǎ'lĭfăt″, –fĭt), the headship of ISLAM. Islam is, theoretically, a theocracy, and its caliph the vicegerent of God. When Mohammed the Prophet died, a caliph [Arabic,=successor] was chosen to rule in his place. The caliph had temporal and spiritual authority, but he was not permitted prophetic power; this was reserved for Mohammed. The first caliph was ABU BAKR. He was succeeded by OMAR, OTHMAN, and ALI. These are the Orthodox caliphs. After Ali's death there was a division in Islam. MUAWIYA became caliph and founded the OMAYYAD dynasty, chiefly by force of arms. Its capital was Damascus. But the SHIITES continued to recognize the descendants of Ali and in 750 won the caliphate for them, massacring the members of the Omayyad family. These Shiite caliphs were of the ABBASID family. Their caliphate is sometimes called the Caliphate of Baghdad. One Omayyad, ABDU-R-RAHMAN I, escaped the general massacre of his family and fled to Spain; there the emirate of Córdoba was set up in 780. This later became the Caliphate of Córdoba, or the Western Caliphate, and persisted until 1031. A third contemporaneous caliphate was established by the Fatimites (see FATIMITE) in Africa and lasted from 909 to 1171. After the fall of Baghdad to the Mongols under Hulagu Khan in 1258, the Abbasids fled to Egypt. From this date the caliphate was virtually ended, since the Abbasids in Egypt had not the slightest power. The Ottomans captured Egypt in 1517; Selim I assumed the title of caliph (by a very flimsy right). The Ottoman sultans then kept the title until the last, Mohammed VI, was deposed. Briefly, he was succeeded by a cousin, but in 1924 the caliphate was abolished altogether. A year later Hussein ibn Ali, king of Arabia, proclaimed himself caliph, but he was forced to abdicate by Ibn Saud. Since then several pan-Islamic congresses have attempted to establish a rightful caliph. See William Muir, *The Caliphate* (2d ed., 1915); Alfred von Kremer, *Orient under the Caliphs* (Eng. tr., 1920); T. W. Arnold, *The Caliphate* (1924); Mohammed Ali, *Early Caliphate* (1947); S. K. Barhsh, *The Caliphate* (1954); P. K. Hitti, *History of the Arabs* (7th ed., 1960).

calisthenics: see GYMNASTICS.

Calistoga (kălĭstō'gù), city (pop. 1,514), W Calif., at the head of the Napa valley N of San Francisco; inc. as a town 1886, as a city 1937. Grapes, prunes, and walnuts are grown in the vicinity. The city is a health resort with nearby hot mineral springs and geysers. Mt. St. Helena and a petrified redwood forest are also in the area.

Calixtines: see HUSSITES.

Calixtus I, Callixtus I (both: kùlĭk'stùs), or **Callistus I, Saint** (kùlĭ'stùs), c.160–c.222, pope (217–222), a Roman; successor of St. Zephyrinus and predecessor of St. Urban I. As archdeacon to Zephyrinus he established the famous Calixtus Cemetery, where all the popes of the 3d cent. except Calixtus himself are buried. His election to the papacy was opposed by HIPPOLYTUS (later antipope), who accused him of monarchianism and of laxness in disciplining repentant sinners. Calixtus

in fact excommunicated the chief monarchianist, SABELLIUS. His other important action, to grant absolution under conditions of true contrition to certain classes of sinners (apostates, murderers, adulterers), considered by many as unforgivable, was important in the development of the Church's doctrine of penance. Calixtus died in the reign of Alexander Severus and may have been a martyr. Feast: Oct. 14.

Calixtus II, Callixtus II, or **Callistus II,** d. 1124, pope (1119–24), a Burgundian named Guy; successor of Gelasius II and predecessor of Honorius II. He was archbishop of Vienne during the INVESTITURE controversy with Emperor HENRY V. When Gelasius died while in exile in France, Calixtus was consecrated pope at Vienne. He immediately summoned a large council at Rheims (1119) which proceeded to anathematize Henry and the antipope that Henry had installed (1118), Gregory VIII. Public reaction sided with the pope and the antipope was imprisoned. Henry, faced by a Church united against him, submitted. He signed (1122) the famous Concordat (see WORMS, CONCORDAT OF) guaranteeing the freedom of the Church in its elections. Thus was the investiture controversy ended and the reform program of Gregory VII realized. Calixtus then called to Rome (1123) the first great ecumenical council of the West (see LATERAN COUNCIL, FIRST) to ratify the achievements of the Hildebrandine reform.

Calixtus III, Callixtus III, or **Callistus III,** 1378–1458, pope (1455–58), a Spaniard (b. Játiva) named Alonso de Borja (Ital. *Alfonso Borgia*); successor of Nicholas V and predecessor of Pius II. He acted as arbitrator between his friend Alfonso V of Aragon and the papacy, and for this he was made a cardinal (1444). Calixtus was elected soon after the fall of Constantinople, and he promptly proclaimed a crusade against the Turks. He spared nothing to aid John HUNYADI, who won a victory with St. JOHN CAPISTRAN at Belgrade (1456). In 1457 Calixtus turned to SCANDERBEG, in Albania, sent him money, and named him captain general of the crusade. Calixtus' reign was embittered by a quarrel with Alfonso, who expected returns, notably the march of Ancona, for his friendship. The pope would not give away church lands and resented Alfonso's failure to help the crusade. Calixtus' nepotism gave the Borgia family its position in Italy. Calixtus was, like other Borgias, an able administrator.

Calixtus, Georgius (jôr'jêùs), 1586–1656, German theologian, whose original name was Georg Callisen. He extended the influence of MELANCHTHON, advocating syncretism, and sought a basis, such as the Apostles' Creed, for uniting Christian churches. Because he tended to minimize the differences in doctrine and to emphasize the importance of Christian living, he was charged by some of the Lutherans with favoring Roman Catholic dogmas and by others with pro-Calvinism. He failed to win the Lutherans to his support at the Conference of Thorn (1645).

Call, Richard Keith, 1791–1862, territorial governor of Florida (1836–39, 1841–44), b. Prince George co., Va. He moved to Kentucky as a youth and served in the War of 1812. Resigning from the army in 1822, he studied law, began practice in

Pensacola, and in 1823 was sent to Congress as territorial delegate. In his first term as governor Call led the campaign against the SEMINOLE INDIANS, commanding at the battles of Wahoo Swamp in Nov., 1836. A dispute with the War Dept. led to his being superseded in command and to his losing the governorship. He then turned Whig and, aiding greatly in the election of W. H. Harrison, was rewarded by being appointed governor again. Call was a leader in the movement for statehood, but was defeated for the governorship in 1845. See biography by H. J. Doherty (1961).

call. In banking, "call money" is money deposited with a bank or loaned by it and, in either case, returnable when called for. With reference to stocks, call money may be an installment of capital for a new concern whose stock has not yet been fully paid up or may be capital for an established concern to cover part of a new issue of shares. Call money may also be a contribution by the shareholders demanded by the person who is liquidating a concern or an option to buy certain stocks at a certain price at a certain date. In this latter sense a "call" is a contract by which one person promises to buy these stocks, while a "put" is a similar promise to sell. A "straddle" or "spread eagle" is a combined option of both calling and putting. Financial call loans are made for an undefined period and are returnable on the demand of the lender. To secure such loans, collateral is usually required. Most of these loans are made to brokers to enable them to pay for stock which they have bought on margin for customers. Domestic banks use call money for secondary reserves, other banks for the employment of international balances, and corporations for investing surplus cash. Thus to a lender, call money is a way of employing funds temporarily idle, while still having the money available for other uses; to a borrower it is a way of adjusting his indebtedness to the daily fluctuations in his needs for funds. New York is the largest call-money market.

calla or **calla lily:** see ARUM.

Callao (käyou'), city (pop. c.130,000), W Peru, just W of Lima. It is a port and a department (14 sq. mi.). One of the best Pacific anchorages in South America, it became a port when Francisco Pizarro founded Lima. Natural protection is afforded by an island and a small peninsula; modern dock facilities are sheltered by breakwaters. The gateway to Lima, Callao has frequently been attacked from the time of the buccaneers, including Sir Francis Drake, through the revolution against Spain, to later foreign wars. It was severely damaged by earthquake in 1940.

Callas, Maria Meneghini (märē'ä měněgē'nē kä'läs), 1923–, Greek-American soprano, b. New York city. She spent her childhood in America but at the age of 13 moved to Greece, where she studied at the Royal Conservatory in Athens. Returning to America in 1945, she refused roles offered her by the Metropolitan Opera in New York because she considered them unsuitable. She made her professional debut in 1947 at Verona. Refusing to accept secondary roles, she rose slowly to prominence. She sang for the first time at La Scala (Milan) in 1950, at Covent Garden (London) in 1952, and at the Metropolitan Opera in 1956. Her contracts have

Maria Callas

been severed with many leading opera houses due to temperamental and artistic disputes. She is known for her dramatic intensity, her dexterity, and her versatility.

Calleja del Rey, Félix María (fä'lěks märē'ä kälyä'hä děl rā'), 1750–1826, Spanish general, viceroy of New Spain (1813–16), conde de Calderón. In command of the post of San Luis Potosí when the revolution under HIDALGO Y COSTILLA broke out, he led a large force into the field and defeated Hidalgo at Aculco and at Calderón Bridge and besieged MORELOS Y PAVÓN in Cuautla (1812). As viceroy Calleja continued to repress revolution, and by the time he left Mexico most of the insurrectionists were defeated. After his return to Spain he held several high posts.

Calles, Plutarco Elías (plōōtär'kō ālē'äs kä'yäs), 1877–1945, Mexican statesman, president (1924–28). He emerged in 1913 from the obscurity of schoolteaching to fight with Álvaro OBREGÓN and Venustiano CARRANZA against Victoriano Huerta. In 1920 he joined Obregón and Adolfo de la HUERTA in the rebellion against Carranza. After Obregón's term as president, Calles, who had been a cabinet member, became the presidential nominee. Adolfo de la Huerta, claiming election fraud,

Plutarco Elías Calles

revolted (Dec., 1923), but Obregón and Calles established their supremacy by force (1924); Calles became president. His administration was notable for both revolutionary zeal and violent reaction. At the outset agrarian reform was prosecuted vigorously but recklessly. Many rural schools were built although teachers were still scarce and underpaid. Material improvements were given special attention; vast road building and irrigation projects were undertaken. The struggle between Church and state reached a new extreme of bitterness. In 1926 the enforcement of anticlerical legislation provoked violence; in 1926–27 the *cristeros*, terrorists whose slogan was "Viva Cristo Rey" (long live Christ the King), took up arms in the states of Colima, Jalisco, and Michoacán. Military chieftains replied by victimizing innocent Catholics, and government officials used the strife for political advantage. At the same time land and petroleum legislation caused a serious dispute with the United States; relations between the two countries improved when Dwight W. Morrow was appointed (1927) ambassador, and the oil question was temporarily settled. Calles created and directed a powerful national army and dissolved the private militia that threatened internal peace. He unified the government and molded the National Revolutionary party into the dominant force in Mexican politics. However, the Calles of humble origins became a power, a landowner, and a financier; he rapidly lost his radical tinge and moved toward dictatorship. Already in control of the labor movement, he made himself the force behind the Callistas, a circle of financiers and industrialists who dominated the country's economy and politics. Thus he became undisputed political chieftain (Jefe Máximo) of Mexico. When Obregón was assassinated (1928) after his reelection to the presidency, Calles appointed Emilio Portes Gil. In 1930 he declared the agrarian reform program a failure. In the same year he engineered the election of Pascual Ortiz Rubio. Two years later he removed him to appoint Gen. Abelardo Luján Rodríguez. The mighty labor union, C.R.O.M. (see LOMBARDO TOLEDANO, VICENTE), was smashed. The conflict with the Church, temporarily subdued (1929) by Morrow, was resumed; priests were openly persecuted. Communist unions, previously used by Calles in his campaign against the C.R.O.M., were ruthlessly repressed, and a fascist organization, the "Gold Shirts," backed by the Callistas, harassed minority groups. As the new champion of conservatism, Calles openly in 1935, opposed the policies of his former protegé, Lázaro CÁRDENAS but was defeated in the contest and in 1936 was exiled. He was allowed to return under an amnesty in 1941.

Calleva Atrebatum: see SILCHESTER.

Callias (kă'lēŭs), fl. 449 B.C., Athenian statesman; he was related to Cimon and also to Aristides. He distinguished himself at the battle of Marathon and was a three-time winner of the Olympic chariot races. Callias was sent to Susa to negotiate for peace c.449 B.C. The result of his work was an agreement usually called the Peace or Treaty of Callias; by it ARTAXERXES I agreed to respect the independence of the Delian League and its members and to send no warships into Greek waters; in return Athens agreed not to interfere with Persian "influence" in Asia Minor, Cyprus, and Egypt. There is doubt that such a treaty was actually ever drawn up; however, peace did exist between Persia and the cities of Greece until the end of the century. According to ancient historians, when Callias returned to Athens he was fined 50 talents for betraying the city. Callias was also supposed to have been one of the negotiators of a treaty between Athens and Sparta (446–445 B.C.) which resulted in 30 years of peace.

Callias, d. c.370 B.C., Athenian leader, one of the generals of the Peloponnesian War. In his old age Callias was one of the ambassadors sent to Sparta with Callistratus to negotiate a peace treaty in 371 B.C. It was ineffective; friction between EPAMINONDAS of Thebes and AGESILAUS II of Sparta became acute. Callias was a rich man and his wealth was ridiculed by his contemporaries, including Aristophanes. His house is the scene of Xenophon's *Symposium* and Plato's *Protagoras*.

Callicrates (kŭlĭ'krŭtēz), 5th cent. B.C., Greek architect. In association with Ictinus he built (447–432 B.C.) the Parthenon at Athens. At Athens also he designed (c.427) the Temple of Nike.

calligraphy, art of writing. Although inscriptions (see INSCRIPTION) remain from almost all times and nations, only in the East has calligraphy been consistently practiced as a fine art. In China, from the 5th cent. B.C., when it was first used, calligraphy has always been considered the equal or even superior to painting. Chinese calligraphy began with a simplified seal script, known as "chancery script," in which the width of the strokes vary and the edges and ends are sharp. The perfection of the brush in the 1st cent. A.D. made possible the stylization of chancery script into "regular script," distinguished by its straight strokes of varying width and clear, sharp corners, and a cursive "running hand." The Japanese value calligraphy as highly as the Chinese. They began to practice it only in the 7th cent. A.D. with the introduction of Buddhist manuscripts from China. Kukai, c.800, invented the syllabic script which was based on Chinese characters. Not only did the pictographic scripts of the Far East give rise to calligraphy; this art is also practiced with the limited letter alphabet of Arabic. The Moslem faith frowns on pictorial representation and reveres the Koran; therefore the Islamic peoples esteem calligraphy as highly as do those of the Far East. The earliest Islamic calligraphy is found in the beautiful Korans, written with black ink or gold leaf on parchment or paper in formal, angular script. Begun by the 8th cent., this script was fully developed by the 10th. Elaborations, such as foliated, interlaced, and other complexities were invented later, but they are used only for decorative work. Korans continued to be copied in austere and monumental letters. In the 12th cent. rounded cursive style was invented and spread throughout Islam. Many different cursive scripts soon developed. Calligraphy decorates mosques and pottery, metalwork and textiles, as well as books.

Callimachus (kŭlĭm'ŭkŭs), 2d half of 5th cent. B.C., Greek sculptor from Athens. He was famous as the maker of the gold lamp in the Erechtheum and a seated image of Hera for a temple at Plataea. There are several Roman copies of his works; one is *Pan and the Three Graces* (Capitoline Mus., Rome). He reputedly originated the Corinthian capital and invented the running drill used for simulating the folds of drapery in marble.

Callimachus, fl. c.265 B.C., Hellenistic Greek poet and critic, b. Cyrene. He was educated at Athens and taught school at Eleusis, a suburb of Alexandria, before obtaining work in the Alexandrian library. He drew up a catalogue, with such copious notes that it was a full literary history. He also wrote criticism and other works in prose, but is most notable as a poet. His works were extraordinarily numerous; it is said that he wrote more than 800. Of these, six hymns (meant only for reading, with no religious use), a number of epigrams, and fragments of other poems survive. His greatest work was the *Aetia*, a collection of legends strung together. Other longer poems of which fragments survive are *The Lock of Berenice, Hecale,* and *Iambi*. His poetry is notable for polish, wit, learning, and inventiveness in form. His literary quarrel with Apollonius of Rhodes is famous.

Callinus (kŭlī'nŭs), fl. 7th cent. B.C., Greek poet. He is the earliest of known elegiac poets. An excerpt from a patriotic exhortation to his fellow Ephesians is the longest of the few fragments of his poetry that survive.

Calliope: see MUSES and ORPHEUS.

calliope (kŭlī'ŭpē; kă'lēōp; cf. the Muse's name), in music, an instrument sometimes called steam organ or steam piano in which steam is forced through a series of whistles controlled by a keyboard. It is usually played mechanically, and its harsh music is a familiar accompaniment of circus parades.

calliopsis: see COREOPSIS.

Callirrhoë: see ALCMAEON.

Callisthenes (kŭlĭs'thŭnēz), c.360–c.327 B.C., Greek historian of Olynthus; nephew of Aristotle. He accompanied Alexander the Great into Asia as the historian of the expedition. At first he likened Alexander to a god, but later he became one of the principal critics of the Orientalizing manners of the court. He was suspected of complicity in a conspiracy against Alexander and put to death; and this turned the Peripatetics, Aristotle's followers, against Alexander. Callisthenes' histories of contemporary affairs in Greece are lost. His fame rests largely on a work of a much later date that was attributed to him—it was the standard biography of Alexander in medieval times.

Callisto (kŭlĭs'tō), in Greek mythology, an attendant of Artemis. Because she forsook her chastity and bore a son, Arcas, to Zeus, she was transformed into a bear by Artemis. According to another legend she was changed into a bear by the jealous Hera. Arcas, while out hunting, was about to kill her when Zeus intervened and transferred them both to the heavens, Callisto becoming Ursa Major [great bear] and Arcas becoming Arcturus.

Callistratus (kŭlī'strŭtŭs), d. c.360 B.C., Athenian statesman and orator. Believing Thebes to be more dangerous to Athens than Sparta, he favored a peace with Sparta. He and CALLIAS in 371 B.C. were the delegates to negotiations on an ineffective peace treaty. His failure to check Thebes led to his impeachment in 366 B.C., but he saved himself with his brilliant defense—an oration that is sup-

posed to have inspired Demosthenes to study rhetoric. After new failure he fled Athens and was condemned *in absentia* for having urged Athens to allow Thebes to occupy Oropus in Boetia. When he returned he was put to death.

Callistus: see CALIXTUS.

Callixtus: see CALIXTUS.

Calloc'h, Jean Pierre (zhã' pyĕr' kälôkh'), 1888–1917, Breton poet. Important in the revival of Breton literature, he wrote in the Vannes dialect of Brittany. His verse, lyrical and sincere, displays a love for the sea and a fascination with death; his chief work, *Ar en deulin* [on both knees] (1925), celebrates the life of Breton fishermen. Calloc'h, who died in the First World War, is often regarded as Britanny's finest poet. He sometimes wrote under the pseudonym Bleimor.

Callot, Jacques (zhäk' kälō'), 1592–1635, French etcher and engraver, b. Nancy. At the age of 12 he was already drawing, and he attempted to run away to Italy. At 16 he was permitted to go to Rome, where he studied engraving. Soon, however, he abandoned this technique and took up etching, at which he became a master. In this medium he introduced the use of a hard varnish ground which allowed both greater flexibility and finesse. For some years he was in the service of Cosimo II de' Medici in Florence. There he created sparkling illustrations of the theater, among them his *Commedia dell' arte* group, reproduced in his *Balli* (1621). On Cosimo's death he returned (1621) to Nancy and under the patronage of the ducal court achieved a wide reputation. He was commissioned (1627) by the Infanta Isabella of Brussels to engrave the siege of Breda and by Louis XIII to etch the sieges of Rochelle and the

One of Jacques Callot's brilliant illustrations from his series of the Commedia dell'arte group.

island of Ré. Famous also are his series *Views of Paris* executed for Louis XIII. Too independent for court favor and deeply impressed by the scenes of carnage he had witnessed in the service of the great, he retired to Nancy, where he executed (1633) his splendid series *Miseries of War*. Callot produced nearly 1,500 plates in a wide variety of styles. His subjects ranged from dazzling views of court life to sympathetic portrayals of paupers, from military scenes to wild fantasies and grotesqueries. See study by Edwin Bechtel (1955).

Calmar: see KALMAR.

Calmet, Augustin (ōgüstĕ′ kälmä′), 1672–1757, French biblical scholar, a Benedictine abbot at Nancy and Sens. His critical commentaries were much studied until the higher criticism changed the technique of biblical criticism in the 19th cent. He also wrote a valuable history of Lorraine.

Calmette, Léon Charles Albert (lāŏ′ shärl′ älbĕr′ kälmĕt′), 1863–1933, French physician and bacteriologist. He was founder and director of the Pasteur institutes at Saigon and at Lille. From 1917 he was affiliated with the Pasteur Institute in Paris. He discovered a serum for snake bite, studied bubonic plague at Oporto, and with Alphonse Guérin introduced B-C-G, a tuberculosis vaccine. He wrote *Recherches expérimentales sur la tuberculose* (1907–14), *Tuberculose chez l'homme et chez les animaux* (1920; Eng. tr., 1923), and *La Vaccination preventive . . . par le BCG* (1927).

Calneh (kăl′nĕ), **1** Place, in S Babylonia, founded by Nimrod with other cities; the word may mean "all of them." Gen. 10.10. **2** Unidentified city, possibly in N Syria. Amos 6.2. It is perhaps the same as **Calno** (kăl′nō), named with Carchemish. Isa. 10.9. Some identify it with Canneh.

calomel (kă′lŭmĕl″, –mŭl), white crystalline powder compounded of mercury and chlorine and occurring to some extent naturally as horn quicksilver. It is used in medicine as a purgative and to eliminate parasitic worms. It also stimulates the flow of bile. Calomel reverts to poisonous bichloride of mercury on exposure to sunlight. Calomel was once a standard household remedy but has largely been replaced by safer drugs.

Calonne, Charles Alexandre de (shärl′ älĕksä′drü dü kälōn′), 1734–1802, French statesman, controller general of finances (1783–87). Faced with a huge public debt and a steadily deteriorating financial situation, Calonne adopted a spending policy to inspire the confidence needed to obtain new loans. Brief prosperity was followed by a ruinous collapse. He then proposed a direct land tax and the calling of provincial assemblies to apportion it, a stamp tax, and the reduction of some privileges of the nobles and clergy. To gain support, Calonne had King Louis XVI call an Assembly of Notables, but the Assembly (1787) refused to consider Calonne's proposals and criticized him bitterly. Dismissed and replaced by LOMÉNIE DE BRIENNE, Calonne fled (1787) to England, where he stayed until 1802. Many of Calonne's official papers have been published and two general works on politics have been translated into English, *Considerations on the Present and Future State of France* (1791) and *The Political State of Europe* (1796).

calorie, the unit measurement of heat quantity in the metric system. The small calorie, called also the gram-calorie or therm, is the quantity of heat required to raise the temperature of one gram of water at its maximum density one degree centigrade. The large calorie, or kilogram-calorie (1,000 small calories), is the quantity of heat required to raise the temperature of one kilogram of water at the temperature of maximum density one degree

centigrade. In physics and chemistry, the term *calorie* is generally employed to indicate the small calorie or gram-calorie. The quantity of heat (given in calories) required to raise the temperature of one gram of any substance one degree centigrade is called the specific heat of that substance. The specific heat of water is, therefore, 1. Since the specific heat of water varies slightly at different temperatures, the calorie is often more accurately defined in terms of the exact temperature rise; e.g., when the measurement represents the amount of heat required to raise the temperature of one gram of water from 14.5°C. to 15.5°C., it is called the 15° calorie. In food chemistry, the kilogram-calorie (large calorie) is often used for convenience. The heat content of food, i.e., the amount of heat energy which a specific food can yield, is stated as being so many calories or kilogram-calories. The value is easily calculated since the amount of heat given up by food when burned as a fuel is the same as the amount of heat evolved by it when undergoing OXIDATION in the body. Calorie values of foods are important in dietetics. One 15° calorie is equivalent to the following: 0.003968 B.T.U.; 4.185 joules; 3.087 foot-pounds; 1.162×10^{-6} kilowatt-hours. The apparatus used to determine the amount of heat (in calories) given off by a substance in combustion or in some other chemical reaction is called a **calorimeter** (kălŭrĭ′mŭtùr). Commonly, it depends for the measurement it gives upon the number of degrees in temperature that a given quantity of water (or other liquid) is raised by the heat generated in the activity under observation, since the amount of heat required to raise one gram of water one degree centigrade is one calorie (and that required for any other liquid is a definite fraction of a calorie). The amount of heat given off by the combustion of a fuel can be determined very accurately in the so-called bomb calorimeter, which consists essentially of a combustion chamber (bomb) set in another chamber filled with water. Upon combustion, the fuel generates heat which is transmitted to the water, raising its temperature. The temperature rise of the water indicates the number of calories given off by the combustion, since the amount of water affected is accurately known. The calorie content of food is tested in this way. Some calorimeters are based upon the principle that ice requires a specific quantity of heat per gram to melt it and are called consequently ice calorimeters. The respiration calorimeter measures the amount of heat generated in animal respiration.

Calovius, Abraham (külō′vĕŭs), 1612–86, German Lutheran theologian, whose original name was Kalan or Calan. He was (1637–43) a professor of theology at Königsberg, then pastor at Danzig, and after 1650 teacher, general superintendent, and finally dean of the theological faculty at Wittenberg. In his many tracts he defended the strict orthodox party against Catholic, Socinian, Arminian, and other views. He particularly attacked the syncretistic doctrines of Georgius CALIXTUS.

Calpe (kăl′pē), ancient name, possibly Phoenician in origin, of GIBRALTAR. It is one of the Pillars of Hercules, at the east end of the Strait of Gibraltar.

Calpurnia (kălpûr′nĕŭ), d. after 44 B.C., Roman matron. The daughter of PISO (L. Calpurnicus Piso Caesoninus), she was married to Julius Caesar in 59 B.C. She was loyal to him despite his many infidelities and his neglect. The picture of her in Shakespeare's *Julius Caesar* is drawn mainly from Plutarch.

Calpurnius (Titus Calpurnius Siculus) (kălpûr'nēŭs), fl. 1st cent. A.D., Roman poet. His *Eclogues* (seven pastorals) imitate Vergil with grace and charm.

Caltagirone (käl″täjērō'nä), city (estimated pop. 45,724), S Sicily, Italy. It has been famous for its majolica since the Arab occupation; terra cotta figures also are made here.

Caltanissetta (käl″tänĕs-sĕt'tä), city (estimated pop. 61,612), capital of Caltanissetta prov., central Sicily, Italy. It is a modern agricultural city, and a most important Sicilian sulphur center.

Calumet (kăl'ūmĕt). **1** Village (pop. 1,139), extreme N Mich., Keweenaw peninsula, in a copper region; inc. 1875 as Red Jacket; renamed 1929. It grew mainly after the development of the Calumet and Hecla copper mine (see AGASSIZ, ALEXANDER). A state park is nearby. **2** Uninc. village (pop. 1,241), SW Pa., SSE of Greensburg.

calumet [Fr.,=reed], the "peace pipe," a long, feathered stem, with or without pipe bowl, which figured in numerous North American Indian ceremonials. Such shafts possessed the highest sacred powers, offering media of communion with the animate powers of the universe and embodying the honor and the source of power of the tribe who possessed them. Every item of their fashioning and decoration was symbolic and varied from tribe to tribe. Calumets were particularly used at the conclusion of peace treaties and in ceremonies of adoption. They served as ambassadors' credentials and were passports of safe-conduct wherever recognized. The pipes were principally used by the Siouan and Algonquian peoples of the Great Plains and in the SE United States. Among the Iroquois, their function was supplanted by wampum. The concept of the "peace pipe" properly belongs to calumet-using groups. However, pipes were used through most of North America, and communal smoking, wherever found, usually carried the guarantees of amity, granted with food sharing. In the Middle West PIPESTONE was much used in making them.

Calumet City, city (pop. 25,000), NE Ill., a suburb S of Chicago near the Ind. line; inc. 1911. Lake Calumet, just north of the city, is connected with Lake Michigan. Various anti-vice crusades have been initiated here.

Calumet Park, village (pop. 8,448), NE Ill., a suburb S of Chicago; inc. 1912.

Calvados (kälvädôs'), department (2,198 sq. mi.; estimated pop. 442,991), in NORMANDY, N France, on the English Channel. It is the most fertile part of Normandy and home of Camembert cheese and Calvados brandy. Iron ore is mined and processed near Caen (the capital). The tourist industry is also important with numerous resorts, such as Deauville, on the Channel.

Calvaert, Denis (käl'värt), 1540–1619, Flemish mannerist painter in Italy, where he was known as Il Fiammingo. He studied in Antwerp and later in Bologna under Prospero Fontana. While a student he assisted in the execution of frescoes in the Vatican. On returning to Bologna he established a

school, counting among his pupils Guido Reni and Domenichino. Most of his carefully drawn works, painted in smooth enamellike colors, are in the churches and national museum of Bologna.

Calvary (kăl'vŭrē) [Latin,=a skull] or **Golgotha** (gŏl'gŭthŭ) [Heb.,=a skull], place, where Jesus was crucified, outside the wall of Jerusalem. Its location is not certainly known. Mat. 27.33; Mark 15.22; Luke 23.33; John 19.17–20. The traditional identification of the site of Calvary was made by St. Helena, when she found what was believed to be a relic of the Cross (see CROSS). The spot is within the Church of the Holy Sepulchre. In the 19th cent. Charles G. Gordon proposed a site near the Damascus Gate; this is called the Garden Tomb or Gordon's Calvary.

Calve, Emma (kälvä'), 1858–1942, French operatic soprano; pupil of Mme Marchesi. She sang in the principal opera houses of Europe and between 1893 and 1904 sang often at the Metropolitan Opera, New York, where her portrayal of Carmen was especially acclaimed. See her autobiography (1922).

Calverley, Charles Stuart, 1831–84, English poet and wit. Expelled from Oxford, he earned academic honors at Cambridge (M.A., 1859). He became famous for the wit and erudition of his light verse, particularly his parodies (published under the initials C. S. C.). A barrister, he suffered an injury in 1867 which curtailed his legal career. His published works include *Translations into English and Latin* (1866) and *Fly Leaves* (1872).

Calvert, Cecilius, 2d **Baron Baltimore** (kăl'vŭrt), c.1605–1675, first proprietor of the colony of MARYLAND. He received the province in 1632 as a grant from the king, in place of his father, George Calvert, who died as the charter was being issued. Cecilius Calvert never visited the province himself, but governed it by deputies until his death, his last deputy being his only son, Charles Calvert. See W. H. Browne, *George Calvert and Cecilius Calvert* (1890); C. C. Hall, *The Lords Baltimore and the Maryland Palatinate* (1902).

Calvert, Charles, 3d **Baron Baltimore,** 1637–1715, second proprietor of Maryland. He was sent over as deputy governor of that province in 1661 by his father, Cecilius Calvert, and at his father's death in 1675 succeeded to the proprietorship. A Catholic faced by an overwhelming Protestant population, he ruled arbitrarily, restricting the suffrage, and filling the offices with his partisans. At the time of BACON'S REBELLION in Virginia there was a similar rebellion in Maryland, which was quickly suppressed. He became involved in a bitter dispute with William PENN over the northern boundary of his grant and in 1684 went to England to defend himself in the controversy. He never returned. His charter was overthrown by a Protestant revolt in 1689, and in 1692 a royal government was established. See C. C. Hall, *The Lords Baltimore and the Maryland Palatinate* (1902).

Calvert, Edward, 1799–1883, English painter and engraver. A great admirer of William Blake, Calvert, along with several of his contemporaries, formed a group around him called the Brotherhood of the Ancients. His art celebrated the life of a primitive society. See Laurence Binyon, *The Followers of William Blake* (1925).

Calvert, George, 1st **Baron Baltimore,** c.1580–1632,

colonizer, grad. Trinity College, Oxford, 1597. In 1606 he became private secretary to Sir Robert Cecil, then a secretary of state. His advance was rapid. In 1609 he became a member of Parliament, in 1613 clerk of the privy council, and in 1619 secretary of state and a member of the privy council. He defended the measures of James I in the House until his resignation in 1625, when he announced himself a Catholic. The king then created him Baron Baltimore. Calvert had been a member of the Virginia Company and a member of the council of the New England Company, but, wishing to found his own colony, he was granted in 1623 the peninsula of Avalon in Newfoundland. He spent much money on a colony which was established there, but it did not prosper, and in 1629 Baltimore petitioned for a grant farther south where the weather was less severe. In 1632 the king granted him the territory N of the Potomac river which became the province of Maryland. Baltimore prepared the charter of his proposed colony, but died before it could be accepted. The grant passed to his son, Cecilius Calvert. See C. C. Hall, *The Lords Baltimore and the Maryland Palatinate* (1902).

Calvert. 1 City (pop. 1,505), SW Ky., SE of Paducah, in a grain and livestock area; inc. 1871. Chemicals are made. **2** City (pop. 2,073), E central Texas, in the Brazos valley and SE of Waco; settled c.1840, inc. 1896. It is the center of a bottom-lands farming and grazing area.

Calverton Park, village (pop. 1,714), E Mo., a suburb NW of St. Louis; inc. 1941.

Calvin, John, 1509–64, French Protestant theologian of the Reformation, b. Noyon, Picardy. Calvin early prepared for an ecclesiastical career; from 1523 to 1528 he studied at Paris. His opinions gradually turned to disagreement with the Roman position, and a demonstrated ability at disputation led him in 1528, at his father's instance to study law at Orléans and Bourges. After his father's death in 1531 he returned to Paris, where he pursued his own predilection—the study of the classics and Hebrew. He came under the humanist influence and became interested in the growing rebellion against conservative theology. He experienced c.1533 what he later described as a "sudden conversion," and he turned all his attention to the cause of the Reformation. As a persecuted Protestant, Calvin found it necessary to travel from place to place, and at Angoulême in 1534 he began the work of systematizing Protestant thought in his *Institutes of the Christian Religion*, one of the great theological works of all time. Completed at Basel in 1536 and later frequently revised and supplemented, the original work contained the basic Calvinist theology. In the *Institutes* Calvin diverged from Catholic doctrine in the rejection of papal authority and in acceptance of justification by faith alone, but many of his other positions, including the fundamental doctrine of predestination, had been foreshadowed by Catholic reformers and by the Protestant thought of Martin Luther and Martin Bucer. In 1536 Calvin was persuaded by Guillaume Farel to devote himself to the work of the Reformation at Geneva, and there Calvin instituted the most thoroughgoing development of his doctrine. At first the Genevans were unable to

accept the austere reforms and departures from established church customs, and in 1538 the opposition succeeded in banishing Farel and Calvin from the city. Calvin went to Basel and then to Strasbourg, where he spent three fruitful years

John Calvin

preaching and writing. By 1541 the Genevans welcomed Calvin, and he immediately set himself to the task of constructing a government based on the subordination of the state to the Church. Once the Bible is accepted as the sole source of God's law, the duty of man is to interpret it and preserve the orderly world which God has ordained. This end Calvin set out to achieve through the establishment of ecclesiastical discipline, in which the magistrates had the task of enforcing the religious teachings of the Church as set forth by the synod. The Genevan laws and constitution were recodified; regulation of conduct was extended to all areas of life. Ecclesiastical discipline was supplemented by a systematized theology, with the sacraments of baptism and the Lord's Supper given to unite man into the fellowship of Christ. Calvin wrote extensively on all theological and practical matters. He was involved in many controversies. Among them were his violent opposition to the Anabaptists; his disagreement with the Lutherans over the LORD'S SUPPER, which resulted in the separation of the Evangelical Church into Lutheran and Reformed; and his condemnation of the anti-Trinitarian views of Michael SERVETUS, which ended in the notorious trial and burning of Servetus in 1553. The extension of Calvinism to all spheres of human activity was extremely important to a world emerging from an agrarian, medieval economy into a commercial, industrial era. Unlike Luther, who desired a return to primitive simplicity, Calvin accepted the newborn capitalism and encouraged trade and production, at the same time rigorously suppressing the abuses of exploitation and self-indulgence. The development of a successful industrial economy was stimulated by the Christian virtues of thrift, industry, sobriety, and responsibility which Calvin preached as essential to the achievement of the reign of God on earth. The influence of Calvinism spread throughout the entire Western world, realizing its purest forms through the influence of

John KNOX in Scotland and through the clergymen and laymen of the Puritan Revolution in England and the Puritan moralists in New England. See R. H. Tawney, *Religion and the Rise of Capitalism* (1922); Georgia Harkness, *John Calvin: the Man and His Ethics* (1931); W. C. Northcott, *John Calvin* (1946); A. T. Davies, *John Calvin and the Influence of Protestantism on National Life and Character* (1946); A. M. Schmidt, *John Calvin and the Calvinist Tradition* (Eng. tr., 1960); H. J. Forstman, *Word and Spirit: Calvin's Doctrine of Biblical Authority* (1962).

Calvin, Melvin, 1911–, American organic chemist and educator, b. St. Paul, Minn., grad. Michigan College of Mining and Technology, 1931, Ph.D. Univ. of Minnesota, 1935. In 1937 he joined the faculty at the Univ. of California, where he became director (1946) of the bio-organic division of the Lawrence Radiation Laboratory and professor (1947) of chemistry. For his work in determining the chemical reactions that occur when a plant assimilates carbon dioxide, Calvin was awarded the 1961 Nobel Prize in Chemistry. His writings include *The Photosynthesis of Carbon Compounds* (with J. A. Bassham, 1962).

Calvinism, term used in several different senses. It may indicate the teachings expressed by John Calvin himself; it may be extended to include all that developed from his doctrine and practice in Protestant countries in social, political, and ethical, as well as theological, aspects of life and thought; or it may be employed as the name of that system of doctrine accepted by "the Reformed churches" (see PRESBYTERIANISM), i.e., the Protestant churches called Reformed in distinction from those professing Lutheran doctrines (see also REFORMED CHURCHES). Early Calvinism differed from Lutheranism in its rejection of consubstantiation regarding the sacrament of the Lord's Supper, in its rigid doctrine of predestination, in its notion of grace as irresistible, and in its theocratic view of the state. Luther believed in the political subordination of the church to the state; Calvinism produced the church-dominated societies of Geneva and puritan New England. Calvinism, stressing the utter sovereignty of God's will, held that only those whom God specifically elects are saved, that this election is irresistible, and that man can do nothing of his own to effect this salvation. This strict Calvinism was challenged by Jacobus ARMINIUS, whose more moderate views were adopted by the Methodists and the "General" Baptists. Calvinism challenged Lutheranism throughout Europe, spread to Scotland, influenced the Puritans of England, and received its expression in the United States in the modified New England theology of the elder Jonathan EDWARDS. The doctrinal aspects of Calvinism receded under the rationalism of the 18th and 19th cent. Today, however, in the Reformed theology of Karl Barth, the Calvinist stress on the sovereignty of God has found new and vital expression. See J. T. McNeill, *The History and Character of Calvinism* (1954).

Calvinistic Methodist Church, Protestant Christian denomination, closely allied to PRESBYTERIANISM. It originated in Wales (1735–36) with the evangelistic preaching of Howell Harris, Daniel Rowlands, and others. In Wales it is considered to be the only denomination distinctly Welsh in origin, and it has developed into the most important of the Welsh nonconformist churches. The "Methodist" societies which evolved under the Welsh revivalists were so organized as to prevent any break with the Established Church. They were for a time associated with the Methodists of England; for some six years, from c.1742, George WHITEFIELD was the leader of the Welsh Calvinists. Those in England who accepted his views, as opposed to the Arminian doctrines taught by John WESLEY, either remained within the Church of England, joined the "Connexion" of the countess of HUNTINGDON, or in time became affiliated with the Congregationalists or Independents. The Welsh Calvinistic Methodists, however, held their own vigorously and grew in numbers. Thomas CHARLES of Bala, who joined them in 1784, was a leader of wide influence in religious and educational work. In 1811 they separated from the Established Church and set up a new church, Presbyterian in polity. In 1823 a confession of faith was adopted. Later, theological schools were founded at Bala and at Trevecca. The Calvinistic Methodist Church was introduced (c.1826) into the United States by Welsh settlers in central New York state. In 1920 it united with the Presbyterian Church in the United States.

Calvo, Carlos (kär'lōs käl'vō), 1824–1906, Argentine diplomat and historian. He spent much of his life in diplomatic service abroad. He edited a collection of Latin American treaties and did other historical work but was most important as a writer on international law, and although influenced by Henry Wheaton, his development of international doctrines broke new paths. His best-known work is *Derecho internacional teórico y práctico de Europa y América* (Paris, 1868; greatly expanded in subsequent editions, which were published in French). In this he expressed the principle known as the **Calvo Doctrine,** which would prohibit diplomatic intervention as a method for enforcing private claims before local remedies have been exhausted. It is wider in scope than the DRAGO DOCTRINE, which grew out of it. The **Calvo Clause,** found in constitutions, treaties, statutes, and contracts, is the concrete application of the doctrine. Used chiefly in concession contracts, the clause attempts to give local courts final jurisdiction and to obviate any appeal to diplomatic intervention.

Calvus: see LICINIUS, gens.

calycanthus, any plant of the genus *Calycanthus*, aromatic shrubs of N North America, Asia, and Australia. An American type, the Carolina ALLSPICE (see PIMENTO), is cultivated for the aromatic fragrance of its flowers.

Calydon (kăl'ĭdŭn), ancient city of S Aetolia, Greece, near the Evenus river and the Gulf of Calydon (Gulf of Patras). It was the scene of the famous Calydonian hunt of legend. This was led by Meleager, prince of Calydon, against a wild boar sent by Artemis to destroy the city for neglecting sacrifice. Among the hunters were Jason, Theseus, Peleus, Nestor, and Atalanta.

Calypso (kŭlĭp'sō), nymph, daughter of Atlas, in Homer's *Odyssey*. She lived on the island of Ogygia and there entertained Odysseus for seven years. She offered to make him immortal if he would remain, but he spurned the offer and continued his journey.

calyx: see SEPAL.

Cam or **Granta,** river rising in Essex, England, and flowing c.40 mi. northward, E past Cambridge, then NE to the Ouse S of Ely. It is called the Granta until it is joined by the Rhee above Cambridge.

cam, mechanical device for producing a reciprocating motion, usually from a rotating shaft. A simple form of cam is a circular disk set eccentrically on a shaft in order to induce (when the shaft rotates) a rising and falling motion in a rod or some other moving part held against its edge. There are cams of many diverse shapes, e.g., oval, elliptical, and scalloped-edged, each shape being designed to induce the particular kind of motion required in a moving part. Cams are widely used in many different kinds of machines.

Camacho, Manuel Ávila: see Ávila Camacho, Manuel.

Camagüey (kämägwā′, kämäwā′), city (pop. c.110,000), E central Cuba. Formerly called Puerto Príncipe, it is an important commercial crossroads on the main railroads and highways. The rich agricultural region surrounding Camagüey produces cattle and sugar cane. Known for its churches and mansions, it has retained much of its Spanish colonial atmosphere.

Camanche (kŭmănch′), town (pop. 2,225), E central Iowa, on the Mississippi and SSW of Clinton. Unusual limestone formations are nearby.

Camargue (kämärg′), island, Bouches-du-Rhône dept., SE France, in the Rhone delta. Once a marshland, it has been reclaimed in part and is used for extensive cattle raising. The cowboys are called *gardiens.*

Camarillo (kă″mŭrē′yō), uninc. town (pop. 2,359), S Calif., E of Oxnard. It is a shipping center for a farm area. The main campus of St. John's College (Roman Catholic; for men; 1926) and a state mental hospital are here.

Camarillo Heights, uninc. village (pop. 1,704), S Calif., E of Oxnard, in an agricultural area.

Camas (kăm′ŭs), city (pop. 5,666), SW Wash., on the Columbia and E of Vancouver; settled 1846, platted 1883, inc. 1906. Large lumber and paper mills are here.

camass or **camas** (both: kăm′ŭs), any species of the genus *Camassia* (or *Quamasia*), hardy North American plants of the LILY family, chiefly of moist places in the far West, where their abundance has given rise to various place names. The bulbs of the common camass (*C. quamash*) were a staple food of Northwestern Indians; it is now cultivated as an ornamental for its showy blue to white blossoms. Camass, or quamash, was the Indian name. An eastern camass is called wild hyacinth. The death camass (*Zygadenus venenosus*), with leaves poisonous to sheep, is similar in appearance but distinguishable by having three styles instead of six.

Cambacérès, Jean Jacques Régis de (zhā′ zhäk′ räzhēs′ dù kōbäsärĕs′), 1753–1824, French revolutionist and legislator. He held moderate opinions and was deputy to the National Convention, member of the Committee of Public Safety and of the Council of Five Hundred, second consul under Napoleon (1799–1804), and archchancellor of the empire. Throughout his career, his chief interest was in developing the principles of revolutionary jurisprudence. He played a major part in the preparation of the CODE NAPOLÉON. In 1808 Cam-

Madonna and Child *by Luca Cambiaso.*

bacérès was made duke of Parma. Minister of justice in the Hundred Days (1815), he was exiled in the Restoration until 1818.

Cambay (kămbā′), town (pop. 51,291), Gujarat state, W India, on the Gulf of Cambay. Once a great port under the Moslem rulers of Gujarat (14th–15th cent.), it lost its importance when the harbor silted up and is now only a local trade center. Until 1948 it was the capital of the former princely state of Cambay. The Gulf of Cambay, an arm of the Arabian Sea, lies between Kathiawar peninsula and Gujarat.

Cambert, Robert (rōbĕr′ kăbĕr′), c.1628–1677, French composer; pupil of Chambonnières. Though his works are not the first French lyric dramas, they are the first real French operas. With the librettist Pierre Perrin (1625–75) he created French RECITATIVE in operas such as *Pomone* (1671), which contains all the elements of later French opera such as short symphonies, airs, and dialogues. Both men founded the first French opera company in 1669, but after losing control of this venture to Jean Baptiste LULLY, Cambert settled in London where he was eventually murdered.

Camberwell (kăm′bùrwŭl, –wĕl), metropolitan borough (pop. 174,697) of London, England. It is largely a residential and park section. The South London Art Gallery is here.

Cambiaso, Luca (lōō′kä kämbyä′zō), 1527–85, leading Italian painter and sculptor of the Genoese school, known also as Luchetto da Genova; son and pupil of Giovanni Cambiaso, a fresco painter. His inventiveness and facile execution in both oil and fresco won him early recognition. His best works are in churches and palaces of Genoa and vicinity. In 1583 he went to Spain, where he worked on the decoration of the Escorial. See illustrated monograph by B. S. Manning and William Suida (1958, in Italian).

Cambio, Arnolfo di: see ARNOLFO DI CAMBIO.

cambium (kăm′bēùm), thin layer of reproductive tissue lying between the bark and the wood of a stem, most active in woody plants. The cambium produces new layers of phloem on the outside and of xylem (WOOD) on the inside, thus increasing the diameter of the STEM. In herbaceous plants the cambium is almost inactive; in monocotyledonous plants it is usually absent. In regions wnere there are alternating seasons, each year's growth laid down by the cambium is discernible because of the contrast between the large wood elements produced in the spring and the smaller ones produced in the summer. These are the annual rings, by which the age of a tree can be established. A tree dies when it is "ringed," i.e., cut through the cambium layer. The cork cambium, which lies outside the phloem layer, produces the cork cells of BARK.

Cambodia (kămbō′dĕú) Fr. *Cambodge* (kăbôj′), constitutional monarchy (c.67,000 sq. mi.; pop. c.4,952,000), SE Asia. The capital is Phnom Penh. Cambodia is bordered by Laos on the north, by South Viet Nam on the east, by the Gulf of Siam on

Cambodia location map

the south, and by Thailand (Siam) on the west. The country is a saucer-shaped alluvial plain drained by the Mekong river and shut off by mountain ranges; the Dangrek mountains form the Thai frontier. The northeast and southwest monsoons govern the dry and the wet seasons respectively. The vegetation is tropical; in the jungles are found elephants, tigers, and buffaloes. Near Phnom Penh the Mekong receives the waters of the Great Lake or TONLE SAP, important for its fisheries. West of the lake is a fertile rice-growing area. Pepper is grown on the southern coastal plains, cotton and tobacco on the banks of the Mekong. Large quantities of rubber are also grown. Three fourths of the country is covered by forest, but inadequate transportation hampers exploitation. Mineral resources are limited. The country's industry is based mostly on processing agricultural, fish, and timber products. Cambodia has been developed in recent years by foreign aid; the United States has built a four-lane

highway linking Phnom Penh with the new seaport of Sihanoukville on the Gulf of Siam, and mainland China has financed the construction of a steel mill and several factories. Cambodia is connected by road systems to Thailand, Laos, and South Viet Nam; waterways are an important supplement to roads. Cambodia, one of the few underpopulated countries of SE Asia, has besides the Cambodians, or Khmers, large minorities of Vietnamese and Chinese, plus Chams, Malays, and hill tribesmen. Hinayana Buddhism is the state religion and about 90 percent of the people are Buddhists; the Chams and Malays are Moslems. Khmer is the national language, but French is widely used. The history of Cambodia began in the 1st cent. A.D. when the Funan empire was established here. By the 3d cent. the Funanese, under the leadership of Fan Shih-man (reign 205–225), had conquered their neighbors and extended their sway to the lower Mekong river. In the 4th cent., according to Chinese records, an Indian Brahman extended his rule over Funan, introducing Hindu customs, the Indian legal code, and the alphabet of central India. In the 6th cent. Khmers from the rival Chen-la state to the north overran Funan. With the rise of the KHMER EMPIRE, Cambodia became dominant in SE Asia. After the fall of the empire (15th cent.), however, Cambodia was the prey of stronger neighbors. To pressure from Siam on the western frontier was added in the 17th cent. pressure from ANNAM on the east; the kings of Siam and the lords of Hué alike asserted overlordship and claims to tribute. In the 18th cent. Cambodia lost three western provinces to Siam and the region of COCHIN CHINA to the Annamese. Intrigue and wars on Cambodian soil continued into the 19th cent., and in 1854 the king of Cambodia appealed for French intervention. A French protectorate was formally established in 1863, and French influence was consolidated by a treaty of 1884. Cambodia became part of the Union of Indo-China in 1887. In 1907 a French-Siamese treaty restored Cambodia's western provinces. In the Second World War, under Japanese occupation, Cambodia again briefly lost these provinces to Siam. After the war, France granted Cambodia a greater degree of self-government within the Federation of Indo-China. There were minor nationalist disturbances, and in May, 1947, Cambodia became a constitutional monarchy under King Norodom Sihanouk. In 1949 the country became an associated state in the French Union, and in Mar., 1953, it declared its complete independence. Early in 1954 Communist Vietminh troops from Viet Nam invaded Cambodia. The Geneva Conference of 1954 led to an armistice agreement providing for the withdrawal of all foreign forces from Cambodia. An agreement between France and Cambodia (Dec., 1954) transferred full sovereignty to Cambodia, which was admitted into the United Nations late in 1955. King Norodom Sihanouk abdicated in March, 1955; his father, Norodom Suramarit, succeeded him. Sihanouk subsequently formed the Popular Socialist party and served as premier. After the king's death in 1960, Norodom Sihanouk was installed in the new office of chief of state. His mother, Queen Kossamak Nearireak, was designated to represent the monarchy. Recent relations

Street in Phnom Penh, Cambodia's capital.

Cambodian country children

View of the Mekong river.

Head of Buddha, Khmer
art (end of 12th century).

Angkor Wat, Cambodian temple complex (12th century).

between Cambodia and Thailand and South Viet Nam have been marked by tension and a series of clashes. A dispute with Thailand over the Buddhist temple of Preah Vihear was settled in June, 1962, when the World Court ruled that it should be returned to Cambodia; Thai forces had occupied the border temple when French troops withdrew from Cambodia in 1954. The United States in 1962 stepped up military aid to Cambodia to strengthen its forces against infiltrating groups of Viet Cong Communist guerrillas. In Aug., 1962, Norodom Sihanouk proposed that the 14 nations that had guaranteed the independence of Laos meet to guarantee the neutrality and independence of Cambodia in its border disputes with Thailand and South Viet Nam. Cambodia maintains a policy of neutrality in the struggle between the West and the Communist nations. See M. F. Herz, *A Short History of Cambodia* (1958); D. J. Steinberg and others, *Cambodia* (1959); Ruth Tooze, *Cambodia* (1962).

Cambodian art and architecture: see ANGKOR and KHMER EMPIRE.

Cambon, Jules Martin (zhül′ märtĕ′ kãbõ′), 1845–1935, French diplomat; brother of Pierre Paul Cambon. He served (1891–96) as governor general of Algeria, where he pursued a conciliatory policy and was largely responsible for the decree (1896) establishing administrative autonomy for Algeria. In 1897 he was made ambassador to Washington, and he mediated the peace preliminaries of the Spanish-American War. He was ambassador at Madrid (1902–7) and at Berlin (1907–14), and from 1920 to 1922 he was chairman of the Council of Ambassadors, the group charged with overseeing the enforcement of the Treaty of Versailles (1919). His political works include *The Diplomatist* (Eng. tr., 1931). See biography by Geneviève Tabouis (Eng. tr., 1938).

Cambon, Pierre Joseph (pyĕr′ zhôzĕf′), b. 1754 or 1756, d. 1820, French financier and revolutionist. A merchant of Montpellier, he became a member of the Legislative Assembly and the Convention, and he guided the financial policy of the Revolution from Oct., 1791, to April, 1795. He refunded the debt after consolidating the royal and Revolutionary debts. Advocating war to "free" Europe, he advanced the policy of exploiting conquered territory. His fiscal program, which failed to halt inflation, was attacked by Robespierre, whose fall was partly caused by Cambon's countercharges. Cambon was distrusted by the Thermidorians, and his career ended after his brief triumph. He was exiled after the Bourbon restoration.

Cambon, Pierre Paul (pôl), 1843–1924, French diplomat; brother of Jules Martin Cambon. Named resident minister to Tunis in 1882, he conceived and organized the new Tunisian protectorate under the bey. As ambassador to England (1898–1920), he helped to create the Entente Cordiale (1904) and the Anglo-Russian agreement of 1907, and he encouraged England to enter the First World War (see TRIPLE ALLIANCE AND TRIPLE ENTENTE). He was one of the most able diplomats in French history.

Camborne-Redruth (kăm′bôrn, –bûrn, rĕd′rōōth), urban district (pop. 36,090), Cornwall, SW England. The former urban districts of Camborne and Redruth, situated 3 mi. apart, were combined in the early 1930s. Camborne mines tin and is the site of Dolcoath Mine, one of the largest in Cornwall but now idle. Redruth mines tin and copper. John Wesley preached to outdoor gatherings near the present mines. At the summit of Carn Brea hill are prehistoric remains.

Cambrai (kămbrā′, Fr. kābrā′), city (estimated pop. 29,567), Nord dept., N France, on the SCHELDT (Escaut) river. It has long been known for its fine textiles and gave its name to cambric, first manufactured here. An episcopal see since the 4th cent. and seat of an archdiocese since the 16th cent., Cambrai and the surrounding county of Cambrésis were ruled by the bishops under the Holy Roman Empire until they were seized by Spain (1595) and by France (1677). Fénelon was archbishop of Cambrai from 1695 to 1715. The original cathedral was destroyed in 1793. Cambrai suffered devastation in both world wars.

Cambrai, League of, 1508–10, alliance formed by Emperor Maximilian I, Louis XII of France, Pope Julius II, Ferdinand V of Aragon, and Ferrara, Mantua, and others against Venice to check its territorial expansion. The republic was soon on the verge of ruin. Its army was defeated by the French at Agnadello (1509); most of the territories it had occupied were lost; and Maximilian entered Venetia. The republic had to make concessions to the pope and to Ferdinand. In 1510 the pope became reconciled to Venice and began forming the HOLY LEAGUE against France. The republic emerged from the war having suffered serious losses, but by no means crushed.

Cambrai, Treaty of, called the **Ladies' Peace,** treaty negotiated and signed in 1529 by Louise of Savoy, representing her son Francis I of France, and Margaret of Austria, representing her nephew Emperor Charles V. The treaty renewed the Treaty of Madrid (see FRANCIS I), but it did not exact the surrender of Burgundy to Charles.

Cambreleng, Churchill Caldom (kăm′bûrlĕng), 1786–1862, U.S. Representative (1821–39), b. Washington, N.C. He moved to New York city in 1802 and became a highly successful businessman, though later, as a Congressman, he was opposed by the mercantile interests. Under Presidents Andrew Jackson and Martin Van Buren, Cambreleng was an influential administration leader in the House, particularly able on economic questions. Defeated for reelection in 1838, he served as minister to Russia (1840–41). He was prominent in the New York constitutional convention of 1846 and in 1847 presided over the state convention of the BARNBURNERS. See A. M. Schlesinger, Jr., *The Age of Jackson* (1945).

Cambria (kăm′brĕŭ) [from Welsh *Cymry*=Welshmen], ancient name of Wales.

Cambrian Mountains, name sometimes given the mountain system of Wales.

Cambrian period (kăm′brĕŭn, kăm′–) [Latin, *Cambria*=Wales], first period of the Paleozoic geologic era (see GEOLOGIC ERAS, table). It was named by Adam Sedgwick, who first studied (1831–35) in NW Wales the great sequence of rocks characteristic of the period. Comprising mainly sedimentary ROCK, i.e., conglomerate, sandstone, shale, and limestone, they were formed in shallow seas that covered large areas of North America, Europe, and Asia. In the United States, Lower Cambrian, or Waucobian, formations are found chiefly in the Appalachian and Cordilleran geosynclines, which were then arms of the sea; the most notable deposits are the sandstone near Waucoba Springs, S Calif., and the thick strata of conglomerate and sandstone of Georgia, Tennessee, and North Carolina. Middle Cambrian, or Albertan, formations are rare in the Appalachian region, which was above water in the Middle Cambrian, but they are found in New Brunswick, near Braintree, Mass., and throughout the Cordilleran region. In the Upper Cambrian, or Croixian, epoch, the shallow seas spread over a great part of the continent, depositing, among other formations, the St. Croix sandstone of Wisconsin and the upper Mississippi valley, some of the Arbuckle limestone of Oklahoma, and the Potsdam sandstone on the northern slope of the Adirondacks and elsewhere. In the USSR the Cambrian beds are remarkable in that they comprise mostly undisturbed and unconsolidated sand and clay despite their great age. The Cambrian rocks are notable as the first to contain many easily recognizable fossils. The known Cambrian fauna—all marine—includes every phylum of invertebrates; the possibility that vertebrate fossils may be found cannot be excluded. The dominant animal was the TRILOBITE, and the various rock series are distinguished according to the different genera of trilobites they contain. Brachiopods, snails, and sponges were also common. The seemingly abrupt appearance of such a highly developed and diversified fauna is best explained by the assumption that more primitive forms flourished during the interval between the close of the Pre-Cambrian era and the beginning of the Cambrian, of which all geologic record has been destroyed by erosion.

Cambridge (kām′-), municipal borough (pop. 95,358), county town of Cambridgeshire, E England, on the Cam (or Granta) river. It is an ancient market town, and while light industries such as the manufacture of agricultural tools, precision instruments, radios, and cement have grown up on the outskirts, the town is most famous as the site of CAMBRIDGE UNIVERSITY. Originally a Roman fort (Camboritum), it became the Grantebrycge of the Saxons, the Cantebrigge (Latin *Cantabrigia*) of the Normans, and the Caumbridge of the later English, finally evolving its present name. Here William I built a castle, which has now disappeared; the town's importance grew with the advent of monks from nearby Ely, who gave it a scholastic and ecclesiastical reputation in the 12th cent. and who formed the nucleus of the university foundations. The present town still maintains much of its medieval atmosphere and appearance. There are many old inns, hostels, and houses and winding streets and narrow passages which have not altered greatly with time. Cambridge abounds in medieval churches, the most important of which are St. Benedict's, the oldest, dating back to the Saxon 10th cent.; St. Edward's (mostly 15th cent.), where Hugh Latimer preached; St. Mary the Great (1478), the university church; and the Church of the Holy Sepulchre, one of the four Norman round churches in England. The annual Stourbridge fair,

one of the largest in medieval England, was held on the outskirts of Cambridge for seven centuries before it was abolished in 1935.

Cambridge. 1 Village (pop. 1,665), co. seat of Henry co., NW Ill., SE of Rock Island, in a farm area; inc. 1861. **2** City (pop. 12,239), co. seat of Dorchester co., Md., Eastern Shore, on the Choptank river, across Chesapeake Bay SE of Annapolis, in a farm area; founded 1684, inc. as a town 1793, as a city 1884. The city is a port of entry, a fishing and yachting port, and a canning center for sea food and vegetables. It also has sawmills and makes clothing and electronic equipment. **3** City (pop. 107,716), a co. seat of Middlesex co., E Mass., on the Charles river and NW of Boston; settled 1630 as New Towne, inc. as a town 1636, as a city 1846. It is the seat of HARVARD UNIVERSITY, Radcliffe College, and MASSACHUSETTS INSTITUTE OF TECHNOLOGY. Cambridge was a gathering place for colonial troops; here, on July 3, 1775, Washington took command. It was the first seat of the Massachusetts constitutional convention of 1780. The birthplace and home of James Russell Lowell, the city has also preserved Longfellow's house as a memorial. Longfellow, Lowell, Mary Baker Eddy, and many other notable people are buried in Mt. Auburn Cemetery. An industrial as well as an educational center, Cambridge manufactures confectionary products, chemicals, machinery, electrical equipment, and rubber goods and has industrial and scientific research organizations. Its printing and publishing industry dates from the 17th cent., when Stephen DAYE established here the first printing press in America. **4** Village (pop. 2,728), co. seat of Isanti co., E Minn., N of Minneapolis and on the Rum river, in a farm area; settled 1856, inc. 1876. A state mental hospital is here. **5** City (pop. 1,090), S Nebr., on the Republican and SW of Kearney, in a grazing area; founded 1874. **6** Village (pop. 1,748), E N.Y., ESE of Saratoga Springs and near the Vt. line; settled c.1761, inc. 1866. Its weekly *Washington County Post* was founded in 1787. **7** Industrial city (pop. 14,562), co. seat of Guernsey co., E central Ohio, ENE of Zanesville, in a farm, coal, natural gas, and clay area; settled 1798, inc. as a village 1837. Its chief manufactures include steel, glass, plastics, and pottery. **8** Town (pop. 1,295), N Vt., in the western foothills of the Green Mts., SW of St. Albans; settled 1783. Lucy Wheelock was born here.

Cambridge Bay, Canadian government post and weather station, on the southeast shore of Victoria Island, Northwest Territories.

Cambridge City, town (pop. 2,569), E central Ind., on the Whitewater river W of Richmond; settled 1813, platted 1836. It is a farm trade center.

Cambridge Platform, declaration of principles of church government and discipline, forming in fact a constitution of the Congregational churches. It was adopted (1648) by a church synod at Cambridge, Mass., and remains the basis of the temporal government of the churches. It had little to do with matters of doctrine and belief. The Congregationalists of Connecticut later subscribed (1708), in the Saybrook Platform, to a more centralized church government, resembling Presbyterianism. See also CONGREGATIONALISM.

Trinity College, Cambridge University.

Cambridge Platonists, school of philosophy, centered at Cambridge Univ. in the latter half of the 17th cent. In reaction to the mechanical philosophy of Hobbes this school revived certain Platonic and Neoplatonic ideas. Chief among these was a mystical conception of the soul's relation to God and the belief that moral ideas are innate in man. Although tending toward mysticism, the school also stressed the importance of reason, maintaining that faith and reason differ only in degree. The assertion of the founder of the school, Benjamin Whichcote, that "the spirit in man is the cradle of the Lord" became the motto for the entire movement. Other leading members were Ralph CUD-WORTH, Henry MORE, and John Smith. See F. J. Powicke, *The Cambridge Platonists* (1925); Ernst Cassirer, *The Platonic Renaissance in England* (Eng. tr., 1953).

Cambridgeshire or **Cambridge,** county (pop. 279,025), 864 sq. mi. (including the Isle of Ely), E England. The county town is CAMBRIDGE. The northern section of Cambridgeshire is known as the Isle of Ely (see ELY, ISLE OF) and is administratively a separate county. Most of the area is alluvial fenland, rising to the low chalky East Anglian range in the south, with the Gogmagog Hills near Cambridge their most conspicuous feature. The main rivers are the Ouse, the Cam or Granta, the Lark, and the Nene. Efforts to reclaim the fens date back, apparently, to the days of Roman occupation, but in the subsequent periods of invasions by Danes, Saxons, and Normans the efforts were abandoned. Cornelius Vermuyden, a Dutchman, completed a vast drainage project in 1653. Since that time the region has been known primarily for its market gardening. Ely (see ELY, CITY OF) has been important as an ecclesiastical center for many centuries. CAMBRIDGE UNIVERSITY, famous for its beautiful buildings as well as its scholars, dates from the early 12th cent.

Cambridge Springs, borough (pop. 2,031), NW Pa., near Lake Erie S of Erie; inc. 1866. It is a farm and resort center and produces condensed milk. Alliance College (coeducational; 1912) is here.

Cambridge University, at Cambridge, England. Originating in the early 12th cent. (legend places its origin even earlier than that of OXFORD UNI-VERSITY), Cambridge was organized into residential colleges, like those of Oxford, by the end of the 13th cent. Its colleges, with their dates of founding, are Peterhouse or St. Peter's (1284), Clare (1326), Pembroke (1347), Gonville (1348, refounded as Gonville and Caius, 1558), Trinity Hall (1350), Corpus Christi (1352), King's (1441), Queens' (1448), St. Catharine's (1473), Jesus (1496), Christ's (1505), St. John's (1511), Magdalene (1542; pronounced môd'lĭn), Trinity (1546), Emmanuel (1584), Sidney Sussex (1596), Downing (1800), Selwyn (1882), and Churchill (1960). The women's colleges are Girton (1869), Newnham (1873), Hughes (1885), and New Hall (1954). Fitzwilliam House (1887) is a center for non-collegiate students. Girton and Newnham were pioneers in university education for women. Though women took university examinations in the 1880s and after 1921 were awarded degrees, their colleges were not admitted to full university status until 1948. Cambridge was a center of the new learning of the Renaissance and of the theology of the Reformation; in modern times it has excelled in science. Its faculties include classics, divinity, English, architecture and fine arts, modern and medieval languages, Oriental studies, music, economics and politics, history, law, moral science, engineering, geography and geology, mathematics, natural sciences, agriculture, archaeology and anthropology, and medicine. Its famous Cavendish Laboratory of experimental physics was opened in 1873; the Cavendish professors have been outstanding names in physics. The chapel of King's College (1446), the Fitzwilliam Museum, and the botanic gardens are notable features of the university. Instruction at Cambridge is similar to the system at Oxford, except that tutors are called supervisors and the degree examination is known as the tripos. Until 1948 Cambridge Univ. sent two representatives to Parliament. The Cambridge Univ. Press dates from the 16th cent. See Edmund Vale, *Cambridge and its Colleges* (1959); *Universities Yearbook.*

Cambuluc: see PEIPING.

Cambuskenneth, abbey, Stirlingshire, central Scotland, near Stirling. It was founded in 1147 by David I and was once one of the richest abbeys in

Scotland. James III and Margaret, queen of Denmark, are buried here.

Cambuslang, parish, Lanarkshire, S central Scotland, a suburb of Glasgow. It owes its development to the coal mines and steel industry of the region.

Cambyses (kămbĭ′sēz), d. 521 B.C., king of ancient Persia (529–521 B.C.), son and successor of CYRUS THE GREAT. He disposed of his brother Smerdis to have unchallenged rule. He invaded Egypt, defeating (525 B.C.) Psamtik at Pelusium and sacking Memphis. His further plans of conquest in Africa were frustrated, and at home an impostor claiming to be SMERDIS raised a revolt. Cambyses died, possibly by suicide, when he was putting down the insurrection. Darius I succeeded him.

Camden, Charles Pratt, 1st Earl: see PRATT, CHARLES, 1ST EARL CAMDEN.

Camden, William, 1551–1623, English scholar, chief historian and antiquary of Elizabethan times. His two chiefs works are *Britannia* (1586) and *Annales rerum Anglicarum et Hibernicarum regnante Elizabetha* [annals of affairs in England and Ireland in the reign of Elizabeth]. He was a conscientious scholar in editing old manuscripts and in collecting materials of antiquarian interest. He was also a teacher (1575–97) and headmaster (1593–97) at Westminster School and helped to revive the study of Anglo-Saxon. He wrote a Greek grammar long popular in English secondary schools and aided Sir Robert Cotton in collecting materials. The Camden Society, organized (1838) for the publication of historical documents, was named in his honor.

Camden. 1 Town (pop. 1,121), co. seat of Wilcox co., SW Ala., SSW of Selma, in a lumbering area; inc. 1841. **2** City (pop. 15,823), co. seat of Ouachita co., S Ark., NNW of El Dorado and on the Ouachita river; settled 1824, inc. 1847. A rail and river shipping point, it produces paper, pottery, furniture, air conditioners, and house trailers. **3** Town (pop. 1,125), central Del., SSW of Dover, in a fruitgrowing region; est. 1783. **4** Resort town (pop. 3,988), S Maine, on Penobscot Bay N of Rockland, in beautiful hilly country; settled 1769, inc. 1791. Textile goods and electrical equipment are made here. A state park is nearby. **5** Industrial city (pop. 117,159), co. seat of Camden co., W N.J., a port of entry on the Delaware opposite Philadelphia; settled 1681, laid out 1773, inc. 1828. The arrival of the Camden and Amboy RR in 1834 spurred the city's growth as a commercial, shipbuilding, and manufacturing center. Some of its present large industries had their beginnings in the 19th cent.—Richard Esterbrook in 1858 opened a steel-pen factory; the Campbell canned-foods company originated in 1869. The electrical equipment industry is more recent. Walt Whitman's home is preserved, and the poet is buried in the city where he lived from 1873. Of interest is the county historical society's museum in Charles S. Boyer Memorial Hall (formerly the Joseph Cooper house; built 1726). Access to Philadelphia is via the Benjamin Franklin Bridge (1926) and the Walt Whitman Bridge (1957). Camden is the seat of the College of South Jersey, a campus of RUTGERS—THE STATE UNIVERSITY. **6** Village (pop. 2,694), central N.Y., NW of Rome, in a farm and dairy area; inc. 1834. Copper wire is made.

7 Village (pop. 1,308), SW Ohio, WSW of Dayton, in a farm area; inc. 1831. **8** City (pop. 6,842), co. seat of Kershaw co., N central S.C., near the Wateree river and NE of Columbia; settled c.1735, inc. 1791. In a longleaf pine and farm area, it is a trade and processing center. Textiles, clothing, candy, and wood products are made. In the CAROLINA CAMPAIGN of the American Revolution, the battles of Camden (Aug. 16, 1780) and Hobkirks Hill (April 25, 1781) were fought in the neighborhood. The city was practically destroyed by fire when the British evacuated it on May 8, 1781. In the Civil War, when it was taken (Feb. 24, 1865) by a part of Sherman's army, it was again partially burned. Since the 1880s Camden has become a winter resort; it has beautiful estates and is well known for hunting, polo, and riding. There are a number of ante-bellum houses. It is the birthplace of Bernard M. Baruch. **9** Town (pop. 2,774), co. seat of Benton co., NW Tenn., W of Nashville and near the Tennessee river; laid out 1836, inc. 1899. Corn, cotton, and peanuts are grown here. Nathan Bedford Forrest Park, with a museum of Civil War relics, is here. **10** Uninc. village (pop. 1,131), E central Texas, NW of Beaumont, in a timber area.

Camdenton, city (pop. 1,405), central Mo., SW of Jefferson City; founded 1929, inc. 1930. It is a resort near Lake of the Ozarks. Lead and calcite mines are in the area.

camel, hoofed ruminant of the family Camelidae. There are two genera, the true camels (genus *Camelus* of Asia) and the South American genus *Lama*, which includes the wild guanaco and vicuña and the domesticated alpaca and llama. The two species of camel are the single-humped Arabian

Bactrian camel

Dromedary

camel or dromedary, *Camelus dromedarius*, a domesticated animal used in Arabia and North Africa, and the Bactrian two-humped camel (*C. bactrianus*) of central Asia. Some wild Bactrian camels exist in Turkistan and Mongolia. The humps are storage places for fat. Camels range in color from dirty white to dark brown and have long necks, small ears, tough-skinned lips, and powerful teeth, some of which are sharply pointed. The camel uses the mouth in fighting. Adaptations to desert life include broad, flat, thick-soled cloven hoofs which do not sink into the sand; the ability to go without drinking for several days—or longer if juicy plants are available; and valvular nostrils lined with hairs for protection against flying sand. Horny pads help to protect the chest, knees, and thigh joints against injury from the hard surfaces on which the camel sleeps. Strong camels usually carry from 500 to 600 lb. and cover about 30 mi. a day. Some Bactrian camels can transport 1,000 lb. A light fleet breed of the Arabian camel or dromedary is used for riding and not for bearing heavy loads. The name dromedary was formerly applied to any swift riding camel. Geologic findings indicate that the camel originated in North America, that one group migrated to Asia and the other to South America, and that both became extinct in North America probably after the glacial period.

camellia (–mĕl′–, –mē′–) [for G. J. Kamel, S. J.], any plant of the genus *Camellia*, evergreen shrubs or small trees native to Asia but now cultivated

Camellia japonica

extensively in warm climates and in greenhouses for their showy white or red blossoms and glossy, dark-green foliage. Camellias are closely related to the tea plant. Several species yield oil from the seeds, e.g., the widely cultivated *C. japonica* (commonly called japonica) and, especially, the Asiatic *C.*

Cameo portrait of Agamemnon (5th century B.C.).

sasanqua, the source of tea-seed oil used in textile and soap manufacture and, if suitably refined, for cooking.

Camelot (kăm′ŭlŏt), in ARTHURIAN LEGEND, the seat of King Arthur's court. The origin of the name is unknown. It has been variously located at Cadbury Camp, Somerset; Winchester; Camelford; and Caerleon.

Camembert cheese (kă′mŭmbâr, Fr. kämăbĕr′), unpressed rennet cheese, drained on straw mats and mold-ripened to a creamy consistency. Made since the late 18th cent. near Camembert village, NW France, it is exported in considerable quantity.

Camenae (kŭmē′nē), in Roman mythology, water nymphs gifted in prophecy. At Rome they had a sacred spring from which the vestals drew water for their rites. In later myth they were identified with the Greek Muses.

cameo (kă′mēō), small relief carving, usually on striated precious or semiprecious stones or on shell. The design, often a portrait head, is commonly cut in the light-colored vein, and the dark one is left as the background. Glass of two colors in layers may be cameo-cut; a famous Roman example is the PORTLAND VASE. The art originated in Asia as a decoration on the reverse of seals. The Greeks were noted for their exquisite designs and cutting on jewelry and on decorations for jewel caskets, vases, cups, and candelabra. The Romans were adept cutters, and Rome remains a center of experts in this art. The art was revived during the Renaissance, and cameo jewelry was a vogue of the Victorian era. Antique pieces are sought by collectors.

The famous "Farnese Dish," a masterwork of Alexandrian cameo art, an allegory carved in sardonyx.

camera, in photography, a light-proof container holding a lens that focuses the image of an object upon either a photographic plate or a film enclosed within. A shutter when opened permits the entrance of light that exposes the photographic film. The simplest form is the pinhole camera, consisting of an opaque box in which a tiny aperture takes the place of a lens. Another simple type is the box camera, comprising a boxlike container, a single lens with fixed focus, a single-speed shutter, and a diaphragm usually at a fixed setting. Roll film is generally employed in the box camera. The folding roll-film camera is equipped with an extensible bellows or other means of adjusting the lens position. The miniature, or candid, camera usually utilizes 35-millimeter film in cartridges and contains a high-speed lens. Press photographers now often prefer this camera or a double-lens reflex camera, using roll film and having separate lenses for focusing and taking pictures, to the cut-film camera with bellows that focuses with both ground glass and coupled range finder and has a wire view finder. Portrait photographers, architectural photographers, and others taking static subjects work with a view camera that uses cut film, has a bellows, focuses on a ground glass, and is used on a tripod. In the usual motion-picture camera the film moves intermittently from one spool to another in such a way that the film is at rest during the actual exposure. A rotating shutter exposes the film. The **camera lucida** (lōō'sĭdù) is an optical instrument that causes a virtual image of an external object to appear upon a plane surface so that the outline may be traced. It is usually used with the microscope, as an attachment to the eyepiece. The **camera obscura** (ŏbskyōō'rù) consists of a light-tight box or chamber with a convex lens at one end and a screen on which an image is produced at the other. It is sometimes used for making drawings and was the prototype of the modern photographic camera.

Camerarius, Rudolph Jacob (kămùrâ'rēùs, Ger. rōō'dôlf yä'kôp kämùrä'rēōōs), 1665–1721, German botanist, a physician. The first to present a clear and definite picture of sex in plants, he based his conclusions on careful experiments and observations. In his account of the work he described the stamen as the male organ and the ovary as the female organ and emphasized their relationship to the formation of seeds. He became a professor at the Univ. of Tübingen in 1688.

Cameron, Andrew Carr, 1834–90, American labor leader, b. Berwick-on-Tweed, England. He worked as a printer in Chicago, where he became interested in the labor movement. In the *Workingmen's Advocate,* which he edited from 1864 to 1877, he strongly advocated independent political action by labor. He helped found the National Labor Union in 1866 and was its delegate to the convention of the International Workingmen's Association in Basel in 1869. He was president of the Chicago Trades Assembly, the Grand Eight Hour League, and the Illinois State Labor Association.

Cameron, Donald, 1695?–1748, Scottish chieftain, known as the Gentle Lochiel. He was the first clan chieftain to join Charles Edward Stuart, the Young Pretender, in the unsuccessful rising of the Jacobites in 1745 and was wounded at Falkirk and Cul-loden. His humanity mitigated the savagery of his clansmen.

Cameron, Sir Ewen or **Evan,** 1629–1719, chief of the highland clan of Cameron after 1647, called the Cameron of Lochiel or just Lochiel. On behalf of Charles II he led his clan against the parliamentarians in 1653, and only in 1658 did he submit to the Puritan general, George Monck. He accompanied Monck to London in 1660 and was knighted by Charles II at the Restoration. A supporter of James II and later one of the leading Jacobites, he brought his clan to the aid of John Graham, Viscount Dundee, in the royalist victory at Killiecrankie (1689) and sent it again to aid the Jacobite rebellion of 1715. Lochiel was a romantic warrior of great strength, and from one of his feats Sir Walter Scott drew his description of the fight between Roderick Dhu and Fitz James in *The Lady of the Lake.*

Cameron, John, c.1579–1625, Scottish scholar and theologian. As teacher, lecturer, and preacher at Bordeaux, Saumur, and other cities on the Continent, he came to be celebrated for his learning and ability. He was appointed (1622) principal of the Univ. of Glasgow by James I of England, but his belief in the divine right of kings and his stand for passive obedience made it impossible for him to remain in this post long. Returning to France after less than a year, he became (1624) professor of divinity at Montauban. Not long afterward he was attacked by an enemy of the doctrine of passive obedience and died. His writings, in Latin and French, were largely concerned with his views on man's free will and the grace of God. Those who held the same opinions were sometimes known as Cameronites and practiced a moderate form of Calvinism. His collected works were published in 1642, with a memoir by Louis Cappel.

Cameron, Richard, d. 1680, Scottish leader of the Cameronians, an extreme group of COVENANTERS. Converted by the field preachers, he was licensed as one of them and became known for his eloquence. Strongly opposing the measures aimed at reestablishing the Episcopal Church in Scotland and objecting to any state control of the church, he led a small company who, in the Sanquhar Declaration, disowned the royal authority of Charles II. A price was set on his head and within a short time he and a little band of supporters were overtaken by royal troops. Cameron and many of his group were killed. Later (1743) the Cameronians, growing in numbers, formed a presbytery, taking the name Reformed Presbyterians. This denomination is still represented by congregations in Scotland, the north of Ireland, and North America, but the greater number united (1876) with the Free Church of Scotland. A body of Cameronians formed the nucleus (1689) of the celebrated Cameronian regiment of the British army. See biography by John Herkless (1896).

Cameron, Simon, 1799–1889, American politician and financier, b. Lancaster co., Pa. From humble beginnings he rose to be a newspaper publisher and branched out into canal and road construction, railroad promotion, banking, and iron and steel manufacturing. All these private interests were admirably served by his talent for politics. At first a Democrat, he was long associated in Pennsylvania with James Buchanan, who later called him "an unprincipled rascal." Cameron was elected (1845) to Buchanan's vacated seat in the U.S. Senate but, defeated for reelection, served only until 1849. In 1856, having joined the new Republican party, he was returned to the Senate when three Democratic legislators also voted for him. To Cameron is attributed that famous definition of an "honest politician" as one who, "when bought, stays bought." At the Republican national convention in Chicago in 1860 he was a candidate for the nomination for President, but after the first ballot supported Abraham Lincoln, first exacting from Lincoln's managers, however, the promise of a cabinet post. Lincoln reluctantly recognized the bargain, made without his knowledge, and Cameron resigned from the Senate to serve (March, 1861–Jan., 1862) as Secretary of War. The President's worst fears were realized as notorious corruption in army contracts and appointments aroused the nation. Lincoln eased him out gracefully by appointing him minister to Russia, but Cameron resigned that post in Nov., 1862. The House of Representatives passed (April, 1862) a resolution of censure against him, but Cameron, never a sensitive man, bounded back in 1867, when, in defeating Andrew H. Curtin for the Senate, he became absolute Republican boss of Pennsylvania. Although he retired from the Senate and from active participation in politics in 1877, the machine he created, later run by his son, James Donald Cameron, Matthew S. QUAY, Boies PENROSE, William S. VARE, and Joseph R. Grundy successively, so dominated Pennsylvania that it was not until Franklin D. Roosevelt's victory in 1936 that the Democrats carried the state in a national election. See L. F. Crippen, *Simon Cameron: Ante-Bellum Years* (1942); B. J. Hendrick, *Lincoln's War Cabinet* (1946).

Cameron, Thomas Fairfax, 3d **Baron Fairfax of:** see FAIRFAX OF CAMERON, THOMAS FAIRFAX, 3d BARON.

Cameron, Verney Lovett, 1844–94, English traveler in Africa, b. Dorsetshire. A naval officer, he served (1868) in the British expedition against Ethiopia and assisted in the suppression of the East African slave trade. He was sent (1873) by the Royal Geographical Society to relieve Livingstone but, finding him dead, recovered his papers, explored and mapped Lake Tanganyika, and proceeded to the Atlantic, the first European to cross equatorial Africa. His expedition was recorded in *Across Africa* (1877). In 1882 he explored the Gold Coast with Sir Richard Burton and was co-author with him of *To the Gold Coast for Gold* (1883).

Cameron. 1 City (pop. 3,674), NW Mo., E of St. Joseph; platted 1855, inc. 1867. It is a railroad and trade center in a farm region. Wallace State Park is nearby. **2** City (pop. 5,640), co. seat of Milam co., E central Texas, SSE of Waco, in a farm area; founded 1846, inc. 1888. **3** City (pop. 1,652), W.Va., in the Northern Panhandle SE of Moundsville; settled 1788.

Cameron, Federal Republic of, country (183,376 sq. mi.; pop. c.4,112,000), W Africa. The capital is Yaoundé. The country comprises the former French Cameroons and the southern section of the British Cameroons. It is bordered on the west by

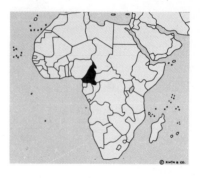

Cameroon
location map

the Gulf of Guinea, on the north and northwest by Nigeria, on the north and northeast by Chad, on the east by the Central African Republic, and on the south by the Congo Republic, Gabon, and Rio Muni. Beyond the coastal swamps and plains the land rises to a densely forested plateau c.1,000 feet above sea level. The interior of the territory is a high plateau (from 2,500 to 4,500 ft.), and forests give way to savanna; the extreme northern regions, near Lake Chad, are dry thorn and bush lands. The highest elevation in the country is Cameroon Mt. (13,350 feet), near the coast. Cameroon is drained by many rivers, among them the Benue, the Temba, the Katsina, and the Cross. The coastal area has an annual average rainfall of 152 in.; in the north annual rainfall averages 31 in. Agriculture is the mainstay of the economy, and Cameroon is one of the world's leading cocoa-producing countries; other exports are coffee, bananas, palm oil, tobacco, and peanuts. Agricultural products are shipped from Douala, the principal seaport. In the north cattle raising is important. The country has a large variety of mineral resources, including gold, diamonds, manganese, bauxite, tin, and mica. Although there is a large aluminum plant at Edéa, agricultural processing remains the chief industry; industrial expansion is hampered by an inadequate transportation system. In the north, where Hamitic and Semitic peoples live, Islam is the predominant religion, whereas in the south and central regions Bantu peoples practice animism; Christianity has made converts here. The official language is French. In early times the region was dominated by many invaders, especially the Fulani, Hausa, Fang, and Kanuri, before it came under German control in the late 19th cent. The Germans advanced into the interior and developed plantations, built roads, and began construction on the port of Douala. For a history of this period and that of the subsequent mandated regions of the Cameroons, see CAMEROONS. In the 1950s guerrilla warfare was waged in the French Cameroons by the Union of the Peoples of the Cameroons, which demanded immediate independence and union with the British Cameroons. France granted self-government to the territory in 1957 and internal autonomy in 1959. At the recommendation of the UN, the trusteeship was ended and independence proclaimed on Jan. 1, 1960. Rioting soon broke out, but President Ahmadou Ahidjo, with the help of the French, restored order.

Wooden figure from Cameroon at left, decorated with colored pearls, representing a deceased ancestor of the owner. Center, native women working a corn mill. At right, savanna landscape of Cameroon.

The republic was admitted to the UN in 1960. Early in 1961, the southern part of the British Cameroons voted in a plebiscite to become a self-governing province in Cameroon, which was then reconstituted as a federal republic. Cameroon is a member of the African-Malagasy Union, and the so-called Monrovia group of African states.

Cameroon Mountain (kă'mŭroͦn) volcanic peak, 13,350 ft. high, Federal Republic of Cameroon. The highest elevation in W Africa, it is the culminating summit of the Cameroon Highlands. The highlands (5,000–10,000 ft. high) are a healthy and fertile region. They stretch for more than 400 mi. northward toward the Benue valley.

Cameroons, Fr. *Cameroun,* Ger. *Kamerun,* former German colony, W Africa, on the Gulf of Guinea and extending N to Lake Chad. Germany's penetration of the area began c.1885, and by 1902 its possession was recognized. Territory of French Equatorial Africa was added in 1911. In the First World War, French and British troops occupied the Cameroons. After the war the territory ceded in 1911 was rejoined to French Equatorial Africa, and in 1919 the remainder of the Cameroons was divided into French and British zones, which became mandates under the League of Nations. In 1946 the mandates were made trust territories of the United Nations. **British Cameroons** (31,150 sq. mi.) consisted of two detached sections lying on the eastern border of Nigeria; the more southerly extended to the coast. **French Cameroons** (166,489 sq. mi.) was administered as a separate territory with the capital at Yaoundé. In 1960 French Cameroons became the Cameroon Republic; in 1961 the southern section of British Cameroons was joined to the Cameroon Republic to form the Federal Republic of Cameroons, while the northern section passed to the Federation of Nigeria.

Camilla (kŭmĭl'ŭ), city (pop. 4,753), co. seat of Mitchell co., SW Ga., S of Albany, in a farm and timber area; inc. 1858.

Camillus (Marcus Furius Camillus) (kŭmĭl'lŭs), d. 365? B.C., Roman hero. He was a patrician who, the Roman historians say, was elected dictator five times (396, 390, 386, 368, 367 B.C.) and on each occasion won a signal victory. He captured Veii, saved Rome from the Gauls, defeated the Aequi

Camillus (detail from a Roman relief)

and Volscians, took Praeneste, and defeated the Gauls at Alba Longa. Modern historians do not accept in full the traditional account of Camillus' victories.

Camillus, village (pop. 1,416), central N.Y., W of

Syracuse, in a farm and dairy area; inc. 1852. Pocket knives and cutlery are made.

Caminha, Pedro Vaz de (pä'drŏ väzh' dù kùmē'nyù), fl. 1500, Portuguese explorer. He sailed in the expedition of Pedro Alvares Cabral and wrote a letter to King Manuel I giving a detailed account of the voyage.

Camisards (kämēsär', kăm'ĭsärdz), Protestant peasants of the Cévennes region of France who in 1702 rebelled against the persecutions which followed the revocation (1685) of the Edict of Nantes (see NANTES, EDICT OF). The name was probably given them because of the shirts which they wore in night raids. Led by the young Jean CAVALIER and Roland LAPORTE, the Camisards met the ravages of the royal army with guerrilla methods and withstood superior forces in several battles. In 1704 Marshal Villars, the royal commander, offered Cavalier vague concessions to the Protestants and the promise of a command in the royal army. Cavalier's acceptance broke the revolt, though others, including Laporte, refused to submit unless the Edict of Nantes were restored, and scattered fighting went on until 1710. See A. E. Bray, *The Revolt of the Protestants of the Cévennes* (1870); H. M. Baird, *Huguenots and the Revocation of the Edict of Nantes* (1895).

Cammack Village, town (pop. 1,355), central Ark., a suburb WNW of Little Rock.

Cammaerts, Émile (ämēl' kä'märts), 1878–1953, Belgian poet. In 1908 he settled in England, becoming a professor at the Univ. of London in 1933. His poetry of the First World War, which appeared in French, was translated and collected in *Belgian Poems* (1915) and *New Belgian Poems* (1916). Later works, in English, include *Upon This Rock* (1943), a poignant character sketch of a son killed in the war, and volumes on Belgian history and culture.

Camões or **Camoens, Luís de** (both: lōōĕsh' dù kùmō'ĭsh), 1524?–1580, Portuguese poet, the greatest figure of Portuguese literature. Born of a poor

Luís de Camões

family of the minor nobility, he gained wide familiarity with classic literature at the Univ. of Coimbra. Always turbulent and impetuous, he did not complete his course. In Lisbon he fell in love—

perhaps with a lady of the court, Dona Caterina de Ataíde, or with the Infanta Maria—and wrote fiery and flawless love poems for his beloved. After some offense had earned him banishment from court in 1546, he served as a soldier in a campaign against Ceuta in Africa, where he lost an eye. Back in Lisbon, he led a riotous life that ended in imprisonment (1552) for wounding a court official. Released in 1553 with the understanding that he would serve in India, he went there over the same route traveled by Vasco da Gama. Apparently he had already begun his most celebrated work, *The Lusiads* [Port. *Os Lusíadas*=sons of Lusus, i.e., the Portuguese], but this journey may have caused him to make Vasco's voyage the central theme of his epic. After fighting in India, he was given an official post at Macao in China. On his way there, he spent more than a year in the Moluccas, but by 1558 charges were brought against him for maladministration at Macao, and he was put aboard a ship for Goa in India. A shipwreck delayed his arrival until 1561. The year 1567 saw him on his way back to Portugal, but he stopped at Mozambique for some time and arrived in Portugal only in 1570. He brought with him the manuscript of *The Lusiads*, published in 1572. This won him a royal pension, albeit meager and sometimes long delayed. His last years were spent in poverty, and in 1580 he died in obscurity, although his epic had begun to enjoy world fame. By 1655 it had appeared in English in a version by Sir Richard Fanshawe. Although modeled on Vergil and showing the influence of Ariosto, it is imitative of neither and is a great epic in its own right. The beauty of its poetry is enlivened by a vigorous and realistic narrative that embraces not only the voyage of Vasco da Gama but also most of Portuguese history; there is a fanciful section describing the reception of Gama and his men on Venus' Isle of Love. Apart from *The Lusiads*, however, Camões's sonnets and lyrics would have won him lasting fame. Although they have largely defied translation, many translations of the epic have been made through the years. See J. D. M. Ford's edition of *The Lusiads* with English notes to accompany the Portuguese text (1946); biography by H. H. Hart (1962).

camomile: see CHAMOMILE.

Camon (kā'mŏn) [Heb.,=standing place], unidentified place. Judges 10.5.

Camorra (kùmô'rù), Italian secret criminal association in Naples and Sicily. Of controversial, probably Spanish, origin, it first came to light in 1830. Its activities spread by intimidation, blackmail, and bribery until Naples was controlled by the organization. In 1901 a league of Neapolitan citizens was organized to break the power of the Camorra, which was finally dissolved after the trial and conviction of 40 members in 1911. The Camorra frequently terrorized Italian immigrants in the United States.

camouflage (kă'mùfläzh), in warfare, the disguising of objects with artificial aids, especially for the purpose of making them blend into their surroundings or of deceiving the observer as to the location of strategic points. The principle, of course, is observed in the world of nature (see PROTECTIVE COLORATION) and has long been used by man. Scientific camouflage was greatly developed in the

Soldier wearing camouflaged helmet.

Latium, central Italy. Mostly abandoned for centuries because of its malarial climate and the lack of water for cultivation, the area has greatly benefited from reclamation works in the 19th and 20th cent. and is now used as pasture land. There are some remains of Roman aqueducts and tombs.

Campagnola, Domenico (dōmā′nēkō kämpänyō′lä), 1500-c.1564, painter and engraver. Although Campagnola's entire artistic career was in Italy, there are documents indicating that he was of German origin. He was a pupil of Giulio Campagnola and of Titian, whom he assisted in the decorating of the Scuola del Santo. He painted chiefly in the churches of Padua. His best-known works are three frescoes in the Scuola del Carmine, Padua; *Four Prophets* (Academy, Venice); and *Holy Family* (Pitti Palace). Campagnola is celebrated also for his engravings, woodcuts, and masterly pen-and-ink drawings, which resemble Titian's. Examples are in the Uffizi and in the British Museum.

Campagnola, Giulio (jōō′lyō), b. c.1482, d. after 1513, Italian painter and engraver. He painted miniatures and altarpieces, but is best known for his finely executed engravings, many of them after the works of Giovanni Bellini and Giorgione.

campaign, political, organized effort to secure nomination and election of candidates for government offices. In the United States, political campaigns center about the nomination and election of candidates for the offices of President and Vice President. In each political party such nominations are made every four years at a national CONVENTION preceding the presidential election. The contending parties are organized with a national chairman at the head of an elaborate system of national, state, and local committees. The size of and diversity within the two major American parties make the campaign for the presidency the chief effective function of each party. Every available means of publicity is enlisted on behalf of a presidential candidate. In recent years radio and television have taken on an increasingly large role in this process of communicating with the voter. Television in particular has been widely used to publicize the candidates' speeches and the political rallies. In 1960 it was the medium of a major innovation in campaign technique when a series of debates between the principal candidates received nationwide television coverage. Financial contributions by corporations, individuals, and federal employees, and expenditures by the national committees

First World War. The French, in particular, used elaborate devices to conceal military objectives and industrial plants. False landscapes were created, using wire screens as a foundation for foliage. Ships were dazzle-painted to conceal their course by distortion of perspective. In the Second World War camouflage was further developed and was used on a large scale by all belligerents. With the development of RADAR and AERIAL PHOTOGRAPHY in the Second World War comouflage diminished greatly in utility. Particularly in the guerrilla campaigns of Southeast Asia, however, camouflage again became important.

Camp, Walter Chauncey, 1859–1925, American football expert, b. New Britain, Conn., grad. Yale, 1880. He was a prominent athlete at Yale, where he was football coach after 1888; later, Camp became athletic director. Often called the father of American football, he had a leading role in developing the game and shaping its rules. Camp originated (1889), with Caspar W. Whitney, the practice of choosing an All-American football team. In the First World War he adapted for use in training camps the calisthenics known as the daily dozen. He wrote more than 30 books on football and physical fitness.

Campagna di Roma (kämpä′nyä dē rō′mä), low-lying region surrounding the city of Rome, in

Campagna di Roma (ancient ruins of the arena of Massentium near the Appian Way).

are restricted by law. Presidential campaigns overshadow and in part determine the outcome of concurrent state and local elections. Local campaigns are administered and waged along the same general lines as the presidential. In England the system of parliamentary government permits the overthrow of the cabinet by a vote of no confidence at any time and necessitates a stronger permanent party organization, since an election is always theoretically imminent. English parliamentary and local elections are never held concurrently; campaigns are short and intensive, and party expenditures are very moderate and are fixed by law. See Ivan Hinderaker, *Party Politics* (1956); V. O. Key, *Politics, Parties and Pressure Groups* (4th ed., 1958); Alexander Heard, *The Costs of Democracy* (1960).

Campan, Jeanne Louise Henriette (Genest) (zhän′ lwēz′ ärēĕt′ kăpä′), 1752–1822, French educator and author. She served as a reader to Louis XV's daughters and as lady in waiting to Marie Antoinette. In 1792 she founded a school for girls at Saint-Germain, which Hortense de Beauharnais attended, and directed it until her appointment (1806) as principal of the academy established by Napoleon at Écouen. She retired in 1814. Among her works, published posthumously, are *Mémoires sur la vie privée de Marie Antoinette* (1823), *Journal anecdotique* (1824), and *Correspondance inédite avec la reine Hortense* (1835).

Campaña, Pedro: see KEMPENER, PIETER DE.

Campanella, Tommaso (tŏm-mä′zo kämpänĕl′lä), 1568–1639, Italian Renaissance philosopher and writer. He entered the Dominican order at the age of 15, and though he was frequently in trouble with the authorities, he never left the Church. Imprisoned in 1599 on the grounds that he was plotting against the Spanish rule of Naples, he

Naples, capital of the Campania on the Bay of Naples, with Vesuvius in the background.

was released in 1626 on the representation of the pope. His best-known work is *Civitas solis* (1623; Eng. tr., *The City of the Sun*), an account of a utopian society which closely follows the pattern of Plato's *Republic*. Though he retained much of scholasticism and insisted on the preeminence of faith in matters of theology, he emphasized perception and experiment as the media of science. His importance, like that of Francis Bacon and

Tommaso Campanella (painting by Francesco Cossa)

Bruno, depends largely on his anticipation of what came to be the scientific attitude of empiricism. For his *Civitas solis*, see Henry Morley, ed., *Ideal Commonwealths* (1890).

Campania (kämpä′nyä), region (5,249 sq. mi.; estimated pop. 4,736,636), S Italy, extending from the Apennines to the Tyrrhenian Sea and from the Garigliano river to the Gulf of Policastro. Including several small islands, the region is divided into the provinces of Avellino, Benevento, Caserta, Naples, and Salerno, all named after their chief cities. Naples is the capital. The coast is mostly high and rocky, with volcanic ridges and the crater of Vesuvius. The plains of Campania have been famous since ancient times for their fertility; the hills are covered with vineyards and orange, lemon, and olive groves. Industries are on a small scale and are mostly clustered along the Bay of Naples. The picturesque and historically rich Bay of Naples has a thriving tourist industry. Various Italic tribes, Greek colonists, Etruscans, and Samnites lived here before the Roman conquest (4th–2d cent. B.C.). After the fall of Rome the Goths and Byzantines occupied the region, which later became part of the Lombard duchy of Benevento (except Naples and Amalfi). In the 11th cent. the Normans conquered the region, and in the 12th cent. it became part of the kingdom of Sicily. Naples soon rose to prominence and after the Sicilian Vespers (1282) became the capital of a separate kingdom. For the later history of Campania, see NAPLES, KINGDOM OF and TWO SICILIES, KINGDOM OF THE. There was heavy fighting around Naples after the Allied landing (Sept., 1943) at SALERNO during the Second World War.

campanile (kămpŭnē′lē, Ital. kämpänē′lä) [Ital. from Late Latin, =bell tower], Italian form of bell tower, constructed chiefly during the Middle Ages. Built in connection with a church or a town hall, it served as a belfry and watch tower and often functioned as a civic or commemorative monu-

The campanile of Florence by Giotto.

ment. The campanile generally stands as a detached unit. At the top is the bell platform, where is concentrated the main architectural emphasis, generally a group of arched openings. Originating in the 6th cent., the campaniles were the earliest church towers in Europe and were generally circular in shape; examples of this type remain at Ravenna. Beginning with the 8th cent., the square plan became the most usual, being constructed in all parts of Italy. The Lombardy section produced the richest development of the campanile. Brick is the material most used, often combined with stone for the cornices and string courses, the latter surrounding the tower at each story level in the Roman examples. The celebrated campanile of Florence, known as Giotto's campanile (1334), is entirely faced in marble and ornamented with sculptures. Also of marble is the leaning tower at Pisa.

campanula: see BELLFLOWER.

Campbell, Alexander (kăm′bŭl), 1788–1866, clergyman, cofounder with his father, Thomas Campbell (1763–1854), of the DISCIPLES OF CHRIST. Of Scottish lineage, both were born in Ireland and educated at the Univ. of Glasgow. Both were Anti-Burgher Presbyterians, a division opposed to the discipline of the main church. In 1807 the father went to America, where he was welcomed among the Scotch-Irish in SW Pennsylvania. His habit of asking all Presbyterians to join his church members in the communion service was contrary to a ruling of the Anti-Burgher synod in which he was preaching, and his action was condemned by his presbytery. Although his synod upheld him, the atmosphere remained so hostile that he and his followers, who were popularly called Campbellites (kăm′bŭlīts, kă′mŭ-), withdrew. In 1809 they formed the Christian Association of Washington, Pa., setting forth its purposes in a "Declaration and Address" which is considered the most important document of the Disciples body. In that year Campbell was joined in America by his son, Alexander, and the other members of his family. In c.1812, having accepted the doctrine of immersion, the Campbells and their followers were invited to join the Baptists. Until c.1827 they were nominally Baptists, but there were differences which caused trouble. Alexander Campbell, who had by this time assumed the leadership, advocated a return to scriptural simplicity in organization and doctrine; his followers became known as Reformers. He founded (1823) the *Christian Baptist* to promote his views and traveled throughout the new Western states, addressing large audiences. He edited (from 1830) the *Millennial Harbinger*, wrote *The Christian System* (1839), and in 1840 founded Bethany College in West Virginia and became its president. Meanwhile, the Reformers had seceded or been forced out of many Baptist churches, and Campbell suggested that they form congregations and call themselves Disciples of Christ. Many of the "Christians," led chiefly by Barton Warren STONE, joined congregations of the Disciples; in 1832 the two leaders agreed to unite their efforts. See Robert Richardson, *Memoirs of Alexander Campbell* (2 vols., 1868–70); D. R. Lindley, *Apostle of Freedom* (1957).

Campbell, Archibald, 1st duke of Argyll, d. 1703.

The leaning tower of Pisa.

Scottish nobleman; eldest son of the 9th earl of Argyll. To recover his father's forfeited estates, he supported first James II (even to the point of embracing Catholicism) and later William III. He is chiefly remembered for his part in instigating, organizing, and carrying out (under John CAMPBELL, earl of Breadalbane) the horrible massacre of the Macdonalds at Glencoe (1692). He was given several offices and made a duke (1701).

Campbell, Archibald, 3d duke of Argyll, 1682–1761, Scottish nobleman; brother of the 2d duke. As lord high treasurer of Scotland (1705) and commissioner for the union (1706), he aided in joining the kingdoms of Scotland and England and was created earl of Islay (1705). He succeeded (1743) his brother as duke of Argyll and served as a Scottish peer in the united Parliament until his death. He was a consistent supporter of George I. He held high offices in Scotland and promoted the trade, industry, and schools of his native land.

Campbell, Archibald, 5th earl of Argyll, 1530–73, Scottish statesman; He and Lord James Stuart (later earl of Murray) became followers of John Knox in 1556 and led troops of the Scottish reformers, the lords of the congregation, against those of the regent, Mary of Guise. Won by Mary Queen of Scots when she arrived in Scotland (1561), he turned from Knox to her until she proposed marrying Lord Darnley. He then tried to enlist Queen Elizabeth's aid against Mary. Failing, he returned to Mary's party and is thought to have had some part in the murder of Darnley. He was in command of Mary's soldiers when they were defeated at Langside in 1568 by the soldiers under Murray, now regent, but he was reconciled with Murray the next year. Becoming a supporter of James VI, he was made lord high chancellor in 1572. He was responsible for the reconciliation between the parties of Mary and James at Perth in 1573.

Campbell, Archibald, 8th **earl of Argyll** and 1st **marquess of Argyll,** 1607–61, Scottish statesman. He became chief of his powerful clan at his father's death (1638). Charles I attempted to win his support, but he stood firmly for Presbyterianism, and at the Pacification of Berwick (1639) he insisted that the "lords of the articles" be chosen by the estates, not by the king. This greatly increased the influence of the Scottish Parliament. Still eager for his support, Charles made him a marquess in 1641, but in the civil war Argyll took the field with the Covenanters and was defeated (1645) by royalists under James Graham, 5th earl of Montrose, at Inverlochy and Kilsyth. After Montrose's defeat a few months later and after the surrender of Charles to the Scots (1646), Argyll was the mediator between the king and the two Parliaments, attempting to secure a Presbyterian settlement in England. He later supported Oliver Cromwell but suffered a serious loss of influence because of the revulsion of feeling in Scotland at the king's execution. Hoping that Charles II could be restored as a Presbyterian king, he turned from Cromwell and crowned (1651) Charles II in Scotland, but Scottish opinion was so at odds about his action that Argyll lost all real power. He was executed for treason at the Restoration. The most powerful Presbyterian leader in Scotland, he pursued, like Cromwell, a practical, if not wholly consistent policy. His *Instructions to a Son* (1661) was written during his imprisonment. See biography by John Willcocks (1903).

Campbell, Archibald, 9th **earl of Argyll,** 1629?–1685, Scottish nobleman; son of the 8th earl. An ardent and active royalist and a Protestant, he opposed extreme measures against the Covenanters and so incurred the enmity of the duke of York (later James II), who was in 1680 high commissioner of Scotland. Argyll was accused of treason and sentenced to death in 1681. He escaped to Holland, was a leader of the rebellion in favor of the duke of MONMOUTH, and was captured and beheaded.

Campbell, Colin, Baron Clyde, 1792–1863, British general. He commanded troops in China (1846) and India (1847–54) and in the famous victory at BALAKLAVA in the Crimean War. For his services in India in suppressing the Sepoy Rebellion he was created baron in 1858. He was made a field marshal in 1862. See biography by Lawrence Shadwell (1881).

Campbell, Colin, d. 1729, Scottish architect, who, in England, became one of the initiators of the Neo-Palladian movement. Campbell's most important contribution to this revival of classicizing architecture was his publication of *Vitruvius Britannicus* (3 vols., 1715, 1717, 1725). These volumes consisted of engravings of classical buildings in England —at first especially those of Inigo Jones, but the later volumes presented designs by Campbell and other contemporary architects. Campbell's major buildings were Wanstead House, Essex (1715–20, destroyed), which incorporated what Campbell claimed to be England's first classical portico; the remodeling of Burlington House, London (c.1717); **and Mereworth Castle, Kent (1723). They derive from obvious Palladian precedents. Through his writings and his executed buildings, Campbell's influence on English architecture was great.**

Campbell, John, 2d **duke of Argyll** and **duke of Greenwich** (grĭ′nĭj), 1678–1743, Scottish general. He entered the army at 16 and became (1703) colonel of the Scottish house guards. For his ardent support of the union of England and Scotland he was created (1705) earl of Greenwich. He served under the duke of Marlborough in the War of the Spanish Succession, in spite of his jealousy of his superior, and rose to be commander in chief in Spain in 1711. On his return to Scotland he actively supported the succession of George I, commanded the army in Scotland which put down the Jacobite rebellion in 1715, and was made duke of Greenwich in 1719. His ambitions brought him high political offices, but he was tactless and too forthright, and his later career was uneven.

Campbell, John, 1st **earl of Breadalbane** (brŭdôl′-bĭn, brĕd-), 1635?–1717, Scottish chieftain. He took part in the royalist rising of 1654 and helped George Monck to further the Restoration. In 1689 he took the oath to William III and was authorized to receive the submission of the clans. The Macdonalds of Glencoe were delayed in taking the oath, and Campbell used this as a pretext for the brutal massacre at Glencoe (1692), destroying that clan (with the collusion of the 1st earl of Stair) to wipe out old scores under the cloak of official action. He was elected to the united Parliament in 1713 but joined the Jacobite rebellion of 1715.

Campbell, John, 4th **earl of Loudoun,** 1705–82, British general. As commander in chief he reorganized (1756–58) the military establishment in America, but was censured for failing to attack Louisburg in the French and Indian Wars. His recall to England ended his career.

Campbell, John, 1st **Baron Campbell,** 1779–1861, English jurist and statesman. He became lord chief justice (1850) and lord chancellor (1859). Appointed (1828) as head of the Real Property Commission, he played a leading role in reforming the real estate laws of England. Campbell sat in Parliament as a Whig from 1830 to 1849. It was partly upon his advice that England recognized the Confederacy as a belligerent in the American Civil War. He wrote *Lives of the Lord Chancellors* (1845–47) and *Lives of the Chief Justices* (1849–57).

Campbell, John, 1653–1728, American editor, b. Scotland. Emigrating to Boston, he was postmaster of the city from 1702 to 1718 and wrote newsletters for regular patrons. In 1704 he started printing these newsletters as a weekly half sheet, devoted mostly to foreign news, entitled the *Boston News-Letter.* Sold to Bartholomew Green in 1722.

it was the first successfully established paper in America despite a small circulation.

Campbell, John Francis, 1822–85, Scottish Gaelic scholar. He is known for *Popular Tales of the West Highlands* (4 vols., 1860–62) and *Leabhar na Feinne* (1872), a collection of Gaelic folk ballads. A meteorologist also, he invented an instrument to record the intensity of the sun's rays.

Campbell, Sir Malcom, 1885–1949, English automobile and speedboat racer, b. Kent. A racing enthusiast from boyhood, Campbell set many speed

Sir Malcolm Campbell

records for motorcycles, airplanes, automobiles, and motorboats and in 1931 was knighted for his accomplishments. Driving his famed automobile *Bluebird* at Bonneville Flats, Utah, in 1935, Sir Malcolm was the first to reach the 300 mi. per hr. mark. He then turned to speedboat racing and in 1939 set a new record of 141 mi. per hr. His son Donald Campbell (1921–) raised the water speed record to 260 mi. per hr. in 1959.

Campbell, Mrs. Patrick, 1865–1940, English actress, whose maiden name was Beatrice Stella Tanner. Remembered today for her association with G. B. Shaw, she was in her day an actress of great beauty and wit. She made her debut in 1888 but achieved her first London success in 1893 in the title role of Pinero's *Second Mrs. Tanqueray*. In 1901 she made the first of her numerous tours to the United States; in 1912 she met Shaw at whose request she created the role of Eliza Doolittle in *Pygmalion*. See her *My Life and Some Letters* (1922) and her correspondence with Shaw (ed. by Alan Dent, 1952).

Campbell, Robert: see ROB ROY.

Campbell, Robert, 1804–79, American fur trader and merchant, one of the mountain men, b. Ireland. He came to the United States c.1824. Having been advised to lead an outdoor life on account of his lungs, he joined (1825) a fur trapping expedition. He trapped and traded in the Rocky Mts. until 1832, when he and William Sublette formed a partnership, which offered competition to the American Fur Company. Suffering reverses, they confined their activities to the mountain territory. The partnership was dissolved in 1842, and Campbell returned to St. Louis, where he amassed a fortune in merchandising, real estate, and banking.

In 1851 and again in 1869 he served as Indian commissioner.

Campbell, Robert, 1808–94, Canadian fur trader and explorer, b. Scotland. In 1832 he was employed by the Hudson's Bay Company, which sent him in 1834 to the Mackenzie river region, where he remained until 1852. He discovered the Pelly river in 1840, descending it in 1843 to its confluence with the Lewes to form the Yukon. Here he established Fort Selkirk. Later (1850–51) he followed the Yukon to its junction with the Porcupine at Fort Yukon. He wrote *The Discovery and Exploration of the Pelly River* (1883).

Campbell, Roy, 1901–57, South African poet. His persuasive and robust poetry, reminiscent of the 19th-century English romantics, includes *The Flaming Terrapin* (1924), *Mithraic Emblems* (1936), and *Flowering Rifle* (1939). A fascist, Campbell lived in Spain and fought with Franco's army in the Spanish civil war. His collected poems were published in 1957. See his autobiography (1952).

Campbell, Thomas, 1763–1854, American clergyman, a founder of the DISCIPLES OF CHRIST. See CAMPBELL, ALEXANDER, his more famous son.

Campbell, Thomas, 1777–1844, English poet, b. Glasgow. He is best known for his war poems "Hohenlinden," "The Battle of the Baltic," and

Thomas Campbell

"Ye Mariners of England." Among his other poems are *The Pleasure of Hope* (1799), *Gertrude of Wyoming* (1809), and *Theodric* (1824).

Campbell, Wilfred (William Wilfred Campbell), 1861–1918, Canadian poet, b. Kitchener, Ont. Although he wrote several historical novels and poetic dramas, his fame rests mainly on his *Lake Lyrics* (1889), a volume of nature poetry. He also edited the *Oxford Book of Canadian Verse* (1913). See his *Poetical Works* (1923).

Campbell, William, 1745–81, patriot officer in the American Revolution, b. Augusta co., Va.; brother-in-law of Patrick Henry. He fought in Lord Dunmore's War (1774) and helped expel the royal governor from Williamsburg in 1776. Campbell and his group of Virginia riflemen in 1780 joined Sevier and Shelby at Kings mt. (see CAROLINA CAMPAIGN), where he was in command. Later

Campbell saw action at Guilford Courthouse, at Eutaw Springs, and in the Yorktown campaign.

Campbell. 1 City (pop. 11,863), W Calif., SW of San Jose; founded 1885, inc. 1952. It is a processing center in a fruit and vegetable area. 2 City (pop. 1,964), SE Mo., near the Ark. line and SE of Poplar Bluff; inc. 1892. It has cotton gins and a sawmill. 3 City (pop. 13,406), NE Ohio, ESE of Youngstown; inc. as a village 1908, as a city 1926. Steel is made here.

Campbell-Bannerman, Sir Henry, 1836–1908, British statesman. He entered Parliament (1868) as a Liberal, was secretary of the admiralty (1882–84) and secretary of state for Ireland (1884), and was knighted (1895). He served (1886, 1892–95) as secretary of state for war and became (1898) party leader in succession to Sir William Harcourt. He led opposition to British policy in the South African War. When the Liberals formed a government (1905), Campbell-Bannerman became prime minister. Before ill-health caused his retirement in 1908 he had furthered many Liberal measures, including that of self-government for the Transvaal and the Orange Free State. See biography by J. A. Spender (1923).

Campbellites: see CAMPBELL, ALEXANDER, and DISCIPLES OF CHRIST.

Campbellsport, village (pop. 1,472), E Wis., SE of Fond du Lac; inc. 1902. A state forest is nearby.

Campbellsville (kăm′bŭlzvĭl), city (pop. 6,966), co. seat of Taylor co., central Ky., SSW of Lexington, in an area of farms, timber, and limestone; inc. 1817. A junior college is here.

Campbellton (kăm′bŭltŭn), city (pop. 9,823), N N.B., Canada, on the Restigouche river near the head of Chaleur Bay. It is a starting point for canoe, fishing (salmon and trout), and hunting trips into the forested interior. Across the river, at Mission Point, is Micmac village.

Campbelltown, uninc. village (pop. 1,061), SE Pa., E of Harrisburg.

Campbeltown (kăm′bŭltŭn, -toun), burgh (pop. 6,525), Argyllshire, W Scotland, on Kintyre peninsula. It is a harbor town, with waterworks and whisky distilleries. Nearby is famous Machrihanish golf course.

Camp Borden, largest military training establishment in Canada, S Ont., NW of Toronto. It covers an area of 20,000 acres and has also an armored-vehicle range at Meaford, to the northwest.

Campeche (kämpā′chä), state (19,672 sq. mi.; pop. 168,219), SE Mexico, on the Gulf of Campeche. Comprising most of the western half of the YUCATAN peninsula, it lies in hot, humid, and unhealthful lowlands. Rainfall in the southwestern sector is heavy. Much of the state is extensively forested, and logwood (called *campeche* in Spanish) is one of the chief exports. Agriculture (especially the growing of sisal hemp) and stock raising are important, and some minerals are exploited. From Campeche as a base Francisco de Montejo led (1531–35) expeditions against the Maya. The coast was a haunt of pirates from the 17th cent. to the 19th. The principal ports are Campeche and Carmen, a small town on an island at the entrace to the Laguna de Términos. **Campeche,** the capital (pop. 31,272), was founded (1540) by the younger

Montejo. Backed by low hills, it is picturesque, with many impressive colonial ruins. There are scenic beaches nearby. It was sacked several times by English buccaneers. The port is shallow, and vessels anchor far out. A railroad connects the capital with Mérida, Yucatan.

Campeggio, Lorenzo (lōrĕnt′sō kämpĕd′jō), 1472?–1539, Italian churchman and diplomat, cardinal of the Roman Church. He had wide repute as a jurist when the death of his wife turned him to the Church (c.1510). In 1512 he became bishop of Feltre, and in 1513 cardinal. He was chosen as legate for the most delicate missions. In 1518 he went to England to secure the adherence of HENRY VIII to an alliance against Turkey. He did not succeed, but he received (1524) the bishopric of Salisbury from Henry, which he held *in absentia* until 1534. In 1528 Cardinal Campeggio went again to England to act with Cardinal WOLSEY as judge in the divorce of KATHARINE OF ARAGON. He followed his instructions to temporize and adjourned the hearing. Cardinal Campeggio was sent to Germany in 1524 to attempt a pacification of the Lutherans, but except for a promise from Charles V to enforce the Edict of Worms he obtained nothing. He was ardently desirous for the reformation of the Church, especially of the papal court and of the administration of the Holy See.

Camperdown (kăm′pùrdoun″), Dutch *Kamperduin* (käm′pùrdoin″) [=the dune of Kamp], locality near the village of Kamp, in North Holland prov., NW Netherlands, on the North Sea. Here, in 1797, the British defeated the Dutch in a naval battle.

Camp Fire Girls, American organization for girls from 7 to 18 years old. It was founded (1910) by Luther Halsey Gulick (1865–1918) and other educators "to perpetuate the spiritual ideals of the home" and "to stimulate and aid in the formation of habits making for health and character." The seven crafts of its program are the home, the creative arts, the outdoors, frontiers (of science), business, sports and games, and citizenship. The Camp Fire members are divided into three age groups—Blue Birds (7 to 10), Camp Fire Girls (10 to 15), and Horizon Clubs (15 to 18). The official organ of the organization is the *Camp Fire Girl.*

Camphausen, Ludolf (lōō′dôlf kämp′houzùn), 1803–90, Prussian statesman and businessman. A leading merchant in Cologne, he headed the liberal ministry appointed by the king in April, 1848, but was forced to resign in June when the assembly moved to the left and the king to the right. He was an important figure at the Frankfurt Parliament.

Camp Hill. 1 Town (pop. 1,270), E central Ala., NE of Montgomery, in a farm area; inc. 1907. 2 Residential borough (pop. 8,559), S central Pa., across the Susquehanna from Harrisburg; founded 1756, in. 1885. Conveying equipment is made.

camphor, white, crystalline solid with a characteristic pungent odor and taste, a compound of carbon, hydrogen, and oxygen, melting at 176°C. and subliming at 204°C. The natural variety, Japan camphor, is obtained by steam distillation of the wood of the camphor tree (*Cinnamomum camphora*) native to China, Japan, and Formosa (its chief source). It is also prepared synthetically from oil of turpentine. Camphor is used in the manufacture of celluloid (mixed with pyroxylin), of some perfumes, of disinfectants, of explosives, of some lacquers, and as a moth repellent. It is used in medicine as a stimulant, a diaphoretic, and an inhalant. Camphor ice is a mixture, containing principally camphor and wax, used for external application. Camphor is practically insoluble in water but soluble in alcohol, ether, chloroform, and other solvents. The alcoholic solution is known as spirits of camphor. The camphor tree is now cultivated in the S United States.

Campi, Giulio (jōō′lyō kăm′pē), c.1500–c.1572, Italian painter and architect, founder of a school of painters at Cremona. He was a pupil of his father, Galeazzo Campi (c.1475–1536), a well-known painter, and of Giulio Romano and studied the works of Correggio and Raphael. Giulio produced many excellent altarpieces and frescoes in Milan, Mantua, and Cremona, the frescoes in the Church of Santa Margherita, Cremona, being entirely his work. Among his pupils were his two brothers, Cavaliere **Antonio Campi** (kävälyä′rä äntō′nyō), b. before 1536, d. 1591, painter, architect, and historian of Cremona, and **Vincenzo Campi** (vēnchän′tsō), 1532–91, whose works consist principally of portraits and still-life pieces. Another brother was **Bernardino Campi** (bĕrnärdē′nō), 1522–c.1590, a painter of great skill with a vigorous and original style, excelling in fresco painting and portraiture. Bernardino's most important work is the series of biblical frescoes in the cupola of San Sigismondo, Cremona, a work of colossal dimensions admirably executed.

Campian, Thomas: see CAMPION, THOMAS.

Campin, Robert (käm′pĭn), 1378–1444, Flemish painter. This artist has also been identified as the Master of Flémalle on the basis of three panels in Frankfurt-am-Main said to have come from the abbey of Flémalle near Liège. Campin was active in Tournai, having become a citizen of that city in 1410 and the dean of the painters' guild in 1423. To him have been attributed the *Mérode Altarpiece* in the Cloisters, New York, a *Nativity* in Dijon, the *Annunciation* and *Marriage of the Virgin* in Madrid, the *Madonna of Humility* in London, and a number of other panels in various collections. Campin's style matured in the fresh climate of one of the mercantile urban centers of Northern Europe, where artistic taste came increasingly to reflect the values of the rising middle class. His works are characterized by a robust and highly developed realism which constituted an important stage in the stylistic evolution leading to the art of Jan van Eyck. It is believed that Roger Van der Weyden was apprenticed in Campin's workshop.

Campina, (kûm′pĕnä), town (pop. 20,733), S central Rumania, in Walachia. A major petroleum center, it also has manufactures of chemicals and oil-drilling equipment. It is connected by oil pipeline with Ploesti and the port of Constanta on the Black Sea.

Campinas (kämpē′nùs), city (pop. c.179,800), SE São Paulo state, Brazil. It is a growing industrial city, the processing and distributing center for a diversified agricultural region, and a major transportation hub. A famed agronomical research institute is here.

Campine (kămpēn′, Fr. käpēn′), Flemish *Kempen* (kĕm′pùn), region in Limburg and Antwerp provs., NE Belgium, and in North Brabant prov., S Netherlands. It is a coal-mining area. Once covered by moors and marshes, it has been partially reclaimed. The chief towns are Hasselt and Turnhout.

Campion, Edmund (kăm′pĕun), c.1540–1581, English Jesuit martyr, educated at St. Paul's School and St. John's College, Oxford. As a fellow at Oxford he earned the admiration of his colleagues and his students and the favor of Queen Elizabeth by his brilliance and oratorical ability. He went (1569) to Dublin to help in the proposed restoration of the university there. Though he had reluctantly taken orders as a Protestant, he had open Roman Catholic leanings and fled in disguise (1571) to England and then to the Continent, where he studied at Douai, joined (1573) the Society of Jesus, and was ordained (1578). In 1580 he and another Jesuit, Robert PERSONS, were sent as Jesuit missionaries to England. Campion's travels were marked by many conversions and did much to guarantee the persistence of Roman Catholicism in England. Copies of his secretly printed pamphlet, *Decem rationes* [10 reasons], against the Protestants, appeared at Oxford in 1581. The long pursuit by the government ended (July, 1581) with the taking of Campion. He was racked three times, but though his body was broken he conducted debates with Protestant theologians brilliantly and won more converts. He defended himself ably against trumped-up charges of sedition but was nevertheless condemned and hanged, drawn, and quartered. He was beatified in 1886. See biography by Evelyn Waugh (1935).

Campion or **Campian, Thomas,** 1567–1620, English poet, composer, and lutenist, a physician by profession. His lyric poetry was set to music by him and other composers in lute song collections and in masques for the English court. His graceful, simple lute songs were published in five Books of Airs (1601–1617). He wrote a treatise on English poetry condemning the use of rhyme, but he used rhyme freely in his own poetry. His treatise *A New Way of Making Fowre Parts in Counterpoint* (1613) has often been republished.

campion: see PINK.

camp meeting, outdoor religious meeting, held usually in the summer and lasting for several days. The camp meeting was a prominent institution of the American frontier. It originated under the preaching of James McGready in Kentucky early in the course of a religious revival (c.1800) and spread throughout the United States. Immense crowds flocked to hear the noted revivalist preachers, bringing bedding and provisions in order to camp on the grounds. The meetings were directed by a number of preachers who relieved each other in carrying on the services, sometimes preaching simultaneously in different parts of the camp grounds. Shouting, shaking, and rolling upon the ground often accompanied the tremendous emotional release which followed upon "conversion," though these extravagances were opposed and discouraged by conservative ministers. Camp meetings were usually held by evangelical sects, such as the Methodists and Baptists, and by the Cumberland Presbyterians and other newer denomina-

An 1830 lithograph of a camp meeting.

tions which developed out of the religious revival. In modified form they continued to be a feature of social and religious life in the region between the Alleghenies and the Mississippi river until comparatively recent times; in a sense, they survive in summer conferences and assemblies, such as the Chautauqua Institution and the Ocean Grove Camp Meeting Association. See C. A. Johnson, *The Frontier Camp Meeting* (1955).

Campoamor, Ramón de (rämōn′ dā kämpōämōr′), 1817–1901, Spanish poet. One of the most popular poets of his time in Spain and Spanish America, he created types of humorous short poems exemplified in the titles *Doloras* (1846), *Pequeños poemas* (1872–74), and *Humoradas* (1886–88). His somewhat prosaic approach to poetry, embodied in the poems, is expressed also in his *Poética* (1883). Less known are the two long poems, *Colón* [Columbus] (1853) and *El drama universal* (1869). Now considered an unimaginative philistine, he has lost his former appeal.

Campobasso (käm″pōbäs′sō), town (estimated pop. 31,398), capital of Campobasso prov. (coextensive with Molise), chief city of Abruzzi e Molise, S Italy. It is an agricultural center with cement, soap, textile, and cutlery manufactures. There is a 15th-century castle.

Campobello (käm″pōbĕ′lō), island, c.8 mi. long and 3 mi. wide, in Passamaquoddy Bay, N.B., Canada, just off the coast of Maine. The island passed to Canada by the Convention of 1817. President Franklin D. Roosevelt had a summer home here for many years.

Campo Formio, Treaty of (käm′pō fōr′myō), Oct., 1797, peace treaty between France and Austria, signed near Campo Formio, a village near Udine, NE Italy, then in Venetia. It generally ratified the preliminary Peace of Leoben, signed at the conclusion of Bonaparte's Italian campaign (see NAPOLEON I). Bonaparte signed for France, Count Cobenzl for Austria. Austria ceded its possessions in the Low Countries (the modern Belgium) to France and secretly promised the left bank of the Rhine. The republic of Venice, invaded despite its attempts to maintain neutrality, was dissolved and partitioned: all Venetia E of the Adige, as well as Istria and Dalmatia, passed to Austria; the present provinces of Bergamo and Brescia went to the

newly founded CISALPINE REPUBLIC; the IONIAN ISLANDS went to France. Emperor Francis II summoned a congress at RASTATT to settle the affairs of the Holy Roman Empire.

Campomanes, Pedro Rodríguez de (pä′dhrō rôdhrē′gäth dā kämpōmä′näs), b. 1723, d. 1802 or 1803, Spanish statesman, economist, and author. As minister under Charles III and briefly under Charles IV he introduced administrative, social, and economic reforms. He wrote on the revival of industry and on the professional education of the working classes.

Campos, Arsenio Martínez de: see MARTÍNEZ DE CAMPOS, ARSENIO.

Campos (käm′pōōs), city (pop. c.90,600), NE Rio de Janeiro state, Brazil, on the Paraíba near its mouth. It is the commercial hub of a rich agricultural region, a transportation center, and a major center of the sugar industry. Sugar refineries and distilleries are here.

Camp Point, village (pop. 1,092), W Ill., NE of Quincy; settled before 1830, inc. 1857.

Campti, village (pop. 1,045), NW La., near the Red River SE of Shreveport; inc. 1903.

Campton, resort town (pop. 1,058), central N.H., in the White Mts. N of Plymouth; settled 1765, inc. 1767. Textiles and wood products are made.

Campulung (kûmpōōlōōng′), town (pop. 18,900), S central Rumania, in Walachia, on the southern slope of the Transylvanian Alps. A commercial center, it produces textiles and paper. It is also a summer resort. Founded in the 12th cent. by German colonists, it became the capital of Walachia in the 13th cent. The town has a 13th-century monastery with a tower and a 14th-century church (restored 17th–18th cent.).

Campus Martius: see *Roman Empire* and *Renaissance and Modern Rome* under ROME.

Camrose, city (pop. 6,939), central Alta., Canada, SE of Edmonton. It is in a mixed farming area and is a railroad center. A provincial normal school and a Scandinavian Lutheran college are here.

Camulodunum: see COLCHESTER, England.

Camus, Albert (älbĕr′ kämü′), 1913–60, French writer, b. Algiers. While a student at the Univ. of Algiers, he formed a theater group and directed,

Albert Camus

adapted, and acted in plays. Shortly after his essay *Noces* appeared (1939), he went to Paris as a journalist. In the Second World War he joined the resistance and was principal editor of the underground paper *Combat*. Noted for his vigorous, clean style, Camus soon gained recognition as a major literary figure. His belief that man's condition is absurd identified him with the existentialists, but he denied allegiance to that group; his works express rather a courageous humanism. His essay *Le Mythe de Sisyphe* (1942; Eng. tr., *The Myth of Sisyphus*, 1955) formulates his theory of the absurd and is the philosophical basis of his novel *L'Étranger* (1942; Eng. tr., *The Stranger*, 1946) and of his plays *Le Malentendu* (1944; Eng. tr., *Cross Purpose*, 1948) and *Caligula* (1944; Eng. tr., 1948). *L'Homme révolté* (1951; Eng. tr., *The Rebel*, 1954), an essay dealing with historical, spiritual, and political rebellion, treats themes found in the novels *La Peste* (1947; Eng. tr., *The Plague*, 1948) and *La Chute* (1956; Eng. tr., *The Fall*, 1957). Other works include the plays *L'États de siège* (1948; Eng. tr., *State of Siege*, 1958) and *Les Justes* (1950 ; Eng. tr., *The Just Assassins*, 1958); journalistic essays; and stories. Camus was awarded the 1957 Nobel Prize in Literature. See studies by Philip Thody (1957), Thomas Hanna (1958), and Germaine Brée (1959).

Cana (kā′nù), ancient town of Galilee. Here Jesus performed His first miracle by turning water into wine at a wedding. John 2.1,11; 4.46,54; 21.2. Two modern towns claim to be the old Cana—Kefr Kenna, NE of, and close to, Nazareth, and Khirbet Kana, N of Nazareth.

Canaan (kā′nùn). **1** Son of Ham and the eponymous ancestor of the Canaanites. Gen. 9.20–27; 10.6,15,19. **2** Territory, the same as ancient Palestine, lying between the Jordan, the Dead Sea, and the Mediterranean and sometimes including Transjordan. It was the Promised Land of the Israelites, and after their delivery from Egypt they subjugated it. Gen. 12.5; Ex. 3.8; Num.13.17,29; 14.45; 21.3; Joshua 22.11,32; Judges 1. The Canaanites are the inhabitants of Canaan and are probably related to the Amorites. In Mark 3.18 the name signifies one of the Zealots. Chanaan is a variant of Canaan. See UGARIT; ASHERAH; BAAL; PHILISTIA; PHOENICIA.

Canaan. **1** Village, Conn.: see NORTH CANAAN. **2** Village, Fla.: see MIDWAY. **3** Town (pop. 1,507), W central N.H., E of Lebanon; settled 1766, inc. 1770. It is a resort town, and a state park is nearby. Wood products are made.

Canada, nation (3,851,809 sq. mi.; pop. 18,238,247), N North America, member of the British Commonwealth of Nations. The capital is OTTAWA. Canada occupies all the continent N of the United States except for Alaska and the tiny French islands of St. Pierre and Miquelon. It is a confederation of 10 provinces—NEWFOUNDLAND, NOVA SCOTIA, NEW BRUNSWICK, PRINCE EDWARD ISLAND, QUEBEC, ONTARIO, MANITOBA, SASKATCHEWAN, ALBERTA, and BRITISH COLUMBIA—but also includes the NORTHWEST TERRITORIES and the territory of the YUKON. Canada is an entirely autonomous political unit. Although the nominal head of the government is the queen of Great Britain and Northern Ireland, her official acts regarding Canada and those of her representative, the governor general, are completely determined by the Canadian ministers, who are responsible to the Canadian Parliament. The confederation government draws its authority from the British North America Act of 1867, which is the Canadian constitution. It is in general outline similar to the Constitution of the United States; the most important difference is that in Canada the powers not expressly granted to the provincial governments are reserved to the government of the confederation. The provinces have power to administer and legislate on matters of property and civil rights, education, and local affairs generally. The Canadian Parliament, consisting of a House of Commons and a Senate, has the general powers of legislation and government. The term *dominion* is still applied, but it has not been strictly accurate since the British Commonwealth was constituted in 1931. Canada and the United States are separated by a transcontinental border, marked in part by the Great Lakes. Canada is bounded on the north by the long coast of the Arctic Ocean from the border of Alaska eastward. Boothia Peninsula and the ARCTIC ARCHIPELAGO thrust far into the Arctic, and Canada has at least nominal sovereignty to the North Pole in this quadrant. In the east Ellesmere Island all but touches the coast of Greenland high in the arctic regions. The north coast of Canada is deeply cut by gigantic Hudson Bay. The extreme northeast edge of the continent is swept by the Labrador current and is very cold. Exploitation has begun in recent years of huge iron ore deposits in this region. Just to the south the cold current mingles with the Gulf Stream, causing the incessant Newfoundland fogs. Nova Scotia (with Cape Breton Island), Prince Edward Island, and New Brunswick compose the Maritime Provs. The enchanting scenery of these provinces makes tourism a leading industry, but fishing is still the mainstay of the economy. HALIFAX and SAINT JOHN are their chief cities. The heart of Old Canada (or New France) was the present province of Quebec. Here the St. Lawrence river opens a way from the Atlantic to the huge North American central plains in the Great Lakes region. The two great cities of the province are QUEBEC and MONTREAL, large ports which receive produce from the interior. Quebec prov. is still the home and cultural stronghold of the French Canadians; neighboring Ontario shows, in contrast, its long British heritage. The cities of Ontario, like those of Quebec, have developed much industry. TORONTO, HAMILTON, LONDON, and WINDSOR, in the region of the E Great Lakes, are linked together and to the west by rail and road. Their industries range from simple food processing to the manufacture of automobiles and heavy machinery. The joint U.S.-Canadian SAINT LAWRENCE SEAWAY AND POWER PROJECT has made the Great Lakes cities ocean ports, greatly increasing their trading capacities in such products as iron ore, wheat, and fuel oil. It has integrated Canada into the trade of the Americas and has increased its international importance as an industrial nation. Like S Quebec, SE Ontario also has much diversified agriculture. At the western end of the Great Lakes are the twin lake ports of PORT

Aerial view of
Parliament buildings in Ottawa.

ARTHUR and FORT WILLIAM, which ship produce received from the prairies. Settlement in Quebec and Ontario is, however, concentrated in the south, for N of the St. Lawrence and the Ottawa rises the LAURENTIAN PLATEAU. This almost uninhabitable region is a land of rocks, small mountain ranges, and rolling country reaching in the north to the BARREN GROUNDS. To a large extent this north country is still a land of the fur trader, for whom the old ports of Rupert House, Fort Albany, York Factory, Port Nelson, and Churchill still operate; in the southern part are areas attracting the sportsman and the vacationer. Development of its mineral resources (aluminum, nickel, gold, silver, copper, platinum, iron, and uranium) is being explored, and its forests yield lumber. To the west of the Great Lakes lie the Prairie Provs., Manitoba, Saskatchewan, and Alberta. They compose one of the great wheatgrowing regions of the world. Lakes of the region, such as Lakes Winnipeg and Manitoba, and rivers such as the Red River of the North, the Saskatchewan, and the Hayes, Nelson, and Churchill, are connected with Hudson Bay; in NW Alberta, the Athabaska and the Peace are connected through Lake Athabaska, the Slave river, and Great Slave Lake with the northern system of the Mackenzie. Settlement is largely centered in the south, and the larger cities (WINNIPEG, REGINA, SASKATOON, EDMONTON, and CALGARY) are situated there. Alberta produces most of Canada's petroleum and also has huge reserves of natural gas and coal. The Rockies of Alberta are notable for majestic beauty, and attract vacationers. British Columbia for the most part is a mountainous region seamed by the Rockies in the east and the Coast Mts. in the west. Important rivers having headwaters in the province are the Columbia, the Mackenzie, and the Yukon, and here the Fraser runs into the Pacific. In the south-

west around the coast and on Vancouver Island is one of the heaviest concentrations of population in Canada. The Pacific fisheries, lumbering, agriculture, and mining have all contributed to the wealth of the region. Its major cities, VANCOUVER, VICTORIA, and NEW WESTMINSTER, have developed industries on the basis of these resources. The north part of the province is still the land of the Indian and the fur trapper. Similar to this region is the neighboring Yukon, which is still largely undeveloped mountain country. The settlements of WHITEHORSE and Skagway are on the Yukon river, and transportation—as in most of the north country—depends on the airplane, though the Yukon has a railroad and is reached by the Alaska Highway. The Northwest Territories have just begun to be developed. The westernmost and most populous of its three districts, Mackenzie dist., has oil wells and refineries. Of its two huge lakes, Great Bear and Great Slave lakes, the former is bordered by uranium and silver mines. The region, however, still has not been thoroughly explored. Even more desolate are Keewatin dist. to the east and Franklin dist. to the north (the arctic islands). Because of Canada's latitude, its winters are generally cold; the climate, however, varies greatly. The central plains have a continental climate, with very cold winters and very hot summers; the north is characteristically arctic; and the winters about the Great Lakes are temperate.

French-British Rivalry to 1760. The signs of imperial rivalry appeared in the first historic explorations (ignoring the obscure activities of the vikings after A.D. 1000) of this vast land. French and British rivalry was to dominate the history of Canada until 1760. John CABOT, under British service touched the east coast in 1497. In 1534 the Frenchman Jacques CARTIER planted a cross

Map of northwestern Canada and adjacent United States (Lambert Conformal Conic Projection)

Top longitude scale: 160° 155° 150° 145° 140° 135° 130° 125° 120° 115° 110° 105° 100° 95° 90° 85° 80°

Grid row letters (left margin): C D E F G H
Latitude (left margin): 65° 60° 55° 50° 45° 40°

Bottom scale: 9 120° 10 115° 11 110° 12 105° 13 100° 14 95°

Longitude West of Greenwich

Bodies of water / regions

Beaufort Sea
Pacific Ocean
Viscount Melville Sound
Amundsen Gulf
Lancaster Sound
Jones Sound
Hazen Strait
Melville Sound
Barrow Str.
M'Clure Strait
McClintock Channel
Queen Maud Gulf
Coronation Gulf
Dolphin and Union Str.
Franklin Str.
Ross Str.
Boothia Gulf
Hecate Strait
Dixon Entrance
Queen Charlotte Sd.
Hudson Bay
Chesterfield Inlet
Baker Lake

Islands / Territories

PRINCE PATRICK I.
BORDEN I.
MACKENZIE KING I.
MELVILLE ISLAND
PRINCE OF WALES ISLAND
BANKS ISLAND
VICTORIA ISLAND
SOMERSET ISLAND
DEVON ISLAND
ELLESMERE ISLAND
BYLOT ISLAND
BAFFIN
CORNWALLIS I.
BATHURST ISLAND
PARRY ISLANDS
BOOTHIA PENINSULA
BRODEUR PENINSULA
SIMPSON PEN.
CHAPMAN

Provinces / States

ALASKA
YUKON
NORTHWEST TERRITORIES
DISTRICT OF MACKENZIE
DISTRICT OF KEEWATIN
DISTRICT OF FRANKLIN
BRITISH COLUMBIA
ALBERTA
SASKATCHEWAN
MANITOBA
WASHINGTON
OREGON
IDAHO
MONTANA
WYOMING
NEVADA
NORTH DAKOTA
SOUTH DAKOTA
IOWA
UNITED STATES

ALEXANDER ARCHIPELAGO
BARANOF
PRINCE OF WALES ISLAND
QUEEN CHARLOTTE ISLANDS
GRAHAM I.
MORESBY I.
VANCOUVER ISLAND

Mountains / features

BROOKS RANGE
MACKENZIE MTS.
SELWYN MTS.
RICHARDSON MTS.
OGILVIE MTS.
PELLY MTS.
CASSIAR MTS.
GRIZZLY BEAR MTS.
MT. SIR JAMES MAC BREN 9062
MT. SMYTHE 9800
MT. WELDON
ROCKY MOUNTAINS
COAST MTS.
ST. ELIAS MTS.
MT. LOGAN 19,850
MT. ST. ELIAS
MT. FAIRWEATHER 15,300
GLACIER BAY NAT. MON.
MT. McKINLEY
MT. WRANGELL
NUTZOTIN MTS.
SHARKTOOTH MTN. 8105
MT. NESSELRODE 8105
CAPEGOAT
SALMON RIVER MTS.
BLUE MTS.
BITTERROOT RANGE
STIKINE

Cities / towns

Barrow
Fairbanks
Whitehorse
Dawson
Mayo
Teslin
Atlin
Watson Lake
Wrigley
Norman Wells
Fort Good Hope
Fort Norman
Fort Simpson
Fort Providence
Fort Liard
Fort Nelson
Fort Vermilion
Ft. Smith
Fort Fitzgerald
Hay River
Yellowknife
Reliance
Rae
Resolution
Aklavik
Inuvik
Sachs Harbour
Cambridge Bay
Coppermine
Port Radium
Bathurst Inlet
Baker Lake
Eskimo Point
Chesterfield Inlet
Churchill
York Factory
Fort Chipewyan
Fort McMurray
Uranium City
Stony Rapids
Fond-du-Lac
Brochet
Lynn Lake
Flin Flon
The Pas
Wabowden
Norway House
Berens River
Island Lake
Grand Rapids
Dauphin
Swan River
Yorkton
Melville
Regina
Weyburn
Estevan
Brandon
Souris
Portage la Prairie
Winnipeg
St. Boniface
Selkirk
Morden
Emerson
Prince Albert
North Battleford
Saskatoon
Swift Current
Medicine Hat
Moose Jaw
Lethbridge
Calgary
Red Deer
Edmonton
Drumheller
Camrose
Lloydminster
Wetaskiwin
Lacombe
Innisfail
Vermilion
Grande Prairie
Peace River
High River
Banff
Cranbrook
Nelson
Trail
Kamloops
Kelowna
Penticton
Vernon
Revelstoke
Golden
Prince George
Quesnel
Williams Lake
McBride
Wells
Smithers
Prince Rupert
Terrace
Kitimat
Vanderhoof
Hazelton
Lillooet
Ashcroft
Hope
Chilliwack
Victoria
Nanaimo
Powell River
New Westminster
Vancouver
Port Alberni
Dawson Creek
Hythe
McLennan
Spirit River
Grande Cache
Hinton
Jasper
Rocky Mountain House

Seattle
Tacoma
Spokane
Yakima
Walla Walla
Olympia
Portland
Salem
Eugene
Bend
Medford
Klamath Falls
Astoria
The Dalles
Pendleton
La Grande
Missoula
Helena
Butte
Great Falls
Havre
Billings
Bozeman
Miles City
Sheridan
Boise
Twin Falls
Pocatello
Idaho Falls
Bismarck
Jamestown
Fargo
Minot
Devils Lake
Grand Forks
Aberdeen
Pierre
Rapid City
Watertown
Sioux Falls
Mitchell
Minneapolis
St. Paul
Austin
Fort Frances
Kenora
Dryden

YELLOWSTONE NATIONAL PARK
WOOD BUFFALO NATIONAL PARK

Rivers / lakes

Yukon
Mackenzie
Peel
Liard
Peace River
Athabasca
Slave
Great Bear Lake
Great Slave Lake
Lake Athabasca
Reindeer L.
Wollaston L.
Cree L.
La Martre
Dubawnt L.
Aberdeen L.
Baker Lake
Yathkyed L.
Lake Winnipeg
Lake Winnipegosis
Lake Manitoba
Cedar L.
Southern Indian L.
Churchill River
Nelson River
Hayes R.
Saskatchewan River
N. Saskatchewan River
S. Saskatchewan River
Columbia
Snake River
Yellowstone R.
Missouri
Fraser River
Nechako
Skeena
Stikine
Colville
Porcupine
Lake of the Woods
Rainy River
Red River
North Magnetic Pole
Arctic Circle

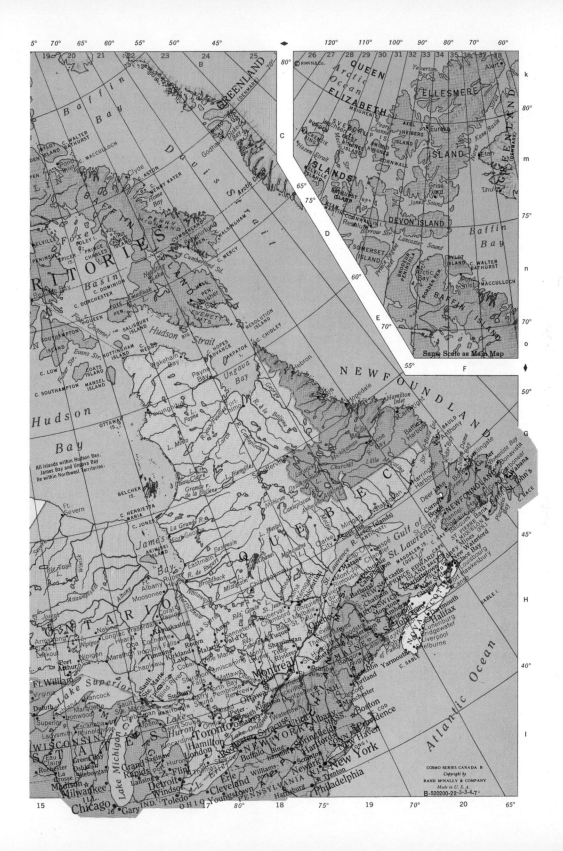

At left, a typical scene from the gold mining center of the Northwest Territories. At right, fishing boats at the Gaspé Peninsula. Fishing is still the mainstay of the economy of the Maritime Provinces.

on the Gaspé Peninsula. The first settlement, founded in 1604 by the sieur de MONTS and Samuel de CHAMPLAIN, was soon removed to Port Royal (now Annapolis Royal, N.S.) in ACADIA. Meanwhile, the English had moved to support their claims under Cabot's discoveries. They attacked Port Royal (1614) and captured Quebec (1629). But Quebec was regained in 1632, and the French under the Company of One Hundred Associates began to exploit the fur trade and establish settlements. The French objective was to establish, by daring penetration of the interior, an enormous but thinly settled empire, in contrast with the relatively dense settlements of the British on the S Atlantic coast. Under a policy initiated by Champlain, the French supported the Huron Indians in their warfare against the Iroquois; a result was that the French colony came near extinction when later in the 17th cent. the Iroquois demolished the Huron and nearly destroyed the French with them. Exploration, however, continued; the Company of One Hundred Associates was replaced by the French royal government (1663), and the colony was now ruled by the royal governor, the intendants, and the bishops. The force exercised by these officers may be seen in the careers of Louis de Buade, comte de FRONTENAC, the greatest of the colonial governors, Jean TALON, the first and greatest of the intendants, and François Xavier de LAVAL, the first bishop of Quebec. There was, however, conflict between the rulers, especially over the treatment of the Indians—the bishop regarding them as potential converts, the governor as means of trade. Meanwhile, both missionaries, such as Jacques MARQUETTE, and traders, such as RADISSON and Groseilliers, were extending French knowledge and influence. The greatest of all the empire builders in the west was Robert Cavelier, sieur de LA SALLE, who descended the Mississippi to its mouth and who envisioned the great empire in the West that was made a reality by men like Duluth, Bienville, Iberville, and Cadillac and by the many *coureurs de bois* and diligent missionaries. But the French did not go unchallenged. The British continued to make claims on Acadia, and the HUDSON'S BAY COMPANY in 1670 began to vie for the lucrative fur trade of the West. When the long series of wars between Britain and France broke out in Europe, it was paralleled in North America by the FRENCH AND INDIAN WARS. The French settlements of Acadia and the seigneuries on the St. Lawrence were threatened. The St. Lawrence valley was a prize for the British, but perhaps even more alluring was the trade of the West and North. The imperial contest came to an end after Gen. James Wolfe defeated Montcalm on the Plains of ABRAHAM, bringing about the fall of Quebec in 1759. Montreal fell in 1760, and the Treaty of Paris in 1763 ended New France and established British rule. The ensuing antagonism between the deep-rooted, Roman Catholic French Canadians and the newly come, Protestant British has persisted, though in diminishing force, to the present day.

To the Confederation. Strong French resentment was aroused by the Royal Proclamation of 1763, which favored the British in the Quebec colony. Many of its provisions, however, were reversed by the QUEBEC ACT (1774), which granted important concessions to the French. This act infuriated the residents of the Thirteen Colonies. In the American Revolution the Canadians remained loyal to the British crown, and the effort of the revolutionists to take Canada failed dismally (see QUEBEC

The almost uninhabitable region of the barren grounds is still a land for the fur trader (at left). At right, a sawmill in British Columbia, Canada's leading province in the lumber industry.

CAMPAIGN). Loyalists from the colonies in revolt (see UNITED EMPIRE LOYALISTS) fled to Canada and settled in large numbers in the Maritime Provs. and Ontario. This period was one of expansion and further exploration. Alexander MACKENZIE made voyages in 1789 to the Arctic Ocean and in 1793 to the Pacific. Mariners also reached the Pacific Northwest, and such men as Capt. James Cook, John Meares, and George VANCOUVER secured for Britain a firm hold on what is now British Columbia. The War of 1812, in which the Canadians and the British soldiers in Canada repulsed several American invasions, did not change the general situation but did lead toward the settlement of the U.S.–Canadian boundary. The New Brunswick boundary (see AROOSTOOK WAR) and the boundary west of the Great Lakes continued in some dispute; but since the War of 1812, except for minor flurries, the long border has been a line of peace. The internal struggle for control between the NORTH WEST COMPANY and the Hudson's Bay Company erupted into bloodshed in the RED RIVER SETTLEMENT, and was resolved by amalgamation of the companies in 1821. The new Hudson's Bay Company then held undisputed sway over RUPERT'S LAND and the Pacific West until U.S. immigrants challenged the British hold over Oregon and obtained the present boundary. In the east the Canada Act of 1791 had divided Lower Canada (present Quebec) from Upper Canada (present Ontario). They and the Maritime Provs. grew from the immigration of Scotch and Irish after 1815. The 1830s saw a democratic movement toward responsible government and the overthrow of the ruling groups (see FAMILY COMPACT). In the Maritime Provs. the movement was successful. In the two Canadas, however, it was only after the

Harvest in Nova Scotia, foremost in agriculture.

separate groups led by Louis J. PAPINEAU in Lower Canada and William Lyon MACKENZIE in Upper Canada had unsuccessfully resorted to rebellion (1837–38) that the British government acted. The two Canadas were brought together by the Act of Union in 1841. Responsible government was achieved in 1849, largely as a result of the efforts of Robert BALDWIN and Louis H. LaFONTAINE. The movement for confederation was given impetus in the 1860s by the need for common defense, the desire for some central authority to forward railroads, and the necessity for a solution to the prob-

CANADA

An Eskimo baby eats a crust of bread while carried in the hood of his mother's parka (Frobisher Bay, N. W. T.).

Mount Robson, 12,972 feet, loftiest peak of the Canadian Rockies.

Peace River country, Northwest Territories.

lem posed by the two new Canadas (now Canada East and Canada West), where rival parties led by John A. MACDONALD and George BROWN had reached an impasse. Proposals were made for a confederation allowing local separation of the Canadas. However, the Maritime Provs., which sought union among themselves, agreed at the Charlottetown Conference of 1864 to admit delegates from the Canadas as well. Two more conferences were held—the Quebec Conference later in 1864 and the London Conference in 1866 in England—before the British North America Act in 1867 made confederation a fact. Nova Scotia and then Prince Edward Island joined only after some reluctance, and Newfoundland did not join until 1948.

The New Nation. The new confederation gained Rupert's Land in 1869, and in 1871 British Columbia agreed to come into the union largely on the promise of a transcontinental railroad. Pushing through the CANADIAN PACIFIC RAILWAY was achieved by the long administration of Macdonald. Objection in the West to lack of political representation and to unfair land-grant and survey laws produced rebellions led by Louis RIEL in 1869–70 and 1884–85, but the West was opened. In 1879 Macdonald adopted the National Policy, a program for building up the nation, partly through protective tariffs. Under the long administration (1896–1911) of Sir Wilfrid LAURIER, immigration to the Prairie Provs. was increased. Today W Canada shows the contributions of peoples from Central and Eastern Europe, Japanese and Chinese, and many other groups. The prairie agricultural empire bloomed. Mining boomed in the Klondike and in the Laurentian Plateau. Large-scale development of hydroelectric resources helped forward industrial development and urbanization. Under the premiership of Robert L. BORDEN, Canada joined Britain in the First World War. The struggle over military conscription, however, deepened the cleavage between French Canadians and their fellow citizens. During the depression that began in 1929, the Prairie Provs. were hard hit by droughts that shriveled the wheat fields. Farmers developed huge cooperatives and also sought to press their interests through political movements such as SOCIAL CREDIT and the CO-OPERATIVE COMMONWEALTH

FEDERATION (now the New Democratic Party). Canada was of great importance in the Second World War, when, under the premiership of W. L. Mackenzie KING, Canada joined the Allies in 1939. Despite economic strain Canada emerged from the war with enhanced prestige and took an active role in the United Nations. Extremely rich in natural resources, Canada has embarked on a policy of vigorous national development. New uranium, iron, and petroleum resources have been exploited; uses of atomic energy have been developed; and hydroelectric and thermal plants have been built to produce electricity for new and expanded industries. Huge pipelines carry oil from Alberta to outlets on the west coast and the Great Lakes, and the trans-Canadian highway crosses the nation from coast to coast. The Conservative government of John G. DIEFENBAKER has maintained in general the nationalist policies of his predecessor, the Liberal Louis ST. LAURENT. A controversy over defense policy in early 1963 caused the government to fall, and the Liberals, under Lester PEARSON, were making a strong bid in the general elections of April, 1963. Classic works on early Canada are those of Francis Parkman. See G. M. Wrong, *The Rise and Fall of New France* (1928); D. G. Creighton, *Dominion of the North* (1944); J. B. Brebner, *The North Atlantic Triangle* (1945); A. R. M. Lower, *Colony to Nation* (1946); Mason Wade, *The French-Canadian Outlook* (1946); Edgar McInnis, *Canada: a Political and Social History* (rev. ed., 1959) and *Canada in World Affairs* (9 vols., 1940–59); J. B. Brebner, *Canada* (1960).

Canada, Lower: see QUEBEC, province.

Canada balsam (bôl'sùm), yellow, oily, resinous exudation from the balsam FIR (*Abies balsamea*) of Canada and the NE United States. It is an oleoresin and a true turpentine rather than a balsam. It has a pleasant odor but a biting taste. Because of its transparency and adhesiveness, retained upon solidification and exposure to air, it is especially valued as a cement for microscope slides and for optical lenses. It is also used in paints and polishes.

Canada Company, chartered in England in 1826 for the purpose of making settlements. The Scottish novelist, John Galt, was the company's representative. Its lands were along the Lake Huron side of the S Ontario peninsula, and its headquarters at Guelph. The type of immigrant obtained by Galt was high, and the first road from Lake Ontario across the Huron tract to Lake Huron was built by the company. In general the Canada Company was one of the most successful colonizing schemes of the period.

Canada First movement, party that appeared in Canada soon after confederation (1867). The purpose was to encourage the growth of nonpartisan loyalty to the new dominion of Canada. In Toronto, in 1874, it founded the *Nation* and the National Club and entered the political field as the Canadian National Association. Although its official career was short-lived, the party's ideals were expressed by Canadian poets and other writers and were absorbed by the older political parties. In this way the Canada First movement had an effect on the development of Canadian nationalism. See W. S. Wallace, *The Growth of Canadian National Feeling* (1927).

Canada jay: see JAY.

Canada rice: see WILD RICE.

Canadian, town (pop. 2,239), co. seat of Hemphill co., extreme N Texas, NE of Amarillo on the Canadian river, in the Panhandle; inc. 1908. Since its founding with the coming of the railroad (1887), it has been chiefly a rail and cattle town.

Canadian, river, c.906 mi. long, rising in E New Mexico in the high plains and flowing E across the Texas Panhandle and most of Oklahoma. It is joined by the North Canadian in E Oklahoma near Eufaula and enters the Arkansas a little farther northeast. Construction was begun on Eufaula Dam in 1956.

Canadian art and architecture. An outstanding early colonial art was French-Canadian wood carving, chiefly of saints and retables for the churches. This art flourished from 1675 (when Mgr Laval established an Ecole des Arts et Métiers) until c.1850. The art perhaps reached its height after the separation from France when, freed from the French Renaissance tradition, it developed a local character beautifully exemplified in such work as that in the Church of the Sainte Famille on Orléans Island and in the Musée provinciale at Quebec. Before 1880 almost the only paintings and drawings produced in Canada were those of the colonial topographers, many of them English army officers. While much of this work is purely documentary, a few men produced interesting and imaginative scenes. Paul KANE, who painted Indians, and Cornelius KRIEGHOFF, who depicted the life of the habitants, were the earliest genre painters. J. A. Fraser, known for his views of the Rockies, was instrumental in founding (1875) the Ontario College of Art, at Toronto. In 1880 the Royal Canadian Academy of Arts (at Montreal) and the National Gallery of Canada (at Ottawa) were

Parliament Hall, Ottawa

founded. The National Gallery has since 1910 played an active part in Canadian life through its traveling exhibits. Its collection is the finest in Canada. Today there are art schools and galleries in Montreal, Quebec, Ottawa, Toronto, Hamilton, Edmonton, Winnipeg, Vancouver, and other cities. In the late 19th cent. the outstanding names were those of the landscapists Daniel Fowler, F. M. Bell-Smith, and Robert Gagen; the portrait painter Robert Harris; and two great cartoonists, J. W. Bengough and Henri Julien. They were followed by a number of fine painters, including George A. Reid, Franklin Brownell, Florence Carlyle, F. McG. Knowles, Horatio WALKER, M. A. de Foy SUZOR-CÔTÉ, William Brymner, Maurice Cullen, Tom THOMSON, and J. W. MORRICE, who is perhaps the most celebrated of Canadian landscapists. In 1920 Franklin Carmichael, Lawren Harris, A. Y. Jackson, Franz H. Johnston, Arthur Lismer, J. E. H. MacDonald, and F. Horsman Varley formed the Group of Seven, dedicated to painting the Canadian scene. They traveled and painted all over the dominion. Their movement did much to awaken the interest of the country at large, and while their school of painting with its emphasis on flat design tended toward a poster style, they did some excellent work. The cultural center of the Seven was Toronto; in Montreal toward the end of the Second World War a new group banded together, including Alfred PELLAN, John Lyman, P. E. Borduas, and J. P. RIOPELLE. Influenced by Matisse, Picasso, and the surrealists, they evolved the *automatiste* movement. Other popular painters, working in a wide variety of styles, are David MILNE, Emily CARR, Pegi Nicol MacLeod, and B. C. Binning. After the decline of French Canadian wood carving, little sculpture was produced until 1900. Philippe HÉBERT, Suzor-Côté, Alfred Laliberté, Tait McKenzie, and Walter ALLWARD are well-established sculptors. Among the later sculptors, Emanuel Hahn, Elizabeth Wyn Wood, and Henri Hébert are notable. The French Canadians have a tradition of fine skill in such decorative arts and crafts as metalworking and rug-hooking. Canadian architecture adheres in the main to foreign trends, especially in the planning of public buildings. From the 18th to the 20th cent., French Renaissance, English Georgian, regency, and Gothic revival designs were successively dominant. A notable example of Gothic revival is found in the buildings of Parliament Hall, Ottawa (begun, 1859). Based on the ideas of H. H. Richardson, well-known structures in the château style are the Château Frontenac (1890), Quebec city, and the Banff Springs Hotel (1913), Banff, Alberta. More recently modern forms have been espoused, e.g., the Electrical Building and Civic Auditorium, Vancouver, British Columbia, and the Shakespearean Festival Theatre, Stratford, Ont. Church and domestic architecture in Canada has consistently shown originality. Particularly in Quebec during the colonial period charming rural stone houses and churches were developed—typically low and rectangular, with steep pitched roofs and uptilting eaves. See studies on art by William Colgate (1943), Graham McInnes (rev. ed., 1950), D. W. Buchanan (1950), and Paul Duval (1954); on architecture by Alan Gowans (1958).

Canadian literature, English. Although it began as an imitative colonial literature, it has steadily developed its own national characteristics. Because of the huge immigrations, first of New England Puritans from 1760 on and later of American Loyalists during the Revolution, Canadian literature followed that of the United States almost until the confederation in 1867. Until after 1800 the rigors of pioneering left little time for the writing or the appreciation of literature. The only notable works were journals, such as that of Jacob Bailey, and the recorded travels of explorers, such as Samuel Hearne and Sir Alexander Mackenzie. The first novelist was John Richardson, whose *Wacousta* (1832) popularized the genre of the national historical novel. With *The Clockmaker* (1836) T. C. Haliburton began his humorous series on Sam Slick the Yankee peddler. Historical novelists writing c.1900 included William Kirby, author of *The Golden Dog* (1877), and Sir Gilbert Parker, author of *The Seats of the Mighty* (1896). The novels of Sara Jeannette Duncan, such as *A Social Departure* (1890), contained both satire and humor. The Rev. C. W. Gordon (Ralph Connor) began with *Black Rock* (1898) a series of novels on pioneer life in W Canada. Animal stories became popular in the works of Ernest Thompson Seton, Sir C. G. D. Roberts, and Margaret Marshall Saunders. Since 1900 Canadian novels have tended toward stricter realism, but have remained predominantly regional. Among the most prominent authors have been Mazo de la Roche, well known for her series on the Whiteoaks of Jalna; Frederick P. Grove, author of *Settlers of the Marsh* (1925), novel of farm life; and Laura Salverson and Nellie McClung, novelists of immigrant and rural life in W Canada. Important novelists during and after the Second World War are Morley Callaghan, Gwethalyn Graham, and Hugh MacLennan. Their novels have focused attention on Canadian city life, social problems, and the large problem of Canadian cultural unity. Stephen Leacock is well known for his humorous essays as well as for his scholarship. Other notable essayists include Sir Andrew Macphail, Archibald MacMechan, and

A Habitant Farm, *painting by Cornelius Krieghoff.*

Lorne Pierce. Genuinely Canadian poetry was late in developing. In the 18th cent. Puritan hymnists such as Henry Alline and refugee Tory satirists such as Jonathan Odell took their models from American colonial or English neoclassical literature. Until after the confederation of 1867 the only poets of note were Charles Sangster, the first to make use of native material, and Charles Heavysege, whose long poetic drama *Saul* was admired by contemporary American poets. Starting c.1880, the "confederation school"—C. G. D. Roberts, Archibald Lampman, Bliss Carman, and Duncan Campbell Scott—began producing a large body of romantic poetry, describing nature and rural life. In 1905, long after her death in 1887, Isabella V. Crawford was recognized as an important poet; she was followed by Emily Pauline Johnson and Marjorie Pickthall. Other poets of the early part of the century included Wilfred Campbell, W. H. Drummond, Francis Sherman, John McCrae, and the greatly popular Robert W. Service. In 1926 E. J. Pratt broke away from the romantic tradition with *The Titans;* his highly original and powerful epics make him easily the greatest poet of Canada. Among many recent poets following the strong tradition wrought by Pratt are Kenneth Leslie, Earle Birney, W. W. E. Ross, Dorothy Livesay, and Anne Marriott. Other poets sharing the modern cosmopolitan tradition of the United States and W Europe are F. R. Scott, L. A. Mackay, A. J. M. Smith, A. M. Klein, and P. K. Page. See R. P. Baker, *History of English-Canadian Literature to the Confederation* (1920); E. K. Brown, *On Canadian Poetry* (rev. ed., 1944); Desmond Pacey, *Ten Canadian Poets* (1958) and *Creative Writing in Canada* (rev. ed., 1961); Univ. of Toronto *Quarterly.*

Canadian literature, French. Except for the narratives of French explorers and missionaries, no notable writing was produced before the British conquest of New France in 1759. Since that time the inspiration of most Canadian writing in French has been the passionate concern of French Canadians to preserve their identity in a country dominated by the English language and cultural tradition and by the Protestant religion. There has been little contact between the two literatures. Until the 20th cent. French literature found its models mainly in writers of France and its themes in nationalism, the simple lives and folkways of the habitants, and the devotion to the Catholic church. The first artistic expression of this spirit was F. X. Garneau's *Histoire du Canada* (1845–48; 2d ed., 1852), still the classic of French Canadian nationalism. It inspired the first nationalistic poet, Octave Crémazie, and the Quebec school of poets, novelists, and historians who began a deliberate effort in 1861 to create a national literature, with such French authors as Hugo and Lamartine as their chief models. The group included Philippe Aubert de Gaspé, J. B. A. Ferland, Louis Honoré Fréchette, Pamphile LeMay, H. R. Casgrain, Antoine Gérin-Lajoie, and Benjamin Sulte. There developed c.1900 a new group of writers, chiefly in Montreal, who tried to achieve the stricter technique and keener artistic perceptions of the Parnassians of France. Some poets, such as Émile Nelligan and Paul Morin, abandoned the national

note for exotic subjects; others, such as Albert Lozeau and Albert Ferland, found inspiration in Canadian nature. About this time men of letters, notably Adjutor Rivard, began a movement to preserve the purity of the French language in Canada. Influential critics were Camille Roy, Henri d'Arles, and Louis Dantin. In the novel, rural inspiration could be seen in the works of Félicité Angers (Laure Conan). A more realistic fiction took impetus from Louis Hémon's *Maria Chapdelaine* (1913), a novel of the peasants of the Lake St. John country. There followed a stream of fiction on habitant life in the backwoods, on the farms, and in the villages, by such native Canadians as Robert Choquette, F. A. Savard, Claude Henri Grignon, Roger Lemelin, and Ringuet. Although some novels were set in cities and a notable author such as Robert Charbonneau explored the psychological defeatism of his characters, the realistic regional novel about the simple Catholic community persisted strongly. Important poets since 1914 include Clément Marchand, whose inspiration is often religious; Alfred DesRochers,. who writes of the life of the soil; and Robert Choquette and Roger Brien, whose romantic lyrics are eloquently individualistic. Following the Second World War there was evidence of a new, less self-conscious spirit. Poets and novelists, trying to settle the vexing problem of language, declared that pure French should be standard with the use of Canadianisms accepted wherever these served a purpose. Although it was still possible to detect the influence of France (often with a lag of 30 years), at midcentury most of the creative writing in Canada had taken its place in the world of letters characterized everywhere by experiment with matter and method. Among the poets of the new trend were Anne Hébert, Alain Grandbois, Fernand Oellette, and Jacques Godbout and Jean Guy Pilon, the last two forming the nucleus of a group in Montreal which started (1959) the literary magazine *Liberté*. The many novelists included Gabrielle Roy, Robert Elie, and Yves Thériault. See criticism of current French Canadian literature in the quarterly *Canadian Literature;* Ian F. Fraser, *The Spirit of French Canada* (1939); Berthelot Brunet, *La Littérature canadienne-française* (1946); Auguste Viatte, *Histoire littéraire de l' Amérique française des origines à 1950* (1954); Gérard Tougas, *Histoire de la littérature canadienne-française* (1960).

Canadian Mounted Police: see ROYAL CANADIAN MOUNTED POLICE.

Canadian National Railways, government owned and operated transportation system in Canada, extending from coast to coast with many branch lines in each province. The system is an amalgamation of several separate enterprises. They were unified in 1923 under a single management, and a considerable part of the original mileage was abandoned.

Canadian Pacific Railway, transcontinental transportation system in Canada and extending into the United States, privately owned and operated in competition with the Canadian National Railways. The construction of a railroad crossing the continent in Canadian territory was one of the conditions on which British Columbia entered the confederation in 1871. After many difficulties and a political scandal, the contracts were awarded in 1880, and the line from Montreal to the Pacific coast was completed in 1885.

Canadian Shield: see LAURENTIAN PLATEAU.

canafistula: see SENNA.

canaigre: see BUCKWHEAT.

Canajoharie (kă″nùjōhă′rē, –hâ′rē), village (pop. 2,681), E central N.Y., on the Mohawk and the Barge Canal, W of Amsterdam; settled c.1730 by Dutch and Germans, inc. 1829. The Van Alstyne House (1749) contains historical papers and relics. Food packing is the chief industry.

Canal, Antonio: see CANALETTO.

canal. Canals were dug for irrigation probably almost as long ago as agriculture began; traces of them have been found in Egypt and in other regions of ancient civilization. The Indians of SW North America irrigated their fields by canals, parts of which still exist in Arizona and New Mexico. Canals for transportation came somewhat later and for long were level or provided with inclines up which barges or boats had to be hauled from one level to the next; locks (see LOCK, CANAL) were first built in Europe, in Italy or Holland. The Grand Canal of China (completed 1289) is the most notable of the early canals. The countries of France, Belgium, Holland, and Germany developed inland waterway systems, connecting their rivers by canals, and thereby furthered their economic and commercial progress. Russia built canals to connect the Baltic with the Black and Caspian seas by a great system of rivers, lakes, and canals, and the Soviet Union built a canal between the White Sea and the Baltic. England, before the building of railroads, had an elaborate network of much-used canals; in the United States the ERIE CANAL was important. A sea voyage often can be shortened or made less dangerous by the building of a canal: for this purpose the SUEZ CANAL, the PANAMA CANAL, and the KIEL CANAL were built. When falls interrupt transportation, as in the Columbia, the Niagara (see WELLAND SHIP CANAL), and the Congo, or where there are shoals, a canal may be built. Drainage may be accomplished by means of a canal—a notable example is the Chicago Drainage Canal (see CHICAGO, river); reclamation of land through drainage canals has been practiced in many countries, as in the drainage of the Florida swamps, the fens of England, and the Zuider Zee in the Netherlands. See T. C. Bridges, *Great Canals* (1936); Robert Payne, *The Canal Builders* (1959); Carter Goodrich, *Government Promotion of American Canals and Railroads, 1800–1890* (1960) and *Canals and Economic Development* (1961).

Canalejas y Méndez, José (hōsā′ känälä′häs ē män′dăth), 1854–1912, Spanish statesman. He was a member of the Cortes, held several cabinet posts, and was premier from 1910 to 1912, when he was assassinated. He founded a more democratic group within the liberal party. Canalejas advocated curbing the power of the religious orders and breaking up the large estates, but achieved neither goal. He was also a notable jurist.

Canaletto (känälät′tō), 1697–1768, Venetian painter, whose real name was Antonio Canal. He studied with his father, Bernardo Canal, a scene painter, and spent several years in Rome. Returning to Venice, he devoted himself to the painting of the Venetian scenes upon which his fame chiefly rests. From 1746 to 1755 he lived in England and produced many fine landscapes, notably those of Eton College. Examples of his works are in most of the large European and American collections. Canaletto is unsurpassed as an architectural painter. His works are finely detailed yet delicate and airy. Among his best works are *View on the Grand Canal* and *Regatta on the Grand Canal* (National Gall., London); *Church of Santa Maria Della Salute* (Louvre); *View of Venice* (Uffizi); and *The Piazzetta, Venice* (Metropolitan Mus.). His nephew and pupil, Bernardo Bellotto, was also called Canaletto. See studies by Vittorio Moschini (Eng. tr., 1956) and W. G. Constable (1961).

Canal Fulton, village (pop. 1,555), NE Ohio, on the Tuscarawas and NW of Canton; founded c.1814, inc. 1840. It is a trade center for a wheat and dairy area.

Canal Winchester, village (pop. 1,976), S central Ohio, on the Ohio and Erie Canal and SE of Columbus; inc. 1866. Glass products are made here.

Canal Zone: see PANAMA CANAL ZONE.

Cananaean (kănùnē′ùn), epithet of St. SIMON.

Canandaigua (kănùndā′gwù), city (pop. 9,370), co. seat of Ontario co., W central N.Y., in the Finger Lakes region, at the north end of Canandaigua Lake and SE of Rochester; settled 1789, inc. 1913. It is a resort and farm trade center, with various industries. The county historical society museum contains a copy of the treaty with the Iroquois Confederacy, signed here in 1794 by Timothy Pickering. The courthouse was the scene of Susan B. Anthony's trial (1873) for voting. A U.S. veterans' hospital is here.

Canandaigua Lake, 15 mi. long and ½ to 1½ mi. wide, W central N.Y., one of the FINGER LAKES.

Canarese (kănùrēz′), variant spelling of Kanarese, a Dravidian language spoken mainly in S India. See LANGUAGE (table).

Canaris or **Kanaris, Constantine** (both: känä′rĭs), 1790–1877, Greek patriot and admiral. He distinguished himself in the Greek War of Independ-

Barge delivery of gasoline on the Erie Canal.

ence, notably at Tenedos, where he destroyed (1822) the flagship of the Turkish admiral. In 1862 he was a leader in the revolution which ousted King Otto and put George I on the Greek throne. He was twice premier (1864–65, 1877).

Canaris, Wilhelm (vĭl′hĕlm känä′rĭs), 1887–1945, German admiral. He occupied various positions in the German navy during and after the First World War. In 1935 he was made chief of the Abwehr [military intelligence]. A conservative, Canaris at first welcomed Hitler, but Hitler's methods and the fear that a new war would destroy Germany drove him into the opposition. The Abwehr became a center of conspiracy against the regime. Dismissed in Feb., 1944, he was arrested shortly after the attempt (July, 1944) on Hitler's life, though he was not directly involved in the plot. He was executed by the Gestapo in April, 1945.

Canarsee Indians (kŭnär′sē), North American Indian tribe of Algonquian linguistic stock. They occupied the western part of Long Island, N.Y., and sold the site of Brooklyn to the Dutch. They paid tribute to the Mohawk, and when they stopped paying and defied the Mohawk, they were almost wiped out.

canary, familiar cage bird of the FINCH family, descended from either the wild serin finch or from the very similar wild canary of the Canary Islands, Madeira, and the Azores and introduced into Europe in the late 15th or early 16th cent. The wild birds are usually gray or green; breeding has produced both plain and variegated birds, mostly yellow and buff but sometimes greenish. Germany is traditionally the center for training and breeding canaries; the Harz mt. and the St. Andreasberg canaries originated there. The birds are trained to sing by exposure to other birds of superior ability or to musical instruments. The song of roller canaries is a series of "tours," a complex set of rolling trills delivered with the bill almost closed; choppers sing with the bill open. Canaries breed rapidly in captivity and with proper care may live to 15 years or more.

Canary Islands, Span. *Islas Canarias*, group of seven islands (2,808 sq. mi.; pop. 803,023), off Spanish Sahara, in the Atlantic Ocean. They comprise two provinces of Spain. Santa Cruz de Tenerife (1,329 sq. mi.; pop. 427,796) includes Teneriffe, Palma, Gomera, and Hierro. Las Palmas (1,565 sq. mi.; pop. 375,227) includes Grand Canary, Lanzarote, and Fuerteventura. The islands, of volcanic origin, are rugged; the highest point is Mt. Teide (12,162 ft.) on Teneriffe. Pliny mentions an expedition to the Canaries in c.40 B.C., and they may have been the Fortunate Islands of later classical writers. They were occasionally visited by Arabs and by European travelers in the Middle Ages. Jean de Béthencourt, a Norman, settled at Lanzarote in 1402 and, with the support of Castile, became its king in 1404. The Guanches, the native inhabitants of the islands, were conquered by 1496, and Spanish dominion was recognized. The Canaries were frequently raided by pirates and privateers. Las Palmas beat off Francis Drake in 1595, but it was ravaged by the Dutch in 1599. In the French Revolutionary Wars, Horatio Nelson was repulsed in 1797 at Santa Cruz. Wine was the main export of the Canaries until the grape blight of 1853. Its place was taken by cochineal until aniline dyes came into general use; sugar cane then became the chief commercial crop. The leading exports are now bananas, tomatoes, and potatoes, grown where irrigation is possible. Fishing on the open sea employs many. The ports are of great importance as coaling stations.

Santa Cruz de Tenerife, Canary Islands.

canary wood or **canary whitewood**, name applied to the timber of the tulip tree (see MAGNOLIA) in some parts of the United States and to an Australian eucalyptus, the Indian mulberry, and two species of the genus *Persea* of the laurel family.

canasta: see RUMMY.

Canastota (kănŭstō′tŭ), village (pop. 4,896), central N.Y., ENE of Syracuse, in a farm region; inc. 1835.

Canaveral, Cape: see CAPE CANAVERAL.

Canberra (kăn′bŭrŭ), city (pop. 43,973), capital of the Commonwealth of Australia, in the Australian Capital Territory, SW Australia. The site of the city was chosen in 1908. Founded in 1913, Canberra became the second capital (succeeding Melbourne) of the commonwealth; the Parliament first met here in 1927. During the Second World War the capital was temporarily shifted back to Melbourne. The city was planned by Walter Burley Griffin of Chicago. Canberra is the seat of the Duntroon Military College, Canberra University College (1929), and the National Museum of Australian Zoology.

Canby, Edward Richard Sprigg, 1817–73, Union general in the Civil War, b. Kentucky, grad. West Point, 1839. He fought in the Seminole War and in the Mexican War. In the Civil War, Canby commanded the Dept. of New Mexico, where he thoroughly repelled the Confederate invasion (1862). He was made a brigadier general of volunteers in March, 1862, and was on special duty in the War Dept. in Washington from Jan., 1863 to March, 1864, except for four months as the efficient commander of New York city during the DRAFT RIOTS of 1863. Canby was promoted major general in

May, 1864, and assigned to command the Military Division of West Mississippi. He captured Mobile in April, 1865, and in May received the surrender of the last Confederate armies. After the war Canby held various commands in the South until 1870, when he was sent to the Dept. of the Columbia on the Pacific coast. He was killed during a peace conference with the MODOC INDIANS. See biography by M. L. Heyman, Jr. (1959).

Canby, Henry Seidel, 1878–1961, American editor and critic, b. Wilmington, Del., grad. Yale, 1899. He taught at Yale from 1900, achieving professorial rank in 1922. He established and edited (1920–24) the *Literary Review* of the New York *Evening Post,* afterwards joining with others to found and edit (1924–36) the *Saturday Review of Literature;* his *Seven Years' Harvest* (1936) is an intellectual diary culled from its files. His critical and literary works include *Definitions* (1st series, 1922; 2d series, 1924), *Classic Americans* (1931), a biography of Thoreau (1939), and *Turn West, Turn East: Mark Twain and Henry James* (1951). His *American Memoirs* (1947), which contains condensations of his *Age of Confidence* (1934) and *Alma Mater* (1936), is personal reminiscences, reflections, and opinions on American life and literature.

Canby. 1 City (pop. 2,146), SW Minn., W of Granite Falls near the S.Dak. line; platted 1876, inc. as a village 1879, as a city 1905. It is a trade center for farm cooperatives. **2** City (pop. 2,168), NW Oregon, near the Willamette river and SW of Oregon City; founded 1873, inc. 1893. It is a trade center of an agricultural area specializing in the growing of flowers and bulbs.

Cancer [Latin, =the crab], in astronomy, a northern constellation which contains the star cluster Praesepe (sometimes known as the "bee hive" and the "manger"). The Tropic of Cancer takes its name from this constellation, which marks the northernmost point of the ecliptic and therefore the time of the summer solstice in the Northern Hemisphere. Cancer, the Crab, is the fourth sign of the zodiac, and the constellation is a zodiacal constellation.

cancer or **carcinoma** (kärsĭnō'mŭ), malignant proliferation of body cells occurring in man and other animal life as well as in plants. Its cause is not yet fully understood, but viruses and prolonged mechanical or chemical irritation are thought to be factors. The rapidly growing cells infiltrate surrounding tissues and by way of the blood and lymphatics may travel to remote sites of the body where metastases, new growths, are initiated. This tendency to spread, which makes cancer so dangerous, is one of the characteristics that distinguishes it from benign tumors. No area of the body, not even the blood (see LEUKEMIA), is immune to cancer. The most common site of cancer in man is the skin, especially those portions exposed to the elements or other irritating factors, e.g., the faces and arms of persons constantly exposed to strong sunlight and the lips of pipe and cigar smokers. Skin that has been scarred or damaged by thermal burns or X-ray treatment is also believed to be predisposed to the development of cancer. It is believed by many investigators that the smoking of cigarettes plays a large role in the development of cancer of the lungs. Whatever the location, the sooner a cancerous condition is recognized and treated, the better the prospect for cure. Skin cancer has the highest ratio of cure since it can be discovered and treated more easily than an internal cancer. The diagnosis and eradication of internal cancer is difficult because signs and symptoms sometimes do not appear until the process is already far advanced. Surgical eradication, wherever feasible, is the best hope of curing cancer. Where this is not possible, treatment with X ray or other radiologic media and with chemical agents is employed. An important factor in early diagnosis, however, is the education of the public to the recognition of signs and symptoms of cancer. Unexplained loss of weight, difficulty in swallowing, change in bowel habits, bleeding from the bowel or pelvic organs, lumps of the breast or skin, ulcerations that do not heal within a reasonable period of time are all signs that should receive prompt medical investigation. Cancer-detection centers have been set up throughout the United States to aid in the early diagnosis and control of malignant growths.

Candace (kăn'dŭsē, kăndā'sē), name of several queens of ancient Ethiopia. One of them made war (c.22 B.C.) on the Roman governor of Egypt, who defeated her and destroyed Napata, her capital. Another Candace is mentioned in the Bible as the queen of the eunuch converted by Philip. Acts 8.27–39.

Candahar: see KANDAHAR.

Candela, Felix, 1910–, Mexican architect, b. Madrid. He studied architecture in Madrid but was forced to flee Spain after the Spanish civil war. Candela went to Mexico in 1939 and set up his own construction firm. He is best known for his design of thin-shelled concrete domes, often in startling shapes. Among the structures which he has helped plan are the Cosmic Ray Pavilion (1950–51) for Mexico's University City; the Church of La Virgen Milagrosa (1953), Mexico city; and Los Manantiales restaurant (1958), Xochimilco.

candelabrum (kăn″dŭlä'brŭm) [Latin], primarily a support for candles, designed in the form of a turned baluster or a tapered column, also a branched CANDLESTICK or a lampstand. Candelabra found in Etruscan and Pompeiian ruins are usually of bronze. Though most used and developed during the Renaissance, the candelabrum originated in Etruria and Rome. From ancient Rome come the tall and monumental candelabra used in temples and public buildings. Of bronze or marble, they had triangular pedestals from which rose columnar shafts, finely sculptured and terminating at the top in a bowl used for holding illuminating oil and incense. With these as inspiration, Italian Renaissance artists produced superb candelabra in richest materials for altars, chapels, and processions. In this period the distinctive form of the candelabrum came also to be a ubiquitous decorative motive, used freely in architectural ornament, tapestry borders, stained glass windows, and furniture. It was even converted (especially in Lombardy) into a definite architectural element, taking the place of a column or colonnette, as in windows of the Certosa at Pavia. See F. W. Robins, *The Story of the Lamp (and the Candle)* (1939).

Candia (kăn'dēŭ), Gr. *Herakleion* (ērä'klēôn), city

(pop. 63,458), on the island of CRETE, Greece. It is a port on the Gulf of Candia (an arm of the Aegean Sea) and the largest city on Crete. It was its capital until 1841. Founded (9th cent.) by the Saracens, it was conquered (961) by the Byzantine emperor Nicephorus II and in the 13th cent. became a Venetian colony. The Venetians, who named the city Candia, fortified it and improved its port. In 1669, after a two-year siege, it was captured by the Turks. The city has a museum of Minoan antiquities which were excavated at the site of ancient Cnossus, just outside of Candia. Among its historic monuments are a cathedral, several mosques, and remains of Venetian walls and fortifications.

candle. The evidence of ancient writings is not conclusive as to the history of the candle; words translated "candle" may have meant "torch" or "lamp" and the "candlestick" was probably a stand for one of these lights. The candle probably evolved from wood, rushes, or cords dipped in fat or pitch. It competed with the lamp in Roman times and was more commonly used in Western civilizations during the Middle Ages. Tallow, beeswax, and vegetable wax such as bayberry in the American colonies, candleberry in the East, and waxberry in South America were supplemented by spermaceti; in the late 18th cent., by stearine c.1825, and by paraffin c.1850. Twisted strands for wicks were replaced (c.1825) by the plaited wick. Candles were commonly made by repeated dipping in melted tallow, by pouring tallow or wax into molds, or by pouring beeswax over the wicks. Most modern candles are machine-made by a molding process. In literature, art, and religion the candle has had a wide range of symbolism; it commonly represents joy, reverence for the divine, and sacrifice (since the candle spends itself). Candles are used in rites especially of the Roman Catholic Church and are blessed on Candlemas Day. The very large paschal candle stands at the Gospel side of the altar; it is blessed and lighted during the Exsultet on the vigil of Easter and is relighted at important ceremonies until Ascension Day.

candleberry: see BAYBERRY.

candlefish: see SMELT.

Candlemas, Feb. 2, in the Roman Catholic and the Anglican churches the feast of the Purification of the Blessed Virgin. In the Eastern Church it is called the feast of the Presentation of Christ in the Temple. The name Candlemas is derived from the procession of candles, inspired by the words of Simeon "a light to lighten the Gentiles" (Luke 2.32). In the Roman Catholic Church the candles for use in the ensuing year are blessed on this day. An old superstition claims that the weather is foretold by the ground hog (see WOODCHUCK) on Candlemas.

candle power: see PHOTOMETRY.

candlestick, support for one or more candles, often with a rim or cup to catch the drip. In early forms such as the Etrurian, the candle was held on a spike or pricket, but the Romans generally used a socket support. When the use of candles was revived in the Middle Ages, the pricket holder was developed in several forms—the single candlestick, the CANDELABRUM, and the corona, a wheellike holder supported on a stand or suspended from the ceiling.

The socket candlestick became common in the 16th cent. except in churches, some of which still use pricket holders, as do many Eastern nations. The symbolical holder with seven branches probably originated as the Jewish tabernacle lampstand of Bible times and was represented as a candelabrum on the Arch of Titus in Rome. Candles passed into the Christian service and symbolism, and the church candleholder became an elaborate and richly wrought device. The chandelier, a suspended multiple holder, was derived from the medieval corona. Wall candlesticks include brackets and sconces.

Candlewood Lake, large artificial body of water, W Conn., N of Danbury. Made in 1926 by a power dam in the Rocky River near its mouth in the Housatonic, it is 15 mi. long and covers 6,000 acres.

Cando (kăn'dōō), city (pop. 1,566), co. seat of Towner co., NE N.Dak., NNW of Devils Lake; named 1884, inc. 1901. It is a trade center for a grain, livestock, and dairy region.

Candy, Ceylon: see KANDY.

candy: see CONFECTIONERY.

candytuft, any plant of the genus *Iberis* of the MUSTARD family, low-growing plants of the Old World. A number of half-hardy annuals and evergreen perennials are cultivated—chiefly in borders and rock gardens—for the flat-topped or elongated clusters of flowers of various colors.

cane, in botany, name for the hollow or woody, usually slender and jointed stems of plants (particularly RATTAN) and for various tall grasses, e.g., SUGAR CANE, sorghum, and also other grasses used in the S United States for fodder. The large or giant cane (*Arundinaria macrosperma* or *gigantea*), a BAMBOO grass native to the United States, often forms impenetrable thickets 15 to 25 ft. high—the canebrakes of the South. The stalks are used locally for fishing poles and other purposes, and the young shoots are sometimes eaten as a potherb.

cane, walking stick. Probably used first as a weapon, it gradually took on the symbolism of strength and power and eventually authority and social prestige. Ancient Egyptian rulers carried the symbolic staff, and in Greece, some gods were represented with a staff in hand. In the Middle Ages, the long staff or walking stick was carried by pilgrims and shepherds. A scepter carried in the right hand symbolized royal power; carried in the left hand of a king the staff was the "hand of justice." The Church, too, adopted the staff for its officials; the pastoral staff (crosier), long with a crooked handle, symbolizes the bishop's office. The word *cane* was first applied to the walking stick after 1500 when bamboo was first used. After 1600 canes became highly fashionable for men. Made of ivory, ebony, and whalebone, as well as of wood, they had highly decorated and jeweled knob handles. They were often made hollow in order to carry possessions or supplies or, most frequently, to conceal a weapon. The late 17th cent. saw the extensive use of oak sticks, especially by the Puritans. The cane continued its rule in men's fashions throughout the 18th cent.; as with the women's fan a set of "rules" became standard for its use. From time to time women adopted the cane, particularly for a short time when Marie Antoinette carried the shepherd's crook. In the 19th cent. the cane became a mark of the professional man; the gold-headed cane was especially favored.

Canea (kŭnē′ŭ), ancient Gr. *Cydonia* (sīdō′nĕŭ), modern Gr. *Khania* (khänyä′), city (pop. 38,467), on the west coast of the island of Crete, Greece. This large seaport on the Gulf of Canea has been the capital of Crete since 1841. One of the oldest Cretan cities, it was conquered (69 B.C.) by the Romans and in A.D. 826 fell under Arab rule. Reconquered (961) by the Byzantines, it became (13th cent.) a Venetian colony. The Turks took it in 1645. The city has a synagogue, a mosque, and several churches. Among its historic sites are medieval fortifications and an old Venetian arsenal.

canella (kŭnĕl′ŭ), plant of the genus *Canella*, tropical aromatic trees. The wild cinnamon (*C. winterana*) grows in the West Indies and S Florida. Canella bark, sometimes called whitewood bark or white cinnamon, is used as a condiment, as a stimulant in medicine, and for flavoring tobacco. The plant is not related to the true cinnamon of Asia.

cane sugar: see SUCROSE.

Caney (kā′nē), city (pop. 2,682), SE Kansas, W of Coffeyville at the Okla. line, near oil fields; founded 1871, inc. 1887.

Caney, El (ĕl känä′), mountain village, SE Cuba, NE of Santiago de Cuba. It was the scene of a hard-fought attack (July, 1898) in the Spanish-American War, in which U.S. and Cuban troops dislodged the Spanish.

Caney Fork, river of central Tennessee rising NW of Crossville and flowing c.144 mi. W and NW to the Cumberland river near Carthage. On the river are the Center Hill Dam (250 ft. high; 2,160 ft. long; completed 1951), impounding Center Hill Reservoir, and the Great Falls Dam (completed 1925).

Canfield, Dorothy: see FISHER, DOROTHY CANFIELD.

Canfield, Richard Albert, 1855–1914, American gambler, b. New Bedford, Mass. A well-known gambling operator in Providence, R.I., Dick Canfield went in the 1880s to New York, where his gambling establishment became famous. The place was closed in 1904 largely through the efforts of W. T. JEROME, district attorney. Canfield was a noted art collector. The solitaire game Canfield was named for him. See biography by Alexander Gardiner (1930).

Canfield, village (pop. 3,252), NE Ohio, SW of Youngstown; surveyed 1798, inc. 1849. It is a trade center for a mine, farm, and timber area.

Can Grande della Scala: see SCALA, CAN FRANCESCO DELLA.

Canisius, Peter: see PETER CANISIUS, SAINT.

Canisteo (kănĭstē′ō), residential village (pop. 2,731), S N.Y., SE of Hornell, in a farm area; settled before 1790, inc. 1873.

Cankar, Ivan (ē′vŏn tsän′kär), 1876–1918, Slovenian poet. One of the great Slovenian literary figures, he was influential in the development of modern satire, symbolic drama, and the psychological novel. The struggle of the outcast poor is a theme of his satirical novel *Bailiff Yerney and His Rights* (1907; Eng. tr., 1930) and many other works. Cankar also wrote satires on politics and culture.

cankerworm, destructive larva of the geometrid moth, called also measuring worm, inchworm, spanworm, and looper. The spring and fall cankerworms, named for the seasons at which the adults emerge from underground pupation, feed on the leaves of orchard and shade trees. The wingless female lays her eggs on the bark, and one control method is the placing of bands of sticky paper around the tree trunks to trap the females before laying. The popular names for these larvae describe their looping movement, the result of having only two or three pairs of abdominal legs. When alarmed, cankerworms drop and hang suspended in mid-air at the end of a long silken thread secreted from their mouths; they ascend this thread after the danger has passed. The English sparrow was originally introduced in the United States to combat the spring cankerworm. For control methods see bulletins of the U.S. Dept. of Agriculture.

canna [Latin,=cane], any plant of the genus *Canna*, tropical and subtropical perennials, grown in temperate regions in parks and gardens for the large foliage and spikelike, usually red or yellow blossoms. Most cultivated cannas are hybrids, but two species are found wild in the S United States, one called Indian shot because of the hard shotlike seeds. *C. edulis*, Queensland arrowroot, is cultivated in the tropics for its rootstock, a commercial ARROWROOT starch.

cannabis: see HEMP.

Cannae (kăn′ē), ancient village, Apulia, SE Italy, scene in 216 B.C. of Hannibal's crushing defeat of the Romans.

Canneh (kăn′ē), unidentified city, apparently in N Syria. Ezek. 27.23. See CALNEH **2**.

cannel coal: see COAL.

Cannelton (kăn′ŭltŭn). **1** City (pop. 1,829), co. seat of Perry co., S central Ind., on the Ohio and NE of Owensboro, Ky.; laid out 1835. **2** Uninc. village (pop. 1,044 including Carbondale), S central W.Va., SE of Charleston.

Cannes (kănz, kăn, Fr. kän), town (estimated pop. 50,192), Alpes-Maritimes dept., SE France. It is a fashionable resort on the French Riviera. Napoleon I landed nearby on his return (1815) from Elba. The international film festival is held here each spring.

cannibalism (kă′nĭbŭlĭzŭm) [Span. *caníbal*, referring to the Carib Indians]. According to all available evidence, the partaking of human flesh was a widespread ritual practice. Only very rarely, under the pressure of such calamities as famine and shipwreck, have human beings resorted to eating their fellow men in order to survive. Various skeletal prehistoric finds suggest that ancient man practiced HEAD-HUNTING and cannibalism, but associated evidence strongly supports the magico-religious theory and the apparent rule that victims for these rites were always sought among alien groups. Various peoples, however, have been known to eat part of their kinsmen's corpses out of respect for the deceased and in order to absorb some magic powers. This aim of vital transfer seems to lie behind all cannibalism and head-hunting. The two practices rarely occur together, and it is believed that the latter may have evolved from the former. Among a few tribes, which may represent a connecting link, the head of the enemy is preserved and the rest of his body or selected parts of it are eaten.

Canning, Charles John Canning, Earl, 1812–62, British statesman; third son of George Canning.

Succeeding to the peerage conferred on his mother, he took his seat as Viscount Canning in the House of Lords (1837) and served as Sir Robert Peel's undersecretary of state for foreign affairs (1841–46) and the 4th earl of Aberdeen's postmaster general (1853). Governor general of India in the SEPOY REBELLION, he was nicknamed "Clemency Canning" for his efforts to restrain revenge against the natives. In 1858 he became India's first viceroy, after the power of government was transferred from the East India Company to the crown. He was created earl in 1859, and retired in 1862. See H. S. Cunningham, *Earl Canning and the Transfer of India* (1892).

Canning, Elizabeth, 1734–73, London servant girl, subject of a famous mystery. She disappeared Jan. 1, 1753, and returned home, cold, dirty, and half starved, after 28 days. She said she had been seized and confined in a garret. A gypsy woman was identified as one of her captors and was sentenced to hang. At the second trial, Elizabeth herself was accused of perjury and banished to America, but her conviction was debated throughout England. See R. Wellington, *The Mystery of Elizabeth Canning* (1940).

Canning, George, 1770–1827, British statesman. Canning was converted to Toryism by the French Revolution, became a disciple of William Pitt, and was his undersecretary for foreign affairs (1796–99). To bring ridicule upon English radicals and Whigs who favored the Revolution, he contributed numerous articles to the *Anti-Jacobin* (1797–98). During the war against Napoleon I, he served as treasurer of the navy (1804–6) and was foreign minister (1807–9). He exerted great influence in military affairs, planned the seizure of the Danish fleet at Copenhagen (1807), and supported the Peninsular War. He resigned (1809) after a duel with Robert Stewart, Viscount CASTLEREAGH, who had charged him with deception. As president of the board of control for India (1816–20) he eschewed conquest, discontinued censorship of the press, and initiated new policies for the appointment of East India Company officials. A friend of Queen Caroline, he resigned when the government attacked her status. Recalled (1822) to the foreign office after Castlereagh's suicide, he reversed previous policy toward the HOLY ALLIANCE and took a stand of forthright opposition. Recognizing England's advantage in the free trade of small independent states, Canning refused to cooperate in the suppression of European revolutions. He protested at the decisions of the Congress of Verona (1822), opposed French intervention in Spain, and foiled joint intervention in Portugal. His policies toward the Spanish colonies in America, whose independence he recognized, led to the promulgation of the MONROE DOCTRINE. He arranged the French-Russian-British agreement, which, after his death, resulted in Greek independence. After the death of Lord Liverpool, he was prime minister (April–Aug., 1827). See biographies by H. W. V. Temperley (1905), Dorothy Marshall (1938), and C. A. Petrie (2d ed., 1946).

Canning, Stratford: see STRATFORD DE REDCLIFFE, STRATFORD CANNING, VISCOUNT.

canning. The process of hermetically sealing cooked food for future use was discovered about the beginning of the 19th cent. by a Frenchman, Nicolas APPERT. The process proved moderately successful and was put into practice in France, England, and Ireland. A patent was taken out in New England c.1815 by Ezra Daggett for the canning of oysters, salmon, lobsters, pickles, jams, and sauces. In 1820 a Boston firm made pickles, jellies, and jam and canned some quinces, currants, and cranberries. About 1847 large quantities of tomatoes were put up for the use of students at Lafayette College, Easton, Pa. During the Civil War considerable amounts of canned meat and of canned tomatoes and other vegetables were in use. The canning of sea food at Eastport, Maine, began in 1843. Salmon was canned on the Columbia river in 1866 and in Alaska in 1872. Today a great variety of fish products are packed; Maine, Massachusetts, Washington, Oregon, California, and Alaska lead in this branch of the industry. Highly specialized machinery, knowledge of bacteriology and food chemistry, and more efficient processes of cooking now combine to make the commercial canning of food an important feature of modern life. The range of products preserved has increased enormously and may be grouped as meat and poultry; fruits and vegetables; fish; oysters, clams, and other shell fish; milk; and preserves, jams, jellies, pickles, and sauces. To these might be added another large class of miscellaneous edibles, such as steamed puddings and brown bread, cooked spaghetti, and the like, the demand for which arises from the phenomenal increase of the small apartment and of part-time housewifery. The emphasis given to the vitamin and other valuable qualities of fruit and some vegetable juices has led to extensive canning. The general principles of commercial and domestic canning are the same, but in the factory more accurate control of procedures is practiced and highly specialized machinery is available. Successful canning requires rapid handling of sound, clean raw material to prevent loss of vitamins, bacterial spoilage, and enzyme changes causing deterioration in the appearance, flavor, and texture of foods. Some foods, especially vegetables, are blanched (scalded) to remove respiratory gases from cell tissue and to facilitate packing. By the hot-seal method or by mechanical means the air is exhausted from the containers, which are then sealed and processed for the time and at the temperature required to cook the food and to attain commercial sterility (destruction of all microorganisms except for some spores). Glass containers were used at first but proved bulky, costly, and brittle. Peter Durand, an Englishman, patented in 1810 the first tin canister, and in 1825 the first American patent was obtained. Early canmaking was slow and expensive; sheets of tin were cut with shears, bent around a block, and the seams heavily soldered. A good tinsmith made only about 60 cans a day. The industry began to assume importance with the invention in 1847 of the stamp can. A machine for shaping and soldering was exhibited in 1876 at the Centennial Exposition at Philadelphia. The open-top can of the 20th cent. with a soldered lock seam and double-seamed ends permits easy cleaning and filling. Body blanks are stamped from tin-plated steel. Cans used for foods which react with metals, causing discoloration (usually harmless), may be coated with a lacquer film. The belief that food must not be left in an opened can is a fallacy. Distension of the ends of cans may indicate dangerous bacterial food spoilage or may result from chemical or physical causes such as improper filling.

Canning Dam, Western Australia, Commonwealth of Australia, in the Canning river. It is 218 ft. high, with a reservoir 24 mi. in circumference.

Cannizzaro, Stanislao (stänĕslä'ō kän-nĕt-tsä'rō), 1826–1910, Italian chemist. From 1861 he was professor at Palermo and from 1871 at Rome, where he was also a member of the senate and of the council of public instruction. He is known for his discovery of cyanamide, for obtaining alcohols from aldehydes by Cannizzaro's reaction, and for distinguishing between molecular and atomic weights. Of fundamental importance was his explanation of how atomic weights may be determined systematically on the basis of Avogadro's law (see AVOGADRO) if an atom of hydrogen is used as a reference standard and the specific heat used in the case of elements whose compounds are not volatile.

Cannock, urban district (pop. 42,186), Staffordshire, W central England. It is a mining town dependent upon the rich coal deposits of Cannock Chase, an infertile moorland nearby.

Cannon, Annie Jump, 1863–1941, American astronomer, b. Dover, Del., grad. Wellesley (B.S., 1884; M.A., 1907). In 1897 she became an assistant in the Harvard College Observatory, where from 1911 to 1938 she was astronomer and curator of astronomical photographs. In the course of her photographic work she discovered 300 variable stars, five new stars, one spectroscopic binary, and many stars with bright lines or variable spectra. She made a bibliography of variable stars which includes about 200,000 references and completed a catalogue of some 300,000 stellar spectra, besides preparing many papers on the subject.

Cannon, George Quayle, 1827–1901, Mormon apostle, b. Liverpool, England. He and his parents were converted to Mormonism in 1840; two years later they emigrated to Nauvoo, Ill., and in 1847 to Utah. In 1850 Cannon founded a Mormon mission in Hawaii. He became an apostle in 1859 and was assigned to England, where for four years he edited the *Millennial Star* and supervised missionary work. He served as a member of the Utah territorial council and as private secretary to Brigham Young, of whose will he was an executor. In 1867 he became editor of the influential *Deseret News*. Cannon was elected (1872) territorial delegate from Utah to Congress, but in 1882 he was refused his seat, under the Edmunds antipolygamy law. In 1888 he suffered imprisonment for practicing polygamy.

Cannon, Joseph Gurney, 1836–1926, speaker of the U.S. House of Representatives (1903–11), b. Guilford co., N.C. He moved to Indiana as a boy, attended Cincinnati Law School, and was admitted to the Illinois bar in 1858. Danville, Ill., ultimately became his home town. Cannon served in Congress from 1873 to 1923, except for the years 1891–93 and 1913–15, when first the Populists and then the Progressives turned him out. As speaker he carried the traditional power of his office to appoint all legislative committees to its ultimate arbitrary extremes, dictatorially ruling the House in the interest of his fellow "Old Guard" Republicans and suppressing minority groups. In March, 1910, insurgent Republicans, led by George W. Norris and supported by all the Democrats, passed a resolution which, by providing that the House itself should appoint the important Committee on Rules with the speaker ineligible for membership, broke Cannon's power. See C. R. Atkinson, *The Committee on Rules and the Overthrow of Speaker Cannon*

Joseph Gurney Cannon

(1911); L. W. Busbey, *Uncle Joe Cannon* (1927); Blair Bolles, *Tyrant from Illinois* (1951); W. R. Gwinn, *Uncle Joe Cannon, Archfoe of Insurgency* (1957).

Cannon Falls, city (pop. 2,055), SE Minn., SSE of Minneapolis. It is a farm trade center.

Cano, Alonso (älōn'sō kä'nō), 1601–67, Spanish baroque painter, sculptor, and architect. He received painting and architecture commissions from King Philip IV. After a rather adventurous life, he became canon and was chief architect of the cathedral at Granada, whose façade (1667) is his architectural masterpiece. He executed both the sculpture and paintings for his monumental altarpieces and did independent religious pictures and portraits. Fine examples of his paintings are *Descent into Limbo* (Los Angeles County Mus.); *Way to Calvary* (Worcester Art Mus., Mass.); and portrait of an ecclesiastic (Hispanic Society of America, New York). His sculptures, including statues of saints in Granada cathedral, are executed with vigor, yet often show great sensitivity. See study by H. E. Wethey (1955).

Cano, Juan Sebastián del (hwän' sävästyän' dĕl), c.1476–1526, Spanish navigator, the first to circumnavigate the globe. Under Magellan he commanded the *Concepción* and after Magellan's death in the Philippines took command of the expedition. From the Philippines to the Molucca islands Cano sailed new waters, arriving in Spain with the *Victoria* and 18 men on Sept. 6, 1522. He set out in 1525 on a second voyage to the Moluccas by Magellan's route, but died while crossing the Pacific.

canoe (kůnōō'), long, narrow watercraft with sharp ends originally used by most primitive peoples. It

Light Eskimo canoes near an iceberg in the Arctic.

Canadians shooting the rapids in a canoe (19th-century painting).

varies in material according to locality and in design according to the use made of it. In North America, where the natives were without horses and where the interlocking river systems were unusually favorable, the canoe in its various types was highly developed. Where large logs were available, it took the form of the hollowed-out log or dugout, especially on the N Pacific coast, where immense trees grew at the water's edge, where an intricate archipelago invited navigation in ocean waters, and where the tribes came to depend to a large extent upon sea life for their food supply. A semiseafaring culture developed here, and the great canoes of the Haida and Tlingit tribes, with high, decorated prows, capable of carrying 30 to 50 Indians, began to resemble in appearance the boats of viking culture. On the northern fringe of the American forest where smaller tree trunks were found and rapid rivers and many portages favored a lighter craft, the bark canoe dominated, reaching its highest development in the birch-bark canoe. At portages this light canoe could be lifted on one's shoulders and easily transported. A third type of primitive canoe is that made from skins, found where trees are lacking. The bullboat of the Plains Indian, little more than a round tub, made of buffalo hides stretched over a circular frame, was its crudest form. A much finer form is the kayak of the Eskimo, made of sealskin stretched over a frame constructed of driftwood or whalebone. In the South Seas canoes were developed for use on long voyages from island to island across the open sea. In the South Seas also ingenious outriggers were developed to give stabilization to the canoe under sail. It was the birch-bark canoe that carried such men as Marquette and Alexander Mackenzie and David Thompson on their journeys, and it was the canoe that carried fur traders out with their goods for the Indians and back with furs; thus it played an important part in early American history. With thickening of settlement, canoeing became less of a means of travel and more of a sport in the better-settled regions. The sport was extremely popular in the late 19th and early 20th cent., and many canoeing clubs were founded. The canoe's popularity waned somewhat later, but wherever possible today summer camps lay emphasis on canoeing. A sort of combination of sport and necessity is the use of canoes by guides in the north woods for taking sportsmen to hunt and fish. Vacation trips in canoes are especially popular in N Maine, the Adirondack region, N Wisconsin, and

N Minnesota, but in any town on a favorable river there are likely to be enthusiastic canoeists. The double-bladed paddle—used among North American natives only by the Eskimo—is almost always in use on wide bodie of water affected by wind and tidal currents. The substitution of canvas for birch bark in making canoes is credited to the Oldtown or Penobscot Indians in Maine; the canvas-covered wooden canoe is sometimes called the Oldtown canoe. All-wood canoes made of basswood or cedar, very popular in Canada, are sometimes called Peterborough canoes after a canoe-making center. Plywood canoes made in Canada and elsewhere have also been popular. The majority of canoes made today, however, are manufactured of a tough but light aluminum alloy. This type of canoe contains an air pocket in either end to ensure flotation. The aluminum canoe used in salt water must be anodized (i.e., covered with zinc chromate or other such protective film before it is painted) to prevent corrosion. Modern canoes are also made of fiber glass, of plastic, and even of a hard-rubber nonsinkable compound. The sail used on the modern canoe is usually the triangular lug sail known as the làteen. The gunter rig also used on canoes has a gaff that on being hoisted extends the height of the mast, thereby making possible a larger mainsail; it is sometimes augmented by a jib. The decked sailing canoe used for racing carries two and sometimes three sails; its navigator uses a sliding seat (frequently called the monkey seat) on which he balances, frequently out over the water on either side, to prevent his craft from heeling over too far; when he does capsize, the canoe, being decked, does not take on water and by means of the sliding seat is quickly righted again. This canoe, clocked at 16 knots or more, and the Samoan canoe (with an outrigger), exceeding 20 knots, were the fastest watercraft under sail until the advent of the catamaran. The outboard motor is increasingly used on the modern canoe. It is affixed to a bracket on either side near the stern or to a square stern provided for it.

canoeing: see BOATING.

canon (kă′nŭn), in Christendom, term of several meanings. Decrees of church councils are usually called canons; since the Council of Trent the expression is especially reserved to dogmatic pronouncements of ecumenical councils. The body of ratified conciliar canons is a large part of the legislation of CANON LAW. A canon is also an official list, as in canonization, i.e., enrollment among the saints, and of the names of books of the Bible accepted by the Church (see OLD TESTAMENT; NEW TESTAMENT; APOCRYPHA; PSEUDEPIGRAPHA). The central, mainly invariable part of the MASS is the canon. The term is also applied in the Western Church to certain persons. There are canons regular, priests living in community under a rule but not cloistered like monks; the Austin, or Augustinian, canons and the Premonstratensians are the best known of these. The priests attached to a cathedral or large church are sometimes organized into a group, or college, and called canons secular; a church having such a group is a collegiate church. Cathedral canons often have diocesan charges or pastoral duties apart from the cathedral. Canons of the Church of England are mostly cathedral canons.

canon, in music, a type of counterpoint employing the strictest form of IMITATION. All the voices of a canon have the same melody, beginning at different times. Successive entrances may be all at the same pitch or at different pitches. Another form of canon is the circle canon, or ROUND, e.g., SUMER IS ICUMEN IN. In the 14th and 15th cent. retrograde motion was employed to form what is known as crab canon, or canon cancrizans, wherein the original melody is turned backward to become the second voice. In the 15th and 16th cent. mensuration canons were frequently written, in which the voices sing the same melodic pattern written in different note values, i.e., to be sung at different speeds. Bach made noteworthy use of canon, particularly in the *Goldberg Variations.* Beethoven, Mozart, Haydn, Schumann, and Brahms wrote canons, and Franck used the device in the last movement of his violin sonata. It is an essential device of SERIAL MUSIC.

Canonchet: see PHILIP (King Philip).

Canon City (kăn′yŭn), city (pop. 8,973; alt. c.5,300 ft.), co. seat of Fremont co., S central Colo., on the Arkansas river above Pueblo, in a fruit, truck-farm, and livestock area. Laid out in 1859 on the site of a blockhouse built (1807) by Zebulòn M. PIKE, it was incorporated in 1872. Coal and gold mines and feldspar and dolomite quarries are nearby. The city has a museum of archaeology and natural history and is the entrance to the ROYAL GORGE. South Canon was annexed to the city in 1950.

Canonicus (kùnŏn′ĭkùs), c.1565–1647, American Indian chief, who ruled the Narragansett tribe when the Pilgrims landed in New England. He granted (1636) Rhode Island to Roger WILLIAMS and because of Williams's influence remained friendly to the whites, despite their aggressive ways. See H. M. Chapin, *Sachems of the Narragansetts* (1931).

canonization (kă″nŭnĭză′shŭn), in the Roman Catholic Church, process by which the name of a person is enrolled among the saints. It is now performed at Rome alone, although in the Middle Ages and earlier bishops everywhere used to canonize. Canonization is not necessary for martyrs, who are considered to be enrolled among the saints on their death, but in recent years the Church has approved the cult of canonized persons only. The process of canonization is a trial (or cause), at which the saint is said to be defended by the Church; a prosecutor is appointed to attack all evidence alleged in favor of canonization. The prosecutor is popularly called *advocatus diaboli* [devil's advocate], his opponent the *advocatus Dei* [God's advocate]. This evidence consists primarily of the proof of four miracles attributable to the saint and proof that the saint's life was exemplary. Beatification, by which a person is called blessed and his cult is approved for localities and orders, requires two miracles. Miracles attributed to saints are considered probable or pious opinions, and Catholics are not required to believe in them. The first solemn canonization seems to have been that of St. Ulrich late in the 10th cent. The method of formal canonization was set by the enactments of Urban VIII that came into force in 1634. See SAINT.

canon law (kă′nŭn), in the Roman Catholic Church, the body of law based on the legislation of the councils (both ecumenical and local) and the popes, as well as the bishops (for diocesan matters). It is the law of the church courts and is to be distinguished from other parts of ecclesiastical law, such as liturgical law. However, when liturgical law overlaps with canon law, the great body of canon law, promulgated in the *Codex juris canonici* [code of canon law] in 1917 (and effective since 1918), prevails, though exceptions to this rule are noted in the code. The code itself, the culmination of centuries of legal growth, consists of 2,414 canons, with an analytical index (at the beginning) and nine appended documents; it superseded all previous compilations. It does not contain all of canon law, which is a living organism, but it is the base of the present-day law, and the study of canon law consists mainly in mastering the code and its application. It lays down rules for the governance and regulation of the clergy and the Church, including such matters as the qualifications, duties, and discipline of the clergy and the administration of the sacraments (more particularly the laws regarding holy orders and the sacrament of marriage). Canon law embraces both general laws applicable in the church universal, such as those on requirements for the priesthood and those on marriage, and local laws applicable only in certain dioceses. The early law grew particularly from the letters of the bishop of Rome that settled matters of ecclesiastical government and discipline from the end of the 1st cent. A.D. Such papal letters and pronouncements are called decretals. Joined to them are the canons of the councils of the Church regarding church discipline and governance. From the 4th cent. this legislation grew profuse, and attempts to collect and correlate the laws began early (see CONSTITUTIONS, APOSTOLIC). These collections were not always authorized and were sometimes not genuine, as in the case of the FALSE DECRETALS. It was not until the middle of the 12th cent. that the great genius of the canon law, GRATIAN, following after Ivo of Chartres, applied the methods of Roman law in bringing order out of the chaos of conflicting and uncoordinated legislation. His *Concordantia discordantanium canonum* (c.1140) or *Decretum Gratiani,* called in English *Gratian's Decree,* became the basis for future compilations of the law. Important among the later additional works were the collections of decretals under Gregory IX, called the *Extravagantes* or *Extra* because they were outside *Gratian's Decree;* the collection issued (1298) by Boniface VIII and called *Liber sextus* [the sixth book] because it added to the five books of decretals promulgated by Gregory; the collection promulgated (1317) by John XXII, drawn mostly from the constitutions of Clement V at the Council of Vienne and called the *Clementinae;* the work commonly called *Corpus juris canonici,* which in 1500 combined all the preceding with the *Extravagantes* of John XXII and the *Extravagantes communes* (decretals from Boniface VIII through Sixtus IV) and was to be the fundamental work in canon law for centuries. The Council of Trent (1545–63, with interruptions) by its decrees concerning the Church and church discipline was a landmark in canon law. Legislation in the Church went on later and arrived again at considerable confusion, which was resolved in 1904 when St. Pius X announced the undertaking of the *Codex juris canonici.* This was drafted by a commission of cardinals headed by Cardinal Gasparri; all the resources of the Church were used to produce this code. In 1917, when the code was finished, a permanent commission of cardinals was set up to interpret it. This code does not apply to Catholics of Eastern rites, who have their own separate codes, approved by the Roman Catholic Church. Canon law has had a profound influence on the law of countries where the Roman Catholic Church has been the state church. In the Middle Ages the church courts had very wide jurisdiction —e.g., in England, control of the law of personal property—and because they were well regulated, they tended to attract many borderline cases that might have been the business of the developing royal courts (see BENEFIT OF CLERGY). The term "canon law" is also used for ecclesiastical law in the Anglican and Protestant Episcopal churches. The Anglican *Constitutions and Canons Ecclesiastical* (1603) was a collection of rulings, not based on the old canon law, but given equal force with the canon law. See T. Lincoln Bouscaren and Adam C. Ellis, *Canon Law* (1946); A. G. Cicognani, *Canon Law* (rev. ed., 1949); Stanislaus Woywod, *Practical Commentary on the Code of Canon Law* (rev. ed., 1949); J. A. Abbo and J. D. Hannan, *The Sacred Canons* (1957); René Metz, *What Is Canon Law?* (1960).

Canonsburg, borough (pop. 11,877), SW Pa., SW of Pittsburgh; settled 1773, laid out 1787, inc. 1802. Radio equipment and metal products are made, and coal is mined nearby. A gram of radium produced here was presented to Mme Curie in 1921, and the town was visited by her. Log Academy (1780), oldest school building W of the Alleghenies, is here. Black Horse Tavern (1794) was the site of the precipitation of the Whisky Rebellion. Roberts House (1804) is an example of the W Pennsylvania manor type.

Canopus (kùnō′pùs), ancient city of N Egypt, 12 mi. E of Alexandria. Canopus, the pilot of Menelaus' ship, died here. In Hellenistic times Canopus was known as a pleasure city for the rich. Vases capped with the figure of a human head, called Canopic vases, were used to hold the viscera of embalmed bodies. The Decree of Canopus, issued here in 238 B.C. and found at Tanis, was of value in studying the ancient Egyptian language. The modern village of ABOUKIR is near the ancient ruins.

Canopus, second brightest star in the heavens. It is the brightest star in Carina, a part of a Southern Hemisphere constellation called Argo Navis, and is known as Alpha Carinae or Alpha Argus. The star is not visible north of lat. 37° N. Only Sirius is brighter than Canopus, but since Canopus is many times more distant it is probably thousands of times greater in mass.

Canosa di Puglia (känō′zä dē pōō′lyä), Latin *Canusium,* town (estimated pop. 35,910), Apulia, S Italy. An agricultural center, it flourished under the Romans and was noted for its wool and its fine vases, many of which have been found in tombs nearby. The Romans fled to Canusium after the disastrous defeat at Cannae (216 B.C.). There are remains of Roman walls, of an amphitheater, and of a gate. The 11th-century Romanesque cathedral has fine sculptured bronze doors and contains the tomb of Bohemond.

Canossa (kùnō′sù, Ital. känôs′sä), village, Emilia-Romagna, N central Italy, in the Apennines. There are ruins of the castle of the powerful feudal

Countess Matilda, Henry IV, and a monk at Canossa (12th-century miniature from Life of Matilda*).*

family which took its name from the place. In the 10th and 11th cent. they ruled over much of Tuscany and Emilia. MATILDA, countess of Tuscany, was the last of the family. In Jan., 1077, the castle was the scene of penance done by Emperor HENRY IV to obtain from Pope Gregory VII the withdrawal of the excommunication against him. The pope was Matilda's guest at the castle, and Henry is said to have stood three days barefoot in the snow before being admitted to the pope's presence. Henry was absolved, but the peace between him and the pope was short-lived. The political implications of this episode inspired Bismarck to coin the phrase "to go to Canossa" (i.e., to submit to the demands of the Roman Catholic Church) in the Kulturkampf.

Canova, Antonio (äntō'nyō känō'vä), 1757–1822, Italian sculptor, leading exponent of the neoclassical school. His influence on the art of his time was enormous. Canova's monumental statues and basreliefs are executed with extreme grace. polish. and purity of contour. His first important commission was the monument (1782–87) to Clement XIV in the Church of the Apostles, Rome, followed by that to Clement XIII (completed 1792) in St. Peter's. He then received an extraordinary number of major commissions from many countries and traveled to Vienna, Paris, and London. An admirer of Napoleon, Canova executed a bust of the emperor from life and several other portraits, including two where Napoleon is represented nude in the guise of a Roman emperor. In 1815 Canova was sent by the pope to Paris in order to recover some of the Italian art treasures that had been looted by the French. For his part in the venture he was made Marchese d'Ischia. His statue (1820) of George Washington for the statehouse at Raleigh, N. C. (destroyed), was dressed in Roman armor. Canova's memorabilia, consisting of sketches, casts, a few oil paintings, and a voluminous correspondence, are divided between the Gipsoteca in Possagno, his birthplace, and the Civic Museum in Bassano. See illustrated monographs (in Italian) by Elena Bassi (1943) and Antonio Muñoz (1957).

Cánovas del Castillo, Antonio (äntō'nyō kä'nōväs dĕl kästē'lyō), 1828–97, Spanish conservative statesman, historian, and man of letters. He led

Monument to Clement XIII by Antonio Canova.

political plans to restore Alfonso XII and was afterward repeatedly premier. The chief figure in stabilizing the restored monarchy, he helped work a political arrangement that rotated power within a narrow group. He was assassinated by an anarchist. His reputation later suffered because of criticism from all sectors of Spanish politics. The editor of *Historia general de España* (18 vols., 1891–99), he also wrote several historical and critical works.

Canrobert, François Certain (fräswä' sĕrtĕ' kärô-bĕr'), 1809–95, marshal of France. After brilliant service in Africa, he returned to Paris and aided Louis Napoleon (later Napoleon III) in the coup d'état of 1851. He served in the Crimean War and distinguished himself in the Italian War of 1859 and in the Franco-Prussian War. He also held political and diplomatic posts and became a senator under the Third Republic.

Canso, fishing town (pop. 1,151), E N.S., Canada, near the entrance to Chedabucto Bay and near Cape Canso, the easternmost point of Nova Scotia peninsula proper. Canso is the western terminus of a number of ocean cables. The harbor was much used by fishing fleets in colonial times and was fortified by the British in 1720. The Gut, or Strait, of Canso, scarcely a mile wide in places, separates Nova Scotia peninsula proper from Cape Breton Island. The strait is much used by sailing vessels and coast steamers. There are fishing villages along its hilly, wooded shores.

Cantabrian Mountains (kăntā'brĕun), N Spain, extending c.300 mi. along the Bay of Biscay from the Pyrenees to Cape Finisterre. The highest peaks are the Peña de Cerredo (8,687 ft.) and the Peña Vieja (8,573 ft.) in the Europa group in the central section. The mountains are rich in minerals, especially coal and iron; the slopes are farmed.

Cantabrigia: see CAMBRIDGE, England.

Cantacuzene (kăn"túkūzĕn') or **Cantacuzino** (kän"-

Antonio Cánovas del Castillo

Francois C. Canrobert

täko͞oze'nô), noble Rumanian family of Greek origin, tracing its descent from the Byzantine emperor JOHN VI (John Cantacuzene). Under Ottoman rule members of the family were among the PHANARIOTS who governed Walachia and Moldavia, and late in the 16th cent. one branch settled in Walachia. A Russian branch of the family held high positions in the army and as governors of Bessarabia. **Serban Cantacuzene,** 1640–88, hospodar of Walachia (1678–88), took part in the Turkish siege of Vienna (1683); he probably was poisoned because of his open pro-Austrian feelings. During his rule Rumanian was substituted for Slavonic as the liturgical language, and the first Rumanian Bible was printed (1688) under his auspices. **George Cantacuzene,** 1837–1913, was head of the Rumanian conservatives and was (1905–7) premier.

Cantacuzene, John: see JOHN VI, emperor.

Cantal (kätäl'), department (2,231 sq. mi.; pop. 177,000), S central France, in AUVERGNE. Aurillac is the capital. The **Plomb du Cantal** (plō" dü kätäl'), an extinct volcano, is the highest peak (6,096 ft.) of the Cantal mountain group.

cantaloupe: see GOURD and MELON.

Cantarini, Simone (sēmō'nä käntärē'nē), 1612–48, Italian painter and etcher, called Il Pesarese and Simone da Pesaro. He closely followed the style of Guido Reni, whose portrait he painted (Bologna). Cantarini was probably more significant as an etcher.

cantata (kùntä'tù) [Ital.,=sung], composite musical form developed in Italy in the baroque period. The term was first used in 1620 to refer to strophic variations in the voice part over a recurrent melody in the bass accompaniment. Gradually the cantata came to contain contrasting sections of recitative and aria separated by instrumental passages, often in the current operatic style. In the second half of the 17th cent. the secular cantata was standardized by Stradella, Alessandro Scarlatti, and other members of the Neapolitan school into two arias with recitatives. This form was very popular through the 18th cent. as a vehicle for virtuoso singing. In France the cantata was adapted by Rameau to contain three arias with recitatives. In Germany the sacred cantata was more popular than the secular. It incorporated extensive choral and instrumental sections. A particular variety, the chorale cantata, utilized the verses of hymns and frequently the hymn tunes in various parts of the cantata. This type, as written by J. S. Bach, opens with a chorus, which is followed by recitatives and arias for each soloist, and then closes with a harmonized chorale. After Bach the cantata became, in general, a diminutive form of the oratorio.

Canterbury, county borough (pop. 30,376), Kent, SE England, on the Stour river at the foot of the North Downs. It was the Durovernum in Roman times and the Cantwaraburh [O.E.,=fort of the Kentish militia] of the Saxons. It has long been the spiritual center of England. In 597 St. Augustine arrived from Rome to convert the island peoples to Christianity. He founded an abbey at Canterbury and became the first archbishop of Canterbury and primate of all England. The early cathedral was several times burned and rebuilt (1011, 1067, 1174). After the murder (1170) of THOMAS À BECKET and the penance of Henry II, Canterbury became famous throughout Europe as the object of pilgrimage, and the *Canterbury Tales* of Chaucer are based upon the stories of these travelers. The present cathedral is a magnificent structure, its architecture embodying the work of several periods and various men (notably Lanfranc and St. Anselm). Noteworthy are the great 15th-century tower (235 ft. high); the long transepts; the screen separating the raised choir from the Perpendicular nave; the east chapel (called the Corona or Becket's Crown), which contains the marble chair in which the archbishops are enthroned; Trinity Chapel, which held the shrine of St. Thomas until 1538, when Henry VIII ordered it destroyed and the accumulated wealth confiscated; the chapel in which French Protestants worshiped in the 16th cent. and where

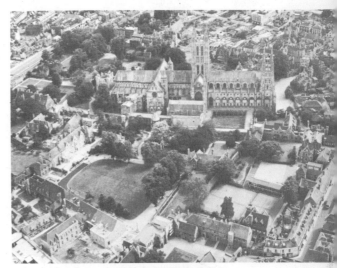

Aerial view of Canterbury and cathedral.

services are still held in the French tongue; the northwestern transept (where a plaque commemorates the exact site of Thomas à Becket's murder); and the tombs of Henry IV and Edward the Black Prince. In the Second World War the cathedral was the object of severe German reprisal raids (June, 1942), which resulted in the destruction of the comparatively new library and many other surrounding buildings, but the cathedral itself received no direct hits. The city of Canterbury is also of great historical interest, having remains of ancient city walls and gate; St. Martin's Church (established before St. Augustine's arrival and known as the Mother Church of England); St. Augustine's Abbey (on the site of the original monastery); the old pilgrims' hostel called the Hospital of St. Thomas; and several fine old inns. Christopher Marlowe was born at Canterbury and was educated at King's School here (of very ancient origin) before going to Cambridge.

Canterbury, farming town (pop. 1,857), E Conn., on

the Quinebaug and NE of Norwich; settled c.1690, inc. 1703. The site of Moses Cleaveland's birthplace is marked. Prudence Crandall had a school for Negro girls here.

Canterbury bells: see BELLFLOWER.

cantharides: see BLISTER BEETLE.

Canticles, another name of the SONG OF SOLOMON.

Cantigny (kätēnyē'), village (estimated pop. 100), Somme dept., N France. Captured by the 1st Division of the U.S. army in May, 1918, Cantigny is the site of a monument commemorating the first offensive operation by American forces in the First World War.

cantilever (kăn'tŭlēvŭr), beam supported rigidly at one end to carry a load along the free arm or at the free end. A slanting beam fixed at the base is often used to support the free end, as in a common bracket. The springboard is a simple cantilever beam, and the cantilever design is often used for canopies, for balconies, for sidewalks outside the trusses of bridges, and for large cranes such as those used in shipyards. By the use of cantilever trusses, obstructing columns are eliminated in theaters. Sometimes the great steel BRIDGE of modern times is constructed on the cantilever principle.

Cantinflas (kän'tēnfläs"), 1911–, Mexican comedian, originally named Mario Moreno. In films he portrays a lovable raffish character, and has achieved an international reputation. In 1941 he organized the Posa Film Company. Often called Mexico's Charlie Chaplin, he specializes in broad gestures and in nonsense talk. He is also well known as a philanthropist.

Cantire: see KINTYRE.

Canton, John, 1718–72, English physicist. He is known for his experiments in magnetism and in electricity (verifying Franklin's results). He invented an electroscope and an electrometer, demonstrated the compressibility of water, and produced Canton's phosphorus (phosphorescent calcium sulfide) by calcining oyster shells with sulfur.

Canton (kăn"tŏn', kăn'tŏn"), Mandarin *Kuangchou*, city (pop. c.1,900,000), capital of Kwangtung prov., S China, on the Canton river delta. It is a large river port and the chief industrial center of S China, with shipbuilding industries, machinery plants, and manufactures of silk, paper, cement, and rubber products. It is also a cultural and educational center with several institutions of higher learning, notably Sun Yat-sen Univ. Canton became a part of China in the 3d cent. B.C. Foreign trade was carried on here for more than a thousand years. Hindu and Arab merchants reached Canton in the 10th cent., and the city became the first Chinese port regularly visited by European traders. In 1511 Portugal secured a trade monopoly, but it was broken by the British in the late 17th cent.; in the 18th cent. the French and Dutch were admitted also. Trading, however, was under onerous restrictions until the treaty of Nanking (1842), which ended the Opium War, opened the city to foreign trade. Following a disturbance, French and British forces occupied Canton in 1856. Later the island of Shameen was ceded to them for business and residential purposes, and this reclaimed sandbank with its broad avenues, gardens, and fine buildings became one of the most attractive sections; it was wholly restored to China in 1946. Canton was the

View along the riverfront of Canton.

seat of the revolutionary movement under Sun Yat-sen in 1911, and here was proclaimed the Republic of China. From Canton the Nationalist armies of Chiang Kai-shek marched northward in the 1920s to establish a government in Nanking. In 1927 Canton was briefly the seat of one of the earliest Communist communes in China. Canton was developed as an industrial center and a modern port—with a great trade to and from Hong Kong—by the Communist regime.

Canton. 1 Town (pop. 4,783), N central Conn., NW of Hartford; settled 1737, inc. 1806. The town includes the industrial village of Collinsville (pop. 1,682), where edged tools have been produced since 1826. **2** Industrial town (pop. 2,411), co. seat of Cherokee co., N Ga., N of Atlanta and on the Etowah river, in an area of farms and marble quarries; inc. 1833. **3** City (pop. 13,588), W central Ill., SW of Peoria, in the Illinois corn belt; founded 1825, inc. 1849. It is a trade and industrial center for a coal and farm area. Among its manufactures are farm implements and work clothes. **4** Town (pop. 12,771), E Mass., SSW of Boston; inc. 1797. Paul Revere operated a copper-rolling mill here. The town has a state hospital school for the physically handicapped. Rubber goods and textiles are produced. **5** City (pop. 9,707), co. seat of Madison co., W central Miss., NNE of Jackson; inc. 1836. It is a trade and processing center in a cotton, truck-farm, and timber area. There are a number of fine old ante-bellum houses. **6** City (pop. 2,562), NE Mo., on the Mississippi and NNW of Hannibal; laid out 1830, inc. 1871. Gloves, fiber-glass boats, and machinery are made. It is the seat of Culver-Stockton College (Disciples of Christ; coeducational; 1853). **7** Village (pop. 5,046), co. seat of St. Lawrence co., N N.Y., on the Grass river and ESE of Ogdensburg; settled 1799, inc. 1845. It is the seat of St. Lawrence Univ. (coeducational; 1856) and of a state agricultural and technical school.

Frederic Remington was born here. **8** Industrial town (pop. 5,068), W N.C., WSW of Asheville. In a timber area, it has pulp and paper mills. **9** City (pop. 113,631), co. seat of Stark co., NE Ohio, on Nimishillen Creek and SSE of Akron; laid out 1806, inc. as a town 1822, as a city 1854. In an important iron and steel area, the city has varied manufactures which include roller bearings, vacuum cleaners, and steel products. William McKinley lived and was buried there. **10** Industrial borough (pop. 2,102), NE Pa., SW of Towanda; settled c.1796, inc. 1864. Its manufactures include wood and paper products and leather goods. **11** City (pop. 2,511), co. seat of Lincoln co., SE S.Dak., on the Big Sioux river and S of Sioux Falls; settled 1868, inc. 1881. It is a trade and shipping point for a livestock and grain region. **12** Village (pop. 1,114), co. seat of Van Zandt co., NE Texas, NW of Tyler; settled 1850. It is a commercial center in a farm and ranch area.

Canton, Chinese *Yueh Kiang* or *Yueh Chiang* (both: yōoâ′ jyäng′), or **Pearl,** Chinese *Chu-kiang* or *Chu-chiang* (both: jōo′ jyäng′), river, S Kwangtung prov., S China. Although only c.110 mi. long, the river, linking Canton to Hong Kong and the sea, is one of the most important waterways of China. Formed at Canton, it flows E and S past Canton and Whampoa to form a large estuary between Hong Kong and Macao. This estuary, called Boca Tigris, was dredged (1949, 1956) and is open to ocean vessels.

Canton Island, area 3.5 sq. mi., central Pacific, one of the Phoenix Islands, c.2,000 mi. SW of Honolulu. Canton was claimed for the United States by American guano companies under the terms of the Guano Act (1856). In 1937 the British also claimed it and built a radio station here. In 1938 the island was formally claimed by the United States and placed under the Dept. of the Interior. In that year, both British and American colonists were brought to Canton. Because of the island's importance as a stopping place on the air route to Australia, the two countries agreed (1939) on joint control of Canton and nearby ENDERBURY ISLAND for 50 years.

Cantonment, uninc. town (pop. 2,499), extreme NW Fla., NNW of Pensacola. Vegetables are packed.

Cantor, Georg (gā′ôrk kän′tôr), 1845–1918, German mathematician, b. St. Petersburg. He studied under Karl Weierstrass and taught (1869–1913) at the Univ. of Halle. He is known for his work on transfinite numbers and the development of set theory, which is the basis of modern analysis. His still controversial approach to the concept of the infinite revolutionized mathematics by challenging the processes of deductive reasoning and led to the present critical investigation of the foundations of mathematics.

Cantor, Moritz Benedikt (mō′rĭts bā′nädĭkt), 1829–1920, German mathematician. He taught (1863–1913) at the Univ. of Heidelberg and was author of a four-volume history of mathematics (1880–1908).

cantor [Latin,=singer], a singer or chanter, especially one who performs the solo chants of a church service. The office of cantor, at first an honorary one, originated in the Jewish synagogues, in which it was early the custom to appoint a lay member to represent the congregation in prayer. The cantilla-

tion of prayers, and later of parts of the Scriptures, was transmitted by oral tradition. The notation of the chants was forbidden. In the 6th cent. poetic prayer forms were developed, and with them more complicated modes, or music, thus necessitating professional cantors. In the early Christian church, cantors known as *precentors* (see PRECENTOR) had charge of the musical part of the service.

Canusium: see CANOSA DI PUGLIA.

Canute (kȧnōōt′, kȧnūt′), 995?–1035, king of England, Norway, and Denmark. The younger son of Sweyn of Denmark, Canute accompanied his father in the invasion of England in 1013 which forced ÆTHELRED to take refuge in Normandy.

Canute

When Sweyn died (1014), the Danes in England swore fealty to Canute, but he withdrew with them to Denmark, where his older brother, Harold, was king. With allies Canute invaded England in 1015, conquered most of Wessex, harried the Danelaw, and conquered Northumbria. After the Danish victory in the battle of ASSANDUN, Canute divided England with EDMUND IRONSIDE, Æthelred's son. When Edmund died, late in 1016, Canute was accepted as sole king. He gave England peace and strove to continue English traditions by restoring the Church to high place and codifying English law. To forestall dynastic quarrels he banished his wife (and their son Sweyn) and married Emma, the widow of Æthelred. His son by Emma was Harthacanute. He maintained a military household of his followers and gave English lands to many Danes. In 1018 he succeeded to the throne of Denmark and was forced to lead several expeditions to assert his rights there and in the Danish provinces in Norway. In 1026 he won a signal victory, and in 1028 he drove out Olaf II of Norway, thus becoming ruler of the three kingdoms. He made his son Harthacanute king of Denmark, and in 1029 he made his son Sweyn king of Norway, with Sweyn's mother as regent. She and Sweyn were driven out by 1035, and Norway was ruled by Olaf's son Magnus. Canute established friendly relations with the Holy Roman Empire and attended the coronation of Conrad II in Rome in 1027. At the end of his reign Canute led an army into Scotland to stop Scottish invasions under Malcolm II. Canute was succeeded by his illegitimate son, Harold Harefoot, then by Harthacanute. The name also appears as Knut. See biography by L. M. Larson (1912).

Canute the Saint, d. 1086, king (1080–86) and patron saint of Denmark. He built churches and cathedrals and raised the bishops to the rank of prince. In 1085 he made an unsuccessful attempt to invade England. Feast: Jan. 19.

Canutillo (kănŭtē′yō), uninc. village (pop. 1,377), extreme W Texas, NNW of El Paso and on the Rio Grande, in an irrigated farm area.

canvas, strong, coarse cloth of cotton, flax, hemp, or other fibers, early used as sailcloth (see SAIL). Made in natural color, bleached, or dyed, it has a wide variety of uses, as for game, duffel, sport, mail and nose bags, tennis shoes, covers, tents, and awnings. Waterproofed with tar, paint, or the like it is called tarpaulin and used to protect boats, hatches, and machinery. Duck is a fine light quality used for summer clothing, awnings, and sails. Artists' canvas is a light, smooth, single-warp texture, specially treated to receive paint. Art or embroidery canvas is an open-mesh type, usually linen, for working in crewels and for needlepoint.

canvasback: see DUCK.

Canyon, city (pop. 5,864), co. seat of Randall co., extreme N Texas, S of Amarillo in the Panhandle; settled 1892, inc. 1906. Near Canyon, Palo Duro Creek and Tierra Blanca Creek form the Prairie Dog Fork of the Red River just above Palo Duro Canyon. The canyon itself, a brilliant gash in the dun plateau of the Llano Estacado, is today viewed by many visitors. It was probably seen by Coronado and was known centuries later to Charles Goodnight and other cattlemen. Canyon is proud of its past as a cow town and handles cattle and wheat today. West Texas State College (coeducational; 1910) has a museum featuring relics of the ranching past.

Canyon de Chelly National Monument, 83,840.00 acres, NE Ariz.; est. 1931. The area contains the ruins of several hundred prehistoric Indian villages, most of them built between A.D. 350 and 1300. There are many pictographs in rock shelters and on cliff faces. Probably the earliest people living in the region were the Basket Makers and the later Pueblo Indians. The spectacular cliff dwellings include Mummy Cave Ruin, with a 3-story tower house.

Canyonville, city (pop. 1,089), SW Oregon, S of Roseburg, in a lumbering region; inc. 1901.

canzone (käntsō′nä) or **canzona** (-nä), in literature, Italian term meaning lyric or song. It is used to designate such various literary forms as Provençal troubadour poems and the lyrics of Petrarch and other Italian poets of the 13th and 14th cent. The term was revived in the 19th cent. by Italian lyric poets, among them Giosuè Carducci.

canzone or **canzona,** in music, a type of instrumental music in Italy in the 16th and 17th cent. Previously the term had been given to strophic songs for five or six voices; usually the canzone had three sections. The instrumental canzone was written in imitation of lute or keyboard transcriptions of French chansons. Frescobaldi used it in a series of fugal sections, each a rhythmic variation of the same theme. The thematic unity of his example was adopted by Froberger and other German composers, and this development led to the fugue. The canzone for instrumental ensemble became, in the hands of Giovanni Gabrieli and his followers, a structure consisting of sections of imitation in duple meter alternating with passages in triple meter.

Canzoneri, Tony, 1908–60, American boxer, b. Slidell, La. Although only 5 ft. 4 in. tall, he became one of the greatest lightweight fighters of all time. He engaged in 20 championship bouts, won the featherweight crown from Benny Bass, and knocked out Al Singer in the first round for the lightweight title in 1930. Canzoneri lost the lightweight crown to Barney Ross in 1933, but he regained the title from Lou Ambers in 1935. Canzoneri also held the junior lightweight and junior welterweight championships. During his professional career he had 177 fights and won 139, including 44 by knockout. He retired in 1939.

caoutchouc: see RUBBER.

cap: see HAT.

Capablanca, José Raúl (hōsä′ räōōl′ käpäbläng′kä), 1888–1942, Cuban chess player, b. Havana. Champion of Cuba at the age of 12, he won the world's championship from LASKER in 1921, retaining the title until he was defeated by ALEKHINE in 1927. His game was almost free from false interpretations

José Raúl Capablanca

of position, and his technique, though facile, was highly refined. See his *My Chess Career* (1920), *Chess Fundamentals* (1931), and *Primer of Chess* (1935); *Capablanca's Hundred Best Games* (ed. by H. Golombek, 1947).

Capac (kā′păk), village (pop. 1,235), SE Mich., WNW of Port Huron; inc. 1873. Peat moss is grown.

Capaneus (kăpŭnē′ŭs), in Greek legend, one of the SEVEN AGAINST THEBES. He defied Zeus by scaling the wall of the city and was killed by a bolt of lightning.

Cap de la Madeleine (käp′ dü lä mädlĕn′), city (pop. 26,925), S Que., Canada, on the north bank of the St. Lawrence river just N of Trois Rivières. There are many factories.

Cape Breton Island (brĕ′tŭn), c.3,600 sq. mi., forming the northeastern part of Nova Scotia, Canada, and separated from the main part by the Gut of

CANSO. The easternmost point is called Cape Breton. The center of the island is occupied by the Bras d'Or salt lakes. Gently sloping in the south, the island rises to rugged hills in the wilder northern part. The inhabitants are mainly of Scottish Highlander descent. There are many summer resorts on the lakes and fishing villages on the coast. In the northeast are the extensive Sydney coal fields on which the important steelworks are dependent. The Cabot Trail, a road for motorists, commemorates the traditional discovery of Cape Breton Island in 1497 by John Cabot. By the Peace of Utrecht (1713) the French retained Cape Breton, and many Acadians migrated here from Nova Scotia, which was ceded to the English. They renamed the island Ile Royale and at LOUIS-BURG established their strong fortress. With the final cession of Canada to the British (1763), Cape Breton was attached to Nova Scotia. It was again independent from 1784 to 1820, with Sydney as its capital.

Cape Canaveral (kŭnă'vŭrŭl), barrier island, E Fla., separating Banana river (a lagoon) from the Atlantic Ocean. It is the site of Patrick Air Force Base and, since 1950, of a major U.S. air force missile testing center. Most of the nation's earth satellites (see SATELLITE, ARTIFICIAL) and SPACE PROBES have been launched from Cape Canaveral, and it has been the site of most of Project Mercury's manned space-flight operations (see ASTRONAUT) On Feb. 20, 1962, John GLENN, the first American to be put into orbital flight, was shot into space from the Cape Canaveral launching pad. Since 1950 the region around Cape Canaveral has grown in population and become the site of many industries related to rockets and guided missiles. Cape Canaveral was renamed Cape Kennedy in 1963 in memory of President John F. Kennedy.

Cape Charles, town (pop. 2,041), E Va., a port of entry on Chesapeake Bay near the tip of the Eastern Shore peninsula; founded 1884, inc. 1886. Fruit, vegetables, and sea food are processed. It was occupied by Federal forces in the Civil War.

Cape Coast, town (pop. c.35,000), capital of the Western Region of Ghana, a port on the Gulf of Guinea. It grew around European forts built in the 17th cent. After 1664 it was the British headquarters and then capital of the country; it was superseded by Accra as capital in 1876. Cape Coast, the oldest educational center, has several well-known schools. There are fisheries.

Cape Cod, sandy peninsula of glacial origin, 65 mi. long and 1 to 20 mi. wide, SE Mass., comprising Barnstable co. It is bounded by Cape Cod Bay, the Atlantic Ocean, Nantucket and Vineyard sounds, and Buzzards Bay. It is a popular resort center, and many people have summer houses here. Cranberries are extensively cultivated, and candle-making and boatbuilding are carried on. Its towns include Provincetown, Barnstable, Falmouth, and Bourne. The name Cape Cod is attributed to Bartholomew Gosnold, who visited these shores in 1602. The Pilgrims put in at the site of Provincetown in Nov., 1620. Fishing towns were founded, and shipping, whaling, and saltmaking were practiced. The Cape Cod Canal (c.18 mi. long), built in 1909–14 and improved by the Federal government in 1927, connects Cape Cod Bay and Buzzards Bay,

A Mariner-Mars launch vehicle on its launching pad at Cape Kennedy.

crossing the town of Bourne. Otis Air Force Base is in the town of Falmouth. Much has been written of the people, history, lore, and scenery of the cape. **Cape Cod National Seashore,** 26,666 acres, est. 1961, contains some of the cape's finest scenery—forests, spectacular sand dunes, fresh-water ponds, rolling heathlands, marshes, and river valleys. Also here are several historical sites. See Thoreau, *Cape Cod* (1865); the many works of Joseph C. Lincoln; H. C. Kittredge, *Cape Cod* (1930); Katharine Dos Passos and Edith Shay, *Down Cape Cod* (rev. ed., 1947); Edith and Frank Shay, *Sand in Their Shoes* (1951).

Cape Colony: see CAPE PROVINCE.

Cape Elizabeth, farming and resort town (pop. 5,505), SW Maine, SE of Portland, along SW Casco Bay; settled c.1630, set off from Falmouth 1765. A state park is nearby.

Cape Fear River, formed SW of Raleigh, N.C., by the junction of the Deep and the Haw rivers and flowing c.202 mi. southeasterly across the piedmont and coastal plains, past Fayetteville and Elizabethtown, to the Atlantic just N of Cape Fear. With three locks and dams, the river is navigable from Wilmington, at the head of its estuary, to Fayetteville.

Cape Girardeau (jĭrär'dō, jĕrûrdō'), city (pop. 24,947), SE Mo., SSE of St. Louis and overlooking the Mississippi; founded 1793 as a trading post, chartered 1843, inc. 1892. Its position on the river, near the confluence of the Ohio, early made it an important port. During the Civil War it was a fort. Today it is an industrial and trade center and manufactures shoes, cement, electrical appliances, and hospital supplies. Southeast Missouri State College (coeducational; 1873) is here. Fort D (1861) and other old buildings are among the points of interest. The city is connected with Illinois by a highway bridge.

Cape jasmine: see MADDER.

Capek, Josef, Czech *Čapek* (chä'pĕk), 1887–1945, Czech writer and painter. He collaborated with his brother Karel and, alone, wrote the utopian play *Land of Many Names* (1923; Eng. tr., 1926) and several novels. *Poems from a Concentration Camp* (1946) were written in Belsen, where he died. As a painter, Josef Capek was first a leading cubist, then a primitivist of repute. In critical works he spoke in praise of the art of children and of primitive peoples.

Capek, Karel, Czech *Čapek*, 1890–1938, Czech playwright, novelist, and essayist. He is best known as the author of two brilliant satirical plays—*R. U.R.* (*Rossum's Universal Robots,* 1921; Eng. tr., 1923), which introduced the word *robot* into the English language, and *The Insect Play* (written with his brother Josef, 1921; Eng. tr., 1923, pub. in the United States as *The World We Live In*). Also noted are the plays *The Makropoulos Secret* (1923; Eng. tr., 1925), an inquiry on longevity, and *Power and Glory* (1937; Eng. tr., 1938), which condemns dictators. He also wrote travel sketches (e.g., *Travels in the North,* Eng. tr., 1939), such fanciful romances as *The Absolute at Large* (1922; Eng. tr., 1927) and *Krakatit* (1924; Eng. tr., 1925), and essays (*Letters from England,* 1923; Eng. tr., 1925). His three volumes of conversations with Thomas G. Masaryk (1928–35; Eng. tr. 1934, 1938) form an outstanding biography, while the three psychological novels *Hordubal* (1934; Eng. tr., 1934), *Meteor* (1934; Eng. tr.. 1935). and *An Ordinary Life* (1935; Eng. tr., 1936) are a worthy climax to a notable career. See study by W. E. Harkins (1962).

Cape Kennedy: see CAPE CANAVERAL.

Capell, Edward (kă'pŭl), 1731–81, English Shakespearean scholar. His 10-volume edition of Shakespeare (1768) was the first to incorporate exact collations of all available old texts. He followed this with a commentary, *Notes and Various Readings to Shakespeare* (3 vols., 1783).

Capella, Martianus (märshēä'nŭs kŭpĕ'lŭ), fl. 5th cent.?, Latin writer, b. Carthage. His one famous work, *The Marriage of Mercury and Philology,* called also the *Satyricon* and *Disciplinae,* is a long allegory about the liberal arts. Philology as here presented is love of learning, and the allegory surveys the seven branches of medieval learning (the seven bridesmaids in the allegory): grammar, dialectic, and rhetoric (the trivium) and geometry, arithmetic, astronomy, and music (the quadrivium). Its popularity in medieval schools was universal. The author is known also as Felix Capella and may have lived in the 4th cent.

Capelle, Eduard von (ā'dooärt fŭn käpĕ'lŭ), 1855–1931, German admiral. As secretary for the navy (1916–18) he reinstituted (1917) unrestricted submarine warfare.

Capello, Bianca (byäng'kä käpĕl'lō), 1548–87, grand duchess of Tuscany (1579–87). Of a noble Venetian family, she eloped (1563) with the Florentine, Pietro Bonaventuri, who was later killed (1569). She was the mistress, then (1579) the wife, of Francesco de' MEDICI. After a banquet the grand duke and his duchess died suddenly, giving rise to rumors that they had been poisoned.

Cape May, city (pop. 4,477), S N.J., at the end of Cape May peninsula; settled in the 17th cent., inc. 1869. It became a popular resort in the mid-19th cent. **Cape May,** southern extremity of New Jersey, has a lighthouse on the point at the entrance to Delaware Bay; c.3 mi. above the point the cape is bisected by a canal (12 ft. deep and 100 ft. wide) constructed by the Federal government in 1942–43 as a war emergency measure to eliminate the longer and hazardous route around the cape. The canal is part of the New Jersey Intracoastal Waterway. In recent years erosion has washed away nearly a fifth of a mile of the cape in the area about Cape May Point (pop. 263).

Cape May Court House, uninc. village (pop. 1,749), co. seat of Cape May co., S N.J., NNE of Cape May city; laid out 1703. A historical museum is here.

Cape Province, formerly **Cape of Good Hope Colony,** province (278,465 sq. mi.; pop. 5,308,839), Republic of South Africa. The capital is Cape Town. Bounded by the Atlantic Ocean in the west and the Indian Ocean in the south and east, it occupies the southernmost tip of Africa, including the Cape of Good Hope, for which it was named. Elevations increase rapidly away from the coast and a high plateau occupies most of the province. It includes the TRANSKEIAN TERRITORIES in the east. Much of the interior (e.g., the Karroo) is quite level and is used for sheep raising, one of the chief activities of the province. Crops, such as wheat, citrus fruits, grapes and tobacco are raised chiefly in the fertile coastal regions. There are rich fisheries off the coast, and diamonds and copper are mined in Namaqualand. Major industries include automobile assembly, textile manufactures, and food canneries. Cape Prov. is served by an excellent road net and by several rail lines which connect its ports, including Cape Town, Port Elizabeth and East London, with the interior. Although the Cape of Good Hope was first circumnavigated (1488) by Bartolomeu Dias, a Portuguese navigator, and later (1497) by Vasco da Gama, European settlement of the region was not established until 1652, when Jan van Riebeeck founded a Dutch victualing station at Table Bay; it subsequently became Cape Town. In the late 17th cent. there was migration of French Huguenots, besides more Dutch settlers. Great Britain temporarily (1795–1803) occupied the Dutch settlements in South Africa, and in 1806 it annexed the territory and named it the Cape of Good Hope Colony. Opposition to British rule led many of the Boer (Dutch) farmers to migrate northward (see TREK). In the South African War (1899–1902) important engagements were fought in the colony, notably at Kimberley and Mafeking. The colony became Cape Province with the establishment (1910) of the Union of South Africa. There are 997,377 Europeans in the province.

caper, common name for the Capparidaceae, a family of tropical plants found chiefly in the Old World and closely related to the mustard family. *Capparis spinosa* is cultivated in the Mediterranean area for the flower buds—capers—which are pickled and used as a condiment. The spider-flower (*Cleome spinosa*) is a common garden annual. The family also includes a few species indigenous to the United States, e.g., the burro-fat (*Isomeris*), a common desert shrub of the Southwest.

Aerial view of the Cape peninsula and Cape Town.

Cape River: see SEGOVIA, river.

Capernaum (kùpûr'nàùm) or **Capharnaum** (kùfär'-nàùm), town, NE Palestine, on the northwestern shore of the Sea of Galilee, closely associated with Jesus' ministry. John 2.12; 6.59; Mat. 11.23; 8; 9; Mark 1; 2; Luke 4; 5. Capernaum is the modern Tell Hum (Israel). A synagogue of the 3d cent. was excavated here and partially restored.

Cape Sable Island (sà'bùl), 7 mi. long and 3 mi. wide, SW N.S., Canada, SW of Shelburne and separated from the mainland by Barrington Passage. Clarkes Harbour (pop. 945), a fishing port, is on the west coast.

Capetians (kùpē'shùnz), royal house of France, which ruled continuously from 987 to 1328. The first historical ancestor was ROBERT THE STRONG, count of Anjou and of Blois. His son, EUDES, count of Paris, was elected (888) king after the deposition of Charles III (Charles the Fat). From 893 to 987 the crown passed back and forth between CAROLINGIANS and Capetians. Eudes's brother, ROBERT I, was chosen king in 922, but died in 923. The title, waived by his son, HUGH THE GREAT, passed to Robert's son-in-law, RAOUL, duke of Burgundy. In 987 Hugh's son, HUGH CAPET (kà'pĭt, kă'pĭt), whose nickname gave the house its appellation, became king. His direct descendants remained on the throne till the death (1328) of Charles IV, when it passed to the related house of VALOIS. The successors of Hugh Capet were Robert II, Henry I, Philip I, Louis VI, Louis VII, Philip II, Louis VIII, Louis IX, Philip III, Philip IV, Louis X, John I, Philip V, and Charles IV. Their reign marked the expansion of royal authority, the revival of towns and commerce, and the beginning of the modern French state. See Robert Fawtier, *The Capetian Kings of France* (1941; Eng. tr., 1960).

Cape Town or **Capetown,** city (pop. c.730,000), SW Cape Prov., parliamentary capital of the Republic of South Africa, on the Atlantic Ocean. The city is situated at the foot of Table Mt. and on the shore of Table Bay. The chief port of the country, it was founded in 1652 by Governor Jan van Riebeeck as a supply station on the Dutch East India Company's sea route to the East. In 1795 the British occupied the city. Returned to the Dutch in 1803, it was captured again by the British in 1806. Cape Town was the capital of the British Cape Colony until South Africa became an independent member of the British Commonwealth in 1910. The beauty and mild climate of the city have made it a warm-weather resort. Among its attractions are the Castle, a fortress dating from 1666; botanical gardens; art galleries; and museums. It is the site of the Univ. of Cape Town and several colleges. The European population numbers c.275,000.

Cape Verde Islands (vûrd), Port. *Ilhas do Cabo Verde,* archipelago (1,560 sq. mi.; estimated pop. 200,000), in the Atlantic Ocean c.300 mi. from the coast of W Africa. A Portuguese possession, it comprises 10 islands, the most important ones being São Vicente and São Tiago. The capital, Praia, is on São Tiago. Of volcanic origin, the islands are rocky, mountainous, hot, and dry. They are used as coaling stations. Coffee, fish, and salt are exported. The archipelago was discovered by the Portuguese in 1460. It was populated with slaves from the Guinea coast and convicts from Portugal. The Negroes and mulattoes today outnumber the whites. The dominant religion is Roman Catholicism. The islands are an overseas province of Portugal, ruled by a governor assisted by two councils. In recent years many islanders have emigrated to the United States seeking work.

Cape York Peninsula, Queensland, Commonwealth of Australia, between the Gulf of Carpentaria and the Coral Sea. It is largely tropical jungle.

Capgrave, John (kăp′grāv), 1393–1464, English author and Augustinian friar. One of the most learned men of his day, he was a distinguished theologian, philosopher, and historian. His writings, many of which have been lost, include a chronicle of England up to 1417 and the Latin works *De illustribus Henricis* [on illustrious men named Henry] and *Nova legenda Angliae* [new legends of England], a rewriting of a collection of lives of English saints by a monk of Tynemouth.

Cap-Haïtien (kăp″-hā′shŭn, –hā′tēŭn, Fr. kăp-äĕsyĕ′), city (pop. c.30,000), N Haiti. A major seaport, it is the second largest city in Haiti. Founded in 1670, it was until 1770 the capital of colonial Haiti, owing its eminence to a good harbor and the development of large sugar plantations in the surrounding lowlands. Le Cap was also the capital of the kingdom ruled by Henri CHRISTOPHE. In spite of earthquakes (especially severe in 1842), bombardments, and almost continual civil strife, it retains some picturesque colonial charm. Cap-Haïtien is a commercial center and exports coffee, cacao, and sugar.

Capharnaum (kủfär′nāủm), the same as CAPERNAUM.

Caphtor (kăf′tôr), home of the Philistines before they came to Canaan. Its inhabitants are called Caphtorim. Gen. 10.4; Deut. 2.23; 1 Chron. 1.12; Jer. 47.4; Amos 9.7. Caphtor is now generally identified with Crete.

capillarity (kăpŭlă′rĭtē), action by which that part of a liquid's surface in contact with a solid is elevated above or depressed below that part of the surface not in contact with the solid. For example, the surface of water in a glass jar is seen to be not level but slightly higher around the edges where the water and the glass are in contact. The reverse is true of mercury, the edges of the surface being depressed. This phenomenon receives its name from the fact that when one end of an open tube of extremely small diameter (called a capillary tube from the Latin *capillus* meaning a hair) is placed vertically in a liquid, the liquid rises in the tube to a level above the level outside (as in the case of water) or is depressed (as in the case of mercury). Capillarity is explained in terms of the effects of two opposing forces: adhesion, the attractive force between the liquid and the solid, which tends to make the edge of the surface rise up on the solid; and cohesion, the attraction of the liquid's molecules for each other, which tends to minimize the total surface of the liquid and hence to depress its edges (see SURFACE TENSION). One of the causes of the upward movement of water in the soil is capillarity.

capillary (kă′pŭlĕ″rē), minute blood vessel, smallest unit of the circulatory system, and one unit of the vast network serving the entire body. Capillaries are the connecting links between arterioles (smallest arteries) and venules (smallest veins). Through the thin capillary walls the nutritive material and oxygen in the blood pass into the body tissues, and the waste matter and carbon dioxide in turn are absorbed from the tissues into the blood stream.

Capistrano, John of: see JOHN CAPISTRAN, SAINT.

Capistrano Beach, uninc. town (pop. 2,026), S Calif., on the Gulf of Santa Catalina NW of San Clemente. Nearby are the San Juan Capistrano Mission and a state park.

capital [Latin,=of the head], the crowning member of a column, pilaster, or pier. It acts as the bearing member beneath the lintel or arch supported by the shaft and has a spreading contour appropriate to its function. The most primitive type, of which examples were found in the Beni Hassan tombs, Egypt, consisted of a square block. In later forms the capital had three well-defined parts, the necking, where it joins the shaft; the echinus, or spreading member above it; and the abacus, or block at the top. In Egypt such types were developed as early as 1500 B.C.: papyrus buds, the lotus, and the palm leaf were used as motives of ornamentation. The Greeks perfected three types belonging to three separate orders of architecture—the DORIC ORDER, the IONIC ORDER, and the CORINTHIAN ORDER—which were also used in slightly modified forms by the Romans. The classic forms of capitals continued in use after the fall of Rome, but the Romanesque and Gothic designers introduced new forms rich in variety: grotesque heads, birds, and animals. In the 15th cent., with the Renaissance, came a return to the classic orders that continued in use until the late 19th and early 20th cent. when the modernists cast out classic decoration.

capital. As originally used in business, capital denoted money that bears interest; but the word now includes the entire stock of goods from which an income is derived. Tools, machines, stores of merchandise, houses, means of transportation, lands, and such paper as stocks and bonds—any materials used to extract, transport, create, or alter goods—can be called capital. Marketable intangibles, as credits, good will, promises, patents, and franchises, are also included by some economists. Capital goods provide for future wants, while consumers' goods provide only for the present. Distinction is also made between capital stocks or circulating capital (raw materials, goods in process, finished goods, and sometimes wages) and capital instruments or fixed capital (machines, tools, railways, factories). Capital may be classed as specialized, such as railway equipment, or unspecialized, such as raw materials having many uses. Capital is thought to arise and accumulate from savings from incomes, scarcity of natural materials, presence of monopolies, previous profits, speculation, and recapitalization. A revolutionary new concept was offered by Karl Marx in *Das Kapital*. For more conservative views, see Irving Fisher, *The Nature of Capital and Income* (1906); F. A. von Hayek, *The Pure Theory of Capital* (1941); F. P. Randall, *Issue, Control, and Regulation of Capital* (1951); B. S. Keirstead, *Capital, Interest, and Profits* (6th ed., 1959); S. S. Kuznets, *Capital in the American Economy* (1961).

capitalism, economic system characterized by private ownership of property, production of goods for private profit, and the institution of bank credit. Generally the capitalist system is also thought of as embodying the concepts of a rational economic man, inheritance, freedom of individual initiative, competition, and the profit motive. Capitalism has existed in at least partial form in the economies of all civilizations, but its modern importance dates from the Industrial Revolution of the 18th cent., when bankers, merchants, and industrialists began to displace landowners in political, economic, and social importance, particularly in Great Britain. Capitalism stresses freedom of individual economic enterprise, but even when, as in the early 19th cent., the economy was least restricted, the ultimate right of the state to supervise and regulate industry and trade was questioned by few. In the 19th and the early 20th cent. the profit motive called into being vast credit, manufacturing, and distributing institutions, and the social and economic effects of capitalism largely transformed world culture. In the middle of the 20th cent. social and industrial reforms in democratic states and the action of totalitarian governments circumscribed the freedom of economic action in formerly free capitalist systems. See FREE ENTERPRISE SYSTEM. See Joseph Schumpeter, *Capitalism, Socialism, and Democracy* (1942); John Chamberlain, *The Roots of Capitalism* (1959); Henry Wallich, *The Cost of Freedom* (1960); Milton Friedman, *Capitalism and Freedom* (1962).

capital levy, form of taxation by which the state takes part of the capital of any person or business, as distinguished from a tax on personal or business income. It is usually applied to all capital above a certain minimum and may be set aside for a specific purpose, such as the sinking of the public debt. It was used by several European nations in financial contingencies arising from the armaments race and the First World War and has been advocated as a measure of social welfare and a deterrent to war profits. Opponents of the capital levy stress the implied penalty to saving. In the Second World War, Great Britain and the United States resorted to tremendous direct taxation to accomplish many of the aims of the capital levy. A special tax on capital gains, at a rate more favorable than the tax rate on earned income, has been a part of the U.S. system since the New Deal. A modified form of capital gains tax was introduced in England in 1962. See I. S. Gulati, *Capital Taxation in a Developing Economy* (1957); A. R. Ilseric, *The Taxation of Capital Gains* (1962).

capital punishment, putting to death by the state. Capital punishment was widely applied in ancient times, and methods included beheading, stoning, drowning, and burning. Death by burning was carried out in Europe as late as the 18th cent., and in England at the beginning of the 19th cent. over 200 crimes still carried the death penalty. Public executions were common until the late 19th cent., and hangings at NEWGATE and TYBURN were notorious spectacles. BECCARIA, Jeremy BENTHAM, and others campaigned against capital punishment. In 1962 Britain, France, Spain, and the Republic of Ireland in W. Europe still retained the death penalty for crimes. Under U.S. law there are six capital crimes: murder, rape, bank robbery, kidnaping, treason, and espionage. By 1962 six states had abolished capital punishment completely—Wisconsin (1853), Maine (1887), Minnesota (1911), Alaska (1957), Hawaii (1957), and Delaware (1958); three others—Michigan, Rhode Island, and North Dakota—never invoke it. Eight states have abolished it and then restored it. See John Laurence, *A History of Capital Punishment* (1960); J. A. Joyce, *Capital Punishment: a World View* (1961).

Capito, Wolfgang Fabricius (kǎ'pǐtō, Ger. vôlf'gäng fäbrē'tsyŏos kä'pētō), 1478–1541, German Protestant reformer, whose original family name was Köpfel. As a well-known humanist, he brought about communication between Erasmus and Luther. Capito worked with Martin BUCER in an attempt to unify the Evangelical churches of Germany, France, and Switzerland.

Capitol, seat of the U.S. government at Washington, D.C. It is the city's dominating monument, built on an elevated site which was chosen by George Washington in consultation with Major Pierre

The Capitol, Washington, D.C.

L'ENFANT. The building as it now stands took many years to build and is the result of the work of several architects. In 1792 a competition was held to select an architect, but William THORNTON gained the President's approval with a plan separately submitted and was appointed. In 1793 the President set the cornerstone, with Masonic rites, and the building was begun. Later three additional architects were employed—E. S. HALLET, George Hadfield (d.1826), and James HOBAN. In 1814 the uncompleted building was burned by the British, and B. H. LATROBE, who had been appointed (1803) surveyor of public buildings, undertook its restoration. He was succeeded in 1818 by Charles BULFINCH, who brought the design to completion in 1830. The building proved inadequate and was greatly enlarged (1851–65) by T. U. WALTER, who added the extensive House and Senate wings at either end and the imposing dome, c.288 ft. in height, which dominates the composition. The building proper is over 750 ft. long, including approaches c.350 ft. wide. In 1960 the east front of the Capitol was extended 32 ft. and the original sandstone façade was replaced by marble. See I. T. Frary, *They Built the Capitol* (1940).

Capitol, in Rome: see CAPITOLINE HILL.

Capitola, city (pop. 2,021), W Calif., on Monterey Bay E of Santa Cruz; inc. 1949. It is a seaside resort. There are nurseries here, and the city is noted for its begonias.

Capitol Heights, town (pop. 3,138), W central Md., a suburb SSE of Washington, D.C.; inc. 1910.

Capitoline Hill or **Capitol,** highest of the seven hills of ancient Rome, historic and religious center of the city. The great temple of Jupiter Capitolinus, on its southern summit, was dedicated in 509 B.C.; it was foremost among the temples and altars of Rome. Destroyed three times by fire, it was last rebuilt by Domitian. On the northern summit of the Capitol was the citadel (arx). On the side overlooking the Forum stood the Tabularium, where

the state archives were kept. Until the 1st cent. A.D., state criminals were hurled to their death from the Tarpeian Rock, on the steep south face of the hill. In the Middle Ages the Capitol remained the political center of Rome. The center of municipal government in Rome is still on the same location. In the 16th cent. Michelangelo designed the present plan. A flight of steps leads to the fine square on top of the hill; on one side of the square is the Palazzo dei Conservatori, on the other, the Capitoline Museum. Both buildings now house collections of antiquities. In the center of the square is the ancient equestrian bronze statue of Emperor Marcus Aurelius.

Capitol Reef National Monument: see NATIONAL PARKS AND MONUMENTS (table).

capitularies (kǔpǐ'chŏŏlĕ"rēz), decrees and written commands of the Merovingian and Carolingian kings of the Franks. Both legislative and administrative, they were the chief written instrument of royal authority. The ordinances were issued by the king alone or by the king and his counselors. Additions to, and alterations of, the customary GERMANIC LAWS required the consent of the tribes concerned or of their representatives. Several capitularies—such as the exemplary *De villis*—dealt with the administration of the royal domains; others dealt with the Church. Most important were the *missi dominici*, addressed by Charlemagne to his officers. These contained instructions for the administration of the empire and instituted far-reaching reforms. Capitularies issued in the late Carolingian period foreshadowed the feudal system and are collected in the MONUMENTA GERMANIAE HISTORICA. The term *capitularies* is applied also to similar documents in other fields.

Capo d'Istria, Giovanni Antonio, Count (kä"pō dē'strēä), Gr. *Joannes Antonios Capodistrias* or *Kapodistrias*, 1776–1831, Greek and Russian statesman, b. Corfu. After administrative work in the Ionian Islands he entered (1809) the Russian service and was Russian foreign minister (1820–22). He refused leadership of the Greek uprising in 1821 but brought Russian influence to bear in favor of the Greeks. In 1827 the Greek national assembly elected him president of Greece. He was a dedicated reformer and gained popularity, but his autocratic methods and Russian affiliations aroused opposition and led to his assassination.

Capodistria (kăpůdǐ'strēů, Ital. käpōdē'strēä), town (estimated pop. 8,210), in NW Yugoslavia, on the Istrian peninsula, in the Gulf of Trieste. It is a fishing port with small shipyards. From the 13th cent. until 1797 it was the capital of ISTRIA under Venetian rule; it passed to Austria, then to Italy in 1919. In 1947 it became part of the Free Territory of Trieste. In 1954 Capodistria was annexed to Yugoslavia. It preserves the aspect of a Venetian town. In the main square are the Romanesque cathedral and campanile, a Gothic loggia, and the pinnacled town hall.

Capone, Al (Alfonso or Alphonse Capone) (kùpō'nē), 1899–1947, American gang leader, b. Naples, Italy. Al Capone was brought up in New York city, where he became connected with organized crime and was involved in murder investigations. In 1920 he moved to Chicago and became a lieutenant to John Torrio, one of the most feared

Capitoline Hill, Rome.

gangsters of the city. They established numerous "speakeasies" in Chicago in the prohibition era and expanded their operations. After several of his enemies were murdered and Torrio fled the city, "Scarface" Capone took control. He became implicated in brutal murders and was known to have received tribute from businessmen and politicians. His crime syndicate—which terrorized Chicago in the 1920s and controlled gambling and vice there—was estimated by the Federal Bureau of Internal Revenue to have taken in $105,000,000 in 1927 alone. Capone was indicted (1931) by a Federal grand jury for evasion of income-tax payments and was sentenced to an 11-year prison term. In 1939, physically and mentally shattered, Capone was released. See biography by F. D. Pasley (1930); Kenneth Allsop, *The Bootleggers and Their Era* (1961).

Caporetto: see KOBARID.

Capote, Truman (käpō'tē), 1924–, American novelist and short-story writer, b. New Orleans. His writings reflect a private, but highly imaginative, wistful world of grotesque, narcissistic, and strangely

Truman Capote

innocent people. His first publication, *Other Voices, Other Rooms* (1948), written with remarkable sensitivity, is the story of a young boy's painful quest for identity. His second novel, *The Grass Harp*, published in 1951, portrays with humor and compassion the plight of a group of courageous misfits who take refuge in a tree house from the cold, practical world. Capote's dramatization of the book was successfully produced the following year. The unique and compelling *A Tree of Night* (1949) and *Breakfast at Tiffany's* (1958) reveal his talent in the short-story form. Capote's other works include the travel sketches *Local Color* (1950), the film script for the hilarious spoof *Beat the Devil* (1953), and the report on his trip to Russia, *The Muses Are Heard* (1956). See Ihab Hassan, *Radical Innocence* (1961).

Cappadocia (kăpŭdō'shŭ), ancient region of Asia Minor, watered by the Halys river (the modern Kizil Irmak), in present E central Asiatic Turkey. The name was applied at various times to territories of varying size. At its greatest extent it stretched from the Halys valley E to the Eu-

phrates, from the Black (Euxine) Sea in the north to the heights of the Taurus and Anti-Taurus ranges in the south. Mostly a high plateau, it was famous for its mineral resources, particularly its copper and iron. In Asia Minor, Cappadocia maintained its local Asiatic traditions in contrast to the Mediterranean seacoast, which was closer to the Aegean culture. Several thousand tablets, written in cuneiform by Assyrian colonists in Cappadocia, have been found at Kültepe (Kanesh); they show that a highly developed trade existed between Assyria and Asia Minor before 1800 B.C. At that time Cappadocia was the heart of an old Hittite state. Later the Persians controlled Cappadocia. It did not yield fully to the conquest of Alexander the Great, and during the 3d cent. B.C. it gradually developed as an independent kingdom. PONTUS now became completely separated from Cappadocia. The kings had their capital at Mazaca (later CAESAREA MAZACA); the only other important cities were Tyana and Melitene, though Iconium was at times in Cappadocia. In the 2d and 1st cent. B.C. the Cappadocian dynasty maintained itself largely by siding with Rome. Invaded in 104 B.C. by Mithridates VI and c.90 B.C. by his son-in-law, Tigranes of Armenia, Cappadocia was restored by Pompey. Antony replaced the king, who had been disloyal to Rome in the Parthian invasion at the time of Julius Caesar, and in A.D. 17 Rome annexed the region as a province. Cappadocia became prosperous. Christianity was introduced

The valley of Goreme in Cappadocia.

early (1st cent. A.D.). The name appears in the Bible, though its importance as a separate region was already declining and later disappeared.

Cappel: see KAPPEL.

Capponi, Gino (jē'nō käp-pō'nē), 1792–1876, Italian historian and educationalist, a marquis. He played an important part in the Risorgimento. His theory of education anticipated the thought of John Dewey. In 1848 he was president of the constitutional government in Tuscany, and he became a senator after the annexation (1860) of Tuscany to the kingdom of Sardinia. Of his historical writings, the history of the Florentine republic (3 vols., 1875) is best known.

Capponi, Piero (pyä´rō), 1446?–1496, Florentine nobleman and diplomat. He served Lorenzo and Piero de' Medici and later the Florentine republic. His firm and courageous attitude toward Charles VIII of France, who wanted to impose harsh terms on the republic, induced the king to grant (1494) more equitable conditions.

Caprera (käprä´rä), small island, off the northeast coast of Sardinia, Italy, in the Strait of Bonifacio. It was the residence of Garibaldi, who is buried here.

Capri (kä´prē), Latin *Capreae*, island (estimated pop. 10,519), in the Bay of Naples off the tip of the Sorrento peninsula, S Italy. There are two small towns, Capri and Anacapri, both much-visited tourist centers. Celebrated for its striking scenery, delightful climate, and luxurious vegetation, the island exports a dry white wine. The Blue Grotto is the most famous of the many caves along its high, precipitous coast. Monte Solaro, the highest point (1,932 ft.), commands a magnificent view. The Roman emperors Augustus and Tiberius built here fine villas, of which there are remains. The local architecture has Roman, Norman, and Moorish features.

Capricornus (kăprĭkôr´nŭs) [Latin, = goat horn], in astronomy, inconspicuous constellation of the Southern Hemisphere lying between Sagittarius and Aquarius. It has been depicted from earliest times either as a goat or as a figure with its fore part like that of a goat and its hind part like the tail of a fish. The Tropic of Capricorn takes its name from this constellation, which marks the southernmost point of the ecliptic and therefore the winter solstice in the Northern Hemisphere. Capricornus is the name of the 10th sign of the zodiac, the Goat, and the constellation is one of the zodiacal constellations.

caprifig: see FIG.

Caprivi, Leo, Graf von (lä´ō gräf´ fŭn käprē´vē), 1831–99, German statesman, whose full name was Georg Leo, Graf von Caprivi de Caprara de Montecuculi. He succeeded (1890) Bismarck as chancellor. Under him the antisocialist law was abrogated and military service was shortened from three to two years. Favoring industrial over agrarian interests, he negotiated (1892–94) a series of reciprocal trade agreements. Agrarian opposition caused his dismissal (1894). Prince Hohenlohe-Schillingsfürst succeeded him as chancellor.

Caprivi Zipfel (käprē´ vē tsĭp´fŭl) [Ger. *Zipfel* = tip, point] or **Caprivi Strip**, territory, 300 mi. long and 50 mi. wide, extending along the northern border of Bechuanaland W to the Zambezi river. A part of South-West Africa, it is named for the German chancellor Graf von Caprivi, who obtained it from Great Britain as part of a general settlement (1890) between the two countries. It gave the former German colony access to the Zambezi.

Capsian culture: see GAFSA.

Captain Cook, uninc. village (pop. 1,687), Hawaii, on the west coast of Hawaii, SSE of Kailua, in a coffee and cattle region. Nearby is the monument to Capt. James Cook (erected 1874), marking the place where the explorer was killed.

Captain Jack (d. 1873), subchief of the MODOC INDIANS and leader of the hostile group in the Modoc war (1872–73). Jack, whose real name was Kintpuash, had agreed (1864) to leave his ancestral home and live on a reservation with the Klamath Indians. He found it impossible to live on friendly terms with his former enemies, and after killing a Klamath medicine man, Jack and a band of followers left the reservation. They resisted arrest (Nov., 1872) and fled into the lava beds in California. Their strong defensive position frustrated numerous attempts by U.S. troops to dislodge them. In April, 1873, a peace commission headed by Gen. E. R. S. CANBY met with Jack and several of his men. At a prearranged signal, Jack shot Canby dead. The army renewed its efforts to capture them and forced the Modocs to take refuge elsewhere. The Indians, who were tired of fighting, began to give themselves up, and on June 1, Captain Jack surrendered. He was taken to Fort Klamath, where on Oct. 3, 1873, he and three of his head men were hanged for the murder of Canby. See biography by D. P. Payne (1938).

Captivity, Exile, or **Babylonian captivity,** in the history of Israel, the period from the fall of Jerusalem (586 B.C.) to the reconstruction in Palestine of a new Jewish state (after 538 B.C.). After the capture of the city some thousands were deported to Mesopotamia, probably selected for their prosperity and importance; the number of those who remained is disputed by scholars. Such deportations were commonplace in Assyrian and Babylonian policy. The exiles kept up close connections with their kinsmen at home, as is clear from Ezekiel, the prophet of the early years of the Exile. In 538 B.C., Cyrus, the new master of the empire, brought in a new attitude toward the nations and decreed the restoration of worship at Jerusalem. The century following this decree was critical in the history of the Jews, for it is the time of their reintegration into a national and religious unit. For parts of the period, Ezra and Nehemiah are the best sources. The prophesied 70 years of captivity were fulfilled when the new Temple was completed in 516 B.C. Jer. 25.11; Dan. 9.2; Zech. 7.5. For the papal captivity at Avignon, see PAPACY.

Capua (kä´pūu̇, Ital. kä´pwä), town (estimated pop. 17,054), in Campania, S Italy, on the Volturno river. It is an agricultural center and occupies the site of ancient CASILINUM. Ancient Capua (which was 3 mi. to the southeast, where Santa Maria Capua Vetere now stands) was a strategic Roman town on the Appian Way. In 216 B.C. it opened its gates to Hannibal; retaken by the Romans, it became the most important center of S Italy. Capua was destroyed (841) by the Arabs; the inhabitants moved to Casilinum and founded modern Capua. Strongly fortified to defend Naples, Capua suffered various sieges, the last one by the Piedmontes (1860). It has an ancient cathedral and a Roman bridge.

Capuana, Luigi (lwē´jē käpwä´nä), 1839–1915, Italian critic and novelist. His activities included teaching, scientific study, and politics. He wrote in almost every genre, but his reputation rests upon his naturalistic novels and criticism. Among his best works are the short stories in *Paesane* [peasant women] (1894), the novel *Il marchese di Roccaverdina* (1901), and his *Studi della letteratura contemporanea* (1879–82). His stories for children include *Nimble Legs* (1903; Eng. tr., 1927) and *Once upon a Time* (1882; Eng. tr., 1892). See study by S. E. Scaglia (1952).

Capuchins (kă′pūchĭnz) [Ital.,=hooded ones], Roman Catholic religious order of friars, one of the independent orders of FRANCISCANS, officially the Friars Minor Capuchin [Latin abbr., O.M.Cap.]. It was founded (1525–28) in central Italy as a reform within the Observants, led by Matteo di Bascio. It is one of the largest orders. Born, like the Jesuits, at the beginning of the Catholic Reformation, the Capuchins became a key feature in church activity, especially in preaching and in missions. With the Jesuits they did much to revive Catholicism in the parts of Europe where Protestantism had prevailed. The Capuchins have been very important in foreign missions; they were early in French Canada. They are conspicuous among Roman Catholic clergy for their beards. See study by Father Cuthbert (1928).

Capulin Mountain National Monument: see NATIONAL PARKS AND MONUMENTS (table).

capybara (kăpĭbä′rù), mammal of Central and much of South America. It is the largest living member

Capybara

of the rodent order, reaching a length of 4 ft. and a weight of 75 to 100 lb. Its brownish hair flecked with yellow is coarse and scanty, and its tail rudimentary. The feet are partially webbed, and there are four thick-nailed toes on the front feet and three on the hind feet. It is an expert swimmer and diver. It eats vegetation and sometimes damages crops. It is hunted for food, its hide is made into gloves, and its bristles are used in brushes. It is also called water hog and carpincho.

caracal (kă′rùkùl) or **Persian lynx,** mammal of the cat family, native to Asia and Africa. By some it is considered a link between the true cats and the true lynxes. It is reddish brown with black-tufted ears. Its total length is about 3¼ ft. It preys on small deer, hares, birds, and other animals; in some regions it is trained to catch such game for man.

Caracalla (kărùkă′lù), 188–217, Roman emperor (211–17), son of Septimius SEVERUS. His real name

Caracalla

was Marcus Aurelius Antoninus, and he was called Caracalla because he wore a Gallic tunic. He was made Caesar in 196 and Augustus in 198, but he resented having to share these honors with his brother Geta and early showed his true character by bringing about the downfall of his father-in-law, the political leader Plautianus, through false reports. After Septimius Severus died, leaving the

Caracal

empire to his two sons, Caracalla murdered (212) the more popular Geta and ordered a general massacre of Geta's followers and sympathizers (including the jurist Papinian). He thus ushered in a reign infamous for cruelty and blood. Caracalla did, however, pacify the German frontier. He also extended Roman citizenship to all free inhabitants of the empire, presumably not out of generosity but to increase his income from taxes in order to meet staggering expenses. He tried to buy popularity with his soldiers and planned an ambitious campaign to extend his father's conquests into old Persia. When leading an expedition in Asia, Caracalla was murdered by MACRINUS, who succeeded him. The famous Baths of Caracalla were erected in his reign.

caracara: see FALCON.

Caracas (kŭrä′kŭs, kŭrä′–, Span. kärä′käs), city (pop. c.1,200,000), N Venezuela, the capital and largest city of Venezuela, in a mountain valley near the Caribbean. It was founded in 1567 as Santiago de León de Caracas by Diego de Losada (d. 1569). With an elevation of c.3,100 ft., Caracas has a healthful and pleasant climate, a factor that made it rather than VALENCIA the economic and political center of Spanish colonization in Venezuela. The older parts of the city are picturesque. With air, rail, and highway connections to La GUAIRA, to W Venezuela, and S to Ciudad Bolívar by road and air, Caracas is the commercial, industrial and cultural hub of the nation. In the wake of the recent oil boom Caracas has expanded prodigiously. Enormous sums of money have been spent on

Arch of the Federation in Caracas.

public works, notably the futuristic University City, school construction, slum-clearance projects, a new aqueduct, and an impressive highway cloverleaf, known to Caracans as "the octopus." A colossal shopping center, the Helicoid, is being built on a hill outside the city. In addition to oil, industries include textile mills, sugar refineries, and meat-packing plants. Key to control of Venezuela, Caracas assumed a leading role in the revolution against Spain. Here independence was advocated in April, 1810, and formally declared in July, 1811. Its almost complete destruction by earthquake on March 26, 1812, did much to blight the revolution led by Francisco de MIRANDA. In Aug. 1813, Simón BOLÍVAR recaptured Caracas, but abandoned it after a crushing defeat in June, 1814. Finally, after his victory at Carabobo (1821) he made a triumphal entry in June, 1821.

Caracci, family of Italian painters: see CARRACCI.

Caracciolo, Francesco (fränchä′skō kärät′chōlō), 1752–99, Neapolitan admiral. He fought the Barbary pirates and served with the British in the American Revolution. He fled with King Ferdinand IV of Naples to Sicily in Dec., 1798, but soon returned and took command of the small fleet of the French-sponsored Parthenopean Republic. When the Bourbons recaptured Naples (1799), Lord Nelson ordered his immediate execution.

Caractacus (kŭrăk′tŭkŭs) or **Caradoc** (kŭrä′dŭk), fl. A.D. 50, British chieftain; son of Cymbeline. He fought for nine years against the Romans, was captured, and was taken to Rome. Claudius, admiring his courage, spared his life.

Caragiali, Ion Luca (yŏn′ lōōkä kärä̆jä′lĭ), 1853–1912, Rumanian author and theatrical manager. In 1888 he became director of the Bucharest National Theater. Among his comedies satirizing Rumanian society are *The Lost Letter* (1884) and *Carnival Adventures* (1885). *False Accusation* (1889) is a tragedy. Caragiali also wrote short stories and novels.

Caraglio, Giovanni Jacopo (jōvän′nē yä′kōpō kärä′lyō), c.1500–1565, Italian engraver and designer, known also as Jacobus Parmensis and Jacobus Veronensis. He was a pupil of Raimondi and achieved distinction as an engraver on copper and, later, as a designer of medals and engraver of gems. His plates, about 70 in number, are chiefly reproductions of works of the Italian masters— Raphael, Titian, Michelangelo, and others.

Caraites: see KARAITES.

Caraman: see KARAMAN.

Caran d'Ache (kärä′ däsh′), pseud. of **Emmanuel Poiré** (ĕmänüĕl′ pwärä′), c.1858–1909, French caricaturist and illustrator. Among his numerous works, those contributed to the periodical *Caricature* are perhaps his finest. The *Album Caran d'Ache* and *Bric-à-brac* contain good examples of his humor and originality.

Carausius (kŭrô′shĕŭs), d. 293, Gallo-Roman military commander. He was stationed in Gaul, but Emperor MAXIMIAN suspected him of conspiring with the Germans and condemned him to death. Carausius fled to Britain and established his rule there, defying attempts to conquer him. Diocletian and Maximian finally recognized (c.289) him as coemperor, and he established his rule in NE Gaul as well as in Britain. In 293, however, Constantius (later Constantius I) defeated him, and he was murdered by one of his own men.

Caravaca (kärävä′kä), town (pop. 21,752), Murcia prov., SE Spain, in Murcia, on the Caravaca river. It is an agricultural center and has textiles and brandy manufactures. The miraculous Cross of Caravaca was formerly kept in the Church of the Most Holy Cross (1617).

Caravaggio, Michelangelo Merisi da (mēkälän′jälō märē′zē dä käräväd′jō) or **Amerigi da Caravaggio** (ä″märē′jē), 1573–1610, Italian painter. His surname Caravaggio came from his birthplace. After an apprenticeship with a mediocre painter in Milan, he arrived in Rome where he eventually became a pensioner of Cardinal Francesco del Monte for whom he produced several paintings, among them the *Concert of Youths* (Metropolitan Mus.). Most of Caravaggio's genre pieces such as the *Fortune Teller* (Louvre) are products of his early Roman years, but after completing the *Calling of St. Matthew* and the *Martyrdom of St. Matthew* (c.1598–99, San Luigi de' Francesi), he devoted himself almost exclusively to religious compositions and portraiture. His violent temper and erratic disposition involved him in several brawls, and in 1606 he fled Rome after killing a young man in a duel. He spent the last four years of his life in Naples, Malta, Syracuse, and Messina. A revolutionary in art, Caravaggio was accused of imitating nature at the expense of ideal beauty. In religious scenes his use of models from the lower walks of life was considered irreverent. He generally worked directly on the canvas, a violation of current artistic procedure. His strong chiaroscuro technique of partially illuminating figures against a dark background was immediately adopted by his contemporaries, and although he had no real pupils, the influence of his art was enormous. Its effect can be seen throughout Europe, from Ribera in Spain to Rembrandt in Holland. See Walter Friedlaender, *Caravaggio Studies* (1955).

Caravaggio, Polidoro Caldara da (pōlēdō′rō käldä′rä), c.1496–1543, Italian painter. His surname Caravaggio came from his birthplace. A student of Raphael, he was responsible for some of the monochrome decorations in the Vatican Stanze as well as for a few of the scenes in the Loggia. After Raphael's death (1520) Polidoro entered upon a career as a decorator of house façades. These chiaroscuro decorations, based on scenes taken from ancient history, survive now mainly through engravings and drawings. Greatly admired in his own time, Polidoro exercised considerable influence on later generations. In 1527 he left Rome, traveling to Naples and Messina. Of his paintings from this period the *Christ on the Way to Calvary* (Naples) is perhaps the most impressive.

caravan, group of travelers or merchants banded together and organized for mutual assistance and defense while traveling through unsettled or hostile country. Caravan trade is associated with the history of the Near East as far back as records of ancient civilizations extend and seems to have been well developed before sea commerce began. It is evident that all trade from one fertile area to another in this region had to be organized from the first, since long distances of desert trail separated settled parts and since local governments could not

Madonna and Child (detail from Michelangelo Merisi da Caravaggio's painting The Flight into Egypt*).*

guarantee protection against tribes eager for loot and pillage. Such wares as jewels, spices, perfumes, dyes, metals, rare woods, ivory, oils, and textiles, chiefly silk, are associated with the trade. Camels were the main carriers from Egypt to Mesopotamia and throughout the Arabian peninsula. They were introduced into North Africa and the Sahara region in the 3d cent. A.D. Donkeys were used in Asia Minor. Trade naturally prospered in the period of the great empires when the caravan routes could be controlled and protected; and it was to secure control of such routes that many wars were fought and conquests made in ancient times. An empire provided for the establishment of caravansaries for the accommodation of travelers along the way. Such improvements facilitated the movement of troops to protect the routes. Cities rose and fell in ancient times in proportion to the rise and fall in the trade of the caravan routes upon which they were located. Basically the trade underwent little change until challenged in modern times by the motor truck and the airplane. Travelers having occasion to cross desert spaces usually joined merchant caravans. Since the advent of Islam, the pilgrimage of the devout to Mecca has given rise to the long pilgrim caravans which are a feature of the pilgrimage season each year. The closest approach to caravan trade in the New World was the wagon-train commerce which developed over the Santa Fe Trail. Caravans still play an important role in the commercial life of certain areas, notably in Sinkiang prov.,

China, in central Asia, in Arabia, and in North Africa. See Mikhail Rostovtzev, *Caravan Cities* (1932); E. W. Bovill, *The Golden Trade of the Moors* (1958).

caravel (kă′rŭvĕl″) or **carvel** (kär′vŭl), three-masted sailing vessel, generally square-rigged with the aftermast lateen-rigged. It had a roundish hull with a high bow and stern. The term "carvel-built" (see BOAT) was derived from its method of construction. The change from bulkier ships to caravels, with their small displacement, enabled the Portuguese in the 15th cent. to take the lead among Western nations in exploring the African coast. The caravel thereafter was of primary importance in the era of expansion and exploration. The *Santa María*, the flagship of Christopher Columbus, was a typical caravel.

caraway (kăr′ŭwā), biennial Old World plant (*Carum carvi*) of the CARROT family, cultivated in Europe and North America for its aromatic seeds. They are small and ovate, with a pleasant spicy flavor, and are used as a condiment; as seasoning of pastry and bread doughs, cabbage, sausage, and some kinds of cheese; and as flavoring for certain liqueurs (as kümmel). The volatile oil expressed from the seeds is a stimulant and a carminative.

Carberry Hill, in Midlothian, SE Scotland, near Edinburgh, scene of an encounter (1567) between the troops of MARY QUEEN OF SCOTS and those of the rebel Scottish lords. Mary surrendered here and remained a virtual prisoner the rest of her life.

carbide, any one of a group of compounds consisting of carbon and one other element, either a metal or boron or silicon. In general, carbides are prepared by heating the metal, metal oxide, or metal hydride with carbon or other carbon compounds; calcium carbide is prepared by heating calcium oxide and coke in an electric arc furnace. Although some carbides, e.g., chromium carbide and silicon carbide, are not affected by water, many are decomposed by it and yield a gas. For example, calcium carbide produces acetylene and is an important commercial source of this gas. Barium carbide also yields acetylene. On the other hand, aluminum carbide reacts to form methane. Some carbides, e.g., SILICON CARBIDE, or carborundum, are almost equal to diamonds in hardness and are used as abrasive materials, and some, e.g., tungsten carbide, for the cutting edges of precision machine tools. Iron carbide is present in steel, cast iron, and some other iron alloys.

Carbo, Cneius Papirius (nē′ŭs pŭpēr′ēŭs kär′bō), d. 82 B.C., Roman political leader. He was consul three times (85 B.C., 84 B.C., 82 B.C.) and one of the leaders of the party of MARIUS. After the death of Marius he and his colleague, CINNA, gathered (84 B.C.) an army to oppose SULLA in Italy. When Cinna was murdered in a mutiny, Carbo became chief commander. Sulla gathered strength as he came slowly N through Italy, and much of Carbo's force deserted. He was defeated at Faventia (modern Faenza) by Q. Caecilius METELLUS PIUS and fled to Africa. He later crossed to Sicily, where he was captured, condemned, and executed by Pompey.

carbohydrate (kärbōhī′drăt), any one of a number of organic compounds of carbon, hydrogen, and oxygen, having (in general) the hydrogen and oxygen in the same atomic ratio as in water (2:1). The carbohydrates are an important group of foods; they supply heat energy and are involved in fat production. In various forms, the carbohydrates are used in industry and commerce. Three main subdivisions of the group are recognized. The monosaccharides include the sugars FRUCTOSE and GLUCOSE. The disaccharides, whose molecules upon HYDROLYSIS yield two molecules of monosaccharides, include LACTOSE, MALTOSE, and sucrose or cane sugar ((see SUGAR). The polysaccharides are represented by such substances as CELLULOSE, DEXTRIN, GLYCOGEN, and STARCH.

carbolic acid or **phenol** (fē′–), colorless (when pure), crystalline solid, melting at 41°C. and boiling at 182°C., a derivative of BENZENE. It exhibits weak acid properties but forms esters with acid anhydrides. With strong alkalies, salts called phenolates are formed. Carbolic acid dissolves in many organic solvents such as alcohol and ether, but in water at room temperature it is only moderately soluble. It is corrosive and poisonous. In medicine it is used as an antiseptic and disinfectant. In industry it is important in the production of certain artificial resins such as BAKELITE, and in the synthesis of many drugs, dyes, weed killers, insecticides and explosives (PICRIC ACID). Carbolic acid is the simplest member of a group of compounds called phenols which are derivatives of benzene and have a hydroxyl (OH) radical attached directly to the benzene ring. Those derived from toluene are called cresols and are used in commercial disinfectants.

carboloy (kär′bŭloi) [portmanteau word from carbon and alloy], an alloy containing cobalt, tungsten, and carbon. This alloy is extremely hard, harder than steel; it is used to cut steel, porcelain, quartz, and other materials. Its hardness is not affected by great heat, and it retains a sharp cutting edge even at red heat.

carbon, nonmetallic element (symbol=C; in group IV A of the PERIODIC TABLE; for physical constants, see ELEMENT, table). The atomic weight of carbon-12 was adopted in 1961 by the International Union of Pure and Applied Chemistry to replace oxygen-16 as the basis for computing the atomic weights of all the elements. One of the most widely distributed and abundant of all the elements, carbon is a constituent of all organic matter. The diamond and graphite are two crystalline forms (see ALLOTROPY). In so-called amorphous carbon, including CHARCOAL, COAL, COKE, lampblack, PEAT, and LIGNITE, the element occurs partly free and partly combined. It has the capacity to act chemically both as a metal and as a nonmetal. With hydrogen, the element forms the extensive class of HYDROCARBON compounds; with oxygen and hydrogen together, CARBOHYDRATE compounds. The study of carbon compounds both natural and synthetic is called organic chemistry. Plastics, petroleum, drugs, animal and plant tissues and secretions, foods, textiles, wood, paper, and many other common substances contain carbon. Fuels (e.g., natural gas), marsh gas, and the gases resulting from the combustion of fuels (e.g., carbon monoxide and carbon dioxide) are compounds of carbon. With oxygen and a metallic element, carbon forms many important carbonates, e.g., calcium carbonate (limestone) and sodium carbonate (soda). Certain active metals unite with it to make industrially important carbides, notably silicon carbide (known as carborundum); calcium carbide, used for producing acetylene gas; and tungsten carbide for rock drills and metal-working tools. Carbon is added to molten iron in the production of steel, and carbon electrodes are widely used in electrical apparatus. The "lead" of the ordinary pencil is graphite mixed with clay. The successful linking in the 1940s of carbon with silicon has led to the development of a vast number of new substances known collectively as the silicones. Some of them, as liquids, are used for lubrication at very low temperatures; others find use as plastics, in insulation, in rubber substitutes, and in waterproofing. Carbon of atomic weight 14, a naturally occurring isotope that can also be produced in a nuclear reactor, is radioactive and has a half life of 5,760 years. It is used extensively as a research tool in tracer studies. A compound synthesized with C-14 is said to be "tagged"; using a geiger counter, it can be followed through a chemical or biochemical reaction. In this way C-14 has been used in the study of such problems as utilization of foods in animal nutrition, catalytic petroleum processes, photosynthesis, and the mechanism of aging in steel. It is used also for determining the age of archaeological specimens (see DATING).

Carbon, Mount, peak, 14,259 ft. high, W central Colo.; highest summit in the Elk Mts. of the Rockies. It is sometimes referred to as Castle Peak.

Carbonari (kärbōnä′rē) [Ital.,=charcoal burners], members of a secret society which flourished in Italy, Spain, and France early in the 19th cent. Possibly derived from Freemasonry, the society originated in the kingdom of Naples in the reign of Murat and drew its members from all stations of life, particularly from the army. It was closely organized, with a ritual, a symbolic language, and a hierarchy. Beyond advocacy of political freedom its aims were vague. The Carbonari were partially responsible for uprisings in Spain (1820), Naples (1820), and Piedmont (1821). After 1830 the Italian Carbonari gradually were absorbed by the RISORGIMENTO movement; elsewhere they disappeared.

carbonate, any one of a group of chemical compounds, either a salt of carbonic acid or, in the case of the organic carbonates, an ester of this acid. The carbonate RADICAL consists of one atom of carbon and three of oxygen ($-CO_3$). Normal carbonates are formed when equivalent amounts of carbonic acid and a base react; if the acid is in excess, bicarbonates or acid carbonates are formed. Other than the ammonium, potassium and sodium salts, the carbonates are insoluble. With the exception of the salts of the ALKALI METALS, they decompose on heating to yield carbon dioxide and the oxide of the metal. A test for carbonates consists of treatment with dilute acid to liberate carbon dioxide, which upon being passed into lime water produces a white precipitate of calcium carbonate. Carbonates occur widely distributed in nature. Some are: barium carbonate, commonly called witherite, which is used for the preparation of other barium compounds; calcium carbonate, found in the shells of animals and as ICELAND SPAR,

LIMESTONE, and MARBLE and in commerce as whiting and putty; iron carbonate, a ferrous compound, known as SIDERITE, the chief source of iron in England, Scotland, and Wales; and magnesium carbonate, occurring as MAGNESITE and, when combined with calcium carbonate, as DOLOMITE. Potassium carbonate constitutes POTASH or pearlash. Sodium carbonate, or SODA, is found in nature, but is usually prepared for commercial use by the SOLVAY PROCESS, which has replaced the LEBLANC PROCESS in the United States. Calcium bicarbonate, which causes "hard" water by changing to insoluble calcium carbonate, produces the STALACTITE and stalagmite formations of limestone caves. Most widely used are sodium carbonate, for making glass and soap; sodium bicarbonate (baking soda) and the hydrated form of sodium carbonate (washing soda) in the household; basic lead carbonate in the WHITE LEAD of paints; and calcium carbonate for the production of LIME.

Carbon Cliff, residential village (pop. 1,268), NW Ill., on the Rock River (here bridged) and E of Moline; inc. 1906.

Carbondale. 1 City (pop. 14,670), S Ill., N of Cairo, in a coal-mine and farm area; founded 1852, inc. 1869. A railroad division point with repair shops, it manufactures work gloves. Southern Illinois Univ. (coeducational; 1869) is in Carbondale, and Giant City State Park and a wildlife refuge are nearby. Memorial Day was inaugurated (1868) here by Gen. John A. Logan. **2** Industrial city (pop. 13,595), NE Pa., on the Lackawanna river and NE of Scranton; settled 1814, inc. 1851. Its important activities are anthracite-coal mining and the manufacture of clothing, metal products, and plastics. Terence Powderly, labor leader, was born here. **3** Village, W.Va.: see CANNELTON.

carbon dioxide, colorless, almost odorless, gaseous compound of carbon and oxygen, the molecule consisting of one atom of carbon and two atoms of oxygen. Carbon dioxide is one and one-half times heavier than air; it neither burns nor supports combustion, is soluble in water volume for volume, and can be liquefied without difficulty under pressure (critical temperature 31.1°C.). Because its aqueous solution exhibits weak acid properties (CARBONIC ACID), the gas is often known in commerce as carbonic acid gas. Carbon dioxide in the solid, or "frozen," state is called DRY ICE or carbon dioxide snow. The chokedamp and afterdamp (see DAMP) of mines, pits or old, unused wells is largely this gas. Carbon dioxide occurs free in nature. It is a constituent of the ATMOSPHERE, being usually more abundant in the air of cities than in that of the country. It is formed in the combustion of carbon or carbonaceous materials such as coal, wood, and fuel oil. The hydrocarbons, used widely as fuels, burn in air, yielding carbon dioxide and water. Carbon dioxide is produced also when a CARBONATE is decomposed by heat or acids. The gas is a product of animal respiration and is also given off in other processes, such as alcoholic FERMENTATION, brought about by the action of yeast. It is a raw material for plant PHOTOSYNTHESIS. In various parts of the world, as in Italy, Java, and the Yellowstone National Park in the United States, it is formed in the ground and issues from fissures. Dissolved in water under pressure, it gives the "sparkle," or effervescence, to natural mineral waters, such as Vichy water. When the pressure is released, the excess gas collects in bubbles and passes upward through the water. The same condition obtains in the common "charged" water of the soda fountain. Carbon dioxide has varied uses. Formed by the action of yeast or baking powder, it causes the rising of bread dough. Some fire extinguishers produce carbon dioxide which, expelled through a nozzle, settles on the flame and smothers it. In one version of this apparatus, the gas is produced by the action of an acid, e.g., sulphuric, upon a carbonate, the two being brought into contact by inverting the extinguisher. Another produces a foam in which bubbles of carbon dioxide are caught and held to prevent diffusion. The gas is used in the SOLVAY PROCESS for the preparation of sodium bicarbonate. The standard test for carbon dioxide is its action with limewater (calcium hydroxide), which in its presence becomes cloudy because of the formation of an insoluble carbonate.

Carbonear (kärbŭnēr'), town (pop. 4,234), E N.F., Canada, on the west coast of Conception Bay and W of St. John's. It is the commercial center of the region. In 1762 the town was captured by the French; it was later recaptured by the English.

Carbon Hill, city (pop. 1,944), NW Ala., NW of Birmingham, in a coal area; inc. 1891.

carbonic acid, weak acid known only in solution, formed when carbon dioxide is dissolved in water. Its molecule is composed of two atoms of hydrogen and the carbonate radical ($-CO_3$). Carbonic acid, being a dibasic ACID, forms two series of salts, the carbonates and the bicarbonates (see CARBONATE). Carbonic acid contributes the sharp taste to a carbonated beverage.

carbonic acid gas: see CARBON DIOXIDE.

Carboniferous period (kärbŭnĭ'fŭrŭs) [Latin,=coal making], fifth period of the PALEOZOIC ERA of geologic time (see GEOLOGIC ERAS, table). The Carboniferous period was marked by vast, coal-forming swamps and a succession of changes in the earth's surface which, continuing into the PERMIAN PERIOD, ended the Paleozoic era. The events of the Carboniferous fall naturally into two divisions, the Mississippian and the Pennsylvanian; in America the break in sequence is so sharp that each division is commonly considered an independent period. In the Lower Carboniferous, or Mississippian, period, the interior of North America was submerged several times by shallow seas, in which were formed limestone, shale, and sandstone. In the Appalachian region, especially in Pennsylvania, great deposits of sandstone and shale were laid down by the erosion products from the eastern coastal highlands. In the Far West the Rocky Mt. region was covered by floods which deposited the Madison limestone and the Redwall limestone of the Grand Canyon. The Lower Carboniferous in Europe, as in America, was a period of submergence and was also one of great volcanic activity. In the British Isles and adjacent areas the mountain limestone was formed; E of the Rhine, the culm shale, sandstone, and conglomerate; and in the USSR, the Coal Measures. The close of the Lower Carboniferous was marked by mountain building in New Brunswick, Nova Scotia, the S Appalachian

region, the SW United States, and Europe. In the Upper Carboniferous, or Pennsylvanian, period, there was at least one great flood; however, the sea level oscillated and caused the formation of great marshes with extensive vegetation that was later transformed into coal. In the E United States great deltas of sediments, now represented by the Pottsville conglomerate, were formed during the early Pennsylvanian. In Kansas, Nebraska, Arkansas, and Texas, the Pennsylvanian beds are chiefly shale, sandstone, and coal; over the Cordilleran region, marine limestone, with little coal; on the Pacific coast from California to Alaska, limestone and shale. The Carboniferous coal fields of North America include the anthracite field of E Pennsylvania; the Appalachian field, from Pennsylvania to Alabama; the Michigan field; the eastern interior field, of Indiana, Illinois, and Kentucky; the western interior and southwestern field, stretching from Iowa to Texas; the Rhode Island field; and the Acadian field of SE Canada. In the Upper Carboniferous of Western Europe, the Millstone Grit, equivalent to the Pottsville conglomerate, is followed by the Coal Measures, which include the Welsh, English, Belgian, Westphalian, and Saar Basin fields. In the Mediterranean region and in the USSR, the Upper Carboniferous resembles that of W North America. The Upper Carboniferous was a period of marked crustal disturbances. In Europe the Paleozoic Alps were thrust up; in Asia, the Altai and Tien Shan; in North America, the Arbuckle and Wichita mts. and the ancestral S Rockies. The Indian peninsula became an active site of deposition; in the Himalayan geosyncline and much of China, mountain building was dominant. Crustal movements in the Andean geosyncline of South America affected the pattern of sedimentation over much of the continent. The plant life of the Carboniferous period was extensive and luxuriant, especially in the Pennsylvanian. It included ferns and fernlike trees; giant horsetails, called calamites; club mosses, or lycopods, such as LEPIDODENDRON and SIGILLARIA; seed ferns; and cordaites, or primitive conifers. Land animals included primitive amphibians, reptiles (which first appeared in the Upper Carboniferous), spiders, millepedes, land snails, scorpions, enormous dragonflies, and more than 800 kinds of cockroaches. The land waters were inhabited by fishes, clams, and various crustaceans; the oceans by mollusks, crinoids, sea urchins, and one-celled lime-making Foraminifera.

carbonite: see COKE.

carbon monoxide, chemical compound, a poisonous, colorless, odorless, tasteless, gas. An oxide of carbon, its molecule consists of one atom of carbon and one of oxygen. Carbon monoxide is lighter than air, is almost insoluble in water, and, under normal pressure, liquefies at $-190°$ C. and solidifies at $-207°$ C. The gas burns in air with a characteristic blue flame, forming carbon dioxide. A constituent of both PRODUCER GAS and WATER GAS, it is widely used as a fuel. It removes oxygen from many compounds and consequently is used in the reduction of metals, such as iron (see BLAST FURNACE), from their ores. The gas is formed by the incomplete combustion of carbon or carbonaceous substances because there is an insufficient

The medieval walled city of Carcassone.

supply of air or at an extremely high temperature in the presence of excess oxygen. It is present in the exhaust of gasoline engines (as in automobiles) and is generated in ordinary coal stoves and furnaces when there is insufficient air owing to faulty draft. Its poisonous properties—it is fatal to man in even extremely small quantities—make it dangerous, especially since its presence cannot be detected easily. Poisoning may occur from the exhaust fumes of an automobile or a similar engine running in a closed room, or from coal gas released by a furnace. Carbon monoxide when inhaled combines with the hemoglobin of the blood and prevents it from taking up and distributing oxygen. The poisoning quickly affects the nervous system causing paralysis, respiratory failure, and death. Carbon monoxide poisoning can be treated by administering artificial respiration to the patient and by supplying him with fresh air.

carbon tetrachloride, chemical compound, a colorless liquid with a pungent odor, comprised of one atom of carbon and four atoms of chlorine. A solvent for fats, oils, and greases, it is used in dry cleaning and, being nonflammable, it is widely employed as a filler for fire extinguishers. Care must be taken when using carbon tetrachloride, for at high temperatures it reacts with steam to form the poisonous gas phosgene. Although toxic when absorbed through the skin, or inhaled in large quantity, carbon tetrachloride is used in medicine against hookworm and other intestinal parasites.

Carborundum: see SILICON CARBIDE.

carbuncle, in geology: see GARNET.

carbuncle (kär′bŭng-kŭl), acute inflammatory nodule of the skin caused by bacterial invasion into the hair follicles or sebaceous gland ducts. It is actually a boil, but one that has more than one focus of infection, i.e., involves several follicles or ducts. Carbuncles occur more often in men because of their more extensive body hair growth. The infection is treated by applying antibiotics systemically and directly to the lesion and by incision and drainage at the proper time.

carburetor. 1 Device, part of a gasoline engine, in which liquid fuel is converted into a vapor and mixed with a regulated amount of air for combus-

tion in the cylinders. Land vehicles, boats, and light aircraft have a float carburetor, in which a float regulates the fuel level in a reservoir from which the fuel is sucked into the intake manifold at a restriction called a venturi. This venturi metering system controls the flow of a continuous pumped spray into the intake manifold downstream from the carburetor. In aircraft designed for violent maneuvers the float is replaced with a diaphragm, and to prevent carburetor icing these high-performance aircraft are fitted with injection carburetors. When there is an individual spray for each cylinder and the injection is an intermittent, timed spurt, or is metered differently, the device is usually called a fuel injector, not a carburetor. **2** Another type of carburetor is used to enrich coal gas and water gas. It varies in size from 4 to 11 ft. in diameter and from 14 to 18 ft. in height and is lined with brick. In it oil or other mixtures of hydrocarbons are mixed with the gas until the desired richness is obtained. The illuminating power of the gas is thus increased.

Carcas (kär′kŭs), king's chamberlain. Esther 1.10.

Carcassonne (kärkäsôn′), city (estimated pop. 37,035), capital of Aude dept., S France, in Languedoc, on the Aude. It is one of the architectural marvels of Europe. The old city, atop a hill and divided from the new city by the Aude river, is a medieval walled city, entirely restored by VIOLLET-LE-DUC in the 19th cent. A stronghold of the ALBIGENSES, it was taken by Simon de Montfort in 1209. The beautiful church of Saint-Nazaire (11th–14th cent.) is located here. On the other side of the river, the "new city" founded in the 13th cent., has manufactures of cloth and trade in agricultural products.

Carchemish (kär′kĭmĭsh, kärkē′mĭsh), city of ancient Syria, NE of modern Alep. It was an important Neo-Hittite city and was prosperous in the 9th cent. B.C. before it was destroyed by the Assyrians. Even then it continued as an important trade center. Here, in 605 B.C., Nebuchadnezzar defeated Necho. 2 Chron. 35.20; Jer. 46.2; Isa. 10.9. Among the remains excavated are sculptured Neo-Hittite reliefs with hieroglyphic Hittite inscriptions. See Sir Leonard Woolley, *Carchemish* (1921).

CARCINOMA

carcinoma: see CANCER.

Carco, Francis (fräsēs′ kärkō′), 1886–1958, French poet and novelist, b. New Caledonia of Corsican parents. His real name was François Carcopino. The bohemian life he cherished is treated in many of his novels, including *Jesus-la-caille* (1914). *L'Homme traqué* (1922; Eng. tr., *The Hounded Man*, 1924), in a bourgeois setting, deals with the same dilemma of man's inevitable fate. Among his verses are *La Bohème et mon cœur* (1912) and *Poèmes en prose* (1948).

cardamom: see GINGER.

Cardamon Hills, range, Kerala state, SW India. It is named for the cardamon growing on its slopes.

Cardano, Geronimo (järō′nēmō kärdä′nō), 1501–76, Italian physician and mathematician. His works on arithmetic and algebra established his reputation. Barred from official status as a physician because of his illegitimate birth, he practiced as a medical astrologer. His major work, *De subtilitate rerum* (1550), on natural history, was perceptive and implied a grasp of evolutionary principles. He described a tactile system similar to Braille for

Geronimo Cardano

teaching the blind and thought it possible to teach the deaf by signs. See study by Henry Morley (1854).

Cárdenas, García López de (gärthē′ä lō′pĕth dä kär′dänäs), fl. 1540, Spanish explorer in the Southwest. A member of the 1540 expedition of Francisco Vásquez de CORONADO, he was selected to lead a party from Cibola (the Zuni country of New Mexico) to find a river of which the Hopi Indians had spoken. After 20 days' march he became the first white man to see the GRAND CANYON of the Colorado. He was not, however, the discoverer of the Colorado itself, for Hernando de ALARCÓN had explored its lower waters a month earlier.

Cárdenas, Lázaro (lä′särō kär′dänäs), 1895–, president of Mexico (1934–40). He joined the revolutionary forces in 1913 and rose to become a general. He was governor (1928–32) of his native state, Michoacán, and held other political posts before he was, with the support of Plutarco E. CALLES, elected president. After a bitter conflict Cárdenas sent (1936) Calles into exile and organized a vigorous campaign of socialization of

Lázaro Cárdenas

industry and agriculture based on the constitution of 1917. Large land holdings were broken up and distributed to small farmers on the EJIDO system, and many foreign-owned properties, especially oil fields, were expropriated. His policy, founded on his determination to make Mexico a modern democracy, became anathema to large landowners, industrialists, and foreign investors, but—himself a mestizo—he won the love of the Indians and of the Mexican working classes and became their hero and champion. Cárdenas relinquished his office at the end of his term, thus acting in consonance with his desire for democratic and orderly constitutional processes and paving the way for his successors, Manuel ÁVILA CAMACHO and Miguel Alemán. Cárdenas was recalled to public service as minister of national defense (1942–45). His political influence as the undisputed leader of the Mexican left wing continued undiminished in the years after the Second World War.

Cárdenas, city (pop. 47,750), W Cuba, a port on Cárdenas Bay. It processes and exports sugar and sisal and has a fishing fleet. Narciso López landed here in 1850.

Cardiff (kär′dĭf), county borough (pop. 256,270), county town of Glamorganshire, S Wales, on the Taff near its mouth on the Bristol Channel. One of the greatest coal-shipping ports in the world, Cardiff has grown largely since the construction of docks by the 2d marquess of Bute in 1839. There are now more than 5 mi. of quays; the port of Cardiff includes the docks at Penarth and Barry. Rail connections with the interior (especially the coal fields) are excellent, and there is a canal to Merthyr Tydfil, with a branch to Aberdare. Besides the export of immense quantities of coal, Cardiff has important ironworks, steelworks, flour mills, and a fishing industry. Cardiff Castle, long the residence of the marquess of Bute, was built in 1090 on the site of a Roman fort. Robert II, duke of Normandy, was imprisoned (1108–34) in the castle. Owen Glendower partly destroyed it in 1404. The city and suburbs suffered damage in concentrated air raids in 1941. In Cathays Park the group of public buildings includes the National Museum of Wales, the law courts, the city hall, Glamorgan county hall, and the University College of South Wales and Monmouthshire (one of the four constituent colleges of the Univ. of Wales). The parish church of St. John dates partly from the 13th and partly from the 15th cent.

Cardigan, James Thomas Brudenell, 7th earl of (kär′dĭgùn), 1797–1868, British general. In the Crimean War he led the disastrous cavalry charge at Balaklava (1854) which Tennyson immortalized in *The Charge of the Light Brigade*. The charge was made on a misunderstood order, and the brigade was destroyed. Quarrels with his officers showed him a vain and contentious man. The cardigan jacket was named for him. See Cecil Woodham-Smith, *The Reason Why* (1953).

Cardigan (kär′dĭgùn), municipal borough (pop. 3,780), county town of Cardiganshire, W Wales, on the Teifi river near its mouth on Cardigan Bay. It is a cattle and dairy center. In 1176 the first eisteddfod was held in Cardigan Castle.

Cardiganshire or **Cardigan**, county (pop. 53,564) 677 sq. mi., W Wales, on Cardigan Bay. The county town is Cardigan, but ABERYSTWYTH is of greater importance. The region is largely one of pleasant, rolling hills, with fertile valleys and a narrow coastal plain. It is noted for its fine cattle. There is also some manufacture of woolens. The county long resisted English influence, and the Welsh language and Welsh customs are preserved here to a large degree.

cardinal [Latin,=belonging to the hinge), in the Roman Catholic Church, a member of the highest body of the Church below the pope. This, the sacred college of cardinals of the Holy Roman Church, is the electoral college of the PAPACY. Its members are appointed by the pope. There are three classes. Cardinal bishops are the bishops of seven sees around Rome (Ostia, Velletri, Porto and Santa Rufina, Albano, Frascati, Palestrina, and Sabina); the first of these in order of creation is dean of the college and ex officio bishop of Ostia in addition to his other see. Cardinal priests are mostly archbishops outside the Roman province; the title "cardinal archbishop"—often applied to these men—simply represents the union of the two dignities in one man. Cardinal deacons are priests with functions in the papal government.

Cardinal priests and cardinal deacons have titles corresponding to churches of the Roman diocese. A cardinal's insignia resemble those of a bishop, except for the characteristic red, broad-brimmed, tasseled hat which is conferred by the pope but not subsequently worn. Cardinals are styled "Eminence." Apart from papal elections, the cardinals have great importance as the privy council of the pope. Hence those who are not bishops away from Rome must live at Rome. They meet with the pope in consistories, public and secret, but most of the business they transact is done in their various jurisdictional capacities. Thus the cardinals in residence at Rome make up a cabinet for the pope, directing the work of the Curia Romana, as the papal administration is called. This is made up of standing committees and courts, the departments of administration divided among them. Since there is no division of powers in the headship of the Church, most organs of the Curia have power to judge, to command, and to legislate. The acts of these bodies are validated by papal approbation, and they therefore bind Roman Catholics as direct pontifical acts. Only the pope himself can speak finally in matters of faith and morals (see INFALLIBILITY). The Curia may be divided into Roman congregations, Roman tribunals, curial offices, and secretariats. A Roman congregation consists of a group of cardinals, headed by a prefect, together with two staffs which transact most of the business—the *congresso* of major officials and a staff of minor officials chosen by competitive examination and assigned to less important affairs. The congregation proper, i.e., the cardinals, makes all major decisions. The following are the Roman congregations (founded by Sixtus V in 1588 and reorganized by Pius X in 1908): Congregation of the Holy Office (see INQUISITION), of which the pope is prefect; Congregation of the Consistory, of which the pope is prefect, for the preparation of agenda for consistories and the regulation of dioceses of the Western Church not under the Propaganda; Congregation of the Sacraments, for legislation on administration of the sacraments and for dis-

Cardinals gathered in the Sistine Chapel in Vatican City for conclave.

pensations concerning them; Congregation of the Council, for the regulation of councils and of benefices, properties, and the like, for dispensations from the commandments of the Church, and for the maintenance of the shrine of Loreto; Congregation of Religious, for all concerns of all seculars and regulars, of both sexes; Congregation for the Propagation of the Faith (the Propaganda), for all concerns of the MISSIONS of the Latin rite; Congregation of the Eastern Church, for all concerns of the Oriental rites in communion with the pope and of every person involved, except for the Russian Catholics, who are under a separate commission; Congregation of Sacred Rites, for all public worship of the Latin rite, for canonizations, liturgical books, and the like; Congregation of the Ceremonial, for liturgical ceremonies involving the pope and the sacred college; Congregation for Extraordinary Ecclesiastical Affairs, virtually a board of assistants to the secretariat of state; Congregation of Studies, for the administration of education, of seminaries, and of ecclesiastical research; Congregation of the Fabric, for the maintenance of St. Peter's Church. Of the Roman congregations, the two whose influence is felt most deeply throughout the Church are probably the Holy Office and the Propaganda. The Roman tribunals are three secret courts, the highest of the Church; each is headed by a cardinal, and its work is handled by trained canonists. They are the Apostolic Penitentiaria, for all cases of conscience appealed by any Catholic to the pope and for the regulation of indulgences; the Apostolic Signatura, the court of final appeal of the Church, considering only cases involving the members of, or appealed from, the Rota; the Sacred Roman Rota, the court of appeal from diocesan courts and the lower court of Vatican City, hearing all cases requiring trial and evidence, except cases of conscience, cases of canonization, and cases involving sovereigns of states (reserved to the pope in person). The curial offices are now to a large extent unimportant and honorary. They are the Apostolic Chancery, to issue bulls of foundations and the like; the Apostolic Dataria, to handle matter concerning candidates for papal benefices, pensions, and the like; the Apostolic Camera, headed by the chamberlain of the Holy Roman Church, to administer the property (except revenue) of the Holy See, notably in the vacancy of the papal see. The secretariats are the secretariat of state, headed by the cardinal secretary of state, who has charge of all matters involving relations with political governments and has for his aid a large staff and the Congregation of Extraordinary Ecclesiastical Affairs, and the secretariat of briefs, in charge of the official Latin correspondence of the pope. Besides these permanent departments there are always some special commissions of cardinals, e.g., for the Russian Church, for the revision of the Vulgate, for biblical study, and for sacred art. The term *cardinal* was formerly applied to important clergymen of all sorts and countries, but in the Middle Ages it was officially restricted to the Roman province. The college of cardinals is the modern derivative of the advisory board of clergymen of the ancient diocese of Rome, used by the pope for advice and transaction of business. Pope

Cardinals near nest.

Sixtus V set the maximum number of cardinals at 70, a tradition maintained for centuries until the pontificate of Pope John XXIII. In 1960 there were 86 cardinals; six of them were American. Pope Pius, in 1946, created the first truly international college of cardinals. See G. D. Kittler, *The Papal Princes* (1960).

cardinal or **redbird,** North American songbird of the FINCH family. In the eastern cardinal the male is bright scarlet with black throat and face; the female is brown with patches of red. Both sexes have crests and red bills. The Arizona, gray-tailed, Louisiana, and San Lucas cardinals frequent the S United States and Mexico. The pyrrhuloxia of the SW United States, gray with red face, crest, breast, and tail, is called gray cardinal or parrotbill.

cardinal flower: see LOBELIA.

carding, process by which fibers are opened, cleaned, and straightened preparatory to spinning. The fingers were first used, then a tool of wood or bone shaped like a hand, then two flat pieces of wood (cards) covered with skin set with thorns or teeth. Primitive cards, rubber covered and toothed with bent wires, are still employed by Navaho women. Modern carding dates from the use of revolving cylinders patented in 1748 by Lewis Paul. A mechanical apron feed was devised in 1772, and Richard Arkwright added a funnel which contracted the carded fiber into a continuous sliver. See COMBING.

Cardington, village (pop. 1,613), central Ohio, SE of Marion, in a rich farm area; founded 1822, inc. 1857.

Cardozo, Benjamin Nathan (kärdō′zō), 1870–1938, American jurist, Associate Justice of the U.S.

Supreme Court (1932–38), b. New York city, grad. Columbia (B.A., 1889; M.A., 1890). He was admitted to the bar (1891) and practiced law until he was elected (1913) to the New York supreme court on a fusion ticket. Cardozo was appointed (1914) to the court of appeals, was elected (1917) for a 14-year term, and in 1927 was elected chief judge of the court, which, largely through his influence, gained international fame. He was prominent in the efforts of the American Law Institute to restate and simplify the law, and he advocated a permanent agency to function between the courts and legislatures to aid in framing effective legislation. He was active in a number of Jewish movements. He was appointed (1932) by President Hoover to the Supreme Court to succeed Oliver Wendell Holmes. Cardozo was one of the foremost spokesmen of sociological jurisprudence, and his views on the relation of law to social change made him probably the most influential of American judges. His philosophy of law and the judicial process was developed in three classics of jurisprudence: *The Nature of the Judicial Process* (1921), *The Growth of the Law* (1924), and *The Paradoxes of Legal Science* (1928). He also wrote *Law and Literature and Other Essays* (1931). See B. H. Levy, ed., *Cardozo and Frontiers of Legal Thinking* (1938); M. E. Hall, ed., *Selected Writings of Benjamin Nathan Cardozo* (1947); biographies by J. P. Pollard (1935) and G. S. Hellman (1940).

Banjamin Nathan Cardozo

cards, playing: see PLAYING CARDS.
Cardston, town (pop. 2,801), SW Alta., Canada, SW of Lethbridge and near the U.S. boundary. It was established in the middle of the 19th cent. by Mormons from Utah under the leadership of Charles Ora Card, son-in-law of Brigham Young. The chief Mormon temple of Canada is here. There are coal mines and stone quarries in the vicinity.
Carducci or **Carducho, Bartolomeo** (bärtōlōmä'ō kärdōōt'chē, kärdōō'kō), 1560–1638, Italian painter, sculptor, and architect in Spain. He studied with Federigo Zuccaro, whom he accompanied (1585) to the court of Madrid. He assisted Tibaldi in decorating the library ceiling of the Escorial and executed some of the cloister frescoes. His master-

piece, *Descent from the Cross*, is in San Felipe el Real, Madrid. His brother **Vincenzo Carducci** (vēnchän'tsō), 1576–1638, succeeded him as court painter to Philip III. Vincenzo is the author of the *Diálogos de la pintura* (1633). The paintings of both brothers, though different in style, are marked by sobriety and an insistence upon moral tone.
Carducci, Giosuè (jōzōōä'), 1835–1907, Italian poet. He was professor of literature at the Univ. of

Giosuè Carducci

Bologna from 1860 to 1904. He was a scholar, an editor, an orator, a critic, and a patriot, although his defection from republicanism brought him into disfavor even with his students. He was awarded the 1906 Nobel Prize in Literature. Carducci ranks with the greatest Italian poets; his verse is classic in design, with a deep and wide range of emotion. His chief works include *Rime* (1857), *Inno a Satana* [hymn to Satan] (1865), *Decennali* (1871), *Nuove poesie* (1873), *Odi barbari* (1877, 1882, 1889), *Rime nuove* (1889; Eng. tr., *New Rhymes*, 1916), and *Rime e ritme* (1898). For translations, see G. L. Bickersteth, *Carducci: a Selection of His Poems* (1913); Maud Holland, *Poems by Giosuè Carducci* (1927). For biography and criticism, see Orlo Williams, *Giosuè Carducci* (1914); R. S. Phelps, *Italian Silhouettes* (1924); John Bailey, *Carducci* (1926); S. E. Scaglia, *Carducci, His Critics and Translators* (1937).
Carducho, Bartolomeo: see CARDUCCI, BARTOLOMEO.
Cardwell, Edward Cardwell, Viscount, 1813–86, British statesman. He entered Parliament (1842) as a supporter of Robert Peel, under whom he was secretary of the treasury (1845) and president of the Board of Trade (1852–55). Under Palmerston he was Irish secretary (1859–61) and chancellor of the duchy of Lancaster (1861–64). While colonial secretary (1864–66) he worked toward federation in Canada. As war secretary (1868–74) under Gladstone, he reformed the British army, abolishing the purchase of commissions, shortening the term of enlistment, and creating a reserve.
Careah (kārē'ù), variant of KAREAH.
Carême, Marie Antoine (märē' ätwän' kärĕm'), 1784–1833, celebrated French cook and gastronomist. He was chef of Talleyrand, Tsar Alexander I, George IV, and Baron Rothschild. His writings

on the culinary art include *La Cuisine française* (1833).

Carencro (kă′rĭnkrō″), village (pop. 1,519), S La., N of Lafayette, in a farm region.

Caretta, town (pop. 1,092), S W.Va., SSW of Welch, near the Va. line.

Carew, George, Baron Carew of Clopton and **earl of Totnes** (kûrōō′, klŏp′tŭn, tŏt′nĭs), 1555–1629, English statesman. Variously a military officer in Ireland, captain for Sir Humphrey Gilbert, and diplomat for Queen Elizabeth I, he was (1600) as lord president of Munster a great aid to the lord lieutenant, Lord Montjoy, in defeating Hugh O'Neill, earl of Tyrone. Under James I, Carew was unable to save his friend, Sir Walter Raleigh, but himself received honors, including his earldom in 1626. An antiquarian, he collected material on the history of Ireland, used later by his secretary, Sir Thomas Stafford, to prepare the important *Pacata Hibernia; or, An Historie of the Late Warres of Ireland* (1633).

Carew, Thomas (kăr′ē, kûrōō′), 1595?–1639?, English author, one of the CAVALIER POETS. Educated at Merton College, Oxford, he had a short diplomatic career on the Continent, then returned to England and became a favorite of Charles I and a court official. He is best known for his courtly, amorous lyrics, such as "Ask me no more where Jove bestows" and "He that loves a rosy cheek," but of equal importance are his "Elegy on the Death of Dr. Donne," and the highly erotic poem, "A Rapture." In his use of metaphysical and classical material, he shows the influence of both John Donne and Ben Jonson. See edition of his works by Rhodes Dunlap (1949); study by E. I. Selig (1958).

Carey, Henry, 1687–1743, English author. After the first collection of his poems appeared in 1713, he turned to writing for the stage. He was primarily a writer of farce comedy, his greatest success being *Chrononhotonthologos* (1734), a burlesque on theatrical bombast. He is best remembered, however, for his songs, in particular the ballad *Sally in Our Alley*.

Carey, Henry Charles, 1793–1879, American economist, b. Philadelphia; son of Mathew CAREY. In 1835 he retired from publishing, where he had done notable work, to devote himself to economics. His *Principles of Political Economy* (3 vols., 1837–40) and *Principles of Social Science* (3 vols., 1858–59) were among the first important American works in the field. Carey opposed the dominant English political economy of the day, particularly the "pessimism" of Ricardo and Malthus, and led in the theoretical development of American economic nationalism. He advocated the protective tariff but believed generally in laissez faire. See study by A. D. H. Kaplan (1931).

Carey, Mathew, 1760–1839, American publisher, bookseller, and economist, b. Dublin. In his Dublin journal he violently attacked English rule of Ireland, was imprisoned for a month, and emigrated (1784) to Philadelphia. There a gift from Lafayette enabled him to establish (1785) the *Pennsylvania Herald*. From Jan., 1787, to Dec., 1792, he edited and published the *American Museum*, making it the leading American magazine of the period. Carey began (c.1790) his career as bookseller

and publisher on a large scale. Through his publication of many authors and through his wide distribution of books, he stimulated the growth of American letters. Although many of his own political pamphlets were controversial, the most famous, *The Olive Branch* (1814), was written during the War of 1812 in an effort to unite the Republican and Federalist parties in support of the war. His copious writings advocating the American protective system are interesting documents for the study of American economic history. The economist Henry Charles Carey was his son. See biography by E. L. Bradsher (1912).

Carey, William, 1761–1834, English Baptist missionary and Orientalist, one of the first Protestant missionaries to India. He helped found the Baptist Missionary Society in 1792 and shortly thereafter went to India. Carey did most of the work in publishing the Bible in many Indian vernaculars. He wrote grammars of the vernaculars and several dictionaries. He became a professor of Sanskrit at Fort William College, Calcutta. See biography by S. P. Carey (8th ed., revised, 1934).

Carey, village (pop. 3,722), NW Ohio, SE of Findlay; platted 1843, inc. 1858. It is a trade and shipping center for a truck-farming area. Rubber products are made, and limestone is quarried.

Carey Land Act, written by Sen. Joseph M. Carey and passed by the U.S. Congress in 1894. The act provided for the transfer of U.S.-owned desert lands to Western states on condition they be irrigated. Settlers were permitted to buy up to 160 acres of this land at 50 cents an acre plus the cost of water rights. Hopes that the act would hasten reclamation and settlement were disappointed.

Cargill, Donald (kär′gĭl), 1619?–1681, Scottish Covenanter. He was a minister in Glasgow from c.1655 to 1662, when he was expelled for denouncing the Restoration and resisting the establishment of the episcopacy in Scotland. After escaping wounded from the battle of Bothwell Bridge (1679), he joined Richard Cameron in the Sanquhar Declaration (1680) against Charles II. Cargill, having excommunicated the king, the duke of York, and others, was arrested and executed.

Caria (kâ′rĕȗ), ancient region of SW Asia Minor, S of the Maeander river, which separated it from Lydia. The territory is in present SW Asiatic Turkey. The Carians were probably a native people, but their region was settled by both Dorian and Ionian colonists. Caria was a center of the Ionian revolt (c.499 B.C.) which was a prelude to the Persian Wars. Some of the communities joined (c.468) the Delian League. In the 4th cent. B.C. the region was united under a dynasty of princes, of whom the most celebrated was MAUSOLUS. Alexander the Great conquered Caria, and it changed hands often in the wars after his death. In 125 it was made a Roman province (part of the province of Asia). Cnidus, Halicarnassus, and Miletus were famous Carian cities.

Carías Andino, Tiburcio (tēbōōr′syō kärē′äs ändē′nō), 1876–, president of Honduras (1933–49). A strong-handed dictator, his term was twice extended by congress. Some improvements were made in communication and education. After Carías announced his retirement in 1948, presidential elections were held. Juan Manuel Gálvez, the government candidate, won easily.

Caribbean Sea (kă″rĭbē′ŭn, kŭrĭ′bēŭn), part of the Atlantic Ocean. It is closed on the west and the south by Central America and N South America and marked off on the north and east from the Gulf of Mexico and the Atlantic proper by the Yucatan peninsula of Mexico and the chain of islands of the West Indies.

Caribbees (kă′rĭbēz), name sometimes applied to the islands of the Caribbean or even to all the West Indies. More specifically the Caribbees are the Lesser Antilles and include the LEEWARD ISLANDS, the WINDWARD ISLANDS, and the VIRGIN ISLANDS.

Carib Indians (kă′rĭb), native people formerly inhabiting the Lesser Antilles, West Indies. They seem to have overrun the Lesser Antilles and to have driven out the ARAWAK about a century before the arrival of Columbus. The original name, Calinago or Calino, was corrupted by Columbus to Caribales and is the origin of the English word *cannibal*. Extremely warlike and ferocious, they practiced cannibalism and took pride in scarification and fasting. Fishing, agriculture, and basket-making were the chief domestic activities; they were expert navigators, crisscrossing a large portion of the Caribbean in their pirogues and small canoes. After European colonization began in the 17th cent., they were all but exterminated. A group remaining on St. Vincent mingled with Negro slaves who escaped from a shipwreck in 1675. This group was transferred (1795) by the British to Roatán island off the coast of Honduras. They have gradually migrated north along the coast into Guatemala. A few Caribs survive on a reservation on Dominica. The Carib, or Cariban, languages are a separate family, believed to have originated in Brazil. The Carib languages spread after the arrival of the Spanish and are found in N Honduras, British Honduras, and N South America.

Cariboo Mountains (kă′rĭbōō), range, c.200 mi. long, E British Columbia, Canada. Its axis is northwest-southeast, roughly parallel with the main Rocky Mt. range to the northeast, from which it is separated by the Rocky Mt. trench, here occupied by the Fraser river. It reaches its greatest altitude probably in Mt. Titan (c.11,750 ft.). In the foothills to the westward is the Cariboo dist., scene of the famous Cariboo gold rush of 1860. Many camps sprang up in the region, and in the next six years much gold was taken out, but afterwards the diggings declined. Many stayed on in the region, and today there are several thousand who make their living by a combination of mining, hunting, and farming. The Cariboo wagon road, built (1862–65) by the government, facilitated the settlement of the interior of the province. It started from Yale on the Fraser, at the head of navigation, and ended in the Cariboo dist. nearly 400 mi. to the northward. See Agnes Laut, *The Cariboo Trail* (1916).

Caribou (kă′rĭbōō), town (pop. 12,464), NE Maine, on the Aroostook and N of Presque Isle; inc. 1859. A port of entry for planes, the town is also a center for winter sports. It is a shipping point for a potato-growing region and processes food.

caribou (kă′rĭbōō), name in America for the genus (*Rangifer*) of deer from which the Old World REINDEER was originally domesticated. Caribou are found in arctic and subarctic regions. They are the only deer in which both sexes have antlers. The broad hoofs support the animal (males may weigh over 300 lb.) on boggy land or snow and have sharp edges which enable it to traverse rocky or frozen surfaces and to dig down to the grass and lichens on which it sometimes feeds. In North America there are two main types: the woodland caribou of the bogs and coniferous forests from Newfoundland to British Columbia, with palmate antlers up to 4 ft. wide; and the barren-ground caribou of the tundra of Alaska and N Canada, which has many-branched, slender antlers and which may undertake mass migrations in search of food.

caricature, a satirical drawing, plastic representation, or description which, through gross exaggeration of natural features, makes its subject appear

Alaskan caribou

Fraser river, Cariboo Mountains.

ridiculous. Although 16th-century Northern painters, such as Holbein, Bruegel, and Bosch, possess
certain elements of caricature, no established tradition of the genre with emphasis on comic aspects
of the individual appears until 17th-century Italy
with the work of the Carracci. In the 18th cent.
caricature flourished in England with the work of
Hogarth, Thomas Rowlandson, and James Gillray,
and it expanded to include political and social as
well as personal satire. This latter trend is more
properly categorized as a step in the development of
the CARTOON. Periodicals of caricature, such as
Charivari (which appeared in France in 1832),
followed by *Punch* in England, *Simplicissimus* in
Germany, and *Puck*, *Life*, and *Judge* in the United
States, were quite popular in the 19th cent. and
featured such artists as Daumier, George Cruik-
shank, John Tenniel, Art Young, E. W. Kemble,
and Daniel Fitzpatrick. Modern caricaturists of
note include David Low, Roland Searle, Max
Beerbohm, Al Hirschfeld, and H. L. BLOCK. Sculpture generally lends itself less well to caricature,
but an exception exists in the series of heads by
Franz Xavier Messerschmidt (1736–83) which
represent exaggerated states of emotion and
character. In literature, caricature has been a

Wayside shrine in Carinthia.

Max Beerbohm's cari-
cature of Winston
Churchill (1912).

popular form since the ancient Greeks. Through
verbal exaggeration and distortion the writer
achieves an immediate, comic, often satiric effect.
No one has made wider use of the literary caricature than Dickens. See study by Werner Hofmann
(Eng. tr., 1957).

Carignan-Salières regiment (kärēnyä'-sälyĕr'), only
complete French regiment ever sent to New
France. The regiment arrived in Canada in 1665
and was over 1,000 strong. It was charged with
making the lower St. Lawrence valley safe from
Indian raids. It had a distinguished record; but it
suffered in Canada from disease and constant
Indian harassment. With its mission completed,
it was ordered back to France in 1668. About half
its members remained as settlers.

carillon, in music: see BELL.

Carinthia (kŭrĭn'thēŭ), Ger. *Kärnten* (kĕrn'tŭn),
province (3,680 sq. mi.; estimated pop. 493,972),
S Austria. Klagenfurt is the capital. Predominantly a mountainous region, it is the southernmost Austrian province, bordering on Italy and
Yugoslavia in the south. The GROSSGLOCKNER,
the highest point in Austria, rises at the Tyrol
frontier in the north. Carinthia has a well-devel-
oped forestry industry, mines (lead, zinc, iron, and
lignite), and farms (especially in the fertile Drava
plain). There is also an active tourist trade,
particularly along the Wörthersee, near Klagenfurt.
In 976 Carinthia, which then included Istria,
Carniola, and Styria, was detached from BAVARIA
and created an independent duchy. Acquired by
Ottocar II of Bohemia in 1269, it fell to RUDOLF
I of Hapsburg and in 1335 became an Austrian
crownland. After 1919 it lost some minor territories to Italy and Yugoslavia. Carinthia, the only
Austrian province with an appreciable cultural
minority, has a Slovene population in the south.

Carinus (Marcus Aurelius Carinus) (kŭrī'nŭs),
d. 285, Roman emperor (283–85). He was the son
of CARUS, who left Carinus as ruler in the West
when he went to the East on a campaign against
the Parthians. On the death of Carus, Carinus
succeeded in the West, and his brother Numerianus
succeeded in the East. After the murder of Numerianus, DIOCLETIAN was chosen (284) emperor in
the East by the soldiers. Carinus set out to defeat

the new claimant and met him in battle. At the moment of victory, however, Carinus was murdered by one of his own soldiers, and Diocletian became sole emperor.

Carisbrooke (kă'rĭzbroŏk), village, on the Isle of Wight, S England, near Newport. There are vestiges of Roman settlement and the ruins of a castle in which Charles I was imprisoned.

Carissimi, Giacomo (jä'kōmō kärēs'sēmē), 1605–74, Italian composer. Most of his life was spent in Rome, where he wrote chamber cantatas in a style that lasted for over a century. His Latin oratorios, of which *Jephtha* is best known, are among the earliest extant examples of true oratorio. Famous as a teacher, he had among his pupils Alessandro Scarlatti.

Carlen, Emilie Smith Flygare-: see FLYGARE-CARLEN.

Carleton: see COFFIN, CHARLES CARLETON.

Carleton, Guy, 1st Baron Dorchester, 1724–1808, governor of Quebec and British commander in the American Revolution. He came to America in 1758 and gave distinguished service in the French and Indian Wars, at Louisburg and Quebec, and in the attack on Havana. After 1766, as lieutenant governor, acting governor, and governor of Quebec, he proved to be a very able administrator. He is given major credit for the QUEBEC ACT of 1774, which was designed to better relations between the British and the French Canadians and was successful. The loyalty of the French Canadians to the British in the American Revolution was at least partly the result of it. On the other hand, it infuriated the colonists in the present United States and helped bring on revolution. When Thomas Gage resigned as commander in chief of British forces in America, the command was divided—Sir Guy Carleton had command in Canada, and Sir William Howe had command farther south. When the patriots in the American Revolution launched their QUEBEC CAMPAIGN, Carleton had few men and had to abandon Montreal, which fell to the forces under Richard Montgomery. Withdrawing to Quebec, Carleton there threw back (Dec. 31, 1775) an attack led by Montgomery and Benedict Arnold and withstood a long winter siege. British reinforcements in the spring enabled him to push the American forces out of Canada to Crown Point, which he took in the autumn of 1776. Disagreements with Lord George Germain led to his being replaced as commander by Gen. John Burgoyne in 1777. Carleton resigned as governor, but he could not leave Canada until 1778, when he was succeeded by Sir Frederick Haldimand. In Feb., 1782, after the Yorktown campaign had already effectively ended the American Revolution, Carleton replaced Sir Henry Clinton as commander in chief of the British forces. His delicate task was to suspend hostilities, withdraw the forces from the New York and Vermont frontiers, and protect the Loyalists—both those who were emigrating to Canada and those who were attempting to reestablish themselves in their old homes. His tact, persistence, firmness, and ability to mingle threat with promise accomplished more than seemed possible. He was again governor of Quebec from 1786 to 1796. High-principled, gentlemanly, and able, Carleton was perhaps the most admirable British colonial commander in America in his time. See biography by A. G. Bradley (new ed., 1926).

Carleton, Mark Alfred, 1866–1925, American botanist, b. Monroe co., Ohio. He was a graduate of Kansas State College of Agriculture. His later experiments on grain rusts at the agricultural experiment station there won attention. His worldwide search for drought-resisting and rust-resisting wheats led to the introduction of many new varieties, of which the Kubanka durum wheat and the red Kharkov winter wheat, both from Russia, proved exceptionally hardy and found wide favor with Western farmers.

Carleton, Will, 1845–1912, American poet, b. Hudson, Mich., grad. Hillsdale College, 1869. He is best known for his sentimental poems of rural life, his most famous being "Over the Hill to the Poorhouse." Among his works are *Farm Ballads* (1873), *Farm Legends* (1875), and *City Ballads* (1885). See biography by A. E. Corning (1917).

Carleton, William, 1794–1869, English author, b. Ireland. His *Traits and Stories of Irish Peasantry* (5 vols., 1830–33) realistically depicts his own rural youth. This was followed by *Tales of Ireland* (1834), *Fardorougha the Miser* (1839), and *The Black Prophet* (1847). See study by Benedict Kiely (1947).

Carleton, village (pop. 1,379), SE Mich., SW of Detroit; inc. 1911.

Carleton College, at Northfield, Minn.; coeducational; chartered 1866 by Congregationalists. It was called Northfield College until 1872 when it was renamed for William Carleton. Among its programs are the Kellogg Foundation for Education in International Relations.

Carlile, Richard (–līl'), 1790–1843, English journalist, reformer, and freethinker. For his radical writings and efforts to secure the freedom of the press, he spent over nine years in prison. He republished suppressed works by Thomas Paine, William Hone, and others, brought out his own *Political Litany* (1817), and while he was imprisoned kept his weekly, the *Republican*, going (1819–26) with the help of his wife and sister. See biography by G. A. Aldred (1923).

Carlin, town (pop. 1,023), N Nev., on the Humboldt river and WSW of Elko; settled 1868, inc. 1927.

Carlinville, city (pop. 5,440), co. seat of Macoupin co., W central Ill., SW of Springfield, in a coal, natural gas, and farm area; settled c.1829, inc. 1837. It is the seat of Blackburn College (United Presbyterian; coeducational; 1857). Mary Hunter Austin was born here.

Carlisle, Charles Howard, 1st earl of: see HOWARD, CHARLES, 1ST EARL OF CARLISLE.

Carlisle, Frederick Howard, 5th earl of: see HOWARD, FREDERICK, 5TH EARL OF CARLISLE.

Carlisle (kärlīl'), county borough (pop. 71,112), county town of Cumberland, N England, near the junction of the Caldew, Eden, and Petteril rivers. It is an important rail center which manufactures textiles and biscuits and holds an important livestock auction. The Roman station Luguvallum (near Hadrian's Wall) which was here was destroyed by the Danes in 875. Carlisle castle, built by William II in 1092, withstood siege by Robert I of Scotland, was taken by the parliamentarians in the civil wars, was again besieged in 1745, and is now used as a barracks. Mary Queen of Scots was imprisoned here in 1568. The cathedral, founded early in the 12th cent., was preceded by an Augustinian priory church. A technical college was founded at Carlisle in 1952.

Carlisle (kärlīl′, kär′līl). **1** Town (pop. 1,514), central Ark., E of Little Rock, in an area producing rice, cotton, and dairy goods; founded 1871. A large cheese plant is here. **2** Town (pop. 1,317), S central Iowa, SE of Des Moines near the Des Moines river. **3** City (pop. 1,601), co. seat of Nicholas co., N Ky., NE of Lexington, in a tobacco region. **4** Rural town (pop. 1,488), E Mass., N of Concord; settled c.1650, inc. 1805. **5** Industrial borough (pop. 16,623), co. seat of Cumberland co., S Pa., SW of Harrisburg; laid out 1751, inc. 1782. Its manufactures include shoes, clothing, railroad equipment, tires, and carpets. In the French and Indian War the Forbes (1758) and the Bouquet (1763) expeditions were organized here. A munitions depot during the Revolution, Carlisle was a headquarters for Washington during the Whisky Rebellion. Molly Pitcher is buried in the Old Graveyard here. The borough was a stop on the Underground Railroad and was attacked in the Civil War by Gen. Fitzhugh Lee. It is the seat today of the United States Army War College and DICKINSON COLLEGE. The **Carlisle Indian School** (Federally supported), founded in 1879 by R. H. PRATT, was the first school of higher education for Indians to be established off a reservation. Its football team, led by Jim THORPE and coached by Glenn WARNER, brought the school nationwide attention. Pratt, who strenuously opposed the Indian Bureau's efforts to establish schools closer to the reservations, was relieved of his superintendency in 1904. The school was closed in 1918.

Carlists, partisans of Don CARLOS (1788–1855) and his successors, who claimed the Spanish throne under the SALIC LAW of succession, introduced (1713) by Philip V. The law (forced on Philip by the War of the Spanish Succession to avoid a union of the French and Spanish crowns) was abrogated by Ferdinand VII in favor of his daughter, who succeeded him (1833) as ISABELLA II. Ferdinand's brother, Don Carlos, refused to recognize Isabella and claimed the throne. A civil war followed, and in the hope of autonomy most of the Basque Provs. and much of Catalonia supported Carlos. The Carlists' conservative and clericalist tendencies gave the dynastic conflict a political character, since the upper middle classes profited from the sale of Church lands and supported Isabella. In 1839 the Carlist commander yielded to ESPARTERO, but in Catalonia the Carlists under Ramón CABRERA continued the struggle until 1840. In 1860 Don Carlos's son, Don Carlos, conde de Montemolín (1818–61), attempting a rising, landed in Catalonia but failed and renounced his claims. These were revived by his nephew, Don Carlos, duque de Madrid (1848–1909), after the deposition (1868) of Isabella. Two insurrections (1869, 1872) failed, but after the abdication (1873) of King AMADEUS and the proclamation of the Spanish republic, the Carlists seized most of the Basque Provs. and parts of Catalonia, Aragon, and Valencia. The ensuing chaos and brutal warfare ended in 1876, over a year after ALFONSO XII, son of Isabella, was pro-

claimed king. Don Carlos escaped to France. In the next half century many defected from Carlist ranks, and several rival groups formed. Pressure against the Church by the second republic (1931–39) helped revive Carlism, an ultraconservative force. The Carlists embraced the Insurgent cause in the Spanish civil war (1936–39). Under the Franco regime Carlism has been significant mainly as an obstacle to plans for restoring the main branch of the BOURBON dynasty.

Carl Junction, city (pop. 1,220), SW Mo., NNW of Joplin; inc. 1863.

Carlōman, 751–71, son of Pepin the Short. He and his brother, CHARLEMAGNE, shared the succession to their father's kingdom, Carloman ruling the southern portion. Attempts to end rivalry between the brothers failed; and when Carloman died, Charlemagne seized his domain. Carloman's wife and children went to the court of DESIDERIUS.

Carloman (kär′lōmăn″), d. 880, king of Bavaria, Carinthia, Pannonia, and Moravia (876–80) and of Italy (877–80), son of LOUIS THE GERMAN and father of Emperor Arnulf. He failed (875) to prevent the assumption of the imperial crown by his uncle, Charles II (Charles the Bald). In 879 he was incapacitated by a paralytic stroke and transferred to his brothers the authority to rule. He was the first German king to become king of Italy.

Carloman, d. 884, French king, son of LOUIS II (Louis the Stammerer). He became joint ruler with his brother LOUIS III in 879. His reign was disturbed by revolts in Burgundy, by the loss (879) of Provence to Boso, count of Arles, and by an invasion of the Normans. Defeated by Louis at the Somme (881), the Normans returned to France after his death, but Carloman checked them at the Aisne; they had agreed to withdraw when he died. He was succeeded as French king by Emperor Charles III (Charles the Fat).

Carloman, d. 754, mayor of the palace in the kingdom of Austrasia after the death (741) of his father, Charles Martel. With his brother, PEPIN THE SHORT, he carried on successful wars against Hunald of Aquitaine, the Saxons, the Swabians, and the Bavarians. The brothers helped St. Boniface reform the Frankish church, bringing church and state into closer relationship. In 747 Carloman retired to a monastery.

Carlos. For Spanish and Portuguese kings thus named, see CHARLES.

Carlos, 1545–68, prince of the Asturias, son of Philip II of Spain and Maria of Portugal. Don Carlos, who seems to have been mentally unbalanced, was imprisoned by his father in 1568 on the eve of a projected flight to the Netherlands. He died shortly afterward. Friedrich von Schiller deliberately idealized his character in his tragedy *Don Carlos,* portraying him as a champion of liberalism, unhappily in love with his stepmother, ELIZABETH OF VALOIS.

Carlos (Carlos María Isidoro de Borbón), 1788–1855, second son of Charles IV of Spain. He was the first Carlist pretender. After his father's abdication he was, with the rest of his family, held a prisoner in France until 1814. A conservative and a devout Catholic, he was supported by the clerical party when he refused to recognize Isabella, daughter of his brother, King FERDINAND VII, as suc-

Carlos

cessor to the Spanish throne. When his niece became queen (1833) as Isabella II, Don Carlos took up arms. Defeated in 1839, he escaped to France and renounced his claim in favor of his son, Don Carlos, conde de Montemolín. See Carlists.

Carlotta (kärlŏ′tú) Span. *Carlota* (kärlō′tä), 1840–1927, empress of Mexico, daughter of Leopold I of Belgium, christened Marie Charlotte Amélie. She married Maximilian, archduke of Austria, on July 27, 1857, and accompanied him when he went to Mexico as emperor (1864). After Napoleon III decided to withdraw the French troops from Mexico and the fate of the empire became apparent, she went to Europe (1866) and sought the aid of Napoleon III and the pope. Her pleas were in vain, and her overwrought mind gave way under the strain. The Mexican empire ended with the execution of Maximilian in 1867, but the unhappy empress survived it 60 years.

Carlow (kär′lō), county (pop. 33,345), 346 sq. mi., SE Republic of Ireland. The chief towns are Carlow, the county town; Bagenalstown, on the Barrow, which forms much of the western boundary of the county; and Tullow, on the Slaney, which crosses the county from north to south. The granitic uplands of the southeast are a conspicuous feature in an otherwise fertile lowland region. Cattle raising, farming, and dairying are the occupations of the region. There are some coal deposits in the west. Organized as a county in the early 13th cent., Carlow was strategically situated on the southern edge of the English Pale. There are remains of medieval castles and ecclesiastical establishments.

Carlow, urban district (pop. 7,707), county town of Co. Carlow, SE Republic of Ireland, on the Barrow river. It is an agricultural market in a dairy region, with sugar refining, flour milling, brewing, and shoe manufacturing. It has a 12th-century castle and is the seat of the Roman Catholic cathedral of the diocese of Kildare and Leighlin. Of strategic importance, Carlow was burned in 1405 and in 1577; in 1778 there was a fierce street battle fought by insurgent United Irishmen.

Carlsbad (kärlz′băd), Ger. *Karlsbad* (kärls′bät), Czech *Karlovy Vary* (kär′lŏvĭ vä′rĭ), city (estimated pop. 45,319), W Bohemia, Czechoslovakia.

A famous health resort, it is one of the best-known spas of Europe. Its hot mineral water is taken particularly for digestive diseases. The city was chartered in 1370 by Emperor Charles IV, who is said to have discovered (1347) its springs.

Carlsbad (kärlz′băd). **1** Resort city (pop. 9,253), S Calif., on the Pacific coast N of San Diego; settled in the 1880s after the discovery of mineral water in the area, inc. 1952. Flowers, fruits, and winter vegetables are grown here. **2** City (pop. 25,541), co. seat of Eddy co., SE N.Mex., on the Pecos river; settled 1888, organized 1889. The region has grazing lands and irrigated farms which yield cotton and alfalfa. The Carlsbad reclamation project, begun in 1906, serves more than 20,000 acres. Carlsbad mines and refines vast quantities of potash and serves the oil industry of neighboring areas.

Carlsbad Caverns National Park, 45,846.59 acres, SE N.Mex., in the foothills of the Guadalupe Mts.; est. as a national monument 1923, as a national park 1930. These limestone caves, with remarkable stalactite and stalagmite formations and tremendous chambers, were discovered c.1900 and have not been completely explored. Seven miles of trail

Temple of the Sun, Carlsbad Caverns National Park.

1129

are electrically lighted. The Big Room, the most majestic of the many chambers, is over a mi. long and encompasses a floor space of 14 acres. Millions of bats inhabit the caves, and their flight, as incredible numbers of bats spiral upward out of the cave, is one of the most interesting attractions.

Carlsbad Decrees, 1819, resolutions of a conference of the ministers of German states, convened and dominated by Prince METTERNICH, the occasion being the murder of August von KOTZEBUE. They provided for uniform press censorship and close supervision of the universities, with the aim of suppressing all liberal agitation against the conservative governments of Germany, particularly in the student organizations (see BURSCHENSCHAFT). The resolutions, ratified by the diet of the German Confederation, remained in force until 1848.

Carlscrona: see KARLSKRONA.

Carlson, Evans Fordyce, 1896–1947, U.S. marine officer, b. Delaware co., N.Y. Enlisting at 16 in the army, he served in the Philippines, in Hawaii, and in France. In the U.S. Marine Corps after 1922, he saw service in Cuba, Nicaragua, Japan, and especially China, where in 1937 he studied guerrilla warfare intensively. Angered by censorship of his reports, he resigned, but in 1941 he applied for recommissioning. During the Second World War he organized and commanded Carlson's Raiders. In 1946 he was promoted brigadier general and retired from service. He wrote *The Chinese Army* (1940) and *Twin Stars of China* (1940).

Carlsruhe: see KARLSRUHE.

Carlstadt, Karlstadt (both: kärl'shtät), or **Karolostadt** (kä′rōlōshtät″), c. 1480–1541, German Protestant reformer, whose original name was Andreas Rudolph Bodenstein. As early as 1516 Carlstadt presented theses denying free will and asserting the doctrine of salvation by grace alone. In 1518 he supported Luther against the attacks of Johann Maier von Eck by maintaining the supremacy of Scripture and in 1519 he appeared with Luther against Eck in the public disputation at Leipzig. He soon became known as the most extreme of the Wittenberg reformers. During Luther's stay at the Wartburg (1521–22) he became the leader at Wittenberg and began to put his radical beliefs into effect. His extreme spiritualization of religion tended to undermine the importance of the church and the sacraments. Upon his return Luther accused Carlstadt of betrayal and restored the more orthodox practices. Accused of revolutionary political activity he fled to Switzerland where he was protected by the Zurich preachers and became professor of theology at Basel.

Carlstadt (kärl'stät), industrial borough (pop. 6,042), NE N.J., SE of Passaic; inc. 1894. Chemicals and plastics are made.

Carlton Club, British political and social club. Founded in 1832, it was long the center of the Conservative party organization. Since the Second World War the club has been primarily social. See study by Sir C. A. Petrie (1955).

Carlyle, Jane Baillie Welsh, 1801–66, English woman of letters; wife of Thomas Carlyle, whom she married in 1826. She possessed a genius for letter writing, manifest in the volumes of her published correspondence (1883, 1924, 1931). See edition of her letters by Trudy Bliss (1950); study by Lawrence Hanson (1952).

Carlyle, Thomas, 1795–1881, English author, b. Scotland. He studied (1809–14) at the Univ. of Edinburgh, intending to enter the ministry, but left when his doubts became too strong. He taught mathematics before returning to Edinburgh in 1818 to study law. However, law gave way to reading in German literature. He was strongly influenced

Thomas Carlyle

by Goethe and the transcendental philosophers and wrote several works interpreting German romantic thought, including a *Life of Schiller* (1825) and a translation (1824) of Goethe's *Wilhelm Meister*. In 1826 he married Jane Baillie Welsh, a well-informed and ambitious woman who did much to further his career. They moved to Jane's farm at Craigenputtock in 1828. There he wrote *Sartor Resartus* (published 1833–34 in *Fraser's Magazine*), in which he told his spiritual autobiography. He saw the material world as mere clothing for the spiritual one. The God of his beliefs was an immanent and friendly ruler of an orderly universe. In denying corporeal reality, Carlyle reflected his revulsion from the materialism of the age. In 1832 Ralph Waldo Emerson went to Craigenputtock and began a friendship with Carlyle which was continued in their famous correspondence. In 1834 the Carlyles moved to London to be near necessary works of reference for the projected *French Revolution*. Finally completed in 1837, the book was received with great acclaim. Although it vividly re-creates scenes of the Revolution, it is not a factual account but a poetic rendering of an event in history. Carlyle extended his view of the divinity of man, particularly in his portraits of the great leaders of the Revolution. In subsequent works he attacked laissez-faire theory and parliamentary government and affirmed his belief in the necessity for strong, paternalistic government. He was convinced that society does change, but that it must do so intelligently, directed by its best men, its "heroes." His lectures, published as *On Heroes, Hero-Worship, and the Heroic in History* (1841), express his view that the great men of the past have intuitively shaped destiny and have been the spiritual leaders of the world. His other works expanded his ideas—*Chartism* (1840); *Past and Present* (1843), contrasting the disorder of modern society with the feudal order of 12th-century England; *Oliver Cromwell's Letters and Speeches* (1845); *Latter-Day Pamphlets* (1850); *Life of John Sterling* (1851); and a massive biography of a hero-king, Frederick the Great, on which he spent the years 1852-65. In 1866 his wife died, and the loss saddened the rest of his life. One of the most important social critics of his day, Carlyle influenced many men of the younger generation, among them Matthew Arnold and Ruskin. His style, one of the most tortuous yet effective in English literature, was a compound of biblical phrases, colloquialisms, Teutonic twists, and his own coinings, arranged in unexpected sequences. See his *Reminiscences* (1881) and numerous collections of his letters and his wife's; biographies by J. A. Froude (4 vols., 1882-84) and D. A. Wilson (6 vols., 1923-34; Vol. VI finished by D. W. MacArthur); studies by Emery Neff (1932), L. M. Young (1935), Eric Bentley (1944), and Julian Symons (1952).

Carlyle, city (pop. 2,903), co. seat of Clinton co., S Ill., on the Kaskaskia river and E of East St. Louis, in a farm and coal area; laid out 1818, inc. 1837. Shoes are made. A state fish hatchery is nearby.

Carmagnola, Francesco Bussone da (fränchäs'kō bōōs-sō'nä dä kärmänyō'lä), c.1380?-1432. Italian CONDOTTIERE. He rendered conspicuous service to Filippo Maria Visconti, duke of Milan, but later fell out with Visconti and entered the service of Venice. After 1425 he commanded Florentine and Venetian forces against Milan. His irresolute conduct of the war led the Venetians to suspect treason, and he was tried by the Council of Ten and was executed.

Carman, Bliss (kär'mūn), 1861-1929, Canadian poet, b. Fredericton, N.B. He studied at the universities of New Brunswick and Edinburgh and at Harvard. While at Harvard (1886-88) he began a friendship with Richard Hovey which later resulted in their joint publication of the series *Songs from Vagabondia* (1894, 1896, 1901). Among numerous volumes of his verse are *Behind the Arras* (1895), the series *Pipes of Pan* (1902-5), and *Echoes from Vagabondia* (1912). The best of these and other poems are collected in *Later Poems* (1921) and *Ballads and Lyrics* (1923). His *Talks on Poetry and Life*, lectures on Canadian literature, was published in 1926. See biography by Odell Shepard (1924); study by James Cappon (1930).

Carman, Harry James, 1884-, American historian and educator, b. Greenfield, Saratoga co., N.Y., grad. Syracuse Univ. (Ph.B., 1909; M.A. and Pd.B., 1914), Ph.D. Columbia, 1919. He was a grade school teacher and a high school principal before becoming an instructor and then an assistant professor at Syracuse Univ. (1914-17). In 1918 he came to Columbia Univ., where he attained professorial rank in 1931. From 1925 to 1931 he was assistant to the dean of Columbia College, and from 1943 to 1950 he was dean. He was appointed a member of the Board of Higher Education of New York city in 1938 and served on the New York State Board of Mediation from 1941 to 1955. Among other works he has written *Social and Economic History of the United States* (2 vols., 1930-34), *Lincoln and the Patronage* (with R. H. Luthin, 1943), *A History of the American People* (with H. C. Syrett, rev. ed., 1962), *A Short History of New York State* (with others, 1957). He has also edited several works concerning early American

agriculture, on which he is a leading authority—Jared Eliot's *Essays upon Field Husbandry in New England* (with Rexford G. Tugwell, 1934), *American Husbandry* (1939), and *Jesse Buel, Agricultural Reformer: Selections from His Writings* (1947). Carman is also the editor of a valuable compilation, *A Guide to the Principal Sources for American Civilization, 1800-1900, in the City of New York* (with A. W. Thompson, 2 vols., "Manuscripts," 1960, and "Printed Sources," 1962).

Carman, town (pop. 1,930), S Man., Canada, on the Boyne river and SW of Winnipeg. It is the center of a farm area.

Carmania, region of ancient Persia: see KERMAN, Iran.

Carmarthen: see CAERMARTHEN.

Carmathians: see KARMATHIANS.

Carmel (kär'mūl), town (pop. 1,442), central Ind., N of Indianapolis.

Carmel, Mount [Heb.=garden land], mountain, NW Israel. It extends c.12 mi. NW from the plain of Esdraelon to the Mediterranean Sea, where it ends in a promontory marking the southern limit of the Bay of Acre. Its highest point is 1,818 ft., and it is one of the most striking physical features of the country. Long an object of veneration, in biblical times it was associated with the lives of the prophets Elijah and Elisha. Isa. 35.2; Amos 9.3; 1 Kings 18. From the mountainside vineyards comes the renowned Mt. Carmel wine. At its foot is the port of Haifa. On its slopes are a Bahaist garden shrine with the tombs of Bab-ed-din and of Abdul Baha and a 19th-century Carmelite monastery.

Carmel-by-the-Sea or **Carmel** (kärměl'), city (pop. 4,580), S Calif., on Carmel Bay and S of Monterey; inc. 1916. It is an artists' and writers' community and has an annual Bach festival. The bay, named

Carmel-by-the-Sea

in 1602 by Carmelite friars in Vizcaíno's expedition, is famed for its beauty. Mission San Carlos Borromeo, the burial place of Father Junípero Serra, is nearby.

Carmelites (kär'mŭlĭts), Roman Catholic order of mendicant friars. They first appear as hermits on Mt. Carmel, Palestine; they were apparently Europeans when their supervision was taken over (c.1150) by St. Berthold. In 1238 they moved to Cyprus, and thence to Western Europe. St. Simon Stock (d. 1265), an Englishman, was their second founder. He transformed them into an order of friars resembling Dominicans and Franciscans and founded convents at Oxford, Cambridge, Paris, and Bologna. They rapidly became prominent in university life. An enclosed order of Carmelite nuns was established. The Carmelites, like other orders, decayed in the 15th cent. They were revived by St. THERESA (of Ávila) and St. JOHN OF THE CROSS in 16th-century Spain. These great contemplatives gave the order a special orientation toward mysticism. Their reformed branch is the Discalced (or Barefoot) Carmelites; it is now more numerous than the Carmelites of the Old Observance. The Discalced Carmelites cultivate the contemplative life, in all aspects, and they have produced many works on mystical theology. St. THERESA (of Lisieux) is the well-known modern Discalced Carmelite. In 1790 the first community came to the United States and settled near Port Tobacco, Md. In 1959 there were 74 communities (most of them Discalced) and 15,000 Carmelite tertiaries in the United States. See E. Allison Peers, *Spirit of Flame* (1944).

Carmel Valley, uninc. village (pop. 1,143), W central Calif., SSW of Salinas.

Carmel Woods, uninc. residential village (pop. 1,043), W Calif., S of Santa Cruz.

Carmen Sylva: see ELIZABETH, queen of Rumania.

Carmi (kär'mī). **1** Father of Achan. Joshua 7.1,18; 1 Chron. 2.7. In spite of textual difficulties this is probably the Carmi of 1 Chron. 4.1. **2** Reuben's son. Gen. 46.9; Ex. 6.14; Num. 26.6; 1 Chron. 5.3.

Carmi (kär'mī), city (pop. 6,152), co. seat of White co., SE Ill., ESE of Mt. Vernon on the Little Wabash; platted 1816, inc. 1819. It is a rail and trade center in a farm and oil-producing area.

Carmichael, uninc. city (pop. 20,455), N central Calif., ENE of Sacramento and on the American river. It has boatyards and nurseries.

carmina burana: see GOLIARDIC SONGS.

Carmona, Antonio Oscar de Fragoso (äntô'nyō ŭshkär' dù frägō'sō kärmō'nù), 1869–1951, Portuguese marshal and political leader. An able soldier, he rose to the rank of general. When Gen. Manuel de Oliveira Gomes da Costa led a successful revolution in 1926, Carmona was made foreign minister in the new government. Shortly afterward he overthrew Gomes da Costa and served (1926–28) as head of the provisional government. Elected president in 1928, Carmona won (1935, 1942, 1949) each successive election. The regime he established was dictatorial, dominated after 1928 by Antonio de Oliveira SALAZAR.

Carmona (kärmō'nä), town (pop. 29,009), Seville prov., SW Spain, in Andalusia. It is an agricultural center. Ferdinand III of Castile took Carmona from the Moors in 1247. It has a Moorish and a Renaissance city gate and the imposing ruins of an alcazar. A Roman necropolis was discovered nearby in 1881.

Carnac (kärnäk'), town (estimated pop. 3,393), Morbihan dept., NW France, in Brittany, at the foot of the Quiberon peninsula. It is the site of remarkable MEGALITHIC MONUMENTS, particularly the MENHIR. The menhirs, some of them 20 ft. high, extend along the coast in 11 parallel rows 1,100 yd. long. They were formerly ascribed to the druids.

Carnaim (kär'naĭm): see ASHTEROTH KARNAIM.

Carnap, Rudolf, 1891–, German-American philosopher, b. Wuppertal, Ph.D. Univ. of Jena, 1921. He taught philosophy at the Univ. of Vienna (1926–31) and at the Univ. of Prague (1931–35). Since coming to the United States he has taught at the Univ. of Chicago (1936–52) and at the Univ. of California at Los Angeles (1954–62). Carnap is one of the most influential of contemporary philosophers; he is known as a founder of LOGICAL POSITIVISM and has made important contributions to logic, semantics, and the philosophy of science. In *Logische Syntax der Sprache* (1934; Eng. tr., *The Logical Syntax of Language,* 1937) he defined philosophy as "the logic of the sciences" and considered it a general language whose only legitimate concern could be to describe and criticize the language of the particular sciences. All propositions were held to be either tautological (embodying logical or mathematical systems), scientific (embodying philosophy properly understood), or nonsensical (embodying the nonverifiable propositions of traditional philosophy). Through an analysis of scientific, logical, and mathematical language he revealed the inadequacies of everyday speech. In recent years Carnap modified this extreme view, which rejects almost all of traditional philosophy. His other works include *Introduction to Semantics* (1942), *Meaning and Necessity* (1947; 2d ed., 1956), *Logical Foundations of Probability* (1950), and *Einfuhrung in die symbolische Logik* (1954; Eng. tr., *Introduction to Symbolic Logic and its Applications,* 1958). See P. A. Schilpp, ed., *The Philosophy of Rudolf Carnap* (1963).

Carnarvon, George Edward Stanhope Molyneux Herbert, 5th **earl of** (kärnär'vùn), 1866–1923, English Egyptologist. With Howard Carter he excavated in the Valley of the Kings from 1906 to 1922. The final and most famous of their discoveries was the tomb of Tut-ankh-amen. Lord Carnarvon died before it was thoroughly explored. He collaborated on the report *Five Years' Explorations at Thebes* (1912).

Carnarvon, Henry Howard Molyneux Herbert, 4th **earl of,** 1831–90, British statesman. As colonial secretary (1866–67) under the earl of Derby he promoted the bill for confederation of the North American colonies and in the same office (1874–78) under Disraeli attempted federation in South Africa. His policy as lord lieutenant of Ireland (1885–86) was conciliatory but failed to stem Irish nationalism. See biography by A. H. Hardinge (1925).

Carnarvon, Wales: see CAERNARVON.

Carnatic (kärnä'tĭk), region, SW India, on the Arabian Sea. The early European settlers sometimes applied the term Carnatic to all of S India. The region was the site of the earliest European settlements in India, those of Portugal. During the 18th cent. the Carnatic plains became the arena for the struggle between Great Britain and France for supremacy in India.

carnation: see PINK.

carnauba, WAX obtained from the wax palm or carnauba (*Copernicia cerifera*) of Brazil. It is secreted by the leaves, apparently in defense against the hot winds and droughts of its native habitat, and the resultant coating is removed by drying and flailing. The hardest, highest-melting natural wax known, its' many commercial uses include the production of polishes, lubricants, phonograph records, plastics, carbon paper, and floor waxes. The United States is the major importer. A similar wax is obtained from the trunk of *Ceroxylon andicola,* the wax palm of the Andes.

Carnavalet (kärnävälä′), municipal museum of Paris, France. Housed in a mansion built by Bullant and by Goujon, who sculptured its beautiful façade, it is situated in the once fashionable Marais. The mansion was bought (1578) by a Breton named Kernevenoy, whose name was corrupted into Carnavalet. It later was the home of Mme de Sévigné.

Carneades (kärnē′ùdēz), 213–129 B.C., Greek philosopher, b. Cyrene. He studied at Athens under Diogenes the Stoic, but reacted against Stoicism and joined the ACADEMY, where he taught a skepticism similar to that of Pyrrho. While denying the possibility of absolute certainty in knowledge, he held that probable knowledge was available to guide the actions of men. He recognized three degrees of probability, and his work anticipated modern discussions of the nature of empirical knowledge.

Carnegie, Andrew (kärnä′gē), 1835–1919, American industrialist and philanthropist, b. Dunfermline, Scotland. His father, a weaver, finding it increasingly difficult to get work in Scottish factories, brought (1848) his family to Allegheny (now Pittsburgh), Pa. Andrew first worked in a cotton mill as a bobbin boy, then advanced himself as a telegrapher, and became (1859) a superintendent for the Pennsylvania RR. He resigned (1865) his railroad position to give personal attention to the investments he had made (1864) in iron manufactures. By 1873 he had recognized America's need for steel and, concentrating on steel production, began his acquisition of firms which were later consolidated into the Carnegie Steel Company. Carnegie's success was due in part to efficient business methods, to his able lieutenants, and to close alliances with railroads. Another factor was his partnership with Henry C. FRICK. Carnegie, concentrating on production rather than stock-market manipulations, further expanded his plants and consolidated his hold in the depression of 1893–97. By 1900 the Carnegie Steel Company was producing one quarter of all the steel in the United States and controlled iron mines, coke ovens, ore ships, and railroads. It was in these circumstances that the U.S. Steel Corp. was formed to buy Carnegie out. He had long been willing to sell—at his own price—and in 1901 he transferred possession for $250,000,000 in bonds and retired from business. He lived a large part of each year after 1887 in Scotland on his great estate on Dornoch Firth. His essay "The Gospel

of Wealth" (1889) set forth his idea that rich men are "trustees" of their wealth and should administer it for the good of the public. Carnegie's benefactions (totaling about $350,000,000) included Carnegie Hall (1892) in New York city, the Carnegie Institution of Washington (1902), the Carnegie Hero Fund Commission (1904), the Carnegie Foundation for the Advancement of Teaching (1905), the Carnegie Endowment for International Peace (1910), and over 2,800 libraries. See his autobiography (1920); biographies by Burton J. Hendrick (1932) and A. F. Harlow (1953); *A Manual of the Public Benefactions of Andrew Carnegie* (1919).

Andrew Carnegie

Carneades

Carnegie. 1 (kär′nŭgē) Town (pop. 1,500), SW Okla., on the Washita river and SW of Oklahoma City, in an agricultural area. Some quarrying and lumbering is carried on. **2** (kärnä′gē) Industrial borough (pop. 11,887), SW Pa., SW of Pittsburgh; inc. 1894. A steel town, it also mines coal and manufactures metal products and chemicals. The Neville House was the home of Gen. John Neville, an officer in the French and Indian and Revolutionary wars. The borough was named for Andrew Carnegie.

Carnegie Corporation of New York, established in 1911 under the N.Y. state laws to administer Andrew Carnegie's remaining personal fortune for philanthropic purposes. Initially endowed with $125,000,000 the residual estate added another $10,000,000 to the foundation. In 1960 its endowment exceeded $261,000,000. Carnegie directed the foundation's activities until his death; in accordance with his early interests he established the policy of grants for free public libraries and church organs. In the years following his death the trustees followed a more general policy leading to "the advancement and diffusion of knowledge and understanding." The foundation has financed many studies in the areas of its main interest—

U.S. education and underprivileged groups; a notable study is that of the American Negro by the Swedish scholar Gunnar Myrdal, completed in 1944. Many funds have been channeled through the other Carnegie foundations, with grants to philanthropic institutions and to colleges and universities. Since 1917 a small portion of the foundation's income has been used for studies within the British Commonwealth.

Carnegie Endowment for International Peace, established 1910 by a gift of $10,000,000 from Andrew Carnegie to "hasten the abolition of international war" and to promote peace. It has financed the publication and distribution of books on international law and relations; the 150-volume economic and social history of World War I and a multivolumed series on Canadian-American relations are two of its major undertakings. It has also engaged in teacher and student exchange programs. In recent years the endowment has focused on the study of international organizations.

Carnegie Institute of Technology, at Pittsburgh; partly coeducational; founded 1900, opened 1905 with funds from Andrew Carnegie, chartered 1912. It includes Margaret Morrison Carnegie College (for women; 1906), College of Engineering, and a noted College of Fine Arts. Among its programs are metal and coal research laboratories and a nuclear research center.

Carnegie Institution of Washington, D.C., chartered 1902 and 1904, organized 1904, endowed by Andrew Carnegie and the Carnegie Corp. to encourage investigation, research, and discovery. Its projects, directed by eminent scientists, lie in the fields of astronomy (with Mt. Wilson Observatory), terrestrial and biological sciences, and historical research. It has units at Baltimore, Boston, Cold Spring Harbor, N.Y., and Stanford Univ.

carnelian (kärnē′lyùn) or **cornelian** (kôr–, kùr–), variety of red CHALCEDONY, used as a gem. It is distinguished from SARD by the shade of red, carnelian being bright red and sard brownish. The red coloring is apparently caused by iron oxide.

Carney, Md.: see PARKVILLE.

Carniola (kärnēō′lù), Croatian *Kranj* (krä′nyù), Ger. *Krain* (krīn), historic region, Slovenia, NW Yugoslavia, formerly an Austrian crownland. Ljubljana was its chief city. It is largely a mountainous area with an overwhelmingly Slovenian population. The history of Carniola is closely linked with that of SLOVENIA. Part of the Roman province of Pannonia, Carniola was settled by the Slovenes in the 6th cent. It became a march or margraviate in the 10th cent. and in 1269 was acquired by Ottocar II of Bohemia. It passed to the Hapsburgs in 1282 and was made (1364) a titular duchy. It was raised to a crownland in 1849 and remained in Austria until 1918. After the First World War Carniola was divided between Italy and Yugoslavia, but the Italian part passed to Yugoslavia in 1947.

Carnion (kär′nēŏn): see ASHTEROTH KARNAIM.

carnival, communal celebration, especially the religious celebration in Roman Catholic countries that takes place just before LENT. Since early times, carnivals have been accompanied by parades, masquerades, pageants, and other forms of revelry that had their origins in pre-Christian pagan rites, particularly fertility rites that were

Carnival celebrations in a south German town.

connected with the coming of spring and the rebirth of vegetation. One of the first recorded instances of an annual spring festival is the festival of Osiris in Egypt; it commemorated the renewal of life brought about by the yearly flooding of the Nile. In Athens, during the 6th cent. B.C., a yearly celebration in honor of the god Dionysus featured a float dedicated to him which was wheeled through the city streets to the accompaniment of songs, dances, and ribald merrymaking. This is the first recorded instance of the traditional use of floats for spring festivals. It was during the Roman Empire that carnivals reached an unparalleled peak of civil disorder and wanton freedom. Developing out of folk celebrations and the Greek mysteries of Dionysus, the major Roman carnivals were the Bacchanalia, the Saturnalia, and the Lupercalia. In Europe the tradition of spring fertility celebrations persisted well into Christian times, particularly in Teutonic regions, where carnivals reached their peak during the 14th and 15th cent. Because carnivals are deeply rooted in pagan superstitions and the folklore of Europe, the Catholic Church found it impossible to stamp them out and ultimately was driven to the position of having to accept many of them as part of Church activity. The immediate consequence of Church influence may be seen in the medieval Feast of Fools, which included a mock Mass and a blasphemous impersonation of Church officials, and the Feast of the Ass, which retained many pagan rites and was at times outrageously bawdy. Eventually, however, the power of the Church made itself felt, and the carnival was stripped of its most offending elements. The Church succeeded in dominating the activities of the carnivals, and eventually they became directly related to the coming of Lent. The

MARDI GRAS (Shrove Tuesday) remains the most typical carnival in the world today. In recent times, the term *carnival* has also been loosely applied to include local festivals, traveling circuses, bazaars, and other celebrations of a joyous nature regardless of their purpose or their season.

carnivorous plants: see BLADDERWORT; PITCHER PLANT; VENUS'S-FLYTRAP.

Carnot, Hippolyte (ēpôlēt' kärnō'), 1801–88, French statesman; son of Lazare Carnot. He shared his father's exile after 1815 and returned to France in 1823. A follower of Claude Henri de Saint-Simon, he participated in the July Revolution of 1830. He came to oppose the July Monarchy and was elected three times as an opposition member of the chamber of deputies. He took part in the radical agitation that led to the February Revolution of 1848 and became minister of education in the provisional government. Entering (1864) the *corps législatif*, he joined the liberal opposition to Napoleon III, after whose downfall he became a member of the constituent assembly (1871) and then a senator for life (1875).

Carnot, Lazare Nicolas Marguerite (läzär' nēkôlä' märgǔrēt'), 1753–1823, French revolutionist, called the great Carnot. A military engineer by training, Carnot became the military genius of the Revolution and was chiefly responsible for the success of the French in the FRENCH REVOLUTIONARY WARS. A member of the Legislative Assembly, the Convention, and the Committee of Public Safety, he made himself almost indispensable through his military knowledge. After the fall of Robespierre he managed to avoid punishment for his own part in the Terror and became a member of the DIRECTORY. The coup d'état of 18 Fructidor (1797) caused Carnot to flee abroad. He returned in 1799 and served as minister of war (1800) and in the Tribunate under Napoleon. In the next few years he wrote several works on mathematics and military engineering; in 1810 appeared his masterpiece, *De la défense des places fortes*, long considered the classic work on fortification. Carnot was the best-known advocate of the principle of active defense. In 1814 he returned to active service and conducted the defense of Antwerp. In the Hundred Days he served as minister of the interior. Exiled after the Restoration, he died in Magdeburg. See biographies by Huntley Dupre (1940) and Marcel Reinhard (2 vols., 1950–52, in French).

Carnot, Nicolas Léonard Sadi (nēkôlä' läônär' sädē'), 1796–1832, French physicist, a founder of modern thermodynamics; son of Lazare N. M. Carnot. His famous work on the motive power of heat (*Réflexions sur la puissance motrice du feu*, 1824) is concerned with the relation between heat and mechanical energy. Carnot devised an ideal engine in which a gas is allowed to expand to do work, absorbing heat in the process, and is expanded again without transfer of heat but with a temperature drop. The gas is then compressed, heat being given off, and finally it is returned to its original condition by another compression, accompanied by a rise in temperature. This series of operations, known as Carnot's cycle, shows that even under ideal conditions a heat engine cannot convert all the heat energy supplied it into mechanical energy; some of the heat energy must be re-

jected. This is an illustration of the second law of thermodynamics. Carnot's work anticipated that of Joule, Kelvin, and others.

Carnot, Sadi, 1837–94, French statesman, president of the Third Republic (1887–94); son of Hippolyte Carnot. As minister of public works (1880–85) and of finance (1886), he remained untainted by the financial scandals of the time. He succeeded Jules Grévy in the presidency; his tenure was disturbed by the agitation for General

Sadi Carnot

Boulanger and by the Panama Canal scandal. He was assassinated by an Italian anarchist. Jean Paul Pierre Casimir-Perier succeeded him.

Caro, Annibale (än-nē'bälä kä'rō), 1507–66, Italian poet, friend of Cellini, Varchi, and Bembo. He is best known for his translation of the *Aeneid* and for his opportunistic poems in praise of opposing royal houses.

Caro or Karo, Joseph ben Ephraim, 1488–1575, eminent Jewish codifier of law, b. Toledo, Spain, d. Safed, Palestine. His literary works rank among the masterpieces of rabbinical literature. Chief among them are *Bet Yosef* [house of Joseph] and *Shulhan Aruk* [the table set], parts of which are still used as the authoritative code for orthodox religious and legal disputes. This code owes its fame and popularity as much to the opposition it aroused and the many commentaries it inspired as it does to its merits.

Caro (kâ'rō), village (pop. 3,534), co. seat of Tuscola co., S Mich., SE of Bay City; settled 1867, inc. 1871. It is a farm trade center, and beet sugar and canned goods are produced. A state hospital is here.

carob (kǎ'rǔb), leguminous evergreen tree (*Ceratonia siliqua*) of the PULSE family, native to Mediterranean regions but cultivated in other warm climates, including Florida and California. The large red pods have been used for food for animal and man since prehistoric times. The pods and their extracted content have numerous common names, e.g., locust bean gum and St.-John's-bread—the latter from the belief that they may have been the "locust" eaten by John the Baptist in the wilderness (Mark 1.6). Carob is used also for curing tobacco, in papermaking, and as a stabilizer in food products. It has been claimed that the seeds were the original of the carat, the measure of weight for precious jewels and metals.

Carol I, 1839–1914, prince (1866–81) and first king (1881–1914) of Rumania, of the house of Hohenzollern-Sigmaringen. He is also called Charles I. A Prussian officer, he was elected to succeed the deposed Alexander John Cuza as prince of Rumania. He reformed the Rumanian constitution and, siding with Russia in the war of 1877–78 against Turkey, obtained at the Congress of Berlin (see BERLIN, CONGRESS OF) full independence for Rumania, which he declared a kingdom in 1881. Exploitation of Rumanian oil fields began in his reign. Economic development, however, did not improve the lot of the peasants, and an uprising in 1907 was cruelly suppressed. Carol's wife was Princess ELIZABETH of Wied. He was succeeded by his nephew Ferdinand.

Carol I

Carol II

Carol II, 1893–1953, king of Rumania, son of King Ferdinand. While crown prince, he contracted a morganatic marriage with Mme Zizi Labrino but divorced her to marry (1921) Princess Helen of Greece. He soon formed a liaison with Mme LUPESCU, with whom he lived in Paris after being forced (1925) to renounce his right of succession. On the death (1927) of King Ferdinand, Carol's son MICHAEL became king, but Carol, having divorced Queen Helen in 1928, returned to Rumania in 1930, supplanted his son, and had himself proclaimed king *de jure* since 1927. A turbulent period began (see RUMANIA). In 1938 Carol constituted a royal dictatorship. A contest between the king and the fascist IRON GUARD was then fought out by assassinations and massacres on both sides. Forced to call on Ion ANTONESCU to form a government (1940), Carol was deposed and fled abroad with Mme Lupescu. Michael once

more became king. In 1947, in Brazil, Carol married Mme Lupescu. He died in Portugal.

carol, popular hymn, of joyful nature, in celebration of an occasion such as May Day, Easter, or especially Christmas. The earliest English carols date from the 15th cent. Carols exist in all Christian nations; many may be from pagan sources. Despite the folk-song character of true carols, many Christmas hymns composed in the 19th cent. have been called carols. The oldest printed carol is the *Boar's Head Carol,* printed in 1521 by Wynkyn de Worde. Carols of French origin are called also noels. See Edmonstoune Duncan, *The Story of the Carol* (1911); Percy Dearmer, Ralph Vaughan Williams, and Martin Shaw, *The Oxford Book of Carols* (1928); R. L. Greene, *The Early English Carols* (1935) and *A Selection of English Carols* (1962).

Carolan, Turlough: see O'CAROLAN, TURLOUGH.

Carol City, uninc. city (pop. 21,749), SE Fla., NW of Miami.

Caroleen, uninc. textile-mill village (pop. 1,168), SW N.C., W of Charlotte.

Carolina, North and **South:** see NORTH CAROLINA and SOUTH CAROLINA.

Carolina Beach, town (pop. 1,192), SE N.C., on the Atlantic coast S of Wilmington. It is a beach resort and fishing town.

Carolina campaign, 1780–81, of the American Revolution. After Sir Henry Clinton had captured CHARLESTON, he returned to New York, leaving a British force under Cornwallis to subordinate the Carolinas to British control. Cornwallis swept north and capped his success in the battle of Camden on Aug. 16, 1780. The American force was completely routed, the gallant Baron de Kalb was mortally wounded, and the American commander, Horatio Gates, fled from the field, outdistancing officers and men in retreat. Patriot defense was broken in the Carolinas, where only the swift and secretly moving guerrilla bands of Francis Marion, Thomas Sumter, and Andrew Pickens harassed the invaders. The American cause spurted upward, however, with the remarkable battle of Kings Mt. (Oct. 7, 1780), where bands of frontier riflemen under Isaac Shelby, John Sevier, and William Campbell surrounded a British raiding party under Patrick Ferguson; the British commander fell, and his men surrendered. This victory prefaced the campaign fought in North Carolina by Gen. Nathanael Greene (who had been appointed to succeed Gates) and his lieutenants, notably Light-Horse Harry Lee and Daniel Morgan. It was Morgan who at the head of a raiding party met and all but annihilated Cornwallis's raiders under Banastre Tarleton at Cowpens (Jan. 17, 1781). Cornwallis pushed north and at Guilford Courthouse (March 15, 1781) won over Greene a Pyrrhic victory; the British had technically won but had to retreat to British-held Wilmington, N.C., and then to Virginia. Greene then joined the guerrilla leaders in freeing South Carolina. Again the Americans were defeated—by Lord Rawdon at Hobkirks Hill (April 25, 1781) and by Col. Alexander Stewart at Eutaw Springs (Sept. 8, 1781)—and again the British had to retreat, returning to Charleston. The campaign was a British failure and was the more a triumph for the patriots because it set the stage for the YORKTOWN CAMPAIGN.

Caroline, Fort: see FORT CAROLINE.

Caroline Affair. In 1837 a group of men led by William Lyon MACKENZIE broke into rebellion in Upper Canada (now Ontario), demanding a more democratic government. There was much sympathy for their cause in the United States, and a small steamer, the *Caroline*, owned by U.S. citizens; carried men and supplies from the U.S. side of the Niagara river to the Canadian rebels on Navy Island just above Niagara Falls. On the night of Dec. 29, 1837, a small group of British and Canadians loyal to the Upper Canadian government crossed the river to the U.S. side where the *Caroline* was moored, loosed her, set fire to her, and sent her over the falls. One American was killed in the incident. Americans on the border were aroused to intense anti-British feeling, and soldiers under Gen. Winfield Scott were rushed to the scene to prevent violent American action. The affair passed over, though it had an aftermath, when one of the men who had taken part in the attack boasted of that fact when he was in the United States and was arrested as a criminal. That matter, too, was smoothed over, but the Caroline Affair and the Aroostook War helped to make relations with Great Britain very tense in the years before the Webster-Ashburton Treaty.

Caroline Islands, archipelago (c.525 sq. mi.; pop. 48,446) W Pacific; included in 1947 in the U.S. Trust Territory of the Pacific Islands under United Nations trusteeship. It comprises two single volcanic islands (Kusaie and PONAPE), three major island groups (PALAU, TRUK, and YAP), some 30 atolls, and numerous islets. The islands are fertile and produce coconuts, sugar cane, and tapioca. There are deposits of phosphate, guano, bauxite, and iron. The chief exports are dried bonito, copra, and tapioca. Most of the natives are Micronesians, and a few are Polynesians. Discovered by the Spaniards in 1526, the islands were under Spanish control from 1886 until after the Spanish-American War, when they were sold (1899) to Germany. They were occupied in 1914 by the Japanese, who in 1922 were given a mandate over them. Japan annexed the group in 1935. In the Second World War, Palau, Truk, Yap, and Ulithi were heavily bombed.

Caroline of Anspach (äns′päk), 1683–1737, queen consort of George II of England, daughter of the margrave of Brandenburg-Ansbach. She married George in 1705 while he was electoral prince of Hanover and bore him three sons and five daughters. After his accession she gave active support to Robert WALPOLE. Her political influence over the king lasted until her death. See biographies by R. L. Arkell (1939) and Peter Quennell (1940).

Caroline of Brunswick, 1768–1821, consort of GEORGE IV of England. The daughter of Charles William Ferdinand, duke of Brunswick, she married George (then prince of Wales) in 1795. She bore him one daughter, but the couple separated in 1796, and Caroline, deprived of her child, lived in retirement for several years and spent some years abroad. Reports to her moral discredit occasioned a commission of inquiry (1806), which found her innocent but imprudent. On the acces-

sion of George IV (1820) she refused to abdicate her rights as queen, and the government instituted proceedings against her in the House of Lords for divorce on the grounds of adultery. Caroline was frivolous and very possibly guilty of the charge, but her persecution by a profligate husband aroused popular sympathy for her, and the bill was dropped. See biography by H. S. Coxe (1939); studies by W. D. Bowman (1930) and Joanna Richardson (1960).

Carolingian architecture and art. In the 8th cent. a gradual change appeared in Western culture and art, reaching its apex under CHARLEMAGNE. The new architecture, inspired by the forms of antiquity, abandoned the small boxlike shapes of the Merovingian period and used instead spacious basilicas often intersected by vast transepts. In some churches, such as Fulda and Cologne, the central nave ended in semicircular apses. An innovation of Carolingian builders, which was to be of incalculable importance for the later Middle Ages, was the emphasis given to the western extremity of the church. The façade, flanked symmetrically by towers, or simply the exterior of a massive complex (westwork), became the focal point of the structure. The function of the westwork is still debated. It had an elevation of several stories, the lowest a vaulted vestibule to the church proper, and above, a room reached by spiral staircases, which may have served as a chapel reserved for high dignitaries. The outstanding structure of the Carolingian period still in existence is the palatine chapel at Aachen, dedicated by Pope Leo III in the year

The palatine chapel at Aachen is an outstanding example of surviving Carolingian architecture.

805. It is centralized in plan and surmounted by an octagonal dome. The throne of the emperor stood overlooking the central space within an upper gallery, which could be reached directly from the imperial apartments. The design of the palatine chapel appears to have been based in part on the 5th-century Church of San Vitale in Ravenna. Other important structures still partly preserved, or known through documentary evidence, include the churches of Saint-Denis, Corbie, Centula (Saint-Riquier), and Reichenau. The best-preserved artistic achievements of the age are works of small dimensions—manuscript illumination, ivory carving, and metalwork. Besides the imperial court, at Aachen, the leading centers of art were the monasteries in Tours, Metz, Saint-Denis, and near Rheims. The earliest liturgical manuscripts of the Carolingian period, such as the Gospel book signed by the scribe Godescalc (written between 781 and 783), are characterized by a tentative and not always successful fusion of ornamental motifs of chiefly Anglo-Saxon and Irish origin and by figures derived from antiquity. Full-page portraits of the four evangelists were often designed. Later Carolingian miniatures show an increasing familiarity with the heritage of late antiquity and in some instances are perhaps influenced by Byzantine art. The manuscripts owe much of their beauty to the new minuscule form of writing, remarkable for its clarity and form. The most-influential work was the Utrecht Psalter, illustrated in a mode of nervous and flickering intensity quite unparalleled in earlier Western art. Closely allied in style to the miniatures were the ivory carvings, many of them originally part of book covers. Metalwork objects are rarer, although literary evidence shows that goldsmiths and enamel workers were active. The large golden altar of Sant' Ambrogio in Milan (executed in 835), the portable altar of Arnulf (now in Munich), several splendid book covers, and other sumptuously decorated objects provide insight into the artistic accomplishments of the period, which ended in the late 9th cent. See A. K. Porter, *Medieval Architecture: Its Origin and Development* (Vol. I, 1909); Howard Saalman, *Medieval Architecture* (1962); Adolph Goldschmidt, *German Illumination* (Vol. I: *Carolingian Period*, 1928); Roger Hinks, *Carolingian Art* (1935).

Carolingians (kăr´ŭlĭn´jĭnz), dynasty of Frankish rulers, founded in the 7th cent. by PEPIN OF LANDEN, who, as mayor of the palace, ruled Austrasia for Dagobert I. His descendants, PEPIN OF HÉRISTAL, CHARLES MARTEL, CARLOMAN (d. 754), and PEPIN THE SHORT, continued to govern the territories under the nominal kingship of the MEROVINGIANS. In 751 Pepin the Short deposed Childeric III and became sole Frankish king. The family was at its height when represented by Pepin's son, CHARLEMAGNE, who was crowned emperor in 800. His empire was divided by the Treaty of Verdun (843) after the death of his son, Emperor LOUIS I, among Louis's three sons. LOTHAIR I inherited the imperial title and the middle part of the empire. LOUIS THE GERMAN founded a dynasty that ruled in Germany till 911, his successors being CHARLES III (Charles the Fat), ARNULF, and LOUIS THE CHILD. The third son of Louis I, CHARLES II (Charles the Bald),

founded the French Carolingian dynasty, which ruled, with interruptions, till 987. Its rulers were LOUIS II (Louis the Stammerer), LOUIS III, CARLO-MAN (d. 884), CHARLES III (Charles the Simple), LOUIS IV (Louis d'Outremer), LOTHAIR (941–86), and LOUIS V. In the Carolingian period were founded the institutions and the historical trends that marked much of the later Middle Ages. Feudal principles were formulated, and a landed economy was firmly established. The kings and emperors worked closely with church officials; Charlemagne became the pope's protector. See Louis Halphen, *Charlemagne et l'empire carolingien* (1949); Heinrich Fichtenau, *The Carolingian Empire* (1949; Eng. tr., 1957); E. S. Duckett, *Carolingian Portraits* (1962).

Carolus-Duran (kärôlüs´-dürä´), whose real name was **Charles Auguste Émile Durand** (shärl´ ōgüst´ āmēl´ dürä´), 1837–1917, French painter. He studied in Lille and Paris and in 1861 won a pension and traveled in Italy and Spain. Best known as the teacher of many famous painters, he became (1905) the director of the Académie de France à Rome. There are numerous portraits by him in the Louvre and a portrait of Mrs. William Astor in the Metropolitan Museum.

Carondelet, Francisco Luis Hector, baron de (kŭrŏndŭlĕt´, Span. fränthē´skō lwēs´ ĕktôr bärōn´ dä kärōndälĕt´), c.1748–1807, governor of Louisiana (1791–97) and West Florida (1791–95), b. Noyelles, Flanders. He married into the Las Casas family, prominent in Spanish colonial affairs. He came to New Orleans from the governorship of Salvador and was unfortunately not well informed as to Louisiana problems. Ignorant of the English language and local customs, and faced with conflicting rumors of American hostility, he became convinced in 1792 that the Americans were planning to invade Louisiana. With unwarranted aggressiveness, he stirred up the Indians of the Southwest, concluding an alliance with the four great tribes and establishing Spanish posts in their territory. He revived intrigues with Kentucky frontiersmen looking toward the establishment of an independent state in the West. Relations between Spain and the United States were severely taxed. After Carondelet was replaced by Manuel Gayoso de Lemos, he was made president of the *audiencia* and governor general of Quito (1799–1807). See A. P. Whitaker, *The Spanish-American Frontier, 1783–1795* (1927).

Carossa, Hans (häns´ kärô´sä), 1878–1956, German poet and novelist. His autobiographical novel *Childhood* (1922; Eng. tr., 1930) and its sequels (1928, 1941) are noted for clear graceful style. *Fuhrung und Geleit* [guidance and companionship] (1933) contains warm vignettes of his literary mentors and friends, among them Mann, Rilke, and Hesse. Other works are *A Roumanian Diary* (1924; Eng. tr., 1929), the novel *Doctor Gion* (1931; Eng. tr., 1933), and volumes of poems (1938, 1949).

carp, hardy fresh-water fish, the largest member of the MINNOW family. A native of Asia, the carp was introduced in Europe and America and has become so well established that it is called the English sparrow of the fishes. The common American carp, also called German carp, is the European carp of which many variations in color and form have de-

Carp

veloped. Carp have four barbels ("whiskers") around the mouth and are usually dark greenish or brown (occasionally yellowish or silvery) with red on some of the fins. Most carp are scaled, although the mirror carp has only a few scattered scales and the leather carp has none. They are bottom-feeders, eating chiefly aquatic plants but also insects and small animals, and their habit of rooting in the mud often makes the water unfit for the feeding and spawning of other fishes. However, they are valued commercially as food fish, especially in Europe, where they are sometimes bred and raised for this purpose. Carp may reach 3 ft. in length and 25 lb. in weight.

Carpaccio, Vittore (vĕt-tō'rä kärpät'chō), c.1450–1522, Venetian painter, influenced by Gentile and Giovanni Bellini. His delightful narrative paintings reflect the pageantry of 15th-century Venice. They also offer a fanciful view of the Orient, gained through contemporary drawings. His style is notable for its rich color, luminosity, and wealth of detail. Among his best paintings are the cycle depicting the life of St. Ursula, the St. George series, the *Presentation in the Temple* (all: Academy, Venice); scenes from the life of St. Stephen (Louvre; Brera, Milan); *Meditation on the Passion* (Metropolitan Mus.); *Saint Reading* and other works (National Gall. of Art, Washington, D.C.). See biography by Pompeo Molmenti and Gustav Ludwig (Eng. tr., 1907).

Carpathians (kärpā'thēŭnz) or **Carpathian Mountains**, Pol. and Ukr. *Karpaty*, Rum. *Carpatii*, major mountain system of central and E Europe, forming an arc, c.930 mi. long, which encloses the Danubian plain in the north and the east. The foothills (Little Carpathians and White Carpathians) rise in Slovakia, N of the Danube at Bratislava, and extend northeast to the Polish-Czechoslovak border. The Northern Carpathians, comprising the BESKIDS and the TATRA, run east along the Polish-Czechoslovak frontier and southeast through W Ukraine; in Rumania they are continued by the Southern Carpathians or the TRANSYLVANIAN ALPS, which prolong the system, extending SW to the Danube at the Iron Gate. The highest peaks are the Gerlachovka (8,737 ft.) in the Tatra and Mt. Moldoveanul (8,316 ft.) in the Transylvanian Alps. Heavily wooded, the Carpathians are rich in minerals and mineral spas.

Carpathian Ukraine: see TRANSCARPATHIAN OBLAST.
Carpathus: see KARPATHOS.
Carpatii: see CARPATHIANS.
Carpeaux, Jean Baptiste (zhä' bätĕst' kärpō'), 1827–75, French sculptor and painter. He studied with François Rude, won the Prix de Rome, and rose to fame with his *Ugolino* (Tuileries), done in Italy under the inspiration of Michelangelo. A favorite of the Second Empire, he received many commissions. Best known is *The Dance* on the façade of the Opéra, Paris. His *Neapolitan Shell-Fisher* and his portrait busts of Napoleon III, Dumas fils, Gérôme, and Empress Eugenie are in the Louvre, along with numerous paintings, including *Bal costumé aux Tuileries, Les Trois Souverains,* and several portraits. The works of Carpeaux exhibit a freedom and force which distinguish them from the banality of his period. See study by Édouard Sarradin (1927, in French).

Carpentaria, Gulf of (kärpŭntâ'rēŭ), arm of the Arafura Sea, indenting the north coast of Australia, between Arnhem Land peninsula and Cape York Peninsula. It has an average width of 300 mi. On its eastern shore is located a vast bauxite deposit.

Carpenter, Edward, 1844–1929, English author, educated at Cambridge. Although ordained in 1869, he became a Fabian socialist in 1874 and renounced religion. Among his works on social reform are *Towards Democracy* (1883–1902), a long unrhymed poem revealing the influence of his friend Walt Whitman; *England's Ideal* (1887); *Civilization: Its Cause and Cure* (1889); and *Love's Coming of Age* (1896). See the autobiographical

The Dream of St. Ursula by Vittore Carpaccio.

My Days and Dreams (1916); study by Tom Swan (1929 ed.).

Carpenter, George Rice, 1863–1909, American educator, b. Labrador, grad. Harvard, 1886. After study abroad, he returned to teach at Harvard (1888–90) and Massachusetts Institute of Technology (1890–93). From 1893 he was professor of rhetoric at Columbia Univ. He wrote a number of textbooks on literature and rhetoric and biographies of Longfellow, Whittier, and Walt Whitman.

Carpenter, John Alden, 1876–1951, American composer, b. Park Ridge, Ill.; pupil of J. K. Paine at Harvard and of Elgar. His music, refined and skillfully written, influenced by French impressionism, often depicts the spirit and the scenes of American life, in such works as the orchestral suite *Adventures in a Perambulator* (1914) and the ballets *Krazy Kat* (Chicago, 1921) and *Skyscrapers* (New York, 1926). A Spanish flavor and jazz, frequently elements in his music, are both found in *Patterns* (1932) for orchestra. Other important compositions are his ballet *The Birthday of the Infanta* (Chicago, 1919), a violin concerto (1937), a concertino for piano and orchestra (1915), songs, symphonies, and chamber music.

Carpenter, Malcolm Scott, 1925–, American astronaut, b. Boulder, Colo. The second American to go into orbital flight around the earth, he made his historic and suspenseful flight on May 24, 1962. In his three-orbit trip he repeated the earlier success of John GLENN. Carpenter's second orbit was under manual control, and during it he discovered that he could make small changes in the capsule's orientation in space by movements of his head and

Malcolm Scott Carpenter

arms. On descending, his capsule, *Aurora 7*, overshot the pickup area by 250 mi., causing nationwide concern for his safety. A commander in the U.S. navy, Carpenter had served with an antisubmarine patrol during the Korean war.

Carpenter, Mary, 1807–77, English educator. She devoted her life to the establishment of schools and institutions and the promotion of educational reforms. In 1835 she organized the Working and Visiting Society, in 1846 opened a "ragged school," and in 1852 founded a juvenile reformatory (see her *Juvenile Delinquents: Their Condition and Treatment,* 1852). Her agitation for reformatory and industrial schools contributed to the passage of the Juvenile Offenders Act (1857) and furthered the movement for free day schools. She made four visits to India after 1866, interesting herself in Indian education, and also lectured in the United States. See J. E. Carpenter, *The Life and Works of Mary Carpenter* (1879).

Carpenter, Rhys, 1889–, American archaeologist and classicist, b. Cotuit, Mass., grad. Columbia, 1908, Ph.D., 1916. He taught classical archaeology at Bryn Mawr (1913–55) and was director of the American School for Classical Studies at Athens (1927–32; 1946–48). His writings include *The Greeks in Spain* (1925), *The Humanistic Value of Archaeology* (1933), *Folktale, Fiction and Saga in the Homeric Epics* (1946), and *Greek Sculpture* (1960).

carpenter's square: see SQUARE, STEEL OR CARPENTER'S.

Carpentersville, village (pop. 17,424), NE Ill., on the Fox river N of Elgin; settled 1834, platted 1851, inc. 1887. Pumps and valves are made.

Carpentier, Alejo (älĕ′hō kärpĕntyâr′), 1904–, Cuban novelist and musicologist. He was professor of music history at the National Conservatory. Regarded as one of the most powerful Spanish-American writers of recent decades, he or his novels pictured the exotic in Caribbean life. Among his works are *Ecue-Yamba-O* (1933), *La música en Cuba* (1946), *Los pasos perdidos* (1953, Eng. tr., *The Lost Steps,* 1956), *El acoso* (1956), and *The Kingdom of This World* (Eng. tr., 1957).

Carpentras (kärpäträs′), town (estimated pop. 15,076), Vaucluse dept., SE France, in Provence. It is an important agricultural market. From 1229 to 1791 it was the capital of the Comtat VENAISSIN. An episcopal see from the 3d cent., Carpentras was ruled by its bishops until the French Revolution. It was here that the long conclave met which elected Pope John XXII.

carpentry, the trade concerned with constructing either a wood building or the wooden portions of any building. It comprises the larger and more structural aspects of woodwork, rather than the delicate assembling which is the field of cabinetmaking and joinery. The craft dates from the earliest use of tools. Though no actual examples of carpentry survive from antiquity, many remains of the earliest known stone architecture exhibit forms which are undoubtedly imitative of still earlier constructions in wood. This is especially apparent in most Asiatic architecture, and certain details of Greek temples are suggestive of carpentry prototypes. Some monumental wood buildings of the 7th cent. still stand in Japan, a country where intricate and beautiful carpentry has prevailed throughout its history. In the United States, expert carpentry has existed ever since the construction of dwellings by the colonists in the first half of the 17th century. Rough carpentry refers to the "framing" of a wood building, namely, the erection of the structural frame or skeleton composed of the

Flemish 15th-century tapestry.

Wool-and-silk tapestry woven in Gobelin (1804).

Closeup showing tapestry-weaving technique.

vertical members or studs, the horizontal members of foundation sills, floor joists, and the like, the inclined members or rafters for the roof, and the diagonal members for bracing. Finished carpentry is the setting in place, over the rough frame, of all finishing members both of exterior and interior, such as sheathing, siding, stairs, the casings of doors and windows, flooring, wainscoting, and trim. In the United States the two traditional types of house framing, frequently combined into one, are the braced frame and balloon frame. The latter, which is the most used, employs continuous vertical studs running from the foundation to the roof plate, is assembled entirely with nails, and can be erected rapidly. The braced frame is the older method. In it the studs are only one story in height, the corners are braced everywhere, and the fitting together is done by mortising and pinning, after which whole sections are raised into place. See also CENTERING. See Gilbert Townsend, *Carpentry* (2d ed., 1945).

carpet and rugs, thick fabrics, usually woolen, mainly for floor coverings. They were formerly woven to protect the body from cold, to spread on a dais or before a seat of honor, to cover a table, couch, or wall, or to form the curtains of a tent. All carpet divides into two classes—handmade and machine made. There is considerable evidence of the existence of hand-woven carpets in antiquity. On the rock tombs of Beni Hassan, Egypt, of c.2500 B.C., men are depicted with the implements of rug weaving. Other evidence of the early use of rugs is seen in the drawings on the ancient palace walls of Nineveh. In that mountainous region of the East stretching from Turkey through Persia and central Asia into China where the fleece of the sheep and the hair of the camel and goat grow long and fine, the art of carpet weaving reached its height early in the 16th cent. The Oriental artist works on a rude hand loom consisting essentially of two horizontal beams on which the warp is stretched; on the lower one the finished carpet is rolled, while the warp unrolls from the upper one. The yarn for the pile, spun and dyed by hand, is cut in lengths of about 2 in. and is knotted about the warp threads, one tuft at a time, after one of the two established ways of tying called the Ghiordes, or Turkish, knot and the Senna, or Persian, knot. When a row of knots has been placed across the width of the loom, two or more weft threads of cotton or flax are woven in and beaten into place with a heavy beater or comb. The tufts or pile thus appears only on the face of the fabric, which when completed is sheared to perfect smoothness. The wool of the sheep, the camel, and the goat was used in the weaving of Oriental rugs, but at least half the warps and wefts and a very large percentage of the pile were of sheep's wool. Beautiful silk rugs interwoven with gold thread were made in the 16th and 17th cent. The quality of the carpet depends on the materials used and the number of knots to the square inch of surface, which may vary from 40 to 1,000. In America the Navahos and other Indian tribes have for generations produced substantial rugs, without pile, woven somewhat in the manner

Navaho woman weaving on primitive hand loom.

of TAPESTRY on primitive hand looms. In the palaces of Montezuma were found remarkable floor coverings which utilized the plumage of birds. The primitive use of rushes or straw has survived in the form of Chinese and Japanese mattings. In 1608 King Henry IV of France established weavers in the Louvre. In 1631 an old soap works, the Savonnerie, near Paris, was converted to carpet weaving, and its name remains attached to one of the finest handmade carpets now made at the Gobelin works. Tapestries for walls and floors were made at Aubusson at an early date. In 1685 the revocation of the Edict of Nantes scattered skilled carpetmakers (mostly Protestants) over Europe. Centers of weaving were established in England, first at Kidderminster (1735), then at Wilton and Axminster. Cheaper, more easily manufactured floor covering soon came into demand, and the making of ingrain began at Kidderminster. The weavers of Flanders had made a loom which produced a pile by looping the worsted warp threads, and this loom, although guarded, was copied by a Kidderminster weaver; soon many looms in England were making Brussels carpet. Axminster was England's headquarters for imitation Oriental or tufted-pile carpet. Up to 1839 all carpets were made on hand looms with such devices and improvements as could be operated by hand or foot power; then Erastus Bigelow's power loom (first used in 1841) revolutionized the industry and made the carpet a commodity for the many instead of the few. A few distinctive types include all carpets both antique and modern —Oriental, European hand-woven, Brussels, Wilton, velvet, Axminster, chenille, ingrain, rag, hooked, straw, fiber. To the first class belong not only the genuine antique Orientals, now rare, but also the modern reproductions. These are dyed with aniline instead of vegetable dyes, much of the yarn being spun and dyed in Europe and shipped to the East to be woven. Many are washed in chlorine solutions to give an effect of age or in glycerine to simulate the luster of fine wool. Commercial methods have somewhat standardized and debased the characteristic ancient patterns, but the modern Orientals are commercially important. Some of the traditional beauties still remain—the deep, rich color and intricate patterns of Persia, the brighter hues and conventionalized figures of Asiatic Turkey, the naïve designs and primitive colorings of Turkistan and the Caucasus, and the symbolic ornament of China. European hand-woven carpets, both Aubussons (tapestry) and Savonneries (pile), are now made in the major Western countries, mostly to special order. Modern commercial carpets are woven on complex and highly specialized machines, a development from Bigelow's power loom. Brussels carpet has a warp and weft of linen, with a pile of worsted yarn drawn into loops by means of wires. It is called 3, 4, or 5 "frame" depending on the number of bobbins carrying different colored warp threads, which make the pattern. Tapestry Brussels is a cheap single-frame sort, either yarn printed or piece printed. Wilton is made on the same principle, except that the loops which form the pile are cut as they are woven into place. Velvet is an equivalent of tapestry Brussels with the pile cut. Axminster (formerly called moquette), similar in effect to

Oriental, uses unlimited colors in design made on machines which loop the tufts, one color at a time, and then interlock the weft about them. Chenille, or chenille Axminster, is made in two stages; first the chenille thread or "fur" is made and then is folded and ironed so that the woolen fibers are like a fringe along a cotton or linen chain. This "fur" is then woven into a strong backing of linen with the nap on the surface. Chenille has a pile often ⅝ of an inch deep and woven up to 30 ft. in width. Ingrain, no longer widely used, is a plain-weave fabric, of two- or three-ply woolen weft on a concealed cotton warp. Rag carpet, first made on household looms, of used rags sewn together for warp, became commercially important in the last years of the 19th cent. Hooked rugs are made of narrow strips of woolen cloth drawn by a pointed hook through a canvas foundation on which a design is indicated. Carpetmaking began in the United States in the colonial period. The first important factory was started at Philadelphia in 1791. After 1804 others were opened in Massachusetts, New York, and New Jersey.

carpetbaggers, epithet used in the South after the Civil War to describe the Northern adventurers who flocked to the South to make money and seize political power in the RECONSTRUCTION period. A few of them were substantial citizens bent on settling in the community, but most were men of the unstable future symbolized by the carpetbags in which they carried their possessions. They came as agents of the Freedmen's Bureau and other Reconstruction organizations, or they individually sought speculative and commercial openings. The carpetbaggers, in collusion with their Southern counterparts, the scalawags, dominated the Republican state governments through their control of the Negro vote. Although some were honest men, the activities of others made the term *carpetbagger* synonomous with the worst type of political corruption.

Carpini, Giovanni de Piano (jōvän′nē dā pyä′nō kärpē′nē), c.1180–1252, Italian traveler and Franciscan monk, b. Pian del Carpini (now Piano della Magione), Umbria. He was a companion of St. Francis of Assisi and spread Franciscan teachings in Germany and Spain. In 1245 he was sent by Pope Innocent IV to the court of the MONGOLS. With a Pole, Friar Benedict, he started from Lyons, went to Kiev, then across the Dnieper to the Don and the Volga, where he found the camp of a Mongol prince. He then traveled across central Asia to the imperial court at Karakorum in Mongolia. A journey of c.3,000 mi. was accomplished on horseback in 106-days. At Karakorum he witnessed the installation (1246) of Jenghiz Khan's grandson as the great khan of the Mongols. Carpini returned to Lyons in 1247, and his careful account of the journey, known as *Liber Tartarorum,* proved invaluable. It is a full record of Mongol manners, history, policy, and military tactics— the first of such works to appear in Europe.

Carpinteria (kär″pǐntŭrē′ú), uninc. town (pop. 4,998), S Calif., on the Pacific coast E of Santa Barbara. It was established in 1863 on the site of an Indian village visited (1769) by Gaspar de Portolá. It is a resort in a lemon-producing area.

Carpocrates (kärpŏk′rŭtēz), fl. c.130–c.150, Alexan-drian philosopher, founder with his son Epiphanes of a Hellenistic sect related to Gnosticism. Epiphanes wrote a treatise, *On Justice,* which advocated communal ownership of property, including women; he died, aged 17, at Cephalonia and was long worshiped as a deity there. The Carpocratians believed that men had formerly been united with the Absolute, had been corrupted, and would, by

Carpocrates

despising creation, be saved in this life or else later through successive transmigrations. Jesus, they held, was but one of several wise men who had achieved deliverance. The sect was notoriously immoral.

Carpus [Gr.,=fruit], man of Troas. 2 Tim. 4.13.

Carr, Edward Hallett, 1892–, English political scientist and historian. Educated at Cambridge, he was a diplomat in London, Paris, and Riga, a professor of international relations (1936–47), and an editor for the London *Times* (1941–46). His works include biographies of Dostoyevsky (1931), Marx (1934), and Bakunin (1937), as well as important studies on international relations and on the Soviet Union. Carr's *History of Soviet Russia* (Vols. I–VI, 1950–59) is the definitive work in English on the Soviet era. Sympathetic yet detached, it is the product of scrupulous scholarship and profound research.

Carr, Emily, 1871–1945, Canadian painter, b. Victoria, British Columbia. She studied (1889–c.1895) at the San Francisco School of Art and later in London and in Paris. In Victoria, she taught painting and visited Indian villages. From her study of totem poles and other Indian art, she developed a powerful style marked by simplified forms and a fauvist intensity of color. She wrote *Klee Wyck* (1941) and *The House of All Sorts* (1944). See her autobiography, *Growing Pains* (1946); study by Ira Dilworth and Lawren Harris (1945).

Carr, Eugene Asa, 1830–1910, American general, b. Concord, Erie co., N.Y., grad. West Point, 1850. In the Civil War he distinguished himself at Wilson's Creek (1861) and Pea Ridge (1862), was made (March, 1862) a brigadier general of volunteers, and fought in the campaigns at Vicksburg (1863) and Mobile (1865). After the war Carr was a well-known cavalry leader and Indian fighter in the West. Promoted brigadier general in 1892, he was retired in 1893.

Carr, Robert: see SOMERSET, ROBERT CARR, EARL OF.

Carrà, Carlo, 1881–, Italian painter. Trained as a decorator, he became associated with the movement known as FUTURISM. He then moved toward a more carefully structured art form, related to cubism. After meeting Chirico in 1916, Carrà became a

Boy and Horse by Carlo Carrà.

Crucifixion by Annibale Carracci.

spokesman of the *scuola metafisica.* A prolific writer on art, he has also exerted considerable influence as a teacher.

Carrabelle, resort city (pop. 1,146), NW Fla., on the Gulf coast SSW of Tallahassee; inc. 1931. A port of entry, it is also a fishing center.

Carracci or **Caracci** (kärät'chē), family of Italian painters of the Bolognese school, founders of an important academy of painting. **Lodovico Carracci** (lōdōvē'kō), 1555–1619, a pupil of Tintoretto in Venice, was influenced by Correggio and Titian. He also studied in Bologna, Padua, and Parma. With his cousins, Agostino and Annibale, and with Anthony de la Tour, he established in Bologna an academy of painting which sought to unite in one system the preeminent characteristics of each of the great masters. The school rapidly became one of the outstanding schools in Italy, and Lodovico remained its head until his death. Its noted pupils include Guido Reni, Francesco Albani, and Domenichino. Excelling as a teacher, Lodovico was also a painter of talent and energy. Excellent examples of his art abound in the churches of Bologna and elsewhere. Among the best are *Sermon of John the Baptist* (Pinacoteca, Bologna) and *Vision of St. Hyacinth* (Louvre). His cousin **Agostino Carracci** (ägōstē'no), 1557–1602, left the goldsmith's trade and studied painting with Prospero Fontana. He also studied engraving, in which he excelled and to which he devoted most of his time, with Domenico Tibaldi and Cornelis Cort. After several years' study in Parma and Venice, he joined his cousin and his brother in the founding of their academy and in the execution of numerous joint painting commissions. In 1597 he went to Rome and collaborated with Annibale in the decorating of the Farnese Palace gallery; he himself executed the admirable frescoes *Triumph of Galatea* and *Rape of Cephalus* (cartoons in the National Gall., London). He died in Parma just after completing his great work, *Celestial, Terrestrial, and Venal Love,* in the Casino. Other notable examples of his art are *The Last Communion of St. Jerome* (Pinacoteca, Bologna), *Adulteress before Christ,* and the masterly engraving of Tintoretto's *Crucifixion.* His brother **Annibale Carracci** (än-nē'bälä), 1560–1609, a pupil of his cousin, Lodovico Carracci, was a painter of unusual skill and versatility. He spent seven years studying the works of the masters, particularly those of Correggio and Parmigiano, in Venice and Parma. Returning to Bologna, he aided in the conducting of the academy school until 1595, when he went to Rome to assist in the decorating of the Farnese gallery. Among his paintings are *Juno before Jupiter, The Triumph of Bacchus,* and *Diana and Endymion,* which show his fine technique and color. Well known among his numerous works are *Christ and the Woman of Samaria* (Brera, Milan); *The Dead Christ* (Louvre); and *The Temptation of St. Anthony* (National Gall., London).

carrageen: see SEAWEED.

Carrantuohill (kă″rŭntōō′ŭl), mountain, 3,414 ft. high, Co. Kerry, SW Republic of Ireland, in Macgillicuddy's Reeks; highest peak in Ireland.

Carranza, Venustiano (kŭrăn′zủ, Span. vănōōstyä′nō kärän′sä), 1859–1920, Mexican political leader. While governor of Coahuila, he joined (1911) Francisco I. MADERO in the revolution against Porfirio Díaz. When Victoriano HUERTA overthrew (1913) President Madero, Carranza promptly took the field against Huerta. Fighting in the north, he was soon joined by other insurgents, notably Álvaro OBREGÓN and Francisco VILLA. Emiliano ZAPATA led a peon uprising in the south. Soon the entire country was aflame. The A.B.C. Powers and the United States tried unsuccessfully to mediate between Huerta and Carranza. Huerta was forced to resign and Carranza took over the executive powers (Aug., 1914). Chaos now took hold of the nation. Carranza and Villa, both ambitious for power, soon fell out. An attempt at reconciliation failed at the Convention of AGUASCALIENTES (Oct., 1914). Villa and Zapata, refusing to recognize Carranza's authority, attacked Mexico city. Between Nov., 1914, and Aug., 1915, the capital changed hands repeatedly between the forces of Villa and Zapata and those of Carranza and Obregón. The United States finally recognized the Carranza regime in Oct., 1915. The U.S. punitive expedition against Villa, however, resulted in much friction between the two governments, and Mexico remained neutral during the First World War. Under great pressure from Obregón, Carranza initiated a reform program embodied in the Constitution of 1917. Provisions affirming national ownership of oil and mineral deposits and the restoration of the *ejido* [common land] system generated discord with the United States and other powers. Ecclesiastical reforms brought Church and government into conflict. Provisions for labor reform constituted a theoretical advance. The Constitution, however, was never vigorously enforced, and there was little pretense of democratic control. Carranza actually repressed labor and agrarian reform, even to the extent of engineering the assassination (1919) of the agrarian leader, Emiliano Zapata. In 1920, when Carranza attempted to prevent Obregón from succeeding as president, Obregón revolted. Carranza fled to Veracruz with a valise containing five million pesos in gold and silver, and was murdered by a local chieftain.

Carranza de Miranda, Bartolomé de (bärtōlōmā′ dä kärän′thä dä merän′dä), 1503–76, Spanish churchman. He joined the Dominicans (1520) and taught at Valladolid. He was active in the first part of the Council of Trent, where he distinguished himself for his vigorous support of the rule that bishops must be resident in their sees. In 1554 Philip II of Spain sent him to England to aid in the restoration of Catholicism. In 1558 he was made archbishop of Toledo (primate of Spain); the same year he attended the dying Charles V. His commentary on the catechism appeared in 1558, and it was apparently from passages in this that he was accused of heresy. He was arrested in 1558 (with King Philip's permission); his case dragged on in Spain until 1564, when the archbishop appealed to Rome. At length, in 1576, he was found not guilty of heresy but was compelled to abjure certain propositions.

Carrara (kŭrä′rŭ, Ital. kär-rä′rä), city (estimated pop. 64,663), in Tuscany, central Italy, near the Ligurian Sea. It is the most important center of the Italian MARBLE industry; the famous Carrara marble is quarried in the nearby Alpi Apuane. With Massa, the city constituted the duchy of Massa and Carrara. Carrara has a fine 12th-century cathedral; the former ducal palace now houses the Fine Arts Academy.

Carrboro, town (pop. 1,997), N central N.C., WSW of Durham. It has lumber and textile mills.

Carrel, Alexis (kǎ′rǔl), 1873–1944, American surgeon and experimental biologist, b. near Lyons, France, M.D. Univ. of Lyons, 1900. Coming to the United States in 1905, he joined the staff of the Rockefeller Institute in 1906 and served as a member from 1912 to 1939. For his work in suturing blood vessels, in transfusion, and in transplantation of organs, he received the 1912 Nobel Prize in Physiology and Medicine. In the First World War he developed with Dakin a method of treating wounds by irrigation with a sodium hypochlorite solution. With Charles A. Lindbergh he invented an artificial, or mechanical, heart—a sterile glass chamber through which is pumped a fluid containing food materials and oxygen—by means of which he kept alive a number of different kinds of tissue and organs; he kept alive for 32 years tissue from a chicken's heart. In 1939 he returned to France. He wrote *Man the Unknown* (1935) and, with Lindbergh, *The Culture of Organs* (1938).

Alexis Carrel

Carreño, Teresa (tärä′sä kärä′nyō), 1853–1917, Venezuelan pianist; pupil of L. M. Gottschalk and Anton Rubinstein. Her debut was made in New York in 1862. She appeared as an opera singer for a brief period, but thereafter continued her piano career, becoming known as one of the greatest women pianists of her time. She composed a festival hymn for the Bolívar centenary, 1883, and was a teacher of Edward MacDowell. See biography by Marta Milinowski (1940).

Carreño de Miranda, Juan (hwän′ kärä′nyō dä merän′dä), 1614–85, Spanish baroque painter. He was a protégé of Velázquez, whom he eventually succeeded as painter to the Spanish court. He is best known for his elegant portraits, of which that of the queen mother, Mariana (Prado), is a fine example. Carreño also painted numerous admirable religious pictures and frescoes for the churches and palaces of Madrid, Segovia, and Toledo.

Carrera, José Miguel (hōsā′ mĕgĕl′ kärä′rä), 1785–1821, Chilean revolutionist. With his brothers,

CARRERA, RAFAEL

Juan José and Luis, he overthrew the revolutionary junta headed by MARTÍNEZ DE ROZAS and dominated Chile until replaced by Bernardo O'HIGGINS in 1813. He again seized control in 1814, precipitating a civil war which facilitated Spanish reconquest of Chile. Later he was forbidden by José de San Martín to reenter Chile. San Martín and O'Higgins ordered the execution at Mendoza of his brothers. Involving Argentina in civil turmoil, Carrera was on the point of invading Chile when he too was captured and beheaded at Mendoza.

Carrera, Rafael (räfäĕl'), 1814–65, president of Guatemala, a *caudillo*. He led the revolution against the anticlerical liberal government of Guatemala, and his ultimate success in 1840 helped to destroy the Central American Federation. Illiterate and of mixed blood, he received unquestioned support from the Indian masses; a conservative devoted to the Church, he recalled the Jesuits and restored the power of the Church in the state. Until his death Carrera dominated Guatemala and was the most powerful figure in Central America, intervening to strengthen, restore, or install conservative governments in the other Central American countries.

Carrera Andrade, Jorge (hôr'hĕ kär-rĕ'rä ändrä'dĕ), 1903–, Ecuadorean poet. His early pro-Indian poems, together with some of his later work, reveal an interest in social revolution, but his writings are not dominated by political themes. As he matured his concern with the purely esthetic aspects of poetry became intensified. He traveled widely and studied Oriental forms of poetry. His lyrics are graceful and charming and reveal a flair for original and often brilliant images. Among his works are *Latitudes* (1934; essays), *Rol de la manzana* (1935), *Registro del mundo* (1940), *La tierra siempre verde* (1955; essays), and *Edades poéticas*

(1958). See translations in *12 Spanish American Poets* (1943) by H. R. Hays; *Secret Country* (1946), a selection of his poems translated by Muna Lee.

Carrère, John Merven (kûrâr'), 1858–1911, American architect, b. Rio de Janeiro. After graduating from the École des Beaux-Arts, Paris, he worked under McKim, Mead, and White in New York, and from 1886 until his death practiced in partnership with Thomas Hastings. The best-known works of Carrère and Hastings are the New York Public Library (completed 1911), which they were awarded in a competition; and the office buildings of the Senate and the House and the Carnegie Institution, Washington, D.C.

Carrhae (kă'rē), Roman name for the ancient Mesopotamian city of HARAN. The name Carrhae is best known because of the battle of Carrhae in 53 B.C. M. Licinius Crassus (see CRASSUS, family) was defeated by the Parthians, who by their archery routed the Roman force.

carriage, a wheeled vehicle, in modern usage restricted to passenger vehicles. Carriages date from the Bronze Age; early forms include the two-wheel cart and four-wheel wagon for goods. The early passenger carriage was a CHARIOT, but Roman road-building activity encouraged the development of other forms. From the fall of Rome, horses and litters were used exclusively until the 12th cent., when goods carts and wagons were gradually reintroduced. The coach, a closed four-wheel carriage with two inside seats and an elevated outside seat for the driver, is believed to have been developed in Hungary and to have spread among the royalty and nobility of Europe in the 16th cent. The hackney coach was introduced in London c.1605. During the 17th cent., coaches became lighter and less ornate and in England the public STAGECOACH became common. France developed the two-wheel forerunner of the chaise, the sulky, and the Cuban *volante*. The numerous forms developed in the 18th cent. include the chariot, a closed carriage with one seat; the landau, a coach whose top folded back from the center in two sec-

Chinese light carriage

Roman chariot

Hansom cab

Brougham

Victoria

Landau

tions; the barouche coach with a folding hood fixed at the back; and the phaeton, usually with low sides. The hansom cab, patented by J. A. Hansom in 1834, was a closed carriage with an elevated driver's seat in back. Lord Brougham based the carriage known by his name on the hansom. The victoria, popular after 1850, was similar to the phaeton but had only one seat for passengers. The carriage-building trade became firmly established in the United States after the War of 1812; the most distinctive model was a light four-wheel buggy with open sides and a folding top.

Carrickfergus (kărĭkfûr′gŭs), municipal borough (pop. 10,211), Co. Antrim, NE Northern Ireland, on the shore of Belfast Lough. A fishing port, it has linen and rayon mills, and rock salt is mined. There are remains of a 12th-century castle; of the walls of the old town, a gateway is still standing. John Paul Jones fought (1778) a victorious battle offshore from Carrickfergus.

Carrick-on-Shannon, county town of Co. Leitrim, N Republic of Ireland. It is a farm market and a center for trout fishing.

Carrick-on-Suir (sho͞or), urban district (pop. 4,667), Co. Tipperary, S central Republic of Ireland, on the Suir, here crossed by a very old bridge. It is a market town and has a castle built in 1309 and remains of a 14th-century abbey.

Carrier, Jean Baptiste (zhã′bätēst′ kärēä′), 1756–94, French revolutionist. An extreme Jacobin, he demanded the establishment of a revolutionary tribunal, and as a Revolutionary representative to Nantes in the Reign of Terror, he instituted NOYADES and committed other atrocities. Though he was denounced to the Convention and recalled to Paris, he temporarily escaped punishment through the fall of Robespierre (July, 1794), but in November he was arrested and executed.

Carriera, Rosalba (rōzäl′bä kär-rēä′rä), 1675–1757, Italian portrait and miniature painter, one of the greatest of her day. At 24 she had achieved a reputation throughout Italy and abroad for her miniatures and crayon portraits. In 1705 she was elected to the Academy of St. Luke (Rome), the Academy of Bologna, and Florence Academy. In 1720 she visited Paris, where she painted the portraits of the young Louis XV, the regent, and other court figures. Returning to Italy, she visited the courts of Modena, Parma, and Vienna, receiving honors and commissions wherever she went. Her portraits are delicate in color and vivacious. She is well represented in most of the European galleries. *Muse Crowned with Laurel* is in the Louvre.

Carrière, Eugène (ûzhĕn′ käryĕr′), 1849–1906, French painter and lithographer, best known for his spiritual interpretations of maternity and family life. His figures and heads emerge from a brownish penumbra, usually with an expression of deep melancholy. Characteristic are his *Crucifixion* and *Maternity* (both: Louvre). He also painted some large canvases for the Sorbonne and the Hôtel de Ville, Paris. The author of many notable portraits, he depicted Verlaine, Daudet, and Edmond de Goncourt (all: Louvre). See studies (in French) by Élie Faure (1908), Gustave Geffroy (1908), and Gabriel Séailles (rev. ed., 1922).

Carrier Mills, coal-mining village (pop. 2,006), S Ill., SW of Harrisburg; inc. 1894.

carrier of disease: see DISEASE CARRIER.

carrier wave: see RADIO.

Carrington, Henry Beebee, 1824–1912, U.S. army officer and historian, b. Wallingford, Conn., grad. Yale, 1845, and afterwards studied at Yale Law School. Carrington ably reorganized the Ohio state militia and subsequently became adjutant general. In the Civil War he helped to save West Virginia for the Union by sending Ohio militia there. Later as chief mustering officer of Indiana, he sent over 100,000 men to the war and was instrumental in quelling the operations of a secret society of Southern sympathizers. After the war, as commander of the Mountain Dist. of the Dept. of the Platte, he led the force which in 1866 attempted to open and guard the Bozeman Trail route to Montana. He planned and built Forts C. F. Smith and Phil Kearney on this route. Blamed for the FETTER-MAN MASSACRE he was later exonerated. After his retirement from the army, Carrington was (1869–78) professor of military science at Wabash College. His *Battles of the American Revolution* (1876), supplemented by a volume of maps (1881), is a standard work. *Ab-sa-ra-ka, Home of the Crows* (1868; 3d ed., revised and enlarged, 1878), written by his first wife, deals with his life on the plains.

Carrington, city (pop. 2,438), co. seat of Foster co., E central N.Dak., NNW of Jamestown, in a dairy, wheat, and livestock area; laid out 1882, inc. 1900.

Carrizo Springs (kûrē′zō, –rĭ′zō), city (pop. 5,699), co. seat of Dimmit co., SW Texas, SW of San Antonio; settled 1862, inc. 1910. Formerly a cow town, it is now the center of an irrigated winter-garden area producing spinach and other truck crops.

Carrizozo (kärĭzō′zō), town (pop. 1,546; alt. 5,425 ft.), co. seat of Lincoln co., S central N.Mex., WNW of Roswell; laid out 1899. The trade and shipping center of a livestock and farm area, Carrizozo is also a health resort.

Carroll, Anna Ella, 1815–93, alleged adviser to Abraham Lincoln in the Civil War. A member of the Protestant branch of the Carroll family of Maryland, she was a press agent for the Know-Nothing movement in the 1850s. It is claimed that Miss Carroll was the "great, unrecognized member of Lincoln's Cabinet," responsible, it is said, for the successful Union strategy of the early Western campaigns and for numerous other decisions on high policy. See biography by Sydney Greenbie and Marjorie Greenbie (1952).

Carroll, Charles, 1737–1832, American Revolutionary patriot, signer of the Declaration of Independence, b. Annapolis, Md. After completing his education in France and England, he returned (1765) and his father gave him a large estate near Frederick, Md., known as Carrollton Manor; he was afterwards styled Charles Carroll of Carrollton. As leader of the Roman Catholic element, he attacked support of the established Anglican church in a series of articles written for the *Maryland Gazette*. He threw himself boldly into revolutionary activities, though he was an extremely wealthy man. In 1776 the Continental Congress appointed him, together with Benjamin Franklin and Samuel Chase, to obtain Canadian support for the Continental cause. His journal is one of the chief sources for study of this vain mission. Carroll served (1776–78) in the Continental Congress; he refused to attend the Federal Constitution Convention (1787), but he later supported the Constitution. He was one of Maryland's first U.S. Senators, serving from 1789 until 1792. The last surviving signer of the Declaration of Independence, he took an interest in early canal and railroad building. See biographies by K. M. Rowland (1898), Joseph Gurn (1932), and E. H. Smith (1942).

Carroll, James, 1854–1907, American bacteriologist and army surgeon, b. Woolwich, England, M.D. Univ. of Maryland, 1891. He went to Canada at 15 and later joined the U.S. army. A member of the Yellow Fever Commission under Walter Reed, he voluntarily submitted to the bite of an infected mosquito, contracted yellow fever, and recovered. This proved the mosquito to be the carrier of the disease. Carroll also proved that the infectious agent is a filterable virus.

Carroll, John, 1735–1815, American Roman Catholic churchman, b. Maryland. He studied as a child with Jesuits at Bohemia, Md., later at Saint-Omer in Flanders, since Catholic secondary education was not allowed in Maryland. He joined the Jesuits in 1753, studied at Liège, and was ordained in 1769. After the suppression of the Jesuits he returned to America and traveled about, ministering to the scattered Catholics. He had a private chapel, for Catholic churches were forbidden by law. He ardently supported the American Revolution and accompanied Benjamin Franklin (always his good friend) on the vain mission to Quebec (1776) to persuade the Canadians to join the Revolutionary cause. Seeing that American Roman Catholics should be free of supervision by the vicar apostolic of London, he led in petitioning Rome for the appointment of a priest with some episcopal powers. In 1784 Father Carroll was made superior of the missions in the United States. In the same year he published a controversial pamphlet, *An Address to the Roman Catholics of the United States of America*, to combat a paper impugning the loyalty of Catholics. In 1790 he was consecrated bishop of Baltimore. He invited the Sulpicians, who opened a seminary at Baltimore, and he founded GEORGETOWN UNIVERSITY. He encouraged many communities and patronized schools throughout his diocese. In 1808 he became archbishop, with suffragans at Boston, New York, Philadelphia, and Bardstown, Ky. His last years were somewhat clouded by misunderstandings with the Catholics in Philadelphia and New York. See biographies by J. G. Shea (1888), P. K. Guilday (1922), and A. M. Melville (1955).

Carroll, Lewis, pseud. of **Charles Lutwidge Dodgson,** 1832–98, English writer and mathematician, b. Daresbury, Cheshire. Educated at Christ Church College, Oxford, he lectured in mathematics there from 1855 until 1881; he was ordained a deacon in 1861. Among his mathematical works, now almost forgotten, is *Euclid and His Modern Rivals* (1879). He is chiefly remembered as the author of the very popular children's books, *Alice's Adventures in Wonderland* (1865) and its sequel *Through the Looking Glass* (1872), both published under his pseudonym and both illustrated by Sir John Tenniel. Carroll developed these stories from tales he told to the

Lewis Carroll

children of Dean Liddell, one of whom was named Alice. Many of his characters—the Mad Hatter, the March Hare, the White Rabbit, the Red Queen, and the White Queen—have become familiar figures in literature and conversation. Though numerous satiric and symbolic meanings have been read into Alice's adventures, the works can be read and valued as simple exercises in fantasy. He also wrote humorous verses, the most popular of them being *The Hunting of the Snark* (1876). Carroll remained a confirmed and hard-working bachelor his whole life. See his complete works (ed. by Alexander Woollcott, 1939); selected letters (ed. by E. M. Hatch, 1933); studies by F. B. Lennon (1945) and Derek Hudson (1954).

Carroll, Paul Vincent, 1900–, Irish playwright. His plays, vigorous commentaries on the conflicts of village life in Ireland, include *Shadow and Substance* (1937), *The White Steed* (1939), *The Wise Have Not Spoken* (1946), and *The Wayward Saint* (1955). See his *Irish Stories and Plays* (1958).

Carroll, city (pop. 7,682), co. seat of Carroll co., W central Iowa, W of Ames; inc. 1869. Turkeys are processed here. Nearby is Swan Lake State Park.

Carrollton. 1 City (pop. 10,973), co. seat of Carroll co., W Ga., WSW of Atlanta and on the Little Tallapoosa river. It is a trade center for a fertile farm area and has textile mills. West Georgia College is here. **2** City (pop. 2,558), co. seat of Greene co., W Ill., NW of Alton; settled 1818, laid out 1821, inc. 1861. It is a farm trade center. **3** City (pop. 3,218), co. seat of Carroll co., N Ky., on the Ohio at the mouth of the Kentucky and NE of Louisville, in a farm area; inc. 1794. The city has tobacco storehouses. A state park is nearby. **4** City (pop. 3,385), W central Md., a suburb NE of Washington, D.C.; inc. 1953. **5** City (pop. 4,554), co. seat of Carroll co., N central Mo., ENE of Kansas City, in a farm area; settled 1818, inc. 1833. There is a monument to Gen. James Shields. A Federal wildlife refuge is nearby. **6** Village (pop. 2,786), co. seat of Carroll co., NE Ohio, SE of Canton; laid out 1815. It was the home of the "fighting McCooks" of Civil War fame. **7** City (pop. 4,242), N Texas, NNW of Dallas, in a blackland cotton and corn region; inc. 1915. A wide range of metal products, aircraft parts, and electronic equipment are manufactured. Many of its residents commute to Dallas.

Carrolltown, agricultural borough (pop. 1,525), S central Pa., in the Alleghenies NW of Altoona; laid out 1840, inc. 1858. Coal is mined.

Carron, village, Stirlingshire, central Scotland, near Falkirk. It has long-established ironworks (c.1760), and electrical equipment is made. The village gives its name to the carronade naval gun, used extensively in the Napoleonic Wars, and to carron oil.

carrot, common name for the Umbelliferae, a family (also called the parsley family) of chiefly biennial or perennial herbs of north temperate regions. Most are characterized by aromatic foliage, a dry fruit that splits when mature, and an umbellate inflorescence (a type of flattened flower cluster in which the stems of the small florets arise from the same point, like an umbrella). The seeds or leaves of many of these herbs have long been used for seasoning or as greens (e.g., ANGELICA, ANISE, CARAWAY, CHERVIL, CORIANDER, CUMIN, DILL, FENNEL, LOVAGE, and PARSLEY). The carrot, CELERY, and PARSNIP are vegetables of commercial importance. The common garden carrot (*Daucus carota sativa*) is a ROOT CROP, probably derived from some variety of the wild carrot (or QUEEN ANNE'S LACE). In antiquity several types of carrot were grown as medicinals, and in Europe carrots have long been grown for use in soups and stews. In the 20th cent. the custom of eating carrots raw as a salad has become widespread. Carrots are a rich source of carotene (vitamin A), especially when they are cooked. Several types of carrot have also been cultivated since ancient times as aromatic plants. Some are still planted as fragrant garden ornamentals, such as the button snakeroot and sweet cicely. A few members of the Umbelliferae have long been known to be lethally poisonous. It was one of these, the poison hemlock, that Socrates was compelled to take. The water hemlock is also poisonous.

Carrucci, Jacopo: see PONTORMO, JACOPO DA.

Carrville, town (pop. 1,081), E central Ala., NE of Montgomery at the southern end of Lake Martin.

Carshena (–shē'–), counselor of Ahasuerus. Esther 1.14.

car sickness: see MOTION SICKNESS.

Carso: see KARST.

Carson, Edward Henry Carson, Baron, 1854–1935, Irish politician. From 1892 to 1921 he was a member of Parliament (first as a Liberal, then a Conservative). A prominent trial lawyer, he was solicitor general from 1900 to 1905. He had long opposed Home Rule for Ireland, and in 1911 he organized military resistance in Ulster against an English attempt to impose it, fearing dominance of Protestant Ulster by the Catholic South. He was diverted only by the First World War, in which he served in two coalition governments. He was made baron in 1921. He violently denounced the creation of the Irish Free State in 1921 but approved the separation of Northern Ireland. See biographies by Edward Marjoribanks and Ian Colvin (3 vols., 1932–37) and H. M. Hyde (1953).

Carson, Kit (Christopher Carson), 1809–68, American frontiersman and guide, b. Madison co., Ky. In 1811 he moved with his family to the Missouri

frontier. After his father's death, he was apprenticed to a saddler in Old Franklin, an outfitting point on the Santa Fe Trail, but in 1826 he ran away, joining a caravan for Santa Fe and continuing on to Taos, N.Mex., which became his home and his headquarters. For the next 14 years he made his living as a teamster, cook, guide, and hunter for exploring parties. In 1842, while returning from St. Louis by boat up the Missouri, he met J. C. FRÉMONT, who employed him as a guide for his Western expeditions of 1842, 1843–44, and 1845. He became famous as a result of Frémont's reports of his skill and courage. After the

Kit Carson

taking of Los Angeles in 1846, he was ordered to Washington with dispatches. In New Mexico he met Gen. Stephen Kearny's troops, and Kearny commanded him to guide his forces to California. When Kearny's men were surrounded in California, Carson, E. F. Beale, and an Indian made their way by night through enemy lines to secure aid from San Diego. In 1847 and again in 1848, Carson was sent east with dispatches. He determined to retire to a sheep ranch near Taos, but depredations by Indians compelled him to continue as an Indian fighter. In 1853 he was appointed U.S. Indian agent, with headquarters at Taos, a position he filled with notable success. At the outbreak of the Civil War he helped organize and commanded the 1st New Mexican Volunteers, who engaged in campaigns against the Apache, Navaho, and Comanche Indians in New Mexico and Texas. At the end of the war he was made a brigadier general, in command (1866–67) of Fort Garland, Colo. See his autobiography (ed. by Blanche C. Grant, 1926; ed. by M. M. Quaife, 1935); biographies by Stanley Vestal (1928) and M. M. Estergreen (1962); E. L. Sabin, *Kit Carson Days* (rev. ed., 1935).

Carson, Rachel Louise, 1907–, American writer and marine biologist, b. Springdale, Pa., M.A. Johns Hopkins, 1932. Her widely known books on sea life— *Under the Sea Wind* (1941), *The Sea Around Us* (1951), and *The Edge of the Sea* (1954)—combine keen scientific observation with rich poetic description. Her *Silent Spring*, which appeared in 1962, is a provocative study of the dangers involved in the use of insecticides.

Carson, Calif.: see NORTH WILMINGTON.

Carson City. 1 Village (pop. 1,201), S Mich., on Fish Creek and NNW of Lansing, in a farm area; settled 1854, inc. 1887. **2** City (pop. 5,163), state capital, and co. seat of Ormsby co., W Nev., in the Carson valley S of Reno; inc. 1875. It was laid out in 1858 on the site of Eagle Station, a trading post established (1851) on the emigrant trail from Salt Lake City to California. It served as a supply station for miners in the valley, achieved importance with the discovery (1859) of the COMSTOCK LODE, and later became the terminus of the railroad carrying ore. In 1861, when the Territory of Nevada was created, the city was made the capital, and in 1864 it became the state capital—largely through the efforts of William Morris Stewart. A U.S. mint, which closed in 1893, is now occupied by the Nevada State Museum. State and Federal offices are here, and the city is a resort and trade center for a mining and agricultural area.

Carson Sink, swampy area, c.100 sq. mi., W Nev., NE of Fallon. It is a remnant of ancient Lake Lahontan, and in it the Carson river is dispersed. The river's course was followed by California-bound travelers in the 1850s and 1860s. Lahontan Dam (162 ft. high; 5,400 ft. long; completed 1915) now conserves most of the river's flow in Lahontan Reservoir for the NEWLANDS PROJECT.

Carstares or **Carstairs, William,** 1649–1715, Scottish statesman and divine. While studying theology at Utrecht, he became a friend of William of Orange (later William III of England). He was imprisoned in Edinburgh (1675–79) for alleged co-authorship of *An Account of Scotland's Grievances* and imprisoned and tortured in London (1682) as a suspect in the Rye House Plot. Shortly before 1688 he was made chaplain to William of Orange, later accompanied him to England, and became so powerful in his efforts to reconcile the new king and the Scottish church and to frustrate the Episcopalian Jacobites that he was nicknamed "the Cardinal." His influence continued under Queen Anne as he worked for the union of England and Scotland, served as principal of the Univ. of Edinburgh from 1703, and was four times moderator of the assembly of the Church of Scotland. See biography by R. H. Story (1874).

Carstens, Asmus Jacob (äs'mŏos yä'kōp kär'stŭns), 1754–98, Danish historical painter and engraver, b. Schleswig, studied in Copenhagen and in Italy. He was influenced by the work of Giulio Romano. Carstens lived chiefly in Germany, where he was a popular professor at the Berlin Academy. Through such pupils as Peter von Cornelius he had a great influence on German historical painting. *Homer Singing* is a characteristic work.

Carstensz, Mount (kär'stŭnz), group of peaks in the Nassau Mts., W central New Guinea. Its highest peak, c.16,400 ft., is the highest on the island. Mt. Carstensz and its adjacent peaks are often called the Carstensz Mountains.

Cartagena (kärtähä'nä), city (pop. c.174,000), N Colombia. A port on the Caribbean, it was founded in 1533 by Pedro de Heredia on an excellent harbor. Cartagena became the treasure city of the Spanish Main, where precious stones and minerals brought down the Magdalena awaited transshipment to

Cartagena seen from the fortress of San Felipe.

Spain. With shady plazas and narrow cobblestone streets, it is one of the most picturesque cities in South America. The harbor was guarded by 29 stone forts, and the city was encircled by a high wall of coral. Nevertheless, buccaneers swooped down on the city, which was sacked in 1544, 1560, and 1586 (this time by Sir Francis Drake). In 1741, in the War of the Austrian Succession, Cartagena heroically withstood a three-month siege by the British, who finally retired. Cartagena was the first of the cities of Colombia and Venezuela to declare (Nov. 11, 1811) absolute independence from Spain. The republic of Cartagena captured SANTA MARTA in 1813, but lost it to royalist forces toward the end of the year. In 1815 it was besieged by the Spanish under Pablo MORILLO and, after a magnificent defense, surrendered. A large part of the population died. After proclaiming an amnesty, Morillo executed hundreds of the survivors. The city was captured by patriot forces on Oct. 1, 1821. The revolution cost Cartagena its supremacy. Later a natural side channel of the Magdalena, the Canal de Dique, silted up, and river traffic began to go to BARRANQUILLA. Some of its former importance was regained by Cartagena in the 20th cent. when a railroad was built to Calamar and an oil pipeline was laid to the fields in the Magdalena basin. Considerable trade comes from the ATRATO valley. Besides oil, exports include gold and platinum.

Cartagena (kärtŭjē'nŭ, Span. kärtähä'nä), Latin *Carthago Nova,* city (pop. 110,979), Murcia prov., SE Spain, on the Mediterranean. An important seaport and naval base, it has a fine natural harbor, protected by forts, and has a naval arsenal. Shipbuilding and metalworking are important occupations. Lead, iron, and zinc are mined nearby, but the rich silver mines exploited in ancient times by Carthaginians and Romans are now almost exhausted. The city was founded by Hasdrubal c.225 B.C. and soon became the chief Carthaginian base in Spain and a flourishing port. Captured (209 B.C.) by Scipio Africanus Major, it continued to flourish under the Romans. The Moors, who took it in the 8th cent., later included it in MURCIA. The Spaniards retook it definitively in the 13th cent. Cartagena was sacked (1585) by Sir Francis Drake and figured later in the Peninsular and Carlist wars. No traces remain of the ancient city. The medieval Castillo de la Concepción, whose ruins are surrounded by fine gardens, commands a splendid view of the city and harbor.

Cartago (kärtä′gō), city (pop. c.18,000), central Costa Rica. Founded in 1563 at the eastern extremity of the central plateau, in a rich coffee-growing region, Cartago was the political center of Costa Rica until liberal dominance after 1821 established SAN JOSÉ as capital. Cartago remained a conservative stronghold. Destroyed by an eruption (1723) of IRAZÚ volcano, it was also severely damaged by earthquakes in 1822, 1841, and 1910. To withstand shock most buildings are low and massive. Cartago's principal church is the scene of annual pilgrimages. Although many colonial traditions survive, Cartago's former glory has vanished.

Carte, Richard D'Oyly (doi′lē kärt′), 1844–1901, English impresario. In 1875 he produced *Trial by Jury*, the first operetta of Sir William Schwenck GILBERT and Sir Arthur Sullivan, and subsequently produced all their other works. In 1881 he built the Savoy Theatre (the first to be lighted by electricity), which the operettas made famous.

cartel, national or international organization of manufacturers or traders allied by agreement to fix prices, limit supply, divide markets, or fix quotas for sales, manufacture, or division of profits among the member firms. In that it may have international scope the cartel is broader than the TRUST, and in that it carries on manufacture it differs from the speculative CORNER or ring. Of German origin, the cartel achieved prominence in the world depression of the 1870s, which coincided with the unification of Germany and the growth of its economy. The existence of cartels is in opposition to classic theories of economic competition and the free market, and they are forbidden by law in many nations. In Germany, however, by the outset of the Second World War nearly all industry was controlled by cartels closely supervised by the government. Participation by American firms in German cartel agreements has been prosecuted by the U.S. government as constituting restraint of trade. Foes of cartels have alleged that they have driven competing firms out of existence, reduced volume of trade, raised prices to consumers, protected inefficient members from competition, and benefited German aggression by furnishing markets, profits, and technical data to Germany before the Second World War. Apologists for cartels claim that they protect the weaker participating firms, do away to an extent with limitations on trade resulting from high tariffs, distribute risks and profits equitably,

stabilize markets, reduce costs, and hence protect consumers. The U.S. government legalized export associations in 1918 and has itself participated in agreements regulating production and international trade in foodstuffs, rubber, and other commodities. The International Trade Organization formed at the end of the Second World War has opposed cartels, but many factors limit its authority. Because they infer the agreement of several governments, cartels in international trade are usually felt to be less harmful than those which tend to create monopolies in the home market for participants. Formal international agreements, involving governments as well as private firms, still control the price, output, and distribution in some industries, notably in diamonds and in oil. Although not referred to as cartels, these agreements have the same general effect on world trade. See also TARIFF. See G. W. Stocking and M. W. Watkins, *Cartels or Competition?* (1948); K. L. Mayall, *International Cartels* (1951); J. P. Miller, *Competition: Cartels and Their Regulation* (1962).

Carter, Elizabeth, 1717–1806, English poet and translator. Under the pen name Eliza she contributed for years to the *Gentleman's Magazine*. One of the group of 18th-century women known as the bluestockings, she was a friend of Johnson, Burke, Reynolds, and Horace Walpole. Collections of her poems appeared in 1738 and 1762. Her translations of Epictetus were published in 1758. See her memoirs (1807); study by Alice C. C. Gaussen (1906); *Bluestocking Letters* (ed. by R. B. Johnson, (1926).

Carter, Henry Rose, 1852–1925, American sanitarian, b. Caroline co., Va., M.D. Univ. of Maryland, 1879. He entered the Marine Hospital Service, and in the campaign to keep yellow fever out of the Southern states he completely reorganized the Federal quarantine service. He organized similar departments in Cuba after the Spanish-American War and in the Panama Canal Zone in 1904. His work *Yellow Fever* was posthumously published in 1931.

Carter, Hodding, 1907–, American journalist, and news publisher, b. Hammond, La., grad. Bowdoin, 1927, Columbia, B. Litt., 1928. After teaching briefly at Tulane Univ., he worked as a newspaperman until starting (1932) his own paper, which was distinguished by its opposition to Huey Long's control of Louisiana. In 1936 he moved to Greenville, Miss., and started another paper. After Second World War service with the army bureau of public relations he returned to his paper to write a series of articles on racial, religious, and economic intolerance that won him the 1945 Pulitzer Prize for distinguished reporting. Particularly cited was his plea for fairness for returning Nisei soldiers. Among his works—both fiction and nonfiction—are *Mississippi* (1942), *Flood Crest* (1947), *Where Main Street Meets the River* (1953), *The Angry Scar: The Story of Reconstruction* (1959).

Carter, Howard, 1873–1939, English Egyptologist. He served (1891–1899) with the Egyptian Exploration Fund and later helped to reorganize the antiquities administration of Upper Egypt. Carter's excavations (1906–22) with Lord Carnarvon in the Valley of the Kings led to the discovery in 1922 of the tomb of Tut-ankh-amen. With A. C. Mace he wrote *The Tomb of Tut.ankh.amen* (Vols. I–II, 1923; Vol. III, 1933).

Carter, Mrs. Leslie, 1862–1937, American actress, b. Lexington, Ky., whose maiden name was Caroline Louise Dudley. After a divorce from her first husband, she became a protégé of Belasco and first appeared (1890) in *The Ugly Duckling.* His *Heart of Maryland* (1895) brought her recognition, and her success continued in his *Zaza* (1899), *Du Barry* (1901), and *Adrea* (1905). Their association ended with her second marriage in 1906, after which her stage popularity somewhat diminished.

Carter, Nick, a fictional detective character in dime novels said to have been created by J. R. Coryell in the 1880s. The firm of Street & Smith, New York, published over 1,000 stories about Nick Carter, written variously by F. V. R. Dey, E. T. Sawyer, G. C. Jenks, and others. The name Nicholas Carter was used as a pseudonym by many authors of dime novels.

Carter, Samuel Powhatan, 1819–91, American naval officer and Union general in the Civil War, b. Elizabethton, Tenn., grad. Annapolis, 1846. In the Civil War he was transferred from the navy to the War Dept., sent to organize Union troops in East Tennessee, made brigadier general of volunteers (May, 1862), and given command of a cavalry division in the Army of the Ohio. Mustered out as brevet major general (1866), he returned to the navy. In 1882 he was made a rear admiral on the retired list. Carter is said to have been the only American who was both a major general and a rear admiral.

Carteret, Sir George (kär′tŭrĭt, –rĕt), c.1610–1680, proprietor of East Jersey (see NEW JERSEY). He served in the British navy, fought for the royalists, and became (1643) lieutenant governor of his native island of Jersey. In 1663, with several others, he was granted the proprietorship of Carolina and in 1664, in conjunction with Lord Berkeley, was granted part of New Jersey. His widow sold his claim to 12 purchasers who joined with 12 others as the 24 proprietors of East New Jersey.

Carteret, John: see GRANVILLE, JOHN CARTERET, 1ST EARL.

Carteret, Philip, 1639–82, first colonial governor of NEW JERSEY. Carteret, commissioned by the proprietor, Sir George Carteret, his fourth cousin, arrived in the province in 1665. He was soon faced with rebellion against quitrents and confused land titles. After the division of New Jersey in 1676, he was made governor of East Jersey. Mounting difficulties with Sir Edmund ANDROS over the right to collect customs duties led to Carteret's imprisonment by Andros and his eventual restoration by the duke of York (later James II).

Carteret (kärtŭrĕt′), borough (pop. 20,502), NE N.J., on Arthur Kill and SSW of Newark; inc. 1906. It processes metals and produces machinery and chemicals.

Carter Lake, town (pop. 2,287), SW Iowa, on an oxbow lake W of the Missouri and WNW of Council Bluffs. Steel products are manufactured.

Cartersville, city (pop. 8,668), co. seat of Bartow co., NW Ga., NW of Atlanta and on the Etowah river, in a piedmont mining area; inc. as a town 1850, as a city 1872. Rubber products and textiles are made here, and lime, manganese, iron ore,

barium, and ochre are mined in the area. Artifacts and other archaeological items of interest have been excavated from the nearby Etowah Indian mounds.

Carterville. 1 City (pop. 2,643), S Ill., SW of Herrin, in a farm and coal-mine area; inc. 1892. **2** City (pop. 1,443), SW Mo., NE of Joplin; laid out 1875, inc. 1882. Its lead-mining activities have declined.

Cartesian coordinates (kärtē′zhŭn) [for René Descartes], values representing the location of a point in relation to two straight lines. The two straight lines are known as axes; the horizontal can be called the *x* axis and the vertical the *y* axis, and the point is located by measuring its distance from each line along a parallel to the other line. In terms of present-day mathematics Descartes used both rectangular (perpendicular) and oblique axes. This work on analytic geometry, or the application of algebra to geometry, was embodied in his *La Géométrie,* one of three sections appended to his essays on the method of science (1637). His was the first published presentation of the fact that a curve can be represented by means of an equation giving the relation between the coordinates (*x*, *y*) of a point on the curve. Descartes advanced generality in mathematics by showing that an infinity of curves can be referred to one system of coordinates. Others, including Pierre de Fermat and Thomas Harriot, developed similar concepts. A common application of coordinate geometry is in the making of graphs. See Descartes's *Geometry* (Eng. tr. by D. E. Smith and M. L. Latham, 1924).

Cartesian philosophy: see DESCARTES, RENÉ.

Carthage (kär′thĭj), ancient city, on the northern shore of Africa, on a peninsula in the Bay of Tunis and near modern Tunis. The Latin name, Carthago or Cartago, was derived from the Phoenician name, which meant "new city" (the old city being Utica). It was founded (traditionally by DIDO) from Tyre in the 9th cent. B.C. The city-state built up trade and in the 6th and 5th cent. B.C. began to acquire dominance in the W Mediterranean. Merchants and explorers went out across the seas, and the wide net of trade brought back great wealth to Carthage. The state was tightly built under an aristocracy of nobles and wealthy merchants. Though a council and a popular assembly existed, these early lost power to oligarchical institutions, and actual power was in the hands of the judges and two elected magistrates. The greatest weakness of Carthage lay in the rivalry of the leading families, who traditionally backed opposing policies. The most important division was between those favoring land expansion and those favoring sea power. The maritime faction was generally in control, and about the end of the 6th cent. B.C. the Carthaginians established themselves on Sardinia, Malta, and the Balearic Islands. The navigator Hanno in the early 5th cent. is supposed to have gone down the African coast as far as Sierra Leone. The statesman Mago arrived at treaties with the Etruscans, the Romans, and some of the Greeks. However, Sicily, which lay almost at the front door of Carthage, was never brought completely under Carthaginian control. The move against the island, begun by settlements in W Sicily, was brought to a halt when the Carthaginian general HAMILCAR (a name which

Ruins of ancient Carthage in the foreground; today's city, a suburb of Tunis, in the background.

recurred in the powerful Carthaginian family usually called the Barcas), was defeated (480 B.C.) by Gelon, tyrant of Syracuse, in the battle of Himera. The Greek city-states of Magna Graecia were thus preserved, but the Carthaginian threat continued and grew with the steadily increasing power of Carthage. Hamilcar's grandson, Hannibal (another name much used in the family), and his colleague, Himilco, destroyed Acragas c.406 B.C. (see AGRIGENTO). SYRACUSE resisted the conquerors, and a century later the campaign (310–307?) of the tyrant AGATHOCLES on the shores of Africa threatened Carthage. After his death, however, Carthage had practically complete control over all the W Mediterranean. In the 3d cent. B.C., Rome challenged that control in the PUNIC WARS (so called after the Roman name for the Carthaginians, Poeni, i.e., Phoenicians). The first of these wars (264–241) cost Carthage all remaining hold on Sicily. Carthage's fatal division of the leading families in the state was shown clearly when the actions of another HANNO, a rival of the Barcas, brought on a great uprising of the mercenaries (240–238) soon after the First Punic War. HAMILCAR BARCA put down the revolt and compensated for the loss of Sicilian possessions by undertaking conquest in Spain, a conquest continued by Hasdrubal. This growth of power again activated trouble with Rome, and the second of the Punic Wars took place (218–201). Though the Carthaginian general was HANNIBAL, Carthage was ingloriously defeated, partly by the Roman generals, FABIUS (d.203) and SCIPIO AFRICANUS MAJOR, and partly by the fatal division in Carthage itself, which prevented Hannibal from receiving proper supplies. After Scipio had won (202) the battle of Zama, Carthage sued for peace. All its warships and its possessions outside Africa were lost, but

Carthage was allowed to continue and expand its lucrative commerce. However, Rome (and particularly CATO THE ELDER) felt even this to be a threat, and the third of the Punic Wars (149–146) ended with the total destruction of Carthaginian power and the razing of the city itself by SCIPIO AFRICANUS MINOR. Romans later undertook to build a new city on the spot in 122, but the project failed. Julius Caesar did found a new city, which under Augustus became an important center of Roman administration. Carthage was later (A.D. 439–533) the capital of the Vandals and was briefly recovered (A.D. 533) for the Byzantine Empire by Belisarius. Although the Arab Hassan ibn Numan, governor of Egypt, practically destroyed the city in 698, the site was populated for many centuries afterward. There are hardly any remains of the ancient Carthage. A few Punic cemeteries, shrines, and fortifications have been discovered, and there are some Roman ruins including baths, an amphitheater, and other buildings. Louis IX of France (St. Louis) died here when on crusade. A chapel in his honor stands on the hill which is traditionally identified as Byrsa Hill, site of the ancient citadel. The Lavigérie Museum is also here. Carthage today is a suburb of TUNIS. See B. H. Warmington, *Carthage* (1960); Colette and Gilbert Charles-Picard, *Daily Life in Carthage at the Time of Hannibal* (Eng. tr., 1961).

Carthage. 1 City (pop. 3,325), co. seat of Hancock co., W Ill., near the Mississippi and E of Keokuk, Iowa; laid out 1833, inc. 1837. It is a farm trade center. Carthage College (Lutheran; coeducational; 1870) is here. The old jail in which the Mormon leader Joseph Smith was killed (1844) by a mob is now the property of the Mormon church and is regarded as a shrine by the many Mormons who annually visit it. **2** Town (pop. 1,043), E central Ind., E of Indianapolis, in a grain and livestock area. **3** Town (pop. 2,442), co. seat of Leake co., central Miss., near the Pearl and NE of Jackson, in a farm and timber area. **4** City (pop. 11,264), co. seat of Jasper co., SW Mo., on the Spring river and near Joplin, in a lead, zinc, and marble area; founded 1842, inc. 1873. It is a shipping center for farm and dairy products. Explosives and clothing are among the city's manufactures. In the Civil War Carthage was the scene of a Confederate victory on July 5, 1861. At nearby Diamond is the George Washington Carver National Monument (210 acres; est. 1951), the site of Carver's birthplace. **5** Village (pop. 4,216), N N.Y., on the Black River and E of Watertown; settled before 1801, inc. 1841. Paper milling is the chief industry. **6** Town (pop. 1,190), co. seat of Moore co., central N.C., SW of Sanford, in a fruit and tobacco area; inc. 1796. **7** Town (pop. 2,021), co. seat of Smith co., central Tenn., on the Cumberland river and ENE of Nashville; founded 1804, inc. 1817. A tobacco center, it also produces cheese and textiles. The Cordell Hull Bridge crosses the river here. **8** City (pop. 5,262), co. seat of Panola co., E Texas, SE of Longview and near the Sabine; founded 1848. It is the site of a large natural-gas field and the source of numerous interstate pipelines. The region also yields oil and pinewood. A junior college is here.

Carthusians (kärthū′zhùnz), small order of monks of the Roman Catholic Church [Lat. abbr.,= O.Cart.]. It was established by St. BRUNO at La Grande Chartreuse (see CHARTREUSE, GRANDE) in France in 1084. The Carthusians are peculiar among orders of Western monasticism in cultivating a nearly eremitical life: each monk lives by himself with cell and garden and, apart from their public worship, scarcely meets the others. No order is more austere. The Carthusian enclosure is called charterhouse in English, and its architecture differs necessarily from that of the Benedictine ABBEY. The CHARTERHOUSE of London was famous, and the CERTOSA DI PAVIA, Italy, is an architectural monument. The Carthusians are devoted mainly to contemplation. In 1960 they numbered 587 members throughout the world. They are unchanging in their rule, their independence, and their original way of life. CHARTREUSE is the well-known liqueur manufactured by Carthusians in France. There are a very few Carthusian nuns following a similar rule.

Cartier, Sir Georges Étienne (zhôrzh′ ātyĕn′ kärtyā′), 1814–73, Canadian statesman, b. Quebec prov. He was called to the bar of Lower Canada in 1835. He took part in the rebellion of 1837 and was forced to flee to the United States, but he returned to Canada in 1838. In 1848 he was elected to the legislative assembly of Canada, where he became a leader of the French Canadians. With Sir John A. MACDONALD, his ally in Upper Canada, he formed the Macdonald-Cartier ministry (1857–62). He was the leading French Canadian advocate of confederation, played a prominent role in the Charlottetown Conference and Quebec Conference of 1864, and was mainly influential in persuading his compatriots to accept the federation proposals. On the other hand, in order to protect the French Canadians, he had insisted on a federal system as

The Certosa di Pavia, famous Carthusian monastery.

against a more centralized form of government. As one of Macdonald's most trusted colleagues, Cartier became minister of militia in the first dominion government. In 1868 he went to England with William McDougall to arrange for the purchase of the Hudson's Bay Company territory. He also had an important part in the projection of the Grand Trunk and Canadian Pacific railroads. See biographies by John Boyd (1914) and A. D. DeCelles (1926).

Cartier, Jacques (zhäk), 1491–1557, French navigator, first explorer of the Gulf of St. Lawrence and discoverer of the St. Lawrence river. He made three voyages to the region, the first two (1534, 1535–36) directly at the command of Francis I and the third (1541–42) under the sieur de Roberval in a colonization scheme that failed. On the first voyage he entered by the Strait of Belle Isle, skirted its barren north coast for a way, and then coasted along the west shore of Newfoundland to Cape Anguille. From there he discovered the Magdalen Islands and Prince Edward Island, and going to the coast of New Brunswick, explored Chaleur Bay, continued around the Gaspé Peninsula, and landed at Gaspé to take possession for France. Continuing to Anticosti island, he turned back with the approach of autumn storms. Hitherto the region had been considered cold and forbidding, interesting only because of the Labrador and Newfoundland fisheries, but Cartier's reports of a warmer, more fertile region in New Brunswick and on the Gaspé and of an inlet of unknown extent stimulated the king to dispatch him on a second expedition. On this voyage he ascended the river to the site of modern Quebec and, leaving some of his men to prepare winter quarters, continued to the Indian village of Hochelaga, on the site of the present city of Montreal, and there climbed Mt. Royal to survey the fertile valley and see the Lachine Rapids and Ottawa river. On his return he explored Cabot Strait, ascertaining Newfoundland to be an island. His *Brief Récit et succincte narration* (1545), a description of this voyage, was his only account to be published in France during his life. On his third trip he penetrated again to the Lachine Rapids and wintered in the same region, but gained little new geographical information. Roberval did not appear until Cartier was on his way home, and Cartier refused to join him. Although Cartier's discoveries were of major geographical importance and the claims of the French to the St. Lawrence valley were based on them, he failed in his primary object, the discovery of the Northwest Passage and natural resources. The region remained virtually untouched until the time of Champlain. The best edition of the voyages is H. P. Biggar, *The Voyages of Jacques Cartier* (1924).

Currier & Ives cartoon (1868), which was captioned "Reconstruction, or a White Man's Government."

Jacques Cartier

Cartier-Bresson, Henri (ărē', –brĕsŏ'), 1908–, French photographer. He is known for his numerous memorable images of 20th-century events, which range from pictorial records of the Spanish civil war to photographs of the coronation of George VI. A prisoner of war in Germany for three years, he escaped to France and in 1944 organized underground photography units. Since 1946 he has photographed many aspects of American life. He is the author of *Decisive Moment* (1952), *People of Moscow* (1955), and *China in Transition* (1956).

cartilage (kär'tŭlĭj) or **gristle,** white flexible semi-opaque substance without blood vessels that forms part of the skeletal system in man and other vertebrates. Temporary cartilage makes up the skeletal system of the fetus and the infant and gradually turns to bone as the body matures. Permanent cartilage remains throughout life, as in the external ear, nose, larynx, and windpipe. It is also present about the joints where it acts as a padding between hard bones and imparts flexibility to the joints. Cartilage is subject to injury and disease.

cartoon. 1 In the fine arts, a full-sized preliminary drawing for a work to be afterwards executed in fresco, oil, mosaic, stained glass or tapestry. Glass and mosaic are cut exactly by the patterns taken from the cartoons while in tapestry the cartoon is inserted beneath the warp to serve as a guide. In fresco painting, the lines of the cartoon are perforated and transferred to the plaster by pouncing. The Italian Renaissance painters developed their designs for fresco and tapestry in full detail in the

cartoons, and such works as Raphael's cartoons for the tapestries of the Sistine Chapel (Victoria and Albert Mus.) or Mantegna's cartoons of the *Triumph of Julius Ceasar* (Hampton Court) are treasured masterpieces. **2** In journalism, any single humorous or satirical drawing employing distortion for emphasis and often accompanied by a caption or a legend. Cartoons, particularly editorial or political cartoons, make use of the elements of CARICATURE. The political cartoon first appeared in 16th-century Germany during the Reformation, the first time such art became an active propaganda weapon with social implications. While many of these cartoons are crudely executed and incredibly vulgar, some, such as Holbein's *German Hercules,* were produced by the best artists of the time. In England, in the 18th cent., the cartoon became an integral and effective part of journalism through the works of Hogarth and Rowlandson. By the mid-19th cent. editorial cartoons had become regular features in American newspapers and were soon followed by sports cartoons and humorous cartoons. The effect of political cartoons on public opinion was amply demonstrated in the elections of 1871 and 1873 when the power of Tammany Hall was broken and Boss Tweed imprisoned largely through the efforts of Thomas Nast and his cartoons for *Harper's Weekly.* In 1922 the first Pulitzer Prize for editorial cartooning was won by Rollin Kirby of the New York *World.* Other Pulitzer Prize winners include John T. McCutcheon (Chicago *Tribune*, 1932), C. D. Batchelor (New York *Daily News*, 1937), Jacob Burck (Chicago *Times*, 1941), Bill Mauldin (*Up Front*, 1945), Rube Goldberg (New York *Sun*, 1948), and Tom Little (Nashville *Tennessean*, 1957). Humorous nonpolitical cartoons became popular with the development of the color press, and in 1893 the first color cartoon appeared in the New York *World.* In 1896 R. F. Outcault originated *The Yellow Kid*, a large single panel cartoon with some use of dialogue in balloons, and throughout the '90s humorous cartoons by such artists as T. S. Sullivant, James Swinnerton, Frederick B. Opper, and Edward W. Kemble began to appear regularly in major newspapers and journals. The single cartoons soon developed into the narrative newspaper COMIC STRIP, although the single panel episodic tradition is still retained, exemplified by humorists such as Charles Addams, Peter Arno, Ted Key, and Virgil Partch. See Stephen Becker, *Comic Art in America* (1959).

Cartouche (kärtōōsh'), 1693–1721, nickname of Louis Dominique Bourguignon, French criminal. His band terrorized the Paris area until his capture. He was broken on the wheel. Cartouche's daring exploits have been celebrated in stories, dramas, ballads, and popular prints.

Cartwright, Edmund, 1743–1823, English inventor and clergyman. He was the inventor of an imperfect power loom which, when finally patented (1785), became the parent of the modern loom. It was the first machine to make practical the weaving of wide cotton cloth. A few of Cartwright's many other inventions were a wool-combing machine (1789), a machine for ropemaking (1792), and a fuel alcohol engine (1797). He cooperated with Fulton on his experiments with steam navigation.

Cartwright, John, 1740–1824, English reformer and pamphleteer; brother of Edmund Cartwright. He had an early career in the navy. He declined to fight the American colonists and wrote *American Independence: the Interest and Glory of Great Britain* (1774). A major in the Nottinghamshire militia (1775–92), he was deprived of his commission in the hysteria at the time of the French Revolutionary Wars. He came to be called the father of reform for his advocacy of universal manhood suffrage, parliamentary and army reform, and abolition of slavery.

Cartwright, Peter, 1785–1872, American Methodist preacher, b. Virginia. He was a circuit rider in Kentucky, Tennessee, Indiana, Ohio, and Illinois for nearly 50 years. In 1846 he was defeated for Congress by Abraham Lincoln. An interest in education led Cartwright to aid in founding Illinois Wesleyan Univ. and Illinois Conference Female Academy (now MacMurray College for Women). The methods and experiences of the pioneer preacher are vividly recorded in his autobiography (1857) and other books. See biography by H. H. Grant (1931).

Cartwright, Sir Richard John, 1835–1912, Canadian politician, b. Kingston, Ont., educated at Trinity College, Dublin. He was elected as a Conservative to the legislative assembly of Canada (1863) and to the first dominion House of Commons (1867), but he later joined the Liberals. He was minister of finance (1873–78) in Alexander Mackenzie's administration. As minister of trade and finance (1896–1911) in Sir Wilfrid Laurier's government, Cartwright was acting prime minister on several occasions. He entered the Senate in 1904. A noted public speaker, he was the Liberal party's spokesman on financial matters and an earnest advocate of trade reciprocity with the United States. See his reminiscences (1912).

Cartwright, William, 1611–43, English author and divine. An ardent royalist and a disciple of Ben Jonson, he had a high reputation in his day both as preacher and as author. In addition to his poems, which are now almost entirely forgotten, Cartwright wrote plays, of which *The Ordinary* (produced 1635?) and *The Royal Slave* (produced 1636) were the most successful. See his works (ed. with an introduction by G. Blakemore Evans, 1951).

Carucci, Jacopo: see PONTORMO, JACOPO DA.

Carus (Marcus Aurelius Carus) (kâ'rùs), d. 283, Roman emperor (282–83). Praetorian prefect under PROBUS, he was made emperor by the soldiers after the murder of Probus. Leaving his son CARINUS in command of the West, Carus and another son, Numerianus, went on a campaign in the East. He defeated the Sarmatians, successfully attacked the Parthians, and took Ctesiphon. Soon afterward he died mysteriously.

Carus, Paul, 1852–1919, American philosopher, born and educated in Germany. For many years he was editor of the *Open Court* and the *Monist*, periodicals devoted to philosophy and religion. His philosophy was monistic, seeking to establish religion on a scientific basis. Among his many works were *Fundamental Problems* (1889), *The Religion of Science* (1893), *The Gospel of Buddha* (1900), *The History of the Devil* (1900), and *The Principle of Relativity* (1913).

Caruso, Enrico (kùrōō'sō, Ital. änrē'kō kärōō'zō), 1873–1921, Italian operatic tenor, b. Naples. The range, power, and vivid coloring of his voice made him one of the greatest singers in the history of the opera. He early gained repute and was well known before his first appearance at the Metropolitan as the duke in *Rigoletto* in 1903. He was there a reigning favorite until his fatal illness began in 1920. He sang more than 50 roles in Italian and French operas. After his death his records continued to swell his fame. His big-voiced singing

Enrico Caruso

of Canio in *I Pagliacci* perhaps won the most rapturous public applause, but roles in the Verdi and Puccini operas and his concerts showed his artistry to better advantage. See biographies by P. van R. Key and Bruno Zirato (1922), Dorothy Benjamin Caruso (1945), and T. R. Ybarra (1953).

Caruthersville (kŭrŭ'dhŭrzvĭl), city (pop. 8,643), co. seat of Pemiscot co., extreme SE Mo., on the Mississippi and NW of Dyersburg, Tenn., in a cotton, farm, and timber region; founded 1794, platted and inc. 1857. It is a cotton-ginning and shipping point; its products include shoes, sand, and gravel.

Carvajal, Francisco de (fränthē'skō dä kärvähäl'), 1464?–1548, Spanish conquistador. For 40 years he fought in European wars before going to Mexico and subsequently to Peru, where he aided Francisco Pizarro. He grew rich from the tributary labor of Indians, thousands of whom died in his mines at Potosí. He supported (1542) VACA DE CASTRO against the revolt of Diego de Almagro the younger, but when the New Laws to protect the Indians were put in force in Peru (1544), he joined the revolt of Gonzalo PIZARRO. He was captured with Gonzalo Pizarro and was executed.

carvel: see CARAVEL.

Carver, George Washington, 1864?–1943, American Negro agricultural chemist, b. Diamond, Mo.,

George Washington Carver

grad. Iowa State College, 1894. Having joined (1894) the staff of Tuskegee Institute, he became (1896) director of the department of agricultural research there, and he retained this post the rest of his life, his work winning him international repute. His efforts to improve the economy of the South included the teaching of soil improvement and of diversification of crops. He discovered hundreds of uses for the peanut, the sweet potato, and the soybean and thus stimulated the culture of these crops. He devised many products from cotton waste and extracted blue, purple, and red pigments from local clay. From 1935 he was a collaborator of the Bureau of Plant Industry. Carver contributed his life savings to a foundation for research at Tuskegee. In 1953 his birthplace was made a national monument. See biographies by Rackham Holt rev. ed., 1963 and Shirley Graham and G. D. Lipscomb (1944).

Carver, John, c.1576–1621, first governor of Plymouth Colony. A native of either Nottinghamshire or Derbyshire, he won considerable wealth as a London merchant. In 1609 he emigrated to Holland, where he soon joined the Pilgrims at Leiden.

His excellent character and his fortune, of which he gave liberally to the congregation, made him a leader. Carver, the chief figure in arranging for the Pilgrim migration to America, secured the backing of merchant friends in London, enlisted a number of capable settlers who came directly from England, and hired and provisioned the *Mayflower* for the journey. After the signing of the Mayflower Compact he was elected (1620) governor for one year and was probably responsible for the choice of the site at Plymouth. On his death, William BRADFORD succeeded him. See G. F. Willison, *Saints and Strangers* (1945).

Carver, Jonathan, 1710–80, American explorer, b. Weymouth, Mass. He served in the French and Indian War and in 1766 was hired by Robert ROGERS to undertake a journey to some of the Western tribes. He journeyed to the Mississippi and up that river to a point several days' journey above the present site of Minneapolis. In the spring of 1767 he returned to Prairie du Chien, where by Rogers's orders he joined the expedition to search out the "Western Ocean." Their journey northwestward being prevented by war between the Sioux and Chippewa, they ascended the Chippewa river and crossed to Lake Superior, the coast of which they followed to Grand Portage. Carver went to London in 1769 with the intention of publishing a narrative of his travels and of pressing claims for compensation for his services, for Rogers, having exceeded his authority in employing Carver, could not pay him. After nine years of struggle and poverty, Carver published the first edition of his *Travels through the Interior Parts of North America in the Years 1766, 1767, and 1768* (1778). The popularity of this book, the first English account of the upper Great Lakes and Mississippi region, is attested by the 32 editions, or more, through which it passed.

Carver, rural town (pop. 1,949), SE Mass., W of Plymouth; settled c.1660, inc. 1790.

Carver Court, uninc. village (pop. 1,818), SE Ala., near Tuskegee.

carving, the art of cutting or abrading designs or figures in relief or in the round in stone (see CAMEO), wood, metal, bone, ivory, and other materials. The tools commonly used in carving include a wide variety of gouges, drills, points, hammers, chisels, and saws. Carving is to be clearly distinguished from such other techniques of the sculptor as modeling or casting, which presuppose a readily malleable material or one which can be liquefied. True carving is always a process of subtraction. (See SCULPTURE and WOOD CARVING.)

Cary, Alice, 1820–71, and **Phoebe Cary**, 1824–71, American writers, sisters, b. Ohio. Their first success came with *Poems of Alice and Phoebe Cary* (1849), after which they moved to New York and became popular in the circle of Horace Greeley. Alice contributed to the leading magazines of the time and was the author of several novels. Phoebe is best known for her religious verse, most notably the famous hymn, "One sweetly solemn thought."

Cary, Henry Francis, 1772–1844, English writer. He translated several classical writers, including Aristophanes and Pindar. His blank-verse rendering (1814) of Dante's *Divine Comedy* is still a standard translation.

Caryatids of the Temple of Apollo in Delphi, Greece.

Cary, Joyce (Arthur Joyce Lunel Cary), 1888–1957, English novelist. In the 1910s he served as an administrator and soldier in Nigeria. Several of his early works, including *Mister Johnson* (1939), reflect his African experiences. Cary is perhaps best known for his two trilogies. The first consists of *Herself Surprised* (1941), *To Be a Pilgrim* (1942), and *The Horse's Mouth* (1944); the second of *Prisoner of Grace* (1952), *Except the Lord* (1953), and *Not Honour More* (1955). These works, full of humor and compassion, convey the sense of the gradual change in the social and political structure of modern England. A collection of his short stories, *Spring Song*, was published posthumously in 1960. See study by Andrew Wright (1958).

Cary, Lucius: see FALKLAND, LUCIUS CARY, 2D VISCOUNT.

Cary, Phoebe: see CARY, ALICE.

Cary. 1 Village (pop. 2,530), NE Ill., near the Fox river and N of Elgin, in a resort and dairy region; settled 1834, platted 1856, inc. 1893. Electronic equipment is made. A center for the artificial breeding of cattle is here. 2 Town (pop. 3,356), central N.C., W of Raleigh; founded 1852, inc. 1870. Mineral products and machinery are made. It is the birthplace of Walter Hines Page. Nearby are the state fairgrounds.

caryatid (kăreă'tĭd) [Gr.,=maid of Caryae, 15 mi. N of Sparta; i.e., dancer at Artemis' shrine there], a sculptured female figure serving as an ornamental support in place of a column or pilaster. It was a frequently used motive in architecture, furniture, and garden sculpture during the Renaissance, the 18th cent., and notably, the CLASSIC REVIVAL of the 19th cent., when caryatids were popular as mantelpiece supports. The motive appeared in Egyptian and Greek architecture; the most celebrated example extant is the Porch of the Caryatids, forming part of the ERECHTHEUM. Here six beautifully sculptured figures, acting as columns, support an entablature on their heads. They are considered the only faultless examples of a form which ranks as somewhat questionable architecturally. Caryatids were used also in two small treasuries (6th cent. B.C.) at Delphi.

Casa, Giovanni della (jōvän'nĕ dĕl'lä kä'zä), 1503–56, Italian cleric and poet. He was archbishop of Benevento and papal nuncio to Venice. He wrote lyric verse, a life of Bembo, and a treatise on etiquette, the *Galateo* (1560; Eng. tr., 1576). His verse is often of great dignity and formal beauty. See Lorna de' Lucchi, *An Anthology of Italian Poems* (1922).

Giovanni della Casa

casaba melon: see MELON.

Casabianca, Louis (kä"sûbēäng'kû, kä"zû-), c.1752–1798, French revolutionist and naval officer, b. Corsica. At ABOUKIR Bay he commanded (1798) the *Orient*, which caught fire. He refused to quit his ship, and his young son refused to desert him. This event is the basis for a poem by Felicia Hemans.

Casablanca (kä"sûbläng'kû, kä"zû-, Span. kä"säbläng'kä), Arabic *Dar el Beida*, city (pop. 960,812), Morocco, a port on the Atlantic Ocean. It is on the site of Anfa, a prosperous town which the Portuguese destroyed in 1468; they resettled it briefly in 1515 under its present name. Almost destroyed by an earthquake in 1755, Casablanca was rebuilt by Mohammed XVI, who fostered its commerce. By 1900 it was an important port of North Africa, and it was occupied by the French in 1907 (see MOROCCO). The port, its facilities greatly improved, handles over two thirds of Morocco's commerce. It exports cereals, leather, wool, and phosphates, and it shelters large fishing fleets. In the Second World

Courtyard of the Great Mosque in Casablanca.

Casablanca conference. Left to right: General Giraud, President Roosevelt, General de Gaulle, Prime Minister Churchill.

War it was the scene of one of the three major allied landings in North Africa (Nov., 1942) and of a conference between Winston Churchill and F. D. Roosevelt (Jan., 1943). About one fifth of the population is European.

Casablanca Conference, Jan. 14–24, 1943, meeting of U.S. President F. D. Roosevelt and British Prime Minister Winston Churchill at Casablanca, French Morocco. A joint declaration pledged that the Second World War would end only with the unconditional surrender of the Axis states. No agreement was reached on the claims for leadership of the rival French generals, Henri H. Giraud and Charles de Gaulle, who also attended the conference.

Casablanca group: see AFRO-ASIAN BLOC.

Casadesus, Robert (käsädäsüs'), 1899–, French pianist, studied at the Paris Conservatory. He was head of the piano department of the American Conservatory at Fontainebleau in 1934 and director of the school for some years after 1945. He made (1935) a concert tour in the United States, where he took up residence in 1940. A distinguished pianist, particularly as a player of French music, he is the composer of concertos, piano pieces, and symphonies. He often appeared in two-piano recitals with his wife, Gaby Casadesus. Their son, Jean Casadesus (1927–), is also a pianist.

Casa Fuerte, Juan de Acuña, marqués de: see ACUÑA, JUAN DE.

Casa Grande (kä'sä grän'dä), town (pop. 8,311), S Ariz., near the Casa Grande Mts. and SSE of Phoenix, in an irrigated farm area. It was named for an excavated Indian pueblo, which is now included in nearby Casa Grande National Monument (472.50 acres; est. 1918).

Casal, Julián del (hōōlyän' dĕl käsäl'), 1863–93, Cuban poet, a friend of Rubén Darío and a leader in *modernismo*. He was thoroughly imbued with the French Parnassian movement. Afflicted with a painful form of tuberculosis, he wrote verse expressing deep pessimism, but he escaped reality by choosing subjects from antiquity and far-off lands, especially Japan. His best-known collections are *Hojas al viento* [leaves in the wind] (1890) and *Bustos y rimas* [busts and rimes] (1893).

Casale or **Casale Monferrato** (käsä'lä mōnfär-rä'tō), city (estimated pop. 38,632), in Piedmont, NW Italy, on the Po. Much wine is produced in the region, and there are important cement industries.

It became the capital of the marquisate of MONT-FERRAT in 1435 and was strongly fortified. In 1703 it passed to the house of SAVOY. The 15th-century citadel is now a barracks.

Casals, Pablo (pä'blō käsäls'), 1876–, Spanish cellist and conductor. He began his career as a cellist in 1895, and in 1905 he formed a chamber trio with

Robert Casadesus

Pablo Casals

Jacques Thibaud (1880–1953) and Alfred Cortot. His career as a conductor began in 1920, when the Orquestra Pau Casals, Barcelona, gave its first concert. In 1901 he made the first of many concert appearances in the United States. In 1939 he settled at Prades in S France, a voluntary exile in protest against the Spanish government. In 1950 he began to conduct annual music festivals in Prades. In 1956 he moved to Puerto Rico, where the following year he inaugurated annual music festivals at San Juan. See Lillian Littlehales, *Pablo Casals* (rev. ed., 1948); Bernard Taper, *Cellist in Exile* (1962). **Casanova, Giovanni Battista** (jōvän′nē bät-tēs′tä käzänō′vä), c.1722–1795, Italian painter, studied in Dresden. He is remembered principally for his designs for Winckelmann's work on ancient monuments. His brother, **Francesco Giuseppe Casanova** (fränchäs′kō jōōzĕp′pä), 1727–c.1802, b. London, was a painter and engraver. He was painter to the king and a member of the Académie royale de Peinture et de Sculpture.

Giovanni Giacomo
Casanova de Seingalt

Giovanni Battista Casanova

Casanova de Seingalt, Giovanni Giacomo (kăzùnō′vù, Ital. jōvän′nē jä′kōmō käzänō′vä dä sängält′), 1725–98, Venetian adventurer and author. His first name also appears as Jacopo. He studied for the church but was expelled from school for immorality. A life of adventure took him all over Europe. He supported himself by gambling, spying, writing, and, especially, by his power to seduce women, and his personal charm affected the foremost persons of his time. Arrested (1755) in Venice, he accomplished the notable feat of escaping (1756) from the "leaden roofs" of the state prison. In Paris, where he enjoyed favor in court circles, he became director of the lottery. In 1785 Casanova retired to the castle of Dux, Bohemia, where his friend Count Waldstein employed him as librarian. A man of learning and taste, with interests ranging from mathematics, poetry, and literary and musical criticism to commercial and political projects, Casanova left many writings.

His memoirs, written in French, became world-famous. Only abridged versions were published until 1960, when the complete memoirs began to appear in French and in German translation. Accurate as to history, the memoirs probably contain much invented personal matter. Other papers, in prose and verse, were released in 1930. See biographies by Édouard Maynial (Eng. tr., 1911), Guy Endore (1929), and Hermann Kesten (Eng. tr., 1955).

Casas, Bartolomé de las: see LAS CASAS.

Casaubon, Isaac (ēzäk′ käzōbō′), 1559–1614, French classical scholar and theologian, b. Geneva. He became professor of Greek at Geneva and at Montpellier and attracted by his learning the notice of Henry IV, who made him royal librarian. Both Catholics and Protestants sought to win Casaubon's support, and both denounced him when he joined the Church of England. In 1610 James I of England made him prebendary at Canterbury and Westminster. He spent the rest of his life in England and was buried in Westminster Abbey. Casaubon's great works are his editions of the classics, particularly Athenaeus and the *Characters* of Theophrastus. Casaubon's diary, *Ephemerides*, was edited by his son, **Florence Étienne Méric Casaubon** (flôrãs′ ätyĕn′ mārēk′), 1599–1671, who was also a classical scholar.

Casca (Publius Servilius Casca Longus) (kă′skù), d. c.42 B.C., Roman politician, one of the assassins of Julius CAESAR. Casca was the first to stab Caesar. He died (presumably by suicide) soon after the battle of Philippi.

Cascade, town (pop. 1,601), E central Iowa, on the North Fork of the Maquoketa river and SSE of Dubuque, in a fertile farm area; settled 1834, platted 1842, inc. 1881.

Cascade Range, northern continuation of the Sierra Nevada extending c.700 mi. through N California, Oregon, and Washington into British Columbia, paralleling the Pacific coast (and the Coast Ranges) 100 to 150 mi. inland. The range shows evidence of volcanic activity in the later geological periods, and all the highest summits are volcanic cones covered with snow fields and glaciers. Some of the most magnificent and better-known peaks are Mt. Shasta (14,162 ft.; Calif.); Mt. Thielsen, Mt. Jefferson, and Mt. Hood (Oregon); Mt. St. Helens, Mt. Adams, Mt. Rainier—the highest, with an altitude of 14,410 ft.—and Mt. Baker (Wash.). The slopes are clothed with fir, pine, and cedar forests, large areas of which are held as national reserves. Three rivers, the Klamath, the Columbia, and the Fraser, cut across the range to the Pacific. See R. O. Case and Victoria Case, *Last Mountains: the Story of the Cascades* (1945).

cascara sagrada (kăskâ′rù sùgrä′dù), dried bark of a buckthorn (*Rhamnus purshiana*) native to North America from British Columbia to N. California and Montana. An extract prepared from the cured bark is used in medicine as a laxative.

Casco Bay (kăs′kō), inlet of the Atlantic, S Maine, with its principal harbor at Portland. Its shores and many islands are irregular in outline, hilly, and beautifully wooded; hundreds of summer estates and resorts are here.

case, in INFLECTION, one of the several possible forms of a given noun, pronoun, or adjective. In

Southern slopes of Mt. Rainier in the Cascade Range.

English, many nouns have two cases, e.g., man (common or nominative) and man's (possessive or genitive), and a few pronouns have three, e.g., *he* (nominative), *him* (objective), *his* (possessive). Latin has six cases: nominative, genitive, dative, accusative, ablative, and vocative. The linguistic ancestor of Indo-European languages had eight cases, the above six plus the instrumental and locative cases. Languages differ in the number of cases and in the range of their meanings; German has four, Russian six, Finnish sixteen. The greatest number of cases observed in a language is fifty-two, found in Tabarasan, a language of the E Caucasus. In Europe, the concept of case was first introduced by the Greeks. Sanskrit grammarians, independently, also established this category. The names of the most common cases derive from Greek by way of Latin translation, as does the term *case* itself. Its original meaning has never been satisfactorily explained.

casehardening: see HARDENING.

casein (kā′sēĭn), white, amorphous protein, constituting about 80 percent of the total PROTEINS in milk. A complex substance containing phosphorus, it is properly called a phosphoprotein. Precipitated by the LACTIC ACID in souring milk it forms the edible curd, acid casein, used widely in adhesives, in cold-water paint, for coating paper, and in printing textiles and wallpaper. Casein precipitated by the enzyme rennin forms the insoluble rennet (or calcium) casein, the chief protein in cheese. Treated with formaldehyde, rennet casein forms casein plastic that is used especially for manufacturing buttons and fountain pens and sometimes as a waterproof coating for paper receptacles.

Case Institute of Technology, at Cleveland; for men; chartered 1880, opened 1881 through a bequest of Leonard Case, Jr.; called Case School of Applied Science until 1947. The Warner and Swasey Observatory and the Nassau Astronomical Station are operated here.

Casella, Alfredo (älfrä′dō käsĕl′lä), 1883–1947, Italian composer, pianist, conductor, and writer on music; pupil of Gabriel Fauré at the Paris Conservatory. He taught piano at the Paris Conservatory (1911–15) and at the St. Cecilia Conservatory, Rome (1915–23). In 1917 he organized a society, later known as Corporazione delle Nuove Musiche, to promote the recognition of contemporary music. He is the author of *The Evolution of Music throughout the History of the Perfect Cadence* (Eng. tr., 1924). His best-known compositions are the ballets *Il convento veneziano* (1912) and *La Giara* (Paris, 1924), the latter based on a novel by Pirandello. Other works are piano pieces, songs, chamber music, orchestral works, and concertos. See his memoirs, *Music in My Time* (Eng. tr., 1955).

Casement, Roger David, 1864–1916, Irish revolutionary. In the course of British consular service (1895–1913) he exposed the atrocious conditions imposed on gatherers of wild rubber in the Congo. His report served as grounds for the extinction (1908) of the Congo Free State. He exposed similar conditions in South America and was knighted for his services. Though an Ulster Protestant Casement became an ardent Irish nationalist. He went to Germany to gain aid for the rebellion of 1916 in Ireland. He was arrested on his return to Ireland when he landed from a German submarine. He was convicted in London of high treason, deprived of knighthood, and hanged. He is regarded by the Irish as a martyr patriot. See biographies by René MacColl (1956) and Peter Singleton-Gates and Maurice Girodias (1959).

Caserta (käzĕr′tä), city (estimated pop. 47,711), capital of Caserta prov., Campania, S Italy. An

Reception hall of the royal palace at Caserta.

agricultural and commercial center, it is noted for its magnificent royal palace (built 1752–74) and gardens. The surrender of the German forces in Italy to the Allies was signed here on April 29, 1945.

Casey (kā′zē, kā′sē), city (pop. 2,890), E Ill., SW of Terre Haute, Ind., in a farm area; inc. 1896.

Caseyville, village (pop. 2,455), SW Ill., E of East St. Louis; inc. 1869.

Casgrain, Henri Raymond (ärē′ rāmō′ käsgrē′), 1831–1904, French Canadian historian. He wrote enthusiastic histories, such as *Légendes canadiennes* (1861), *Pélerinage au pays d'Evangeline* (1887), *Les Pionniers canadiens* (1876), and *Montcalm and Wolfe* ("Makers of Canada" series; rev. ed., 1926).

Cashew leaves, apple, and nut.

cash, popular term for ready MONEY. In commerce and banking the term is used in contradistinction to commercial paper. To "cash" such paper means to convert it into currency. In bookkeeping terms like petty cash and cashbook, the word has the same meaning. "Cash payment" is opposed to "credit," though cash payment may be made in coin, in notes, or by check.

Cashel (kă′shúl) [Irish,=castle], urban district (pop. 2,679), Co. Tipperary, S central Republic of Ireland. An agricultural market now, it was the ancient capital of the kings of Munster and was the stronghold of Brian Boru. The Rock of Cashel, rising 300 ft. in the center of the town, has the ruins of the 14th-century St. Patrick's Cathedral, a round tower (10th cent.), an ancient cross, and Cormac's Chapel (12th cent.). Below the Rock are the ruins of Hore Abbey (1272). Cashel is the seat of a Roman Catholic archbishop and of an Anglican bishop.

cashew (kủshōō′, kăsh′ōō), tropical American tree (*Anacardium occidentale*) of the SUMAC family, valued chiefly for the cashew nut of commerce. The tree's acrid sap is used in making a varnish that protects woodwork and books from insects. The fruit is kidney-shaped, about an inch in length, and has a double shell. The kernel, which is sweet, oily, and nutritious, is much used for food in the tropics after being roasted to destroy the caustic juice. It yields a light-colored oil said to be the equal of olive oil and is utilized in various culinary ways by the natives. In the West Indies it is used to flavor wine, particularly Madeira, and is imported into Great Britain for this purpose. The nut grows on the end of a fleshy, pear-shaped stalk, called the cashew apple, which is white, yellow, or red, juicy and slightly acid, and is eaten by the native people or fermented to make wine.

Cashmere, India: see KASHMIR.

Cashmere, farm trade town (pop. 1,891), central Wash., on the Wenatchee river and near Wenatchee, in an apple area; settled 1881, platted 1892, inc. 1904. A historical museum here has exhibits of Indian and pioneer life.

Casilinum (kăsĭl′nŭm), ancient town, Campania, S Italy. Founded (c.600 B.C.) probably by the Etruscans, it became (5th cent. B.C.) the capital of the Samnites. Under the Romans it was an important military station controlling the bridge of the Appian Way over the Volturno river. It was destroyed by the Saracens in the 9th cent. A.D.; the inhabitants of nearby CAPUA moved here soon after and changed its name from Casilinum to Capua.

Casimir I (Casimir the Restorer) (kă′sŭmēr), Pol. *Kazimierz Odnowiciel*, c.1015–1058, Polish ruler, duke of Poland (c.1040–1058), son of MIESZKO II. He succeeded in reuniting the central Polish lands under the hegemony of the Holy Roman Empire, but he was never crowned king. His son and successor was Boleslaus II.

Casimir II, 1138–94, Polish ruler (1177–94), youngest son of Boleslaus III. A member of the PIAST dynasty, he drove his brother Mieszko III from power at Cracow in 1177 and became the principal duke of Poland. At the Congress of Leczyca (1180) the nobility and clergy, in return for privileges he had granted them, vested hereditary rights as rulers of Cracow in Casimir's descendants. Casimir himself was never crowned king.

Casimir III

Casimir III (Casimir the Great), Pol. *Kazimierz Wielki*, 1310–70, king of Poland (1333–70), son of Ladislaus I and last of the PIAST dynasty. He brought comparative peace to Poland. By the congress of Visegrad (1335) he promised to recognize the suzerainty over Silesia of John of Luxemburg, king of Bohemia; in return John renounced all claim to the Polish throne. In 1339 Casimir officially acknowledged John's power. By the Treaty of Kalisz (1343) with the Teutonic Knights, Casimir consolidated his territories, and later he acquired much of the duchy of Galich-Vladimir (see GALICH). He strengthened the royal power at the expense of the nobility and clergy; codified Polish law in the Statute of Wislica, alleviating the lot of the peasants (hence he was "king of the peasants"); improved the condition of the Jews; encouraged industry, commerce, and agriculture; and founded (1364) the Univ. of Cracow. Casimir was succeeded by his Angevin nephew, King Louis I of Hungary.

Casimir IV (Casimir Jagiello), 1427–92, king of Poland (1447–92). He became (1440) ruler of Lithuania and in 1447 succeeded his brother Ladislaus III as king of Poland. He united the two nations more closely by placing them on equal footing. With the Second Peace of Torun (1466) he ended a 13-year war with the Teutonic Knights. Calling (1467) the first Polish diet, he confirmed the privileges of the aristocracy. His marriage to an Austrian Hapsburg enabled his son Ladislaus to become king of Bohemia and later king of Hungary as Uladislaus II. Casimir was succeeded by his sons John I (1492–1501), Alexander I (1501–5), and Sigismund I (1506–48).

Casimir-Perier (käzēmēr′-pěryä′), name assumed after 1873 by **Auguste Casimir Victor Laurent Périer** (ōgüst′, vēktôr′ lōrä′), 1811–78, French statesman; son of Casimir PÉRIER. He was minister of the interior (1871–72). His son **Jean Paul Pierre Casimir-Perier** (zhä′ pôl′ pyěr′), 1847–1907, served as premier in 1893 and created the ministry of colonies. In 1894 he succeeded Sadi Carnot as president of the French republic. A moderate republican, he was attacked by the increasingly important left-wing parties and resigned early in 1895. Félix Faure succeeded him.

casino or **cassino** (both: kŭsē′nō), card game played with a full deck by two to four players. Four cards are dealt to each player, and four open cards are dealt to the table. Each player in turn must take in cards by matching his cards with cards of corresponding indices on the table (he may take two or more totaling his card's value); "build," add to one or more table cards to total the index value of a card remaining in his hand (there are other building variations); or "trail," lay a card face up on the table. The game ends after all the cards of the deck are dealt in successive hands of four cards each. The object is to take the greatest number of cards (counting 3 points) and the greatest number of spades (counting 1 point), the 10 of diamonds or big casino (2 points), the 2 of spades or little casino (1 point), and the aces (counting 1 point each). Casino probably originated in Italy.

Casiphia (kăsĭf′ēŭ, kăsĭf′ŭ), place, on the way from Babylon to Jerusalem. Ezra 8.17.

Casiquiare (kässēkyä′rä), river, S Venezuela. Also called the Canal Casiquiare, it is a branch of the Orinoco and flows c.100 mi. SW to the Río Negro, thus linking the Orinoco and Amazon basins.

Casket Letters: see MARY QUEEN OF SCOTS.

Caskets or **Casquets,** group of dangerous rocky isles in the English Channel near Alderney.

Caslon, William (kăz′lŭn), 1692–1766, English type founder. He worked first in London as an engraver of gunlocks. The use of the "old-style" types designed by him was discontinued for many years while "modern" types of John BASKERVILLE and others were preferred, but the merits of Caslon's types were rediscovered, and their standing is registered in the printers' maxim, "When in doubt, use Caslon." The individual letters are less impressive than those of Baskerville and Giambattista

BODONI, but they have the merit of combining marvelously into legible words and pages in which no detail of line or variation in "color" distracts a reader's attention from an author's meaning. In Caslon's "old-style" type, the contrast of light and heavy lines is not stressed as in "modern" type, and the serifs are inconspicuous, and at the tops of roman lowercase letters they are sloping; they are not decorations, but are mere aids to the eye in recognizing the letters.

Casluhim (kăs'lūhǐm, kăslū'–), ancient unidentified tribe. Gen. 10.14; 1 Chron. 1.12.

Caso, Alfonso (älfōn'sō kä'sō), 1896–, Mexican archaeologist. He is an authority on the ancient high civilizations of Mexico. During the 1920s and '30s he directed explorations at MITLA and MONTE ALBÁN. Among his many books and articles are *La religion de los Aztecas* (1936, Eng. tr., *The Religion of the Aztecs*, 1937), *Thirteen Masterpieces of Mexican Archeology* (Eng. tr., 1938), and *The Aztecs: People of the Sun* (Eng. tr., 1958).

Caspar: see WISE MEN OF THE EAST.

Casper, city (pop. 38,930), co. seat of Natrona co., E central Wyo., on the North Platte river and NW of Cheyenne; founded 1888 with the coming of the railroad, inc. 1889. It is a rail, distributing, and processing center in an oil and livestock area, with important wool and livestock markets, large oil refineries, and many oil-affiliated industries. The first well was tapped at Salt Creek field (1890); the Teapot Dome and Big Muddy fields followed, and Casper boomed. Wells in the Lost Soldier field of Sweetwater co. brought another boom in 1948. At this fording place on the Oregon Trail the Mormons in 1847 established a ferry, which was in the 1850s superseded by Platte Bridge. A junior college is here. Nearby are Hell's Half Acre, an eroded area; Independence Rock, a granite landmark on the Oregon Trail; the site of old Fort Caspar (a clerk's error accounts for the later spelling of the name); and Casper Mt. (c.8,000 ft. high), with a recreational area. Near Casper the Kendrick project of the Bureau of Reclamation comprises c.24,000 irrigated acres. The project has two dams in the North Platte—Seminoe Dam (295 ft. high; 530 ft. long; completed 1939), with a power plant and storage reservoir, and Alcova Dam (265 ft. high; 763 ft. long; completed 1938), with a power plant. Operated in conjunction with the Kendrick project are Pathfinder Reservoir, part of the NORTH PLATTE PROJECT, and Kortes Dam, part of the MISSOURI RIVER BASIN PROJECT. See A. J. Mokler, *History of Natrona County, Wyoming, 1888–1922* (1922).

Caspian, city (pop. 1,493), N Mich., SW Upper Peninsula, near the Wis. line S of L'Anse, in a lake region; inc. as a village 1918, as a city 1949.

Caspian Gates: see DERBENT.

Caspian Kara-Kum: see KARA-KUM.

Caspian Sea, Latin *Mare Caspium* or *Mare Hyrcanium*, salt lake, area c.163,800 sq. mi., USSR and Iran, between Europe and Asia, the largest inland body of water in the world. The larger part lies in Soviet territory; only the southern shore belongs to Iran. The Caspian Sea is at 92 ft. below sea level; it reaches its maximum depth (c.3,200 ft.) in the south. The Caucasus rises from its southwestern shore, and the Elburz mts., parallel to its

southern coast. It receives the Volga, Ural, Kura, and Terek rivers, but it has no outlet. The rate of evaporation is particularly high in the eastern inlet called KARA-BOGAZ-GOL, which is exploited for its salt. Variation in evaporation accounts for the great changes in the size of the sea in the course of history. Large projects are under way for raising its level. The chief ports on the Caspian are BAKU, the oil center, and ASTRAKHAN, at the mouth of the Volga. Oil is shipped across the Caspian from Baku to Astrakhan, from where it continues on the Volga. The Caspian is also of great importance for its fisheries and sealeries. The northern part of the sea is the chief source of beluga caviar.

Casquets: see CASKETS.

Cass, Lewis, 1782–1866, American statesman, b. Exeter, N.H. He established (1802) himself as a

Lewis Cass

lawyer in Zanesville, Ohio, and was U.S. marshal for Ohio from 1807 to 1812. In the War of 1812 Cass's command was included against his will in the forces which Gen. William Hull surrendered to the British at Detroit in Aug., 1812. Cass later fought with distinction at the battle of the Thames (Oct. 5, 1813). Left in command at Detroit, Cass was also appointed governor of Michigan Territory, a post he filled ably for 18 years (1813–31). Made Secretary of War in 1831, he favored removal of the Indians beyond the Mississippi and supported President Andrew Jackson in the nullification crisis. Minister to France (1836–42) and U.S. Senator from Michigan (1845–48, 1849–57), Cass was the Democratic candidate for President in 1848, but because of the defection of the antislavery Democrats led by Martin VAN BUREN, who became the candidate of the FREE-SOIL PARTY, he lost the election to the Whig candidate, Zachary Taylor. President James Buchanan made (1857) Cass his Secretary of State, but he resigned in Dec., 1860, in protest against the decision not to reinforce the forts of Charleston, S.C. See biography by F. B. Woodford (1950).

Cassander (kùsăn'dùr), 358–297 B.C., king of Macedon, one of the chief figures in the wars of the DIADOCHI. The son of Antipater, he was an officer under Alexander the Great, but there was ill feeling between them. After his father's death, Cassander engaged in vigorous warfare against Antipater's successor as regent, Polyperchon. He was successful, and by 318 he had a preponderant influence in Macedonia and Greece. Alexander's mother, Olympias, challenged this and put Philip III, Alexander's half brother, and many others to death. Cassander pursued her, crushed her army, and condemned her to death (316). Later, to strengthen his claim to the throne, he married Alexander's half sister, Thessalonica, and in 311 he murdered Alexander's widow, Roxana, and their son. He resisted the efforts of Antigonus I to rebuild the empire and was one of the coalition that defeated Antigonus and Demetrius at Ipsus in 301. Secure in his position, he founded the cities of Thessalonica and Cassandreia (on the site of Potidaea) and rebuilt Thebes.

Cassandra (kúsăn'drú), in Greek legend, Trojan princess, daughter of Priam and Hecuba. She was given the power of prophecy by Apollo, but because she would not accept him as a lover, he changed her blessing to a curse, causing her prophecies never to be believed. Seeking refuge from the Greeks, she was dragged from the temple of Athena and violated by the Locrian Ajax. After the Trojan War she was the slave of Agamemnon and was killed with him by his wife Clytemnestra.

Cassandre, Adolphe Mouron (ädôlf' mōōrō' käsä'drú), 1901–, French poster artist, b. Russia. His first poster was published in 1922; by 1923 he was well known as the artist of *Bûcheron* [woodcutter], a poster made for a cabinetmaker. Later posters included designs for tennis matches, fairs, magazines, wines, shoes, horse races, steamships, and railways. Cassandre's originality and clarity have made his designs classics of advertising and have influenced the development of the graphic arts.

Cassandreia: see POTIDAEA.

Cassano d'Adda (käs-sä'nō däd'dä), town (estimated pop. 10,560), in Lombardy, N Italy, on the Adda. It is an agricultural and industrial center. Here the French under Vendôme defeated the imperialists under Eugene of Savoy in 1705 (see SPANISH SUCCESSION, WAR OF THE). It was also the site of the victory (1799) of the French general Moreau over the Russians under Suvarov.

Cassatt, Mary (kúsăt'), 1845-1926, American figure painter and etcher, b. Pittsburgh. Most of her life was spent in France, where she was greatly influenced by her great French contemporaries, particularly Manet and Degas, whose friendship and esteem she enjoyed. She early allied herself with the impressionists. Motherhood was her favorite subject. Her pictures are notable for their refreshing simplicity, vigorous treatment, and pleasing color. She excelled also as a pastelist and etcher, and her dry points and color prints are greatly admired. She is well represented in the public and private galleries of the United States. Her best-known pictures include several versions of *Mother and Child* (in the Metropolitan Mus.; Mus. of Fine Arts, Boston; Worcester, Mass., Art Mus.); *Lady at the Tea-Table* (Metropolitan Mus.); *Modern Women,* a mural painted for the Women's Building of the Chicago exposition; and a portrait of the artist's mother. See Forbes Watson, *Mary Cassatt* (1932).

cassava (kúsä'vú) or **manioc** (mă'nĕŏk), any plant of the genus *Manihot* of the SPURGE family. The roots, which resemble sweet potatoes and are eaten in much the same way, yield cassava starch, a staple food in the tropics. The cassava is native to Brazil and has long been cultivated there by the Indians as a major food source. Cassava roots are also fermented to make an alcoholic beverage, are the source of TAPIOCA or Brazilian arrowroot, and are utilized in other ways, e.g., for cotton sizing and laundry starch. Most cassava flour is made from *M. esculenta*, sometimes called bitter cassava because of the presence in the raw roots of prussic acid in sufficient quantities to be deadly. This poison is dispelled by cooking. Some species with a lesser acid content, called sweet cassava, are edible raw and can be used for fodder.

Cass City, village (pop. 1,945), S Mich., on the Cass river and E of Bay City; settled 1866, inc. 1883. It is a farm trade center that makes automobile parts.

Cassel, Gustav (gōō'stäf kä'súl), 1866–1945, Swedish economist and authority on international monetary problems. He was a delegate to many world economic conferences and wrote valuable papers on foreign exchange. Among his books are *Money and Foreign Exchange after 1914* (1922), *Fundamental Thoughts on Economics* (1925), and *On Quantitative Thinking in Economics* (1935).

Portrait of Mademoiselle C. by Mary Cassatt.

Abbey of Monte Cassino

Cassel (käsĕl′), town (pop. 2,680), Nord dept., N France, near Dunkirk. Dating from Roman times, it was a medieval fortress. Here in 1328 Philip VI of France defeated the Flemings. Here also the French defeated (1677) William of Orange (later William III of England) in the Dutch Wars.

Cassel, Germany: see KASSEL.

Casselberry, town (pop. 2,463), central Fla., NE of Orlando.

Casselton, city (pop. 1,394), SE N.Dak., W of Fargo; inc. 1883. It is a commercial and railroad center in a grain-raising region.

cassia: see CINNAMON and SENNA.

Cassian (kă′shŭn), 360–435, leader in monasticism in the West, named John Cassian. He settled at Marseilles (415) and established religious houses for men and for women. He was attacked for Semi-Pelagianism (see PELAGIANISM), but he was trusted in Rome. His *Collations,* spiritual writings for monks, and his *Institutes,* on monasticism, had critical influence on the thought of St. Benedict, St. Gregory, and hence on all Benedictines, in matters touching ascetic and mystical life. He wrote against Nestorianism. See study by Owen Chadwick (1950).

Cassini, Giovanni Domenico (jōvän′nē dōmā′nēkō käs-sē′nē), 1625–1712, French astronomer of Italian origin. At the summons of Louis XIV he took charge in 1671 of the observatory at Paris and organized its activities. He discovered four of the satellites of Saturn and described the structure of Saturn's ring, noting the division in the ring; determined the rotation of Mars; cooperated in determining the solar parallax; and is claimed to have made the earliest systematic observation of zodiacal light. His son, grandson, and great-grandson succeeded him in turn as head of the observatory.

Cassino (käs-sē′nō), town (estimated pop. 21,245), in Latium, central Italy, in the Apennines, on the Rapido. At the end of 1943 the town and the nearby abbey of MONTE CASSINO were strongly defended by the Germans blocking the Allied advance to Rome. After five months of repeated concentrated ground attacks and Allied attempts to divert German troops by landings at ANZIO, the German positions were finally captured in May, 1944. The town was reduced to rubble, and the cathedral and the Church of Santa Maria (8th cent.) were completely destroyed; now Cassino is a rebuilt, modern city.

cassino: see CASINO.

Cassiodorus (Flavius Magnus Aurelius Cassiodorus Senator) (kăshōdō′rŭs), c.487–c.583, Roman statesman and author. He held high office under Theodoric the Great and the succeeding Gothic rulers of Italy, who charged him with putting into official Latin their state papers and correspondence. These he later collected as *Variae epistolae* (Eng. tr. by Thomas Hodgkin, 1886). After retiring to his estate he founded two monasteries; in one of these the monks devoted leisure time to copying old

Cassiodorus (11th-century illustration)

manuscripts, which were thus preserved. Among Cassiodorus' works were his *History of the Goths,* preserved in the abridgment by JORDANES, and a treatise on orthography.

Cassiopeia, in Greek mythology: see ANDROMEDA.

Cassiopeia, in astronomy, a prominent northern constellation, visible above the horizon throughout the night. Five bright stars in the constellation form a rough W in the sky. Some see in this formation the shape of a chair known as Cassiopeia's Chair.

Cassirer, Ernst (ĕrnst' käsēr'ừr), 1874–1945, German philosopher. He was a professor at the Univ. of Hamburg from 1919 until 1933, when he went to Oxford; he later taught at Yale and Columbia. A leading representative of the Marburg Neo-Kantian school, Cassirer's early work was devoted to the critical-historical study of the problem of knowledge. This was presented in his monumental *Das Erkenntnisproblem in der Philosophie und Wissenschaft der neueren Zeit* (3 vols., 1906–20) and *Substanzbegriff und Funktionsbegriff* (1910; Eng. tr., *Substance and Function*, 1923). In his chief work *Philosophie der symbolischen Formen* (3 vols., 1923–29; Eng. tr., *Philosophy of Symbolic Forms*, 1953–57) he applied the principles of the Kantian philosophy toward the formation of a critique of culture. All cultural achievements such as language, myth, and science are the results of man's symbolic activity. This led Cassirer to a new conception of man as the "symbolic animal." Cassirer wrote many other studies on science, myth, and various historical subjects. These include two written in English: *An Essay on Man* (1944) and *Myth of the State* (1946).

Cassius (kă'shừs), ancient Roman family. There were a number of well-known members. **Spurius Cassius Viscellinus** (spyŏŏ'rēừs, vĭsừlĭ'nừs), d. c.485 B.C., seems to have been consul several times. In 493 B.C. he negotiated a treaty between Rome and the Latin cities on terms of equality. In 486 he proposed that land be distributed equally among the Roman and the Latin poor (see AGRARIAN LAWS). It is said that the patricians, outraged at the suggestion, accused Cassius of royal aspirations and had him executed. A descendant, **Quintus Cassius Longinus** (kwĭn'từs, lŏnjĭ'nừs), d. 45 B.C., won a reputation for greed and corruption when he was a quaestor in Spain (54 B.C.). He and ANTONY, as tribunes in 49 B.C., vetoed the attempts of the senate to deprive Julius CAESAR of his army. When the senate overrode the tribunes on Jan. 7, 49 B.C., Cassius and Antony fled to Caesar, who crossed the Rubicon and began the civil war. After Caesar's triumph, Cassius was given (47 B.C.) a post in Farther Spain. There was a rebellion against him, and Caesar had to come from Italy to put it down. Cassius died in a shipwreck. Best known of all was **Caius Cassius Longinus** (kā'ừs, kī'ừs), d. 42 B.C., leader in the successful conspiracy to assassinate Julius Caesar. He fought as a quaestor under M. Licinius Crassus (see CRASSUS, family) at CARRHAE in 53 B.C. and saved what was left of the army after the battle. He supported Pompey against Caesar, but was pardoned after the battle of PHARSALA. He was made (44 B.C.) peregrine praetor and Caesar promised to make him governor of Syria. Before the promise could be fulfilled, Cassius had become ringleader in the plot to kill Caesar. The plot involved more than 60 men (including M. Junius Brutus, P. Servilius Casca, and L. Tillius Cimber) and was successfully accomplished in the senate on the Ides of March in 44 B.C. When the people were aroused by Antony against the conspirators, Cassius went to Syria. He managed to capture DOLABELLA at Laodicea and coordinated his own movements with those of Brutus. Antony and Octavian (later AUGUSTUS) met them in battle at Philippi. In the first engagement Cassius, thinking the battle lost, committed suicide. Another of the conspirators was **Caius Cassius Parmensis** (pärmĕn'sĭs), d. 30 B.C. He fought at Philippi and later with Sextus Pompeius. He later sided with Antony in the naval battle off Actium and was killed by order of Octavian.

Cassius Dio Cocceianus: see DION CASSIUS.

Cassivellaunus (kă″sĭvĭlô'nừs), fl. 54 B.C., British chief, recognized as leader in the struggle against the invasion of Julius Caesar in 54 B.C. Caesar crossed the Thames into Cassivellaunus' home country. Aided by discontented British tribes, Caesar attacked Cassivellaunus in his strong fort in the marshes and drove the Britons out with heavy losses. After an unsuccessful attack against the Roman ship camp, Cassivellaunus sued for peace, which Caesar granted in return for hostages and annual tribute.

Cass Lake, village (pop. 1,586), N central Minn., on the west shore of Cass Lake, SE of Bemidji, in a lumbering, dairy, and lake resort region; inc. 1899. It was named for Lewis Cass, who explored the region in 1820. The Ojibwa Indian agency is here. A forest experiment station and tree nursery are nearby.

cassone (käs-sō'nā), the Italian term for chest or coffer, usually a bridal or dower chest, highly ornate and given prominence in the home. Major artists such as Uccello and Botticelli painted cassone panels, and prominent sculptors were also employed to carve elaborate chests. The cassone was usually decorated with mythological or historical episodes. It became one of the first means of bold secular expression in Renaissance art. See Paul Schubring, *Cassoni* (1915, in German).

Cassopolis (kừsŏ'pừlĭs), resort village (pop. 2,027), co. seat of Cass co., SW Mich., NE of South Bend, Ind., in a farm area; settled 1831, inc. 1863. Trailers are made. There are Indian garden beds and mounds in the vicinity.

cassowary (kăs'ừwâr″ē), flightless, swift-running, pugnacious forest bird of Australia and the Malay

Cassowary

Last Supper by Andrea del Castagno.

Archipelago, smaller than the related ostrich and emu. The plumage is dark and glossy and the head and neck unfeathered, wattled, and brilliantly colored, with variations in the coloring in different species. The head bears a horny crest.

Cassville. 1 City (pop. 1,451), co. seat of Barry co., SW Mo., SE of Joplin; platted 1845, inc. 1847. A resort and fishing center in the Ozarks, it is also a shipping point for a fruit, dairy, and poultry region. Confederate sympathizers in the Missouri General Assembly met here in 1861 and passed an ordinance of secession. Roaring River State Park is nearby. **2** Village (pop. 1,290), extreme SW Wis., on the Mississippi and NW of Dubuque, Iowa, in an agricultural area; inc. 1882. A state park is nearby.

Castagno, Andrea del (ändrä′ä dĕl kästä′nyō), c.1423–1457, major Florentine painter of the early Renaissance. His first recorded painting (1440; now destroyed) brought him fame in spite of its disconcerting subject. Castagno painted the effigies of hanged men, enemies to the Florentine regime. Two years later he was in Venice, frescoing the ceiling of the chapel in San Zaccaria. He returned to Florence and c.1445 began the cycle of the *Passion of Christ* for the church of Sant' Apollonia. Best known of these scenes is the *Last Supper.* Castagno combined a rigorous perspective with harsh, metallic lighting which greatly intensified the drama of the scene. He decorated the hall of the Villa Pandolfini with heroic figures, including Pippo Spano, Dante, Petrarch, and Boccaccio. Here the influence of Donatello can be felt, particularly in the vitality and plastic rendering of forms. In the Annunziata church there is a powerful conception of the *Savior and St. Julian.* His last dated work is the equestrian statue of Niccolò da Tolentino in the cathedral. Other examples of his art are *David* (National Gall. of Art, Washington, D.C.) and the *Resurrection* (Frick Coll., New York).

Castaldi, Pamfilo (päm′fēlō kästäl′dē), c.1398–c.1490, Italian humanist and printer. He was the first printer of the city of Milan. He is credited by some, on insufficient evidence, with the invention of movable type. See GUTENBERG, JOHANN.

Castalia (kăstā′lyù), in Greek mythology, spring on Mt. Parnassus. Named for a nymph, it was sacred to the MUSES and was said to give poetic inspiration to those who bathed in it.

Castalion or **Castellio, Sébastien** (kăstāl′yùn, kăstĕl′yō), 1515–63, French Protestant theologian. Castalion was with Calvin at Strasbourg and Geneva until, after doctrinal differences, he moved to Basel. He obtained a chair of Greek literature in the university there. Castalion is known for his defense of religious toleration in the preface to his Latin translation of the Bible (1551). In 1554 he published, under the pseudonym Martinus Bellius, *Concerning Heretics* (Eng. tr., 1935), in which he protested the execution of Servetus. The name also appears as Castellion and Châtillon. See Stefan Zweig, *Right to Heresy* (1936).

castanets, percussion instruments known to the ancient Egyptians and Greeks, possibly of Oriental origin. They are made of two small matching pieces of hard wood or ivory, joined at the inner edge and used with a thin strap in the player's hand; they are snapped together between the palm and fingers. Many Spanish dancers use castanets in each hand, to mark rhythm only.

caste [Port. *casta*=basket], hereditary social division. The caste is a closed group whose members are severely restricted in their choice of occupation and in degree of social participation. Marriage outside the caste is prohibited. Social status is determined by the caste of one's birth and may only rarely be transcended. Certain religious minorities may voluntarily constitute a quasi-caste within a society, less apt to be characterized by cultural distinctiveness than by their self-imposed social segregation. A specialized labor group may operate as a caste within a society otherwise free of such distinctions (e.g., the ironsmiths in parts of tribal Africa). In general, caste functions to maintain status quo in a society. Nowhere is caste better exemplified by degree of complexity and systematic operation than in India. The Indian term for caste is *jati*, which generally designates a group varying in size from a handful to many thousands. There are thousands of such *jatis* and each has its distinctive rules, customs, and modes of government. In order to validate their claim to highest status, the Hindu Brahman priests classified (about A.D. 200) the *jatis* into four major divisions or *varnas:* the Brahmans, said in the Laws of MANU to have sprung from the head of Brahma; the Kshatriyas, or warriors, from his arms; the Vaisyas, farmers and merchants, from his belly; and the Sudras, or laborers, from his feet. The untouchable, or PARIAH, is, under this classification, on the lowest level of the Sudra division. These divisions may correspond to what were formerly large, undifferentiated social classes. Indian castes are rigidly differentiated by rituals and beliefs which pervade all thought and conduct (see DHARMA). So widely do castes at social extremes differ in habits of everyday life and of worship, that only the close intergrading of intervening castes and the intercaste language communities serve to hold them within the single framework of Indian society. The explanation that Indian castes were originally based on color lines to preserve the racial and cultural purity of conquering groups is inadequate historically to account for the physical and cultural variety of such groups. Castes may reflect distinctiveness of religious practice, occupation, locale, culture status, or tribal affiliation, either exclusively or in part. Divergence within a caste on any of these lines will tend to produce fission which may, in time, result in the formation of new castes. Every type of social group as it appears may be fitted into this system of organizing society. The occupational barriers among Indian castes have been breaking down steadily under economic pressures since the 19th cent., but social distinctions have been more persistent. Attitudes toward the untouchables only began to change in the 1930s under the influence of Gandhi's teachings; since India's independence, various legislative measures have been enacted against untouchability. See J. H. Hutton, *Caste in India* (1951); McKim Marriott, ed., *Village India* (1955).

Castelar y Ripoll, Emilio (ämē'lyō kästälär' ē rēpō'lyû), 1832–99, Spanish statesman and author. A professor of history and philosophy at the Univ. of Madrid and a republican leader, he was foreign minister and then head of the government (1873–74) in the brief republic that followed the abdication of King Amadeus. Under Alfonso XII he was a member of the Cortes and became reconciled to the monarchy itself, although he remained in the political opposition. He wrote historical, political, and literary works.

Castel Gandolfo (kästěl' gändōl'fō), town (estimated pop. 4,685), in Latium, central Italy, in the Alban Hills. Overlooking Lake Albano, it possibly occupies the site of ancient Alba Longa. Castel Gandolfo is the papal summer residence. The papal palace (17th cent.), its magnificent gardens, and the Villa Barbarini enjoy extraterritorial rights. The Church of St. Thomas of Villanova was designed by Bernini.

Castellammare di Stabia (kästěl″lämä′rä dē stä′-byä), city (estimated pop. 61,788), in Campania, S Italy, on the Bay of Naples. It has mineral springs used since Roman times and is also a commercial and industrial center, with navy yards founded in 1783. Ancient Stabiae, near here, was a favorite resort of the Romans; it was buried in the eruption of Mt. Vesuvius in A.D. 79. The royal villa, Quisisana, built in 1310 and rebuilt in 1820, is now a hotel.

Castellani, Sir Aldo, 1877–, British-Italian bacteriologist, b. Florence, Italy. He demonstrated the cause and mode of transmission of sleeping sickness (with Sir David BRUCE and David Nabarro, 1903), discovered the spirochete of yaws (1905), and did other original work in bacteriology and in parasitic diseases of the skin. He also lectured in tropical medicine in London and Ceylon, was professor of tropical medicine at Tulane Univ. and at Louisiana State Univ., and founded in Rome the Royal Institute for Tropical Diseases. With A. J. Chalmers he wrote *Manual of Tropical Medicine* (1910; 3d ed., 1919). He was knighted in 1928. See his autobiography (1960).

Castellio or **Castellion, Sébastien:** see CASTALION, SÉBASTIEN.

Castello or **Castelli, Bernardo** (běrnär'dō kästěl'lō, –těl'lē), 1557–1629, Italian painter of the Genoese school; pupil of Cambiaso, whose style he imitated. He was the friend of Tasso and made the designs for *Jerusalem Delivered*, some of which were subsequently engraved by Agostino Carracci. Castello executed numerous works in the churches of Genoa. His son, **Valerio Castello** (välär'yō), 1625–59, painter of historical scenes, was influenced by Procaccini and Correggio, but created a fine style of his own. He executed many frescoes of high merit for the churches and monasteries of Genoa. His best-known painting is *The Rape of the Sabines* (Genoa).

Gardens of the papal palace in Castel Gandolfo.

Castello, Giovanni Battista (jōvän'nē bät-tēs'tä kästěl'lō), c.1509–c.1569. Italian painter and architect; called *Il Bergamasco* to distinguish him from Bernardo Castello who also worked in Genoa. Giovanni was born near Bergamo where many of his works still exist. After a trip to Rome, Castello returned to Genoa, where he worked with Luca Cambiaso on the Palazzo Imperiale. Giovanni's propensity for grotesque decorations is best seen in the Palazzo Pallavicino (now the Palazzo Cataldi-Garega). In his capacity as an architect, he designed (c.1560–1563) a palace for the Pallavicino, his patrons. In 1567 he went to Spain where he became architect and painter to Philip II.

Castello, Valerio: see CASTELLO, BERNARDO.

Castello-Branco, Camillo: see CASTELO BRANCO, CAMILO.

Castellón de la Plana (kästělyōn' dä lä plä'nä), city (pop. 59,671), capital of Castellón de la Plana prov., E Spain, in Valencia, 3 mi. from its Mediterranean port of Grao. Reconquered from the Moors by James I of Aragon in 1233, it suffered in the uprising (16th cent.) of the comuneros and in the Peninsular War (19th cent.).

Castelnau, Michel de (mēshěl' dù kästělnō'), c.1520–1592, French diplomat and soldier. He early attracted the favorable notice of the cardinal of Lorraine (Charles de Guise) and performed important services for Anne, duc de Montmorency, and King Henry II. In the religious wars he went on missions to England, Scotland, the Netherlands, and Savoy, and fought in the royal army; from 1575 to 1585 he served as ambassador to England. Upon his return he fell out with the Guises and rendered valuable services against the LEAGUE to Henry III and Henry IV. Although a Catholic, he favored a policy of moderation toward the Huguenots. He left valuable memoirs.

Castelo Branco, Camilo (kämē'lō kästě'lō bräng'kō), 1826?–1890, Portuguese novelist. His tempestuous life was filled with incidents almost as improbable as those in his profuse, sentimental novels. They are rescued from oblivion only by a singular poetic purity of style; typical are *Os misterios de Lisboa* (1854) and *Amor de perdiçao* (1862). He spelled his name Camillo Castello-Branco and was visconde de Correia Botelho.

Castel Sant' Angelo (kästěl' säntän'jälō), **Hadrian's Mausoleum,** or **Hadrian's Mole,** massive construction on the right bank of the Tiber in Rome. Originally built (A.D. 135–39) by Emperor Hadrian as a MAUSOLEUM for himself and his successors, it was later decorated and fortified as a place of refuge for the popes and was connected to the Vatican by a secret passage. It was used as a fortress and prison until 1870; it is now a museum.

Castiglione, Baldassare, Conte (bäldäs-sä'rä kōn'tä kästēlyō'nä), 1478–1529, Italian statesman attached to the court of the duke of Milan and later in the service of the duke of Urbino. His famous *Libro del cortegiano* (1528; Eng. tr., *The Courtier*, 1561), a treatise on etiquette, social problems, and intellectual accomplishments, is one of the great books of its time. It gives a picture of 15th- and 16th-century court life. See Ralph Roeder, *The Man of the Renaissance* (1933).

Castiglione, Giovanni Benedetto (jōvän'nē bänädět'tō), 1610?–1670, Italian painter and engraver of the Genoese school, called Il Grechetto. In his later years Castiglione was court painter at Mantua. He is best known for his landscapes and rural scenes with animals, but he also painted portraits and religious works, such as the *Nativity* (Genoa). His pictures are full of life and movement, the color rich and glowing. Castiglione's etchings, numbering about 70 and reflecting the influence of Rembrandt, are among the best produced in Italy during his century. The treatment of light and shade, as in his paintings, is particularly fine.

Castiglione delle Stiviere (kästēlyō'nä děl'lä stēvyä'rä), town (estimated pop. 9,384), in Lombardy, N Italy. Here Napoleon Bonaparte and Augereau defeated the Austrians in 1796.

Castile (kästēl'), Span. *Castilla* (kästē'lyä), region and former kingdom, central and N Spain, traditionally divided into Old Castile (Span. *Castilla la Vieja*), in the north, and New Castile (Span. *Castilla la Nueva*), in the south. Old Castile (19,390 sq. mi.; pop. 4,210,817) comprises the provinces of Ávila, Burgos, Logroño, Santander, Segovia, and Soria, named after their chief cities. New Castile (27,933 sq. mi.; pop. 2,218,884) comprises the provinces and cities of Ciudad Real, Cuenca, Guadalajara, Madrid, and Toledo. The endless, bleak landscape of Castile has an austere beauty. The region includes most of the high plateau of central Spain, across which rise the rugged Sierra de Guadarrama and the Sierra de Gredos, forming a natural boundary between Old Castile and New Castile. The upper Duero, the Tagus, and Guadiana rivers form the chief basins. The soil of Castile, ravaged by centuries of erosion, is poor, and the climate severe. Old Castile has grain growing and sheep raising; in more fertile areas, especially in New Castile, olive oil and grapes are produced. Scattered forests yield timber and naval stores. Agricultural methods are largely primitive, and irrigation, introduced by the Moors, has progressed little since their time. Of the industries which flourished in the 14th and 15th cent. (particularly wool and silk textiles), few have survived the expulsion of the Moriscos. Mineral resources, except for the rich mercury mines of ALMADÉN, are of minor economic importance. The name Castile derives from the many castles built here by the Christian nobles early in the reconquest from the Moors (8th–9th cent.). Old Castile at first was a county of the kingdom of LEON, with Burgos its capital. Its independent-minded nobles, notably FERNÁN GONZÁLEZ, secured virtual autonomy by the 10th cent. Sancho III of Navarre, who briefly annexed the county, made it into a kingdom for his son, FERDINAND I, in 1035. Leon was first united with Castile in 1037, but complex dynastic rivalries delayed the permanent union of the two realms, which was achieved under FERDINAND III in 1230. The Castilian kings played a leading role in the fight against the Moors, from whom they wrested New Castile. At the same time they had to struggle against the turbulent nobles and were involved in dynastic disputes which plunged the country into civil war (see ALFONSO X). PETER THE CRUEL limited the vast privileges of the nobles, but they were permanently curbed only late in the 15th cent. In 1479, after ISABELLA I had defeated the dynastic pretensions of Juana la Beltraneja, a per-

Castel Sant'Angelo

Still Life and Biblical Scene by Giovanni Benedetto Castiglione.

Toledo, one of Castile's major cities on the Tagus river.

Conte Baldassare Castiglione (painting by Raphael Santi)

sonal union of Castile and Aragon was established under Isabella and her husband Ferdinand II of Aragon (FERDINAND V of Castile). The union was made permanent with the accession (1516) of their grandson, Charles I (later Emperor Charles V), to the Spanish kingdoms. Charles. who nominally shared the rule of Castile with his insane mother, Joanna, until her death in 1555, suppressed the uprisings of the COMUNEROS in Castile (1520–21; see CHARLES V, emperor). Castile became the core of the Spanish monarchy, centralized in Madrid, its capital after the 16th cent. Its dialect became the standard literary language of Spain, and its history was merged with that of Spain. The character of its people—proud and austere—has become typical of the whole Spanish nation.

Castile, village (pop. 1,146), W N.Y., SSE of Batavia, in a farm area noted for its apples; settled 1816, inc. 1877. It is a summer resort. A state park is nearby.

Castilla, Ramón (rämōn′ kästē′yä), 1797–1867, president of Peru (1845–51, 1855–62). He fought under Antonio José de Sucre in the revolution against Spain (1821–24) in Peru and took part in the civil wars that followed. An army general, energetic and resolute, he twice eliminated his rivals by armed force to become president. He developed the guano, saltpeter, and nitrate industries, helped to reorganize finances, abolished slavery in Peru, and promulgated (1860) a new constitution which became the basis of future Peruvian government. Although he overlooked considerable administrative corruption, Castilla brought unwonted order and a measure of prosperity to the republic.

Castillejo, Cristóbal de (krēstō′bäl dā kästēlyä′hō), c.1490–1550, Spanish poet of the Renaissance. As secretary to the king of Bohemia, brother of Emperor Charles V, he visited Vienna and other European cities. His poems are grouped under the titles *Obras de amores* [works of love] and *Obras morales y de devoción* [moral and devotional works]. His *Diálogo de mujeres* (1544) is a noted description of the vices and virtues of women. He championed the traditional Spanish as against the Italian verse form.

Castillo de San Marcos National Monument: see SAINT AUGUSTINE, Fla.

Castillon-la-Bataille (kästēyō″ lä bätäy′), town (estimated pop. 3,077), Gironde dept., SW France, in Guienne, on the Dordogne. An ancient port, it has a wine and liqueur trade. Here, in 1453, the French defeated the English in the final great battle of the Hundred Years War. It was formerly called Castillon or Castillon-et-Capitourlan.

Castine (kăstēn′), town (pop. 824), S Maine, on a peninsula in East Penobscot Bay; inc. 1796. It includes Castine and North Castine villages. The Plymouth Colony had a trading post near the present Castine village after 1626; a few years later the French seized the post, and thereafter the area, known as the Penobscot, changed hands several times between the French, Dutch, British, and Americans. The town is named after the French adventurer Baron Jean Vincent St. Castin or Castine who "ruled" it for 30 years after 1667. The British, whose permanent settlement began in 1760, held the town in the Revolution and in the

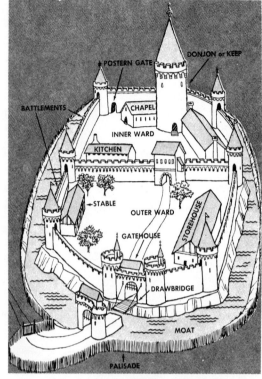

Diagram of a medieval European castle.

War of 1812. Part of Fort George (built by the British in 1779) is preserved; the French Fort Pentagoet is marked. Fort Madison (1811; rebuilt in the Civil War) is still standing as well as a number of interesting old houses. The town is the seat of the Maine Maritime Academy.

casting: see FOUNDING and PLASTER CASTING.

cast iron: see IRON.

Castle, Vernon, 1887–1918, English dancer, originally named Vernon Castle Blythe. He studied civil engineering, but turned to the stage and made his debut in 1907. In 1911 he married Irene Foote (1893–, b. New Rochelle, N.Y.), and in Paris (1912) their versions of such dances as the "Texas Tommy" and the "Grizzly Bear" brought them fame. The team originated the "Castle walk," the one-step, and the "hesitation" waltz, and Mrs. Castle introduced bobbed hair and the slim, boyish figure to the ballroom and the world of fashion. See Irene Castle, *Castles in the Air* (1958).

castle, type of fortified dwelling characteristic of the Middle Ages. FORTIFICATION of towns had been devised since antiquity, but in the 9th cent. feudal lords began to develop the private fortress-residence known as the castle. It served the twofold function of residence and fortress because of the conditions of medieval life, in which war was endemic. The site of the castle was preferably a defensible eminence. England and France, in gen-

Castle Azay-le-Rideau, department Indre-et-Loire, France.

eral, did not afford such inaccessible locations as did the Rhine valley in Germany. The castle of Western Europe was a Norman creation, an outgrowth of the 10th- and 11th-century mound castle, which consisted of a great artificial mound of earth, the motte, surrounded by a dry ditch, or fosse, and surmounted by a wooden blockhouse and its encircling palisade. Until well into the 12th cent., the only English development was the occasional substitution of a massive masonry keep inside the palisade—a form typified in the Tower of London. Great changes soon took place as the science of siegecraft (see SIEGE) was evolved; provisions were made for an aggressive defense. A type which became the model for many English and Norman castles was the formidable castle built at Arques in Normandy by Henry I of England. A square donjon, or keep, was set against the strong outer walls of masonry; the entrance was protected by a double gate, two flanking round towers, and advanced earthworks. The place enclosed by the outer circuit of walls was usually divided into two courts, or baileys, by a palisade. Subterranean passages made detection of mining operations easy. In the Near East the Crusaders developed great castles with double circuits of curving outer walls and towers or turrets to overlook all sections of the wall. The form of these castles had an influence throughout the Continent and the British Isles. Thus early in the 13th cent. the medieval castle, a mixture of Norman, English, and Byzantine elements, reached its full flower, as typified in the Château Gaillard on the Seine in France and Alnwick and the Conisborough in England. In general, the castle was planned for security; the living quarters were rude, poorly lighted, and without provisions for comfort. Typically, the keep contained the living quarters of the lord and his family, the rooms of state, and the prison cells. Two independent systems of walls, each a fortress in itself, extended around the keep; the sections of the walls were flanked by towers, usually round, and the principal entrance was protected by strong gate towers, the massive gateway, with its PORTCULLIS and drawbridge, and the barbican, or advanced outwork.

Castle of Segovia, Spain.

The defenders operated from galleries at the tops of walls and from the flat roofs of towers, whose battlements were provided with embrasures and machicolations for shooting and dropping missiles on the attackers. The fully developed castle was thus marked by successive series of defenses; the fall of the outer works did not necessarily mean the loss of the entire castle. With the use of gunpowder and consequent perfection of ARTILLERY, the castle lost its military importance. The manor house replaced the castle as the residence of the wealthy landowner, but the architectural influence of the castle has persisted even to the present day, when crenelations and towers are still found in country houses. See also CHÂTEAU; G. T. Clark, *Medieval*

Military Architecture of England (1884); Hugh Braun, *The English Castle* (1936); Sidney Toy, *History of Fortification from 3000 B.C. to A.D. 1700* (1955).

Castlebar, urban district (pop. 5,482), county town of Co. Mayo, W Republic of Ireland. It is the market for a cattle-raising and potato-growing area. The manufacture of hats and the curing of bacon are two of the town's industries.

Castlebay, village, on Barra, in the Outer Hebrides, off NW Scotland. Its harbor is the rendezvous of a herring fleet in early summer. There are the ruins of a castle, whose owner is said to have refused Noah's hospitality because he had a boat of his own.

Castle Clinton National Monument: see BATTERY, THE.

Castleford, municipal borough (pop. 40,345), West Riding of Yorkshire, N England, at the junction of the Aire and the Calder. Chartered as a municipal borough in 1955, it has glassworks, chemical works, and collieries. The site of an ancient Roman town lies within its borders.

Castle Garden: see BATTERY, THE.

Castle Hills, city (pop. 2,622), S Texas, within the confines of San Antonio; inc. 1952.

Castlemaine, Barbara, countess of: see CLEVELAND, BARBARA VILLIERS, DUCHESS OF.

Castle Peak: see CARBON, MOUNT.

Castle Pinckney, fortification at the harbor entrance of Charleston, S.C. Built in 1797 when war with France seemed imminent, it was named for Charles Cotesworth Pinckney.

Castlereagh, Robert Stewart, 2d Viscount (kǎ′sùlrā), 1769–1822, British statesman, b. Dublin. Entering the Irish Parliament in 1791 and the British Parliament in 1793, he became Tory chief secretary for Ireland in 1797. He was largely responsible for suppressing the Irish rebellion of 1798 despite French aid to the rebels. Having worked for the Act of Union of England and Ireland (1800), he resigned with William Pitt in 1801 when George III refused to allow Catholic Emancipation. President of the India board of control after 1802, he was later (1805, 1807–9) secretary of war. In that office during the crisis of Great Britain's struggle with Napoleon I, he planned the reorganization of the army, the Peninsular War against the French, and the effective coordination of British land and sea power, and after early disasters he succeeded in putting Arthur Wellesley (later duke of Wellington) in command. The opposition of his colleague, George CANNING, to Castlereagh's policies flared into a serious quarrel. Castlereagh accused Canning of political betrayal, and they fought (1809) a duel. Canning was wounded and both resigned. As foreign secretary (1812–22) under Lord Liverpool, Castlereagh helped to organize the successful coalition against Napoleon I, partly by secret treaties promising territorial changes. Going himself to Chaumont (1814), he obtained that "concert of Europe" later confirmed by the QUADRUPLE ALLIANCE. He advocated a moderate peace settlement for France, including restoration of the Bourbon monarchy, and the limitation of France to her pre-war boundaries. His other objectives were the establishment of a free Poland and a German confederation to prevent Russian expansion. Castle-

reagh condoned the ascendancy of conservative and even repressive European governments as the best way of maintaining peace. He bore the brunt of blame for suppressive actions to curb unrest in England, though, as leader of the Commons, he defended but did not originate them. He became (1821) the 2d marquess of Londonderry on his father's death. Before his death by suicide Castlereagh modified his policy and began to protest the intervention of the Holy Alliance into the domestic affairs of other nations to prevent liberal revolutions. One of the foremost statesmen of his time, Castlereagh was cold in personality and lacked ability as an orator; he never gained an easy popularity. See biography by J. D. R. Marriot (1936); H. A. Kissinger, *A World Restored* (1957).

Castle Rock. 1 Town (pop. 1,152; alt. 6,000 ft.), co. seat of Douglas co., central Colo., S of Denver, in a farm area; inc. 1881. **2** Town (pop. 1,424), SW Wash., on the Cowlitz river and N of Longview, in a farm and timber area; settled in the 1880s, inc. 1890.

Castle Shannon, borough (pop. 11,836), SW Pa., just S of Pittsburgh; inc. 1919. Cement is made.

Castleton, village, Derbyshire, central England, in the Peak district, NE of Buxton. On a nearby hill is the Castle of the Peak, or Peveril Castle, built by William Peveril, natural son of William I. The castle is the scene of part of Scott's *Peveril of the Peak*.

Castleton, town (pop. 1,902), W Vt., in the Lake Bomoseen summer resort area, W of Rutland; chartered 1761, settled 1770. The Green Mountain Boys met in a tavern here before attacking Ticonderoga. The town is the seat of a state teachers college. Slate roofing is made here.

Castleton-on-Hudson, village (pop. 1,752), E N.Y., on the Hudson and S of Albany; settled c.1630 by Dutch, inc. 1827. Paper products are made.

Castletown, town (pop. 1,700), on the southeast coast of the Isle of Man, Great Britain. It is an old town, formerly capital of the island, a seaport, and the site of a 14th-century castle and of King William's College, a public school for boys.

Castor and Pollux, in classical mythology, twin heroes called the Dioscuri; sons of LEDA and Zeus or Tyndareus. Pollux is the Latin name for the Greek Polydeuces. Castor excelled as a horseman and Pollux as a boxer. They were great warriors and were noted for their devotion to each other. When Castor was killed by Lynceus, Pollux, in accordance with the classical tradition that one of every set of twins is the son of a god and thus immortal, begged Zeus to allow his brother to share his immortality with him. Zeus arranged for the twins to divide their time evenly between Hades and Heaven, and in their honor he created the constellation Gemini. According to one legend the Dioscuri were patrons of mariners and were responsible for SAINT ELMO'S FIRE. They were especially honored by the Romans, on whose side they were said to have appeared miraculously during the battle of Lake Regillus.

castor oil, yellowish fixed oil expressed from the seed of the castor bean or castor oil plant (*Ricinus communis*). Probably native to tropical Africa, the plant now grows wild and also under cultivation in most tropical and temperate regions. In the tropics it is treelike, but in colder areas it is an annual often grown for its decorative effect. Its leaves are palmately compound with from 5 to 12 dentate or serrated lobes. The oil content of the seeds varies from about 20 to 50 percent. After the hulls are removed the seeds are cold-pressed. Medicinal castor oil is prepared from the yield of the first pressing; this is used as a purgative and laxative. Oil from the second pressing is used as a lubricant for machinery, as a softening agent in making artificial leather, in the dressing of genuine leather, in brake fluids, and in paints and plastic materials. The residue can be used as fertilizer and, after the poisonous substance, ricin, is removed, as cattle feed. Other products having similar properties and uses have been gradually replacing castor oil.

Castracani, Castruccio (kästroōt′chō kästräkä′nē), 1281–1328, duke of Lucca. His early life was spent in exile. After his return he was made captain (1316) then lord of Lucca (1320) for life. He led the Ghibellines of all Tuscany, waged long wars against Florence, and conquered Volterra, Pistoia, and the Lunigiana. In 1327 Emperor Louis IV recognized him as duke of Lucca. After quelling a rebellion in Pistoia, he was threatening Florence itself when he died. His principality disappeared with him.

Castren, Matthias Alexander, Swed. *Castrén* (mätě′äs ălěksän′dùr kästrän′), 1813–52, Finnish philologist, one of the first scholars to study the Finno-Ugric languages. He was long a professor at the Univ. of Helsingfors (now Helsinki).

Castries (kä′strēz, kä′strēs, kästrē′), town (pop. c.25,000), capital of SAINT LUCIA, British West Indies. It has an excellent landlocked harbor.

Castriota, George: see SCANDERBEG.

Castro, Cipriano (sēprēä′nō kä′strō), 1858?–1924, president of Venezuela (1901–8). In 1899 he usurped the government, overthrowing Andrade. Called the Lion of the Andes by his followers, he was a stern and arbitrary *caudillo*, who nevertheless materially advanced his country. Castro's administration is notable because of the financial claims (see VENEZUELA CLAIMS) made by several foreign powers and his defiance of them. He retired briefly in 1906 in favor of Juan Vicente GÓMEZ, but after violent differences, Castro again assumed power. In 1908 he went to Europe. Gómez immediately deposed him and took control. Castro died in exile.

Castro, Fidel (fē′děl), 1927–, Cuban revolutionist and political leader. A young lawyer, Castro openly criticized the dictatorship of Fulgencio BATISTA Y ZALDÍVAR in 1952. On July 26, 1953, he led an attack on an army post in Santiago de Cuba but had to surrender and was imprisoned. Released during a general amnesty, he went to Mexico where he organized the 26th of July movement. In 1956 he set out with a group of rebels and landed in SW Oriente prov. Castro and 11 others, including his brother Raúl and Ernesto GUEVARA, survived the initial encounter and hid in the mountains of the SIERRA MAESTRA, where they built up a following and led the increasingly effective guerrilla campaign that toppled the Batista regime on Jan. 1, 1959. Widely hailed as a liberator, Castro soon proved to be extraordinary as a demagogue and reckless as a statesman. As premier he perempto-

Fidel Castro

rily juggled both the cabinet and the presidency. In a remarkably short time he destroyed the old army structure and replaced it with a revolutionary militia. Castro also proceeded to collectivize agriculture, to expropriate all native and foreign industry, and to promote close ties with the USSR and Communist China. By constantly denouncing "Yankee imperialism," by aligning himself and the Cuban revolution with the underprivileged peoples of Latin America, Asia, and Africa, and by dramatizing the symbols of his struggle against Batista, Castro kept alive his image as a folk hero while relentlessly uprooting the Cuban social order and replacing it with a police state along Soviet lines. In Dec., 1961, he flatly stated that he was a Marxist-Leninist. Initially his influence with liberals throughout the hemisphere was enormous, but it declined after 1960. During the kaleidoscopic administrative changes of 1960–62 Castro's power was somewhat curtailed, but his status as head of the revolution was unquestioned. Bitterly assailed by thousands of former supporters, he weathered the cancellation of the U.S. sugar quota, the rupture of diplomatic relations with the United States and similar diplomatic rebuffs from 15 Latin American nations, the Bay of Pigs invasion (April, 1961), an economic blockade, a protracted domestic food crisis, and an unexpected compromise by the USSR in the 1962 crisis over missile bases in Cuba. In 1963, nevertheless, Castro's position had weakened and his once extraordinary prestige had dwindled dramatically. (For a chronicle of events, see CUBA). See Theodore Draper, *Castro's Revolution: Myths and Realities* (1962).

Castro, Inés de, or **Inez de Castro** (both: ī′něz dù kä′strō, Port. ēnäsh′ dù käsh′trō), d. 1355, Galician noblewoman, a celebrated beauty and a tragic figure. She was called *Colo de Garça* [heron throat] for her grace. She came (1340) to Portugal as a lady in waiting to Constance of Castile, wife of the heir to the Portuguese throne, Dom Pedro (later PETER I). He fell in love with her. Though his father, Alfonso IV, banished her from court, the prince continued to see her. After Constance died (1345), he established a household with her at Coimbra, where they lived an idyllic life, and she bore him four children. Her brothers, however, gained political influence and awakened the opposi-

White Persian cat

Manx cat

Siamese cat

come with grief and anger, led a rebellion. Peace was restored, and the prince promised to forgive the murderers. When he became (1357) king, however, he recovered two from Castile and executed them horribly; the third escaped. He announced that he had been secretly married to Inés and had two tombs made and installed at Alcobaça showing the life story of Inés in marble. It is not true that he had her disinterred and crowned as queen, but that story was immortalized in a drama of Juan Ruiz de Alarcón. The romantic story of the love affair has been a favorite theme of Portuguese writers and has been much used by Spanish and other writers also.

Castro, Rosalía de, 1837–85, Spanish poet and novelist. The verse of her *Cantares gallegos* (1863) was the first significant poetry in Galician since the 13th cent.; it refined the lyrical and musical appeal of Galician folk songs. The melancholy *Follas novas* (1880) was followed by the despairing verse, in Castilian, of *En las orillas del Sar* (1884; Eng. tr. *Beside the River Sar*, 1937). Her sensitive and compassionate poetry reveals deep psychological insight, and her fine craftsmanship has exerted considerable influence on modern poets. Her novels of Galician life include *La hija del mar* (1859) and *El caballero de las botas azules* (1867).

Castro, Vaca de: see VACA DE CASTRO, CRISTÓBAL.

Castro, Greece: see KASTRON.

Castro Alves, Antônio de (äntō′nyō dē käs′trō äl′vǐs), 1847–71, Brazilian poet. A disciple of Victor Hugo, he came to fame with *Espumas flutuantes* [tossing spume] (1871). His poems are nationalist and socially conscious. Best known is *O navio negreiro* [the slave ship].

Castrogiovanni: see ENNA.

Castro Valley, uninc. city (pop. 37,120), W Calif., SE of San Francisco and E of San Francisco Bay. It has light industry and farms.

Castroville. 1 Uninc. town (pop. 2,838), W Calif., NW of Salinas; founded 1864. It is a center of a vegetable-growing region. **2** Town (pop. 1,508), SW Texas, WSW of San Antonio; settled 1844. It is noted for its quaint old houses and churches.

Castro y Bellvís, Guillén de (gēlyän′ dä käs′trō ē bĕlvēs′), 1569–1631, Spanish dramatist, best known of the Valencian group of playwrights of the Golden Age. Three of his plays dramatize episodes from *Don Quixote*. His masterpiece, *Las mocedades del Cid*, is a historical drama which furnished Corneille with the material for his play *Le Cid*.

cat, carnivorous mammal of the family Felidae, which includes large wild species such as the leopard, tiger, and lion as well as the 30 breeds of small domestic cats (*Felis catus*). All cats have rounded, bullet-shaped heads, short faces, large eyes, sensitive whiskers, erect, pointed ears, tongues coated with sharp papillae, and short, wide jaws equipped with long canine and strong molar teeth. Most have long tails. They have five toes on the forefeet and four on the hind feet, all with retractile claws. Cats have been domesticated since prehistoric times, and were venerated in ancient Egyptian and Norse religions. The cat has often been associated with superstition, probably because of its apparent independence and aloofness; during the Middle Ages cats were burned alive and crucified as witches. However, depopu-

tion of powerful advisers of Alfonso IV. Three of those advisers persuaded the king that Inés must be removed to preserve the legitimate succession to the throne. It is said that the king himself went with the purpose of destroying her but was moved by the pleas of her children. The three advisers, unmoved, later persuaded the king anew and with his permission murdered Inés. The prince, over-

lation of cats led inevitably to plagues of rats and mice, and the cat was reinstated as an invaluable and efficient destroyer of these pests—for which its acute senses well equip it. Cat breeds may be classified as long- and short-haired; the latter are generally more slender and active than the former. The common short-haired cats are believed to be descended from a mixture of tame African and wild European species; the long-haired cats seem to have originated in Asia. The first long-haired cats were the Angoras, but they have interbred with the Persians to such an extent that the original strain no longer exists. Other long-haired varieties are the Burmese, the Tibetan temple cat, and the large Maine cat. The Manx cat is tailless and short-haired; it comes from the Isle of Man but probably originated in Asia, where there are other tailless cats. The Siamese cat is a fawn-colored short-haired breed with seal brown, or, rarely, blue markings. Short-haired breeds also include the blue or Maltese cats, the Abyssinian ticked cat, with fur like that of a wild rabbit, the extremely small Paraguayan cat, and the rare Mexican hairless cat. In crosses between any of these breeds and the common cat, the characteristics of the latter almost invariably predominate. Black, white, blue, red, cream, smoke, chinchilla, and shaded silver cats are known, as well as red, brown, or silver tabbies (marked with darker stripes, as in watered silk), and tortoise-shells with patches of red, black, and yellow. See Carl van Vechten, *The Tiger in the House* (1936); Doris Bryant, *Care and Handling of Cats* (1944); L. H. and H. G. Fairchild, *Cats and All about Them* (1947); M. G. Denlinger, *Complete Book of the Cat* (1948); I. M. Mellen, *A Practical Cat Book* (1950); M. O. Howey, *The Cat in the Mysteries of Religion and Magic* (1955).

catacombs (kăt'–), burial places of the early Christians, arranged in extensive subterranean vaults and galleries. They served incidentally for refuge from persecution and for religious services. Catacombs exist at Rome, Naples, Chiusi, Syracuse, and Paris, at Alexandria and Susa in N Africa, and in Asia Minor and other areas inhabited by the early Christians. Those at Rome are the most important and extensive. Though among Greeks and Romans cremation was the rule, there was no bar against burial for Christians, and the catacombs were not constructed in secrecy. Ordinances forbade interment within the city precincts, and all the Roman catacombs consequently are outside the city gates. They lie from 22 to 65 ft. beneath ground level and occupy a space estimated at more than 600 acres, though much of this is in several levels, one above another. The oldest remains date from the 1st cent. A.D., and construction continued till the early 5th cent. Excavated exclusively in those places where the subsoil tufa or soft rock possessed the suitable granular structure, they consisted primarily of narrow passages, generally about 3 ft. wide. Excavated from the rock, and lining the

Niches in the catacombs of Santa Priscilla in Rome.

Decoration and symbolic frescoes (4th century) on the walls of a cubicle in the catacombs of St. Peter and Marcellino in Rome.

walls of these passages, are the *loculi*, or recesses, of the proper depth to contain the bodies. These niches, arranged one above another in tiers, were sealed after the burials with slabs of marble or terra cotta which bore painted or incised inscriptions. Some passages gave access to separate chambers or *cubicula*, usually about 12 ft. square but sometimes circular or polygonal, which were privately owned family vaults or contained the tomb of a martyr. In these the bodies were often in carved sarcophagi which stood within arched niches, and the rooms were used for the liturgy; that is, they became underground churches. The walls and ceilings were plastered, and sometimes open shafts for lighting extended to the ground above. In some catacombs are seen larger rooms and even rooms arranged in groups; in the catacombs of Sant' Agnese such a group forms a miniature church. In addition, the intricate underground corridors undoubtedly served as the best possible refuges from anti-Christian violence. The spreading of the catacombs, the joining together of separate areas, and the cutting of passages, one above the other, in as many as five successive levels, eventually produced burial places of labyrinthine character. The walls and ceilings of plaster were customarily painted with fresco decorations, and in these can be studied the actual beginnings of Christian art. Religious subjects started to appear in the 2d cent., and the earlier

frescoes confined themselves to the use of symbols. In Rome the remains of Jewish catacombs also are found. Even after official recognition of Christianity in 313, burials continued, through a desire for interment near the martyrs; in addition the catacombs became shrines of pilgrimage. The invasions of Goths, Vandals, Lombards, and Saracens meant the plundering of the catacombs and the robbing of their graves for the bones of saints. Several popes worked at restoring these sacred places and revived worship at the tombs of the martyrs, but by the 8th cent. the bodies had been mainly transferred to churches; by the 10th cent. the catacombs, filled with debris, were well forgotten. In 1578 they were rediscovered. Their preservation and maintenance have since been under control of the papacy. In the Roman liturgy the requirement that Mass be said in the presence of lighted candles and over martyrs' relics is a conscious reminiscence of worship in the catacombs. Exhaustive publications based upon researches in the catacombs were produced by the archaeologist G. B. de Rossi (d. 1894). The catacombs discovered in the vicinity of Rome in 1956 and 1959 contained frescoes of notable historical interest.

Catalan art. In Catalonia and the territories of the counts of Barcelona, art flowered in the early Middle Ages and continued to flourish through the Renaissance. Some of the finest surviving altar-panel paintings of the Romanesque period are Catalan. Many of these are preserved in the Museo del Parque, Barcelona, together with numerous frescoes transferred from the apses of Romanesque churches. The small churches, often bare of sculptural ornament, were elaborately painted throughout, although usually only the decoration of the apse has survived. A fine example from Santa María del Mar, Barcelona, is in the Museum of Fine Arts, Boston. Superb examples of architectural sculpture also exist in many Catalan churches of the period. Also Romanesque is the famous illuminated Bible from the abbey of Farfa, now in

Struggle Between Angels and Devils *(detail from a 15th-century Catalan painting)*.

St. Martin of Tours *(13th-century Catalan painting on wood)*

the Vatican. Catalan art shares most of the characteristics of the international Romanesque style. A more obviously regional character is found in the Catalan painting of the 14th cent. and in the work of Ferrer Bassa and Jaime Serra, although Sienese influence is noteworthy. With the 15th cent., particularly in the paintings of Jaime Huguet, of Jaime, Rafael, and Pablo Vergós, and of other masters, the school reached its maturity in a profuse and highly decorative religious art of great beauty. Only with Luis Dalmáu in the middle of the century did direct Flemish influence appear, and it never gained ascendancy. The great period of Catalan painting as such closed with the 15th cent., although the province has never ceased to produce great individual artists. Several prominent artists of the 20th cent. were of Catalonian origin, notably Juan Gris, Joan Miró, and Salvador Dali. See Chandler R. Post, *A History of Spanish Painting* (9 vols., 1930–47), Vol. VII.

Catalan language (kăt′ůlăn, –lůn), one of the Romance languages of the Indo-European family. It is spoken mainly in NE Spain (Catalonia and Valencia) and in a small region of S France. See LANGUAGE (table).

Catalan literature, like the Catalan language, developed in close connection with that of Provence. In both regions the rhymed songs of the troubadours flourished as an art form from the 11th to the 14th cent. In the 13th cent. court chroniclers gave a fixed form to Catalan prose, and the language became an expressive literary medium in the works of the great Ramon LULL. At the end of the 14th cent. the art of the troubadours began to wane, and in the 15th cent. the influence of the great Italian masters—Dante and Petrarch—was strong, particularly on the work of the poet Auziàs MARCH. From the rise of Castile during the Renaissance Catalan literature was eclipsed until the 19th cent., when it experienced a marked revival. The great writers of this period were the dramatist Angel GUIMERÀ and the poet Mosèn Jacinto VERDAGUER. In the 20th cent. Catalan literature flourished. The realistic regional novel had first-rate exponents in Narcis Oller (1846–1930), Joaquim Ruyra (1858–1939), Prudenci Bertrana (1867–1941), and Catalina Albert i Paradis (1873–?), who wrote under the pseudonym Victor Català. Joan Maragall (1860–1911) was regarded by Miguel de Unamuno as the best lyric poet of the Iberian peninsula. A unique and exotic note was the esthetic dilettantism advocated by Eugenio d'ORS. Later poets of note were Josep Carner and Charles Riba. After the end of the Spanish civil war the regime of Francisco Franco persecuted Catalan authors and imposed a ban on Catalan books and publications, but Catalan writers continued their work in exile and Catalan literary life continued to lead an underground existence.

catalepsy, psychogenic state characterized by a loss of consciousness accompanied by rigidity of muscles that keeps limbs in any position in which they are placed. Attacks are of varying duration, from several minutes to days.

Catalina Island: see SANTA CATALINA.

Catalan altar panel (13th century) with scenes from the life of Archangel Michael.

The Annunciation (1346 Catalan oil mural by Ferrer Bassa).

Folk dance festival, Tarragona province, Catalonia.

Perelada Castle, Gerona province, Catalonia.

catalogue, descriptive list, on cards or in a book, of the contents of a library. Assur-bani-pal's library at Nineveh was catalogued on shelves of slate. The first known subject catalogue was compiled by Callimachus at the Alexandrian Library in the 3d cent. B.C. The library at Pergamum also had a catalogue. Early in the 9th cent. A.D. the catalogues of the libraries of the monastery at Reichenau and of the abbey at Saint-Riquier, N France, had summaries of works catalogued. In 1472 the monastic library at Clairvaux was recatalogued and one of the earliest union catalogues was made—of the contents of 160 Franciscan monastery libraries in England. In 1475 the Vatican librarian, Platina, catalogued that library's 2,527 volumes. About 1660 Clement, librarian of the Bibliothèque du Roi under Louis XV, compiled a subject catalogue and inventory of manuscripts. The printing of the British Museum catalogue was begun by Panizzi as keeper (1837–56) of printed books. Charles A. Cutter devised the modern dictionary catalogue (with author, title, and subject arranged in one alphabet) for the Boston Athenaeum library. In 1901 the Library of Congress began the practice of printing their catalogue entries on cards 3 by 5 in. and distributing them to other libraries for a small fee. The National Union Catalogue, begun in 1952 by the Library of Congress, collates the card catalogue entries of most large American libraries and prints the results in book form. See American Library Association, *Cataloging Rules* (2d ed., 1949); Archer Taylor, *Book Catalogues: Their Varieties and Uses* (1957).

Catalonia (kătŭlō′nēŭ), Span. *Cataluña* (kätälōō′-nyä), region (12,332 sq. mi.; pop. 3,925,779), NE Spain, stretching from the Pyrenees at the French border southward along the Mediterranean. It comprises four provinces, named after their capitals, BARCELONA, GERONA, LÉRIDA, and TARRAGONA. Barcelona is the historical capital. Mostly hilly, the region produces cereals, olive oil, and one third of the wines of Spain. The hydroelectric power furnished by the Ebro, Segre, and Cinca rivers has helped to industrialize Barcelona and Gerona provs. The chief industrial products are textiles, automobiles, airplanes, locomotives, and foundry and other metallurgical products. Trade has been active along the Catalan coast since Greek and Roman times. The history of medieval Catalonia (which, like Castile, took its name from its many castles) is that of the counts of Barcelona, who emerged (9th cent.) as the chief lords in the Spanish March founded by Charlemagne. United (1137) with ARAGON through the marriage of Count RAYMOND BERENGAR IV with Petronella of Aragon, Catalonia nevertheless preserved its own laws, its cortes, and its own language (akin to Provençal). CATALAN ART flourished in the Middle Ages. In the cities, notably Barcelona, the burgher and merchant classes grew very powerful. Catalan traders rivaled those of Genoa and Venice, and their maritime code was widely used in the 14th cent. Catalan merchants, and adventurers such as Roger de Flor, were largely responsible for the expansion of the house of Aragon up to the 15th cent. Catalonia failed in its rebellion (1461–72) against JOHN II of Aragon, and after the union (1479) of Aragon and Castile, Catalonia declined because of the centralizing policy of the Spanish kings, the shifting of trade routes, and the consequent loss of commercial income. Agitation for autonomy was always strong. In the Thirty Years War, Catalonia rose with French help against PHILIP IV, and in the War of the Spanish Succession it sided with Archduke Charles against Philip V, who in reprisal deprived it of all its privileges. In the 19th and 20th cent. it consistently supported the Carlists and all other movements which opposed the central government. After the peaceful revolution of 1931 and the ad-

Panorama of Catania.

vent of the Spanish republic, the Catalans established a separate government, first under Francisco MACIÁ, then under Luis COMPANYS, which in 1932 won autonomy from the Spanish Cortes. A revolution (1934) for complete independence failed, but in 1936 autonomy was restored. In the civil war of 1936–39 Catalonia sided with the Loyalists and suffered heavily. Barcelona was for a time (Oct., 1938–Jan., 1939) the Loyalist capital. Catalonia finally fell to Francisco Franco in Feb., 1939, and it was fully incorporated into his centralized state. See also CATALAN ART and CATALAN LITERATURE.

catalpa: see BIGNONIA.

catalysis (kǔtǎ′lǔsĭs), the changing of the speed of a chemical reaction. The change is brought about by the introduction of some substance, called variously the **catalyst,** catalytic agent, or contact agent. Positive catalysts increase the speed of a reaction and negative catalysts decrease the speed. It is now believed that the catalyst takes some part in the chemical reaction, but after the reaction is completed the catalyst can be recovered unchanged chemically, although its physical properties may be somewhat altered. Water acts in some cases as a catalyst since many substances, which when dry do not react, will enter into chemical reaction when in solution. The temperature at which a reaction takes place can be lowered by the use of a catalyst. When potassium chlorate is heated to its melting point, oxygen is not evolved, but when a catalyst, manganese dioxide, is introduced, oxygen is immediately and plentifully given off. In the contact process, a commercial process for the preparation of sulphuric acid, a catalyst (usually either finely divided platinum or ferric oxide) is used to speed up the reactions involved. Platinum (gauze) is used as a catalyst in the preparation of nitric acid by the oxidation of ammonia. Hydrogen and nitrogen are combined to form ammonia in the Haber process using finely divided iron as a catalyst. Various other substances, such as copper and nickel, exhibit catalytic

action in other processes. Enzymes act as catalysts in the digestion of food and in other processes, causing chemical changes to take place in their presence. Certain poisons apparently retard a reaction, acting as negative catalysts. Other substances prevent the decomposition of compounds at ordinary temperatures, acting thus as negative catalysts. The exact way in which catalysts act is little understood.

Catamarca (kätämär′kä), city (pop. c.29,000), NW Argentina. Founded in 1683, Catamarca is an old colonial city with a famous shrine to Our Lady. It is an agricultural and mining center and is located in an oasis that produces wine, cotton, and livestock.

catamount: see PUMA.

Catanduanes (kätändwä′näs), island (552 sq. mi.; pop. c.100,000), SE of Luzon, the Philippines. The capital is Virac. Hemp and coconuts are grown, and there are manganese and copper mines.

Catania (kǔtä′nēû, Ital. kätä′nyä), city (estimated pop. 344,786), capital of Catania prov., E Sicily, Italy, at the foot of Mt. Etna. Rebuilt after a severe volcanic eruption in 1669 and after earthquakes in 1169 and 1693, it is a busy port and a large commercial and industrial center (flour mills, sulphur refineries, asphalt factories). Founded (8th cent. B.C.) by Chalcidian colonists, it was a flourishing Greek town and later a Roman colony. In 1862, Garibaldi organized here his expedition to Rome which was stopped at Aspramonte. It was heavily damaged in the Second World War. There is a fine cathedral (12th and 18th cent.), a castle built by Emperor Frederick II, a university (founded 1444), and an observatory.

Catanzaro (kätändzä′rō), city (estimated pop. 69,179), capital of Catanzaro prov., Calabria, S Italy, on a hill above the Ionian Sea. There are flour mills and distilleries. Founded (10th cent.) by the Byzantines, it was famous until the 17th cent. for its velvets and damasks.

catapult (kǎ′tŭpŭlt″), machine used to throw missiles in ancient and medieval warfare. There were two major types in wide use. One, a large cross-bow, shot spears at a low trajectory (see BOW AND ARROW). The other type threw large stones, pots of boiling oil, and greek fire at a high trajectory and was used for attacking or defending fortifications. Catapults were widely employed in SIEGE warfare, but with the introduction of artillery in the 14th cent. they passed from use. However, in the 20th cent. a form of catapult was reintroduced as a means of launching aircraft from warships.

cataract, in medicine, opacity of the lens of the eye or its capsule affecting the vision. In the young, cataracts are generally congenital or hereditary;

Cataract brought on by advanced age.

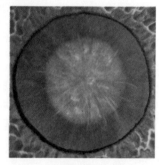

Typical example of a congenital cataract.

later they are usually the result of degenerative changes brought on by advanced age or systemic disease (diabetes). They may also be caused by injury, extreme heat, X rays, exposure to nuclear radiation, inflammatory disease, or toxic substances. Advanced cataracts are treated by surgical removal of the lens.

Catargiu, Lascar (kätärjōō'), 1823–99, Rumanian statesman, of an ancient Walachian family. Unsuccessful as Conservative candidate (1859) against Alexander John Cuza for the rule of Moldavia, he became leader of the Conservative opposition. He was twice premier of Rumania (1871–76, 1891–95) and effected financial and agrarian reforms.

catarrh (kùtär'), inflammation of any mucous membrane accompanied by profuse discharge, e.g., eye catarrh or intestinal catarrh. The word *catarrh* usually refers to chronic irritation of the nasal passages with discharge of secretions. Catarrh may be caused by dust or fumes or bacterial invasion.

Catasauqua (kătùsô'kwù), borough (pop. 5,062), E

Pa., on the Lehigh river and N of Allentown; inc. c.1853. Metal products, textiles, and clothing are made here.

catastrophism (kùtǎs'trùfĭzùm), in geology, the doctrine that at intervals in the earth's history all living things have been destroyed by cataclysms, e.g., floods or earthquakes, and replaced by an entirely different population. The theory, popularly accepted from the earliest times, was attacked in the 18th cent., notably by James Hutton, who may be regarded as the precursor of the opposite doctrine of uniformism. Catastrophism, however, was more easily correlated with religious doctrines, e.g., the Mosaic account of the Flood, and remained for some time the interpretation of the earth's history accepted by the great majority of geologists. It was systematized and defended by Cuvier, whose position as the greatest geologist of his day easily overbore all opposition. In the 19th cent. it was attacked by George Poulett Scrope and especially by Sir Charles Lyell, under whose influence the contrary doctrine gradually became more popular.

Catatumbo (kätätōōm'bō), river, c.210 mi. long, flowing from the Colombian Andes E across NW Venezuela to Lake MARACAIBO. Navigable in its lower course and with a railroad from the head of navigation to Cúcuta, it is the chief outlet for the upper Maracaibo basin and NE Colombia. Numerous oil derricks dot its banks.

Catawba, river: see WATEREE, river.

Catawba Indians (kùtô'bù), North American Indian tribe of Siouan stock, occupying a region in South Carolina. A large and powerful group, they waged incessant but unsuccessful war against the Cherokee and the tribes of the Ohio river valley, sending war parties great distances. Fighting and epidemics of smallpox reduced them to a small group in the 18th cent. A few survivors are in South Carolina.

Catawissa (kătùwĭs'ù), borough (pop. 1,824), E Pa., near the Susquehanna river S of Bloomsburg; laid out 1787, inc. 1892. Metal products are made.

catbird: see MIMIC THRUSH.

catch crop, any quick-growing crop sown between seasons of regular planting to make use of temporary idleness of the soil or to compensate for the failure of a main crop. It may be such rapid-maturing vegetables as radishes, onions grown from sets, or spinach (planted between rows of slower growing crops), quick-growing crops such as rye, millet, or buckwheat, or an annual legume, such as soybean, which is valuable as fodder or, when plowed under, increases the soil's fertility. See COVER CROP.

catchfly: see PINK.

catchment area or **drainage basin,** area drained by a stream or other body of water. The limits of a given catchment area are the heights of land—often called watersheds—separating it from neighboring drainage systems. The amount of water reaching the river, reservoir, or lake from its catchment area depends upon the size of the area, the amount of precipitation, and the loss through evaporation (determined by temperature, winds, and other factors and varying with the season) and through absorption by the earth or by vegetation; absorption is greater, of course, when the soil or rock is permeable than when it is impermeable. A permeable layer over an impermeable layer may act as a natural reservoir, supplying the river or lake in very dry seasons. The catchment area is one of the primary considerations in the planning of a reservoir for water-supply purposes.

Cateau, Le (lù kätō'), town (estimated pop. 8,457), Nord dept., N France, in French Flanders. It was formerly known as Le Cateau-Cambrésis. It has textile, metallurgical, and brewing industries. MATISSE was born here, and there is a museum containing much of his work. In the First World War the town was the scene of heavy fighting.

Cateau-Cambrésis, Treaty of (kätō'-kābräzē'), 1559, concluded at Le Cateau, France, by representatives of HENRY II of France, PHILIP II of Spain, and ELIZABETH I of England. It put an end to the 60-year conflict between France and Spain begun with the ITALIAN WARS, in which HENRY VIII and later MARY I of England had intermittently sided against France. The terms were a triumph for Spain. France restored Savoy, except Saluzzo, to Duke EMMANUEL PHILIBERT, acknowledged Spanish hegemony over Italy, and consented to a rectification of its border with the Spanish Netherlands. CALAIS, however, was confirmed in French possession by England. Henry II's sister, Margaret, was given in marriage to Emmanuel Philibert of Savoy; Henry's daughter, Elizabeth of Valois, was given to Philip II of Spain.

catechism (kă'tŭkĭzŭm) [Gr.,=oral instruction], originally oral instruction in religion, later written instruction. Catechisms are usually written in question and answer form. Almost as old as Christianity, they were used especially for the instruction of converts and children. Popular in the later Middle Ages, they assumed even greater significance in the Reformation through Luther's emphasis on the religious education of children. His Small Catechism (1529) is still the standard book of the Lutheran church. The greatest Calvinist catechism was the Heidelberg Catechism (1563). It was revised at Dort (1619) and was used in Dutch and German Reformed churches; other catechisms are the Longer and Shorter Catechisms of 1647 and 1648, drawn up to supplement the Westminster Confession; they are used in the Presbyterian churches. The Anglican catechism in the Book of Common Prayer is comparatively short. A catechism long in use in the Roman Catholic Church was that prepared by the Jesuit Peter Canisius which appeared in 1556. The catechism of the Council of Trent, a document of high authority issued in 1566, is not really a catechism but a manual of instruction for use by the clergy. The best-known Catholic catechism in England is the Penny Catechism, adopted by the bishops of England and Wales; that in the United States is the Baltimore Catechism.

catechu (kă'tŭchōō) or **cutch,** extract from the heartwood of *Acacia catechu,* a leguminous tree of the pulse family native to India and Burma. Catechu is a fast brown dye used for various shades of brown and olive, including the familiar khaki, and also in tanning. White cutch is a synonym for gambier, a leaf extract of a shrub (*Uncaria gambir*) of the madder family, similarly used. Both varieties, because of their astringent properties, have been used medicinally for intestinal disorder and hemorrhage. As dyes, they are being supplanted by synthetic types.

categorical imperative: see KANT, IMMANUEL.

category, a philosophical term which literally means predication or assertion. It was first used by Aristotle, whose 10 categories formed a list of all the ways in which assertions can be made of a subject. In Kant the 12 categories constitute an exhaustive list of the a priori forms through which the understanding knows the phenomenal world. The term has also been used in many other senses by various philosophers.

Catena, Vincenzo di Biagio (vēnchän'tsō dē byä'jō kätä'nä), c.1470–1531, Venetian painter. His early work reflects the influence of Giovanni Bellini, such as the two paintings of *Madonna and Child with Saints* in the Walters Art Gallery, Baltimore, and the Academy, Venice. In his later period Catena followed closely the style of Giorgione. The best works of this period are *The Doge Loredan Kneeling before the Madonna* (Correr Mus., Venice); *The Martyrdom of St. Christina* (Church of Santa Maria Mater Domini, Venice); and *Christ Giving the Keys to St. Peter* (Gardner Mus., Boston). See monograph by Giles Robertson (1954).

Caterham and Warlingham (kă'tùrŭm, wôr'lĭngŭm), urban district (pop. 34,808), Surrey, S England. It has a military station.

caterpillar: see LARVA.

catfish, family of fresh-water fish related to the SUCKER and MINNOW families and like them having

Brown catfish

a complex set of bones forming a sensitive hearing apparatus. Catfish are omnivorous feeders and are valuable as scavengers. They are named for the barbels ("whiskers") around their mouths and have scaleless skins, fleshy, rayless posterior fins, and sharp defensive spines in the shoulder and dorsal fins. They are also able to produce sounds by means of the air float (see FISH). Some species, e.g., the stone and tadpole catfishes and the mad tom, can inflict stings from poison glands in the pectoral spines. Catfish are usually dull-colored, though the small (3–4 in.) mad tom of E North American streams is brightly patterned. Danube catfish called wels or sheatfish reach a length of 13 ft. and a weight of 400 lb. The South American catfishes show great diversity: there are small, delicate species armored with bony plates; parasitic types that live in the gills of other fish; and one catfish of the E Andes in which the pelvic fins are modified into suckers that enable it to cling to rocks. In Africa are found an electric species (see ELECTRIC FISH) and the Nile catfish, which swims upside down to feed at the water's surface and has a white back and a dark belly, the reverse of the normal coloration. Of the 30 American species the largest and most important is the blue or Mississippi catfish, an excellent food fish weighing up to 150 lb. Best known is the smaller (up to 20 lb.) channel catfish, with a deeply forked tail and slender body. The stone cat (10 in. long) is found in clear water under logs and stones, where the eggs are deposited. The bullheads or horned pouts are catfish of muddy ponds and streams, feeding on bottom plant and animal life. Bullheads have square or slightly rounded tails, are mottled yellowish in color, and may reach 1 ft. in length and 2 lb. in weight. The black, yellow, and brown bullheads are common in the waters of the central and eastern states. There are no catfish in the Pacific except for the introduced white catfish. Marine catfish found during the summer in bays and harbors of the Atlantic and Gulf states include the 2-ft. gaff-topsail catfish, named for its long, ribbon-like pectoral and dorsal fins, and the smaller sea catfish, a very common "trash" fish. The males of both these species carry the fertilized eggs in their mouths (and therefore do not eat) until well after the young hatch, a period of two months. In certain other species the eggs are embedded in the underside of the female. Some tropical catfish survive dry seasons by burrowing into the mud or by crawling overland in search of water.

catgut or **gut,** cord made from the intestines of various animals (sheep and horses especially, but not cats). The membrane is chemically treated, and slender strands are woven together into cords of great strength, which are used for stringing musical instruments such as the violin and the harp. Roman strings, imported from Italy, are considered the best for musical instruments. Catgut is also used for stringing tennis rackets and for some surgical sutures.

Cathari (kă′thŭrĭ) [Gr.,=pure], generic name for the widespread dualistic religious movement of the Middle Ages. Carried from the Balkans to Western Europe, it flourished in the 11th and the 12th cent. as far north as England, and it was known by various names and in various forms, e.g., the BOGOMILS and the ALBIGENSES. Catharism was descended from GNOSTICISM and MANICHAEISM and echoed many of the ideas of MARCION. The Cathari tended to reject not only the outward symbols of Catholicism, such as the sacraments and the hierarchy, but also the basic relationship between God and man as taught by Christianity. Instead, the Cathari believed in a dualistic universe, in which the God of the New Testament who reigned over spiritual things was in conflict with the evil god (or Satan) who ruled over matter. Asceticism, absolute surrender of the flesh to the spirit, was to be cultivated as the means to perfection. There were two classes of the Cathari, the believers and the Perfect. The believers passed to the ranks of the Perfect on acceptance of the *consolamentum.* This, a sort of sacrament, was a laying on of hands. The Catharist concept of Jesus

resembled modalistic MONARCHIANISM in the West and ADOPTIONISM in the East. Persecution, such as that by the INQUISITION, and the efforts of popes like Innocent III wiped out Catharism by the 15th cent.

Cathay (kăthā′), medieval name for China, derived from the Khitai, the founders of the Liao dynasty. It was popularized by Marco Polo and usually applied only to China N of the Yangtze river. S China was sometimes called Mangi.

Cathcart, William Schaw Cathcart, 1st Earl, 1755–1843, British general and diplomat. He served in both the American Revolution and the French Revolutionary Wars. As ambassador to Russia (1813–21) he performed his greatest service in bringing that power into the last coalition against Napoleon. Already a member of the Scottish peerage, Cathcart was created an English viscount in 1807 and an earl in 1814.

cathedral (–thē′drŭl) [Gr.,=seat, i.e., episcopal throne], the church in which a bishop presides. The designation is not dependent upon the size or magnificence of a church edifice but is entirely a matter of its assignment as the church in which the bishop shall officiate. The great structures of the 13th and 14th cent. are the culminating expression of GOTHIC ARCHITECTURE. By its mass and its lofty towers, the cathedral was often the most conspicuous structure of a city, and it served as a center, not only for the religious life, but in many cases for the more important matters of secular life. Great cathedrals have been built in modern times, modern in their planning and construction but generally adhering closely to medieval styles of architecture. Among these are the Cathedral of St. John the Divine and St. Patrick's Cathedral, New York city; the cathedral in Washington, D.C.; and the cathedral in Liverpool, England. Among the most important medieval cathedrals are the following: *France*: Amiens, Beauvais, Bourges, Chartres, Le Mans, Paris, Rouen, Rheims, Strasbourg; *England*: Canterbury, Durham, Ely, Lincoln, Peterborough, Salisbury, Wells, Westminster Abbey, Winchester, York; *Germany*: Bonn, Cologne, Ulm, Worms; *Belgium*: Antwerp, Brussels, Louvain, Ypres; *Italy*: Como, Florence, Milan, Monreale, Orvieto, Pisa, Siena; *Spain*: Ávila, Burgos, Barcelona, Salamanca, Seville, Toledo; *Sweden*: Lund, Uppsala. See J. H. Harvey, *English Cathedrals* (2d ed., 1957); Martin Hürlimann, *French Cathedrals* (2d ed., 1961).

Cathedral City, uninc. village (pop. 1,855), S Calif., E of Riverside in the Coachella Valley. It is a desert resort in an area producing fruits and vegetables.

Cather, Willa Sibert, 1876–1947, American novelist and short-story writer, b. Winchester, Va. Her family moved to the Nebraska prairie frontier when she was nine. Much of her best writing captures the spirit of the pioneering life of the Midwest in the 1880s and '90s. After graduating from the Univ. of Nebraska in 1895, she worked as a journalist and as a teacher in Pittsburgh. In 1904 she went to New York. The publication of *The Troll Garden* (1905), her first collection of short stories, led to her appointment in 1906 to the editorial staff of the muckraking *McClure's Magazine.* After the publication of her first novel, *Alexan-*

The Martyrdom of Saint Catherine (monochrome painting by Guido Mazzoni).

der's Bridge (1912), she left McClure's and devoted herself to creative writing. O Pioneers! (1913) was the first of her novels dealing with the roughness and strength of frontier life. After it came The Song of the Lark (1915), My Ántonia (1918), and A Lost Lady (1923). She turned in later novels to New Mexico in Death Comes for the Archbishop (1927), to 17th-century Quebec in Shadows on the Rock (1931), in both books blending history with religious reverence and loving characterizations. Other volumes—Youth and the Bright Medusa (1920), My Mortal Enemy (1926), and The Old Beauty and Others (1948)—present her highly skilled shorter fiction. Her intense interest in the craft of writing is shown in the essays of Not under Forty (1936) and On Writing (1949). Her own mastery of the craft, her lucidity and control, and her warm humanity made her one of America's outstanding novelists. See biography by E. K. Brown (completed by Leon Edel, 1953); studies by J. H. Randall (1960) and E. A. Bloom and L. D. Bloom (1962).

Catherine, Saint, 4th cent.?, Alexandrian virgin martyr. Nothing certain is known of her. According to tradition she was learned. She was condemned to die on the wheel and was saved by a miracle, but later beheaded. Her principal shrine is the great monastery of Mt. Sinai. Attributes: sword, crown, palm, wheel, and book. The marriage of St. Catherine to Christ, a popular Renaissance subject, represents symbolically the dedication of her virginity. Feast: Nov. 25.

Catherine I, 1683?–1727, empress and tsarina of Russia (1725–27). Of Livonian peasant origin, Martha Skavronskaya was a domestic when she was captured (1702) by Russian soldiers. As mistress of Aleksandr D. MENSHIKOV she met Emperor Peter I (Peter the Great), who made her his mistress. After her conversion from the Lutheran to the Orthodox Church (when she changed her name from Martha to Catherine), Peter, who had divorced his first wife, married her (1711). In 1724 he had her crowned empress and joint ruler. Her loyalty and devotion to her difficult husband were remarkable. When Peter died without naming a successor, Menshikov and the imperial guards raised Catherine to the throne. Her policy was dominated by Menshikov. Peter II succeeded her; her daughter Elizabeth became empress in 1741.

Catherine II or **Catherine the Great,** 1729–96, empress and tsarina of Russia (1762–96), daughter of Christian Augustus, prince of Anhalt-Zerbst. She emerged from the obscurity of her relatively modest background when, in 1744, Empress Elizabeth of Russia, partly on the recommendation of Frederick II of Prussia, chose her as the wife of the future PETER III. Accepting the Orthodox faith, she changed her original name, Sophie, to Catherine. Her successful effort to become completely Russian made her popular with important political elements who opposed her eccentric husband. Neglected by the tsarevich, Catherine read widely, especially in Voltaire and Montesquieu, and informed herself of Russian conditions. In Jan., 1762, Peter succeeded to the throne, but he immediately alienated powerful groups with his program and personality. In June, 1762, a group of conspirators headed by Grigori ORLOV, Catherine's lover, proclaimed Catherine autocrat, and shortly afterward Peter was murdered. Catherine began her rule with great projects of reform. She drew up

Catherine II

a document based largely on the writings of BECCARIA and Montesquieu to serve as a guide for an enlightened code of laws. She summoned a legislative commission (with representatives of all classes except the serfs) to put this guide into law, but she disbanded the commission before it could complete the code. Some have questioned the sincerity of Catherine's "enlightened" outlook, and there is no doubt that she became more conservative as a result of the peasant rising (1773–75) under PUGACHEV. As a result, the nobility's administrative power was strengthened when Catherine reorganized (1775) the provincial administration to increase the central government's control over rural areas. This reform established a system of provinces, subdivided into districts, which endured until 1917. In 1785 Catherine issued a charter which made the nobility a corporate body, freed nobles from taxation and state service, made their status hereditary, and gave them absolute control over their lands and peasants. Another charter, issued to the towns, proved of little value to them. Catherine extended serfdom to parts of the Ukraine and transferred large tracts of state lands to favored noblemen. The serfs' remaining rights were strictly curtailed. She also encouraged colonization of ALASKA and of areas gained by conquest. She increased Russian control over the Baltic provinces and the Ukraine. Catherine attempted to increase Russia's power at the expense of her weaker neighbors, Poland and Turkey. In 1764 she established a virtual protectorate over Poland by placing her former lover Stanislaus Poniatowski on the Polish throne as STANISLAUS II. Eventually Catherine secured the lion's share in successive partitions of Poland among Russia, Prussia, and Austria (see POLAND, PARTITIONS OF). Catherine's first war with Turkey (1768–74; see RUSSO-TURKISH WARS) ended with the Treaty of Kuchuk Kainarji, which made Russia the dominant power in the Middle East. Catherine and her advisers developed a program known as the Greek project. This provided for a partition of Turkey's European holdings by Russia, Austria, and other countries. However, her attempts to break up the Ottoman Empire met with only partial success. In 1783 she annexed the Crimea. Her triumphal tour of S Russia, accompanied by POTEMKIN, her chief instrument in her Eastern policy, provoked the Turks to renew warfare (1787–92). The Treaty of Jassy (1792) confirmed the annexation of the Crimea and Russia's firm hold on the northern coast of the Black Sea. Catherine also extended Russian influence in European affairs. In 1778 she acted as mediator between Prussia and Austria, and in 1780 she organized a league to defend neutral shipping against England. Catherine increased the power and prestige of Russia by skillful diplomacy and by acquiring a belt of land that brought Russia's western boundary into the heart of central Europe. An enthusiastic patron of literature, art, and education, Catherine wrote memoirs, comedies, and stories, and corresponded with the French Encyclopedists, including Voltaire, Diderot, and Alembert (who were largely responsible for her glorious contemporary reputation). She encouraged some criticism and discussion of social and political problems until the French Revolution made her an outspoken conservative and turned her against all who dared criticize her regime. Although her morals were extremely lax, of her many lovers only Orlov, Potemkin, and P. L. Zubov (1767–1822) had any real influence. She was succeeded by her son Paul I. See biographies by Kazimierz Waliszewski (Eng. tr., 1894) and Katharine Anthony (1925). See also G. S. Thomson, *Catherine the Great and the Expansion of Russia* (1947);

G. P. Gooch, *Catherine the Great and Other Studies* (1954); M. E. von Almedingen, *Catherine, Empress of Russia* (1961).

Catherine de' Medici (dĭ mĕd′ĭchē, dä mä′dēchē), 1519–89, queen of France, daughter of Lorenzo de' Medici, duke of Urbino. She was married (1533)

Catherine de' Medici

to the duke of Orléans, later King Henry II. Neglected during the reign of her husband and that of her eldest son, Francis II, she became regent for her second son, CHARLES IX, in 1560. In the conflicts of the time, with the aid of her chancellor Michel de L'HÔPITAL, she at first adopted a conciliatory policy toward the Huguenots. The outbreak (1562) of the Wars of Religion (see RELIGION, WARS OF) led her to an alliance with the Catholic party under François de Guise and to negotiations with Philip II of Spain. When the growing influ-

Saint Catherine of Siena

ence of COLIGNY over Charles IX began to threaten her power, she plotted Coligny's assassination. The attempt having failed, she took part in planning the massacre of SAINT BARTHOLOMEW'S DAY (1572). After the accession of her third son, HENRY III, she vainly tried to revive her old conciliatory policy. See Edith Sichel, *Catherine de' Medici and the French Reformation* (1905) and *The Later Years of Catherine de' Medici* (1908); Paul Van Dyke, *Catherine de Médicis* (1922); Ralph Roeder, *Catherine de' Medici and the Lost Revolution* (1937).

Catherine Howard, queen of England: see HOWARD, CATHERINE.

Catherine of Aragon: see KATHARINE OF ARAGON.

Catherine of Braganza (brägăn'zŭ), 1638–1705, queen consort of Charles II of England, daughter of John IV of Portugal. She was married to Charles in 1662. As part of her dowry England secured Bombay and Tangier. Unpopular in England for her Roman Catholic faith, she also had to suffer the humiliation of her husband's infidelities and the disappointment of her own childlessness. In 1678 she was accused by Titus OATES of a plot to poison the king, but was protected from the charge by Charles himself. After William III's accession she returned to Portugal, where she supported the commercial Treaty of Methuen with England, and in 1704 she acted as regent for her brother, Peter II.

Catherine of Siena, Saint (sēĕ'nŭ), 1347–80, Italian mystic and diplomat, a member of the third order of the Dominicans. The daughter of Giacomo Benincasa, a Sienese dyer, Catherine from early childhood had mystic visions and practiced austerities; she also showed the devotion to others and the winning manner that characterized her life. From the age of about 19, Catherine devoted herself to the poor and the sick, not sparing her own frail health. In 1370, in response to a vision, she began to take part in the public life of her time, sending letters to the great of the day. She went to Avignon and exerted decisive influence in inducing Pope GREGORY XI to end the "Babylonian captivity" of the papacy and return to Rome in 1376. As papal ambassador to Florence, she helped bring about peace between Florence and the Holy See. In the Great Schism, she adhered to the Roman claimant and helped to advance his cause. In 1375 she is supposed to have received the five wounds of the stigmata, visible only to herself until after her death. She was the center of a spiritual revival almost everywhere she went. A formidable family of devoted followers gathered around her. Her mysticism contains overwhelming love for humanity as well as love for God. Though she never learned to write, she dictated hundreds of letters and a notable mystic work, commonly called in English *The Dialogue of Saint Catherine of Siena* or *A Treatise on Divine Providence* (or both as title and subtitle), which has been much used in devotional literature. She was one of the major religious figures of the Middle Ages. Feast: April 30. The accounts of her life collected by her followers were used in a biography by her confessor, Fra Raimondo da Capua (1398). See *Saint Catherine as Seen in Her Letters* (ed. by V. D. Scudder, 1905); biographies by Alice Curtayne (1929), Johannes Jorgenson (Eng. tr., 1938), and Sigrid Undset (Eng. tr., 1954).

Catherine of Valois (văl'wä, Fr. välwä'), 1401–37, queen consort of Henry V of England, daughter of Charles VI of France. She is also called Catherine of France. Married in 1420, she bore Henry a son who was to be Henry VI. Catherine later married the Welsh Owen Tudor; from them the Tudor kings of England were descended.

Catherine Parr, queen of England: see PARR, CATHERINE.

Catherine Tekakwitha (tĕk"äkwĭth'ŭ), 1656–80, American Indian holy woman, b. Auriesville, N.Y. Her name is sometimes given as Kateri Tegakouita. She was the daughter of a Mohawk chief and was baptized a Roman Catholic at the age of seven by a Jesuit missionary. Her tribesmen jeered and stoned her for her adopted faith, and she eventually went to a missionary settlement in Canada. Piety led her to the severest asceticism. The movement for her beatification began in the 1930s, and in 1961 it was publicly advanced before the pope. Many miracles have been attributed to her intercession. See biography by M. C. Buehrle (1954).

Catherine the Great: see CATHERINE II.

cathode: see ELECTRODE.

cathode ray: see ELECTRON; ELECTRODE; X RAY.

cathode ray tube, electron tube that produces electron beams from a cathode (see ELECTRODE) at one end and projects them on a fluorescent screen at the other to form a visual trace or picture. Nearly all cathode ray tubes use hot cathodes in a vacuum and high-anode voltages to accelerate the electron beam. When the electron beam impinges on the fluorescent screen it leaves a dot of light. The beam is focused and deflected by either electrostatic or electromagnetic fields from devices within or immediately surrounding the tube. The beam forms its image by being swept (deflected) very rapidly horizontally and vertically over the tube face. A wide range of cathode ray tubes are made both for monochromatic (single color) and multicolor displays. Their principal uses are in television receivers, radar and sonar receivers, and oscilloscopes.

Catholic Apostolic Church, religious community originating in England c.1831 and extending later to Germany and the United States. It was founded under the influence of Edward IRVING; its members are sometimes called Irvingites. Because of their prophetic gifts, 12 apostles (including Henry Drummond) were in 1835 set aside as officers. They were expected to survive until the second coming of Christ, but the last of them died in 1901. Over each congregation is an angel, or bishop, assisted by elders, deacons, and others. The ministry is not professional. Symbolism and mystery of worship characterize the elaborate liturgy. Much emphasis is given to the second coming of Christ. See P. E. Shaw, *The Catholic Apostolic Church* (1946).

Catholic Church (kă'thŭlĭk) [Gr.,=universal], the body of Christians, living and dead, considered as an organization. It is common for Christian groups to identify their particular churches (exclusively or not) as the Catholic Church. The word *catholic* was first used c.110 to describe the Church by St. Ignatius of Antioch. In speaking of the time before the Reformation, Catholic is technically used to mean orthodox (i.e., those accepting the decrees of Leo I and the Council of Chalcedon). Today in

English it usually means the Roman Catholic Church. Protestants use the words in their original sense to designate the Christian Church taken as a whole.

Catholic Emancipation, term applied to the process by which Roman Catholics in the British Isles were relieved in the late 18th and early 19th cent. of civil disabilities. They had been under oppressive regulations placed by various statutes dating as far back as the time of Henry VIII (see PENAL LAWS). This process of removing the disabilities culminated in the Catholic Emancipation Act of 1829 (and some subsequent provisions), but it had begun a number of years before. Priest hunting, in general, ended by the mid-18th cent. In 1778 English Catholics were relieved of the restrictions on land inheritance and purchase. A savage reaction to these concessions produced the Gordon Riots (see GORDON, LORD GEORGE) of 1780, and the whole history of Catholic Emancipation is one of struggle against great resistance. In 1791 the Roman Catholic Relief Act repealed most of the disabilities in Great Britain, provided Catholics took an oath of loyalty, and in 1793 the army, the navy, the universities, and the judiciary were opened to Catholics, though seats in Parliament and some offices were still denied. These reforms were sponsored by William PITT (1759–1806), who hoped thereby to split the alliance of Irish Catholics and Protestants. But Pitt's attempt to secure a general repeal of the Penal Laws was thwarted by George III. Pope Pius VII consented to a royal veto on episcopal nominations if the Penal Laws were repealed, but the move failed. In Ireland the repeal of POYNINGS'S LAW (1782) was followed by an act (1792) of the Irish Parliament relaxing the marriage and education laws and an act (1793) allowing Catholics to vote and hold most offices. By the Act of Union (1800) the Irish Parliament ceased to exist, and Ireland was given representation in the British Parliament. Now, since the Irish were a minority group in the British legislature, many English ministers began to advocate Catholic Emancipation, influenced also by the decline of the papacy as a factor in secular politics. Irish agitation, headed by Daniel O'CONNELL and his Catholic Association, was now successful in securing the admission of Catholics to Parliament. In 1828 the TEST ACT was repealed, and O'Connell, though still ineligible to sit, secured his election to Parliament from Co. Clare. Alarmed by the growing tension in Ireland, the duke of WELLINGTON, the prime minister, allowed the Catholic Emancipation Bill, sponsored by Sir Robert PEEL, to pass (1829). Catholics were now on the same footing as Protestants except for a few restrictions, most of which were removed in 1866, 1891, and 1926. The Act of SETTLEMENT is still in force, however, and Catholics are excluded from the throne, from the offices of regent, lord chancellor, and keeper of the great seal, from offices connected with the Established Church, and from a few university places. See studies by Bernard Ward (1911), Denis Gwynn (1928, 1929), and J. A. Reynolds (1954).

Catholic League, in French history: see LEAGUE.

Catholic University of America, at Washington, D.C.; Roman Catholic; coeducational, the only U.S. pontifical university; founded 1887 and opened 1889. It includes a college of arts and sciences; schools of canon law, sacred theology, and social science.

Catiline (Lucius Sergius Catilina) (kă'tĭlĭn), c.108 B.C.–62 B.C., Roman politician and conspirator. At first a conservative and a partisan of Sulla, he was praetor in 68 B.C. and governor of Africa in 67 B.C. The next year he was barred from candidacy for the consulship by accusations of misconduct in office, charges which later proved false. Feeling with some justice that he had been cheated, he concocted a wild plot to murder the consuls. He and the other conspirators were acquitted (65 B.C.). Catiline became more bitter than ever against the conservatives and began to advocate popular demagogic proposals. When in 63 B.C. he ran again for consul, he found CICERO, the incumbent, and the conservative party anxious to stop his election at any cost. Catiline was defeated, but this time he decided to try for the consulship by force. He sent money for the troops in Etruria and spread lavish promises in Rome. Cicero became alarmed and on Nov. 8, with facts gained from Catiline's mistress, accused him in the senate (*First Oration against Catiline*). Catiline fled to Etruria. The conspirators remaining in the city did not cease activities, but even approached the ambassadors of the Allobroges. The ambassadors reported the whole plot to Cicero, who arrested the conspirators and arraigned them in the senate on Dec. 3. On Dec. 5 they were condemned to death and executed, in spite of a most eloquent appeal from Julius CAESAR to use moderation. Cicero's haste and summary behavior were illegal, and it was on a charge (by CLODIUS) of executing these Roman citizens without due process of law that he was exiled. Catiline did not surrender; he fell in battle at Pistoia a month later. The prime sources for Catiline's conspiracy are Cicero's four orations against him and Sallust's biography of him. Both of these are prejudiced and unreliable. Catiline's treason may be partly explained, though not condoned, by the ruthless and devious means used against him. The affair did little credit to any concerned, except for the honest and patriotic Cato the Younger and possibly for Julius Caesar, who made a daring plea to a vindictive and ruthless majority on behalf of the conspirators whom he scorned. See E. G. Hardy, *The Catilinarian Conspiracy* (1924).

Catinat, Nicolas (nēkōlä' kätēnä'), 1637–1712, marshal of France. The son of a magistrate, he was conspicuous in his age for winning promotion by merit rather than by wealth or descent. In the War of the Grand Alliance he commanded against Victor Amadeus II of Savoy, whom he defeated in N Italy at Staffarda (1690) and at Marsaglia (1693). Early in the War of the Spanish Succession, he opposed Prince Eugene in Italy, but after reverses he was replaced by Villeroi. He retired in 1705 and later wrote his memoirs.

Cat Island: see SAN SALVADOR, island.

Catlettsburg, city (pop. 3,874), co. seat of Boyd co., E Ky., on the Ohio at the mouth of the Big Sandy near Ashland; settled 1808.

Catlin, George, 1796–1872, American traveler and artist, b. Wilkes-Barre, Pa. He was educated as a lawyer and practiced in Philadelphia for two years but turned to art study and became a portrait painter in New York city. In c.1832 he went west to study and paint the Indians, and after executing numerous portraits and tribal scenes he took his collection to Europe in 1839. In 1841 he published *Manners, Customs, and Condition of the North American Indians*, in two volumes, with about 300 engravings. Three years later he published 25 plates, entitled *Catlin's North American Indian Portfolio*, and, in 1848, *Eight Years' Travels and Residence in Europe*. From 1852 to 1857 he traveled through South and Central America and later returned for further exploration in the Far West. The record of these later years is contained in *Last Rambles amongst the Indians of the Rocky Mountains and the Andes* (1868) and *My Life among the Indians* (ed. by N. G. Humphreys, 1909). Of his 470 full-length portraits of Indians and tribal scenes, the greater part constitutes the Catlin Gallery of the National Museum, Washington, D.C., while some 700 sketches are in the American Museum of Natural History, New York city. His observations of the Indians have been questioned as to complete accuracy. He was the first white man to see the Minnesota pipestone quarries, and pipestone is also called catlinite. See Lloyd Haberly, *Pursuit of the Horizon* (1948); Harold McCracken, *George Catlin and the Old Frontier* (1959); Robert Plate, *Palette and Tomahawk: the Life of George Catlin* (1962).

Catlin, village (pop. 1,263), E Ill., SW of Danville, in a farm and coal-mine region; inc. 1873.

catlinite: see PIPESTONE.

catnip or **catmint,** strong-scented perennial herb (*Nepeta cataria*) of the MINT family, native to Europe and Asia but naturalized in the United States. A tea of the leaves and flowering tops has long been used as a domestic remedy for various ailments. Catnip is best known for its stimulating effect on cats.

Catoche, Cape (kätō'chä), extremity of Yucatan peninsula, SE Mexico. It was the first Mexican land seen by the Spanish (1517).

Catonsville (kä'tŭnzvĭl), uninc. city (pop. 37,372), N Md., a suburb W of Baltimore. A state hospital and park are nearby.

Cato Street Conspiracy: see THISTLEWOOD, ARTHUR.

Cato the Elder (kā'tō) or **Cato the Censor,** Latin *Cato Major* or *Cato Censorius*, 234–149 B.C., Roman statesman and moralist, whose full name was Marcus Porcius Cato. He fought in the Second Punic War and later served as quaestor (204), aedile (199), praetor (198), consul (195), and censor (184). He was renowned for his devotion to the old Roman ideals—simplicity of life, honesty, and unflinching courage. He inveighed against extravagance and new customs, but his policy was not aimed at repression but rather at reform and rebuilding of Roman life. He sought to restrict seats in the senate to the worthy and undertook much building, including repair of the city sewers. Sent on an official visit to Carthage in his old age, he returned stern with disapproval of Carthaginian ways and told the senate to destroy Carthage. He thus helped to bring on the Third Punic War, in which Carthage was destroyed. Probably his detestation of luxury and "cultivated" ways inspired the deep hatred that he had for the Scipio family. He himself deliberately affected a rustic appearance

and rustic manners. However, he complacently accepted class division and treated his servants harshly. He wrote many works, most of which are now lost. Probably the most influential was his history of early Rome. His *De agri cultura* or *De re rustica*, translated as *On Farming*, is a practical treatise which offers valuable information on agricultural methods and country life in his day.

Cato the Elder

Cato the Younger

Cato the Younger or **Cato of Utica,** Latin *Cato Minor* or *Cato Uticensis*, 95 B.C.- 46 B.C., Roman statesman, whose full name was Marcus Porcius Cato; great-grandson of Cato the Elder. Reared by his uncle M. Livius Drusus, he early showed an intense devotion to the principles of the early republic. He had one of the greatest reputations for honesty and incorruptibility of any man in ancient times, and his Stoicism put him above the graft and bribery of his day. His politics were extremely conservative, and his refusal to compromise made him unpopular with certain of his colleagues. He was from the first a violent opponent of Julius CAESAR and, outdoing CICERO in vituperation of the conspiracy of CATILINE in 63 B.C., tried to implicate Caesar in that plot, though maintaining his fairness to all. As a result he was sent (59 B.C.) to Cyprus by CLODIUS in what amounted to exile. He and his party supported POMPEY after the break with Caesar. He accompanied Pompey across the Adriatic and held Dyrrhachium (modern Durazzo) for him until after the defeat at Pharsala. Then he and Q. C. Metellus Pius Scipio (see SCIPIO, family) went to Africa and continued the struggle against Caesar there. Cato was in command at Utica. After Caesar crushed (46 B.C.) Scipio at THAPSUS, Cato committed suicide, bidding his people make their peace with Caesar. Cicero and M. Junius BRUTUS (Cato's son-in-law) wrote eulogies of him while Caesar wrote his *Anticato* against him; the noble tragedy of his death has been the subject of many dramas. He became the symbol of probity in public life.

Cats, Jacob (yä′kŏp käts′), 1577–1660, Dutch poet. A lawyer, he served as pensionary of Dordrecht (1623) and Holland (1636–51) and was ambassador to England. His didactic and moralizing poems discuss home life from marital ethics to table manners. Cats's main repute is as teacher and spokesman of Dutch Calvinist culture.

cat's-eye, gem stone that displays a thin band of reflected light on its surface when cut *en cabochon* (with a curved face) and polished. Its name is derived from its supposed resemblance to the eye of a cat. The optical effect, known as chatoyancy, is caused by the reflection of light from very thin, closely spaced filaments or cracks in parallel arrangement within the stone. True cat's-eye, a variety of CHRYSOBERYL from Ceylon, is the most valuable, but some quartz and tourmaline that display chatoyancy are also used as gems. A golden-yellow species called tiger's-eye is a type of naturally altered crocidolite asbestos.

Catskill (kăt′skĭl), village (pop. 5,825), co. seat of Greene co., SE N.Y., on the Hudson and S of Albany; settled in the 17th cent. by Dutch, inc. 1806. Connected with Hudson, N.Y., by the Rip Van Winkle Bridge, it is a gateway to Catskill Mt. resorts and to the Catskill Forest Preserve. Its manufactures include cement products and clothing. Thomas Cole lived and painted here.

Catskill Aqueduct, SE N.Y., carrying water to New York city from the Esopus and Schoharie watersheds in the Catskill Mts. It was planned in 1905, and the first part of the project was completed in 1917. The waters of Schoharie Creek (impounded at Schoharie Reservoir by Gilboa Dam) are sent via the 18-mile Shandaken Tunnel (opened 1924) to Esopus Creek. Some 15 mi. below the south end of the tunnel, at Ashokan Reservoir (created by Olive Bridge Dam in Esopus Creek), the 92-mile Catskill Aqueduct begins. It delivers water to Kensico Reservoir near White Plains and to Hillview Reservoir in Yonkers, whence it is distributed to the boroughs of New York through tunnels cut in solid rock. The Catskill Aqueduct passes under the Hudson river at Storm King mt. at a depth of 1,114 ft. The Narrows of New York Bay are crossed by a steel pipe to Silver Lake, Staten Island, a distance of 120 mi. from the beginning of the aqueduct at Ashokan Reservoir.

Catskill Mountains, range of the Appalachian Mts., SE N.Y., chiefly in Greene and Ulster counties and just W of the Hudson, to which they descend abruptly in places. The region, which is well wooded and rolling, with deep gorges and many beautiful waterfalls, is drained by the headstreams of the Delaware river and by Esopus, Schoharie, Rondout, and Catskill creeks. Most of the summits are c.3,000 ft. above sea level; Slide Mt. (4,180 ft.) and Hunter Mt. (4,040 ft.) are the highest. Close to New York city, the area is a popular summer and winter resort. Ashokan Reservoir is a source of the metropolitan area's water supply. Catskill Forest Preserve (236,011.34 acres) embraces some of the most impressive scenery of the range, including the region of the Rip Van Winkle legend.

Catt, Carrie (Lane) Chapman, 1859–1947, American suffragist and peace advocate, b. Ripon, Wis., grad. Iowa State College, 1880. She was superintendent of schools, Mason City, Iowa, 1883–84. In 1885 she married Lee Chapman, a journalist (d. 1886), and in 1890, George Catt, an engineer (d. 1905). From 1890 to 1900 an organizer for the National American Woman Suffrage Association, she became its president in 1900. She led the campaign to win suffrage through a Federal amendment to the Constitution. After the ratification of the Nineteenth Amendment (1920), she organized the League of Women Voters for the education of women in politics. At the Berlin convocation of the International Council of Women she helped organize the International Woman Suffrage Alliance, of which she was president from 1904 to 1923. After 1923 she devoted her efforts chiefly to the peace movement. With Nettie R. Shuler she wrote *Woman Suffrage and Politics* (1923). See biography by M. G. Peck (1944).

cattail or **reed mace,** any plant of the genus *Typha*, perennial herbs found in almost all open marshes. The cattail (also called club rush) has long narrow leaves, sometimes used for weaving chair seats, and a single tall stem bearing two sets of tiny flowers, the male flowers above the female. The pollinated female flowers form the familiar cylindrical spike of fuzzy brown fruits; the male flowers drop off and

Cattail

leave a naked stalk tip. The starchy rootstock can be used for food.

Cattaraugus (kătŭrô′gŭs), village (pop. 1,258), W N.Y., S of Buffalo; settled 1851, inc. 1882. The Cattaraugus Indian Reservation is nearby.

Cattaro: see KOTOR.

Cattermole, George, 1800–1868, English watercolor painter and illustrator. He painted a wide variety of subjects with notable success and was equally successful as an illustrator. He was a close friend of Dickens, Thackeray, and Browning.

Cattermole is represented in most of the important British galleries.

cattle, ruminant animals of the family Bovidae, to which the buffalo, bison, yak, and zebu also belong. Western or European domestic cattle (genus *Bos*) are thought to be descended from the AUROCHS and a smaller breed, the Celtic shorthorn. Cattle were first brought to the Western Hemisphere by Columbus on his second voyage. Wealth has sometimes consisted chiefly of cattle and has been measured by them; the word *pecuniary* is derived from the Latin *pecus*, cattle, and the words *cattle, chattel*, and *capital* are related. Breeding for improvement of beef and dairy qualities was practiced by the Romans but was not established on scientific principles until the middle of the 18th cent. by Robert Bakewell in England. The principal beef breeds include the ABERDEEN ANGUS and HEREFORD. The principal dairy breeds include the AYRSHIRE, BROWN SWISS, DUTCH BELTED, GUERNSEY, HOLSTEIN-FRIESIAN, and JERSEY. The chief dual-purpose breeds include the DEVON, POLLED SHORTHORN, RED POLLED, and SHORTHORN. Associations have been formed by breeders interested in improving the various breeds. The nomenclature of cattle is as follows: a bull-calf becomes a bull, and a castrated steer becomes an ox; a heifer-calf grows into a heifer and finally becomes a cow. See also BEEF and DAIRYING. See publications of the U.S. Dept. of Agriculture; C. W. Towne and E. N. Wentworth, *Cattle and Men* (1955).

cattleya: see ORCHID.

Catton, Bruce, 1899–, American historian, b. Petoskey, Mich. He studied at Oberlin College and then entered upon a varied career as a journalist (1926–42) and public official (1942–52). After 1952 he devoted himself to full-time literary work, serving as an editor since 1954 (senior editor, 1959) of the *American Heritage* magazine. In 1954 he received the Pulitzer prize for his historical work, *A Stillness at Appomattox* (1953). Other works include *The War Lords of Washington* (1948), *Mr. Lincoln's Army* (1951), *Glory Road* (1952), *U. S. Grant and the American Military Tradition* (1954), *This Hallowed Ground* (1956), *Grant Moves South* (1960), and *The Coming Fury* (1961).

Catullus (Caius Valerius Catullus) (kŭtŭ′lŭs), 84? B.C.-54? B.C., Roman poet, b. Verona. Of a well-to-do family, he went c.62 B.C. to Rome, where he had access to literary and fashionable circles. There, he and other young writers formed a cult of youth. He fell deeply in love, probably with Clodia, and wrote to his beloved, addressed as Lesbia (to recall Sappho of Lesbos), a series of superb little poems that run from early passion and tenderness to the hatred and disillusionment that overwhelmed him after his mistress was faithless. Of the 116 extant poems attributed to him, three (18–20) are almost certainly spurious. They include, besides the Lesbia poems, poems to his young friend Juventius; epigrams, ranging from the genial to the obscenely derisive; elegies; a few long poems, notably "Attis" and an epithalamium on Thetis and Peleus; and various short poems. His satire is vigorous and flexible, his light poems gay and full-bodied. He was influenced by the Alexandrians and drew much on the Greeks for form and meter, but his genius outran all models. Catul-

lus is one of the greatest lyric poets of all time. Two of the most popular of his poems are the 10-line poem, touching and simple, which ends, "frater ave atque vale" [hail, brother, and farewell], and "On the Death of Lesbia's Sparrow." A collection of his poems in English translation was edited by W. A. Aiken (1950). See Tenney Frank, *Catullus and Horace* (1928); F. A. Wright, *Three Roman Poets* (1938).

Catulus (kă′chŏŏlŭs), family of ancient Rome, of the Lutatian gens. **Caius Lutatius Catulus** (kā′ŭs, kĭ′ŭs, lōōtā′shŭs) was consul in 242 B.C. He won the great Roman naval victory over Carthage off the Aegates (modern Aegadian Isles) that ended the First Punic War. **Quintus Lutatius Catulus** (kwĭn′tŭs), d. 87 B.C., was consul in 102 B.C. His colleague in the consulship was MARIUS, and the two of them went north to oppose a Germanic invasion. He had to retreat before the Cimbri until Marius returned from Gaul. The two then defeated the Cimbri near Vercelli in 101 B.C. He later opposed Marius in the Social War and favored Sulla. Proscribed by the Marians, he either committed suicide or was killed. He was the patron of a literary circle and was himself a writer and a philosopher. Cicero praises his oratory. His son, also **Quintus Lutatius Catulus**, d. c.60 B.C., was consul in 78 B.C. He opposed the constitutional changes sought by LEPIDUS (d. 77 B.C.), and when Lepidus led a revolt, Catulus and Appius CLAUDIUS defeated him. Catulus was censor in 65 B.C. He was the leader of the archconservative group. He led the minority opposing the conferring of unusual powers on Pompey by the Manilian Law in 66 B.C., and he was one of the bitterest opponents of Julius Caesar.

Cauca (kou′kä), river, rising near Popayán, W Colombia. It flows c.600 mi. N to the Magdalena through the Colombian Andes. It is navigable in its lower course and drains a fertile valley, a superb agricultural region, which also has minerals.

Caucasia: see CAUCASUS.

Caucasian and **Caucasoid:** see RACE.

Caucasian Gates: see DARYAL.

Caucasus (kô′kŭsŭs), Rus. *Kavkaz* (kŭfkäs′), region and mountain system, S central European USSR. The mountain system extends c.750 mi. from the mouth of the Kuban river on the Black Sea SE to the Apsheron peninsula on the Caspian Sea. As a divide between Europe and Asia, the Caucasus has two major divisions—North Caucasia and Transcaucasia. North Caucasia begins at the MANYCH DEPRESSION and runs into the main range, the Greater Caucasus. This is a series of chains running east-southeast, including Mt. Elbrus (18,481 ft.), the Dykh-Tau (17,050 ft.), the Koshtan-Tau (16,850 ft.), and Mt. Kazbek (16,541 ft.).' The Greater Caucasus is crossed by several passes, notably the MAMISON and the DARYAL, and by the GEORGIAN MILITARY ROAD and the OSSETIAN MILITARY ROAD, which connect North Caucasia with the second major section, Transcaucasia. This region includes the southern slopes of the Greater Caucasus and the depressions that link them with the Armenian foothills. North Caucasia, part of the RSFSR, includes KRASNODAR TERRITORY (with ADYGE AUTONOMOUS OBLAST), STAVROPOL TERRITORY (with the Cherkess Autono-

Rich oil fields of Baku, one of the major cities of the Caucasus region.

mous Oblast), KABARDINO BALKAR AUTONOMOUS SOVIET SOCIALIST REPUBLIC, North Ossetian Autonomous SSR, DAGESTAN AUTONOMOUS SOVIET SOCIALIST REPUBLIC, and parts of the Rostov and GROZNY oblasts. Transcaucasia includes the GEORGIAN SOVIET SOCIALIST REPUBLIC (including the ABKHAZ AUTONOMOUS SOVIET SOCIALIST REPUBLIC, the ADZHAR AUTONOMOUS SOVIET SOCIALIST REPUBLIC, and the South Ossetian Autonomous Oblast), the AZERBAIJAN SOVIET SOCIALIST REPUBLIC (including the NAKHICHEVAN AUTONOMOUS SOVIET SOCIALIST REPUBLIC and the MOUNTAIN-KARABAKH autonomous oblast), and the ARMENIAN SOVIET SOCIALIST REPUBLIC. Over 40 languages are spoken by the ethnic groups of the entire region. The Ossetians, Kabardinians, Circassians, and Dahestani are the major groups in North Caucasia. The Armenians, Georgians, and Azerbaijani are the largest groups in Transcaucasia. The Kura and Rion river valleys have traditionally been the main thoroughfares of the Caucasus. Now the Rostov-Makhackala RR links North Caucasia with Transcaucasia, and there is a line connecting Rostov and Armavir with the port of Batum, beyond the Caucasus. In Transcaucasia the main line cuts through the center of the region from Baku, Tiflis, and Kutais, and there are lines along the Turkish border and the Caspian Sea. Oil is the major product in the Caucasus, with fields at Baku, Grozny, and Maikop. There is an oil pipeline from Baku, on the Caspian, connecting with Tiflis and Batum, on the Black Sea, and a pipeline from the fields at Grozny to the port of Makhackala. Iron and steel are produced at Rustavi from the ores of Azerbaijan. Manganese is mined at Chiatura, and there are ferro-manganese plants at Zestafoni. Coal is mined, and Novorossiisk produces concrete. Power for these industries is produced at several large hydroelectric stations. On the mountain slopes, covered by dense pine and deciduous trees, there is stock raising. In the valleys, citrus fruits, tea, cotton, grain, and live-

stock are raised. Along the Black Sea coast between Anapas and Sochi there are many resorts and summer homes. PYATIGORSK and KISLOVODSK are notable among the health and mineral resorts in North Caucasia. Major cities in the Caucasus are BAKU, ERIVAN, Grozny, ORDZHONIKIDZE, (formerly Dzaudzhikau), TIFLIS, Krasnodar, Novorossiisk, Batum, Kirovabad, Leninakan, and Kutais. The Caucasus figured greatly in the legends of ancient Greece; Prometheus was chained on a Caucasian mountain, and Jason and his Argonauts sought the Golden Fleece at Colchis. Persians, Khazars, Arabs, Huns, Turko-Mongols, and Russians have invaded and migrated into the Caucasus and have given the region its ethnic and linguistic complexity. The Russians assumed control in the 19th cent. after a series of wars with Persia and Turkey. The people of Georgia and Armenia, then predominantly Christian, accepted Russian hegemony as protection from Turkish persecution. In Azerbaijan, Dagestan, and the historic region of CIRCASSIA, the people were largely Moslem. They bitterly fought Russian penetration and were pacified only after the Shamyl uprising. In the Second World War the invading German forces launched (July, 1942) a major drive to seize or neutralize the vast oil resources of the Caucasus. They penetrated deeply, but in January, 1943, the Russians launched a winter offensive and by October had driven the Germans from the region. The romantic beauty of the Caucasus is celebrated in Russian literature by many poets, most notably in Pushkin's poem "Captive of the Caucasus," Lermontov's novel, *A Hero of Our Time*, and Tolstoy's novels, *The Cossacks* and *Hadji Murad*.

Caucasus Indicus: see HINDU KUSH.

Cauchon, Pierre (pyĕr′ kōshŏ′), d. 1442, bishop of Beauvais, France, president of the ecclesiastic court that convicted (1431) JOAN OF ARC at Rouen. His violent partisanship for the English made a fair trial impossible. His procedure was repudiated by the Church in the rehabilitation trial (1456) of

Joan. See W. P. Barrett, *The Trial of Jeanne d'Arc* (1931).

Cauchy, Augustin Louis, Baron (ōgüstē' lwē' bärō' kōshē'), 1789–1857, French mathematician. He was professor simultaneously (1816–30) at the École polytechnique, the Sorbonne, and the Collège de France in Paris. While a political exile (1830–38) he taught at the Univ. of Turin. He returned to the Sorbonne in 1848. Besides his influential work in every branch of mathematics (especially the theory of functions, integral and differential calculus, and algebraic analysis) he contributed to astronomy, optics, hydrodynamics, and other fields. Among his nearly 800 publications are works on the theory of waves (1815), algebraic analysis (1821), infinitesimal calculus (1823, 1826–28), differential calculus (1827), and the dispersion of light (1836).

caucus: see CONVENTION.

Cauda: see CLAUDA.

caudillo (kôdēl'yō, Span. koudhē'yō, –dhē'lyō) [Span.,=army chieftain], term applied to a type of Hispanic American political leader who arose with the wars of independence. *Caudillos* have varied greatly in character, methods, and aims, but they share certain characteristics. The *caudillo* is frequently a mestizo, whose political platform is of little consequence, but whose personal magnetism commands the blind allegiance of the masses. He is daring and skilled in military matters. Although he almost invariably becomes an oligarch, he often begins his career by opposing the white plutocracy and sometimes the power of the Church. In the eyes of the peasants, he is often a messiah. Although *caudillo* rule tends to be based on rigid discipline, it is also brutal, arbitrary, and unchecked by any system of constitutional rights. Some famous *caudillos* have been Juan Manuel de ROSAS and Juan Facundo QUIROGA of Argentina, Francisco Solano LÓPEZ of Paraguay, Gabriel GARCÍA MORENO of Ecuador, Porfirio DÍAZ and Francisco VILLA of Mexico, and Rafael Leonidas TRUJILLO MOLINA of the Dominican Republic.

Caudine Forks (kô'dĭn), narrow passes in the Apennines, S Italy, on the road from Capua to Benevento. Here, in 321 B.C., the Samnites routed a Roman army and forced it to pass under a yoke.

Caughnawaga (kä'näwä'gù), village, S Que., Canada, on the St. Lawrence opposite Lachine. It was founded (1667) as a refuge for the Iroquois converts to the Christian faith. It is still an Iroquois village, though in 1890 it abandoned government by tribal chief in favor of municipal law.

Caulaincourt, Armand Augustin Louis, marquis de (ärmä' ōgüstē' lwē' märkē' dù kōlēkōōr'), b. 1772 or 1773, d. 1827, French diplomat and general, created duke of Vicenza by Napoleon. He became (1802) Napoleon's aide-de-camp, and as ambassador to Russia (1807–11) he opposed the emperor's war policy. He accompanied Napoleon as aide-de-camp in the Russian campaign and on his two-week dash from Russia to Paris (1812). Caulaincourt was foreign minister when Napoleon abdicated in 1814 and again during the Hundred Days. His remarkable memoirs of the years 1812–15 were first published in 1933 and appeared in English as *With Napoleon in Russia* (1935) and *No Peace with Napoleon!* (1936).

cauliflower (kô'lĭ–), variety of CABBAGE, with an edible head of condensed flowers and flower stems. Broccoli is the horticultural variety (*botrytis*); both were cultivated in Roman times.

Caupolicán (koupōlēkän'), d. 1558, leader of the Araucanian Indians who fiercely resisted the Spanish conquest of Chile. He attempted to carry on the reconquest begun by LAUTARO and won a victory over Pedro de Valdivia. After a heroic but futile battle to keep the Spanish from recapturing Concepción, Caupolicán was forced to retreat into the forest. Here he was surprised, captured, tortured, and killed. His fame rests partly on *La Araucana*, the epic poem of Ercilla y Zúñiga.

Caus or **Caux, Salomon de** (both: sälōmō' dù kō') 1576–1626, French engineer and physicist, educated in England. From 1614 to 1620 he was engineer to the Elector Palatine, Frederick, at Heidelberg. Because of his *Les Raisons des forces mouvantes avec diverses machines* (1615), an early exposition of the principle of steam power, he has been considered the originator of the steam engine.

causality, relationship between the cause and its effect. The scientific conception that given stimuli under controlled conditions must inevitably produce standard results is generally accepted by philosophers. Systems vary, however, in the degree of emphasis that they place on the role of chance in changing a situation. Hume felt that in causal relations we have no evidence of any power exerted by the cause on the effect. Kant thought the notion of cause a fundamental category of understanding, while others argue a strictly mechanical theory of causality. The introduction of the principle of indeterminacy into modern physics has necessitated a modification of traditional concepts.

caustic, substance which acts upon organic material, burning or corroding it. Caustic SODA (sodium hydroxide), as well as caustic POTASH (potassium hydroxide), is a caustic ALKALI. Silver nitrate, called caustic silver or lunar caustic, is commonly used in medicine.

cautery, the searing or destruction of living animal tissue by any method of burning. In olden days, cauterization of open wounds, even those following amputation of a limb, was performed with hot irons; this served to close off the bleeding vessels as well as to discourage infection. In modern times cautery is used only on small lesions, e.g., to close off a bleeding point in the nasal mucous membrane or to eradicate a wart or other benign lesion. This is accomplished either by the application of a caustic substance such as nitric acid, or by the use of an electrically charged platinum wire (electrocautery).

Cauto (kou'tō), longest river in Cuba, rising in the Sierra Maestra. It is c.150 mi. long and flows NW and W to the Caribbean just N of Manzanillo.

Cauvery (kô'vùrē), river, S India, rising in the Western Ghats. About 475 mi. long, it flows east, then southeast, to empty into the Bay of Bengal below Pondicherry. Sometimes called the Ganges of the South, it is sacred to Hindus. The scenic falls near Sivasamudram furnish most of the hydroelectric power in S India. It is sometimes spelled Kaveri or Kavery.

Caux, Salomon de: see CAUS, SALOMON DE.

Cavaignac, Louis Eugène (lwē' ûzhĕn' kävänyäk'), 1802–57, French general. He distinguished himself in the French conquest of Algeria, especially by his defense (1836) of the fortress of Tlemcen. He was promoted (1844) to general. After the outbreak of the February Revolution in 1848, he became governor general of Algeria. Elected to the national assembly, he returned to Paris and was appointed minister of war. He used his dictatorial powers to quell the threatened rising of the working classes in the JUNE DAYS. In the presidential election he was badly defeated by Louis Napoleon (later NAPOLEON III). Arrested after the coup d'état of 1851, he was soon released but, refusing to swear allegiance to Napoleon III, held no further office.

Cavalcanti, Guido (gwē'dō kävälkän'tē), c.1255–1300, Italian poet; friend of Dante. He belonged to the White faction in the struggle of the Guelphs in Florence and was exiled to Sarzana. There he fell ill and died soon after his recall. Much of his best verse is in the *Canzone d'amore* [song of love]. For translations, see his *Sonnets and Ballate*, tr. by Ezra Pound (1912) and Lorna de' Lucchi, *An Anthology of Italian Poems* (1922).

Cavalcaselle, Giovanni Battista (jōvän'nē bättēs'tä kävälkäsĕl'lä), 1820–97, Italian art critic and writer. He studied painting at the Academy of Venice and traveled extensively through Italy studying its art treasures. He participated in the Revolution of 1848 and escaped to England, where he remained for several years. While there he produced in collaboration with Joseph A. Crowe their first joint work, *Early Flemish Painters* (1856). Cavalcaselle returned to Italy in 1857 and subsequently served as director of fine arts in Rome. The writings of Crowe and Cavalcaselle include the still basic *History of Painting in Italy* (3 vols., 1864–66).

Cavalier, Jean (zhä' kävälyä'), 1681?–1740, a leader of the CAMISARDS. From his home in the Cévennes region of France, he fled to Geneva (1701) when persecution of the Protestants became intolerable, but he returned when he knew that the Protestants were about to rebel. As chief leader of the Camisards, he showed remarkable military genius. In 1704 he made peace with Marshal Villars and received from Louis XIV a commission as colonel and a pension. The peace was repudiated by his followers because it did not restore the Edict of Nantes. Distrustful of the king, Cavalier fled from France. He fought for the duke of Savoy and later for England in Spain against the French. His later years were spent in Great Britain, where he was given a pension, made major general, and appointed governor of the isle of Jersey. The *Memoirs of the Wars of the Cévennes*, published in 1726 and dedicated tó Lord Carteret, is attributed to Cavalier.

Cavalier, city (kăvŭlēr'), (pop. 1,423), co. seat of Pembina co., extreme NE N.Dak., on the Tongue river and NNW of Grand Forks; founded 1875, inc. 1885. It is a processing center for a livestock, dairy, and farm region.

cavalier, in general, an armed horseman. In the English civil war the supporters of Charles I were called Cavaliers in contradistinction to the ROUND-HEADS, the followers of Parliament. The royalists used the designation until it was replaced by TORY.

Cavaliere, Emilio del (āmē'lyō dĕl kävälyä'rā),

c.1550–1602, Italian composer. His sacred dramatic work *La rappresentazione di anima e di corpo* (Rome, 1600) was a forerunner of oratorio, and his recitatives were the first monodies. His name also appears as Emilio de' Cavalieri.

Cavalieri, Francesco Bonaventura (fränchä'skō bōnäväntōō'rä kävälyä'rē), 1598–1647, Italian mathematician, a Jesuit priest. Professor at Bologna from 1629, he invented the method of indivisibles (1635) which foreshadowed integral calculus.

Cavalieri, Lina (lē'nä), 1874–1944, Italian operatic soprano. After her debut in Lisbon in 1900 she achieved great success throughout Europe and in the United States in the lyric French and Italian roles, renowned as much for her great beauty and fiery temperament as for her light, pleasant voice. She sang with the Metropolitan Opera Company (1906–8) and with Oscar Hammerstein's Manhattan Opera Company (1909–10).

Cavalier poets, a group of secular poets at the court of Charles I. Their poetry embodied the life and culture of upper-class pre-Commonwealth England, mixing sophistication with naïveté, elegance with raciness. They wrote finely finished verses, expressed with wit and directness, on the courtly themes of beauty, love, and loyalty. Their poetry shows their indebtedness to both Ben Jonson and John Donne. Robert Herrick, Richard Lovelace, Sir John Suckling, and Thomas Carew were the leading writers of the group.

cavalla: see POMPANO.

Cavalli, Pietro Francesco (pyä'trō fränchä'skō kävál'lē), 1602–76, Italian composer, whose real name was Caletti-Bruni; pupil of Monteverdi, whom he succeeded as choirmaster of St. Mark's, Venice. He wrote many operas, including *Didone* (1641), *Giasone* (1649), *Serse* (1654), and *Ercole Amante* (1662), all of which show the full development of the *bel canto* aria.

Cavallini, Pietro (pyä'trō kävál-lē'nē), c.1250–c.1330, Italian painter and mosaicist. Working in a classical style, he had an important influence on the art of Cimabue and Giotto. His surviving works are frescoes in Santa Cecilia, Rome, and in Santa Maria Donnaregina, Naples. He designed some beautiful mosaics in the Church of Santa Maria in Trastevere, Rome.

cavalry (kă'vŭlrē), mounted troops trained to fight from horseback. Cavalry was used by the ancient Egyptians, but it was more extensively employed by the ancient Hittites, Assyrians, Babylonians, and Persians. Some of the Greek city-states had mounted troops, but the typical Greek force was heavy infantry. Since saddles were not introduced until the time of Constantine I and stirrups seem to have been a contribution of the Franks, cavalry was at a disadvantage against well-disciplined infantry at the time when Rome reached the height of greatness, though the Romans did use regiments of horsemen. Cavalry was particularly useful in scouting and in pursuing a routed enemy. The first wide and expert use of cavalry in Europe was that of the invaders from the East, the Huns, Avars, Magyars, and Mongols. In medieval Europe the mounted knight became the typical warrior, and cavalry dominated in the incessant small wars. With the reintroduction of mass fighting at the end of the Middle Ages, infantry came

Lieutenant Colonel Theodore Roosevelt (in light uniform) and the 1st Volunteer Cavalry (Rough Riders) during the Spanish-American War, 1898.

to the fore again. The use of firearms did much to enhance the importance of infantry. Cavalry, however, was still of great value because of its mobility, its rapid striking power, and its usefulness in pursuing a defeated enemy from the field. Cavalry was prominent in the armies of Louis XIV and Frederick II (Frederick the Great), and particularly with Napoleon the cavalryman became the elite of the fighting forces, though most of the actual fighting was done by the infantry. Gaily uniformed cuirassiers, dragoons, hussars, and lancers were features of European armies of the 19th cent., and most of these forces were recruited from the nobility and the landed gentry. Cavalry was of great value during the 19th cent. on the African, American, and British-Indian frontiers, where mobility was essential in fighting lightly armed natives. It was also much used in the U.S. Civil War. Its value, however, began to wane with the introduction of automatic weapons, such as the machine gun, at the end of the 19th cent. Furthermore, in the First World War, because of the trench warfare, cavalry was only used in small numbers on the plains of Eastern Europe and the Near East. Cavalry was employed at the beginning of the Second World War by the Poles and the Russians against the Germans. However, cavalry as a force in modern warfare disappeared with the introduction of highly mobile tank units. In 1946 the U.S. army abolished the cavalry as a separate arm of the service, merging what remained of it with the armored forces.

Cavan (kă'vŭn), county (pop. 56,597), 730 sq. mi., N Republic of Ireland. The county town is Cavan. It is a hilly region of lakes (Lough Oughter chief among them) and bogs, and the climate is extremely damp and cool. Most of the soil is clay. The Erne is the principal river, and the Shannon has its source in Cavan. Although agriculture is the chief occupation, less than a third of the area is under cultivation, and that mostly in very small farms. Manufactures are negligible. Cavan was organized as a shire of Ulster prov. in 1584.

Cavan, urban district (pop. 3,207), county town of Co. Cavan, N Republic of Ireland. It is a farm

market and the seat of the Roman Catholic bishop of Kilmore and the Anglican bishop of Kilmore.

Cave, Edward, 1691–1754, English publisher. He founded (1731) the *Gentleman's Magazine*, the first modern English magazine. He gave Samuel Johnson his first regular literary employment when he printed (1741–44) in his periodical Johnson's parliamentary reports, "Debates in the Senate of Magna Lilliputia." He later published other works of Johnson.

cave, a hollow, either above or below ground. Caves may be formed by the chemical and mechanical action of a stream upon soluble or soft rock, of rain water seeping through soluble rock to the groundwater level, or of waves dashed against a rocky shore. Volcanic action (accompanied by the formation of gas pockets in lava or the melting of ice under lava) and earthquakes or other earth movements are also sources of cave formation. Limestone regions almost invariably have caves; some of these are notable for their STALACTITE AND STALAGMITE formations or for their magnitude and unearthly beauty. Some caves were the means of preserving both the remains of prehistoric man and animals and indications of man's early culture. Speleology, the scientific study of caves and their plant and animal life, contributes to knowledge of adaptation and evolution. Some cave animals lack sight, and both plants and animals living where light is excluded show loss of pigment. Among famous caves in the United States are CARLSBAD CAVERNS NATIONAL PARK (N.Mex.), MAMMOTH CAVE NATIONAL PARK (Ky.), and Wind Cave National Park (Black Hills, S.Dak.); LURAY CAVERNS (Va.); and WYANDOTTE CAVE (Ind.) In Europe there are celebrated caves in Belgium, Dalmatia, Gibraltar, CAPRI, and Sicily, at POSTOJNA, and in England (KENT'S CAVERN and Kirkdale). The caves of the Pyrenees and the Dordogne are famed for their prehistoric paintings (see PALEOLITHIC ART), and those of AJANTA, India, and TUNHWANG, China, for their Buddhist frescoes. Fingal's Cave in the basalt of the Hebrides off Scotland is one of the many caves about which there are legends. The caves of Iceland and Hawaii are volcanic. See also CAVE DWELLER. See F. B. Folsom, *Exploring American Caves* (rev. ed., 1962); Roy Pinney, *The Complete Book of Cave Exploration* (1962).

cave art. Although prehistoric ROCK CARVINGS AND PAINTINGS have been found all over the world the Paleolithic masterpieces of Western Europe remain preeminent. They were the first of their kind to be discovered and the only ones found in deep meandering caves. The first find at Altamira, Spain, in 1879, revealed tremendous artistic merit. Later discoveries in the Iberian Peninsula, S Italy, and the Dordogne region of France, including the celebrated Lascaux cave, reveal a vigorous realistic art that reached its zenith during the Magdalenian phase (see PALEOLITHIC PERIOD). Polychrome techniques, foreshortening, and shadowing were used, and some cave surfaces were utilized to show relief. The accuracy of animal portrayal in such details as hoofs and trunk lobation has been invaluable to paleozoologists. The predominance of animal figures and the fact that many paintings are found in distant passages where the artist could have worked only by artificial illumination, suggest that the paintings had a religious purpose and were used in magical rites to induce successful hunting. See G. Baldwin Brown, *The Art of the Cave Dweller* (1928); Henri Breuil, *Four Hundred Centuries of Cave Art* (Eng. tr. 1952).

Cave fish

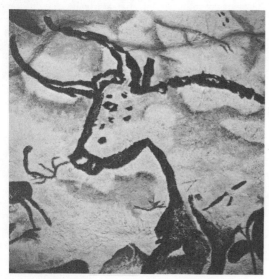

Drawing from a wall in the cave at Lascaux.

Cave City, town (pop. 1,418), S Ky., NE of Bowling Green, in a natural gas region. It is a center for visitors to the state's famous limestone cave region, which includes MAMMOTH CAVE NATIONAL PARK and the Diamond Caverns.

Cavedone, Giacomo (jä′kōmō kävädō′nä), 1577–1660, Italian painter, of the Bolognese school. He assisted Guido Reni in Rome, but his reputation as a master of color and composition was won through his paintings in the churches of Bologna.

cave dweller. Man has made use of caves and rock shelters wherever they are found. Cave remains have provided most of the known data on man during the PALEOLITHIC PERIOD. These indicate most frequent occupation during periods of severe climate, such as the Mousterian phase. They are widespread in Europe and contain famous examples of PALEOLITHIC ART. Stone-using peoples were not the only ones to exploit caves; not until the 2d and 3d cent. A.D., during the Iron Age, did cave dwelling find its greatest development in Britain. The troglodytes, known to classical writers, are assumed to have dwelt in caves along the Red Sea. Caves, often artificial, have been utilized as funeral and religious sites since ancient times all over the world. Corpses, mummies, and cremated remains are often laid, suspended or buried in caves. The Egyptian rock-cut tombs and temples are famous, and so are the Buddhist and Hindu cave temples of India (see AJANTA). Christian churches were built in Near Eastern caves.

cave fish, member of a family of a few species of small fish found in the swamps and in the subterranean streams of limestone regions of the S United States. The normal species, which superficially resembles the toothed minnows, is called the rice-ditch killifish. The cave fish differs in having ridges with tactile papillae on the sides of the body, as do the true blindfishes. The small blindfish, about 2 in. long, is colorless and has vestigial eyes hidden under the skin. The Mammoth Cave blindfish attains a length of 5 in.

Cavell, Edith (kă′vŭl), 1865–1915, English nurse. She was matron of the Berkendael Medical Insti-

Edith Cavell

tute in Brussels, which became a Red Cross Hospital upon the outbreak of the First World War. Nurse Cavell was arrested by the German authorities and pleaded guilty to a charge of harboring and aiding Allied prisoners and assisting some 130 to cross the Dutch frontier. She was shot Oct. 11, 1915, despite the efforts of Brand Whitlock, U.S. minister to Belgium, to secure a reprieve. See biography by Helen Judson (1941).

Cavendish (kă′vŭndĭsh), pseud. of **Henry Jones,** 1831–99, English card-game expert, b. London. Jones studied medicine, practiced in London, and retired in 1868. He became a leading authority on card games and was the first man to formulate a system of playing whist. He was the author of *Principles of Whist: Stated and Explained by "Cavendish"* (1862) and later wrote books on billiards, lawn tennis, and croquet.

Cavendish, George 1500–1561?, English gentleman-usher to Cardinal Wolsey. His biography of Wolsey, written in 1557, remained in manuscript until 1641 and first appeared in entirety in Christopher Wordsworth's *Ecclesiastical Biography* (1810). One of the great books of the English Renaissance, this work was long attributed to Cavendish's brother William, but in 1814 Joseph Hunter clearly established its authorship. See S. W. Singer, ed., *The Life of Cardinal Wolsey* (1825).

Cavendish, Henry, 1731–1810, English physicist and chemist, b. Nice. He was the son of Lord Charles Cavendish and grandson of the 2d duke of Devonshire. He was a recluse, and most of his writings were published posthumously. His great contributions to science resulted from his many and accurate experiments in divers fields. His conclusions were remarkably original. His chief researches were on heat, in which he determined the specific heats for a number of substances (although these heat constants were not recognized or so called until later); on the composition of air; on the nature and properties of a gas which he isolated and described as "inflammable air" and which was later called by Lavoisier HYDROGEN; and on the composition of water, which he demonstrated to consist of oxygen and his "inflammable air." In his *Electrical Researches* (pub. 1879) he anticipated some of the discoveries of Coulomb and Faraday. His experiments to determine the density of the earth led him to state it as 5.448 times that of water. His *Scientific Papers* were collected in two volumes (*Electrical Researches* and *Chemical and Dynamical*) in 1921. See biography by A. J. Berry (1960).

Cavendish, Thomas, 1560–92, English navigator. He commanded a ship in the flotilla under Sir Richard Grenville sent (1585) by Sir Walter Raleigh to establish the first colony in Virginia. In command of three vessels he sailed from England (1586) on a voyage round the world (the third to be made), crossing from the coast of W Africa to Patagonia, where he discovered a fine harbor which he named Port Desire. He ravaged Spanish towns and shipping on the west coast of South America and thence continued his journey by way of the Philippines, East Indies, and Cape of Good Hope, returning to England in 1588 after a voyage of more than two years. A second circumnavigation which commenced in 1591 ended disastrously; his fleet of five ships was dispersed, and he died at sea.

Cavendish, William: see NEWCASTLE, WILLIAM CAVENDISH, DUKE OF.

Cavendish, town (pop. 1,223), SE Vt., on the Black River and E of Ludlow; settled 1769. It includes the village of Proctorsville (pop. 476), where Redfield Proctor was born.

Cavendish Laboratory: see CAMBRIDGE UNIVERSITY.

Caventou, Joseph Bienaimé (zhôzěf' byěnämä' kävätōō'), 1795–1877, French chemist. He was professor at the École de Pharmacie, Paris. With P. J. Pelletier he isolated strychnine, brucine, and quinine (from cinchona bark).

Caves of a Thousand Buddhas: see TUNHWANG.

Cave Spring, city (pop. 1,153), NW Ga., near the Ala. line SW of Rome; settled 1826, inc. 1852. Limestone caves attract tourists. Georgia School for the Deaf (1847) is nearby.

caviar or **caviare** (kǎ'vēär) [Turkish], the roe of various species of sturgeon prepared as a piquant table delicacy, especially in Russia. The ovaries, when removed from the fish, are beaten to loosen the eggs, which are then freed from fibers, fat, and membrane by being passed through a sieve. The liquor is pressed off, and the eggs are salted and sealed in small tins or kegs. "Fresh" caviar made in winter from high-grade eggs, mildly salted, is scarce and expensive. Less choice varieties are cured with 10 percent salt. The eggs, black, green, brown, and the rare yellow or gray, may be tiny grains or the size of peas. The Russian caviar comes from the vicinity of the Black and Caspian seas, from the Danube provinces, and elsewhere. In the United States an imitation of sturgeon caviar is produced from the roe of other fish, such as paddlefish, whitefish, and cod.

Cavite (kävē'tä), city (pop. 42,137), SW Luzon, the Philippines, SW of Manila, on a small peninsula in Manila Bay. It is important as a naval base and trade center. After the Spanish-American War in 1898, the United States established a major naval base at Sangley Point just opposite the city proper. After the Philippines acquired independence it was agreed (1947) that the United States would retain the base for a 99-year period.

Cavour, Camillo Benso, conte di (kämĕl'lō bän'sō

Camillo Benso,
conte di Cavour

kōn'tē dē kävōōr'), 1810–61, Italian statesman, premier of Sardinia (1852–59, 1860–61). The active force behind King VICTOR EMMANUEL II, he was responsible more than any other man for the unification of Italy under the house of Savoy (see RISORGIMENTO). Of a noble Piedmontese family, he entered the army early but resigned in 1831 and devoted himself to politics. In 1847 he founded the Liberal daily, *Risorgimento*, in which he pressed King Charles Albert to grant a constitution and to make war on Austria. A member of parliament after 1848, he became minister of agriculture and commerce and (1852) premier. He reorganized the

CAVY

administration and finances, reformed the army, and won for Sardinia a place among the powers through participation in the CRIMEAN WAR. In 1858, by an agreement reached at Plombières, he won the support of Napoleon III for a war against Austria, promising in exchange to cede Savoy and Nice to France. Austria was maneuvered into declaring war (1859), but Cavour refused to accept the separate armistice of VILLAFRANCA DI VERONA between France and Austria and resigned. He returned to office in 1860. In that year Tuscany, Parma, Modena, and the Romagna voted for annexation to Sardinia, and Giuseppe GARIBALDI overran the Two Sicilies. Cavour met the delicate situation boldly and by his superior statesmanship avoided foreign intervention in favor of the dispossessed dukes and of the pope. Sardinian troops were sent into the Papal States, which, with the exception of Latium and Rome, were annexed to Sardinia. The annexation (1860) of the Kingdom of the Two Sicilies was consummated with the abdication (1861) of Francis II. Cavour's labors were crowned two months before his death, when the kingdom of Italy was proclaimed under Victor Emmanuel II. See W. R. Thayer, *The Life and Times of Cavour* (1911); D. Mack Smith, *Cavour and Garibaldi, 1860* (1954).

cavy (kā′vē), name of the GUINEA PIG and of a number of related South American rodents. The wild cavies are usually a uniform shade of brown and

Spotted cavy

are tailless. One of the large species is the Patagonian cavy, a long-legged, harelike animal which reaches a length of about 2½ ft. Other forms are the Bolivian cavy, the Peruvian cavy (said to have been domesticated by the Incas), the restless cavy of Brazil, and the capybara. Some cavies are hunted for food in South America.

Cawdor (kô′dùr), parish, Nairnshire, NE Scotland, SW of Nairn. Cawdor Castle, built in 1454 and later, is represented by Shakespeare, following tradition, as the scene of the slaying (1040) of Duncan by MACBETH.

Cawnpore (kôn′pôr), city (pop. 705,400), SW Uttar Pradesh state, N India, on the Ganges river. A major industrial center, it produces chemicals, textiles, leather goods, and food products. It is also a transportation hub. Cawnpore was a village until its cession (1801) to the British by the Nawab of Oudh. During the SEPOY REBELLION (1857), Nana Sahib, whose claim to a pension had been rejected, slaughtered the entire British garrison, including women and children. There is an agricultural college nearby. Cawnpore is also known as Kanpur.

Caxton, William, c. 1421–1491, English printer. He served apprenticeship as a mercer, became a member of the Company of Mercers of London, and

William Caxton

from 1463 to 1469 was at Bruges as governor of the Merchants Adventurers in the Low Countries. He learned printing in Cologne in 1471–72, and at Bruges in 1475 he and Colard Mansion printed *The Recuyell of the Historyes of Troye*, the first book printed in English. In 1476 he returned to England, and at Westminster in 1477 he printed *Dictes or Sayengis of the Philosophres*, the first dated book printed in England. He printed three books in Bruges and many in Westmister. He was the translator, from French, Latin, and Dutch, of some of the books that he printed, and for some he wrote original prologues, epilogues, and additions. One of the type faces used by Caxton is the original Old English type. The size of this type of Caxton's (14 point) is known as English. WYNKYN DE WORDE, his successor as a printer, was his assistant at Westminster, and the printers Richard Pynson and Robert Copland refer to Caxton (possibly figuratively) as their master. See William Blades, *The Biography and Typography of William Caxton* (1877); H. R. Plomer, *William Caxton, 1424–1491* (1925); N. S. Aurner, *Caxton* (1926); G. P. Winship, *William Caxton and His Work* (1938).

Cayce, city (pop. 8,517), central S.C., SSW of Columbia; inc. 1914. Fiberglass boats, chemicals, and concrete and metal products are among its manufactures.

Cayenne (kīĕn′, kāĕn′), city (pop. c.14,000), capital of French GUIANA, at the mouth of the Cayenne river. Cayenne was founded by the French as early as 1643, but was wiped out by an Indian massacre and not permanently settled until 1664. Built on

1198

Cayenne island, it has a shallow harbor, and deep-draft ships must anchor some distance out. The chief export is gold. Long the center of French penal settlements in Guiana, it has a population partially made up of descendants of prisoners. It gave its name to **Cayenne pepper,** a very sharp condiment made from the fruit of plants of the genus *Capsicum* of the nightshade family, found on the island in profusion.

Cayes, Haiti: see AUX CAYES.

Cayey (kiā'), town (pop. 19,738), E central Puerto Rico. A sugar, tobacco, and poultry center with clothing factories, it is set in the mountain chain Sierra de Cayey, which makes the climate cool and pleasant. Outside the town is the U.S. military reservation, Henry Barracks.

Cayley, Arthur (kā'lē), 1821–95, English mathematician. He was called to the bar in 1849. In 1863 he was appointed first Sadlerian professor of mathematics at Cambridge. His researches, which covered the field of pure mathematics, included especially the theory of matrices and the theory of invariants. The algebra of matrices was the tool Heisenberg used in 1925 for his revolutionary work in quantum mechanics. The concept of invariance is important in modern physics, particularly in the theory of relativity. Cayley's collected papers were published in 13 volumes (1889–98).

Caylus, Anne Claude Philippe de Tubières, comte de (än' klōd' fēlēp' dù tübyěr' kŏt' dù kälüs'), 1692–1765, French archaeologist and collector of antiquities. He traveled in Europe and Asia and became known as an etcher and as a patron of the arts. His collections are in the Louvre. Among his writings is *Recueil d'antiquités égyptiennes, étrusques, grecques, romaines, et gauloises* (7 vols., 1752–67). He claimed that he had rediscovered the method of encaustic painting on wax.

Caylus, Marie Marguerite, comtesse de (märē märgürět' kŏtěs' dù), 1673–1729, French writer; niece of Mme de Maintenon. A noted beauty and wit, she was lauded for her performance at Saint-Cyr in Racine's *Esther.* Her *Souvenirs* (1770), edited by Voltaire, describe the court of Louis XIV with vivacity and taste.

Cayman Islands (kā'mùn), archipelago (c.90 sq. mi.; pop. c.8,800), British West Indies, NW of Jamaica. Formerly a dependency of Jamaica, the islands—Grand Cayman, Little Cayman, and Cayman Brac—are now administered as a separate colony. The population is mostly Negro. The islanders build ships for local use and export such items as green turtles, turtle shells, and shark skins. There is a considerable tourist trade.

Cayuga Heights, residential village (pop. 2,788), W central N.Y., on Cayuga Lake just N of Ithaca; inc. 1915.

Cayuga Indians: see IROQUOIS CONFEDERACY.

Cayuga Lake (kāyōō'gú, kī–, kù–), 38 mi. long and 1 to 3½ mi. wide, W central N.Y., longest of the FINGER LAKES. It is connected by canal and by the Seneca river with the Barge Canal to the north. Cornell Univ. and Wells College overlook Cayuga with its clifflike banks; near the southern end are Taughannock Falls, 215 ft. high.

cayuse: see MUSTANG.

Cayuse Indians (kiūs'), North American Indian tribe, occupying W Oregon and W Washington.

They were closely associated with the Nez Percé, and early explorers mistook them for the same stock. They were of Waiilatpuan linguistic stock, and the mission established among them by Marcus WHITMAN was called Waiilatpu. In 1847 the Cayuse, apparently blaming the missionaries for an outbreak of smallpox, attacked the mission and killed the Whitmans and their helpers. The white settlers then declared war and subdued the Cayuse. They were placed on a reservation in 1855. A small horse bred by them gave the name cayuse to all Indian ponies.

Cazenovia (kăzúnō'věù), resort village (pop. 2,584), central N.Y., on Cazenovia Lake SE of Syracuse, in a farm area; settled 1793, inc. 1810. A junior college is here, and a state park is near.

Cazin, Jean Charles (zhä' shärl' käzē), 1841–1901, French painter, etcher, and ceramist. Cazin studied in London, where he came under the influence of the Pre-Raphaelites. His landscapes are low-keyed; his biblical scenes are peopled by French peasants. Examples of his art are in the Metropolitan Museum and in Berlin.

Cb, formerly chemical symbol of the element columbium, now called NIOBIUM.

C battery: see BATTERY, ELECTRIC.

Cd, chemical symbol of the element CADMIUM.

Ce, chemical symbol of the element CERIUM.

Ceará (sēärä'), state (c.57,000 sq. mi.; pop. c.3,337,-900), NE Brazil. FORTALEZA, sometimes also called Ceará, is the capital. The state rises from a narrow, sandy coastal plain to the semiarid uplands of the interior (the SERTÃO), where livestock is raised. Cotton, sugar, and coffee are grown along the coast and, under irrigation, in the interior. The state has suffered heavily from periodic droughts, and large-scale migrations are common during the dry season. Numerous dams and reservoirs were built in recent years. Important extractive industries include carnauba wax, oiticica oil, and salt in the coastal area. There is a growing fishing industry. Deposits of uranium and copper were discovered recently. Ceará shared in the Brazilian sugar-growing hegemony and was part of the region occupied by the Dutch in the 17th cent. The state is famous for its traditional handicrafts, which include wood carving and fiber weaving.

Cebu (sāboo'), island (1,702 sq. mi.; pop. 1,350,130), one of the Visayan Islands, the Philippines, between Leyte and Negros. Primarily agricultural, it produces sugar cane, corn, tobacco, coconuts, and hemp. Coal, oil, and gold are exploited. The capital and chief port is Cebu (pop. 201,362), on the east coast, with a harbor sheltered by Mactan island. Cebu city is the trade center of the Visayan Islands, the second most important city in the Philippines, and one of its oldest settlements. Founded in 1565 as San Miguel by López de Legaspi, Cebu city was the first permanent Spanish settlement in the Philippines. It was capital of the Spanish colony until 1571. It has a bishop's palace, a cathedral, and a church with a noted jewel-encrusted gold statue of the Holy Child. Severely damaged in the Second World War and by typhoons in 1949 and 1951, Cebu city has been rebuilt.

Cecco d'Ascoli (chāk'kō dä'skōlē), 1257–1327, Italian astrologer, mathematician, poet, and physician, whose real name was Francesco degli Stabili, b. Ascoli. A teacher of astrology at several institutions in Italy, he was professor of mathematics and astrology at the Univ. of Bologna (1322–24). Accused of heresy, largely because of an attack on Dante's *Divine Comedy*, he was burned at the stake. His chief work was *L'acerba*, an allegorical didactic poem of encyclopedic range.

Cecere, Gaetano (chĭchĕ′rē), 1894–, American sculptor, b. New York city, studied at the American Academy in Rome. His works include the John Stevens monument at Summit, Mont., war memorials in Princeton, N.J., and Plainfield, N.J., and the monumental statue of Lincoln for the Lincoln Memorial Bridge, Milwaukee, Wis.

Cech, Svatopluk, Czech *Čech* (svä′tôplŏŏk′ chĕkh′), 1846–1908, Czech poet and novelist. His strong Pan-Slavism and his love for democracy and freedom made him the most popular poet of his day. His political beliefs animate many of his writings. Cech's powerful epics include *The Adamites* (1873), *Zizka* (1879), and *Vaclav of Michalovice* (1880). He also wrote idyllic verse on Czech country life, notably *In the Shade of the Linden Tree* (1879), and satirical novels, including the utopian *Excursion of Mr. Broucek to the Moon* (1886). See Paul Selver, *Anthology of Czechoslovak Literature* (1929).

Cecil, Edgar Algernon Robert, 1st **Viscount Cecil of Chelwood** (sĭ′sŭl), 1864–1958, British statesman, known in his earlier life as Lord Robert Cecil; third son of the 3d marquess of Salisbury. A Conservative who held several ministerial posts, Cecil gained fame largely through untiring advocacy of internationalism. He collaborated with President Woodrow Wilson and Gen. J. C. Smuts in drafting the League of Nations Covenant. His efforts for international peace were recognized by the 1937 Nobel Peace Prize. See his autobiography, *A Great Experiment* (1941).

Cecil, Robert: see SALISBURY, ROBERT CECIL, 1ST EARL OF.

Cecil, Robert Arthur Talbot Gascoyne-: see SALISBURY, ROBERT ARTHUR TALBOT GASCOYNE-CECIL, 3D MARQUESS OF.

Cecil, William: see BURGHLEY, WILLIAM CECIL, 1ST BARON.

Cecilia, Saint, 2d or 3d cent., Roman virgin martyr. An ancient and famous account of her life is factually valueless. As patroness of music, she is represented at the organ. St. Cecilia is the subject of one of the *Canterbury Tales*, of a song by Dryden, and an ode by Pope. Cecily is an English form of her name. Feast: Nov. 22.

Cecrops (sē′krŏps), in Greek mythology, founder and first king of Athens. A primeval being, he was half man and half serpent. As a maker of laws, he abolished human sacrifice, established monogamy, and initiated burial of the dead.

Cedar, river rising in SE Minnesota and flowing c.300 mi. southeast across Iowa to join the Iowa river at Columbus Junction. It drains an agricultural region, passing Charles City, Cedar Falls, Waterloo, and Cedar Rapids.

cedar, name for a number of trees, mostly coniferous evergreens. The true cedars belong to the small genus *Cedrus* of the PINE family. All are native to the Old World from the Mediterranean to the Himalayas, although several are cultivated else-where as ornamentals, especially the cedar of Lebanon (*C. libani*). This tree, native to Asia Minor and North Africa, is famous for the historic groves of the LEBANON mts., frequently mentioned in the Bible. The wood used in building the Temple and the house of Solomon (1 Kings 5, 6, and 7) may, however, have been that of the deodar cedar (*C. deodara*), native to the Himalayas. It has fragrant wood, durable and fine grained, and is venerated by the Hindus, who call it Tree of God. The name cedar is used (particularly in America, where no cedars are native) for other conifers, e.g., the JUNIPER (red cedar), ARBORVITAE (white cedar), and others of the CYPRESS family. Several tropical American trees of the genus *Cedrela* of the mahogany family are also called cedars.

Cedar Breaks National Monument: see NATIONAL PARKS AND MONUMENTS (table).

Cedarburg, city (pop. 5,191), E Wis., on the Milwaukee river N of Milwaukee; settled 1845, inc. as a village 1848, as a city 1885. A farm trade center, it also makes metal products. Nearby is Wisconsin's only remaining covered bridge.

Cedar City, town (pop. 7,543; alt. c.5,800 ft.), SW Utah, at the base of the Wasatch Mts. E of the Escalante Desert; inc. 1868. With nearby Parowan, it was founded in 1851 by the Mormon "iron mission" sent to develop coal and iron deposits. Today it is a center of iron-ore mining, ranching, and tourist trade. ZION NATIONAL PARK, BRYCE CANYON NATIONAL PARK, and Cedar Breaks National Monument (6,172.20 acres; est. 1933), containing a 2,000-feet-deep amphitheater formed by erosion, are nearby. The College of Southern Utah, a branch of Utah State Univ., is here.

Cedar Creek, small tributary of the North Fork of the Shenandoah river and N of Strasburg, Va. It was the scene of a Civil War battle (Oct. 19, 1864) in which P. H. SHERIDAN defeated J. A. EARLY.

Cedar Falls, city (pop. 21,195), N Iowa, on the Cedar river just above Waterloo; settled 1845, laid out 1853, inc. 1854. With the coming of the railroad (1861), it developed as a milling center. Pumps and farm machinery are among its products. The city is the seat of State College of Iowa and of the Evangelical Campgrounds, scene of the Interdenominational Bible Conference.

Cedar Grove. 1 Town (pop. 1,569), S W.Va., on the Kanawha river and SE of Charleston, in a coal-mining region; settled 1773, inc. 1902. The site of Booker T. Washington's boyhood home is nearby. **2** Village (pop. 1,175), E Wis., SSW of Sheboygan, in a dairy and farm area; inc. 1899.

Cedar Hammock, uninc. town (pop. 3,089), SW Fla., S of Bradenton.

Cedar Hill, city (pop. 1,848), N Texas, SW of Dallas, in a farm area. Television parts and furniture are made.

Cedarhurst, residential village (pop. 6,954), SE N.Y., on SW Long Island, SE of Jamaica; settled 1680, inc. 1910.

Cedar Key, island off W Fla., NNW of St. Petersburg. Nearby is a group of smaller islands known as the Cedar Keys, containing a Federal wildlife refuge.

Cedar Lake, uninc. town (pop. 5,766), NW Ind., SSW of Gary on Cedar Lake, in a farm area.

Cedar Mountain: see BULL RUN, SECOND BATTLE OF.

Cedar Rapids, city (pop. 92,035), co. seat of Linn co., E central Iowa, on the Cedar river and NW of Davenport; settled 1838, laid out 1841 as Rapids City, renamed and inc. as a town 1849, as a city 1856. One of the state's principal commercial and industrial cities, it is a distributing and rail center for an extensive agricultural area. The city has railroad shops, is supplied with power by the Cedar river, and has manufactures of cereals, communication equipment, farm and road machinery, syrup, and plastic products. Coe College (United Presbyterian Church; coeducational; 1881), a large Masonic library (1884), an art gallery (with paintings by Grant Wood), and the landscaped Municipal Island (site of the courthouse and a neoclassic war memorial building) are here. Nearby are a state park and some settlements of the Amana Society.

Cedar Springs, village (pop. 1,768), S Mich., NE of Grand Rapids; settled 1859, inc. 1871. It is a farm and resort trade center.

Cedartown, industrial city (pop. 9,340), co. seat of Polk co., NW Ga., WNW of Atlanta near the Ala. line, in the piedmont region; inc. 1854. A Cherokee settlement was here earlier. Cedartown's main industrial growth stems from the establishment of textile and tire-cordage plants here in the 1920s. Chemicals are also made.

Cedarville. 1 Uninc. village (pop. 1,095), SW N.J., SSE of Bridgeton, in a truck–farming region. **2** Village (pop. 1,702), SW Ohio, S of Springfield; settled 1805, inc. 1843.

cedar waxwing: see WAXWING.

Cedarwood Park, uninc. village (pop. 1,052), E N.J., on the Metedeconk and SSW of Asbury Park.

Cedron (sē′–). **1** The same as KIDRON. **2** Place, near Jamnia, fortified against the Maccabees. 1 Mac. 15.39–41; 16.9.

Cefalù (chāfälōō′), town (estimated pop. 12,775), N Sicily, Italy, on the Tyrrhenian coast. It is a commercial and fishing center. Its famous cathedral, started in 1131 by Roger II, king of Sicily, is one of the finest examples of Norman architecture in Sicily.

Ceiba, La (lä sä′bä), city (pop. c.22,800), N Honduras. A port on the Caribbean, it is the banana exporting headquarters of the Standard Fruit and Steamship Company. Located at the foot of Peak Bonito (alt., 5,000 ft.), it has fine beaches and is a point of departure for the Bay Islands.

Celaenae (sĭlē′nē), ancient city of Asia Minor, in Phrygia, near the source of the Maeander river, in present W central Turkey. In the days of the Persian Empire, Cyrus the Great had a palace here, and Xerxes I built a fort. Alexander the Great conquered the city in 333 B.C. Seleucus I moved the inhabitants to neighboring Apamea. Modern Dinar is on the site.

Celakovsky, Frantisek, Czech *František Čelakovsky* (frän′tĭshĕk chĕ′läkôfskĭ), 1799–1852, Czech folklorist and poet. A disciple of Herder and a romantic Pan-Slavist, he collected (1822–27) Slavic popular poetry and later imitated it in his own verses, *Echoes of Russian Song* (1829) and *Echoes of Czech Song* (1830). At Breslau he became (1841) the first professor of Slavic languages in a Central European university.

celandine: see POPPY.

Cathedral of Cefalù

Native fishing village near Macassar, Celebes.

Celanese, uninc. village (pop. 1,500), NW Ga., NE of Rome.

Celano, Thomas of: see THOMAS OF CELANO.

Celaya (sälä′yä), city (pop. 34,426), Guanajuato, central Mexico. Founded in 1570, it is the center of a rich farming region. There are numerous industries. The Church of Nuestra Señora del Carmen [Our Lady of Mt. Carmel], built (1803–7) and decorated by Francisco Eduardo de TRESGUERRAS, is an unusual structure showing Persian influence. Often involved in Mexican wars, Celaya was the first city to be captured (Sept. 28, 1810) by Hidalgo y Costilla. Here, in 1915, Álvaro Obregón decisively defeated Francisco VILLA.

Celebes (sĕ′lùbēz), island (c.71,695 sq. mi.; pop. including offshore islands 7,079,349), largest island in E Indonesia, E of Borneo, from which it is separated by Macassar Strait. Macassar is its chief city and port; other important towns are Menado, Gorontalo, and Palopo. Extremely irregular in shape, it is comprised of four large peninsulas separated by three gulfs—Tomini on the northeast, Tolo on the southeast, and Boni on the south. The terrain is almost wholly mountainous, with the highest peak Mt. Rantemario (c.11,286 ft.) on the south peninsula. There are numerous lakes, of which Towuti (30 mi. long and 15 mi. wide) is the largest, and Tondano, with its waterfall, the most beautiful. In the interior are large forests of valuable timber. Animals include the babirusa (resembling swine) and the small wild ox called anoa, found only in the Celebes. Among the natural resources are gold, silver, diamonds, coal, nickel, and iron. There are trepang and mother-of-pearl fisheries, and in the coastal areas are grown copra, coffee, and nutmeg, all of which are exported. The inhabitants are Malayan, except for the tribes (sometimes called Alfuros) in the interior, who are seminomadic. Among the Malayan tribes are the Bugis, who are known as seafaring traders, and the Macassars; both groups are Moslem. In the north are the Minahassa, who are Christians. The Portuguese first visited the Celebes in 1512 and settled in Macassar in 1625. The Dutch expelled the Portuguese in 1660 and governed the island as part of the Netherlands East Indies until 1946 when the state of East Indonesia (including Celebes) was founded. In 1950 the Celebes, also called the Sulawesi, became one of the 10 provinces of the newly created republic of Indonesia; it now constitutes North and South Sulawesi provs. The **Celebes Sea** is north of the island, between it and the Philippine Islands.

Celebrezze, Anthony J. (sŭlŭbrē′zē), 1910–, U.S. Secretary of Health, Education and Welfare (1962–), b. Anzi, Italy (while his parents were visiting the country), grad. Ohio Northern Univ. (LL.B. 1936). He practiced law in Cleveland until 1950, when he was elected to the state senate. From that position he was elected mayor of Cleveland in 1953 and was reelected four times. In the 1961 election he received almost three quarters of the total vote and carried every ward in the city. His long experience in education and welfare recommended him to President Kennedy who appointed him to the cabinet in 1962 to succeed Abraham A. Ribicoff.

Céleron de Blainville, Pierre Joseph (pyĕr′ zhōzĕf′ sālŭrō′ dù blĕvēl′), 1693–1759, French Canadian soldier, b. Montreal. He was commandant at Michilimackinac (1734–42), Detroit (1742–43, 1750–53), Niagara (1744–46), and Crown Point (1746–47). In 1739–40 he led a detachment south to what is now Tennessee to cooperate with Bienville in a campaign against the Chickasaw Indians and was decorated for his conduct. His most famous service was as leader of the expedition sent by the governor of New France in 1749 to take official possession of the Ohio valley and warn English traders to leave. An English translation of his Ohio journal appeared in the *Collections* of the State Historical Society of Wisconsin.

celery [Ital. from Gr.,=parsley], biennial plant (*Apium graveolens*) of the CARROT family, of wide distribution in the wild state throughout the north temperate Old World and much cultivated also in America. It was first cultivated as a medicinal, then (during the Middle Ages) as a flavoring, and finally as a food, chiefly for soups and salads. The seeds are still used for seasoning. Celeriac is a variety cultivated chiefly in N Europe for the large edible turniplike root.

celesta (sĭlĕ′stù), keyboard musical instrument patented in 1886 by Auguste Mustel of Paris. It consists of a set of steel bars fastened over resonators and struck by hammers operated from the keyboard. The compass is four octaves upward from middle C. Its tone is delicate and ethereal. Tchaikovsky, in his *Nutcracker Suite*, was one of the first composers to write for it.

Celestina, La (lä thälästē′nä), Spanish novel written in dramatic form. Known to have been published in 1499 as *Comedia de Calisto y Melibea*, it probably appeared earlier. Later it came to be called *La Celestina*, after the principal character, an old woman whose artful devices make it possible for Calisto and Melibea to conduct a love affair against the will of the girl's parents. Authorities disagree as to how much of the novel is the work of Fernando de ROJAS. Called by some the first European novel, the story contains germs of the Spanish picaresque novel and of the theater of Lope de Vega. Its rejection of medieval morality, its frank investigation of sensuality, and its psychological portrayals struck new notes. The novel was widely translated and read. The first complete English translation (1631) was by James Mabbe. See study by Stephen Gilman (1956).

Celestine I, Saint (sĕ′lùstĭn), d. 432, pope (422–32), an Italian; successor of St. Boniface I and predecessor of St. Sixtus III. The opposition of St. Cyril of Alexandria to NESTORIANISM inspired both sides to write to the pope, who judged that Nestorius should be excommunicated if he refused to retract. To the Council of Ephesus, Celestine sent legates with orders not to discuss, but to judge. Celestine also advanced orthodoxy in the West by suppressing Semi-Pelagianism in Gaul and by sending Germanus of Auxerre to Britain. Feast: July 27.

Celestine V, Saint, 1215–96, pope (elected July 5, resigned Dec. 13, 1294), an Italian (b. Isernia) named Pietro del Murrone; successor of Nicholas IV and predecessor of Boniface VIII. Celestine's election ended a two-year deadlock among the cardinals over a successor to Nicholas IV. Although he was known for his austere life as a hermit and for his extremist followers, who called themselves Celestines, he proved a most ineffectual pope and an easy prey to opportunists. King Charles II of Naples quickly dominated him and kept the pope in Naples. Celestine granted privileges and offices to all who asked for them, turned the duties of his office over to a committee of three cardinals, and kept to his cell. His reign was so chaotic that he himself abdicated after only five months and ordered a new election. His successor, Boniface VIII, canceled his official acts and, to avert possible schism among Celestine's ardent followers, kept Celestine in confinement until his death. Celestine was canonized in 1313. Feast: May 19.

celestite (sĕ′lùstĭt) or **celestine** (sĕ′lùstĭn, -tĭn), mineral appearing in blue-tinged or white orthorhombic crystals or in fibrous masses. The natural sulphate of strontium, it is important as a source of strontium and of certain of its compounds, e.g., strontium hydroxide, used in refining beet sugar, and strontium nitrate, used in red signal flares. It occurs in England, in Sicily, and in the United States on islands in Lake Erie and also in Pennsylvania.

celibacy (sĕ′lĭbùsē), voluntary refusal to enter the married state, with abstinence from sexual activity. It is one of the typically Christian forms of ASCETICISM. In ancient Rome the VESTAL virgins were celibates, and successful MONASTICISM has everywhere been accompanied by celibacy as an ideal. Among ancient Jews the ESSENES were celibates. In the Judaism of postexilic times sexual activity in the married state was lawful and good; otherwise it was unlawful. This rule remained in Christianity. But the mainstream of Christian tradition from the start has interpreted the Gospels and Epistles as teaching that voluntary celibacy, especially virginity, is peculiarly meritorious. 1 Cor. 7. In the Eastern churches, monks and nuns are celibates, but the ordinary parish clergy are married; generally they must be married before ordination and may not remarry. Eastern bishops are widowers or celibates, hence they are usually from monasteries rather than parishes. In the West, celibacy has been common among the parish clergy since the 3d cent., and as time passed, the Holy See became the bulwark of celibacy of the secular clergy. The chief problem of reformers in the early Middle Ages was to end concubinage among them—marriage of the clergy had fallen into disrepute, and violations were of the laws of chastity rather than of marriage. In the 12th cent. the most stringent laws were made, and by the time of the Reformation popular opinion tolerated neither concubinage nor marriage in the clergy. The Roman Catholic Church in the Roman rite allows no sacerdotal marriage, but the clergy of Eastern rites united with the pope are often married before ordination. Protestants have rejected voluntary celibacy as an ideal. A standard apologetic explanation of the Western discipline of celibacy for parish priests is that marriage would prevent the priest from giving his complete attention to his parish.

Celina. 1 (sùlĭ′nù) City (pop. 7,659), co. seat of Mercer co., W Ohio, SW of Lima; settled 1834, inc. as a village 1861. On Grand Lake (Lake St. Marys), it is a summer resort with some industry. **2** (sùlē′nù) Town (pop. 1,228), co. seat of Clay co., N Tenn., on the Cumberland at the mouth of the Obey, NE of Nashville; inc. 1909. Dale Hollow Dam (200 ft. high; 1,717 ft. long; completed 1953) is on the Obey nearby. **3** (sĕ′lǐnù) Town (pop. 1,204), N Texas, N of Dallas; settled 1879, inc. 1906. It is a trade center in a blackland farm area.

Céline, Louis Ferdinand (lwē′ fĕrdēnā′ sālēn′), 1894–1961, French author, whose real name was Louis Ferdinand Destouches. A physican, Céline wrote sensationally misanthropic novels; *Journey to the End of Night* (1932; Eng. tr., 1934) was followed by *Death on the Installment Plan* (1936; Eng. tr., 1938). *Mea Culpa* (1937; Eng. tr., 1937) is his renunciation of Communism. His later works were fascistic.

Celje (tsĕ′lyĕ), city (pop. 16,487), E Slovenia, Yugoslavia. An industrial center, it manufactures agricultural machinery, textiles, and chemicals. Founded (1st cent. A.D.) by Emperor Claudius, it was the seat (1341–1456) of the powerful Slovenian counts of Celje (or Cilli). It has a 13th-century monastery, a 16th-century palace, and a castle.

cell, in biology, the unit of structure and function of which all plants and animals are composed. The cell is the smallest unit in the living organism that is capable of carrying on the essential life processes: sustaining metabolism for the production of energy and reproducing for the self-perpetuation of the organism. There are many unicellular organisms (e.g., BACTERIA and PROTOZOA) in which the single cell performs all the life functions. In higher organisms, a division of labor has evolved in which groups of cells have differentiated into specialized TISSUES, which in turn are grouped into organs and organ systems. Because almost all cells are microscopic, knowledge of the component cell parts has increased correspondingly with the development of the microscope and other specialized instruments and of allied experimental techniques. The basic substance of the living cell is PROTOPLASM. In both plant and animal cells the protoplasm is differentiated into the cytoplasm; the cell membrane, which surrounds it; and the nucleus, which is contained in it. In plant cells there is in addition to the membrane a thickened cell wall, usually composed chiefly of CELLULOSE secreted by the cytoplasm. Included in the cytoplasm are many discrete bodies (called organelles), vacuoles containing cell sap, and inert granules and crystals. The most important of the organelles are the chloroplasts (occurring only in the cells of green plants) and the mitochondria. Both these organelles are the "power plants" of life that supply the organism with energy. The chloroplasts convert energy from sunlight by PHOTOSYNTHESIS; the mitochondria extract energy by breaking down the chemical bonds in molecules of complex nutrients during oxidation and respiration (see ATP). Other organelles in the cytoplasm are the lysosomes, which contain digestive enzymes; the centrosomes, which function during cell division; the Golgi body, whose function is still unclear; and, in plants primarily, other plastids in addition to the chloroplasts. The cytoplasm also contains the endoplasmic reticulum, a highly convoluted membrane believed to be responsible for the transmission of substances from outside the cell to the nucleus. It also appears to be the means by which the nucleus communicates with the rest of the cell, in its capacity as "director" of the cell's total activity. The nucleus itself, separated from the cytoplasm by a nuclear membrane, consists of nuclear sap in which are bathed one or more nucleoli (apparently the sites of nuclear protein synthesis) and the long filaments of chromatin that coil tightly into CHROMOSOMES during MITOSIS. The chromatin directs the metabolic functions of the whole cell and, during cell division, passes on its "code" to the new cell by exactly replicating itself. Among the contributors to early knowledge of cells through their use of the microscope were Anton van LEEUWENHOEK, Robert HOOKE, and Marcello MALPIGHI. In the 19th cent. Matthias J. SCHLEIDEN and Theodor SCHWANN developed what is now known as the "cell theory." The very careful observations made

CELL

by these and other men were primarily of the physical and mechanical attributes of the cell. Just as scientists now realize that atoms cannot be thought of only as physical units of matter but must also be described as manifestations of energy, so living cells too must be viewed as more than a complicated architecture of physical "building blocks" or components. It is now known that many processes, such as the passage of substances across the cell membrane, are a series of chemical and electrostatic phenomena rather than purely mechanical functions. The study of the cell is called cytology; the study of its chemical processes is cytochemistry. See R. W. Gerard, *Unresting Cells* (1940); C. P. Swanson, *The Cell* (1960).

cell, in electricity, a source of electric current, in which the flow of current is caused by chemical action resulting in the conversion of chemical energy to electrical energy. A cell consists essentially of two dissimilar substances (a positive ELECTRODE and a negative electrode) which conduct electricity and a third substance (an ELECTROLYTE) which acts chemically upon the electrodes. A group of several such cells connected together is called a battery. One simple form of cell consists of a glass jar (battery jar) containing a dilute solution of sulfuric acid into which are introduced the electrodes of the cell, here a strip of copper and a strip of zinc. When the two electrodes are connected externally by a conductor, such as a piece of copper wire, a current of electricity flows through the wire. The explanation of this phenomenon lies in the activity within the cell. The sulfuric acid and zinc react, the zinc plate diminishing in size as the action proceeds; the copper is unaffected, but clinging to it and escaping into the air around it are bubbles of a gas (hydrogen). The bubbles, collecting rapidly in great numbers, form a protective covering over the copper plate and interfere with the cell's action —a condition called polarization. In the chemical action, the hydrogen of the acid is displaced by the zinc, negative charges (see ELECTRON) being left on the zinc plate. The hydrogen ions migrate to the copper plate, where, each ION receiving an electron, they become atoms and join in pairs to form the hydrogen molecules given off. The electrons received by the hydrogen ions at the copper plate have traveled through the external conductor (the wire) from the zinc to the copper. It is apparent, then, that the electrons flow through the wire from the negative (zinc) plate to the positive (copper) plate, or in a direction opposite to that of the conventional "electric current." There are several kinds of cell, differing in electrode material and electrolyte. The voltage or electromotive force (abbreviated emf) depends upon the activity of the substances used, but is not affected by the size of electrode or quantity of electrolyte. The cells made by Alessandro Volta and by Galvani are of historic significance. The Bunsen cell is a double-fluid cell having electrodes of zinc (−) and carbon (+), solutions of sulfuric acid and fuming nitric acid, and an emf of 1.94 volts. The chromate cell (double fluid also) uses zinc (−) and carbon (+) for electrodes and a solution of sulfuric acid and one of potassium dichromate and sulfuric acid and has an emf of 2

volts. The Daniell cell (double fluid) has zinc (−) and copper (+) electrodes, a solution of sulfuric acid and a saturated solution of copper sulfate, and an emf of 1.06 volts (variations in voltage are obtainable with other solutions). One type of Grove cell uses zinc (−) and platinum (+) electrodes and a solution of sulfuric acid and one of fuming nitric acid and has an emf of 1.93 volts (other types range down to 1.61 volts). The Leclanché cell is a single-fluid cell having zinc (−) and carbon (+) electrodes, a solution of ammonium chloride, and an emf of 1.46 volts. Similar to the Leclanché cell is the common dry cell, so called because the electrolyte is in the form of a paste. The cell consists of a zinc (−) cylinder closed at one end and lined throughout with a layer of absorbent material; a central core of carbon (+); and a closely packed mixture of carbon granules and manganese dioxide, which is saturated with a solution of ammonium chloride (sal ammoniac). The open end of the zinc cylinder is sealed off with pitch. The emf of the cell is about 1.5 volts. The Weston normal cell is the legal standard of emf. It consists of an electrode of cadmium amalgam (−) in a saturated cadmium sulfate solution and a mercury electrode (+) in a paste of mercurous sulfate and cadmium sulfate. It has an emf of 1.0183 volts at 20°C. See ELECTRIC CIRCUIT.

cella (sĕ′lù), that portion of a Roman temple which was enclosed within walls, as distinct from the open colonnaded porticoes which formed the rest of it. It corresponds to the NAOS in Greek temples. The cella housed the statue of the deity to whom the temple was dedicated and was also used as a treasury. Sometimes it extended the whole width of the building, instead of being kept entirely within free-standing colonnades. The cella was generally a single chamber, but there were sometimes two chambers, or even three, as in the temple of Jupiter, on the Capitoline Hill.

Celle (tsĕ′lù), city (pop. 57,239), Federal Republic of Germany, in Lower Saxony, N Germany, on the Aller river. It has oil refineries and produces machinery, chemicals, and textiles. Celle was chartered in 1294. Its castle was the residence of the dukes of Brunswick-Lüneburg until 1705. It was in the Prussian province of Hanover.

Cellini, Benvenuto (chĕlē′nē, Ital. bānvānōō′tō chāl-lē′nē), 1500–1571, Italian sculptor, metalsmith, and author. His remarkable autobiography, written between 1558 and 1562, reads like a picaresque novel. It is, in fact, one of the most important documents of the 16th cent. Cellini tells of his escapades with the frankness and consummate egoism characteristic of the Renaissance man. He was born in Florence, the son of a musician; he studied music until his 15th year, when he was apprenticed to a goldsmith. Banished from Florence after fighting a duel, he went from town to town working for local goldsmiths and in 1519 went to Rome. Under the patronage of Pope Clement VII he became known as the most skillful worker in metals of his day, producing medals, jewel settings caskets, vases, candlesticks, metal plates, and ornaments. Imprisoned on false charges, he worked at the court of Francis I at Paris after his release. He returned to Florence in 1545 and remained until his death in 1571. The decorative quality of his work,

1204

Ganymede Carried Off by an Eagle *(sculpture by Benvenuto Cellini).*

its intricate and exquisite detail and workmanship, are typical of the best of the period. Unfortunately, most of his works have perished. The famous gold and enamel saltcellar of Francis I and the gold medallion of *Leda and the Swan* (both in the Vienna Mus.) and two gold cups in the Metropolitan Museum are perhaps the best examples of those remaining. His sculptures, most of them executed in the later Florentine period, include the colossal bronze bust of Cosimo I (Bargello); the bronze bust of Altoviti (Gardner Mus., Boston); the *Nymph of Fontainebleau* (Louvre); the life-size *Crucifixion*, a white marble Christ on a black cross (Escorial); and the renowned *Perseus with the Head of Medusa* (Loggia dei Lanzi, Florence), a beautifully wrought bronze statue surmounting a marble pedestal lavishly adorned with statuettes and carvings. See translation of the autobiography by J. A. Symonds (1888; many later editions).

cello or **'cello:** see VIOLONCELLO.

celluloid [from *cellulose*], transparent, colorless synthetic PLASTIC made by treating cellulose nitrate with camphor and alcohol. The paste thus obtained can be colored and either rolled into sheets of any thickness or molded into the desired form. Celluloid was the first important synthetic plastic and was widely used as a substitute for more expensive substances, as ivory, amber, horn, and tortoise shell. It is highly flammable and has been largely superseded by newer plastics with more desirable properties. It is used for combs, brush handles, billiard balls, knife handles, buttons, and other useful objects.

cellulose, the chief constituent of the CELL walls of plants. Chemically it is an inert carbohydrate. Raw cotton is composed of 91 percent pure cellulose; other important natural sources are bast fibers (e.g., flax, hemp, and jute), whole stems (straws), and wood. Cellulose has been used for the manufacture of paper since the 2d cent. Insoluble in water and other ordinary solvents, it exhibits marked properties of absorption. Cellulose derivatives—synthetic compounds formed as esters or ethers by the reaction of cellulose with acids, alkalies, anhydrides, or alkyl halides—are of great commercial importance. They include guncotton, fully nitrated cellulose, used for explosives; celluloid (the first plastic), the product of cellulose nitrates treated with camphor; collodion, a thickening agent; and cellulose acetate, used for plastics, lacquers, and nonflammable photographic film. The manufacture of textiles such as RAYON and other synthetic fabrics from cellulose esters or directly from cellulose itself and the production of cellophane are done by the VISCOSE PROCESS. See Emil Heuser, *Chemistry of Cellulose* (1944); William Haynes, *Cellulose: the Chemical that Grows* (1953); Emil Ott, ed., *Cellulose and Cellulose Derivatives* (2d ed., 1954).

Celman, Miguel Juárez: see JUÁREZ CELMAN.

Celoron (sĕ'lûrùn, –ōn″, –ŏn″), village (pop. 1,507), W central N.Y., on Chautauqua Lake, W of Jamestown; inc. 1896.

Celsius, Anders (än'dûrs sĕl'sēùs), 1701–44, Swedish astronomer. While professor of astronomy in the Univ. of Uppsala (1730–44), he traveled through Germany, France, and Italy, visiting great observatories. At Nuremberg in 1733 he published a collection of 316 observations of the aurora borealis that were made by himself and, others. While in Paris he was instrumental in bringing about an expedition organized by the French Academy for the measurement of an arc of the meridian in Lapland, in 1736. Celsius was a member of the expedition. He supervised the building of an observatory at Uppsala in 1740 and became its director. In 1742 he invented the centigrade (or Celsius) thermometer. His works include *De observationibus pro figura telluris determinanda* (1738).

Celsius, Olaf (ō'läf), 1670–1756, Swedish botanist and Orientalist. He wrote a two-volume work, *Hierobotanicon*, on the plants of the Bible (many of which, to his day, had been known only by their Hebrew names), and compiled a catalogue of the plants of Sweden. His greatest contribution to science, perhaps, was the aid and encouragement he gave Linnaeus. Anders Celsius was his nephew.

Celsus (sĕl'sùs), 2d cent., Roman philosopher, an aggressive antagonist of Christianity. His works have been lost, but the substance of his *True Discourse* is given by Origen in his *Against Celsus.*

Celsus, Aulus Cornelius, fl. A.D. 14, Latin encyclopedist. His only extant work, *De re medicina*, consists of eight books on medicine believed to have been written A.D. c.30. He was not esteemed as a scientist in his time, but his was one of the first works to be rediscovered and printed (Florence, 1478) during the Renaissance and was very influential, largely because of its splendid Latin style. It was translated by James Grieve in 1756 and by W. G. Spencer in 1935. Celsus' first name is also written Aurelius.

Celt (sĕlt) or **Kelt** (kĕlt). **1** One who speaks a Celtic language or who derives his ancestry from an area where a Celtic language was spoken; i.e., one from Ireland, the Scottish Hebrides and Highlands, the Isle of Man, Wales, Cornwall, or Brittany. See LANGUAGE (table). **2** A member of a group of peoples first found early in the 2d millennium B.C. in SW Germany and E France. The Celts were a group of tribes speaking Indo-European dialects. Armed with iron weapons and mounted on horses, they spread rapidly over Europe, crossing into the British Isles, moving S over France, Italy, and Spain, fighting the Macedonians, and penetrating into Asia Minor, where they raided Hellenistic centers. They introduced the newly developed iron industries. Their wealth from trade and from raiding helped to maintain their dominance over Central Europe during the Iron Age. The LA TÈNE culture is probably derived from the Celtic. Greek influences that stimulated Celtic culture included the introduction of the chariot and, somewhat later, of writing. Art flourished in richly ornamented styles. The Celts lived in semifortified villages, with a tribal organization that became increasingly hierarchical as wealth was acquired. Priests, nobles, craftsmen, and peasants were clearly distinguished, and the powers of the chief became kinglike. The Celts believed in a daemonic universe and relied on the ministry of the DRUIDS. Western European folklore is derived mainly from the Celts. By the 4th cent. B.C. they could no longer withstand the encroaching Germanic tribes, and they lost most of their holdings in the north and in W Germany. From this time on, Celtic history becomes confused with that of the many unsettled tribes in Europe. Celtic language and culture were variously dispersed among peoples of little historical identity, and until this century historians obscured the very important differences among these groups by naming them all Celts. More confusion has resulted from the designation of a Celtic subrace. This type of light-eyed, dark-haired or red-haired, long-headed individual is most common in Celtic-speaking countries, but usually among the non-Celtic speakers. The term *Celtic* is actually a cultural one, unrelated to physical heredity. It implies a cultural tradition maintained through many centuries of common history in the same general area. See also IRON AGE. See T. G. E. Powell, *The Celts* (1958); A. D. Rees and Brinley Rees, *Celtic Heritage* (1961).

Celtes, Conradus Protucius (kŏn′rädŭs prō′tōŏt-sēŭs kĕl′tŭs), pseud. of **Konrad Pickel** (kôn′rät pī′kŭl), 1459–1508, German scholar and humanist. He traveled widely, lectured at several universities, became librarian to Maximilian I, and founded various societies dedicated to classical learning. He was made (1487) first German poet laureate. Of his works, didactic, lyric, and dramatic, his odes in the manner of Ovid and Horace are noteworthy. Celtes discovered the works of the nun HROSWITHA VON GANDERSHEIM.

Celtic languages, subfamily of the Indo-European languages, spoken on the British Isles and in Brittany. See LANGUAGE (table).

cement, a building material composed of lime, silica, aluminum, and iron oxide, heated to approximately 2900°F. and ground to a fine powder. It is mixed with water and aggregates (crushed stone, sand, and gravel) to form CONCRETE. In ancient Rome a volcanic product found at Pozzuoli on the Bay of Naples (hence called pozzuolana) was used in building, notably in the Pantheon. Cement was little used in the Middle Ages. In the 18th cent.

Richly decorated Celtic cauldron.

John Smeaton in rebuilding the Eddystone lighthouse found that pure lime (burned limestone) was not as good for a building that must stand in water as limestone mixed with clay. Both Joseph Packer in 1791 and Edgar Dobbs in 1810 were granted patents in England for manufacturing cement made of lime and clay. The invention of Portland cement by Joseph Aspdin c.1820 led to a much greater use of concrete for hydraulic structures, such as dams and bridges. A few years later, on the Rondout Creek, New York, a limestone was discovered which made a cement even stronger than Portland. This cement, called Rosendale, was made and shipped from kilns near Kingston for many years; it was used in building the Brooklyn Bridge and the Croton Dam. The quicker-drying quality and greater strength of an improved Portland cement subsequently made this product more popular, and today only a small percentage of the cement produced in the United States is natural cement. Bituminous cements are made from natural asphalt or coal tar. When mixed with small stones they afford a durable paving and road material. Gypsum cement (plaster of Paris) is commonly employed in making casts and in the interior of buildings. Various forms of cement have been used since very ancient times.

cemetery, place for burying the dead. Among primitive peoples, collective burial plots are rare; graves are more often dug inside or near the house of the deceased. Group burials have been found in Paleolithic caves, and fields of prehistoric grave mounds or barrows (see BARROW) dot parts of Europe, Asia, and N America. In the ancient Near East, graves were often grouped around temples and sanctuaries. In Greece, a *necropolis* or "city of the dead" lined the roads leading out of a town, and the same practice was followed by the Romans. The word *cemetery* was first applied to the early Christian burials in the Roman CATACOMBS and found general usage in the 15th cent. Belief in resurrection made chapel crypts and churchyards desirable for burial, but overcrowding and the rise of settled urban centers made it necessary to establish plots of consecrated ground outside the city limits. Graveyards of all periods tend to reflect the familial and class groupings of their living society.

Among the many beautiful and historic cemeteries of Europe are the Père-Lachaise at Paris and the Campo Santo at Pisa. Noteworthy American cemeteries are ARLINGTON NATIONAL CEMETERY, which contains the tomb of the UNKNOWN SOLDIER; Mt. Auburn in Cambridge, Mass., one of the earliest municipal cemeteries in the United States; and the elaborately designed Forest Lawn Memorial Park of Glendale, Calif. The National Park Service also maintains cemeteries (see NATIONAL PARKS AND MONUMENTS, table). See also FUNERAL CUSTOMS; GRAVE; TOMB.

Cenchrea (sĕn′krĕŭ) or **Cenchreae** (–krē-ē″), port of ancient Greece, on the Saronic Gulf, ESE of Corinth. Acts 18.18; Rom. 16.1.

Cenci, Beatrice (bäätrē′chä chän′chē), 1577–99, Italian noblewoman, tragic figure of the late Renaissance. Her father, Francesco Cenci (1549–98), was a Roman noble noted for his viciousness. In 1595 he imprisoned Beatrice and her stepmother Lucrezia in a lonely castle; his cruel treatment finally led Beatrice, with the complicity of her

*Beatrice Cenci
(by Guido Reni)*

stepmother, her brothers, and her lover, to procure his murder. After a famous trial (1599) the conspirators were put to death. This tragedy, often cited as an example of the corruption of 16th-century Rome, is the subject of, among other works, Guerrazzi's novel *Beatrice Cenci* and Shelley's tragedy *The Cenci*. In the Barberini Palace, Rome, is a painting by Guido Reni sometimes said to represent her. See Corrado Ricci, *Beatrice Cenci* (1923; Eng. tr., 1925).

Cenis, Mont (mō sŭnē′), Ital. *Moncenisio* (mōnchānē′zyō), Alpine pass, on the French-Italian border. About 6,831 ft. high, it is one of the great invasion routes in Italian history. Napoleon I built a new road here in 1810. The Mont Cenis railroad tunnel (c.8 mi. long) was built in 1871 and connects Turin, Italy, with Chambéry, France, via Modane, France.

Cennini, Cennino (chän-nē′nō chän-nē′nē), c.1370–1440, Florentine painter, follower of Agnolo Gaddi. None of his paintings is now extant. He is most famous for having written the *Libro dell' arte* (written 1400?; Eng. tr., *The Craftsman's Handbook*, 1933). This treatise marks a transition between medieval and Renaissance concepts of art. Closely

following the tradition of Giotto, he offers detailed advice about the established technique of painting. At the same time, Cennini was one of the first to call for imagination in art and to advocate the elevation of painting from artisanship to the fine arts.

Cenozoic era (sēnŭzō′ĭk, sĕ–) [Gr.,=recent life], fifth and last grand division of geologic time (see GEOLOGIC ERAS, table). Because of the disturbances of the late MESOZOIC ERA, the geography of North America at the beginning of the Cenozoic was substantially the same as it is today. The only areas liable to marine flooding were the Atlantic and Gulf coasts and a small area on the Pacific coast. It is in the Cenozoic era that man appeared. The life of this era has been dominated by the mammals, which were most numerous in the TERTIARY PERIOD and have declined, with the exception of a few specialized types, in the QUATERNARY PERIOD. The elapsed portion of the Cenozoic is about 70,000,000 years, less than half the estimated duration of the Mesozoic. See also GEOLOGY.

censor (sĕn′sŭr), title of two magistrates of ancient Rome (from c.443 B.C. to the time of Domitian). They took the census (by which they assessed taxation) and supervised public behavior. They also had charge of public works and filled vacancies among the senators and knights. A *nota censoria* was a mark placed on the roll of citizens against the name of a citizen failing to maintain a standard of civic duty. CATO THE ELDER was a famous censor.

Censorinus (sĕnsōrī′nŭs), fl. c.238, Roman grammarian. He wrote *De die natali* [on the day of birth], an essay partly astrological, partly chronological, which affords much information on ancient ways of reckoning time.

censorship, official prohibition or restriction of any type of expression believed to threaten the political, the social, or the moral order. It may be imposed by governmental authority, local or general, by religious authority, or occasionally by a powerful private group. It may be applied to the press, the theater, the mails, speech, dance, art, literature, photography, the cinema, radio, or television. Censorship is either preventive or punitive, according to whether it is exercised before or after the expression has been made public, as through publication or performance. The practice has been known since ancient times, in both the East and the West. It has been particularly thoroughgoing under autocratic and heavily centralized governments from the Roman Empire to the totalitarian states of the 20th cent., especially Fascist Italy, Nazi Germany, and the Communist nations. In other countries censorship is accepted as inevitable and unchallenged in times of war, but has been imposed to varying degrees in peacetime. In the Middle Ages the attempts to uproot heresy and the establishment of the Inquisition were closely related to censorship, as are the modern instances of book burning. The absolute monarchs of the 17th and 18th cent. imposed strict controls, and because the Reformation had resulted in reshuffling of the relations of CHURCH AND STATE, these controls were used to persecute opponents of the established religion of a particular state, Catholic or Protestant. A form of book banning, not technically censorship, was adopted by the Roman Catholic Church in the INDEX, a list of publications which the faithful are forbidden to read. Paradoxically, in the lands under Calvinist domination (such as Geneva, Scotland, and England of the Puritan period), where the ideals of personal liberty and freedom from economic and political exactions blossomed, regulation of private conduct and individual opinion was rigorous, and censorship was strong. These attitudes and practices were transplanted to the theocratic settlements of New England, and it has been customary to trace intensive censorship of morals in the United States to these New England sources. The so-called Puritanical restrictions were, however, quite in key with the prudish refinement fostered by bourgeois societies in the 19th cent., and their persistence rested on many circumstances. Attempts to channel or suppress political freedom of the press in the American colonies were recurrent; a notable example was the trial of John Peter ZENGER. The Bill of Rights in the U.S. Constitution guarantees freedom of the press, of speech, and of religion. Nevertheless, there have been examples of obvious and official political censorship, notably in the actions taken under the Sedition Act of 1798 (see ALIEN AND SEDITION ACTS), suppression of abolitionist literature in the antebellum South, and local attempts to repress "radical" attacks upon American politico-economic institutions in the late 19th and the 20th cent. Long before the First World War there were vigilant attacks, such as those by Anthony COMSTOCK, on what was reckoned obscene literature, and the U.S. Post Office expanded somewhat its ban on shipment of obscene literature and art, but it was after the First World War that public controversy raged most fiercely over censorship. One variety of censorship that was much attacked and much defended was the effort to keep out of schools and colleges textbooks and teaching that might be deleterious to what was termed the American form of government or might promote "foreign isms" (see ACADEMIC FREEDOM). The weakening hold of conventional sexual morality had brought frankness into literature and art, and defenders of the conventional code and proponents of artistic freedom alike sometimes found it hard to distinguish between artistic achievement and pornography. The result was a series of battles over particular occurrences of censorship. The producers of motion pictures, dependent for success upon widespread public approval, somewhat reluctantly adopted a self-regulatory code of morals (see HAYS, WILLIAM HARRISON), which was more or less enforced for many years. Trade organizations and local, state, and Federal boards of censorship also pronounced upon the cinema, and some private and religious groups (notably the Catholic Legion of Decency) set up boards to guide voluntary censorship. All these have been attacked as reactionary institutions stifling art. Controversy was perhaps most fiery over the suppression or attempted suppression of books. In a long series of incidents, some of the more noticeable were: the short-lived furor over James Branch Cabell's novel, *Jurgen;* refusal of importation rights for James Joyce's *Ulysses* until the ban was lifted by a Federal Circuit Court judge in 1933, years after the book was universally recognized as a work of world-wide importance; refusal to permit distribution of D. H. Lawrence's *Lady Chatterley's Lover* in

unexpurgated form until another Federal Court decision (1959); and the eruption of state prosecutions after Henry Miller's *Tropic of Cancer* was published in the United States (1961). See also PRESS, FREEDOM OF THE See Robert Cushman, *Civil Liberties in the United States* (1956); R. P. McKeon, Robert Merton, and Walter Gellhorn, *The Freedom to Read* (1957); Robert Downs, *The First Freedom* (1960); Robert Haney, *Comstockery in America* (1960).

census, periodic official count of the number of persons and their condition and of the resources of a country. In ancient times, as with the Jews and Romans, such enumeration was mainly for taxation and conscription purposes. The introduction of the modern census—a periodic and thorough statistical review—is variously claimed by French Canada (1665), Sweden (1749), the United States (1790), and others. The first English census was taken in 1801. The Belgian census of 1846, directed by Adolphe QUETELET, was the most influential in its time because it introduced a careful analysis and critical evaluation of the data compiled. Most Westernized countries now take a census every 5 or 10 years. Scientific census taking in the United States began with the decennial census of 1850, when the scope and methods were greatly improved by making the individual the unit of study and adding information about the structure of the population as well as its members. In 1902 the permanent Bureau of the Census was established in the Dept. of Commerce.

centaur (sĕn'tôr), in Greek mythology, a creature half man and half horse. The centaurs were fathered by IXION or by Centaurus, who was Ixion's son. They were uncouth and savage, but some, such as CHIRON, became friends and teachers of men. They were followers of Dionysus.

Centaurus (sĕntô'rŭs), constellation of the Southern Hemisphere. It is known especially for its star Alpha Centauri, which is visually the third brightest star in the sky (only Sirius and Canopus are brighter). Alpha Centauri is one of the two stars nearest to our solar system. Its distance is about 4.3 light-years. Proxima Centauri, a faint star in Centaurus, is about the same distance away.

Centennial Exposition, International, held in Philadelphia from May to Nov., 1876, to celebrate the 100th anniversary of the Declaration of Independence. The buildings, in Fairmount Park, included the Main Building, covering 20 acres, Machinery Hall, Agricultural Hall, Horticultural Hall, and Memorial Hall, many state buildings, and buildings of 37 foreign countries. The total number of those attending in 159 days was 9,910,966. This was the first of a series of world's fairs which the United States was to hold, and it set a high standard. Particularly did it exhibit in graphic manner the technical advances and industrial growth of the nation. Memorial Hall, a Renaissance structure of granite, became part of the Pennsylvania Museum of Art.

Center. 1 Town (pop. 1,600; alt. c.7,641 ft.), S Colo., NW of Alamosa, in a farm area; inc. 1907. **2** City (pop. 4,510), co. seat of Shelby co., E Texas, NE of Nacogdoches near the Sabine; founded 1866, inc. 1903. In the pine woods, it makes wood and metal products and processes poultry.

center, in politics, a party following a middle course.

The term was first used in France in 1789, when the moderates of the National Assembly sat in the center of the hall. The Catholic group in Prussia assumed the name Center in 1859, also because of the location of its seats, and a similar Center party was formed after 1871.

Centerdale, R.I.: see NORTH PROVIDENCE.

Centereach, uninc. residential town (pop. 8,524), SE N.Y., central Long Island, NNW of Patchogue.

centering, the framework of wood or of wood and steel built to support a masonry arch or vault during its construction. The centering itself must be rigidly supported, either by posts from the ground

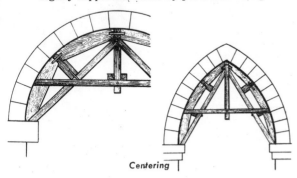

Centering

or by trusses when piers are available to receive their ends. After the centering is built, the setting of the masonry proceeds equally from the ends or sides toward the central point, where the keystone of the arch or the crowning blocks of the vault are finally wedged into position. The centering is removed after setting in the case of arches where the shape is dependent on the cement or concrete, but in other instances, e.g., where dressed stone is used with a lime mortar joint, it is better to remove the centering before setting, so that gravity will control the disposition of the stones. The removal of the centering is a delicate operation, since the placing of undue pressure on one part endangers the whole structure. The Romans built vast domes and vaults of concrete with the aid of wood centerings and of integral brick ribs within the vault itself. Arches of steep rise may sometimes be built without centering. Brunelleschi is said to have dispensed with it in constructing the steep dome of the cathedral at Florence. Today centering is often replaced by inflatable plastic balloons.

Center Line, city (pop. 10,164), SE Mich., a suburb NNE of Detroit; inc. as a village 1925, as a city 1935. Automobiles, metal products, and missile parts are made.

Center Moriches (mŭrĭ'chĕz), uninc. resort town (pop. 2,521), SE N.Y., on the south shore of Long Island, E of Patchogue and on Moriches Bay.

Center Point, town (pop. 1,236), E central Iowa, near the Cedar river and NNW of Cedar Rapids; settled 1839.

Centerport, uninc. resort town (pop. 3,628), SE N.Y., on the north shore of W Long Island, ENE of Huntington.

Centerville. 1 City (pop. 12,769), SE Ill., SSE of East St. Louis; inc. 1957. **2** Town (pop. 2,378), E Ind., WSW of Richmond. It is a processing point for a farm and dairy area. **3** City (pop. 6,629), co. seat of Appanoose co., S central Iowa, SW of Ottumwa, in a coal area; platted 1846, inc. 1855. It has varied manufactures. A community junior college is here. Nearby is Sharon Bluffs State Park. **4** Uninc. town (pop. 3,398 including Dublin Gulch), SW Mont., NNE of Butte. This industrial suburb has many copper mines. **5** Village (pop. 3,490), SW Ohio, a suburb S of Dayton; inc. 1879. **6** Agricultural borough (pop. 5,088), SW Pa., on the Monongahela and S of Pittsburgh; settled 1766, laid out 1821, inc. 1895. Coal is mined. **7** Town (pop. 1,678), co. seat of Hickman co., central Tenn., on the Duck river and SW of Nashville, in a farm and phosphate-mining area; inc. 1911. **8** Town (pop. 2,361), N Utah, near Great Salt Lake and N of Salt Lake City. It is a farm community in an irrigated area served by the Weber basin project.

centigrade scale: see TEMPERATURE.

centipede (sĕn'tụ̄pēd), land ARTHROPOD of the class Chilopoda. Centipedes have long, flattened bodies composed of many segments, most of which each bear one pair of legs (in the millipede there are two). Though the name centipede means hundred-legged, the average is actually 35 pairs. The head bears a pair of antennae and two groups of simple eyes. The appendages of the first body segment are a pair of poison claws which inject a fluid secreted by the poison glands into the prey (insects and worms), paralyzing them. Centipedes move swiftly and are chiefly nocturnal; they are very sensitive to touch. They are found in moist places, e.g., under decaying logs. Most centipedes are 1 to 8 in. long, but some tropical species reach 18 in. The house centipede has long, delicate legs and compound eyes. It feeds on roaches, clothes moths, and other insects. Centipede bites are painful but not dangerous to man.

Centipedes

Central. 1 Town (pop. 1,075), SW N.Mex., near Silver City, in an area of copper, zinc, and lead mines. A U.S. veterans' hospital is nearby. **2** Town (pop. 1,473), NW S.C., WSW of Greenville; inc. 1875. Textiles and concrete products are made. A junior college is here.

Central African Republic, country (238,200 sq. mi.; pop. c.1,227,000), central Africa. The capital is Bangui. The republic was formerly the overseas

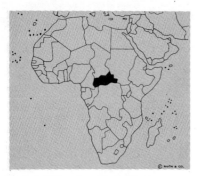

Central African Republic location map

Village near Bangui.

territory of Ubangi-Shari in French Equatorial Africa. It is bordered by the Republic of the Congo and the Congo Republic on the south, by the Republic of Sudan on the east, by Chad on the north, and by the Federal Republic of Cameroon on the west. The country is a landlocked plateau (elevation c.2,000 ft.), mainly covered by savanna; in the south there are dense tropical forests and in the east semidesert topography prevails. It is drained by numerous rivers, of which the Ubangi and the Shari are the largest. There is much farming; cotton, coffee, and peanuts are raised and exported. Lumbering is also important. There is some mining of gold and of industrial diamonds. The country has no railroads and only 3,000 miles of all-weather roads exist; rivers are the chief form of transportation. The population is divided into four main Negro groups: the Mandjia-Baya, the Banda, the M'Baka, and the Zandé. They are mainly animists, but Christianity has made some inroads. French is the official language, but Sangho is widely spoken. The region was first settled (1887) by the French, who organized the territory as a colony in 1894. It was united administratively with Chad in 1906 and incorporated into French Equatorial Africa in 1910. Chad was later made a separate colony. Much of the area was leased to European concessionaires, and their abuses led to rebellions by the Africans in 1928, 1935, and 1946. The population gave active support to the Free French forces during the Second World War. A nationalist movement forced the French to grant the colony increasingly greater autonomy in the 1950s. In 1958 Ubangi-Shari voted to join the French Community, and in December of that year it became the Central African Republic. Full independence was attained on Aug. 13, 1960, and the new country was admitted to the United Nations the following month. David Dacko was elected the first president. It is a member of the Union of Central African Republics, an economic, technical, and cultural association, and of the African-Malagasy Union, which comprises 12 former French colonies. The Central African Republic also belongs to the so-called Monrovia group of African states. See Virginia Thompson and Richard Adloff, *The Emerging States of French Equatorial Africa* (1960).

Central America, narrow strip of land between North America proper and the Isthmus of Panama, which separates the continent from South America. Central America lies between the Isthmus of Tehuantepec and the Isthmus of Panama. Though geographically it includes several Mexican states and the territory Quintana Roo, the term generally applies to five republics, COSTA RICA, GUATEMALA, HONDURAS, NICARAGUA, SALVADOR, and one colony, BRITISH HONDURAS; PANAMA is often included. See CENTRAL AMERICAN FEDERATION.

Location map of Central America, showing the route of the Inter-American Highway.

Central American Federation or **Central American Union,** political confederation (1825–38) of the republics of Central America—Costa Rica, Guatemala, Honduras, Nicaragua, and Salvador. United under a captaincy general in Spanish colonial times, they gained independence in 1821 and were briefly annexed to the Mexican empire formed by Agustín de Iturbide. Subsequently they joined in a loose federal state, appointing as first president (1825–29) Manuel José Arce (d. 1847), who was succeeded by the liberal leader, Francisco MORAZÁN (1830–

38). Political and personal rivalries between liberals and conservatives, poor communication, and the fear of the hegemony of one state over another led to dissolution of the congress (1838) and the defeat (1839) of Morazán's forces by Rafael CARRERA. In 1842 Morazán made an abortive attempt to reestablish the federation from Costa Rica. Later efforts by Nicaragua, Honduras, and Salvador failed. The attempts of Justo Rufino BARRIOS (1885) and José Santos ZELAYA (1895) only increased existing enmities. At the Central American conference of 1922–23 the U.S. recommendation of a union was not favorably received, partly because of earlier U.S. policies in Panama and Nicaragua. Nevertheless, geography, history, and practical expedience are factors that constantly encourage union. In 1951 the organization of Central American States was formed to help solve common problems, and in 1961 the five nations moved toward the establishment of a common market. See T. L. Karnes, *The Failure of Union: Central America, 1824–1960* (1961).

Central Asiatic Railroad: see TRANS-CASPIAN RAILROAD.

Central Australia: see NORTHERN TERRITORY.

central bank. Although the term was hardly known before 1900, the concept of central banking is at least 200 years older. The BANK OF ENGLAND, founded in 1694, gradually became the prototype of later central banks. Another early central bank was the Swedish Riksbank. The weakness of state banks in the United States after the lapse of the BANK OF THE UNITED STATES gradually caused the evolution of central banking practices here. The National Banking Act of 1863 led to the abolition of note issues by state banks; the FEDERAL RESERVE SYSTEM, established in 1913, forced uniform practices on member banks and furnished a central reserve. Every economically developed nation today possesses the equivalent of a central bank with the general purpose of acting as fiscal agent for the government and of constituting the "lender of last resort" for the banking system of the country. Among the subsidiary functions of central banks are the creation of money and the regulation of its use and volume; regulation of the discount rate and advances to commercial banks; purchase and sale of government obligations; check clearances among the member banks; regulation of the ratio of reserves to deposits in member banks; partial or total monopoly of note issue; and correspondence with central banks of other nations. The Federal Reserve System's governing board is charged with regulation of the rate of margin in stock-market trading; it may exert considerable control over the extension of consumer credit by commercial banks. In general, central banks do not exercise the ordinary functions of commercial banks toward depositors. See M. H. de Kock, *Central Banking* (3d ed., 1954).

Central City. 1 Town (pop. 250; alt. c.8,560 ft.), co. seat of Gilpin co., N central Colo., in Clear Creek Canyon W of Denver; inc. 1886. It boomed after the discovery of gold in 1859. Although some mining is still carried on in the area, Central City is now a "ghost town." The past is revived annually with a summer play and music festival in the stone opera house (opened 1878; owned since 1931 by the

Univ. of Denver), where in its heyday nearly every noted player of the time appeared. The Teller House (1872), famous frontier hostelry, is next door. See Caroline Bancroft, *Gulch of Gold* (1958). **2** Village (pop. 1,422), S central Ill., N of Centralia; inc. 1857. **3** Town (pop. 1,087), E central Iowa, NNE of Cedar Rapids. It ships poultry and dairy products. **4** Town (pop. 3,694), W Ky., S of Owensboro; settled as Morehead's Horse Mill, renamed after 1870 when the railroad reached here. It is the trade center of a coal, oil, timber, and farm area. **5** City (pop. 2,406), co. seat of Merrick co., E central Nebr., on the Platte and WNW of Lincoln; platted 1864. Poultry and meat products are processed. Nearby was the site of Lone Tree Ranch, stopping place on the Overland Trail. **6** Borough (pop. 1,604), SW Pa., SE of Johnstown; inc. 1918.

Central Falls, industrial city (pop. 19,858), N R.I., NE of Providence; inc. 1895. Its chief manufactures are apparel, textiles, and machinery. Many of the people are of French Canadian descent.

Central Heights, uninc. town (pop. 2,486), SE Ariz., E of Phoenix and near Globe.

Centralia (sĕntrā'lĕu). **1** City (pop. 13,904), S Ill., E of St. Louis; platted 1853, inc. 1859. It is an industrial and shipping center of a fruit, farm, coal, and oil area. The city has railroad repair shops, and its products include heaters, candy, and clothing. A junior college is here. **2** City (pop. 3,200), N central Mo., SE of Moberly, in a grain region; laid out 1857, inc. 1868. Lumber and metal products are made. The city was the scene of a raid by Confederate guerrillas in 1864. **3** Borough (pop. 1,435), E Pa., S of Bloomsburg; inc. 1866. Anthracite coal is mined here. **4** City (pop. 8,586), SW Wash., S of Seattle and near the Chehalis river; platted 1875, inc. 1889. It is a railroad junction and a farm trade center, with large lumber and food-processing industries. A junior college and the county fairgrounds are in Centralia. A violent clash between townspeople and organized lumber workers occurred here on Nov. 11, 1919.

Central Intelligence Agency (CIA), independent executive bureau of the U.S. government established by the National Security Act of 1947. It replaced the wartime OFFICE OF STRATEGIC SERVICES (1942–45), the first U.S. intelligence agency. In 1946 President Truman set up an agency to gather and report strategic facts from abroad. The CIA reports to the President and to the National Security Council, his advisory body. For secrecy, the CIA was given (1949) special powers under the Central Intelligence Act; its director may spend the agency's funds without accounting for them, and the size of its staff is never divulged. Employees, exempt from civil service procedures, may be hired, investigated, or dismissed as the CIA sees fit. To safeguard civil liberties in the United States, however, the CIA is denied domestic police powers; for operations in the United States it must enlist the services of the Federal Bureau of Investigation. Faulty intelligence reports prior to the Korean war led (1950) to the appointment of General Walter Bedell Smith as director. Allen Welsh DULLES, a veteran intelligence agent who was director from 1953 to 1961, strengthened the agency and emboldened its tactics. The CIA has been criticized for taking an active role in the internal affairs of foreign countries to thwart the spread of communism. In 1960 the USSR brought down a reconnaissance airplane over its territory (see ESPIONAGE); the pilot admitted he was a CIA employee. The agency was heavily involved in the 1961 invasion of Cuba, the failure of which deeply embarrassed the United States; President Kennedy reactivated a supervisory committee to insure that the CIA would execute policies rather than make them. Dulles retired and was replaced by John Alex McCone. See Andrew Tully, *CIA: the Inside Story* (1962).

Central Park. **1** Uninc. town (pop. 2,676), E central Ill., S of Danville. **2** Uninc. village (pop. 1,622), W Wash., on the Chehalis river just E of Aberdeen.

Central Park, 840 acres, largest park on Manhattan island, New York city, between 59th and 110th streets and Fifth Avenue and Central Park West. The land was acquired by the city in 1856 and was improved after the plans of F. L. Olmsted and Calvert Vaux; 185 acres were devoted to lakes and ponds; extensive planting was done, and bridle paths, walks, and roads were laid out. There are a number of playgrounds and other recreational facilities. The Metropolitan Museum of Art stands in the park; other points of interest include the formal conservatory garden, a zoo, a children's zoo, an Egyptian obelisk popularly known as "Cleopatra's Needle," the Mall (where concerts are given), and the reservoir. In an open-air theater (completed 1962) Shakespearean dramas and other plays are presented free of charge.

Central Point, city (pop. 2,289), SW Oregon, NW of Medford; inc. 1889. In an irrigated farm and livestock region, it also grows fruit and has a lumbering industry.

Central Powers, in the First WORLD WAR, the coalition of Germany, Austria-Hungary, Bulgaria, and the Ottoman Empire.

Central Provinces and Berar: see MADHYA PRADESH.

Central Treaty Organization, (CENTO), international governmental organization, formed in 1955 for the military defense of the Middle East. At the start of 1963 members were the United Kingdom, Turkey, Iran, and Pakistan; the United States, not directly a member, was pledged to cooperate. Originally known as the Middle East Treaty Organization, the association was based on the Baghdad Pact of 1955 between Turkey and Iraq. After Iraq left the organization in 1959, the name was changed to CENTO. The CENTO powers are also pledged to economic and social cooperation in the Middle East.

Central Utah Project, NE and N central Utah, planned by the Bureau of Reclamation to gather water from the streams in the Uinta Mts. and carry it across the Wasatch Range to the thickly populated Salt Lake valley by a system of dams, reservoirs, aqueducts, and canals. The initial phase of the project was authorized by Congress in 1956, and work was begun in 1959 near Vernal. The project will provide hydroelectric power, water for industrial and domestic use, and irrigation for c.160,000 acres of land. It is one of several participating projects in the extensive COLORADO RIVER STORAGE PROJECT.

Central Valley, uninc. town (pop. 2,854), N Calif., NNE of Redding, in a farm and timber region. It was founded in 1938 when construction began on the CENTRAL VALLEY PROJECT. Nearby Shasta Lake, impounded by the SHASTA DAM on the Sacramento river, is a recreation area.

Central Valley project, central Calif., for utilization of water resources of the region. There were projects and plans of a limited nature earlier, but it was not until 1935 that the program of the U.S. Bureau of Reclamation was initiated after congressional authorization. The general scheme is to use the abundant waters of the Sacramento river in the north to benefit the abundant farmlands of the San Joaquin Valley in the south. The program has as its purposes flood control, improvement of navigation, development of hydroelectric power, irrigation, supply of water for cities and industries, protection of lands in the Sacramento delta region from seawater penetration, and the propagation and preservation of fish and wildlife. The initial units will irrigate more than 282,000 new acres and will supplement c.938,000 acres of cultivated land. Among the units in the first stage are SHASTA DAM (completed 1945) and the smaller Keswick Dam (159 ft. high; 1,046 ft. long; completed 1950) on the Sacramento; FRIANT DAM (completed 1942) and its reservoir, Millerton Lake, on the San Joaquin; the Madera Canal (completed 1945) northward 36 mi. from Friant Dam; the Friant-Kern Canal (completed 1951) southward c.150 mi. from Friant Dam; the Delta Cross Channel (completed 1951), using the water of the Sacramento to fight soil salinity in the delta; the Contra Costa Canal (completed 1948), taking Sacramento water 48 mi. to a reservoir at Martinez and supplying water to the farms and industries of Contra Costa co. in the delta; a pumping plant at Tracy to take water from the Delta Cross Channel and supply the Delta-Mendota Canal; the Delta-Mendota Canal (completed 1951) to take the water c.120 mi. roughly parallel to the San Joaquin and supply to that river at the Mendota pool; and a steam power plant at Antioch. Recent developments have been started on the Trinity and the American rivers. The program in its entirety embraces other numerous dams, reservoirs, and power plants, not yet constructed. The U.S. Corps of Engineers has contributed much to development by such units as the Pine Flat Dam (430 ft. high; 1,820 ft. long; completed 1954) on Kings river in the southern part of the Central Valley and the Folsom Dam (340 ft. high; 10,200 ft. long; completed 1955) on the American river. See Robert de Roos, *The Thirsty Land* (1949) and U.S. Bureau of Reclamation, *Central Valley Project* (1961).

Centre, town (pop. 2,392), co. seat of Cherokee co., NE Ala., NE of Gadsden, in a farm region; settled c.1840, inc. 1937.

Centre Hall, borough (pop. 1,109), central Pa., ENE of State College, in a resort area; inc. 1885.

Centreville. **1** Town (pop. 1,981), central Ala., SSW of Birmingham and near the Cahaba river, in a timber and cotton area. Talladega National Forest is nearby. **2** Town (pop. 1,863), co. seat of Queen Annes co., Md., Eastern Shore, S of Chestertown, in an agricultural area; founded c.1788, laid out 1792, inc. 1794. Canning is done. **3** Town (pop. 1,229), SW Miss., SSE of Natchez near the La. line; inc. 1880.

centrifugal force and **centripetal force:** see FORCE.

centrifuge (sĕn'trŭfūj), device using the principle of centrifugal FORCE to separate substances of different density. It is applied commonly in the separation of two liquids of different weights or of a liquid and a solid. The centrifuge consists of a fixed base or frame and a rotating part in which the mixture is placed and then turned by means of a crank or motor. One type is widely used for the separation of the solid and the liquid parts of blood. Test tubes containing blood specimens are set in the rotating part in holders so arranged that when the rotary motion begins the test tubes swing into a slanted or a horizontal position with the open ends toward the axis of rotation; the heavier solid part of the blood is thrown outward into the bottom of the tube and the lighter liquid part comes to the top. Similarly other mixtures of substances with different weights, including mixtures in which the differences are very small, can be separated into their components. Another common type of centrifuge is the cream separator. The separation of uranium 238 from uranium 235 is accomplished by centrifuging. The first successful centrifuge was built in 1883 by Carl G. P. de Laval, Swedish engineer, whose design was used chiefly for cream separators. The ultracentrifuge, devised in the 1920s by Theodor SVEDBERG, found wide application in scientific research. Using an optical system with it to observe sedimentation rates, Svedberg determined accurately the molecular weights of substances including proteins and viruses. The ultracentrifuge has attained speeds of 1.5 million revolutions per second.

centumviri (sĕntŭm'vĭrĭ) [Latin,=a hundred men], in ancient Rome, a court of a varying number of men which heard civil cases having to do with land and property claims. Each Roman tribe was represented in it. Under the empire the centumviri had to deal chiefly with inheritance. The last mention of them is in A.D. 395.

Century, uninc. town (pop. 2,046), extreme NW Fla., at the Ala. line N of Pensacola.

century plant: see AMARYLLIS.

Ceos: see KEOS.

cephalic index (sŭfă'lĭk) [Gr.,=head], the numerical ratio of the breadth of the head to its length. Expressed as a percental number, it provides the simplest description of the geometric relation of two dimensions. The index is obtained by dividing the maximum width of the cranium by its maximum length and multiplying by 100. In ANTHROPOMETRY, the cephalic index has been the favored measurement and has sometimes been over-valued, particularly when used as a basis for race classification. It has been shown that the physical and mechanical conditions which control the relationship of the parts measured are not in themselves stable, and the significance of cephalic indexes must depend on correlation with other factors. An index up to 74.9 is considered dolicocephalic or long-headed, while 80 or more indicates the broad-headed or brachycephalic type. The middle range is termed mesocephalic. The cranial index is the same ratio taken on a skull.

Cephalonia (sĕfŭlō'nyŭ), Gr. *Kephallenia* (kĕfä-lēnē'ä), island (c.300 sq. mi.; pop. 39,790), Greece, the largest of the IONIAN ISLANDS. It has an irregular coastline and is largely mountainous, rising to c.5,315 ft. at Mt. Aenos, which in ancient times was crowned by a temple to Zeus. Argostoli, a port, is its main town and exports the local products. Sheep raising and fishing are important occupations. An ally of Athens in the Peloponnesian War and later a member of the Aetolian League, Cephalonia fell under Roman rule in 189 B.C. After the division of the Roman Empire, it was held by Byzantium until its occupation (1126) by Venice. It subsequently was ruled by several Italian families, was seized by the Turks (1479), and was ceded (1499) to Venice, which held it until the Treaty of Campo Formio (1797). Its subsequent history is that of the Ionian Islands. In 1953 the island was devastated by earthquakes of such force that Mt. Aenos was split.

cephalopod: see MOLLUSK.

Cephalus (sĕ'fălŭs), in Greek mythology, husband of Procris. Cephalus and Procris swore eternal fidelity, but Eos, who had fallen in love with Cephalus, persuaded him to test Procris. Cephalus disguised himself and offered to pay her to commit adultery. When Procris yielded, Cephalus angrily deserted her. Later they were reconciled; but then Procris became suspicious and followed Cephalus one night while he was hunting. Mistaking Procris for an animal, he killed her. Cephalus wandered for many years but was unable to escape his grief. Finally he leaped to his death from a precipice.

Cephas (sē'fŭs), Jesus' nickname for St. Peter.

Cepheus, in astronomy, constellation of the Northern Hemisphere, lying partly in the Milky Way on the side of the pole star diametrically opposite Ursa Major. It is an inconspicuous constellation; lines connecting the principal stars form a rough square and an isosceles triangle with one side of the square as its base. Notable stars in the constellation are a deep red star called by Sir William Herschel the "garnet" star and two double stars, one of which is also a variable star. From this variable star (visible to the naked eye) a class of stars, the Cepheid variables, derive their name.

Cephisodotus (sĕfĭsŏ'dŭtŭs), Gr. *Kephisodotos*, fl. 4th cent. B.C., two Greek sculptors. The elder, the master and probably the father or the brother of Praxiteles, is noted for the statue *Irene and Plutus* (*Peace and Wealth*). The original was erected on the Areopagus at Athens c.372 B.C. to celebrate the victory of Timotheus over the Spartans. The best copy is in Munich. Cephisodotus the Younger, a son of Praxiteles, continued the Praxitelean tradition into the early 3d cent. B.C.

Cephissus (sĭfĭ'sŭs), Gr. *Kephisos* (kēfēsôs'), name of three Greek rivers. **1** Rising in Mt. Pentelikon and flowing SW past Athens into the Saronic Gulf. **2** Rising in the Patera mts. in Attica and flowing c.17 mi. generally SE into the Saronic Gulf. **3** Rising on the slopes of Mt. Parnassus in Boeotia and flowing c.71 mi. through central Greece into the Euboic Gulf.

Ceram (sērăm'), island (c.7,191 sq. mi.; pop. including offshore islands 720,169), E Indonesia, W of New Guinea, the largest of the Moluccas. Its chief port and town is Wahai. Traversed by a central mountain range rising to more than

10,000 ft., the island is c.210 mi. long and c.40 mi. wide. Its inhabitants are like those of the Celebes. Copra, resin, sago, and fish are the major commercial products. Oil is exploited in the northeast near Bula. Portuguese missionaries were active here in the 16th cent. In the early 17th cent. Dutch trading posts were opened; and until 1949 Ceram was a Dutch possession. Variants of the name are Seran and Serang.

Ceramic Gulf: see CERAMICUS SINUS.

ceramics (sŭră'mĭks) includes all forms of POTTERY, from crude EARTHENWARE to the finest PORCELAIN. The term is especially used for handmade objects, such as figurines, animals, or flowers.

Ceramicus Sinus (sĕrŭmī'kŭs sī'nŭs) or **Ceramic Gulf** (sŭră'mĭk), ancient name of the Gulf of Kos or of Kerme, SW Turkey, an inlet of the Aegean Sea. The celebrated city of Halicarnassus, capital of Cappadocia, was on the gulf.

Cerano, Il: see CRESPI, GIOVANNI BATTISTA.

Ceraunian Mountains (sīrô'nĕùn), coastal range, S Albania, extending c.70 mi. from the Greek border to the Strait of Otranto. It rises to c.6,687 ft. in Mt. Cike and ends in the Linguetta (anc., *Acroceraunia*), a cape. The territory about the mountain range has long been under dispute. The range is sometimes called the Acroceraunian Mts.

Cerberus (sûr'bùrùs) in Greek mythology, many-headed dog with a mane and a tail of snakes; offspring of Typhon and Echidna. He guarded the entrance of HADES. One of the 12 labors of HERCULES was to capture him.

Cerdic (kûr'dĭk, sûr'–), d. 534, traditional founder of the kingdom of Wessex. A Saxon, he and his son Cynry are said to have landed on the southern coast of Hampshire near Wiltshire in 495. Little is certain about him save that later West Saxon kings traced their descent from him through his son Cynry and his grandson Ceawlin.

Cerealis: see CERIALIS.

cerebellum: see BRAIN.

cerebral palsy, congenital disorder affecting the motor nervous system. Its cause is believed to be a developmental fetal defect of the brain or injuries sustained during the birth process. Spasmodic weakness of the extremities, especially the legs, is the most common manifestation. Those more severely affected have difficulty in speech as well, and sometimes difficulty in swallowing. Children with cerebral palsy are usually brighter than they appear; their seeming slowness is often attributable to physical handicap and difficulty of expression. Curare and other muscle relaxants relieve the spasticity only temporarily. Muscle reeducation, speech training, and corrective orthopedic measures can help those afflicted to lead a more normal life.

cerebrospinal meningitis: see MENINGITIS.

cerebrum: see BRAIN.

Ceredo (sĕr'ĭdō), town (pop. 1,387), W W.Va., W of Huntington near the Ky.–Ohio line; founded 1857. Glassware is made here.

Ceres (sĕr'ēz), in Roman religion, goddess of grain; daughter of Saturn and Ops. She was identified by the Romans with the Greek DEMETER. Her worship was connected with that of the earth-goddess and involved not only fertility rites but also rites for the dead. Her chief festival was the Cerealia,

Ceres
(antique sculpture)

celebrated on April 19, and her most famous cult was that of the temple on the Aventine Hill. There is much argument about the origins and nature of her cults.

Ceres (sĕr'ēz), city (pop. 4,406), central Calif., SSE of Modesto, in a fruitgrowing area; inc. 1918. Nearby is the unincorporated village of Ceres Northwest (pop. 1,126).

cereus: see CACTUS.

Cerialis or **Cerealis** (Petillius Cerialis or Petillius Cerealis) (both: sīrēā'lĭs), fl. A.D. 70, Roman general, a partisan of Vespasian against Vitellius. Vespasian sent him in A.D. 70 to put down the revolt of the Gauls and Germans under CIVILIS. In A.D. 71 he went to Britain as governor. Nothing more is known of him after A.D. 74.

Cerignola (chārēnyō'lä), city (estimated pop. 54,205), in Apulia, S Italy. It is a large agricultural center. Nearby, in 1503, the Spanish under Gonzalo Fernández de Córdoba defeated the French under Louis XII (see ITALIAN WARS).

Cerinthus (sĭrĭn'thùs), fl. A.D. c.100?, an Ephesian religious leader, possibly of Jewish origin. He held tenets influenced by Gnosticism and similar to those of the Ebionites. He taught that the Christ descended into Jesus at His baptism and left Him again before the Passion.

cerium (sĕr'ēùm) [for the planetoid Ceres], one of the more common metallic elements of the RARE EARTHS (symbol = Ce; for physical constants, see ELEMENT, table) resembling iron in color but much less hard. It is ductile and malleable. It does not tarnish in dry air, but is affected by moisture. When heated it burns with a brilliant flame to form the oxide (ceria) which exhibits incandescence and is used in making lamp mantles (see WELSBACH MANTLE). Certain compounds of cerium are used in medicine, e.g., cerium oxalate, which is commonly employed as an antiemetic in seasickness. The element forms alloys with other metals, the alloy of cerium (70 percent) and iron (30 percent), for example, being used in cigar and gas lighters. Minute particles of this alloy ignite in the air when scratched from the surface of the larger mass. The element is prepared by the electrolysis of the chloride. Recognized in 1803 in the oxide (ceria) as a new metal by M. H. Klaproth and by J. J. Berzelius and Wilhelm Hisinger, it was obtained in a very impure state by C. G. Mosander and by Friedrich Wöhler some 30 years later, and not until 1875 was the nearly pure metal obtained by W. F. Hillebrand and T. H. Norton. Cerium is in group III B of the PERIODIC TABLE.

Cernauti: see CHERNOVTSY, Ukraine.

Cernuda, Luis (lwĕs' thärnōō'dhä), 1904–, Spanish poet. An instructor at the Univ. of Toulouse, he fled Spain after the Spanish civil war. His works include *La realidad y el deseo* [reality and desire] (1936; expanded ed., 1940), a collection of his delicate surrealist verse; and *Oknos el affarero* (1943), a prose lyric. He has also written studies on contemporary Spanish poetry (1957) and on English lyric poetry (1958).

Cernuschi, Henri (chĕrnōō'skē), 1821–96, Italian politician and economist. A strong republican, he was a leader in the Milan revolt of 1848 in support of Garibaldi. In 1850 he went to France, where he became a director of the Bank of France. Cernuschi vigorously advocated BIMETALLISM and is said to have coined the word. His writings include many pamphlets on the subject, notably *Silver Vindicated* (1876).

Cerré, Jean Gabriel (zhä' gäbrēĕl' sĕrä'), 1734–1805, frontiersman and trader in the American Midwest, b. Montreal, Canada. By 1755 he had established a fur-trading post at Kaskaskia, Ill., where for many years he was a prominent and powerful figure. He outfitted many traders and hunters for the Missouri region and maintained close relations with the Indians. The British made efforts to gain his support in the American Revolution, but he allied himself with the patriots and gave George Rogers Clark provisions and financial aid. Later

he moved to St. Louis, where his influence was maintained until his death.

Cerro de Pasco (sĕ'rō dä päs'kō), city (pop. c.19,300), central Peru. At an altitude of 13,973 ft., it is one of the highest cities in the world. It is as bleak and barren as its environs, but the fabulous silver mines, which, according to tradition, were discovered in 1630, have made it world renowned. When silver deposits declined late in the 19th cent., the exploitation of other metals, chiefly copper, again made Cerro de Pasco Peru's leading mining center. From the nearby Minasraga mines comes about 80 percent of the world's supply of vanadium. A railroad and highway connect the city with Lima.

Cerro Gordo, village (pop. 1,067), central Ill., E of Decatur, in a farm area; inc. 1873.

Cerro Gordo (sĕ'rô gôr'dhō), mountain pass, E Mexico, on the road between Veracruz and Jalapa, site of a decisive battle (April 17–18, 1847) of the Mexican War. Santa Anna, having established himself firmly at and behind the pass, attempted to halt the advance of Gen. Winfield SCOTT from Veracruz to Mexico city. Though the Mexicans thought their position impregnable, the Americans were able to rout the weak left flank and take the pass from the rear. Santa Anna was defeated, and Jalapa occupied. Capt. Robert E. Lee (who scouted out a route for the flanking movement) and Lt. U. S. Grant took part in the battle.

Certosa di Pavia (chärtō'zä dē pävē'ä), former Carthusian abbey of Pavia. One of the most magnificent of all monastic structures, it has been maintained as a national monument since 1866. The church forming its nucleus was begun in the style of the Italian Gothic in 1396 by Gian Galeazzo Visconti, duke of Milan. Hardly more than the nave was executed in this style, since the Renaissance, diffusing its new taste, quickly dominated the design of the edifice. The facade seems to have been commenced in 1491 by a group of architects

Steel engraving of the Battle of Cerro Gordo.

and sculptors under the leadership of Giovanni Antonio Amadeo; it was finished in the mid-16th cent. Built of rich marbles and profusely ornamented with fine sculptural decorations, it is one of the masterpieces of Renaissance decorative design. The two large arcaded cloisters are of richly ornamented terra cotta. The main choir was badly damaged in the Second World War but was restored between 1953 and 1959.

cerussite (sĕr′ŭsīt), colorless to white or gray mineral, sometimes yellowish or greenish, transparent to opaque, very brittle, crystallizing in the orthorhombic system and occurring also in granular and massive form. It is a carbonate of lead formed by the action of carbonate and bicarbonate solutions on galena. It is an important ore of lead widely distributed throughout Europe and the United States and found associated with galena and other lead minerals.

Cervantes Saavedra, Miguel de (sûrvăn′tēs, Span. mēgĕl′ dā thĕrvän′täs sä″ävä′dhrä), 1547–1616, Spanish novelist, dramatist, and poet, author of *Don Quixote de la Mancha*, b. Alcalá de Henares. Little is known of his youth. He went to Italy in

Miguel de Cervantes
Saavedra

1569, enlisted (1570) in the army, and fought in the naval battle of Lepanto (1571), receiving a wound that permanently crippled his left arm. While returning to Spain in 1575 he was captured by Barbary pirates and was sold as a slave, eventually becoming the property of the viceroy of Algiers. He was ransomed in 1580, at a cost that brought financial ruin to his family and to himself. As a government purchasing agent in Seville (1588–97), he proved less than successful; his unbusinesslike methods resulted in deficits, and he was several times imprisoned. His first published work was an effusive pastoral romance in prose and verse, *La Galatea* (1585). Between 1582 and 1587 he wrote more than 20 plays, only two of which survive. He was 58 at the publication of Part I of his masterpiece, *Don Quixote* (1605; Part II, 1615). As a superb burlesque of the popular romances of chivalry, *Don Quixote* was an immediate success; a spurious Part II was published in 1614, probably spurring Cervantes on

to completion of the work. Later generations have sometimes seen *Don Quixote* as a satire on unrealistic extremism, an exposition of the mishaps of idealism in a corrupt world, or a plea for widespread reform. Regardless of its major emphasis, the work gave to the world an unforgettable description of the transforming power of illusion, and it had an indelible effect on the development of the European novel. In it Don Quixote, a country gentleman who has read too many chivalric romances, and the peasant Sancho Panza, as his squire, set forth on a series of extravagant adventures. The whole fabric of 16th-century Spanish society is laid out with piercing yet sympathetic insight, and the addled idealism of Don Quixote and the earthy acquisitiveness of Sancho serve as catalysts for incidents humorous and pathetic. The contrast of its characters, the excellence of its tales, and its great portrayal of human nature have contributed to the enduring influence of *Don Quixote*. In later years Cervantes wrote other works of fiction, including *Novelas ejemplares* (1613), 12 original tales of piracy, gypsies, and human passions, drawn from his own experience and molded by his mature craftsmanship. Some of these stories alone suffice to prove him one of the great literary masters. The notable translation of *Don Quixote* is that by Samuel Putnam (1949). See studies by A. F. Calvert (1905), James Fitzmaurice-Kelly (1913), Rudolph Schevill (1919), and A. F. G. Bell (1947).

Cervera y Topete, Pascual (päskwäl′ thĕrvä′rä ē tōpä′tä), 1839–1909, Spanish admiral. When the SPANISH-AMERICAN WAR began (1898), he was given command of the Atlantic fleet. He reached the harbor of Santiago de Cuba, where he was blockaded by the American fleet from May until July 3. Then, in an attempt to run the blockade, he was utterly defeated and captured. After his release he was tried and absolved from responsibility for the disaster.

Cervetri: see CAERE.

Cervin, Mont, or **Monte Cervino:** see MATTERHORN.

Cerynean hind (sĕrĭnē′ŭn), in Greek mythology, golden-horned hind sacred to Artemis. The fourth labor of Hercules was to capture the hind.

Cesalpino, Andrea: see CAESALPINUS, ANDREAS.

Cesarean section: see CAESAREAN SECTION.

Cesari, Giuseppe, Cavaliere d'Arpino (jōōzĕp′pä chä′zärē kävälyä′rä därpē′nō), 1568–1640, Italian late mannerist painter. Cesari's best works are the frescoes in the Capitol and in the Borghese Chapel, Church of Santa Maria Maggiore, Rome. Other works are *Adam and Eve Expelled from Paradise* (Louvre); a self-portrait (Uffizi); and *Perseus and Andromeda* (Metropolitan Mus.).

Cesena (chāzā′nä), city (estimated pop. 76,133), in Emilia-Romagna, N central Italy. Now primarily an agricultural center, it flourished (1379–1465) under the MALATESTA family, who built the beautiful library (now containing almost 400 manuscripts) and the cathedral.

Cesis (tsā′sĕs, -zēz), Ger. *Wenden* (vĕn′dŭn), town (pop. c.13,900), N Latvian SSR. It is an agricultural market town. Founded in 1209, it was the seat of the Livonian Knights until it passed to combined Lithuania-Poland in 1561. Attacked (1577) by Ivan the Terrible, the fortress was blown up by its own garrison. Cesis went to Sweden in 1629, to Russia in 1721. Here, in 1919, the Latvians defeated a German free corps under Rüdiger von der Goltz. Ancient castles give the town a romantic air. Variant spellings are Tsesis and Zehsis.

cesium (sē'zēŭm) [from Latin,=bluish-gray], rare, silver-white, soft-as-wax, metallic element [symbol=Cs; for physical constants, see ELEMENT, table], most active of the metals. It tarnishes so quickly and actively in air that it must be kept in kerosene. Cesium is in group I A of the PERIODIC TABLE. It is a member of the ALKALI METALS, resembling especially rubidium and potassium and forming similar compounds—with bromine, chlorine, and iodine and with the sulphate, carbonate, and nitrate radicals. It reacts with water to form a hydroxide which is a very strong BASE. Because of its chemical activity, cesium is never found free in nature but is always combined with other elements in compounds. It is a constituent of pollux, or pollucite, a rare mineral occurring in the United States in Maine and on the island of Elba. Combined with chlorine as a chloride, it is widely distributed—but in minute quantities—in mineral springs. The element is prepared by electrolysis of a fused cyanide out of contact with air. It is used in radio tubes and the electric eye. In 1860 Bunsen and Kirchhoff discovered the element (the first to be discovered by the use of the SPECTROSCOPE) and named it for the two bright blue lines of its spectrum.

Ceska Lipa, Czech *Česká Lípa* (both: chě'skä lē'pä), Ger: *Böhmisch-Leipa* (bū'mĭsh-lī'pä), city (pop. c.12,900), in N Bohemia, Czechoslovakia. A railway junction, it manufactures railroad cars, mining equipment, and electrical instruments. The city has an old castle and an Augustinian monastery.

Ceske Budejovice: see BUDWEIS.

Cesky Les: see BOHEMIAN FOREST.

Cesky Tesin: see TESCHEN.

Céspedes, Carlos Manuel de (kär'lōs mänwĕl' dā sā'spädhäs), 1819–74, Cuban revolutionist, b. Bayamo. He completed his education in Spain and there took part (1843) in a revolution led by Juan Prim. On returning (1868) to Cuba he raised the standard of revolt by proclaiming the demands of Cuban liberals. The TEN YEARS WAR followed. He was elected president by the revolutionists (1869), but other leaders, notably Ignacio Agramonte, disagreed with him, discontent increased, and he was deposed (1873). He was killed, probably by Spanish soldiers.

Céspedes, Carlos Manuel de, 1871–1939, president of Cuba (1933), b. New York city; son of Carlos Manuel de Céspedes (1819–74). He actively participated in the revolution of 1895 and the Spanish-American War. When Gerardo MACHADO was overthrown in Aug., 1933, Céspedes became provisional president, but was forced to resign after a coup (Sept. 5) by a student junta supporting Ramón GRAU SAN MARTÍN.

Céspedes, Pablo de (pä'blō dā thäs'pädhäs), 1538–1608, Spanish artist, poet, and scholar. He studied for the priesthood and subsequently studied painting with Federigo Zuccaro in Rome. There he spent some 20 years and won a considerable reputation as painter, architect, and sculptor. On his return to Spain in 1577 he was appointed canon of the Córdoba Cathedral, where the best of his surviving works remain, including his famous *Last Supper*. He was the author of a comparison of ancient and modern painting, of a work on the Córdoba Cathedral, and of treatises on architecture.

cesspool, cistern dug or built to receive sewage. Cesspools may be of watertight construction or of the leaching type and in either case must be emptied periodically. When watertight they should not be located nearer than 200 ft. from any surface well or spring or less than 60 ft. from any cistern or drinking-water supply. The vault or pit should be kept as dark as possible, and the sides should extend sufficiently above the ground to prevent the access of vermin or small animals. It should also be flyproof. Cesspools called septic tanks are sometimes connected with a drain through which the liquid flows into adjoining ground, while the solid sewage is retained and decomposed by anaerobic bacteria. A leaching cesspool is constructed so that its porous sides, ends, and bottom readily allow the liquid material to soak through the ground. Leaching cesspools always represent a danger where wells are used for the water supply.

cestus or **caestus:** see BOXING.

Cetatea-Alba: see BELGOROD-DNESTROVSKY.

Cetewayo, Cetywayo (both: sĕtĭwä'ō, –wī'ō, kĕ–), or **Ketchwayo** (kĕchwī'ō), c.1836–1884, king of the Zulu. Cetewayo gained ascendancy in 1856, when he defeated in battle and killed his younger brother, who was the favorite of their father, Umpanda. On his father's death in 1872 Cetewayo took over. He was determined to resist European advances in his territory, and in Dec., 1878, he rejected British demands that he disband his troops. The British attacked in 1879, and after losing two engagements they utterly defeated Cetewayo at Ulundi. After a period of exile he was reinstated (1883) in rule over part of his former territory. Discredited by his defeats in the eyes of his subjects, Cetewayo was soon driven out of Zululand to die in exile.

Cetinje (tsĕ'tĭnyĕ), town (pop. 9,345), S Montenegro, Yugoslavia, near the Adriatic. It grew around a monastery founded in 1485. Until 1945 it was the capital of Montenegro. The monastery, the burial place of the Montenegrin princes, and the former royal palace (now a museum) remain.

Cette: see SÈTE.

Cetywayo: see CETEWAYO.

Ceuta (sū'tù, Span. thäoō'tä), city (pop. 59,936; 6.5 sq. mi.), Spanish possession, NW Africa, on the Strait of Gibraltar. Built on a Phoenician colony, the city was held by Romans, Vandals, Byzantines, and Arabs (711). Taken by Portugal (the first permanent European conquest in Africa), it passed (1580) to Spain. It has remained Spanish despite several attacks, notably a prolonged siege (1694–1720) by the Sultan Moulay Ismail. Ceuta, with its large harbor and ample wharves, is an important port of call and a fishing port.

Cévennes (sāvĕn'), mountain range, S France, limiting the Massif Central toward the south and east. The Cévennes proper occupy the central section of a mountainous arc (average height 3,000 ft.), swinging generally NE from the Montagne Noire (NE of Toulouse) to Mont Pilat in VIVARAIS (SW of Lyons). Between the Cévennes proper and the Montagne Noire arè the Causses—barren limestone plateaus intersected by deep chasms and ravines. The Loire, Allier, Lot, Tarn, Aveyron, Hérault, Gard, and Ardèche rivers all radiate from the Cévennes or the Causses. Mont Lozère (5,584 ft.) is the highest peak of the Cévennes proper; Mont Mézenc, in Vivarais, rises to 5,753 ft. The cultivation of silkworms and silk manufacture are characteristic industries of the area. Exploitation of coal in the Grand' Combe-Bessèges area has activated industry at Alès, making this area the most progressive in the Cévennes. Intensive sheep raising in the interior has worsened erosion. The population of the Cévennes, then largely Protestant, long resisted the revocation (1685) of the Edict of Nantes (see CAMISARDS).

Ceylon (sēlŏn'), anc. *Taprobane*, island (25,322 sq. mi.; pop. c.10,167,000), in the Indian Ocean, SE of India. Officially named Sri Lanka, Ceylon is an independent state within the British Commonwealth of Nations. Its capital is Colombo. The pear-shaped island is 140 mi. across at its widest

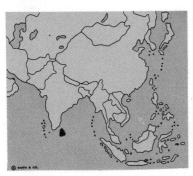

Ceylon location map

point and 270 mi. long. The narrow northern end is almost linked to SE India by ADAM'S BRIDGE, a chain of shoals that are submerged at places but remain an obstacle to navigation. The island comprises a level low-lying plain, which occupies the north and a broad band around the entire coast, and a mountainous section (where once existed large deposits of semiprecious and precious stones) in the south. The mountains rise in several peaks, among them ADAM'S PEAK (7,360 ft.) and Pidurutalagal (8,291 ft.), the highest point on the island. Ceylon has a generally uniform subtropical climate. The average lowland temperature is 80°F. but humidity is high. Rain, largely carried by monsoons, is adequate without irrigation except in the north. The country's economy remains predominantly agricultural, with about 5 million acres under cultivation. Tea and rubber from highland plantations and coconuts from the coastal plain provide the bulk of the island's exports, while rice, fruit, and vegetables are grown for local consumption. Graphite mining is the principal mineral industry, and there are deposits of mica, limestone, and iron ore. Textiles, cement, and varied light manufactures are produced in Ceylon. The island's swift rivers have considerable hydroelectric potential, which is being developed with foreign assistance. Although coastal lagoons provide many sheltered harbors, only S Ceylon lies on the main world shipping routes; the port of Colombo, on which most of the county's railroads and, to some extent, its road system converge, handles most of the foreign trade. After Colombo, the other principal cities are Dehiwala-Mount Lavinia, Jaffna, Kandy, Moratuwa, Galle, and Trincomalee. The population of Ceylon is composed mainly of Singhalese, who are Hinayana Buddhists; Hindu Tamils make up a large minority, and there are smaller groups of Moslem Moors, Burghers (descendants of Dutch and Portuguese colonists), and

Hindu temple in Colombo.

Tea pickers on a Central Ceylon tea estate.

Elephants being washed in the Kandy river.

Eurasians. The most ancient of the inhabitants were probably the ancestors of the Veddas, an aboriginal people (c.3,000) now living in remote mountain areas. They were conquered in the 6th cent. B.C. by the Singhalese, who were originally from N India; the ancient Hindu epic *Ramayana* probably reflects this conquest. The Ceylon chronicle *Mahavamsa* relates the arrival of Vijaya, the first Singhalese king, in 483 B.C. The Singhalese settled in the north and developed an elaborate irrigation system. They founded their capital at ANURADHAPURA, which, after the introduction of Buddhism from India in the 3d cent. B.C., became one of the chief centers of that religion in the world; a slip of the pipal tree under which Buddha attained enlightenment at Buddh Gaya was planted at Anuradhapura. The Temple of the Tooth at KANDY as well as the Dalada Maligawa are sacred Buddhist temples. Buddhism stimulated the fine arts in Ceylon; its classical period was from the 4th to 6th cent. The proximity of Ceylon to S India resulted in many Tamil invasions. The CHOLA of S India conquered Anuradhapura in the early 11th cent. and made POLLONARRUA their capital. The Singhalese soon regained power, but in the 12th cent. a Tamil kingdom arose in the north and the Singhalese were driven to the southwest. Arab traders, drawn by Ceylon's spices, appeared in the country in the 12th and 13th cent.; their descendants are the Moslem Moors. The Portuguese conquered the coastal areas in the early 16th cent. and implanted the Roman Catholic religion. By the mid-17th cent. the Dutch had taken over the Portuguese possessions and the rich spice trade. In 1795 the Dutch possessions were occupied by the British, who made Ceylon a crown colony in 1798. In 1815 the island was brought under one rule for the first time when the central area, previously under the rule of Kandy, was conquered. Under the British, Ceylon was modernized; tea, coffee, and rubber plantations were developed and schools, including a university, were opened. A movement for independence arose in Ceylon during the First World War. The constitution of 1931 granted uni-

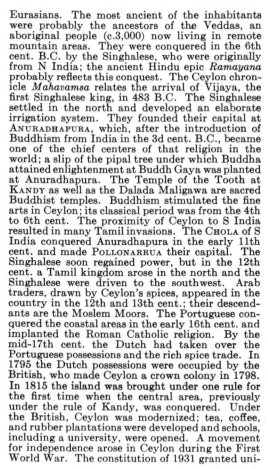

Kandyan performing a native ritualistic dance.

Worshippers in the ancient temple of Pollonarrua.

versal adult suffrage to the Ceylonese, but demands for independence continued and in 1946 a more liberal constitution was enacted. Full independence was finally granted to the island on Feb. 4, 1948, with dominion status in the British Commonwealth. In 1950 delegates of eight countries of the British Commonwealth of Nations met in Colombo and adopted the Colombo Plan. for economic aid to S and SE Asia. Sir John Kotelawala was premier (1953–56) until the defeat of his United National party. The Ceylon Freedom party won, and S. W. R. D. Bandaranaike became premier. Riots in 1958 between Singhalese and the Tamil minority over demands by the Tamils for recognition of their language as the alternate official language and the establishment of a separate Tamil state under a federal system resulted in severe loss of life. In Sept., 1959, Prime Minister S. W. R. D. Bandaranaike was assassinated, and in 1960 his widow, Sirimavo Bandaranaike, became prime minister. The Federal party of the Tamils was outlawed in 1961 following new disorders. Early in 1962 the government announced a plot to assassinate Mrs. Bandaranaike; high military and police officers were quickly arrested. Ceylon nationalized (1962) certain Western business facilities and became involved in a dispute with the United States and Great Britain over compensation. In international affairs Ceylon remains neutral, receiving aid from the West, mainland China, and the USSR. See Harry Williams, *Ceylon* (1951); Sydney D. Bailey, *Ceylon* (1952); A. J. Tresidder, *Ceylon* (1960); W. H. Wriggins, *Ceylon: Dilemmas of a New Nation* (1960); E. F. C. Ludowyk, *The Story of Ceylon* (1963).

Cézanne, Paul (pôl′ säzän′), 1839–1906, French painter, an outstanding figure in modern art, b. Aix-en-Provence; son of a banker. From early childhood he was friendly with Emile Zola, until the latter developed a scathing characterization of the artist in his novel, *L'Oeuvre* (1886). Cézanne went to Paris in 1861; there he met Pissarro, who was a strong influence in his early development. He divided his time between Provence and the environs of Paris until his retirement to Aix in 1899. Cézanne's early work is marked by a heavy use of the palette knife, from which he created thickly textured and violently deformed shapes and scenes of a fantastic, dreamlike quality. Although these impulsive paintings exhibit few of the features of his later style, they anticipate the expressionistic idiom of the 20th cent. Through Pissarro, he came to know Manet and the impressionist painters. He exhibited at the impressionist show of 1874 but later diverged from the impressionist mode of expression and developed a firmer structure in his paintings. Cézanne did not seek to give a pictorial replica of nature, but rather to find formal visual equivalents. Accenting the vertical, horizontal, and diagonal elements found in nature, he also purified natural shapes into more geometric forms. He developed a new type of spatial pattern. Instead of adhering to the traditional focalized system of perspective, he portrayed objects from shifting viewpoints. He created vibrating surface effects from the play of flat planes against one another and from the subtle transitions of tone and color. Cezanne worked in oil, watercolor, and drawing with equal success. From his hand issued forth controlled but forceful still lifes, landscapes, bathers, and portraits, which have been of fundamental importance for the development of modern art. There are fine collections of his paintings in the Louvre; the Metropolitan Museum and the Museum of Modern Art, New York; and the Barnes Foundation, Merion, Pa. See biographies

Paul Cézanne
(self-portrait)

by Gerstle Mack (1935) and John Rewald (Eng. tr., 1948); studies by Roger Fry (1927) and Meyer Schapiro (1952).

Cf, chemical symbol of the element CALIFORNIUM.

Chaadayev, Piotr Yakovlevich (pyô′tŭr yä′kŭvlyĭvĭch chädä′yĕv), 1794–1856, Russian philosopher. An aristocrat by birth, he was converted to Roman

Catholicism. In 1836 the first of his *Philosophical Letters* appeared in the Moscow *Telegraph*. Its devastating attack on Russian institutions, such as autocracy, the Church, and serfdom, created a sensation. Chaadayev was declared insane and was confined to his home. His vigorous writings helped clarify the basic opposition of the SLAVOPHILES AND WESTERNIZERS.

Chabanel, Noël (St. Noël Chabanel) (nôĕl' shäbä-nĕl'), 1613–49, French missionary in North America, a Jesuit. He entered the Society of Jesus in 1630, came as a missionary to New France in 1643, and labored among the Huron Indians. He was captured by the Iroquois and put to death. Chabanel was canonized in 1930 with other missionaries (including Isaac Jogues and Jean de Brébeuf) and laymen. As a group they are known as the Martyrs of North America. Feast: Sept. 26 or (among the Jesuits) March 16.

Chabannes, Antoine de, comte de Dammartin (ätwän' dù shäbän' kõt' dù dämmärtē'), c.1411–1488, French general in the Hundred Years War; brother of Jacques de Chabannes. He served with Joan of Arc, fought as a captain of ÉCORCHEURS, and took part in the PRAGUERIE revolt (1440). Pardoned by Charles VII, he was appointed to various offices and presided over the committee that procured the conviction of Jacques Cœur. After the accession (1461) of Louis XI he was imprisoned. He escaped and joined (1465) the League of the Public Weal against LOUIS XI, but was pardoned once more and became one of the king's most trusted officers.

Chabannes, Jacques de (zhäk'), c.1400–1453, French general in the Hundred Years War. With his brother, Antoine de Chabannes, he served under Joan of Arc and took part in the PRAGUERIE revolt (1440). Pardoned by Charles VII, he distinguished himself in the expulsion of the English from Normandy and Guienne.

Chabas, Paul Émile (pôl' ämel' shäbäs'), 1869–1937, French academic painter. He is remembered chiefly for his nude, *September Morn*, which created a sensation when it was exhibited in 1912. It was sold to a Russian, hidden during the Russian Revolution, and in 1935 rediscovered in a private collection in Paris. It is now owned by the Metropolitan Museum.

Chablis (shäblē'), village (estimated pop. 1,655), Yonne dept., central France, in BURGUNDY. It is famous for the WINE named for it. There is a remarkable early Gothic church (12th cent.).

Chabot, Philippe de (fēlēp' dù shäbō'), also known as **Amiral de Brion** (brēō), 1480–1543, count of Charny and of Buzançois, admiral of France. After a successful campaign (1536) in Savoy and Piedmont, he was, through the intrigues of Anne, duc de MONTMORENCY, accused and convicted (1541) of misconduct in office, but he was pardoned by King Francis I. Chabot was instrumental in arranging the voyages of Giovanni da VERRAZANO.

Chabrias (kā'brēŭs), d. 357 B.C., Athenian general, one of the principal commanders of the Delian League. He was a professional soldier and served not only for Athens, but also for Evagoras of Cyprus and the kings of Egypt in their wars on the Persians. He was particularly renowned for the naval victory of the Athenians over Sparta at Naxos in 376 B.C. He was involved with Callistratus in the negotiations allowing the Thebans to occupy the Athenian city of Oropus, but he was acquitted of blame in 366. He was killed on the punitive expedition sent against Chios when Chios tried to withdraw from the Delian League.

Chabrier, Alexis Emmanuel (älĕksēs' ĕmänuĕl' shäbrēä'), 1841–94, French composer. His best-known works are an orchestral rhapsody, *España* (1883); an opera, *Le Roi malgré lui* (1887); and piano pieces. His vivid sense of harmonic and orchestral color and his musical drollery and humor were admired by the French impressionists and by Satie.

Chaco (chä'kō) or **Gran Chaco** (grän), extensive lowland plain, central S America, sparsely populated, divided among Paraguay, Bolivia, and Argentina. Some of the highest temperatures in the southern continent are reached here. To the north of the Pilcomayo river and to the west of the Paraguay is the section known as the Chaco Boreal, most of which belongs to Paraguay. This is arid desert land, dotted with swamps in the rainy season and with stretches of dense forest in which the QUEBRACHO abounds. The Chaco Central, in Argentina S of the Pilcomayo, has much the same aspect. The plains grow increasingly arid toward the west, but the eastern part—the Chaco Austral and the region W of the Paraguay river—is the only habitable section of the Chaco. The discovery of oil in a narrow strip of the barren section of the Chaco Boreal, at the foot of the Bolivian Andes, precipitated the **Chaco War**, 1932–35, between Bolivia and Paraguay. This territory of the Chaco had been disputed since 1810. Technically the Chaco was intended to be part of Bolivia since it had been part of the *audiencia* of Charcas, but Bolivia paid little attention to this wasteland and Paraguayan settlers opened up the region while Paraguayan soldiers pushed back the wild Indians. Thousands of Paraguayan colonists brought wealth to Paraguay by gathering quebracho and raising cattle. Paraguay was not disposed to give up the lands, and Bolivia needed access to the Paraguay river to ship oil to the sea; a clash was inevitable and disastrous. Over 100,000 lives were lost, and the war was concluded in 1935 only when both sides were exhausted. After three years of negotiation following the end of hostilities, the six mediating nations (Argentina, Brazil, Chile, Peru, Uruguay, and the United States) presented a treaty which was signed by Paraguay and Bolivia in 1938. Three quarters of the disputed Chaco Boreal went to Paraguay; at the same time Bolivia was granted a corridor to the Paraguay river, the privilege of using Puerto Casado, and the right to construct a Bolivian port.

Chaco Canyon National Monument: see NATIONAL PARKS AND MONUMENTS (table).

Chad (chăd, chäd), Fr. *Tchad*, republic (c.496,000 sq. mi.; pop. c.2,800,000), N central Africa. The capital is Fort Lamy. A landlocked country, it borders the Central African Republic on the south, the Republic of Sudan on the east, Libya on the north, and Cameroon, Niger, and Nigeria on the west. S Chad is wooded savanna—rich in wild animals—which becomes brush country near Lake Chad, whence the country takes its name. The

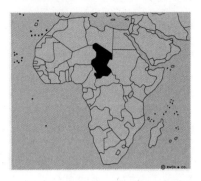

Chad
location map

north is a desert that merges with the S Sahara. The economy is agricultural and pastoral, with cotton and cattle the chief exports. Sodium is the only mineral export, but tungsten and other minerals have been found in the arid Tibesti mts. in the north. Other products include rice, ivory, hides, ostrich feathers, and dates. Chad's isolation and the absence of transportation facilities hamper trade and economic development. In the north the population is mainly Arab and the Moslem Fulani, Hausa, and Wadians. In the south are Bantu peoples, including Saras, Massa, and Moudang; they are mainly animists but some are Christians. The official language of Chad is French. Arab traders penetrated the region of Chad in the 7th cent., and Arab historians mention the area. The invaders weakened the Negro Wadai and Bagirmi empires, and some tribes were converted to Islam. British explorers first entered the area in 1822. The French advanced into the region in 1890, and in 1900 they defeated Rabah Amoney, the last of the Africans to oppose French conquest. In 1913 the area was organized as a colony, and although part of French Equatorial Africa, it remained under military rule. Chad was later linked administratively with Ubangi-Shari. In 1920, however, it again became a separate colony. Chad became a republic in the French Community in 1958. Under the leadership of François Tombalbaye, the first premier and president of the republic, Chad attained full independence on Aug. 11, 1960; it was admitted to the UN the following month. Chad is a member of the Union of Central African Republics and of the African-Malagasy Union. It also belongs to the so-called Monrovia group of African states. See Virginia Thompson and Richard Aldoff, *The Emerging States of French Equatorial Africa* (1960).

Chad, Lake (chăd, chäd), central Africa. It is on the NE border of Nigeria, but the greater part lies in the Republic of Chad. The size varies from 5,000 to 9,000 sq. mi. according to season, but the lake was formerly much larger. Rumors of the existence of the lake reached the ancient Greeks, but it was not visited by Europeans until the early 19th cent. The Shari river is the chief affluent of Lake Chad, which has no outlets.

Chadbourn, town (pop. 2,323), S N.C., WNW of Wilmington near the S.C. line; inc. 1883. It is a marketing and shipping center in a tobacco and strawberry area.

Chadderton, urban district (pop. 32,494), Lancashire, N England, near Manchester. In the cotton-mill district, it manufactures pharmaceuticals.

Chadds Ford: see BRANDYWINE, BATTLE OF.

Chadron (shă′drŭn), city (pop. 5,079), co. seat of Dawes co., NW Nebr., near the S.Dak. line N of Alliance, in a livestock and grain area of the Great Plains region; founded 1885. It is a railroad division point and manufactures flour, feed, and milk products. A state teachers college is here. The Museum of the Fur Trade is nearby.

Chadwick, Sir Edwin, 1800–1890, English social reformer. For many years an assistant to Jeremy Bentham, Chadwick applied his utilitarianism to the reform (1834) of the Poor Law and to the development of public-health measures. He was largely responsible for the passage of the Public Health Act of 1848 which established a board of health. His chief writings were collected and edited by B. W. Richardson as *The Health of Nations* (1887). See Samuel Finer, *The Life and Times of Sir Edwin Chadwick* (1952).

Chadwick, Florence May, 1918–, American distance swimmer, b. San Diego, Calif. She began swimming at the age of six, and four years later she swam the San Diego Bay Channel, the first child to do so. On Aug. 8, 1950, she broke Gertrude Ederle's 24-year record for English Channel swims by women. Florence Chadwick covered the 20 miles from France to England in 13 hr. 20 min. She also swam (Sept., 1951) from England to France, the first woman to swim the channel in both directions. In 1952 she became the first woman to swim the 21-mile Catalina Channel off Long Beach, Calif.

Chadwick, George Whitefield, 1854–1931, American composer, b. Lowell, Mass., studied in Germany. In 1882 he joined the faculty of the New England Conservatory of Music, of which he was director from 1897 until his death. His chief compositions are the overtures *The Miller's Daughter* (1884) and *Rip Van Winkle* (1879); the opera *Judith* (1901); and especially *Symphonic Sketches* (1908) and the song *A Ballad of Trees and the Master* (1899). Though much influenced by German music, Chadwick's best works have been described as having Yankee humor and impudence.

Chadwick, Sir James, 1891–, English physicist,

Sir James Chadwick

grad. Manchester Univ., 1908. He worked at Manchester under Ernest Rutherford on radioactivity. He was assistant director of radioactive research in the Cavendish Laboratory, Cambridge (1923–35), professor at the Univ. of Liverpool (1935–48), and master of Gonville and Caius College, Cambridge (1948–58). For his discovery of the NEUTRON in 1932 he received the 1935 Nobel Prize in Physics. He was knighted in 1945.

Chadwick, Lynn, 1914–, English sculptor. After studying architecture, he began his career as a sculptor in 1945, at first making wire constructions. In 1955 he turned to triangular works of greater mass, largely abstract but with anthropomorphic suggestions. Several of his works are in the Museum of Modern Art, New York.

Chaeronea (kĕrŭnē'ŭ), ancient town of Boeotia, Greece, in the Cephissus river valley and WNW of Thebes. The Athenians and Thebans were defeated here (338 B.C.) by the Macedonians under Philip II. Here Sulla defeated (86 B.C.) the army of Mithridates VI of Pontus under Archelaus. It was the birthplace of Plutarch.

Chaffee (chă'fē), city (pop. 2,862), SE Mo., SW of Cape Girardeau, in a farm and timber area; laid out 1837, inc. 1906. It is a trade center, with small industries.

chaffinch: see FINCH.

Chagall, Marc (märk' shŭgäl'), 1889–, Russian painter, whose name is also spelled Shagall. In 1907 he left his native Vitebsk for St. Petersburg, where he studied under L. N. Bakst. Going to Paris in 1910, he began to assimilate cubist characteristics into his expressionistic style. He is considered a forerunner of surrealism. After serving in the First World War, he was for a time minister of arts of Vitebsk prov. In 1922 Chagall returned to France, where he has spent most of his life, except for the years of the Second World War, when he stayed in the United States. His main subject matter is drawn from Jewish life and folklore; in some of his pictures he employs flower and animal symbols. Another favorite theme is that of his first wife, Bella, with whom the artist is often lyrically represented floating through the air. Among his better known works are *I and the Village* (1911; Mus. of Modern Art, New York) and *The Rabbi of Vitebsk* (Art Inst., Chicago). He designed the sets for the ballets *Aleko* (1942) and *Firebird* (1945). His twelve stained glass windows, symbolizing the tribes of Israel, were exhibited to enthusiastic crowds in Paris and New York city before being installed (1962) in a synagogue in the Hadassah-Hebrew Univ. Medical Center, Jerusalem. Much of Chagall's work is rendered with an extraordinary formal inventiveness and a deceptive naïveté. His autobiography, *Ma Vie* (1931), was first published in Paris and translated into many languages (Eng. tr., 1960). Chagall has illustrated numerous books, including *Illustrations for the Bible* (with an appreciation by Meyer Schapiro, 1956). See Bella Chagall and Marc Chagall, *Burning Lights* (Eng. tr., 1962); study by J. J. Sweeney (1946).

Chagrin Falls (shŭgrĭn', shăg'rĭn), residential village (pop. 3,458), NE Ohio, on the Chagrin river and SE of Cleveland; founded c.1834. Pharmaceuticals and paper bags are made here.

Chahar (chä'här), Mandarin *Ch'a-ha-erh*, former province (109,527 sq. mi.), N China. In 1952 it was abolished as a province, and its region was mainly included in the Inner Mongolian Autonomous Region. Changkiakow was the capital of Chahar. The Chinese, who constitute a majority of the population of the Chahar region, are concentrated in the southern tip of the territory, which contains Changkiakow and lies between two sections of the Great Wall. This area, economically the most important, includes the eastern terminus of the main road to the Mongolian People's Republic and is well connected by rail. Kaoliang, wheat, and corn are raised in its fertile loess soil. The rest of the region, mainly inhabited by Mongolian nomads, is a high, almost barren plateau, where livestock raising and animal trapping are the chief economic activities; horses, hides, fur, and wool are exported.

Chaillé-Long, Charles (shäyā'-lông'), 1842–1917, American soldier and African explorer, b. Princess Anne, Md. After serving in the Civil War, he was commissioned (1869) in the Egyptian army under Gen. C. G. Gordon. Chaillé-Long explored the Victoria Nile and was awarded a medal by the American Geographical Society. In 1875 he crossed the Congo-Nile divide to the Bahr-el-Ghazal re-

Fish in the Street by Marc Chagall.

gion. He returned to America, graduated from the Columbia Law School, and became (1887–89) consul general and secretary to the legation in Korea. His travel narratives in English include *The Three Prophets* (1884), *My Life in Four Continents* (1912), and *Central Africa: Naked Truths of Naked People* (1876). Among his writings in French are *Les Sources du Nil* (1891), *L'Égypte et ses provinces perdues* (1892), and *La Corée ou Tschösen* (1894).

Chaillu, Paul Belloni du: see DU CHAILLU.

Chain, Ernst Boris, 1906–, English biochemist, b. Berlin, Germany. In 1933 he left Germany and went to England, where he conducted research at Cambridge from 1933 to 1935 and at Oxford from 1935; he lectured (1936–48) in chemical pathology at Oxford. In 1951 he became director of the International Research Centre for Chemical Microbiology, Istituto Superiore de Sanità, Rome. He was professor of biochemistry at the Univ. of London from 1961. For his work on PENICILLIN, Chain shared with Sir Alexander FLEMING and Sir Howard FLOREY the 1945 Nobel Prize in Physiology and Medicine.

chain, flexible series of connected links used in various ways, especially for the transmission of motive power, for hoisting (see PULLEY), and for securing or fastening. Commonly, mechanical energy from a motor or other source applied to a sprocket wheel is conveyed by means of an endless chain to another sprocket wheel for driving a mechanism. Examples of such an arrangement are found in bicycles, motorcycles, and conveyor belts. The chain in this application is so designed that each consecutive link fits over a sprocket, the distance between links being called the pitch. The relative speed of the wheels varies according to the number of sprockets on each. Types of chains for the transmission of power include the detachable-link chain, whose members are simple rectangles with connecting hooks; the pintle chain, in which the links have a round bar (pintle) that fits into two sockets of the next link and is held in place by a cotter pin; the block chain, comprising blocks of metal connected by side plates; and others, which incorporate roller bearings at their points of connection. The coil chains used in hoists and for locking or fastening purposes are of the open-link type, comprising solid interlocked rings, or of the stud-link type, in which a stud, or bar, across the link keeps the chain from kinking. For commercial use chains of wrought iron, mild steel, or cast steel are commonly employed.

chain gang: see CONVICT LABOR.

chain store: see STORE.

Chaka (shä'kä), d. 1828, paramount chief (1818–28) of the Zulus. He organized an army of some 40,000 tribesmen, and after reducing many enemy tribes to vassalage, he subjugated all of what is now Natal. Chaka was murdered by his half brother, Dingaan. His name is also spelled Shaka.

Chalcedon (kăl'sĭdŏn, –dŭn, kălsē'dŭn), ancient Greek city of Asia Minor, on the Bosporus. It was founded by Megara on the shore opposite Byzantium in 685 B.C. Taken by the Persians and recovered by the Greeks, it was later a possession of the kings of Bithynia, from whom it passed (A.D. 74) to Rome. The Council of Chalcedon was held here in A.D. 451. The site is now occupied by suburbs of Istanbul.

Chalcedon, Council of, fourth ecumenical council, convened in 451 by Pulcheria and Marcian, empress and emperor of the East, to settle the scandal of the Robber Synod and to discuss Eutychianism (see EUTYCHES). It deposed the principals in the Robber Synod and destroyed the Eutychian party. Its great work, however, was its *Definition* regarding the nature and person of Jesus Christ. Based upon the formulation given by Pope St. Leo I in his famous *Tome* to Flavian, it declared (contrary to the view taken by Eutychianism) that the sec-

ond Person of the Trinity has two distinct natures —one divine and one human. It was also proclaimed that these two natures exist inseparably in one person. This definition became the test of orthodoxy in East and West. The Roman Catholic Church has never admitted a decree of the council that made the patriarch of Constantinople single head of the Church in Eastern Europe.

chalcedony (kălsĕ'dŭnē, kălsŭdō'nē) [from Chalcedon], form of quartz the crystals of which are so minute that its crystalline structure cannot be seen except with the aid of a microscope. Chalcedony has a waxy luster and is translucent to transparent. The name chalcedony is applied more specifically to white, gray, blue, and brown varieties. Some varieties differing in color because of the presence of impurities are AGATE, BLOODSTONE, CARNELIAN, CHRYSOPRASE, JASPER, ONYX, SARD, and SARDONYX.

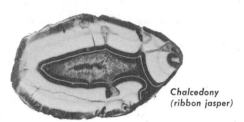

Chalcedony (ribbon jasper)

Chalcidice (kălsĭ'dĭsē), Gr. *Chalkidike* or *Khalkidiki* (both: khälkēdhē'kē), peninsula, NE Greece, projecting into the Aegean Sea from SE Macedonia. Its southern extremity terminates in three peninsulas: Kassandra (anc. Gr. *Pallene*) in the west, Sithonia in the center, and ATHOS in the east. The Athos peninsula was cut by a canal built by Xerxes I. OLYNTHUS and POTIDAEA were the chief towns in antiquity; Polygyros is the present administrative center. The region is largely mountainous, dry, and agricultural. Olive oil, wine, wheat, and tobacco are its chief products. In antiquity it was famous for its timber. It was named for CHALCIS, which established colonies here in the 7th and 6th cent. B.C. In the 4th cent. B.C., Chalcidice was conquered by Philip II of Macedon, and in the 2nd cent. B.C. by Rome. The subsequent history of Chalcidice is essentially that of the city of SALONICA.

Chalcis (kăl'sĭs), Gr. *Chalkis* or *Khalkis* (both: khälkēs'), city (pop. 24,745), Greece, on the island of EUBOEA. It trades in local products. The chief city of ancient Euboea, it was settled by the Ionians and early in its history it became a commercial and colonizing center. It established (8th–7th cent. B.C.) colonies on the Chalcidice peninsula and in Sicily. Chalcis was subdued by Athens (c.506 B.C.) and led the revolt of Euboea against Athens in 446 B.C. Again defeated, it came under Athenian rule until 411 B.C. In 338 B.C. it passed to Macedonia. Aristotle died here. In succeeding centuries it was used as a base for the invasion of Greece. In the Middle Ages it was named Negropont by the Venetians, who occupied it in 1209. It passed to the Turks in 1470. There are several medieval buildings erected by the Venetians and the Turks.

Chalcol (kăl'kŏl), the same as CALCOL.

Chalcopyrite

chalcopyrite (kăl″kŭpĭ′rīt, kăl′kōpĭ′rīt) or **copper pyrites** (pīrĭ′tēz, pŭ–), brass-yellow mineral with irridescent and black streaks. It is a sulphide of copper and iron, sometimes containing gold and silver and also selenium and thallium. It crystallizes in the tetragonal system but is usually found in the massive form. Chalcopyrite is of primary origin and occurs in igneous and metamorphic rock. It is an important ore of copper and is widely distributed in the United States, Canada, South America, Africa, and Europe.

Chaldaea or **Chaldea** (both: kăldē′ů), properly the southernmost portion of the valley of the Tigris and the Euphrates. Sometimes it is extended to include Babylonia and thus comprises all S Mesopotamia, as in the Bible (e.g., Gen. 11.28; Jer. 50.10). The Chaldaeans were a Semitic people who first came into southern Babylonia c.1000 B.C. With the death of Assur-bani-pal (626), Nabopolassar seized the throne and established a new Babylonian or Chaldaean empire. The empire flourished under Nabopolassar's son Nebuchadnezzar II, but it declined rapidly thereafter and came to an end when Babylon fell to Cyrus the Great in 539 B.C. The study of astronomy and astrology

Royal family (ancient clay tablet found in Chaldaea).

was developed in this period, and Chaldaea came to mean simply "astrologer," as in Dan. 1.4 and among the Romans. The term is also understood in the Bible to mean Aramaean.

Chaldean rite: see NESTORIAN CHURCH.

Chaldee (kăldē′), term erroneously applied to bib-

lical Aramaic. The Chaldeans in fact spoke the same language as the Babylonians and Assyrians, i.e., Akkadian.

Chaleur Bay (shŭlŏŏr′), inlet of the Gulf of St. Lawrence, between New Brunswick and the Gaspé Peninsula, Canada. It is c.85 mi. long and 15 to 25 mi. wide and is a submerged valley of the Restigouche river, which enters at its head. The bay is a famous fishing ground—cod, herring, mackerel, and salmon—and there are many Acadian fishing villages on both coasts. The headlands are high and bold and the scenery is romantic. The bay was discovered and named by Cartier in 1534.

Chalfant, borough (pop. 1,414), SW Pa., SE of Pittsburgh; inc. 1910.

Chalfont (chôl′fŏnt″, chäl′–), borough (pop. 1,140), SE Pa., SW of Doylestown; inc. 1901. Chemicals are among its products. It is the traditional burial place of the Delaware Indian chief Tamanend or Tammany.

Chalfont Saint Giles (chăl′fŭnt sŭnt jĭlz′, chä′fŭnt), village, Buckinghamshire, central England, E of High Wycombe. Here is the cottage in which John Milton lived at the time of the great plague.

Chalgrin, Jean François (zhä′ fräswä′ shälgrĕ′), 1739–1811, French architect. He studied under Servandoni and in Italy as a winner of the Grand Prix de Rome (1758). He rebuilt (1777) part of the Church of St. Sulpice in Paris. His most influential work was the Church of St. Philippe-du-Roule, in which he reintroduced a basilica plan to French ecclesiastical architecture. He also enlarged the buildings of the Collège de France and altered the palace of the Luxembourg, after the Revolution, to serve as headquarters for the Directory. In 1806 he was commissioned by Napoleon to design a commemorative arch to the victorious armies of France, and the executed scheme for the ARC DE TRIOMPHE DE L'ÉTOILE was chiefly Chalgrin's, though he died shortly after commencement of the actual construction.

Chalgrove (chăl′grōv), village, Oxfordshire, central England, SE of Oxford. It is memorable for the civil war battle (1643) in which John Hampden was mortally wounded.

Chaliapin, Feodor Ivanovich (fyô′důr ēvä′nůvĭch shŭlyä′pēn), 1873–1938, Russian operatic bass, b. Kazan, of humble parents. He went through years of hardship before he gained notice as a singer in St. Petersburg, then won an international reputation. After the Russian Revolution he was a lauded "artist of the people," but disagreement with the Soviet government caused him to remain outside Russia after 1921, though he maintained stoutly that he was not anti-Soviet. At the Metropolitan he sang first—rather unsuccessfully—in 1907–8 and later—with immense adulation—from 1921 to 1929. His concerts, including popular Russian music, were highly successful everywhere. His tremendous physique, his gusto, and his superb ability as a naturalistic actor were jointed with a powerful and supple voice to make him one of the greatest actor-singers of all time. The role for which he was most famous was Boris in Moussorgsky's *Boris Godunov*, but he also won enormous praise as Ivan the Terrible in Rimsky-Korsakov's *Maid of Pskov*, in the title role of Boito's *Mefistofele*, and as Mephistopheles in Gounod's *Faust*. See his

*Feodor Chaliapin
as Boris Godunov*

autobiographies, *Pages from My Life* (Eng. tr., 1927) and *Man and Mask* (Eng. tr., 1932).

chalice (chă'lĭs) [Latin,=cup], ancient name for a drinking cup, retained for the eucharistic or Communion cup. Celebrated examples are the Great Chalice of Antioch (Syriac), of embossed silver, excavated there in 1910 and attributed to the first century, and an elaborately ornamented chalice found in 1868 at Ardagh, Ireland, and believed to be Celtic work of the 9th or 10th cent. See GRAIL, HOLY.

chalk, calcium carbonate mineral, similar in composition to limestone, but softer. It is characteristically a marine formation and sometimes occurs in great thickness; the chief constituents of these chalk deposits are the shells of minute foraminifera. Chalk has been laid down in all periods of geologic time, but most of the best-known deposits, e.g., the cliffs of the English Channel, date from the Cretaceous period. Chalk is used in the manufacture of putty, plaster, cement, quicklime, mortar, and rubber goods and also for blackboard crayons. Harder forms are used as building stones. Soils containing an excessive proportion of clay are frequently dressed with chalk.

Chalkley, Thomas (chô'klē), 1675–1741, Quaker mariner and missionary preacher, b. England. He made his home after 1701 in Philadelphia, Pa. He traded chiefly with the West Indies, navigating his own ship, and made preaching tours up and down the colonies from New England to the Carolinas and also through England, Scotland, and Wales. His journal (1747), simple in style and elevated in thought, was widely read by many generations of Quakers.

Chalk River, Canadian government research establishment, S Ont., on the south shore of the Ottawa river and W of Ottawa. It is operated by the National Research Council of Canada for the Atomic Energy Control Board.

Challenger expedition, 1872–76, British scientific expedition in charge of Professor C. Wyville Thomson. In the corvette *Challenger* it cruised 68,900 nautical miles, making physical and biological surveys of the Atlantic and Pacific oceans. The results were published in 50 volumes of *Reports* (1880–95). See H. N. Moseley, *A Naturalist on the "Challen-*

ger" (1879); Sir C. Wyville Thomson, *Voyage of the "Challenger"* (1877).

Challoner, Richard (chă'lŭnŭr), 1691–1781, English Roman Catholic prelate. Brought up a Protestant, he became a Roman Catholic in his teens. He was ordained in 1716. In 1730 he returned from Douai to England, where he worked among his coreligionists and was widely known for the number of conversions he made. In 1738 he had to leave England because he published an open reply to an anti-Catholic pamphlet by an Anglican. In 1739 Challoner was appointed coadjutor of the vicar apostolic in London. He was consecrated bishop of Debra *in partibus infidelium* in 1741. The rest of his life he spent working among his people (after 1758 as vicar apostolic) in the face of great difficulties. From 1765 to 1780 a series of efforts was set afoot to molest English Catholics, and Bishop Challoner was involved; in the Gordon riots (1780) he had to flee London for his life. He was an indefatigable writer. He revised the Douay version of the Bible, his revision being the one chiefly used by English-speaking Catholics since. His chief learned works are on English Catholicism since the Reformation; they did much to preserve the memory of English Catholics. He wrote a number of devotional works. Bishop Challoner's translations of the *Imitation of Christ* were standard.

Chalmers, Thomas (chä'mŭrz, chô'-), 1780–1847, Scottish preacher, theologian, and philanthropist, leader of the Free Church of Scotland. His preaching and his interest in philanthropic work during his ministry (1815–23) in Glasgow brought wide recognition. In 1823 Chalmers became professor of moral philosophy at St. Andrews Univ.; in 1828, professor of theology at Edinburgh. His Bridgewater treatise (1833) *On the Adaptation of External Nature to the Moral and Intellectual Constitution of Man* brought him a number of honors. Chalmers took a leading part (1843) in organizing the Free Church of Scotland, formed when, after much friction between Church and state and trouble over patronage, 470 clergymen withdrew from the Established Church. His foresight had planned for the rapid organizing of the Free Church of Scotland, of which he was the first moderator. He was principal (1843–47) of the New College (Free Church) at Edinburgh. His published works fill 34 volumes. See biographies by M. O. W. Oliphant (1893), Adam Philip (1929), and Hugh Watt (1943).

Chalmette National Historical Park: see NATIONAL PARKS AND MONUMENTS (table).

Châlons-sur-Marne (shälŏ'-sür-märn'), city (estimated pop. 40,659), capital of Marne dept., NE France, in Champagne, on the Marne. It is a commercial and industrial center, processing paper, wine, and beer. Here, in 451, the Huns under Attila were defeated by Aetius. Although badly damaged in both World Wars, it still retains its cathedral (13th–17th cent.) and many remarkable Gothic churches.

Chalon-sur-Saône (-sŏn'), town (estimated pop. 37,399), Saône-et-Loire dept., E central France, in Burgundy, on the Saône and the Canal Central. It is an inland shipping center with a large wine and grain trade and with machine manufactures. Dating from pre-Roman times, it was the capital of King Guntram of Burgundy (6th cent.) and the scene of several church councils, notably the council convoked by Charlemagne in 813.

Chalukya (chä′lŏŏkyú), S Indian dynasty, c.550–1200, founded in the W Deccan by Pulakesin I. His son, Pulakesin II (c.608–c.642), expanded his domain while defending his northern frontier against Harsha. The dynasty was eclipsed following the death of Pulakesin II but was revived (973–1200) under the Chalukyas of Kalyani. The history of the kingdom was largely one of war with the Cholas and defense against the incursions of the Turks and Arabs who were plundering N India.

chalybite: see SIDERITE.

Cham (käm), pseud. of **Amédée de Noé** (ämädä′ dü nŏä′), 1819–79, French caricaturist and lithographer. He abandoned a military career to produce over 4,000 designs, many of them caricatures and sketches of French and Algerian life.

Chamalhari (chämälhä′rē, –hŭ′rē) or **Chomo Lhari** (chŏmŏlhŭ′rē, chŏmúlhä′rē), peak, 23,930 ft. high, on the border of Bhutan and Tibet, in the Himalayas. It is sacred to the Tibetans.

Chamavi: see GERMANS.

Chambal (chŭm′bùl), river rising near Indore, Madhya Pradesh, W central India. About 650 mi. long, it flows northeast and then southwest to join the Jumna.

chambered nautilus: see NAUTILUS.

Chamberlain, Arthur Neville: see CHAMBERLAIN, NEVILLE.

Chamberlain, Sir Austen (Sir Joseph Austen Chamberlain), 1863–1937, British statesman; son of Joseph Chamberlain and half brother of Neville Chamberlain. He entered upon a 45-year parliamentary career in 1892. He was chancellor of the exchequer (1903–6), secretary of state for India (1915–17), a member of the war cabinet (from April, 1918), and again (1919–21) chancellor of the exchequer. During his tenure in the latter office he secured parliamentary assent to the policy of imperial tariff preference first advocated by his father. He succeeded Bonar Law as Conservative leader in 1921 and helped negotiate the treaty with the Irish Free State. From 1924 to 1929 he held his most important post, as foreign secretary. The LOCARNO PACT of 1925 was largely his work. The same year (with Charles G. Dawes) he was awarded the Nobel Peace Prize. He last held a cabinet position in 1931, but continued to be influential in Commons until his death. See his *Down the Years* (1935), *Politics from Inside* (1936), and *Seen in Passing* (1937); Sir Charles Petrie, *Life and Letters of Sir Austen Chamberlain* (1939–40).

Chamberlain, Houston Stewart, 1855–1927, Anglo-German writer, b. England. The son of a British admiral, he was educated in France and in Germany, where he settled, married Richard Wagner's daughter, and became a German citizen. His chief work, *Foundations of the Nineteenth Century* (1899; Eng. tr., 1911), is a major document of racist doctrine. Aristocratic and anti-Semitic, Chamberlain glorified the Teutons and credited them with all modern achievement. His ideas on "racial purity" were reshaped as the racist policies of Adolf Hitler.

Chamberlain, Joseph, 1836–1914, British statesman. After a successful business career, he entered

local politics and won distinction as reform mayor of Birmingham (1873–76). He served under Gladstone as a Liberal president of the Board of Trade (1880–85), but in 1886 he resigned and joined the Liberal-Unionists who opposed Home Rule for Ireland. In 1887 as commissioner to the United States, he settled the fisheries dispute between that country and Canada. He became leader of the Liberal-Unionists in the House of Commons in 1891. Here and as colonial secretary (1895–1903) he advocated social reforms at home and in the colonies and a vigorous colonial policy aimed at imperial expansion, cooperation, and consolidation. His negotiations with President Kruger of the Transvaal republic failed, and he was unjustly blamed for the aggressive acts that precipitated the South African War (1899–1902). He was foremost in reconciling the Boers after the war, even going to Africa for that purpose. Since England's ancient commercial monopoly had been

Joseph Chamberlain

destroyed mainly by German and American competition, Chamberlain advocated a tariff giving preference to imperial products. He resigned in 1903 to spend three years trying, through the Tariff Reform League, to "educate" England. His proposal to abandon England's traditional free trade split his Liberal-Unionist-Conservative bloc, resulting in its defeat in the elections of 1906. Ill-health ended his public life in 1906, but his tariff policy was adopted (1919 and 1932) within the lifetime of his sons Austen and Neville. See E. E. Gulley, *Joseph Chamberlain and English Social Politics* (1926); biography by J. L. Garvin and J. Amery (4 vols., 1932–51; to 1903·only); W. L. Strauss, *Joseph Chamberlain and the Theory of Imperialism* (1942).

Chamberlain, Sir Joseph Austen: see CHAMBERLAIN, SIR AUSTEN.

Chamberlain, Joshua Lawrence, 1828–1914, Union general in the Civil War, b. Brewer, Maine, grad. Bowdoin, 1852, and Bangor Theological Seminary, 1855. He taught at Bowdoin from 1855 to 1862, when he became lieutenant colonel in the 20th Maine Infantry. Chamberlain was awarded the Congressional Medal of Honor for his defense of Little Round Top at Gettysburg (1863), and in

June, 1864, Grant promoted him brigadier general of volunteers on the field for his gallantry before Petersburg. He was governor of Maine (1867–71) and president of Bowdoin (1871–83). He wrote *The Passing of the Armies* (1915), which deals with the final campaigns in the East. See biography by W. M. Wallace (1960).

Chamberlain, Neville (Arthur Neville Chamberlain), 1869–1940, British statesman; son of Joseph Chamberlain and half brother of Sir Austen Chamberlain. He studied commerce, metallurgy, and engineering design as a young man, and after seven years on his father's sisal plantation in the Bahamas, he returned to Birmingham to enter upon a

Neville Chamberlain

business career. In 1911 he was elected to the Birmingham city council, became lord mayor in 1915, and during the First World War served for a time as director general of labor recruiting. In 1918, in his 50th year, he was elected a Conservative member of the House of Commons. In 1923 he became chancellor of the exchequer and later (1924–29) served as minister of health. In the crisis of 1931 he resumed his position as chancellor of the exchequer, an office he held until he succeeded Stanley Baldwin as prime minister on May 28, 1937. The period of "appeasement" of the Axis Powers which followed came to be symbolized by Chamberlain and his ever-present umbrella. That policy reached its apogee on Sept. 30, 1938, when, after long negotiations, he signed the MUNICH PACT. Continued German aggression and the invasion of Czechoslovakia the following March brought a stiffening of British policy. Chamberlain continued in office after the outbreak of war, but the British debacle in Norway in April, 1940, forced Chamberlain, who was confronted with increasing Conservative and unanimous Labour opposition, to resign (May 10). He continued in Winston Churchill's government as lord president of the council until ill-health forced his resignation on Oct. 3. He died a few weeks later. See biography by Keith Feiling (1946).

Chamberlain, Owen, 1920–, American nuclear physicist and educator, b. San Francisco, grad. Dartmouth College, 1941, Ph.D. Univ. of Chicago, 1948. From 1942 to 1946 he worked for the Manhattan Engineering District (which built the atomic bomb), first at Berkeley, Calif., and then at Los Alamos, N.M. He taught (1948) at the Univ. of California and became professor of physics there in 1958. He shared with Emilio SEGRÈ the 1959 Nobel Prize in Physics for their joint work in the discovery of the subatomic particle called the antiproton.

Chamberlain, Wilton Norman (Wilt Chamberlain), 1936–, American basketball player, b. Philadelphia. At the Univ. of Kansas he was twice named to the All-American basketball team. Chamberlain left (1958) college to join the Harlem Globetrotters. After 1959 he broke almost every scoring record in professional basketball. With his great height (over 7 ft. 1 in. tall) and unusual athletic agility, "Wilt the Stilt," as Chamberlain is called, was the top scorer in his first three years in the league. Among the records he holds are the most points (100) scored in one game and the most free throws (28) in one game.

Chamberlain, city (pop. 2,598), co. seat of Brule co., S S.Dak., on the Missouri river and SE of Pierre, in a livestock and grain area; platted 1880, inc. 1882. An early ferrying point for passengers and freight on the river, the city has become a trade and recreation center. Crow Creek and Lower Brule Indian reservations are nearby.

Chamberlain's Men, Elizabethan theatrical company for which Shakespeare wrote his plays and served as actor. Organized in 1594, they performed at the Globe Theatre and at the Blackfriars Theatre. Under the patronage of James I they became c.1603 the King's Men. The members shared in the ownership of the theater and the profits, and usually all took part in the performances. Richard BURBAGE and Will KEMP were the most famous players. The most important rival company was the ADMIRAL'S MEN.

Chamberlin, Thomas Chrowder, 1843–1928, American geologist, b. Mattoon, Ill., grad. Beloit College, 1866. He was professor of geology at Beloit (1873–82), president of the Univ. of Wisconsin (1887–92), and professor of geology and director of the Walker Museum at the Univ. of Chicago (1892–1919). Chamberlin was chief geologist of the geological survey of Wisconsin (1873–82) and the founder (1893) of the *Journal of Geology.* While studying glaciation and climates in past geologic time he noted defects in the NEBULAR HYPOTHESIS of LAPLACE that led him to formulate, with F. R. Moulton, American astronomer, the PLANETESIMAL HYPOTHESIS. Chamberlin wrote *The Geology of Wisconsin* (1873–82), *A Contribution to the Theory of Glacial Motion* (1904), *A General Treatise on Geology* (with Rollin D. Salisbury, 1906), *The Origin of the Earth* (1916), and *Two Solar Families* (1928). *The General Treatise,* in various editions and abridgments, is standard in schools and colleges. His son, **Rollin Thomas Chamberlin,** 1881–1948, geologist, made a special study of gases in rocks and was an authority in several fields, including glaciology, and historical, structural, and dynamic geology. He is noted for his method for the prevention of coal-dust explosions in mines. From 1928 he edited the *Journal of Geology.*

chamber music, ensemble music for small groups of

instruments, with only one player to each part. Its essence is individual treatment of parts and the exclusion of virtuosic elements. Originally played by amateurs in courts and aristocratic circles, it began to be performed by professionals only in the 19th cent. with the rise of the concert hall. In the broadest sense it existed as early as the Middle Ages. The *ricercare* and the concerted *canzone* of the 16th cent. are properly chamber music, although unlike later forms they were not for specific instruments but were usually performed by voices and whatever instruments were at hand. During the baroque period the chief type was the trio SONATA. About 1750 the string quartet with its related types—trio, quintet, sextet, septet, and octet—arose. As developed by Haydn and Mozart the quartet became the principal chamber-music form. It was used by Beethoven and Schubert, whose quartets are the last of the classical period, and by the chief composers of the romantic period —Mendelssohn, Schumann, Brahms, Dvorak, Franck, d'Indy, and Reger. In the early 20th cent. the coloristic possibilities of the quartet were exploited by Debussy and Ravel. More recently the different forms of chamber music have been used extensively for experiments in atonality, percussive rhythms, and serial techniques by such composers as Schoenberg, Bartok, Webern, Berg, Stravinsky, Sessions, and Piston. See D. F. Tovey, *Essays in Musical Analysis: Chamber Music* (1944); H. E. Ulrich, *Chamber Music* (1948); W. W. Cobbett, *Cyclopedic Survey of Chamber Music* (new ed., 3 vols., 1963).

chamber of commerce, local association of businessmen organized to promote the welfare of their community, especially its commercial interests. Each chamber of commerce usually has a board of directors elected by the members, and work is done through committees. Among the activities frequently carried on by these committees are industrial surveys and efforts to attract new industries to the city, housing surveys, efforts to provide parking space and promote safety, and advertising the advantages of the city to tourists and to organizations as a convention site. The *chambre de commerce* of Marseilles (1599) was the first organization to use the name; the idea spread through France in the 17th and 18th cent. The first to be formed in Great Britain was on the island of Jersey in 1768. In America the first was the Chamber of Commerce of the State of New York, organized in 1768. By 1870 there were 40 in U.S. cities. The local chambers are federated in the Chamber of Commerce of the United States (founded 1912), which maintains at its Washington, D.C., headquarters a technical staff and lobbies in the interests of its member organizations. Its organ is the *Nation's Business*. The International Chamber of Commerce has its headquarters in Paris. See also TRADE ASSOCIATION.

Chambers, Sir Edmund Kerchever, 1866–1954, English literary critic and Shakespearean scholar. He wrote *The Mediaeval Stage* (1903), *The Elizabethan Stage* (1923), *Arthur of Britain* (1927), and studies of S. T. Coleridge (1938) and Matthew Arnold (1947).

Chambers, Ephraim, c. 1680–1740, English encyclopedist. A French translation of his *Cyclopedia* (2 vols., 1728) inspired the work of D'Alembert and Diderot in their *Encyclopédie*. See ENCYCLOPEDIA.

Chambers, Robert (1802–71): see CHAMBERS, WILLIAM.

Chambers, Robert, 1881–1957, American physiologist, b. Erzurum, Turkey, grad. Univ. of Munich (Ph.D., 1908). He taught (1923–28) at Cornell Univ. Medical College and was research professor of biology at New York Univ. from 1928. Chambers developed the micromanipulator for the dissection and injection of living cells and tissues. By producing lesions in single cells growing in tissue culture, he was able to study the reactions of the damaged cells to various physical and chemical stimuli.

Chambers, Sir William, 1723–96, English architect, b. Gothenburg, Sweden. He traveled extensively in the East Indies and in China, where he made the many drawings of gardens and buildings which were later published. He studied architecture in France and Italy and established (1755) his practice in England where he designed decorative architecture for Kew Gardens. From the founding (1768) of the Royal Academy to the end of his life, Chambers was a dominant figure in its councils. His *Treatise on the Decorative Part of Civil Architecture* (1759) became a standard and influential work on classic design. The foremost official architect of his day in England, he continued the neo-Palladian tradition which he adapted to the prevailing classical taste. His chief work, Somerset House, is an extensive block of government offices, begun in 1776. He also had charge of various alterations at Trinity College, Dublin, and designed additions to Blenheim Palace, the observatory in Richmond Park, and casinos in many parks of the nobility. He became private architect to King George III and was made (1782) surveyor general. Chambers was buried in Westminster Abbey.

Chambers, William, 1800–1883, and **Robert Chambers,** 1802–71, English authors and publishers, b. Scotland. Their firm of W. and R. Chambers is best known for *Chambers's Edinburgh Journal*, which William started in 1832 and for which both brothers wrote, and *Chambers's Encyclopaedia* (10 vols., 1859–68), which has gone through several editions. Robert published several books on history and in geology, including the anonymous *Vestiges . . . of Creation* (1844), a forerunner of Darwin's *Origin of Species*. William, always interested in public improvement, was lord provost of Edinburgh, 1865–69.

Chambersburg, industrial borough (pop. 17,670), co. seat of Franklin co., S Pa., SW of Harrisburg; settled 1730, laid out 1764, inc. 1803. It is a trading center for a fertile agricultural area. Metal products, machinery, clothing, and food products are manufactured. Chambersburg was the headquarters of the abolitionist John Brown in 1859, and the town was burned (1864) by the Confederates under Harry GILMOR. It is the seat of Penn Hall Junior College (for women) and Wilson College (Presbyterian; for women; 1869). Caledonia State Park is nearby.

Chambéry (shäbārē'), town (estimated pop. 32,139), capital of Savoie dept., E France, in the Alpine trough. An archiepiscopal see from the 5th cent., it was the historic capital of Savoy. A communica-

Château Chambord

tions and industrial center, it manufactures leather products, machinery, and clothing. Nearby is the house (the Charmettes) made famous by the sojourn of J. J. Rousseau and Mme de Warens.

Chambiges (shăbēzh′), family of French architects or master masons of the 15th and 16th cent. **Martin Chambiges** (märtē′), d. 1532, took part in the designing of three great cathedrals—Sens (from 1489 to 1499), Troyes (its west front), and Beauvais, where he was employed on the choir (1506), remaining in charge of its construction until his death. In these works he was assisted by his son, **Pierre Chambiges** (pyĕr′), d. 1544, whose most important work is the château of Saint-Germain-en-Laye. Pierre worked at Chantilly for the Montmorencys (1525–30) and perhaps also on the Hôtel de Ville.

Chamblee (chămblē′), city (pop. 6,635), NW Ga., NNE of Atlanta; inc. 1922.

Chambly (shăblē′), town (pop. 3,737), S Que., Canada, on the Richelieu river and E of Montreal. **Chambly Fort** was first built in 1665 and was a strategic point in the defense of New France against the English and the Iroquois. It was captured by the invading Americans in 1775 and burned when they retired in 1776. In 1880 the Canadian government undertook its restoration.

Chambord, Henri Charles Ferdinand Marie Dieudonné, comte de (ärē′ shärl′ fĕrdēnā′ märē′ dyûdônā′ kŏt′ dù shăbôr′), 1820–83, BOURBON claimant to the French throne, posthumous son of Charles Ferdinand, duc de BERRY. His original title was duke of Bordeaux. His grandfather, Charles X, abdicated in his favor in 1830, and he is known to the legitimists as Henry V, though he never held the throne. He accompanied Charles into exile and spent most of the rest of his life at Frohsdorf, Austria. In 1832 his mother, Caroline de BERRY, made an unsuccessful attempt to overthrow Louis Philippe. Efforts to reconcile his claims with those of the Orleanist pretender, Louis Philippe Albert d'ORLÉANS, after the February Revolution of 1848, met with little success. In 1871, after the fall of the Second Empire, Chambord's prospects improved, and in 1873 the Orleanist pretender relinquished his claims in Chambord's favor. However, his stubborn adherence to the Bourbon flag and to ultraroyalist principles destroyed his chance of recognition. He died without issue, and his claims passed to the house of Bourbon-Orléans.

Chambord (shăbôr′), village (pop. c.266), Loir-et-Cher dept., N central France, on the Cosson, a tributary of the Loire. Its huge Renaissance château was built by Francis I. Particularly remarkable is the central stairway, built in two separate overlapping spirals so that a person mounting the stairs would not meet a person descending them. The château was used especially by Louis XIV and by Stanislaus I of Poland. Louis XV gave it in gratitude to Maurice de Saxe, and Napoleon I gave it to Marshal Berthier. In 1821 Chambord was presented, by national subscription, to the duke of Bordeaux, who later took the title count of Chambord. In 1932 it was bought back by the state.

chameleon (kùmē′lyùn), small, slow-moving arboreal lizard of Africa and S Asia. Changes in its skin color are governed not by the color of its back-

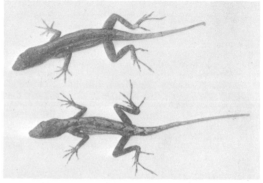

Chameleons

1230

ground but by hormonal and nervous reactions to stimuli such as light intensity, temperature change, and excitement. These reactions involve changes in the location and exposure of pigments in the skin. Old World chameleons are covered with granular scales, and have prehensile tails and opposable digits for efficient grasping. The sticky tongue can be shot far out to capture insects. The eyes, which move independently, are covered by thick lids with a small central opening. The much smaller American chameleon, or anole, also capable of changing color, is a member of another family, related to the iguana.

Chamfort, Sébastien Roch Nicolas (sȧbästyē′ rōk′ nēkōlä′ shȧfôr′), 1740–94, French writer of maxims and epigrams. His acute observations on literature, morals, and politics made him popular at court, despite his republican beliefs. In the Reign of Terror Chamfort was denounced, and he committed suicide.

Chamillart or **Chamillard, Michel** (both: mēshĕl′ shämēyär′), 1651–1721, French statesman. He was named controller general of finances (1699), minister of state (1700), and minister of war (1701). To raise funds Chamillart resorted to the sale of offices and titles, loans, lotteries, manipulation of the currency, and anticipation of revenues. To these means he added a wartime capitation tax, imposed in 1695–98 and again after 1701, but he could not meet the mounting expenses of the government, especially after the War of the SPANISH SUCCESSION began. The deficit and the national debt grew huge, and VAUBAN censured the disorder of the tax system. Chamillart resigned the finances to Nicolas DESMARETS in 1708 and gave up the ministry of war in 1709.

Chaminade, Cécile Louise Stéphanie (sȧsēl′ lwēz′ stäfänē′ shämēnäd′), 1857–1944, French composer and pianist; pupil of Godard in composition. She composed a lyric symphony, *Les Amazones* (1888), and graceful, pleasant songs and piano pieces such as *Scarf Dance* from her highly successful ballet, *Callirhoë* (Marseilles, 1888).

Chamisso, Adelbert von (Louis Charles Adelaide de Chamisso), (ä′dûlbĕrt fŭn shŭmĭ′sō), 1781–1838, German poet and naturalist, b. France. He served as page at the court of William II and, after army service and travels, became keeper of the royal botanical gardens. He edited (1804–6) the *Musenalmanach* and was a member of Mme de Stael's circle. His sentimental poetic cycle *Frauenliebe und Leben* (1830) was set to music by Schumann. *Peter Schlemihls wundersame Geschichte* (1814), his tale of a man who sold his shadow to the devil, has become legend. He also wrote plays, an account of his travels in the Pacific (1836), and a work on linguistics (1837).

chamois (shă′mē), hollow-horned, hoofed mammal related to the antelope and found in the mountains of Europe and the E Mediterranean countries. It is about the size of a large goat and is light brown with a black tail, a black back stripe, and black markings on its face. The erect horns have terminal hooks pointed backward. Its hoofs can cling to rocky surfaces, and it leaps with agility. It ranges to the snow line in summer. The skin was the original chamois leather, but the name is now applied also to leather made from the skins of

Chamois

other animals. The chamois has been introduced into New Zealand.

chamomile or **camomile** (both: kăm′ûmīl) [Gr.,= ground apple], name for various related plants of the COMPOSITE family, especially the perennial *Anthemis nobilis*, the English or Roman chamomile, and the annual *Matricaria chamomilla*, the German or wild chamomile. Both are European herbs with similar uses. The former has an applelike aroma and is the chamomile most frequently grown for ornament (often as a ground cover) and for "camomile tea," made from the dried flower heads, which contain a volatile oil. The oil from the similar flowers of the wild chamomile was most often used medicinally, particularly as a tonic; today its chief use is as a hair rinse.

Chamonix (shämōnē′), town (estimated pop. 5,699), Haute-Savoie dept., E France, at the foot of MONT BLANC, in the beautiful Chamonix valley. The principal base for the ascent of Mont Blanc and for visiting the MER DE GLACE, it is a popular summer and winter resort. It has the highest (12,605 ft.) aerial cable car in the world and is linked by tunnel with Courmayeur, Italy.

Chamorro, Emiliano (ämēlyä′nō chämô′rô), 1871–, president of Nicaragua (1917–20, 1926). A conservative army chief, Chamorro supported the revolt (1909) against José Santos Zelaya. Originally at odds with the United States, he was a signer of the Bryan-Chamorro Treaty, which granted the United States an option on the NICARAGUA CANAL. He opposed all liberal regimes, including that of Anastasio Somoza.

Champa, the kingdom of the Chams, which flourished in Viet Nam from the 2d cent. A.D. till the 17th cent. It was probably of Indian cultural origin, and at its greatest extent occupied ANNAM as far north as the Porte d'Annam. In its early period, Champa mainly warred with China and was forced to change its capital several times; late in the 9th cent. its capital became Indrapura, in the neighborhood of Hué, and the later capital was Vijaya, farther south. Champa repeatedly made war on its stronger neighbor, Annam; it was sometimes allied and sometimes opposed to the KHMER

EMPIRE. In the 12th cent. the Chams invaded Cambodia and sacked Angkor; subsequently they fell for a time under Khmer rule. Decisively defeated by the Annamese in 1472, the Chams were forced to yield most of their territory N of Tourane. In the 17th cent. the rest of the Cham kingdom fell to the Annamese, and the remnants of the people were scattered. Chams still form small, impoverished minorities in South Viet Nam, but in Cambodia a large colony prospers. Although most of those in Annam worship Hindu gods, those of Cambodia are Moslems. Ruins of Cham temples, adorned with bas-reliefs and with statues, are found in S Annam. See Georges Maspero, *The Kingdom of Champa* (Eng. tr., 1949).

Champagne, Philippe de: see CHAMPAIGNE.

Champagne (shămpān', Fr. shäpä'nyù), region and former province, NE France, consisting mainly of the departments Aube, Marne, Haute-Marne, Ardennes, and part of Yonne. The region is almost, but not fully, coextensive with the former province of Champagne and BRIE. Abutting in the west on the Paris basin, Champagne is a generally arid, chalky plateau, cut by the Aisne, Marne, Seine, Aube, and Yonne rivers. Agriculture, except in the Ardennes dept., is mostly confined to the valleys. The plateau is cut from northwest to southeast by crests into several areas. Further east, bordering on Lorraine, is the so-called Champagne Humide [wet Champagne], largely agricultural, and the Langres Plateau. In the center is the Champagne Pouilleuse [Champagne badlands], a bleak and eroded plain, traditionally used for sheep grazing; Troyes and Châlons-sur-Marne, its principal towns, are located in fertile valleys and are centers of the wool industry. A narrow strip along the westernmost crest is extremely fertile, and the small area around RHEIMS and EPERNAY furnishes virtually all the champagne wine exported by France. Other fertile districts are around RETHEL and SENS. The central and open situation of Champagne has made it a major European battlefield from the invasion by Attila's Huns, whom Aetius defeated at Châlons in 451, to the First World War, which left vast areas scorched. Yet the same geographic position gave the towns of Champagne a commercial prosperity in direct contrast to the bleakness of the countryside. The county of Champagne passed to the counts of BLOIS in the 11th cent. After 1152 the main branch of the house held Champagne, which had been considerably increased; upon the counts large parts of France, including Blois, Touraine, and Chartres, were dependent. In 1234 THIBAUT IV inherited the crown of Navarre from his uncle Sancho VII; Navarre remained in the family until the death (1305) of Joan of Navarre, who married King Philip IV of France in 1286. Her son, who inherited Champagne, incorporated it into the royal domain in 1314, when he became king of France as Louis X. The bishoprics of Rheims and Langres were added later. During the rule of the counts Champagne was a virtually independent state. At the Fairs of Champagne, held at Troyes, Provins, Lagny-sur-Marne, and Bar-sur-Aube, merchants from England, the Low Countries, France, Burgundy, and Italy met six times each year. Special laws regulated the trade and had a profound influence on later commercial

Cathedral at Rheims.

customs throughout Europe—the troy weight for precious metals still is used. Prosperity in the capital, Troyes, and the other towns was accompanied by cultural brilliance, culminating in the work of CHRESTIEN DE TROYES and in the Gothic cathedral at Rheims. With its incorporation into France, Champagne declined in prosperity, but the sudden and continuing popularity of its sparkling wine, which began in the 18th cent., restored it somewhat. More recently efforts have been made to reforest the area and to reclaim it from erosion.

champagne (shămpān'), celebrated sparkling white wine made from grapes grown in the old French province of Champagne. The best champagne is from that part of the Marne valley whose apex is Rheims, the center of the industry. Champagne was reputedly developed by a monk, Dom Pérignon, in the 17th cent. It is a blend of grapes from different vineyards, hence is named for the vintners and shippers responsible for each blend. The small, slightly acid grapes are laboriously cultivated. After the first fermentation the wine is blended; it undergoes a secondary fermentation, then is drawn off into bottles reinforced to withstand high internal pressure, and is sweetened to induce further fermentation. The carbonic acid retained in the bottle after the final fermentation renders champagne sparkling. The wine is matured in the labyrinthine tunnels of the old chalk quarries of Rheims. The sediment formed is collected on the cork by tilting the bottle neck downward and frequently rotating it by hand. The wine in the neck of each bottle is then frozen, the cork removed, and the sediment, in a small piece of ice, is blown out. The space left is filled with the proper "dosage" of cane sugar dissolved in wine and usually fortified with cognac. *Brut* champagne is theoretically not sweetened; extra dry champagne, very lightly. An American wine called champagne is made in New York and California.

Champaign (shămpān'), city (pop. 49,583), E central

Ill., ENE of Springfield and adjoining URBANA with which it is allied economically; founded 1854. inc. 1861. It is a railroad (with repair shops), commercial, and industrial center in a rich farm area. Metal products, academic apparel, and electrical equipment are made. The campus of the Univ. of Illinois (see ILLINOIS, UNIVERSITY OF) lies between Champaign and Urbana.

Champaigne or **Champagne, Philippe de** (both: fēlēp′ dü shäpä′nyü), 1602–74, French painter, b. Brussels, of Flemish parents. In 1621 he went to Paris, where he worked with Poussin on the Luxembourg Palace. In 1628 he became painter to the queen, Marie de′ Medici. For her and for Richelieu he executed many religious paintings, still to be seen in French churches, and numerous fine portraits. From 1640 on he became absorbed in the Jansenist movement and has been called the painter of Port-Royal. His later work is characterized by sober realism, simplicity, and austerity. His best-known paintings include his frescoes at Vincennes and in the Tuileries and his portrait of his daughter, a nun at Port-Royal, and that of Richelieu (both: Louvre). Basing his portrait style on patterns established by Rubens and Van Dyck, he rendered his subjects with an air of static majesty.

Champ-de-Mars (shä-dü-märs′), former parade ground of Paris, France, between the École militaire and the Seine. Here, at the Fête de la Fédération (July 14, 1790), Louis XVI took an oath to uphold the new constitution. On its vast grounds several expositions were held, notably that of 1889, when the EIFFEL TOWER was erected here.

Champeaux, William of: see WILLIAM OF CHAMPEAUX.

Championnet, Jean Étienne (zhä′ ätyĕn′ shäpyŏnĕ′), 1762–1800, French general in the FRENCH REVOLUTIONARY WARS. In command of the Army of Rome, he captured Naples from the Second Coalition in 1799 and set up the PARTHENOPEAN REPUBLIC. However, he got into trouble with the Directory and was recalled in disgrace. Subsequently he commanded the Army of the Alps; unable to win success with this badly organized unit, he resigned. He died shortly after.

Champlain, Samuel de (shămplän′, Fr. sämüĕl′ dü shäplĕ′), 1567–1635, French explorer, the chief founder of New France. After serving in France under Henry of Navarre (King Henry IV) in the religious wars of the period, he was given command of a Spanish fleet sailing to the West Indies, Mexico, and the Isthmus of Panama. He described this three-year tour to the French king in a *Bref Discours* (first published in 1859). In 1603 he made his first voyage to New France as a member of a fur-trading expedition. With a pinnace he explored the St. Lawrence river as far as the rapids at Lachine, and after his return to France he described his voyage in *Des sauvages* (1603). With the sieur de Monts, who had a monopoly of the trade of the region, Champlain returned in 1604 to found a colony, which landed at the mouth of the St. Croix river. In 1605 the colony transferred across the Bay of Fundy to Port Royal (now Annapolis Royal, N.S.), and in the next three years Champlain explored the New England coast S to Martha's Vineyard, discovering Mt. Desert Island and most of the larger rivers of Maine; he for the first time made detailed charts of the coast. After revocation of the sieur de Monts's privileges, the colony had to be abandoned, and through the efforts of Champlain a new one was established on the St. Lawrence river. In 1608, in the ship *Le Don de Dieu*, he brought his colonists to the site of Quebec, where they started what was to be the capital of a great colony. In the spring of 1609, accompanying a war party of Huron Indians against the Iroquois, Champlain discovered the lake which bears his name, and near Crown Point, N.Y., the Iroquois were met and routed by French firearms. This incident is believed responsible for the later hatred of the French by the Iroquois. In 1612 he returned to France, where he received a new grant of the fur-trade monopoly. Returning in 1613, he set off on a journey to the Western lakes. He reached only Allumette Island in the Ottawa river that year, but in 1615 he went with Étienne Brulé and a party of Huron Indians to Georgian Bay on Lake Huron, returning southeastward by way of Lake Ontario. Accompanying another Huron war party to an attack on an Onondaga village in present New York, Champlain was wounded and forced to spend the winter with the Indians. Thereafter he made no more explorations, but devoted all his time to the welfare of the colony, of which he was the virtual governor. He helped to persuade Richelieu to found the Company of One Hundred Associates, which was to take over the interests of the colony. In 1629 Quebec was suddenly captured by the English, and Champlain was carried away to four years of exile in England; there he prepared the third edition of his *Voyages de la Nouvelle France* (1632). When New France was restored to France in 1632, Champlain returned. In 1634 he sent Jean NICOLET into the West, thus extending the French explorations and claims as far as Wisconsin. He died on Christmas Day, 1635, and was buried in Quebec. His works were issued by the Champlain Society

Samuel de Champlain

Jean Étienne Championnet

(1922–36) with English and French texts. See C. W. Colby, *The Founder of New France* (1915); biographies by Ralph Flenley (1924), L. H. Sharp (1944), and Morris Bishop (1948).

Champlain (shămplān'), village (pop. 1,549), extreme NE N.Y., N of Plattsburgh, near Lake Champlain; settled 1789, inc. 1873. Close to the Quebec boundary, it is a port of entry.

Champlain, Lake, 107 mi. long and ½ mi. to 14 mi. wide, forming part of the N.Y.–Vt. border and extending into Quebec. It lies in a broad valley between the Adirondacks and the Green Mts. A link in the Hudson-St. Lawrence waterway, the lake is connected with the Hudson (at Fort Edward) by the Champlain division of the Barge Canal; the Richelieu river connects the lake with the St. Lawrence. Lake George drains into it through a narrow channel, and many islands dot its surface, including Grand Isle, ISLE LA MOTTE, and VALCOUR ISLAND. The region is noted for its beautiful scenery and has many resorts; Plattsburgh, N.Y., and Burlington, Vt., are the largest cities on the lake's shores. The lake, discovered by Samuel de Champlain in 1609, was the scene of battles in the French and Indian War and the American Revolution at CROWN POINT and TICONDEROGA, of a naval engagement in 1776, and of the important American victory of Thomas MACDONOUGH in the War of 1812. See Walter Hill Crockett, *A History of Lake Champlain: a Record of More than Three Centuries, 1609–1936* (1937); Frederic F. Van de Water, *Lake Champlain and Lake George* (1946); and Harrison Bird, *Navies in the Mountains: the Battles on the Waters of Lake Champlain and Lake George, 1609–1814* (1962).

Champlin (chăm'plĭn), village (pop. 1,271), SE Minn., on the Mississippi and NNW of Minneapolis, in a potato-growing region.

Jean François Champollion

Champollion, Jean François (zhã' fräswä' shäpôlyŏ'), 1790–1832, French Egyptologist. Though he died while still young, he accomplished much and is considered the founder of the science of Egyptology. When he was 24 his two-volume work on the geography of ancient Egypt appeared. In 1821 by use of the ROSETTA STONE he established the principles for deciphering the Egyptian hieroglyphics. He became director of the Egyptian museum at the Louvre and professor at the Collège de France. He is sometimes called Champollion le Jeune to distinguish him from his elder brother, who gave him his early training. **Jean Jacques Champollion-Figeac** (zhäk', –fēzhäk'), 1778–1867, was an archaeologist, a professor at Grenoble, a curator of manuscripts at the Bibliothèque nationale, a professor of paleography at the École des Chartes, and librarian at the Palace of Fontainebleau.

Champs Élysées (shä zälēzä'), avenue of Paris, France, leading from the Place de la CONCORDE to the Arc de Triomphe. It is celebrated for its tree-lined beauty, its commodious breadth, the elegance of its cafés, theaters, and shops, and the fountain display at its center. The avenue, built and named by Louis XV, led through open country until the early 19th cent.

Chanaan (kā'nŭn), variant of CANAAN **2.**

Chanakkale (khänäk'kälä), Turk. *Canakkale,* city (pop. 44,662), capital of Canakkale prov., NW Turkey, on the Asiatic shore of the Dardanelles. Famous for its fine pottery, it also trades in grain. An old fortified place, it has a 15th-century fort, which the Turkish army still uses. The town and fort were bombarded in 1915 during the Gallipoli campaign. Near here is the mouth of the historic AEGOSPOTAMOS river and the ruins of the ancient towns of ABYDOS and SESTOS.

Chancay (chänkī), archaeological site in central Peru, center of the ancient Cuismancu empire. Culturally influenced by the CHIMU, the Cuismancu dominated less territory and were not as powerful. Nonetheless they built large cities and were more advanced than their southern neighbors, the Chincha (see ICA). The Cuismancu were conquered by the Inca in the 15th cent.

chance, in mathematics: see PROBABILITY.

chancel [Latin, =latticework], primarily that part of the church close to the altar and used by the officiating clergy. In the early churches it was separated from the nave by a low parapet or open railing (*cancellus*), its name being thus derived. San

Chancel of San Clemente in Rome.

Clemente at Rome has one of the few preserved examples. With the development of the choir, additional space was taken, between the SANCTUARY and the nave, for the accommodation of the canons and singers. The chancel rail was moved forward, and the entire space then became known as the choir, although it is also termed the chancel; there is no strict differentiation in the usage. In the Middle Ages the chancel rail was replaced by lofty choir screens (see ROOD), especially in English cathedrals and in monastic churches.

Chancellor, Richard, d. 1556, English navigator. When, largely under the inspiration of Sebastian Cabot, a group of men in England undertook to finance a search for the Northeast Passage to Asia, Chancellor was chosen as second in command under Sir Hugh Willoughby. They sailed in 1553, and Chancellor and Stephen Borough, in the *Edward Bonaventure,* managed to get through dangerous arctic waters to the White Sea. Chancellor then traveled overland across Russia to Moscow at the invitation of Ivan IV. His negotiations prepared the way for trade with Russia and the formation of the Muscovy Company. On the return from a second voyage to Russia he was shipwrecked, and he perished off the coast of Scotland. Since Willoughby had earlier come to grief, it was Stephen Borough who continued the work of opening the northern route to Russia for the Muscovy Company.

Chancellorsville, battle of, in the Civil War, May 2–4, 1863. Late in April, 1863, Joseph Hooker, commanding the Army of the Potomac, moved against R. E. Lee, whose Army of Northern Virginia (less than half the size of Hooker's) had remained entrenched on the S side of the Rappahannock river after the battle of FREDERICKSBURG. Hooker, with four corps, crossed the river above Fredericksburg and took up a strong position near Chancellorsville, a locality 10 mi. W of Fredericksburg; he sent John Sedgwick, with two corps, to cross below Chancellorsville. Although outflanked, Lee did not retreat but, leaving 10,000 men under Jubal A. Early to watch Sedgwick, moved on Hooker, who fell back to a defensive position in the wilderness around Chancellorsville. Lee attacked on May 2: T. J. (Stonewall) JACKSON led his 2d Corps on a brilliant 15-mile flanking movement against the Union right, while Lee, with his small remaining force, feinted along the rest of the line. Jackson fell upon and routed the surprised Federals but, unfortunately for the South, was mortally wounded by his own men. The next day the Confederate wings united (James Ewell Brown STUART succeeding Jackson) and drove Hooker back further. Hooker failed to use his superior forces, but called for Sedgwick, who drove Early from Marye's Heights (May 3) and reached Salem Church, 5 mi. W of Fredericksburg. There part of Lee's force joined Early and repulsed Sedgwick, May 4–5. Sedgwick and Hooker then withdrew across the river. Chancellorsville, Lee's last great victory, led to his invasion of the North in the GETTYSBURG CAMPAIGN. See John Bigelow, *The Campaign of Chancellorsville* (1910); E. J. Stackpole, *Chancellorsville: Lee's Greatest Battle* (1958).

chancery: see EQUITY.

Chanchan (chän′chän′), ruins of an ancient Indian city near Trujillo, N Peru. The city was probably begun in the period A.D. 800–1000, and it is estimated that it once contained 200,000 people. Chanchan is accepted generally as the capital of the CHIMU, a pre-Inca civilization. It is on a large plain of the coastal desert, which was made arable by ambitious and extensive irrigation works. Covering c.11 sq. mi. the city comprised at least 10 self-contained, walled-in units. The walls, built of adobe brick, are decorated with relief designs.

chancre: see SYPHILIS.

Chandernagor (chŭn″dŭrnŭgôr′), town (pop. 49,900), West Bengal state, E India, on the Hooghly river and N of Calcutta. Founded by the French in 1686, it was of great commercial importance until the 19th cent. It was ceded by the French and became part of India in 1951.

Chandigarh (chŭn′dēgŭr), city (pop. c.40,000), capital of Punjab state, NW India. It is a new administrative city, designed by Le Corbusier and built largely in the 1950s.

Chandler, Albert Benjamin, 1898–, U.S. baseball commissioner (1945–51) and politician. b. Corydon, Henderson co., Ky., grad. Transylvania College, 1921, and Univ. of Kentucky law school, 1924. "Happy" Chandler was a lawyer in Versailles, Ky., when he went into politics. He served as lieutenant governor (1931–35), governor (1935–39), and U.S. Senator (1939–45), before becoming baseball commissioner. He retired after major league club owners refused to renew his contract. In 1955–59 Chandler was again governor of Kentucky.

Chandler, Charles Frederick, 1836–1925, American chemist, b. Lancaster, Mass., educated at Harvard and at the Univ. of Göttingen (Ph.D., 1856). He was professor of chemistry at Union College, Schenectady (1857–64). In 1864, with Thomas Egleston, he established the Columbia Univ. School of Mines, serving there as professor of chemistry (until 1911) and as dean (1864–97). Chandler was also associated with the College of Pharmacy of the City of New York, serving as vice president (1894–99, 1904–22) and president (1900–1904), and with the College of Physicians and Surgeons (professor, 1876–97). A founder and twice president of the American Chemical Society, he was one of America's first great industrial chemists and was a specialist in sugar refining and petroleum refining. As the first public-health chemist of the New York city board of health (1867–73) and as president of the board (1873–83) he inaugurated far-reaching reforms. Chandler was influential in establishing the state board of health.

Chandler, Raymond Thornton, 1888–1959, American detective-story writer, b. Chicago, educated in England. After serving with the Canadian forces in the First World War, he engaged in several businesses in California and wrote for magazines before the publication of *The Big Sleep* (1939). With *Farewell, My Lovely* (1940) he became known for his individual style of writing "tough" detective fiction. After *The High Window* (1942) and *The Lady in the Lake* (1943) he wrote motion picture scenarios for several years. His later works include *The Little Sister* (1949), *The Long Goodbye* (1953), and *Playback* (1958). The private detective Philip Marlowe appears in all Chandler's works.

Chandler, Zachariah, 1813–79, U.S. Senator from

Michigan (1857–75) and Secretary of the Interior (1875–77), b. Bedford, N.H. He moved to Detroit in 1833 and through merchandising, land speculation, and banking became a millionaire. Mayor of Detroit (1851–52), he helped organize and was long the boss of the Republican party in Michigan. Old Zack, as he was called, was an able and uncompromising abolitionist, also distinguished for his uncouth manners. A leading radical Republican, most closely associated with Benjamin F. WADE, he was a member of the congressional committee on the conduct of the war and violently opposed Lincoln's Reconstruction program, later adopted by Andrew Johnson. With the radicals victorious over Johnson, he remained a powerful figure in the Senate until he was turned out by the Democratic landslide of 1874. He then entered the cabinet, a typical Grant appointee, and was also chairman of the Republican National Committee in the disputed election of 1876. See biography by W. C. Harris (1917); T. H. Williams, *Lincoln and the Radicals* (1941).

Chandler. 1 Town (pop. 9,531), S central Ariz., in the Salt River Valley; founded 1912, inc. 1920. It produces cotton, alfalfa, and citrus fruit. Williams Air Force Base is nearby. **2** Town (pop. 1,784), SW Ind., NE of Evansville, in a farm and coal-mine area. **3** City (pop. 2,524), co. seat of Lincoln co., central Okla., NE of Oklahoma City; settled 1891. It is a trade center for a farm area noted especially for pecans.

Chandos, Sir John, d. 1370, English soldier and administrator of English territories in France. A friend of Edward the Black Prince, he won distinction in the Hundred Years War by his performance at Poitiers (1356) and by his capture (1364) of Bertrand Du GUESCLIN at Auray. In the Spanish campaign of the Black Prince he again defeated and captured (1367) Du Guesclin at Nájera. He was mortally wounded in a battle with Gascon nobles at Lussac.

Chandragupta, name of two Indian emperors. See SANDRACOTTUS and GUPTA.

Chanel, Gabrielle (gäbrēĕl′ shănĕl′), 1883–, French fashion designer and perfume manufacturer. She began her career as a milliner and became established also as a dress designer after 1920. Later her interests expanded, and textiles, costume jewelry, and perfumes were produced under the Chanel label. A fashion leader for almost half a century, she achieved great variety in style while insisting on simplicity and comfort.

Chaney, Lon (chā′nē), 1883–1930, American cinema actor, b. Colorado Springs, Colo. A master of the art of make-up to distort his face and body, he is best remembered for his work in horror films, most notably *The Hunchback of Notre Dame* and *The Phantom of the Opera.*

Changan: see SIAN.

Changarnier, Nicolas (nēkôlä′ shägärnyä′), 1793–1877, French general and politician. He served in Algeria and was briefly (1848) governor general of Algeria, succeeding Cavaignac. Elected to the national assembly in 1848, he resigned after the rising of the June Days to head the Paris national guard. Later the regular army troops in Paris were added to his command. A monarchist and Orleanist, Changarnier came to oppose the policies of Louis Napoleon and was exiled after the coup d'état of

1851. He returned in 1859 and took part in the defense of Metz (1870) in the Franco-Prussian War. Again elected a deputy in 1871, he opposed a republic. He was made a senator in 1875.

Changchow or **Ch'ang-chou** (both: jäng′-jō′), city (pop. c.296,500), S Kiangsu prov., E central China, on the Grand Canal. It is an agricultural market and industrial center with silk, rice, and flour mills and machine manufactures. Changchow became industrialized in the late 19th cent. It was called Wutsin prior to 1949.

Changchun or **Ch'ang-ch'un** (both: chäng′-chŏŏn), city (pop. c.950,000), capital of Kirin prov., China, on the South Manchurian RR. It is an industrial center, with engineering plants, automobile manufacturing, sawmills, and food processing. As Hsinking [Chinese, = new capital], it was the capital of the former state of Manchukuo (1932–45). During this period the city was rebuilt along modern lines.

changeling, in popular superstition, a fairy child substituted for a human baby. It was believed that evil fairies stole healthy unbaptized infants and left in their stead a fairy child. Hence, sickly and peevish babies were sometimes called changelings.

change of life: see MENOPAUSE.

change ringing: see BELL.

Chang Hsueh-liang (chäng′ shŭĕ′-lyäng′), 1898–, Chinese general. On the death (1928) of his father, CHANG TSO-LIN, he succeeded as military governor of Manchuria. He was then known as Chang Hsiao-liang but later changed his name. He supported Chiang Kai-shek against a rebellious northern army in 1929–30 and was made vice commander in chief of all Chinese forces and a member of the central political council. Ousted by the Japanese from Manchuria, he suffered loss of prestige. In 1936, with the help of Chinese Communists, he had Generalissimo Chiang kidnaped at Sian, allegedly to compel cooperation between the Kuomintang and the Communists and to force a declaration of war against Japan. The generalissimo was released unconditionally a few weeks later. Chang, tried and sentenced for his part in the affair, was pardoned but was kept in unofficial custody.

Changkiakow (chäng′jyäkou′), Mandarin *Chang-chiak'ou,* city (pop. c.425,000), formerly capital of Chahar prov., N China. It is in the southern part of the province, near a gateway of the Great Wall. Changkiakow is well connected by road and rail, is a major trade center for Mongolia and N China, and is the meeting place of caravans traveling from Peiping to Ulan Bator. An important military center under the Manchu dynasty, it somewhat declined after the opening (1905) of the Trans-Siberian RR. In 1928 it became capital of the province. Kalgan is the Mongolian name of the city.

Changkufeng (chŭngkŏōfĕng′), hill, SE Asiatic RSFSR, near the intersection of the borders of Siberia, Korea, and Manchuria. It was the scene of heavy border fighting between Japanese and Soviet troops during July and Aug., 1938.

Changpai or **Ch'ang-pai** (both: chäng′bī′), mountain range, Manchuria, largely in NE China and partly in N Korea. The tallest peak, Paitou Shan, is over 9,000 ft. high. The range is covered by forests up to c.5,000 ft. and is the source of the Yalu, Tumen, and Sungari rivers.

Changsha or **Ch'ang-sha** (both: chäng′shä′), city

(pop. c.500,000), capital of Hunan prov., China, on the Siang river. It is a major trade and industrial center, an important stop on the Peiping-Canton RR, and a river port. It has numerous metal refineries, cotton mills, glassworks, and porcelain works. It was founded in the early 3rd cent. B.C. and has long been noted as a literary and educational center. As Tanchow it was the capital of the Chu kingdom (10th cent.). It became a treaty port in 1907. Mao Tse-tung was educated here, and in 1927 it was the scene of a Chinese Communist uprising, led by Mao. Changsha is the birthplace of many notable Chinese literary figures and statesmen, including Chia Yi, a Han dynasty essayist, and Tseng Kuo-fan, a 19th-century diplomat and general. Changsha was the seat of an American-sponsored medical school.

Changshu (jäng′shōō) or **Ch'ang-shu** (chäng′shōō), town (pop. c.101,400), S Kiangsu prov., E central China. It is an agricultural center.

Changteh or **Ch'ang-tê** (both: chäng′dŭ′), city (pop. c.85,000), NW Hunan prov., China, on the Yuan river. Formerly a treaty port, it is now a large agricultural market center.

Chang Tso-lin (chäng′ tsō′-lĭn′, jäng′), 1873–1928, Chinese general. Chang was of humble birth. As the leader of a group of Manchurian brigands, he assisted (1904–5) the Japanese in the Russo-Japanese War. He occupied various military posts under the Chinese republic. From his appointment (1918) as inspector general of Manchuria to his death he controlled Manchuria, and from 1920 on he constantly warred to extend his rule southward; his most formidable rival for power was Wu Pei-fu. Chang died when the train in which he was retreating to Mukden before the Kuomintang army was bombed. His son, CHANG HSUEH-LIANG, succeeded to control of Manchuria.

Chankiang (chän′jyäng′), Mandarin *Chan-chiang*, Cantonese *Tsamkong*, official Chinese name for the former French territory of Kwangchowan (325 sq. mi.) on Kwangchow Bay, S Kwangtung prov., China. It was leased from China in 1898 for 99 years but was returned in 1945. Its chief city, Fort-Bayard, was renamed **Chankiang** (pop. c.269,000) and since 1955 has been developed as a major seaport by the Communist regime. It is an industrial and trade center and a railway hub.

Channel Islands or **Norman Isles,** Fr. *Îles Normandes*, archipelago (pop. 104,398), 75 sq. mi., off the coast of Normandy, France, in the English Channel. The main islands are JERSEY, GUERNSEY, ALDERNEY, and SARK, and there are a number of smaller islands, including Herm, Jethou, Minquiers, and Ecrehou, all belonging to Great Britain. The mild and sunny climate (35–40 in. rainfall a year) and the fertile soil have made the islands chiefly agricultural and pastoral. Large quantities of vegetables, fruits, and flowers are shipped to English markets. The famous breeds of cattle are kept pure by local laws. The islands are a favorite resort of tourists and vacationers. The islands are divided into two administrative bailiwicks. One of them, Jersey, has more than half the total population and the chief town of the islands, St. Helier. The other, Guernsey, includes all the islands except Jersey. Each bailiwick has its own lieutenant governor appointed by the crown, its own chief magistrate, and its own judicature. The inhabitants are mostly of

Norman descent, but in Alderney the stock is mainly English. The English language is spoken everywhere and is coming to supersede French as the official language. A Norman patois and Norman customs are still maintained by the natives. Christianization took place in the 6th cent., largely through the efforts of St. Helier and St. Sampson. In the 10th cent. the isles were granted to the duke of Normandy. At the Norman Conquest they were joined to the English crown and remained loyal to King John and England in 1204 when Philip II of France confiscated the duchy of Normandy. The French attempted unsuccessfully to reestablish control in the 14th cent. and later. In the Second World War, after the evacuation of some 10,000 military and civilian personnel, the islands were occupied (1940) by German forces, who surrendered to the British after the end of the war.

Channel Islands National Monument: see NATIONAL PARKS AND MONUMENTS (table).

Channel Lake, uninc. village (pop. 1,969), NE Ill., W of Antioch, in a resort region.

Channel-Port aux Basques (pôrt″ ō băsk′), town (pop. 4,141), SW N.F., Canada, a port on Cabot Strait. In 1945 Channel and Port aux Basques were incorporated into a single town. The town is an ice-free port and is connected by mail ships with North Sydney, N.S., and by rail with St. John's. It is a center for cod and halibut fishing, with cold-storage plants.

Channing, Edward, 1856–1931, American historian, b. Dorchester, Mass.; son of William Ellery Channing (1818–1901). Educated at Harvard (B.A., 1878; Ph.D., 1880), he was a notable teacher there from 1883 until his retirement in 1929, holding a professor's rank from 1897. Channing wrote *English History for American Readers* (with Thomas W. Higginson, 1893); *The United States of America, 1765–1865* (1896; 2d ed., 1930; reprinted 1941); *Guide to the Study and Reading of American History* (with Albert B. Hart, 1896; revised and augmented ed. by Channing, Hart, and Frederick J. Turner, 1912), an excellent brief bibliography of American history; *Students' History of the United States* (1898; 5th ed., revised, 1924); and *The Jeffersonian System, 1801–1811* ("American Nation" series, 1906). Most of these books were, however, either incidental to, or preparation for, the great work to which Channing devoted most of his life—*A History of the United States* (6 vols., 1905–25), embracing the years from 1000 to 1865. Based throughout on the author's extensive knowledge of the sources, remarkably accurate in fact, and excellently written, it is generally considered one of the finest histories of the United States ever produced by one man, and the final volume on the Civil War won a Pulitzer Prize in 1926.

Channing, William Ellery, 1780–1842, American Unitarian minister and author, b. Newport, R.I., grad. Harvard, 1798, and later studied theology there. At 23 he was ordained minister of the Federal St. Congregational Church in Boston, where he served until his death. He was a leader among those who were turning from Calvinism, and his sermon at Jared Sparks's ordination in Baltimore (1819) earned him the name "the apostle of Unitarianism." In 1820 he organized the Berry St. Conference of Ministers, which in 1825 formed the American Unitarian Association. Channing's plea was for humanitarianism and tolerance in religion rather than for a new creed. Not only a great preacher but a lucid writer, Channing influenced many American authors, including Emerson and other transcendentalists and Holmes and Bryant. Channing was not by nature a controversialist and never allied himself with the abolitionists, but his writings on slavery helped prepare for emancipation. In his denunciations of war, his discussion of labor problems, and his views on education, he was in advance of his time. His works (6 vols., 1841–43) passed through many editions. See his *Life . . . with Extracts from His Correspondence* (ed. by W. H. Channing, 3 vols., 1848); biographies by J. W. Chadwick (1903) and M. H. Rice (1961).

Channing, William Ellery, 1818–1901, American author, b. Boston; nephew of William Ellery Channing. A noted transcendentalist, he was the close friend of Emerson and Thoreau. His poems, *Poems* (1843), *The Woodman* (1849), among others, were criticized for their careless composition. Perhaps his most successful work was his biography of Thoreau (1873).

chansons de geste (shäsŏ′ dü zhĕst′) [Fr.,=songs of deeds], a group of epic poems of medieval France which flourished from the 11th through the 13th cent. Varying in length from 1,000 to 20,000 lines, assonanced or (in the 13th cent.) rhymed, the poems were composed by trouvères and were grouped in cycles about some great central figure such as Charlemagne. The origin of the form is disputed, but probably the first chansons were composed after the year 1000 by the joint efforts of wandering clerks and jongleurs to attract pilgrims to shrines where heroes of the chansons were supposedly buried. Sung by wandering jongleurs to the accompaniment of a primitive viol, they spread to England, Germany, Italy, and Iceland. The earlier chansons—epic, aristocratic, and militantly Christian—passed as real history to their medieval listeners, though much of the material was legendary. Some later chansons utilize fantastic adventure or reflect bourgeois elements. The oldest extant chanson and also the best and most famous, is the *Chanson de Roland* (c.1098–1100; see ROLAND); others are *Raoul de Cambrai, Huon de Bordeaux, Aliscans,* and *Renaud de Montauban.* See U. T. Holmes, *A History of Old French Literature* (1948).

chant, general name for one-voiced, unaccompanied, liturgical music. Usually it refers to the liturgical melodies of the Orthodox, Roman Catholic, and Anglican branches of Christianity. Roman Catholic chant, commonly called Gregorian or PLAIN SONG, is diatonic, modally organized (see MODE), and has a free rhythm determined by the text. Anglican chant is a harmonized, metrical adaptation to English texts of the Gregorian method of psalm singing, in which a short melody is adjusted to the length of different psalm verses by repeating one tone, the recitation tone, for any number of words in the text. The texts of Anglican chant, used in many Protestant churches, are from the Book of Common Prayer.

Chantaburi (chän″túbúrē′) or **Chantabun** (chän″-túbōōn′), town (pop. 10,649), capital of Chantaburi prov., SE Thailand, near the Gulf of Siam. It is an agricultural trade center, growing rice, pepper, and coffee. Precious gems (principally rubies and sapphires) are mined nearby. Originally part of the Khmer Empire, the town passed to Thailand in 1576. It was occupied by French forces from 1893 to 1905.

chanter: see BAGPIPE.

chantey or **shanty** (both: shăn′tē), work song with marked rhythm, particularly one sung by a group of sailors while hoisting sail or anchor or pushing the capstan. Often it has stanzas sung by a leader, the chanteyman, with a chorus repeated after each by the entire group. Similar songs are sung by shore gangs and lumbermen, and all are related to the work chanting of group labor all over the world, such as the barcaroles of Italian boatmen or the Oriental rope chants. Many universally known chanteys, such as *Way, Haul Away* and *Wide Missouri,* are of American origin. See R. R. Terry, *The Shanty Book* (1921–26); D. W. Bone, *Capstan Bars* (1932); J. C. Colcord, *Songs of American Sailormen* (1938).

Chantilly (shăntĭ′lē, Fr. shätēyē′), town (estimated pop. 7,065), Oise dept., N France. In the 18th cent., Chantilly gained renown for its fine lacework and the beauty of its porcelain. It is now a fashionable horse-racing center. The château, rebuilt in the 19th cent., contains the famous art museum of Condé.

Chantilly (shăntĭ′lē), locality, NE Va., scene of a Civil War battle (Sept. 1, 1862), in which Union troops, retreating after the second battle of BULL RUN, checked Stonewall Jackson.

Chantrey, Sir Francis Legatt, 1781–1841, English sculptor, famous for his portrait busts and statues. Among his many well-known works are equestrian

The château at Chantilly, France.

statues of Wellington and George IV (London); and a statue of George Washington (Statehouse, Boston).

Chanukah: see HANUKKAH.

Chanute, city (pop. 10,849), SE Kansas, on the Neosho and NW of Pittsburg; settled c.1870, formed by the consolidation of four contiguous towns and inc. 1872. A market center for a rich agricultural region, it has railroad repair shops, oil refineries, and plants manufacturing clothing and airplane parts. Nearby is the site of a mission (1824–29), the first in Kansas.

Chany (chŭnē′), salt water lake, 1,280 sq. mi., S central Asiatic RSFSR, Novosibirsk oblast, in the Baraba Steppe. The CHULYM river flows into the lake.

Chanzy, Antoine Eugène Alfred (ātwän′ ûzhĕn′ älfrĕd′ shäzē′), 1823–83, French general. After service in Algeria, Italy, and Syria, he was refused a major command in the FRANCO-PRUSSIAN WAR, but following the fall of the empire he was put in command of the Army of the Loire and opposed the Prussians with great skill. Chanzy was elected to the national assembly. Captured by the Commune of Paris in 1871, he was detained for several days. Chanzy was later governor general of Algeria (1873–79) and ambassador to Russia (1880–81), and in 1875 he was made senator for life. Nominated for president without his approval in 1879, he received a large vote in the election.

Chaoan or **Ch'ao-an** (both: chou′än′), city (pop. c.170,000), E Kwangtung prov., China, at the head of the Han river delta. It is also called Chaochow. It is the trade center for the Han river valley and has manufactures of textiles, machinery, and porcelain.

Chaochow: see CHAOAN.

Chao Phraya (chou′ präyä′) or **Menam** (mănăm′), river, rising in headwaters at the Burma-Laos border and crossing Thailand from north to south, the chief river of that kingdom. It is c.140 mi. long and flows in a tortuous course past Chainat, Angthong, Nontburi, and Bangkok to the Gulf of Siam at Samutprakan. The lower Chao Phraya is a union of four streams; it enters the Gulf of Siam through several outlets, interconnected by canals that serve for both irrigation and communication. The valley of the river is the main rice-producing area of Thailand.

Chaos (kā′ōs), in Greek mythology, vacant, unfathomable space. From it arose all things, earthly and divine. There are various legends explaining it. In the Pelasgian creation myth, EURYNOME rose out of Chaos and created all things. In the Olympian myth, GAEA sprang from Chaos and was the mother of all things. Eventually the word chaos came to mean a great confusion of matter out of which a supreme being created all life.

Chapais, Sir Thomas (shäpä′), 1858–1946, Canadian politician and historian, b. Quebec prov., grad. Laval Univ.; son of Jean Charles Chapais (1811–85). Thomas Chapais became professor of history at Laval Univ. He was appointed to the legislative council of Quebec in 1892, became speaker in 1895, and president of the executive council in 1896. In 1919 he was appointed to the Canadian Senate, and in 1930 he represented Canada in the Assembly of the League of Nations. He was a leader in the

newer school of French Canadian historians, his most notable works being his biographies *L'Intendant Talon* (1914), *The Great Intendant* (1914), and *Montcalm* (1911), and his *Cours d'histoire du Canada* (8 vols., 1919–34).

Sir Thomas Chapais

Chapala (chäpä′lä), lake, c.50 mi. long and 8 mi. wide, W Mexico, mostly in Jalisco but partly in Michoacán. It is the largest lake in the country. Set in a huge land depression, Lake Chapala is fed by the LERMA river, which flows into it from the east, and is drained by the Santiago, which flows out by the northeastern corner. It is a popular scenic resort. Fishing is an important native occupation. In the last 10 years the waters have been receding at an alarming rate; studies have been initiated to determine an effective conservation program.

chaparral (chăpŭrăl′), type of plant community in which shrubs are dominant. It occurs usually in regions having from 10 to 20 in. of rainfall annually, which are thus drier than forest regions and less dry than deserts. Where the rate of evaporation is high, chaparral may be found where the rainfall is well above 20 in. Generally chaparral country has most of its rainfall in the winter. The vegetation includes both evergreen and deciduous forms, the dominant species varying in different areas. Chaparral is well exemplified in parts of the W and SW United States, although similar growth is found in many parts of the world. Climax areas (see ECOLOGY) are well represented by the largely deciduous growths in Colorado, E Utah, and N New Mexico. A subclimax area extends from South Dakota to Texas and through part of the Great Basin. Among the chief species of plants in these regions are Gambel oak (*Quercus utahensis*), mountain mahogany (*Cercocarpus parvifolius*), the squawbush (*Rhus trilobata*), the western chokeberry (*Prunus demissa*), the western serviceberry (*Amelanchier alnifolia*), and mesquite (*Prosopis glandulosa*). Evergreen shrubs are characteristic of the chaparral found in the southern half of California, especially near the coast, and extending into Nevada and Arizona. Among the dominant forms are several species of buckthorn (*Ceanothus*), manzanita (*Arctostaphylos tomentosa* and *A.*

pungens), and the holly-leaved cherry (*Prunus ilicifolia*). A species of scrub oak (*Quercus dumosa*) is the chief deciduous form. Chaparral growth is sometimes so dense that it is almost impenetrable.

chapbook, one of the pamphlets formerly sold in Europe and America by itinerant agents, or "chapmen." The price of a chapbook was low—in England often a penny. Like the broadside, the chapbook was usually anonymous and undated. The text commonly was addressed to such readers as those who purchase tabloid newspapers. Students of the popular taste of the 16th, 17th, and 18th cent. find source material in the chapbooks. The term is occasionally used to refer to old manuscripts showing national character through the use of vernacular expressions.

Chapei: see SHANGHAI.

chapel, subsidiary place of worship. It is either an alcove or chamber within a church, a separate building, or a room set apart for the purpose in a secular building. A movable shrine containing the *cappa*, or cloak, of St. MARTIN was first called a *cappella*; hence a sanctuary that is not called a church. Though the churches of the early Middle Ages possessed only the single altar of the apse, chapels became necessary with the increase of relics and of devotions at altars sacred to numerous saints. At first they appeared as minor apses, flanking the main apse. After the 10th cent. in order to accommodate the increasing number of pilgrims, a complex series of radiating chapels was developed behind the high altar. In the 13th cent. chapels were added to the side-aisle bays of choir and nave. In England the strongly projecting transepts provided the favored space for a relatively small number of chapels. In France the Lady Chapel (dedicated to the Virgin) is the central chapel of the *chevet* and is sometimes larger than the others, while in England it occurs directly behind the high altar. Peculiar to English cathedrals are the small chantry chapels, mostly of the 14th and 15th cent., either built and endowed by individuals for their private Masses or serving to enclose the tombs of bishops and other churchmen. From earliest times, members of royalty had the right to an independent private chapel. Such are the separate building of the Sainte-Chapelle, Paris; St. George's Chapel at Windsor; and Henry VII's magnificent chapel at Westminster, London. In addition, there were royal mortuary chapels, the most celebrated being that of Charlemagne (796–804), at Aachen, since converted into a cathedral. Numerous lords of medieval castles and manor houses established private chapels, over which episcopal jurisdiction was enforced as completely as possible. The two main chapels at the Vatican are the Pauline Chapel (1540), designed by Antonioda SANGALLO for Paul III, and the Sistine Chapel (1473), built by Sixtus IV and celebrated for its great fresco decorations by MICHELANGELO and other masters. Two of the most famous French modern chapels (built in the 1950s) are the chapel at Vence designed by Matisse and the one at Ronchamp by Le Corbusier; both are freestanding buildings.

Chapelain, Jean (zhä′ shäplĕ′), 1595–1674, French poet. His *Pucelle* (1656) was a poem on Joan of Arc. Chapelain was a founding member of the French Academy, for which he composed the paper which made a celebrated and futile attack upon *Le Cid* of Pierre CORNEILLE.

Chapel Hill, town (pop. 12,573), central N.C., NW of Raleigh, at the edge of the piedmont; founded 1792. It is the seat of the Univ. of North Carolina (see NORTH CAROLINA, UNIVERSITY OF).

Chaplin, Charlie (Charles Spencer Chaplin), 1889–, cinema actor, director, producer, writer, and com-

Interior of the Sistine Chapel.

Charlie Chaplin in Modern Times.

poser, b. London, England. At an early age he appeared in London music halls. In 1910 he joined a pantomime troupe and, while on a tour of the United States, he attracted the attention of Mack Sennett. It was with the Keystone Company (1914–15) that he created the famous figure with the trick derby, minute mustache, baggy trousers, oversized shoes, awkward walk, and bamboo cane. In 1918 he became an independent producer with the completion of his own studios. His films were released through United Artists, which he founded (1920) together with D. W. Griffith, Douglas Fairbanks, and Mary Pickford. He often composed his own background music. His most notable films include *The Gold Rush, The Kid, The Circus, City Lights, Modern Times, The Great Dictator* (the first film in which he spoke), *Monsieur Verdoux,* and *Limelight.* Chaplin's creative ability is shown mostly in his portrayal of lovable tramps. He is an English citizen; after tax difficulties with the U.S. government he moved in 1952 to Switzerland. The controversial film *A King in New York* made (1957) in England was not shown in the United States. See his book *My Trip Abroad* (1922); biographies by Parker Tyler (1947), Peter Cotes and Thelma Niklaus (1951), R. J. Minney (1954), and Charles Chaplin, Jr. (1960).

Chaplin, Ralph, 1878–1961, American writer, b. Chicago. After working as a commercial artist, he joined (1911) the Industrial Workers of the World and contributed articles to its publications. As a "Wobbly," Chaplin participated in the strikes at Lawrence, Mass., and Paterson, N.J. In 1914 he wrote *Solidarity Forever,* perhaps the most famous of the many I.W.W. songs. As editor of the I.W.W. paper he bitterly opposed American participation in the First World War. With other I.W.W. leaders Chaplin was convicted (1918) of subversive activities in denouncing the war, and spent four years in jail. While confined he wrote many poems concerned with his life as an I.W.W. worker. See his autobiography, *Wobbly: the Rough and Tumble Story of an American Radical* (1948).

Chapman, George, 1559?–1634, English dramatist, translator, and poet. His great contributions to English literature are his poetic translations of Homer's *Iliad* (1612) and *Odyssey* (1614–15). In Homer, Chapman found a perfect vehicle for determining his heroic man. However, it is in his tragedies that his philosophical dogma is most fully expressed. Chapman was a classical scholar, and his work shows the influence of the Stoic impassivists, Epictetus and Seneca. In his best-known tragedies, *Bussy D'Ambois* (1607) and *The Conspiracy and Tragedy of Byron* (1608), the hero is destroyed by his inability to control his inward passions and resist outward temptation. Chapman wrote and collaborated on nearly a dozen comedies, the most notable being *All Fools* (1605) and *Eastward Ho!* (1605), the latter written with Ben Jonson and John Marston. Included among his other works are several metaphysical poems, a completed version of Marlowe's *Hero and Leander* (1598), and translations of Petrarch and Hesiod.

Chapman, John, 1774–1845, American pioneer, more familiarly known as Johnny Appleseed, b. Massachusetts. From Pennsylvania—where he had sold or given saplings and apple seeds to families migrating westward—he went c.1800 to present Ohio sowing apple seeds as he went. For over 40 years Johnny Appleseed continued to wander up and down in Ohio, Indiana, and W Pennsylvania visiting his forest nurseries to prune and care for them and to aid hundreds of settlers to establish orchards of their own. His ragged dress, eccentric ways, and religious turn of mind attracted attention, and he became a familiar figure to settlers. Scores of legends were told of him after he died. However, it was verified that in the War of 1812 he sped 30 mi. to summon American troops to Mansfield, Ohio, thus forestalling a raid by Indian tribes who were allied with the British. He died near Fort Wayne, Ind. See biographies by H. A. Pershing (1930) and Robert Price (1954).

Chapman, John Jay, 1862–1933, American essayist and poet, b. New York city, grad. Harvard. He was admitted to the bar in 1888 but after 10 years abandoned law for literature. A friend of William James and other Boston intellectuals of the time, Chapman was a fiery and pertinent observer of his environment. He wrote *Emerson and Other Essays* (1898), *Memories and Milestones* (1915), *Greek Genius and Other Essays* (1915), *Songs and Poems* (1919), and *New Horizons in American Life* (1932). He also edited (1917) the letters of his son, Victor Chapman. See biography by M. A. DeW. Howe (1937); study by R. B. Hovey (1959).

Chapman, Maria (Weston), 1806–85, American abolitionist, b. Weymouth, Mass. In 1834 she became a close associate of William Lloyd Garrison, helped organize the Boston Female Anti-Slavery Society, and for several years was treasurer of the Massachusetts Anti-Slavery Society. She edited (1877) the autobiography of her friend Harriet Martineau.

Chapman, city (pop. 1,095), central Kansas, ENE of Abilene, in a wheat and dairy region; settled 1868, inc. 1883.

Chapmanville, town (pop. 1,241), SW W.Va., SW of Charleston and on the Guyandot river.

Chappe, Claude (klōd' shăp'), 1763–1805, French engineer. He developed an ocular telegraph, i.e., one using signals on posts placed within sight of each other. It was first used between Paris and Lille in 1794 and was a predecessor of the modern telegraph.

Chappell (chă'pŭl), village (pop. 1,280), co. seat of Deuel co., W Nebr., W of North Platte and on a tributary of the South Platte, in a wheat-growing Great Plains area; platted 1884.

Chaptal, Jean Antoine (zhă' ătwän' shăptäl'), 1756–1832, French chemist, statesman, and economist. Professor of chemistry at Montpellier, he was minister of the interior (1801–9) and director general of commerce and manufactures (1815) under Napoleon I, who created him count of Chanteloup. He established the first French trade school, constructed an important network of canals and roads, and pioneered in the application of chemistry to industry.

chapter house, a building in which the chapter of the clergy meets. Its plan varies, the simplest being a rectangle. At Worcester, the Norman builders created a circular chapter house (c.1100), with vaulting springing from a central pillar. Subsequent examples, adopting this central support for their vaulted roofs but frequently polygonal in plan, are among the most distinctive achievements of the English Gothic builders. Those at Salisbury, Wells, and Westminster Abbey (1250) are octagonal, while that at Lincoln is decagonal. At York, the octagonal room (c.1300) exhibits a departure in that it dispenses with the central column and is covered with a vaulted wooden roof.

Chapultepec (chäpōōl′tăpĕk′) [Aztec,=grasshopper hill], rocky eminence S of Mexico city; site of bitter fighting in the Mexican War. Originally developed as a playground for Aztec emperors, a castle was built late in the 18th cent. to serve as a summer home for the Spanish viceroys. It became the traditional home of the rulers of Mexico. Heavily fortified, it was the scene of spectacular fighting in the Mexican War. After Santa Anna's blunders had intensified hostilities, Gen. Winfield Scott, in his advance on Mexico city, ordered the storming of Chapultepec on Sept. 12, 1847; it fell the next day. However, the heroic defenders— particularly the "boy heroes" from the adjoining military college who preferred death to surrender —became for Mexicans a symbol of glory. Both Emperor Maximilian and, later, Porfirio Díaz beautified the grounds and embellished the castle. In 1937 Cárdenas, then president, declared it a museum of colonial history and ethnography. The Inter-American Conference on the Problems of War and Peace, which met here in 1945, is commonly called the Chapultepec Conference (see PAN-AMERICANISM).

Chapultepec, Act of: see PAN-AMERICANISM.

char: see SALMON.

characin (kăr′ŭsĭn), large and diverse family of 700 species of fresh-water fishes, related to the carp and the catfish. Characins are found in Africa and in tropical America, especially in the Amazon. Most species are active and predacious—e.g., the no-

Characin

torious piranhas or caribes, which with their powerful jaws and razor-sharp triangular teeth are capable of killing men and cattle. One species of characin, the 4-inch Mexican tetra, or sardina blanca, found in the Rio Grande, is used in aquariums. A small Mexican species of stream characin is interesting for the stages of blindness it exhibits: those which live far back in caves are eyeless; those found near the entrance have imperfect eyes; and the specimens living in open water have normal eyes. A cross of a blind with a normal specimen produces offspring with varying degrees of eye degeneracy.

charade (shŭräd′), verbal, written, or acted representation of the syllables of a word from which a whole word is to be guessed. Winthrop M. PRAED wrote many of the well-known charades, and a good description of the acted charade is found in Thackeray's *Vanity Fair*. In the United States a charade acted in dumb show (usually called simply "the game") had considerable popularity in the 1930s and 1940s.

Charashim (kăr′ŭ–) [Heb.,=craftsmen; cf. Neh. 11. 35], unidentified valley, Palestine, probably near Lydda. 1 Chron. 4.14.

Charcas (chär′käs), Spanish colonial *audiencia* and presidency in South America, known also as Upper Peru and Chuquisaca. Charcas roughly corresponded to modern Bolivia but included parts of present Argentina, Chile, Peru, and Paraguay, a territorial expanse leading to disputes and wars after independence had been won. It was established in 1559 and was attached to the viceroyalty of Peru until joined (1776) to the newly created viceroyalty of La Plata. The prosecutor of Charcas, José de Antequera y Castro, led (1721) the first major creole uprising against viceregal authority. The city of SUCRE was sometimes called Charcas.

charcoal, substance, largely pure CARBON, obtained by burning organic material in the absence of air (destructive DISTILLATION). The most common variety, wood charcoal, was formerly prepared by piling wood into stacks, covering it with earth or turf, and setting it on fire. The noncarbonaceous elements in the wood passed off as vapors into the air, some of the carbon was utilized as fuel, and the remaining carbon was converted into charcoal. In factories the wood is raised to a high temperature

Storming of Chapultepec, September 13, 1847.

in an iron retort, and the industrially important by-products, including METHYL ALCOHOL, ACETONE, and ACETIC ACID, are saved. Synthetic production of acetic acid and methyl alcohol has largely replaced the distillation method. Charcoal obtained from bones is called bone black, animal black, or animal charcoal. Being almost pure carbon, charcoal yields a larger amount of heat in proportion to its volume than is obtained from a corresponding quantity of wood; as a fuel it has the further advantage of being smokeless. It is used also in the manufacture of explosives. Because of its porous structure charcoal is a highly efficient agent for the ADSORPTION of gases and of solids from solution. It is used in sugar refining, in water purification, in the purification of factory air, and in gas masks. By special heating or chemical processes the adsorptive property can be greatly increased; charcoal so treated is known as activated charcoal.

Charcot, Jean Baptiste (zhä′ bätěst′ shärkō′), 1867–1936, French neurologist and explorer in the antarctic region; son of Jean Martin Charcot. He became director of clinics at the Univ. of Paris in 1896, but soon gave up medicine for exploration. In two voyages (1903–7, 1908–10) he surveyed the coast of Antarctica from Palmer Peninsula to Charcot Land, obtaining valuable scientific data. After 1920 Charcot made seven scientific voyages to Greenland aboard his ship, the *Pourquoi Pas?*. In 1935 he came out of retirement for a final expedition to Greenland. Crashing into a reef, Charcot went down with his celebrated ship off the coast of Iceland. His antarctic voyages were recorded in his *Le Pourquoi Pas? dans l'antarctique* (1910; Eng. tr., *The Voyage of the Why Not? in the Antarctic*, 1911).

Charcot, Jean Martin (märtě′), 1825–93, French neurologist. He developed at the Salpêtrière in Paris the greatest clinic of his time for diseases of the nervous system. He made many important observations on these diseases, described the characteristics of the condition known as *tabes dorsalis*, differentiated multiple sclerosis and *paralysis agitans*, and wrote on many neurological subjects. Charcot's insight into the nature of hysteria is credited by Sigmund Freud, his pupil, as having contributed to the early psychoanalytic formulations on the subject. See biography by Georges Guillain (1959).

chard: see ARTICHOKE and BEET.

Chardin, Jean Baptiste (zhä′ bätěst′ shärdě′), 1699–1779, one of the finest French painters of the 18th cent. In 1728 he became a member of the Académie royale de Peinture et de Sculpture and was its treasurer for over 20 years. While the Academy still advocated heroic episodes or history painting as the highest form of art, Chardin chose to paint simple still lifes and domestic interiors. His ability to evoke textures, such as those of vegetables, fruit, and wild game, is unsurpassed, and his muted tones, delicate touch, and compositional skill have always been admired. The Louvre has many of his oils and pastel portraits, including *Benediction* and *Return from Market*. *Blowing Bubbles* and a portrait of *Mme Chardin* are at the Metropolitan Museum. Other paintings are in the National Gallery of Art, Washington, D.C., and in the Museum of Fine Arts, Boston.

Chardon (shär′dŭn), village (pop. 3,154), co. seat of Geauga co., NE Ohio, ENE of Cleveland; settled 1812, inc. 1872. It is a maple-syrup and sugar center.

Chardzhou (chŭrjô′ōō), city (pop. c.66,000), capital of Chardzhou oblast, N central Turkmen SSR, on the Amu Darya river. An inland port, it has shipyards and is a cotton and silk manufacturing center. Chardzhou was founded in the late 19th cent. as a fortress.

Charente (shärät′), department (2,306 sq. mi.; estimated pop. 313,635), W France. Part of the former provinces of Angoumois and Saintonge, its capital is ANGOULÊME. It is an agricultural and dairying region, with brandy distilled at COGNAC.

Charente, river, rising W of Limoges, France. Some 220 mi. long, it flows W to the Atlantic past Angoulême, Cognac, Saintes, and Rochefort. Along its western course are the celebrated vineyards from which cognac is made.

Charente-Maritime (–märētěm′), department (2,792 sq. mi., estimated pop. 447,973), W France, on the Atlantic coast, formerly Charente-Inférieure. It occupies the former provinces of SAINTONGE and AUNIS. La Rochelle is the capital.

Chares (kâ′rēz, kā′–), 3d cent. B.C., Greek worker in bronze from Lindus, Rhodes; pupil of Lysippus. He was the sculptor of the COLOSSUS OF RHODES and is said to have founded the Rhodian school of sculpture. No known works have survived.

chargé d'affaires: see DIPLOMATIC SERVICE.

Charing Cross (chàr′ĭng, châr′–), square at the west end of the Strand, Westminster metropolitan bor-

Return from Market by Jean Baptiste Chardin.

CHARIOT

Chaldaean chariot from Ur.

Nike, driving a quadriga, chariot drawn by four horses (4th-5th-century Greek vase painting).

ough, London, England, near Trafalgar Square. One of the Eleanor Crosses (see ELEANOR OF CASTILE) was erected here. Charing Cross station is one of London's busiest terminals. Charing Cross Hospital is nearby.

chariot (chă'rēŭt), the earliest and simplest type of carriage and the chief vehicle of the ancients. It was known among the Babylonians before the introduction of horses c.2000 B.C., being drawn at first by asses. The chariot and horse introduced into Egypt c.1700 B.C. by the Hyksos invaders doubtless contributed to their military success. Simultaneously the use of the chariot spread over the Near East, chiefly as a war machine. The Assyrians are credited with introducing chariots with scythes mounted on the wheels as weapons, a type later adopted by the Persians. In Greece and Rome the chariot was never used to any extent in war, possibly because of generally unfavorable topography. It was, however, prominent in games and processions, becoming in Rome the inevitable carriage of the triumphal procession. Here also the chariot races of the circus were developed. The ancient chariot was a very light vehicle, drawn by two or more horses hitched side by side. The car was little else than a floor with a waist-high semicircular guard in front. British chariots were open in front, had a curved wall behind, often had seats, and sometimes had scythes on the wheels.

Charites: see GRACES.

Chariton (shă'rĭtŭn), city (pop. 5,042), co. seat of Lucas co., S central Iowa, W of Ottumwa; inc. 1857. It is a farm trade and coal-mining center with railroad shops and factories producing men's clothing and industrial machinery. Red Haw Hill State Park is nearby.

charity, public, organized relief of human disease, poverty, and misery. Among the Greeks and Romans public charity was devoted chiefly to those holding full citizenship. It was early connected with religion, as among the Hebrews and, from them, among the Christians and later the Moslems. The Christian Church was the main dispenser of charity in the Middle Ages, supplemented by the guilds. Later, national and local governmental agencies, as well as many private agencies, took over much of the charitable activity of the Church. First of the extensive state efforts was the Elizabethan POOR LAW of 1601, which attempted to classify dependents and provide special treatment for each group on the local (parish) level. During the Industrial Revolution, many entrepreneurs considered the theory of state charity to violate the concepts of laissez faire, and therefore opposed it. Exceptions were such men as Robert OWEN, who believed that public charity was essential but that its implementation should be undertaken cooperatively rather than as a function of the state. Today, the degree to which the state dispenses and administers public charity varies from country to country. Generally speaking, Britain and the Scandinavian countries are termed "welfare states" because of the very large degree of governmental involvement in the field of public charity and the breadth of their social welfare legislation. Private philanthropies and charitable organizations, however, continue to operate in these countries in many areas of public welfare. In Communist countries, public charity is dispensed and administered exclusively by the state. In the United States public charity has come more and more under state and Federal control, although philanthropic agencies still play a major role. Modern public charities may be listed as the care of destitute adults; the treatment of the defective, insane, feeble-minded, and criminal; the care of the sick in hospitals and dispensaries and through visiting nurses; the care of destitute, neglected, and delinquent children; the care and relief of needy families; and supervisory, educational, and constructive activity such as is provided by the SETTLEMENT HOUSE. Dispensation of public charity has been assumed also by international relief bodies such as the RED CROSS and agencies of the United Nations such as the International Refugee Organization and the UN High Commission for Refugees. See Robert Asher, *United Nations and the Promotion of the General Welfare* (1957); Alfred de Grazia, *American Welfare* (1961); National Conference on Social Welfare, *Social Welfare Administration* (1961); A. C. Marts, *Man's Concern for His Fellow-man* (1961).

Charlack (shär′lăk), village (pop. 1,493), E Mo., a suburb NW of St. Louis; inc. 1945.

Charlemagne (shär′lŭmăn) (Charles the Great or Charles I) [O.Fr.,=Charles the great], 742–814, emperor of the West (800–814), Frankish king (768–814). Elder son of PEPIN THE SHORT and a grandson of Charles Martel, he shared with his brother Carloman in the succession to his father's kingdom. At Carloman's death (771), young Charles was proclaimed sole king of the Franks. When war broke out between DESIDERIUS, king of the Lombards, who had been persuaded to support the claims of Carloman's two young sons, and Pope ADRIAN I, who had refused support, Charles intervened (773) on the side of the pope. At Rome he was received by Adrian as patrician of the Romans (a title he had received with his father in 754), and he confirmed his father's donation to the Holy See. Shortly afterward he took Pavia and assumed the iron crown of the Lombard kings. In 778 he invaded Spain; he was repulsed by the Moors at Saragossa but kept Navarre and the "Spanish March," including Pamplona and Barcelona. Charles's struggle with the pagan Saxons, whose greatest leader was WIDUKIND, lasted from 772 till 804. By dint of forced conversions, wholesale massacres, and the transportation of thousands of Saxons to the interior of the Frankish kingdom, Charles made his domination over Saxony complete. He also warred successfully against the Avars and the Slavs, advancing as far east as Pomerania. Meanwhile the new pope, LEO III, was threatened with deposition by the Romans and in 799 appealed to Charles. Charles hastened to Rome to support Leo, and on Christmas Day, 800, was crowned emperor by the pope. The pretext for his coronation was his refusal to recognize IRENE as empress of the East. In 812 Charles ceded Venice and Dalmatia to the Byzantine emperor, Michael I, who then recognized his imperial dignity. The end of Charles's reign was troubled by the raids of Norse and Danish pirates (see NORSEMEN), and Charles took vigorous measures for the construction of a fleet, which his successors neglected. His land frontiers he had already protected by the creation of marches. In his government he continued and systematized the administrative machinery of his predecessors. He permitted conquered peoples to retain their own laws, which he codified when possible, and he issued many CAPITULARIES (gathered in the MONUMENTA GERMANIAE HISTORICA). A noteworthy achievement was the creation of a system by which he might personally supervise his administrators in even the most distant lands; his *missi dominici* were personal representatives with wide powers who regularly inspected their assigned districts. He maintained contact with the lesser magnates through annual consultative assemblies. He tried to help the poorer freemen by reducing their military obligations and by removing their obligation to attend county assemblies. He strove to educate the clergy and

Coronation of Charlemagne by Pope Leo III at Rome in A.D. 800 (illumination from the 14th century).

Statue of Charlemagne on one of the towers of the cathedral at Zurich. This memorial dates from A.D. 1300.

exercised more direct control over the appointment of bishops. Like the Byzantine emperors, he acted as arbiter in theological disputes by summoning councils, notably that at Frankfurt (794), where ADOPTIONISM was rejected and the decrees of the Second Council of Nicaea were condemned. He stimulated foreign trade and entertained friendly relations with England and with Harun al-Rashid. In 813 Charlemagne designated his son LOUIS I as his imperial consort and successor and crowned him at Aachen, thus founding the Carolingian dynasty of emperors (see CAROLINGIANS). Charlemagne's court at AACHEN was the center of a considerable intellectual quickening. The palace school, under the leadership of ALCUIN, became particularly famous, but of greater significance were the numerous schools for children of all classes, established throughout the empire during Charles's reign. The preservation of classical literature was due almost entirely to his initiative. Prominent figures of the Carolingian renaissance, other than Alcuin, included PAUL THE DEACON, EINHARD, and Peter of Pisa. Charlemagne himself, though scarcely to be considered educated by later standards, showed great taste for learning and strove for purity in his Latin. In his daily life he affected the simple manners of his Frankish forebears, wore Frankish clothes, and led a frugal existence, except for his habit of keeping several wives and concubines. He was beatified after his death and in some churches has been honored as a saint. His physical appearance probably differed vastly from the bearded and patriarchal figure of the legend. Indeed, Charlemagne's actual achievements and prestige were of such magnitude that later generations enlarged them to fantastic proportions. Surrounded by his legendary 12 peers, he became the central figure of a cycle of romance. At first, legend pictured him as the champion of Christendom; later he appeared as a vacillating old man, almost a comic figure. His characterization in the *Chanson de Roland* (see ROLAND) has impressed itself indelibly on the imagination of the Western world. The vogue of the Charlemagne epic ebbed somewhat after the Renaissance, but was revived again in the 19th cent. by Victor Hugo and other members of the Romantic school. Charlemagne's creation (or recreation) of an empire was the basis of the theory of the HOLY ROMAN EMPIRE; it was his example that Napoleon I had in mind when he tried to assume his succession in 1804. Einhard wrote a contemporary biography of Charlemagne. See works by Harold Lamb (1954) and Richard Winston (1954); Heinrich Fichtenau, *The Carolingian Empire* (1949; Eng. tr., 1957). For the literary aspect, see Thomas Bulfinch, *Legends of Charlemagne* (1863), and J. L. Weston, *The Romance Cycle of Charlemagne and His Peers* (1901).

Charleroi (shärlûrwä'), town (estimated pop. 25,491), Hainaut prov., SW Belgium, on the Sambre river and the Charleroi-Brussels Canal. The industrial center of a coal-mining region, it manufactures steel, glass, machinery, and chemicals. It was of strategic importance in the wars of the 17th and 18th cent. The Germans won a battle (1914) here in the First World War. Charleroi is noted for its modern public buildings.

Charleroi (shärlûroi', shär'lûroi), borough (pop. 8,148), SW Pa., S of Pittsburgh and on the Monongahela; laid out 1890, inc. 1892. Glass and mining machinery are produced.

Charles I, emperor and Frankish king: see CHARLEMAGNE.

Charles II or **Charles the Bald,** 823–77, emperor (875–77), king of the West Franks (843–77), son of Emperor LOUIS I by a second marriage. The efforts of Louis to create a kingdom for Charles were responsible for the repeated revolts of Louis's elder sons which disturbed the latter part of Louis's reign. When LOTHAIR I attempted to reunite the empire after Louis's death, Charles and LOUIS THE GERMAN marched against their brother and defeated him at Fontenoy (841). Reaffirming their alliance in 842 (see STRASBOURG, OATH OF), they signed (843) with Lothair the Treaty of Verdun, (see VERDUN, TREATY OF), which divided the empire into three parts. The part roughly corresponding to modern France fell to Charles. He was almost continuously at war with his brothers and their sons, with the Normans, and with rebellious subjects. When Charles's nephew LOTHAIR, king of Lotharingia, died in 869, Charles seized his kingdom, but was forced by the Treaty of MERSEN (870) to divide it with Louis the German. In 875, at the death of his nephew Emperor Louis II, Charles secured the imperial crown. His reign witnessed the growth of the power of the nobles at the expense of the royal power and thus marked the rise of local feudalism. Charles's chief adviser was Archbishop HINCMAR.

Charles III or **Charles the Fat,** 839–88, emperor (881–87), king of the East Franks (879–87), king of the West Franks (885–87), son of LOUIS THE GERMAN, at whose death he inherited Swabia (876). In 886, when he went to relieve Paris, which was besieged by the Normans, he ransomed the city instead of fighting and allowed the Normans to ravage Burgundy. He was deposed in 887 and was succeeded in Germany by ARNULF and briefly in France by EUDES.

Charles IV, 1316–78, emperor (1355–78) and German king (1346–78), king of Bohemia (1346–78). The son of JOHN OF LUXEMBURG, he was educated at the French court and fought the English at Crécy, where his father's heroic death made him king of Bohemia. Pope CLEMENT VI, to whom he had promised far-reaching concessions, helped secure his election (1346) as antiking to Emperor LOUIS IV. Louis's death (1347), the popular desire for peace, which was fostered by the ravages of the Black Death, and the absence of a strong leader to unite the opposition enabled Charles to make good his claim to the crown by 1349. Germany being restored to peace (1354), he was crowned emperor in Rome on Easter Sunday, in 1355, by the papal legate (the pope was then residing at Avignon). In 1356 he promulgated the Golden Bull (see ELECTORS), by which the method of electing an emperor was fixed. Charles rounded out his family possessions by acquiring, through skillful diplomacy, the margraviate of Brandenburg (1373) and by adding to his territories in Silesia and Lusatia. Though he had virtually renounced imperial pretensions in Italy through his treaty with Clement VI, Charles

supported the plans of Urban V to return the
papacy from Avignon to Rome. His intervention
in Italy (1368), however, was chiefly a pretext for
extorting tribute from the cities in exchange for
their freedom. To strengthen his dynasty, he had
his son WENCESLAUS elected German king (1376).
The election necessitated bribing the electors, and
Charles imposed high taxes to raise the money. The
taxes led to a revolt by a league of Swabian cities.
Charles obtained (1378) peace by granting concessions, but the league's struggle with the nobles
troubled the early reign of Wenceslaus. Charles
embellished his capital, Prague, where many landmarks bear his name, founded (1348) the university
at Prague (the oldest in Central Europe), and rebuilt the Cathedral of St. Vitus. By introducing
new agricultural methods and by expanding industries, he fostered economic life. He drew up a
code of laws, the *Maiestas Carolina* (1350)—which
was, however, rejected by the nobles—and he protected the lower classes by giving them courts in
which to sue their overlords. With the Church he
always sought to maintain friendly relations. As
Holy Roman emperor, his reputation rests mainly
on the Golden Bull, which, though it confirmed the
weakness of the imperial power, provided a stable
constitutional foundation for its exercise. See
biographies by G. G. Walsh (1924) and Bede Jarett
(with a translation of Charles's autobiography,
1935).

Charles V, 1500–1558, emperor (1519–58) and, as
Charles I, king of Spain (1516–56), son of PHILIP I
and JOANNA of Castile, grandson of Ferdinand V of

Charles V

Aragon, Isabella of Castile, Emperor Maximilian I,
and Mary of Burgundy. He inherited an empire on
which "the sun never set." The Netherlands, Luxembourg, Artois, and Franche-Comté came to him
on the death (1506) of his father. Aragon, Navarre,
Granada, Naples, Sicily, Sardinia, Spanish America, and joint kingship with his mother (who was
insane) over Castile devolved upon him at the
death (1516) of Ferdinand V; from Charles's accession the Spanish kingdoms remained united. On
the death (1519) of Maximilian I he inherited the
Hapsburg lands and was elected emperor. Born
and raised at Ghent, Charles was brought up as a
Fleming. His aunt, MARGARET OF AUSTRIA, was
regent for him in the Netherlands. She and his
tutor, Adrian of Utrecht (later Pope ADRIAN VI),
were the chief influences on the youth. Arriving in
Spain in 1517, Charles was distrusted as a foreign-
er. His brusque dismissal of Cardinal Jiménez, his
hasty appointments of Flemish favorites to high
offices, and his departure (1520) for Germany to be
crowned heightened the resentment. He won the
imperial elections against his chief rivals, FRANCIS
I of France and HENRY VIII of England, through
the support given him by a surge of German nationalism. However, Charles sought to become the
leader of a universal empire, not of a German national state. His imperial dreams were encouraged
by GATTINARA, whose influence replaced that of
Charles's Flemish advisers.

Struggle for Empire. The chief problems Charles
faced were the Protestant REFORMATION in Germany, his conflict with the papacy, and the advance of the Ottoman Turks. All three were exploited by Francis I. Shortly after his election
Charles began his lifelong struggle with France (see
also HENRY II of France and ITALIAN WARS), which
required immense expenditures. In 1520 he signed
with Henry VIII the Treaty of Gravelines, which
undid the results of the meeting on the FIELD OF
THE CLOTH OF GOLD, and in 1521 he invaded N
Italy, then controlled by France. The fiscal onus
rested on Spain and provoked violent reaction.
Toledo, Segovia, and other Castilian cities revolted
in the brief war (1520–21) of the *comuneros*. A bold
program for limiting the royal power and violent
class warfare marked the rising, which was put
down by the battle of Villalar and by the execution
of Juan de PADILLA and other leaders. Charles
later won the reliable loyalty of his Spanish subjects. In Germany, at the fateful Diet of WORMS
(1521), he secured a satisfactory compromise regarding the REICHSREGIMENT but unyieldingly opposed the doctrines of Martin LUTHER. In his written opinion Charles declared himself ready to stake
his dominions, friends, blood, life, and soul on the
extinction of heresy. Late in May, 1521, he signed
the Edict of Worms, outlawing Luther and his followers, and entered a secret alliance with Pope
LEO X. The emperor and the pope agreed that
Protestantism must be suppressed, but the papacy
was concerned with the threat to its temporal
power and its independence stemming from imperial domination of Italy. Unfortunately, Charles's
plan for a dynastic world-state required full papal
support. In Italy, Charles seemed triumphant
when Francis I, captured (1525) at Pavia, signed

the humiliating Treaty of Madrid (1526). When Francis repudiated it and persuaded Pope CLEMENT VII to join the anti-imperial League of Cognac, Charles sent to Italy a German army composed mostly of Lutherans. Its first commander, FRUNDS-BERG, was succeeded by Charles de BOURBON, who led the semi-mutinous host to Rome (1527). The ensuing sack of Rome (the "German Fury") was disavowed by the emperor, who nevertheless profited from the outrage by extorting large sums from the pope. The Treaty of CAMBRAI with France and the Peace of Barcelona with the pope (both in 1529) confirmed Charles's position in Italy and secured his coronation as emperor at Bologna (1530). Charles was the last German emperor to be crowned by the pope. His brother Ferdinand, king of Bohemia and Hungary (later Emperor FERDINAND I), was elected king of the Romans in 1531. Charles, who had awarded him the Austrian duchies in 1521, delegated increasing authority to him in Germany, then torn by religious and social struggles. The rebellion (1522–23) of Franz von SICKINGEN was followed by the more serious PEASANTS' WAR (1524–26), and the Swabian League in 1531 made way for the Lutheran SCHMALKALDIC LEAGUE. The Reformation progressed, and the breach between Catholics and Protestants widened. Before dealing with the religious problem, Charles had to make peace abroad. Francis I, allied with Sultan SULEIMAN I, having renewed warfare, Charles allied himself (1543) with Henry VIII and in 1544 forced Francis to make peace at CRÉPY. A truce with Turkey, however humiliating, gave Charles and Ferdinand some respite. At last the way opened for the Catholic REFORMATION, ardently desired by Charles and forwarded by St. Ignatius of Loyola, when the Council of Trent (see TRENT, COUNCIL OF) convened in 1545. Turning on the Protestant princes of Germany, Charles split their ranks by winning over MAURICE of Saxony and others, attacked the Schmalkaldic League in 1546, defeated JOHN FREDERICK of Saxony at Mühlberg (1547), and captured PHILIP OF HESSE. He was at the height of his power. At the Diet of Augsburg (1547) he secured the incorporation of the Netherlands into the Hapsburg hereditary possessions and forced through the Augsburg Interim (1548), the compromise profession of doctrine he now tried to impose on the Protestants with the help of Spanish troops. In 1552 Maurice of Saxony changed sides again, called in Henry II of France, and even attempted to capture Charles at Innsbruck.

Withdrawal from Power. Balked in his efforts to recapture METZ from the French and realizing the necessity of compromising with Protestantism, Charles preferred to empower Ferdinand to treat, and he left Germany never to return. Ferdinand negotiated the religious Peace of Augsburg (see AUGSBURG, PEACE OF), but war with France ended only after Charles's death, with the Treaty of CATEAU-CAMBRÉSIS (1559), a triumph for Spain. Charles now began a series of abdications which left the Hapsburg dominions divided between Austria and Spain. In 1554 he gave Naples and Milan to his son Philip, whom he married to Queen MARY I of England; in 1555 he turned over the Netherlands to Philip, and in 1556 he made him king of

Spain and Sicily as Philip II. In 1556 also he practically surrendered the empire to Ferdinand, and in 1558 he formally abdicated as emperor. Though he retired (1556) to the monastery of Yuste, he took an active interest in politics until his death. Two of his natural children were Don JOHN OF AUSTRIA and MARGARET OF PARMA. During Charles's rule the Spanish Empire was tremendously expanded by the conquest of Mexico by CORTÉS and of Peru by Francisco PIZARRO and by the expeditions of De SOTO, CORONADO, PONCE DE LÉON, and Sebastian CABOT. MAGELLAN circumnavigated the globe under Charles's auspices. In Italy, Spanish power had become paramount. Even England seemed about to fall to Spain through Philip's marriage, and Charles's own marriage with Isabella of Portugal brought the Portuguese crown to Philip in 1580. Yet Charles failed in his purpose to return the Protestants to the Church, and the human and financial cost of constant warfare drained Spanish resources. Moreover, Charles's attempt to fuse the dynastic and imperial traditions was in opposition to the theory of the national state then developing in Western Europe. His integrity, strength of will, and sense of duty were conspicuous. His appearance has been made familiar by two portraits by TITIAN. The classic works on Charles V are the biography by Karl Brandi (1937; Eng. tr., 1939) and R. B. Merriman, *The Rise of the Spanish Empire*, Vol. III (1926).

Charles VI, 1685–1740, emperor (1711–40), king of Bohemia (1711–40) and, as Charles III, king of Hungary (1712–40), brother and successor of Emperor Joseph I. Charles was the last emperor of the direct Hapsburg line. By the peace of Szatmar he ended (1711) the rebellion of Francis II RAKOCZY in Hungary. Before his accession he claimed the succession of Charles II of Spain, thus bringing on the War of the SPANISH SUCCESSION. The treaties of 1713–14 (see UTRECHT, PEACE OF) gave Austria most of the Spanish possessions in the Low Countries and in Italy, but left Spain with Charles's rival, PHILIP V of Spain. Philip's attempts to overthrow the settlement resulted (1718) in the formation of the Quadruple Alliance of England, France, the Netherlands, and the emperor. The Treaty of The Hague (1720) repeated the terms of 1713–14, except that Charles obtained Sicily from Savoy in exchange for Sardinia. The War of the POLISH SUCCESSION again involved Charles in war with France and Spain. The Treaty of Vienna (1738) gave Sicily and Naples to Spain, Parma and Piacenza to Austria, and Tuscany to Francis, duke of Lorraine (later Emperor FRANCIS I), who had married (1736) Charles's daughter, MARIA THERESA. Without male issue, Charles made his own succession the chief of his many dynastic preoccupations. His last years were consumed by efforts to secure European recognition of the PRAGMATIC SANCTION of 1713, by which he sought to insure the succession of his daughter to the Hapsburg lands. Though the Pragmatic Sanction was guaranteed by the Treaty of Vienna, the succession was contested on his death (see AUSTRIAN SUCCESSION, WAR OF THE). In his early wars, Charles was well served by Prince EUGENE OF SAVOY. By the Treaty of Passarowitz (1718) Eugene won for Hungary the Banat and N Serbia from the Turks. A less well-conducted

Charles VI

campaign, begun in alliance with Russia in 1737, ended with the separate Treaty of Belgrade (1739), which restored most of Eugene's conquest to the sultan. Charles was a patron of learning and the arts, particularly of music. A mercantilist, he encouraged commerce and industry. His union of Hungary with Austria and Bohemia laid the foundation of the Austro-Hungarian monarchy.

Charles VII, 1697–1745, emperor (1742–45) and, as Charles Albert, elector of Bavaria (1726–45). Having married a daughter of Emperor Joseph I, he refused to recognize the PRAGMATIC SANCTION of 1713 by which Emperor Charles VI (his wife's uncle) reserved the succession to the Hapsburg lands for his daughter, MARIA THERESA. On Charles VI's death (1740) he advanced his own claim and joined with Frederick II (of Prussia), France, Spain, and Saxony to attack Maria Theresa (see AUSTRIAN SUCCESSION, WAR OF THE). In 1742 he was elected emperor, but Bavaria was overrun by Austrian troops. Shortly before his death he regained his territories. Francis I, husband of Maria Theresa, was elected emperor to succeed him.

Charles I, 1887–1922, last emperor of Austria and, as Charles IV, king of Hungary (1916–18), son of Archduke Otto and grandnephew and successor of Francis Joseph. He married ZITA of Bourbon-Parma. The death (1914) of his uncle, FRANCIS FERDINAND, made Charles heir to the throne. He showed skill as a commander in the First World War. After his accession he put out peace feelers. His correspondence with his brother-in-law, Prince SIXTUS OF BOURBON-PARMA, justified French claims to Alsace-Lorraine. The Allies published (April, 1918) the correspondence, thus causing friction between Austria and Germany and diminishing Charles's popularity. Charles vainly tried to save the Austro-Hungarian monarchy by proclaiming (Oct. 16, 1918) an Austrian federative state. Hungary and Czechoslovakia declared their independence, and on Nov. 3 Charles had to consent to the unconditional surrender in the armistice concluded with General Armando Diaz. On Nov. 11 Charles abdicated as emperor of Austria, and on Nov. 13 as king of Hungary; early in 1919 he and his family went into exile in Switzerland. After the triumph of the monarchists in Hungary in 1920, he attempted unsuccessfully to regain that throne in March, 1921, and again in October, when the regent, HORTHY, had Charles arrested. Charles was exiled to Madeira and there died of pneumonia. His son, Archduke Otto, inherited his claim to the throne. See biography by Herbert Vivian (1932).

Charles I, 1600–1649, king of England, Scotland, and Ireland (1625–49), second son of James I and Anne of Denmark, b. Dunfermline. He was made duke of Albany, became heir to the throne on the death of his brother Henry (1612), and was made prince of Wales in 1616. The negotiations for his marriage to the Spanish infanta were unpopular in England, and Charles himself turned against Spain after his unhappy visit to Madrid (1623), in the company of George Villiers, 1st duke of BUCKINGHAM, when he tried to arrange the affair personally. Aside from these negotiations, he took little part in politics before he succeeded (1625) his father as king. A shy and dignified figure, he was popular at that time, but immediately offended his Protestant subjects by his marriage to the Catholic HENRIETTA MARIA, sister of Louis XIII of France. Charles's favorite, Buckingham, was unpopular, and the foreign ventures under Buckingham's guidance were unfortunate, particularly the unsuccessful expedition to Cádiz (1625) and the attempt to aid French Protestants by sending a fleet to Ré (1627–28). Nor would Parliament willingly grant money to help Charles's sister, Elizabeth of Bohemia, and the Protestants in the Thirty Years War. The reign quickly resolved itself into the bitter struggle for supremacy between the king and Parliament that is called the PURITAN REVOLUTION.

The Struggle with Parliament. The House of Commons, and many of the lords, were Puritan in sympathy, while Charles was an advocate of episcopacy. Parliament had the whip hand in its control of money grants to the king and adopted the tactic of withholding grants until its grievances were redressed. The Parliament of 1625 refused money, demanded ministers it could trust, and was soon dissolved by Charles. That of 1626 was dissolved when it started impeachment proceedings against Buckingham. Charles, to meet his needs for money, resorted to quartering troops upon the people and to a forced loan, which he attempted to collect by prosecutions and imprisonments. Forced

Charles I (detail, painting by Anthony van Dyck).

to call Parliament again in 1628, he was compelled to agree to the PETITION OF RIGHT, in return for a badly needed subsidy. Charles prorogued Parliament when it declared that his continued collection of customs duties was a violation of the Petition. Although Buckingham was assassinated (1628), the parliamentary session of 1629 was bitter. It closed dramatically with a resolution condemning unauthorized taxation and attempts to change existing church practices. Charles then governed without Parliament for 11 years, which were marked by popular opposition to strict enforcement of the practices of the Established Church by Archbishop William LAUD and to the ingenious devices employed by the government to obtain funds. The royally controlled courts of high commission and Star Chamber waged a harsh campaign against nonconformists and recusants, and large emigrations to America, of both Puritans and Catholics, took place. The trial (1637–38) of John HAMPDEN for refusal to pay ship money greatly increased public indignation. Meanwhile Charles's deputy in Ireland, Thomas Wentworth, earl of STRAFFORD, was carrying out a wide program of reforms through his oppressive policy of "Thorough."

The Supremacy of Parliament. Conditions in England reached a crisis when Charles attempted (1637) to force episcopacy upon the Scots, an attempt which was violently· opposed by the COVENANTERS and which resulted in the BISHOPS'

WARS. Unable to wage war effectively, Charles summoned (1640) the so-called Short Parliament, which demanded redress of grievances before granting funds and was dissolved. Another attempt to carry on the war without Parliament failed, and the famous Long Parliament was summoned (1640). Under the leadership of John PYM, John Hampden, and Sir Henry VANE (the younger), Parliament secured itself against dissolution without its own consent and brought about the death of Strafford, the abolition of the courts of high commission and Star Chamber, and the end of unparliamentary taxation. Charles professed to accept the revolutionary legislation, though he was known to hold strong views on the divine right of monarchy. Parliament's trust in the king was further undermined when his queen was implicated in the·army plot to coerce Parliament, and Charles was, quite unjustly, suspected of complicity in the Irish massacre (1641) of Protestants in Ulster. In 1641 Parliament presented its Grand Remonstrance, calling for religious and administrative reforms and reciting in full its grievances against the king. Charles repudiated the charges, and his unsuccessful attempt to seize five opposition leaders of Commons in violation of traditional privilege was the fatal blunder that precipitated civil war.

Civil War and Defeat. There were no decisive victories until Charles was defeated at Marston Moor (1644) and Naseby (1645). In 1646 he gave himself up to the Scottish army and in 1647, left behind in England, fell into the hands of Parliament. He was ultimately taken over by the English army leaders, who were now highly suspicious of Parliament. He escaped once to Carisbrooke, on the Isle of Wight, but was treated there as a prisoner, and his attempted coalition between royalists and Presbyterians was broken by the army. Parliament, now reduced in number by Pride's Purge and controlled by his most powerful enemies, established a special high court of justice (see REGICIDES), which tried Charles and convicted him of treason for levying war against Parliament. He was beheaded on Jan. 30, 1649. To the royalists he became the martyred king who wrote the EIKON BASILIKE. By his opponents he was considered a double-dealing tyrant. He had been unable to understand or control the intense religious passions and rapid political development of his age. Whether or not a straightforward and liberal policy toward Parliament and Puritanism would have prevented the war, certainly such a policy was temperamentally impossible for Charles. He had listened to unwise advice and indulged in dangerous halfway measures that undermined confidence in him. His political necessities led him to violate a concept of constitutional government that was rapidly gaining ground in the minds of a powerful group of his subjects, although his own view of the constitution was by no means so indefensible as the 19th-century historians maintained. See S. R. Gardiner, *History of England, 1603–1642* (10 vols., 1883–84) and *History of the Great Civil War* (1893); Godfrey Davies, *The Early Stuarts* (1937); H. Ross Williamson, *Charles and Cromwell* (1946); Evan John, *King Charles I* (1952).